The Four Prohibitions of Acts 15 and Their Common Background in Genesis 1–3

The Four Prohibitions of Acts 15 and Their Common Background in Genesis 1–3

Elena Butova

WIPF & STOCK · Eugene, Oregon

THE FOUR PROHIBITIONS OF ACTS 15 AND THEIR COMMON BACKGROUND
IN GENESIS 1–3

Copyright © 2018 Elena Butova. All rights reserved. Except for brief quotations in critical publications or reviews, no part of this book may be reproduced in any manner without prior written permission from the publisher. Write: Permissions, Wipf and Stock Publishers, 199 W. 8th Ave., Suite 3, Eugene, OR 97401.

Wipf & Stock
An Imprint of Wipf and Stock Publishers
199 W. 8th Ave., Suite 3
Eugene, OR 97401

www.wipfandstock.com

PAPERBACK ISBN: 978-1-5326-5305-6
HARDCOVER ISBN: 978-1-5326-5306-3
EBOOK ISBN: 978-1-5326-5307-0

Manufactured in the U.S.A.

Contents

List of Tables and Figures | vii
Acknowledgments | ix
Abbreviations | x
Introduction | xiii

Chapter 1 History of the Interpretation of the Apostolic Decree | 1
- Manuscript Variants of the Lukan Account of the Apostolic Decree   1
- Patristic Interpretation of the Text of the Apostolic Decree   14
- The Dominance of the Ethical Form of the Apostolic Decree   39
- Turning from the Ethical Form of the Apostolic Decree to Its Jewish Roots   44
- Methodology of the Present Study   65
- Chapter Summary   67

Chapter 2 Exegetical Study of the Apostolic Decree in Its Narrative Context | 69
- The Exegetical Study of the First Account of the Apostolic Decree in Acts 15:1–21   69
- Exegesis of the Second Lukan Account of the Apostolic Decree, Acts 15:22–35   112
- The Third Lukan Account of the Apostolic Decree, Acts 21:17–26   123
- Chapter Summary   140

Chapter 3 Biblical and Theological Context of the Apostolic Decree | 142
- Basic Theological Concepts Developed on the basis of Genesis 1:24—3:24   142
- New Testament Extra-Lukan Echoes of the Content of the Apostolic Decree   184
- Chapter Summary   223

CONTENTS

Chapter 4 The Literary Context of the Apostolic Decree in Luke-Acts | 225
- The Roles of Ritual and Universal Law in Luke-Acts   225
- Uncleanness of the Gentiles   257
- Rethinking the Role of Priestly and Levitical Ministry   277
- Chapter Summary   279

Chapter 5 **Summary and Conclusion** | 281
- Achieving the Main Goals of the Study   281
- Results of the Study   289

Appendix 1 Comparative Study of Manuscripts with Lukan Accounts of the Apostolic Decree | 291

Appendix 2 Diagrams of the Passages Studied in Chapter 3 | 293

Appendix 3 Diagrams of the Passages Studied in Chapter 4 | 318

Bibliography | 339

List of Tables

Table 1   Comparative Study of 1 Cor 8:1–13 and Rom 14:1—15:6 | 216

Table 2   Comparative Study of Passages in Mark 1:29–31 and Luke 4:38, 39 | 250

List of Figures

Figure 1   Unit one—Acts 15:1, 2 | 72

Figure 2   Unit two—Acts 15:3–5 | 76

Figure 3   Unit three—Acts 15:6–11 | 80

Figure 4   Central (C) Narrative Link—Acts 15:12 | 89

Figure 5   Unit four—Acts 15:13–21 | 91

Figure 6   Additional Diagram 1—Acts 15:19, 20 | 103

Figure 7   Additional Diagram 2—Acts 15:21 | 110

Figure 8   Unit five Narrative Frame—Acts 15:22–23a | 112

Figure 9   Unit five—Acts 15:23b–29 | 115

Figure 10   Concluding (C') Narrative Link—Acts 15:30–35 | 120

Figure 11   Part 1—Acts 21:17, 18 | 124

Figure 12   Part 2—Acts 19, 20a | 126

Figure 13   Part 3—Acts 21:20b–22 | 127

Figure 14   Part 4—Acts 21:23, 24 | 134

Figure 15   Part 5—Acts 21:25 | 136

Figure 16   Part 6—Acts 21:26 | 138

Figure 17   Gen 2:7 | 162

Figure 18   Ps 103:29, 30 | 177

Figure 19   1 Cor 10:23b | 188

Figure 20   1 Cor 5:1 | 192

Figure 21   Acts 11:5 | 273

Acknowledgments

I WOULD LIKE TO EXPRESS my heartfelt gratitude to Dr. Steven Thompson, who provided caring and thoughtful supervision for this work. Dr. Thompson spared no effort to improve this research.

He made available not only his encyclopedic knowledge of biblical theology, but also his resources and personal library and most of all he instilled his love for academic excellence.

My warm thanks go to Assoc. Prof. Robert McIver for laying a good foundation for my study at the very beginning and taking me into the world of Greek syntax, which was valuable in my exegesis. His invaluable, constructive criticism and friendly advice during the research were very important and I am most appreciative for the learning opportunities he provided. I also thank Dr. Kayle de Waal, who provided follow-up for my final proposal and made important comments at the early stage of my research.

I am also sincerely grateful to staff at Avondale College of Higher Education, especially Prof. Tony Williams, who encouraged me in my studies by his optimistic attitude; Roberta Matai for helping me to work with advanced computer technologies; and library workers for making available all the facilities necessary for the research. These people patiently dedicated countless hours to helping me complete this thesis to the highest academic standards.

Finally, I am really thankful to my husband, Pr. Vadim Butov, who inspired me to engage in this academic marathon; he served as inspirer, reader and advisor on practical aspects of this research.

Abbreviations

AB	Anchor Bible
AJS Review	Association for Jewish Studies Review
ANF	Ante-Nicene Fathers
ApOTC	Apollos Old Testament Commentary
AUSS	Andrews University Seminary Studies
BBR	Bulletin for Biblical Research
BECNT	Baker Exegetical Commentary on the New Testament
BSac	Bibliotheca Sacra
CBQ	Catholic Biblical Quarterly
ECF	Early Church Fathers
ITQ	Irish Theological Quarterly
JBL	Journal of Biblical Literature
JES	Journal of Ecumenical Studies
JETS	Journal of the Evangelical Theological Society
JSNT	Journal for the Study of the New Testament
JSOT	Journal for the Study of the Old Testament
JTS	Journal of Theological Studies
HTR	Harvard Theological Review
LCL	Loeb Classical Library
NovT	Novum Testamentum
NPNF	Nicene and Post-Nicene Fathers
NTS	New Testament Studies
ResQ	Restoration Quarterly

SNTW	Studies of the New Testament and Its World
TOTC	Tyndale Old Testament Commentaries
TynBul	*Tyndale Bulletin*
VT	*Vetus Testamentum*
WBC	World Biblical Commentary
WTJ	*Westminster Theological Journal*
WUNT	Wissenschaftliche Untersuchungen zum Neuen Testament
WW	*Word and World*

Introduction

According to Acts 15, the decision of the Jerusalem Council postulated that the Jewish ritual law[1] is unnecessary for salvation, nevertheless four prohibitions were enjoined on believers. This decision of the Jerusalem Council (the so-called Apostolic Decree) poses the following questions:

1. What kind of laws were under discussion by the apostles?
2. Why were those laws viewed as no longer relevant?
3. Why were the four prohibitions viewed as still binding?
4. Why were only these four chosen?
5. Were the four prohibitions of temporary or permanent validity?
6. Was there any temporal limitation to the validity of the four prohibitions?

None of the various explanations found in the secondary literature provides firm ground for all four prohibitions of the Apostolic Decree (in shortened form referred to as, the Decree). The present study proposes a common ground for all four prohibitions of Acts 15:20. The purpose of the study is to show that the four prohibitions are based on the patterns of true worship established on the principles of the natural law of God in Gen 1–3.

The thesis aims to discover and analyze the parts of the whole issue and then to reinterpret the parts (accumulated data) in light of the whole issue, forming a hermeneutical loop. Consequently, the first aim is to find the original form of the Decree and the known ways of interpreting it. The second is to differentiate the structure of the Decree and its close context, which allows the researcher to reconstruct the historical context in order to separate the apostolic message itself from the cultural context in which it was formulated. The third aim is to state the broader biblical and theological context of the Decree for which a number of theological concepts of universal scope need to be employed. These concepts are the creation–fall–re-creation paradigm, the patterns of the natural law of God reflected in Gen 1–3 account, and the worship

---

1. This term was chosen according to classification of the laws of Torah provided by Gane, ed., *Leviticus, Numbers*, 306.

motifs as a part of temple theology. The fourth aim is to identify these theological concepts in Luke-Acts and reveal their significance for Luke's theology.

The above aims can be crystallized into the following four goals or tasks for the researcher:

1. To describe the history of the interpretation of the Apostolic Decree, to find the original reading of the Decree, and to develop methods of interpretation that reveal a common basis for all four prohibitions in their original form. This requires investigation of the history of the interpretation of the Decree, beginning with the Greek manuscript traditions, then its history in the works of relevant church fathers, and finally in the post-Reformation critical studies of Acts, including current studies.

2. To provide a detailed exegetical study of three Lukan accounts of the Decree in Acts 15:1–21; 15:22–35; and 21:17–26, using semantic diagrams which allow and, with the help of inductive logic, aid in revealing the meaning of each passage.

3. To describe the basic theological concepts developed on the basis of Genesis 1:24—3:24 and show their connections to the four prohibitions of the Decree, and to investigate whether extra-Lukan New Testament occurrences of the prohibitions also fit theological concepts developed on the basis of Gen 1–3.

4. To note whether references to ritual and natural law appear elsewhere in Luke's two-volume work, and also differentiate between ritual and natural laws.

The significance of the present research is evidenced by two decades of scholarly debate about the best common basis for the four prohibitions. The present research demonstrates that it is possible to root all four prohibitions in the theological concepts developed on the basis of Gen 1–3.

The originality of the present research consists of inductively developing ideas based on the passage structures displayed in the form of semantic diagrams. The role of these diagrams is to isolate and highlight the fundamental ideas of the diagramed passages and reveal their inner logic. The revealing presence of midrashic structures in Acts 15:10–21 is one of the most important outcomes of this method. The presence of midrash based on Gen 1–3 supports the thesis that the four prohibitions of the Decree are connected to and based on biblical concepts formed on a level even deeper than the flood narrative in Gen 9, namely on the level of the creation-fall account of Gen 1–3.

1

History of the Interpretation of the Apostolic Decree

THIS CHAPTER REVIEWS THE history of the efforts to find the Old Testament origin of the Apostolic Decree. Starting with the variant readings found in the preserved manuscripts of Acts, the discussion will extend to include a detailed summary and critique of current views. Section 1 of this chapter reports on a search for the original reading among the manuscript variant readings, and analyzes the variant readings for what they reveal about how the Apostolic Decree was being interpreted in the earliest years of Christianity. The variant readings of the Decree are classified in Appendix 1. Section 2 focuses on patristic quotations of the Decree, which reveal the stages of the transmission of the texts and the appearing of the variant readings. Section 3 describes the period of the dominance of the ethical form of the Apostolic Decree including the stage of its mediaeval interpretation, that of the Reformers, and its critical study.

Section 4 of this chapter is dedicated to the contemporary search for the Jewish roots of the Apostolic Decree and provides a classification and review of the most significant interpretations of the content of the Decree since 1950. This section also explains the premises and necessity for the present research on this topic. Section 5 describes the research methodology employed in the study.

Manuscript Variants of the Lukan Account of the Apostolic Decree

To start the survey of the rationale behind the four prohibitions in Acts 15 one needs to recover the earliest written forms of the Decree and its interpretations. The variety of manuscript variant readings, the quantity of patristic quotations of the Decree, and patristic commentaries on the Decree allow the reconstruction of some early Christian traditions behind the text of the Decree.[1] The manuscript traditions include three aspects: 1) three Lukan accounts of the Decree (Acts 15:20, 29; 21:25) and extra-Lukan NT occurrences of the matters of the Decree (in Pauline writings and the book of

---

1. The data of the patristic interpretation of the Decree will be discussed in section 2 of this chapter.

Revelation);[2] 2) manuscript variants reflecting the process of transmission of the text of the Decree during five centuries of Christianity;[3] 3) information about Christianity provided by selected non-Christian sources.[4]

The primary and earliest evidence of the Apostolic Decree in written form is found in Acts 15:20, 29 and Acts 21:25. These verses contain the Lukan account of the event, and provide the following information: historical context and cause of the dispute, verbal proposal of the Decree in Acts 15:19–21, and its written form in 15:29. Luke informs readers that the apostolic letter existed as a freestanding document, which Paul, Barnabas (from the Antiochene side), Judas and Silas (from Jerusalem side) carried to Antioch and read to the congregation (Acts 15:30).[5] It is also known from Luke's description that the church in Antioch found the message of the letter to bring encouragement and gladness (Acts 15:31). The original letter is no longer extant, so we are dependent on the Lukan version of the event and the Decree.

The Apostolic Decree survives in three types of text: Western, Alexandrian and proto-Alexandrian (Neutral).[6] The Western text is preserved in Codex Bezae (D 05). The Alexandrian text is preserved in ℵ 01 and B 03 (also in $\mathfrak{P}$74, A 02, C 04, Ψ). The proto-Alexandrian text is preserved in $\mathfrak{P}$45. This variety of readings calls for a comparative study of two main traditions preserved in D 05 and B 03 in order to discover the earliest one.

The Western Text Preserved in D 05

The originality of D 05 is argued by Josep Rius-Camps and Jenny Read-Heimerdinger.[7] They believe that the language of D 05 reflects the earliest fixed and unrevised form of Acts. It is assumed from the fact that D 05 was commonly cited in the works of Greek fathers and "formed the basis of the standardized texts of the early versions," namely, the *Latin Vulgate* and the *Syriac Peshitta*.[8] They argue that "two early textual clusters or text-types (B 03 and D 05) were functioning from perhaps as early as the second century."[9]

---

2. Lukan variant readings of the Decree will be discussed in chapter 2 and extra-Lukan NT occurrences of the Decree in Chapter 3.

3. Manuscript variant readings of the Decree will be discussed in section 1.1 of this chapter.

4. Selected non-Christian sources will be discussed in paragraph 1.2 of this chapter.

5. This study assumes that the original text of the Decree was preserved by Luke, the collaborator of the apostle Paul, and that it survived in the manuscripts of Acts, along with its genuine historical and cultural settings.

6. This classification of text types of the passages with the Decree was made by the present researcher according to the Westcott-and-Hort critical reconstruction, which is cited by Metzger, *Text of the New Testament*, 131–35.

7. Rius-Camps, Ropes, and Epp support the earlier dating for D 05, about 400 CE.

8. Rius-Camps and Read-Heimerdinger, eds., *Message of Acts in Codex Bezae*, 1:5.

9. Black, *Rethinking New Testament Textual Criticism*, 34–41.

However, the dating of D 05 is controversial.[10] It is bilingual—Greek in the left column and Latin on the right.[11] The text is arranged in irregular lines, which were intended to follow the units of sense.[12] The Greek text was written in uncials defined by Ropes as "Old Uncial Text."[13] The fact that D 05 had been chosen by the church as an authoritative carrier of original data can be evidence of its selection from the range of available manuscripts on the basis of doctrinal issues rather than antiquity. The selection of the one ms among others is also an attempt at redaction or even censorship. The doctrinal "correctness" could also be seen in the fact that the church fathers often cited D 05.

Another argument of Rius-Camps is that the data in D 05 "are more abundant and more cohesive" and "demonstrate sustained rather than spasmodic use."[14] Also D 05 "displays more complete and more complex allusion to the Scripture."[15] D 05 text "is less dramatic in speaking about tension or disagreement" in the church.[16] Thus, according to D 05 people from Judea (those who start to contradict Paul in the Antiochine church) sent Paul to elders in Jerusalem "in order to be judged in submission to them *(to the church leaders)* over this question."[17]

These features at first sight give a sense of a late revision, assuming the existence of a church hierarchy even at that early stage, which could hardly come from the quill of Luke himself. It can alert one who understands that Luke was less likely to provide the widened historical arrangement for his contemporary readers, especially on the basis of Jewish life well-known at the time, before the church split from Judaism.[18] This also betrays an attempt to endow the church with impeccable authority and unity.

10. Petzer, "History of the New Testament."

11. Parker states that the text of D 05 appeared due to evolution. "The evidence lies in differences between the columns, where the Latin often seems to be a witness to a form of Greek text which lies somewhere between the form in 03 and that in 05." Parker, *Introduction* , 289.

12. Parker, *Introduction*, 288. Here Parker argues that Acts in D 05 was derived by scribe from other bilingual copies. It suggested that D 05 had precursors ($\mathfrak{P}$38, $\mathfrak{P}$48, $\mathfrak{P}$69 and 0171). Aland's opinion, cited by Black, ed., *Rethinking Textual Criticism*, 38–39. Unfortunately none of these three manuscripts contains the apostolic letter. Presence of it might provide the evidences of originality or corruption in later written D 05.

13. Cited by Parker, *Introduction*, 288.

14. Rius-Camps and Read-Heimerdinger, eds., *Message of Acts*, 1:25.

15. Rius-Camps and Read-Heimerdinger, eds., *Message of Acts*, 1:25. According to Rius-Camps D 05 provides details derived not only from Septuagint, but also "from legends and teachings that become associated with the original scriptural account and that were regarded to some degree as authoritative." He states that D 05 also provides data for the historical reconstruction.

16. Rius-Camps and Jenny Read-Heimerdinger, eds., *Message of Acts*, 3:177.

17. Rius-Camps and Read-Heimerdinger, eds., *Message of Acts*, 3:174–75. The words in italics are added.

18. Rius-Camps stated that the Alexandrian Text in B 03 transmits a less theological and more chronological view of history, and that it regularly removes indications of a Jewish or spiritual perspective in what can be described as a tendency to "'historicize' the text." Rius-Camps and Read-Heimerdinger, eds., *Message of Acts*, 1:43.

Another fundamental disagreement of D 05 with B 03 appears in Acts 15:1. Here B 03 has the dative article before Moses to show that the demand for the circumcision was given with the explanation of its necessity. This reading assumes that the demand for circumcision had been imposed on the Gentiles according to the law of Moses. The same verse in D 05 names Moses without an article, and in the genitive case. It changes the meaning and looks like a demand to apply not only to circumcision, but to all other rites from the Mosaic law as well.[19] However, D 05 itself in 15:2 states that circumcision alone was a matter of debate in Antioch.[20] Thus only circumcision is mentioned without reference to the rest of the Mosaic tradition. Thus D 05 tends to show that all Mosaic laws were discussed at once and cancelled by the following Decree.

Rius-Camps and Read-Heimerdinger interpret the phrase ὅτι ἀφ' ἡμερῶν ἀρχαίον in 15:7 as "from the days of old" and interpret it as "a reference to the beginning of the history of Israel."[21] Another time the interpretation of the phrase is suggested as "ever since ancient times."[22] Contrastingly, B 03 contains in 15:7 the phrase "from the early days," which is viewed as a reference only to "the early days of the Church."[23] At this point Rius-Camps' opinion seems to follow the original meaning of Peter's exposition. It presumes that God had a plan for the Gentiles in the beginning, which may refer even to the time of creation.

According to D 05 Peter ends his speech with the words of Moses in (Exod 17:2).[24] This rightly noticed reference to Moses can be understood as an attempt by Peter to transfer the situation in the early church into the well-known pattern of Exodus. It could help him to link disobedience to Moses in the past and disobedience to Christ in the present. From this point the exclamation νῦν οὖν τί πειράζετε τὸν θεὸν together with following ἀλλὰ διὰ τῆς χάριτος τοῦ κυρίου Ἰησοῦ πιστεύομεν σωθῆναι καθ' ὃν τρόπον κἀκεῖνοι can be understood as a set of double contrasts between the grace of God and evil condition of an unbelieving heart, as well as between tempting God and relying upon him in faith.

---

19. Rius-Camps and Read-Heimerdinger, eds., *Message of Acts*, 3:174.

20. Rius-Camps and Read-Heimerdinger, eds., *Message of Acts*, 3:177. This disagreement between verses 1 and 2 suggests that the text in D 05 meaningly avoids the article before the name of Moses in order to hit all cultic Jewish rites.

21. Rius-Camps and Read-Heimerdinger, eds., *Message of Acts*, 3:186. Rius adds that ἀπό with the aorist ἐξελέξατο has sense "as from, as early as."

22. Rius-Camps and Read-Heimerdinger, eds., *Luke's Demonstration to Theophilus*, 500–501.

23. Rius-Camps and Read-Heimerdinger, eds., *Message of Acts*, 3:201. However, here Rius notes that "the succession of three aorist verbs - ἐξελέξατο . . . ἀκοῦσαι . . . πιστεῦσαι - expresses the timeless nature of God's plan."

24. Rius-Camps and Read-Heimerdinger, eds., *Message of Acts*, 3:203, 205. It might be an allusion on extreme lack of faith, when someone cannot even see the divine revelation in miracles by which God attested the acceptance of the Gentiles. It is "the last time that mention will be made in Acts of "signs and wonders", when so far they have accompanied all the main characters," like Moses (7:36), Jesus (2:22; 4:30), the apostles (2:43; 5:12), Stephen (6:8), Paul and Barnabas (14:3).

Rius-Camps' argues that in 15:13–15 James' phrase Συμεὼν ἐξηγήσατο does not refer to the words of Peter. This remark of James was followed by the complex quotation of the prophets. Surprisingly, he sees the name "Simeon" in James' speech as a reference to Simeon the Just.[25] This interpretation seems doubtful as it is based only on one exceptional reading of D 05 in contrast to common textual tradition of ℵ 01, B 03 and 𝔓74.

Significant interpolation in D 05 appears in 15:17, 18. Here, instead of regular conclusion at the end of prophetic composition, λέγει κύριος ποιῶν ταῦτα γνωστὰ ἀπ᾽ αἰῶνος, D 05 reads λέγει κύριος ποιήσει ταῦτα γνωστὸν ἀπ᾽ αἰῶνος ἐστιν τῷ κυρίῳ τὸ ἔργον αὐτοῦ. Here D 05 divides the phrase and places the γνωστὸν ἀπ᾽ αἰῶνος ἐστιν τῷ κυρίῳ τὸ ἔργον αὐτοῦ as an independent sentence which reflects an emphatic declaration of James.[26] According to Rius-Camps, James stated, in this manner, that the inclusion of the Gentiles in the people of God's name "is part of the eternal plan of the Lord."[27] Thus the wording of D 05 once again differs from ℵ 01, B 03 (and additionally from C 04, Ψ, 33, 81) and matches with minor alterations A 02 (fifth century) and 𝔓74 (seventh century).

Discussing the variant readings of these verses, Metzger states that ταῦτα is the ending word of the Amos quotation and the following words γνωστὰ ἀπ᾽ αἰῶνος belong to James and not to quotation. However Metzger admits that the wording in vv. 17–18 looks "so elliptical an expression that copyists made various attempts to recast the phrase, rounding it out as an independent sentence."[28] This fact may also suggest that the scribes were aware of a possible meaning of the verse focusing on the plan of God from eternity.

Finally the supporters of D 05 do not explain the absence of πνικτός. Rius-Camps supports its omission with a range of patristic literature.[29] The word is similarly absent in D 05 from the apostolic letter (15:29) and from James' speech to Paul (21:25). He argues that even from the Jewish point of view the prohibitions of the Decree "can only be ethical: the defilement brought on by disobeying them is permanent."[30] However, many scholars view the ethical form of the four prohibitions in light of the Holiness Code of Lev 17–18. The presence of πνικτός in the list of prohibitions would seem

25. Rius-Camps and Read-Heimerdinger, eds., *Message of Acts*, 3:188. Rius believes that James cited Prophets not from the Torah, but from Simeon the Just, who had summarized the interpretation of Torah. He comes to this conclusion because D 05 uses the future form οὕτως συμφωνήνουσιν where B 03 uses present form συμφωνοῦσιν. See also Rius-Camps and Read-Heimerdinger, eds., *Luke's Demonstration to Theophilus*, 659 n. 206.

26. Rius-Camps and Read-Heimerdinger, eds., *Message of Acts*, 3:189.

27. Rius-Camps and Read-Heimerdinger, eds., *Message of Acts*, 3:211.

28. Metzger, *Textual Commentary on the Greek New Testament*, 379.

29. He notes the same omission has a range of patristic support (Ir1739mg.lat, Tert Hiermss, Ambrosiaster, Augustine). Rius-Camps and Read-Heimerdinger, eds., *Message of Acts*, 1:189.

30. Rius-Camps and Read-Heimerdinger, eds., *Message of Acts*, 3:213. Here he understands that by their nature the prohibitions are deeper than the rules for good behavior. He connects them to Leviticus 17–20.

naturally rooted in Torah and required not only by Jewish cult but also by permanent moral standards. Probably the early Christians would not view it differently to Torah, especially if one takes in account the fact that they had only Jewish Scriptures (Torah, Prophets and Psalms) and quoted them (as it seen in Acts 15).

The omission of πνικτός gives the Decree an ethical form. To insert it would seem odd. This could be the reason for the medieval correctors of D 05 making an intentional change to the text. If this omission was made from a semantic perspective, it appears to be motivated because of doctrinal considerations.[31] The alteration of text does not usually clarify the original meaning. Altering the text usually happens when the meaning of the text has been lost, or is unacceptable. This adjustment of a reading to express some non-original ideas always results in loss of meaning, and makes the altered text not a witness, but a hermeneutic product.

Rius-Camps views the variant readings as a result of alteration to Alexandrian readings, when the church decided to harmonize the mixed table fellowship for Jewish Christian and Gentiles (in Paul's experience 1 Cor 8:1–4, 7–13). He believes that "the reference to πνικτός introduces a dietary issue relevant for table fellowship into the list of James' concerns."[32] His suggestion looks doubtful because not only the Alexandrian, but also the proto-Alexandrian reading of 𝔓45 includes πνικτός.[33] All these witnesses are earlier than D 05. Moreover, the prohibition of πνικτός seems to have sense for James, as will now be explained. Thus, the Decree in D 05 tends to provide a shortened ethical form instead of the cultic form preserved in 𝔓45 or the ambivalent form in 𝔓74, A 02, B 03, E 06, L and Ψ.

The contrast between the attitudes of Peter and James towards the law in 15:21 is explained by D 05 apologists as James' "prior acceptance of Judaism," while Peter insisted on liberating the Gentiles from its burden.[34] However, the believers during the time before the destruction of Jerusalem usually identified themselves with Jewish hopes for salvation. James repeats some of Peter's thoughts and refers to the prophets, which reveals that the apostles shared the same opinion concerning salvation of the Gentiles. The phrase in Acts15:11 presupposes the affirmative answer of the congregation. It means that the congregation consisting of Jewish believers had in mind that the salvific event is a result of God's mercy towards his people of any origin.

The D 05 reading of 15:23 γράψαντες . . . διὰ χειρὸς αὐτῶν is viewed by supporters to state that the letter reporting the apostolic decision "was actually written by Judas and Silas ('through their hand'), rather than simply delivered by them."[35] The

---

31. Metzger, *Text of New Testament*, 200–202.

32. Rius-Camps and Read-Heimerdinger, eds., *Message of Acts*, 3:214.

33. The 𝔓45 witness of 250 CE contains πνικτός, omits τῆς πορνείας and can be classified as the cultic reading.

34. Rius-Camps and Read-Heimerdinger, eds., *Message of Acts*, 3:215, 216. For them, James had gone "against Peter's position with regard to the status of the Law" and offered a compromise.

35. Rius-Camps and Read-Heimerdinger, eds., *Message of Acts*, 3:191.

structure of this sentence is seen in the following diagram: ἔδοξεν — ἐκλεξαμένους — πέμψαι — γράψαντες. Here, the verb δοκέω in v. 22 is used impersonally with the infinitive πέμψαι and relates to it.[36] The aorist participle γράψαντες, as well as the aorist participle ἐκλεξαμένους "should be understood as supplementary participles" to aorist ἔδοξεν, which is the main verb in v. 22.[37] Thus, the apostles, who ἔδοξεν were also those who γράψαντες and ἐκλεξαμένους. The election of messengers and writing of the letter have to be attributed to the apostles and elders, not to Judas and Silas. So, the apostles had written the letter by their own hands, while Judas and Silas delivered it, when it was written.[38]

The discussion about the absence of a plural article before ἐπάναγκες in 15:28, 29 in D 05 brings Rius-Camps to the conclusion "that ἐπάναγκες begins a new sentence, listing the content of τούτων."[39] It helps readers to distinguish "between the decision of the Holy Spirit (μηδὲν . . . βάρος) and that taken by the assembly (πλὴν τούτων· ἐπάναγκες <ἐστιν> ἀπέχεσθαι . . .)."[40] Further he states that "some aspects of the Jerusalem decree are contrary to the Spirit."[41] However, this omission was taken by Metzger as a possible instance of haplography.[42]

Moreover, if the sentence stops after πλὴν τούτων the thought looks disrupted. The addition of the "necessary" after a full stop breaks the logical chain between "all" in the previous sentence and the four matters excluded from the "all" in the following sentence. One then needs to define what the pronoun τούτων refers to? The phrase μηδὲν πλεῖον ἐπιτίθεσται ὑμῖν βάρος πλὴν τούτων meaning "do no greater burden . . . except that" has to provide a supplementary unit where D 05 has the end of the sentence. The supplementary unit is presupposed by the comparative sense of μηδὲν πλεῖον.

According to context it should be a comparison between the burdensome situation in the past and the better situation at present. Thus, the phrase translates "no greater burden to be placed on you except that." In this location the phrase of D 05 μηδὲν πλεῖον ἐπιτίθεσται ὑμῖν βάρος πλὴν τούτων can refer to following ἐπάναγκές and prohibitions, or can refer to previous verses (15:1, 2 and 24). This thought is also possible because the letter starts with "since we heard that some people . . ." and one supposes that the apostolic answer to Antioch should provide the regulation for that problem.

---

36. McIver, *Intermediate New Testament Greek Made Easier*, 62.

37. McIver, *Intermediate New Testament Greek Made Easier*, 62.

38. The diagram of this passage can be found in section 2.1.1 of chapter 2.

39. Rius-Camps and Read-Heimerdinger, eds., *Message of Acts*, 3:193. According to D 05 the new sentence begins with ἐπάναγκες and followed by the infinitive ἐστιν.

40. Rius-Camps and Read-Heimerdinger, eds., *Message of Acts*, 3:193.

41. Rius-Camps and Read-Heimerdinger, eds., *Message of Acts*, 3:228.

42. Metzger, *Textual Commentary on Greek NT*, 386. Rius-Camps to the contrary believes that the presence of the article in B 03 was the result of dittography.

If μηδὲν πλεῖον ἐπιτίθεσται ὑμῖν βάρος πλὴν τούτων in D 05 refers to the demands of Mosaic law imposed by some people from Judea in 15:1, 2, 24, then the meaning of the sentence is: "The decision of the Holy Spirit and of ourselves is to place no greater burden upon you except *the demands of the ritual law*." This meaning cannot be accepted. Then, "more than that" can be linked to the following prohibitions. This link has support from other witnesses fitting them in one sentence, but D 05 divides them by a full stop. If the meaning connects two phrases in one unit, then the full stop placed between them brings perplexity. Together with the omission of πνικτός and addition of the negative form of the Golden Rule, the variant reading in D 05 seems to be merely an attempt to mask the original meaning of the Decree due to doctrinal presuppositions.

Finally, in 15:29 D 05 adds the relative pronoun ὧν before the list of three prohibitions and the negative form of the Golden Rule. Thus D 05 "refers to a more complex package, than a list of wrongdoing."[43] This relative pronoun ὧν together with all insertions just proves the earlier presumption that D 05 intentionally constructs the reading according to the doctrinal interpretation and can suit no more than a periphrastic purpose. Rius-Camps calls the prohibitions "essential requirements for Gentiles" and describes Luke as unhappy with the outcome of the council. For him the Decree brought in "the confusion of the binding nature of the legal demands, on the one hand, and the freedom given by the Holy Spirit, on the other."[44]

According to Rius-Camps the prohibitions caused little joy in the Antiochine church.[45] He assumes this from the comparison of "great joy" of brethren in Phoenicia and Samaria, when they heard about the conversion of the Gentiles to God, to the humble term "rejoiced," describing the reaction in Antioch, when its brethren heard the apostolic letter. The comparison seems awkward because the people in different places and cultures (as seen in Samaria, Phoenicia and Antioch) could express a different intensity of emotions, especially if the causes of joy differed.

Arguments Against the Originality of the Western Text in D 05

An alternative view on the origin and nature of D 05 has been was expressed by Kurt Aland, Bruce Metzger and David Parker.[46] Parker views D 05 as neither Alexandrian nor Western in text type, but as a periphrastic text, and a product of stages of growth.[47]

---

43. Rius-Camps and Read-Heimerdinger, eds., *Message of Acts*, 3:194.
44. Rius-Camps and Read-Heimerdinger, eds., *Message of Acts*, 3:221.
45. Rius-Camps and Read-Heimerdinger, eds., *Message of Acts*, 3:227–28.
46. Aland, Metzger, and Parker support the later dating of D 05.
47. In evidence Parker identifies a number of different emphases of D 05, such as "anti-Judaic tendencies; a greater interest in the role of the Holy Spirit; a greater interest in one or more of the Apostles; a minimizing of the significance of women in the life of early Christianity." Parker, *Introduction*, 298–99.

According to Parker, D 05 had been compiled from different sources in approximately 400 CE. Then "a number of correctors were responsible for changes to the manuscript in the fifth to seventh centuries, and the manuscript had some leaves supplemented at Lyons in the ninth century."[48] Bruce Metzger also believes that the D 05 readings "can scarcely be original."[49] He supports his opinion by quoting Kurt Aland about the Western text type: "Only five out of more than forty Greek papyri from the second and third centuries show any influence from the D-text (and these five witnesses belong to the second half of the third century)."[50] Metzger agrees with Aland that "the D-text arose during the second half of the third century, when the Church was free from persecution (i.e. from A.D. 260 to 303)."[51] The fact that D 05 is 6.6% longer than B 03 suggests that D 05 is unlikely to have the earliest readings, because for the scribe it was easier to omit the word, than deliberately make the process of copying longer.[52]

A discussion about variant readings of Acts 15:20 comes to the conclusion that "the least unsatisfactory solution of the complicated textual and exegetical problems of the Apostolic Decree is to regard the fourfold decree as original (foods offered to idols, strangled meat, eating blood, and unchastity—whether ritual or moral)."[53] Despite this, D 05 variant readings were widely spread in Europe for centuries. It influenced the understanding of the Apostolic Decree and most likely led scribes to modification in the direction of its ethical form. The discussion in 1.1.3 suggests an explanation for why the D 05 readings became so widely spread across Europe. However, now we turn our attention from the ethical form of the prohibitions in D 05 to their cultic form, as preserved in 𝔓45.

Proto-Alexandrian (Neutral) Text Type

Papyrus Chester Beatty I or 𝔓45 contains readings which in many places differ from D 05. This ms is dated to first half of the second century.[54] Westcott and Hort found that Acts in 𝔓45 conforms to what they called the Neutral (proto-Alexandrian) text type. Some scholars believe that 𝔓45 preserves the earliest form of Acts and the Decree, less

---

48. Parker, *Introduction*, 144–46, 288–89. Thus Parker finds that D 05 had ten correctors differentiated during the process of copying.

49. Metzger, *Textual Commentary on Greek NT*, 381. Here Metzger discusses the variant reading of the four prohibitions in the Apostolic Decree in D 05 and Alexandrian reading. He explains that idolatry, murder, and adultery were banned in the universal sense by the Law of God and had no need in additional application on the Gentiles by the letter. Especially it seems strange to start the list of universal taboos with "to abstain from . . ."

50. Cited by Metzger, *Text of New Testament*, 293.

51. Metzger, *Text of New Testament*, 293.

52. Rius-Camps and Read-Heimerdinger, eds., *Message of Acts*, 16; and Black, ed., *Rethinking Textual Criticism*, 28–30.

53. Metzger, *Textual Commentary on Greek NT*, 382.

54. Metzger, *Text of New Testament*, 37.

corrupted by copying than other text types. Yet 𝔓45 shows that even between 250 and 400 CE there were several variant readings of the Decree.

Acts 15:29 and Acts 21:25 are missing from 𝔓45, yet the evidence for existence of Acts 15:29 in 𝔓45 could be provided by quotations from it in patristic literature. Moreover, τῆς πορνείας is missing from 𝔓45 15:20. Origen's commentary made according to 𝔓45 (see Origen, *Contra Celsum*, viii.29), as well as *vg ms Vigilius* and *Gaudentius* witness the omission of τῆς πορνείας in 15:29.[55] It is known that Origen usually cited the New Testament by memory echoing some catch-words of the cited text. After that his amanuensis provided full quotation from the Scripture.[56] So the amanuensis had to copy the quotation from the *ms* which Origen referred to. Since Origen's quotation of Scripture omits τῆς πορνείας in 15:29, we can imagine that Origen had access to 𝔓45 or related text, and that text included 15:29. It suggests that in the third century the cultic form of the Decree was well known to the Eastern church fathers and accepted as the original reading.[57]

Alexandrian Text Type Manuscripts (Ambivalent Readings)

Now the remaining manuscripts containing the Decree come up for discussion. The data for this paragraph are displayed in Appendix 1. From the comparative study in Appendix 1 it becomes clear that both ambivalent and cultic readings are supported by the earliest witnesses. Yet, the ambivalent form of the Decree has stronger support. The ethical view, on the contrary, is supported only by D 05, limited minuscules, and patristic literature.

The threefold tradition of 𝔓45 omits καὶ τῆς πορνείας in 15:20, but contains καὶ τοῦ πνικτοῦ. The passages 15:29 and 21:25 do not exist. This papyrus is the earliest witness to the proto-Alexandrian text type. Yet, the two earliest codices ℵ 01 and B 03 (fourth century), and codices A 02 and C 04 (fifth), as well as E 06 (sixth) and 𝔓74 (seventh) contain the fourfold tradition.[58] This reading also is reflected in L and Ψ dated by ninth to tenth century. It is unlikely that L and Ψ represent the earliest readings, but they witness the wide geographical distribution of the fourfold tradition. It appears that in the fourth century the fourfold reading of the Decree was well-known and accepted as original in the Middle East and in Rome.

The same reading had been in use in Egypt (Alexandria) just one century later. There it was assumed to be the original reading, A 02 was based on it and kept in

---

55. Metzger, *Textual Commentary on Greek NT*, 380. Metzger dates the Origen's writings with citations from the New Testament by 253–54 CE. Metzger, *Text of New Testament*, 88–89.

56. Metzger, *Text of New Testament*, 87–88.

57. The witnesses with Alexandrian type of text were usually quoted in works of Clement of Alexandria, Origen, John Chrysostom, Cyril of Jerusalem, Amphilochius, Socrates of Constantinople, Diodore, Dydimus and Severian.

58. Dating of papyri follows Metzger, *Text of New Testament*, 37, 41.

the Alexandrian library for centuries. The text with minor alterations in Ψ found in Mount Athos also extends the geographical distribution of the fourfold tradition. This evidence points to one common predecessor. Consequently, that archetypal text had to exist before 350 CE, namely, before the appearance of ℵ 01 and B 03. The geographical distribution of copies presumes several decades for the transmission of the material (from some unknown geographical area to Sinai, Rome, Alexandria and Mount Athos). So, the autograph had to be a single ms, which was located centrally between those geographical areas. The major witnesses (ℵ 01, A 02, B 03) in Acts belong to the Alexandrian text type, which is also frequently followed by 𝔓74 in Acts.[59] This may suggest that the churches in Alexandria were the centre of distribution of copies.

All these lines of evidence support the acceptance of the ambivalent reading of the Decree as the original. This has support from C 04, E 06, L and Ψ which preserve the fourfold tradition. These texts add in Acts 21:25: Κρίναντες μηδὲν τοιοῦτο τηρεῖν αὐτούς εἰ μὴ φυλάσσεσθαι αὐτούς. This addition indicates that James himself explained his attitude towards the Mosaic law as unnecessary for the Gentiles. Thus, C 04 partially preserved the interpretation of the Decree which existed in fifth century. This additional phrase was chronologically the latest extension of the text (the earliest *ms* which contains it is C 04, dated fifth century). Metzger defines this manuscript in the following manner: "Its text is of less importance than one might have assumed from its age. It seems to be compounded from all the major text-types, agreeing frequently with the later Koine or Byzantine type, which most scholars regard as the least valuable type of New Testament text."[60] The additional wording in C 04 perfectly matches the phrase of D05 and it seems that D 05 assimilated the phrase from C 04.[61]

Furthermore, E 06 (sixth), L and Ψ (ninth–tenth) more likely contain the result of the same fifth century correction as they preserve the Byzantine text type and share one common feature. Thus, E 06 is the only codex reading in Acts 21:25 καὶ τοῦ πνικτοῦ instead of καὶ πνικτὸν. It seems that the corrector repeated by memory the well-known phrase of Acts 15:20 and 29. This variant reading could be considered an unintentional error.[62]

The minuscules also contain some differences in readings which are probably the result of the latest transformation of uncial letters in cursive writing.[63] A number of minuscules support the fourfold reading in Acts 15:20. They are 33, 36, 81, 181, 307, 323, 453, 610, 614, 1175, 1241, 1409, 1505 1678, 2344 and with a negligible difference in 945, 1739, 1891. Among them there is the famous minuscule 33 called "the queen of

---

59. Metzger, *Text of New Testament*, 41, 249–50.

60. Metzger, *Text of New Testament*, 49.

61. It was stated that D 05 had several correctors making changes in its text between fifth and ninth centuries CE. Parker, *Introduction*, 288–89.

62. Metzger, *Text of New Testament*, 192–93.

63. These changes witness the period of variant readings of the Apostolic Decree at the time of the medieval church, which is to be described in section 3.4 of this chapter.

the cursives," dated ninth century (it agrees with A 02 and B 03 and does not contain any omissions from or additions to the Alexandrian reading of the Decree).[64]

Minuscules of the tenth century (181, 307, 1175, 1739, 1891) also provide a fourfold reading, but 1739 and 1891 (and later 323 and 945) add the negative form of the Golden Rule at the end of a phrase which differs from that in D 05.[65] Parker sees the text of 1739 as a later development of D 05: "It too omits πνικτοῦ and reads grammatically more sophisticated καὶ ἂν μὴ θέλωσιν αὑτοῖς γενέσθαι ἑτέροις μὴ ποιεῖν. This polish suggests a development of the version found in 05."[66] In addition, the majority of witnesses written in between the eleventh and fourteenth centuries still preserve the fourfold reading in Acts 15:20 without any alterations.[67]

The majority of minuscules (33, 323, 945, 1241, 1505, and 1739) keep the fourfold tradition, including καὶ πνικτοῦ in Acts 15:29. Three minuscules (81, 614 and 1175) have in Acts 15:29 the plural form (πνικτῶν).[68] At the same time they preserve, in 15:20, the singular (πνικτοῦ).[69] The reading of Acts 15:29 in these three witnesses is in agreement with in ℵ 01, A 02, B 03 and C 04 and was accepted by Nestle-Aland 28 as original. Consequently, one can recognize that even between the tenth and thirteenth centuries the original reading of 15:29 had been preserved in some manuscripts and seems not to be influenced by unintentional changes.

However, manuscripts 323, 945, 1739 and 1891 add the negative form of the Golden Rule after καὶ τῆς πορνείας in wording similar to D 05, with the alteration of θέλετε into θέλητε. Minuscule 614 differs at this point in 15:29.[70] On one hand 614 has similarities with 323, 945, 1739 in v. 20 and on the other hand with the wording D 05 in v. 29, and looks like a mix of readings.[71] Thus, one can recognize the tendency

---

64. This text is an excellent representative of the Alexandrian type, although in Acts "it shows also the influence of the Koine or Byzantine type." Metzger, *Text of New Testament*, 62.

65. The phrase in 1739 and 1891 (as well as minuscle 945 (eleventh) and minuscle 323 (twelfth)) starts after καὶ τῆς πορνείας (in D 05 it starts after αἵματος), contain in καὶ ὅσα ἂν μὴ θέλωσιν ... instead of καὶ ὅσα μὴ θέλουσιν ... in D 05 (here the particle ἂν is the indicator of contingency), αὑτοῖς instead of ἑαθτοῖς, and ends with ποιεῖν instead of the imperative form ποιεῖε in D 05. Thus the phraseology of 1739 and 1891 betray the latest rewording of the negative form of the Golden rule found in D 05. Metzger sees that the ancestor of 1739 was written in the fourth century. Metzger, *Text of New Testament*, 65.

66. Parker, *Introduction*, 286.

67. It is reflected in minuscule 2344 (eleventh), minuscules 36, 610, 1241, 1505 (twelfth), in 614 (thirteenth) and 453, 1409, 1678 (fourteenth).

68. Minuscule 81 dated eleventh century represents in Acts the Alexandrian text type. Minuscule 614 dated thirteenth century contains a large number of pre-Byzantine readings, many of them of the Western type of text. Metzger, *Text of New Testament*, 63–64. Minuscule 1175 dated tenth century.

69. Metzger provides dating for this text. Metzger, *Textual Commentary on Greek NT*, 386. The reading with πνικτοῦ is exceptional.

70. The addition of the golden rule in 614 starts after καὶ τῆς πορνείας like D 05 in 15:29, and finishes with ποιεῖε like D 05, but contains αὑτοῖς unlike D 05 and γενέσται (instead of γίνεσται in D 05).

71. This text seems to be copied from an ancestor which had mixed type of text by dictation as it reflects the errors of hearing. Metzger defines this type of text as pre-Byzantine with influence of

in the majority of minuscules of ninth and twelfth centuries to repeat the wording of v. 20 in v. 29. This could be a result of misinterpreting πνικτός which in the ninth century did not make any clear theological sense for the scribes.

The text in Acts 21:25 was most influenced by the attempts of correctors. Most of the variant readings in minuscules at this point fall into three patterns. The first pattern (33, 1409 and 2344) preserves the fourfold tradition without any additions to the text. The second pattern (945, 1739, 1891 and 36, 181, 307, 453, 614, 1678) keeps the list of four prohibitions of the Decree, but adds a phrase before it. In 945, 1739, 1891 this additional phrase is κρίναντες μηδὲν τοιοῦτο τηρεῖν αὐτούς ἀλλὰ φυλάσσεσθαι. In 36, 181, 307, 453, 614, 1678 the phrase is κρίναντες μηδὲν τοιοῦτο τηρεῖν αὐτούς εἰ μὴ φυλάσσεσθαι αὐτούς. The third pattern is in 1175, which follows the threefold tradition, omitting καὶ πορνείαν and has no additions regarding the cancellation of the Mosaic law. From this fact one can conclude that even in the tenth century the reading of the Decree could reflect the cultic text form. This provides further evidence that the Decree originally contained four prohibitions rooted in the cultic regulations of Torah.

However, a variety of the minuscules after the fourth and fifth centuries shows the tendency to change the meaning of the Decree into the ethical form. The earliest manuscripts preserve the four prohibitions without any additional elaboration.[72] Thus, the uncials, except D 05, support the fourfold reading. The most authoritative of them (ℵ 01, A 02 and B 03) more easily understood as referring to the laws of Torah rather than to Christian ethics. The omission of τῆς πορνείας from 15:20 of 𝔓45 shows a tendency to view the Decree in a cultic way.[73] These uncials have support from the minuscules 33, 81 and 1409, also with a tendency to a cultic threefold form in 1175.

The earliest evidence of departure from the cultic understanding of the Decree to the ethical one appears in the fifth century in D 05, where both 15:20 and 29 omit καὶ τοῦ πνικτοῦ and add the negative form of the Golden Rule.[74] Moreover, D 05 in 21:25 includes the phrase κρίναντες μηδὲν τοιοῦτο τηρεῖν αὐτούς εἰ μὴ

Western reading. Metzger, *Text of New Testament*, 64.

72. Alexandrian witnesses in ℵ 01, A 02 and B 03 contain the fourfold reading without the addition of the Golden Rule in 15:20, 29 or 21:25. The fourfold tradition appears also in C 04, E 06, L and Ψ with insertion of an additional phrase only in 21:25. However this phrase could be derived from one common ancestor with D05 if one keeps in mind that C 04 was contemporary to D 05 and was influenced by Western readings. Later E 06, L and Ψ inherited the same wording.

73. Metzger mentions P. H. Menoud's view that the original form of the Decree was twofold to which the 𝔓45 added καὶ τοῦ πνικτοῦ from kashrut, while the Western tradition interpreted it in the ethical way adding καὶ τῆς πορνείας and the negative form of the Golden Rule. Metzger argues against the hypothetical twofold Decree. He states that no manuscript was found to support this hypothesis. Moreover, "the fact that in 15:20 πνικτοῦ precedes καὶ τοῦ αἵματος is hardly compatible with the theory that the addition was made in order to clarify and extend the meaning of αἵματος." Metzger, *Textual Commentary on Greek NT*, 381–82.

74. It is noteworthy that D 05 is the only codex which omits καὶ τοῦ πνικτοῦ in all three verses of Acts and adds a form of the Golden Rule.

φυλάσσεσθαι αὐτούς, giving the impression that the following list of prohibitions were the temporary rudiments of Mosaic law. This inclusion later influenced the reading of Acts 21:25 in C 04, E 06, L and Ψ.

Subsequent attempts to fit the prohibitions of the Decree into the ethical explanation take place in minuscules 323, 945, 1739 and 1891 with the addition of the negative form of the Golden Rule. Furthermore, as mentioned above, 945, 1739 and 1891 together with 36, 181, 307, 453, 614, 1678 also imported the additional phrase into Acts 21:29. All these changes became the common tendency from the tenth century onwards. There were no manuscripts with readings similar to 𝔓45, ℵ 01, A 02 or B 03 produced between the twelfth and fourteenth centuries. Instead, the dominant Western reading in Europe, based on a preference for D 05, expressed the ethical form of the Decree. This preference was the result of the patristic tradition, which influenced the correctors of D 05.[75] The dominance of one reading above others for centuries resulted in a loss of the original meaning of the Decree.

Patristic Interpretation of the Text of the Apostolic Decree

The purpose of this section is to argue that many of the variant readings of the Decree represent intentional alterations of the text, which took place in the third and fourth centuries as the result of Jewish-Christian polemic which was partly preserved by the church fathers.

Causes of Anti-Jewish Polemic in the Early Christian Church

During first three Christian centuries many exegetical works written by Christian apologists contained something *adversus Iudaeos*.[76] It happened in spite of the fact that the church originally consisted entirely of Jewish Christians, and was built on the foundation of Old Testament prophecies and teaching.[77] Early Christians depended on Jewish exegetical practice and knowledge.[78] Moreover, for some time, "the very boundaries between Jewish and Christian practice remain blurred and porous."[79]

---

75. Patristic literature which formed the tradition of the ethical interpretation of the Decree will be discussed in the section 3 of this chapter.

76. Horbury, *Jews and Christians*, 201.

77. Chadwick, *East and West*, 3.

78. Horbury, *Jews and Christians*, 205, 219. He observes "great similarities between the forms of midrashic and later patristic literature."

79. Fonrobert, "Jewish Christians, Judaizers, and Christian Anti-Judaism," 237.

The First Cause of Anti-Jewish Polemic

The first cause of anti-Jewish polemic was a constant and increasing Jewish hatred toward the Christian movement. Pliny, a non-Christian author, noted the increasing distinction between Jews and Christians.[80] It was also reflected in works of Celsus of the second CE and Porphyry of the third CE that the Christians, whose religion originated in Judaism and who have built their doctrines on Jewish laws, finally turned away from practicing Jewish laws.[81] Christians depended on Judaism in matters of morality, especially in "three moral concepts—love, sexual purity and avoidance of idolatry."[82] Christians tended to minimize the Old Testament's validity in the epoch of the New Testament.[83] They replaced reading the law in synagogues by reading lectionaries, and insisted on demarcation between Christians and Jews. The anti-Jewish polemic of this early period can be identified as apologetic, "written in 'defence' of the new faith of the Christians."[84]

Although the church fathers of the second century predominantly cited the fourfold form of the Apostolic Decree verbatim, they developed the new theological pattern of Christianity itself.[85] This influenced the church to deny the Jewishness of the apostles. The apologetic works of Tertullian and Cyprian against the Jews reflect this.[86] At the same time, the new theological pattern did not deny the laws of Torah, but viewed them as fulfilled in Christ. Since the Jews rejected Christ, their customs were presumed by Christian apologists as rebellious against God. At the same time in *Dialogue with Trypho* Justin Martyr expresses a belief that those "who have been persuaded by . . . to observe the legal dispensation along with their confession of God in Christ, shall probably be saved."[87] Controversy came to its climax in *Peri Pascha*, the work of Melito of Sardis,

---

80. Räisänen, *Rise of Christian Beliefs*, 247.

81. Lieu, *Neither Jew Nor Greek?*, 14–15. In addition, one may note that the Jerusalem Council solution in Acts 15 was given to explain the reason why Christians viewed the keeping of the entire Mosaic code as unnecessary.

82. Guy, *Introducing Early Christianity*, 32. Pliny the Younger shows that Christians refused to worship pagan gods and the emperor, bound themselves by an oath not to commit any wrongdoings including adultery (*ne adulteria committerent*), and practiced table fellowship at their assemblies with food "of an ordinary and innocent kind" *ad capiendum cibum promiscuum tamen et innoxium* (Letter 96, LCL William Melmoth translation). The mentioning of "innocent" food might be chosen to defend Christians against wrong accusations of cannibalism.

83. Horbury, *Jews and Christians*, 205–6.

84. Jacobs, "Jews and Christians,", 175.

85. Clement of Alexandria quotes Acts 15:20 according to Alexandrian text type and Tertullian in his *Apology* refers to matters mentioned in the Alexandrian reading of the Decree.

86. Apologetic works included Tertullian, *Adv. Jud.*, and Cyprian, *Test*. Also Aristo of Pella, *A Disputation of Jason and Papiscus concerning Christ* (assumed as written by 135 CE), was mentioned by Celsus and Origen.

87. Justin, *Dialogue with Trypho*, 47 (ANF 1:218). It is noteworthy that the dialogue was based on real interviews and represented contemporary understanding of the topic.

dated to the second half of the second century.[88] Here Melito justified the punishment, by death, that had fallen upon the rebellious Jewish nation.

During anti-Jewish polemic in the second century Orthodox Christianity "wrenched the scriptures from the Jews."[89] For this aim, "ethical teachings of the Bible were lavishly used and assimilated to the new law of Jesus," while the "irrational" commandments were abandoned.[90] During controversy even the Pentateuchal passages on diet and ritual were symbolically interpreted.[91] At the same time Lucian, who lived between 120 and 200 CE, pictured Christians as those who can excommunicate one "for eating some forbidden food (probably meat of the idolatrous sacrifices)."[92] This reveals that the Christian writers did not deny the laws of Torah, but explained them as fulfilled in Christ and no more applicable in literal sense for practical use. Consequently, even in the second century CE there were signs of the common Christian practice not to keep Jewish ritual laws in the way Jews did.

The Second Cause of Anti-Jewish Polemic

The second cause of anti-Jewish polemic was persecutions from Gentile Rome, in many cases triggered by the Jews.[93] In those cases the church fathers referred to the Decree in apology for Christian purity in the face of persecutions, pagan immorality, and idol worship. Also, there were many gnostic sects which represented Christian faith in a way unacceptable to both Jews and Gentiles, provoking enmity. They practiced either extremely liberal or extremely ascetic lifestyles based on a revelation of "gnosis." Thus, Marcion doubted that the deficient law, some parts of which need to be cancelled, was imposed by God.[94] The *Gospel of Truth* rejects the Jewish background of Christianity, replacing it with the Christian revelation pattern.[95] Two other gnostic

---

88. Lieu, *Neither Jew Nor Greek*, 13.

89. Räisänen, *Rise of Christian Beliefs*, 281. See also polemic described in Ehrman, "Text as Window," 366–67.

90. Räisänen, *Rise of Christian Beliefs*, 281. He states that as a result of anti-Jewish polemic "circumcision of the flesh was replaced with circumcision of the heart, observance of the law with obedience to moral command."

91. Horbury, *Jews and Christians*, 221. In the writings of church fathers the laws of purity and diet seemed to be fulfilled by the Messiah. The Jews who rejected Messiah thus were contradistinguished by their practical application of the laws. This process of demarcation from Judaism made Christians ignorant of the literal interpretation of the laws.

92. Lucian, *Passing of Peregrinus*, 18–19.

93. Jacobs, "Jews and Christians," 175. He notes that the Jews in the Roman Empire "prayed against Christians, met them acrimoniously in the marketplace of religious ideas, and even cheered as they were tortured and executed by unsympathetic Roman authorities."

94. Räisänen, *Rise of Christian Beliefs*, 279–80. Both Marcion and Ptolemy interpreted the Jewish scriptures at the point of extreme disregard of their value. At the same time Räisänen states that Marcion was "less anti-Jewish than were his orthodox opponents."

95. Räisänen, *Rise of Christian Beliefs*, 278.

texts of that time, the *Apocryphon of John* and *Hypostasis of the Archons*, overturn some OT narratives to remove the Jewish tradition from them.[96] In the middle of the second century Celsus recognizes the diversity as "one of the principal marks of the Christian movement" of his time.[97]

Along with extreme practice, which allowed partaking of any food, there was a radical approach of some Gnostics avoiding any meat in their diet.[98] So-called Montanists, Marcionites, and Encratites kept an ascetic vegetarian diet.[99] Because of their theological views those groups were marginalized by the growing number of Orthodox. However, the diversity of practices was not reduced in the first two centuries, but was increasing.

The Orthodox apologists insisted that not the whole law, but only some parts of the law were canceled. They believed that it did not change the plan of God, which people misunderstood from the beginning. It was assumed that "God's moral law is permanently valid, whereas the 'irrational' part of the law had only a temporal purpose."[100] Among the irrational parts of the law the church fathers viewed the ritual law as well as the dietary laws of Torah. This view was expressed by Tertullian who stated that the dietary laws, "were imposed on the Jews because of their gluttony."[101]

At the same time, Justin Martyr viewed the dietary laws as God's institution, when he says to the Jews, "God by the mouth of Moses commanded you to abstain from unclean and improper and violent animals."[102] He traces the content of the Apostolic Decree to Noah's time pointing out that God gave an order to Noah "to eat of every animal, but not of flesh with the blood, which is *dead*."[103] Thus, he links the dietary laws not only to Moses, but also to Noah. Yet Orthodox Christianity came to a covenantal *nomism* under an angle different from the OT. The "irrational" parts of the law had been removed, some were reinterpreted by the moral commands of Jesus, some spiritualized, and the law of the OT was replaced by the "law of Christ."[104]

---

96. Räisänen, *Rise of Christian Beliefs*, 278.

97. Chadwick, *From Apostolic Times*, 4.

98. McGowan, "Food, Ritual, and Power," 150. The avoiding of meat and wine in a diet of early Christians was due to their prominence in pagan worship as an object of sacrifice. The liberal approach of Gnostics was based on superior knowledge and belief that the idol is nothing and that sacredness of sacrifice partaken with this meat would not pollute it as a food. It differs from Paul's view, when he stated that freedom of diet can defile in Cor 8:7, 10, 13; 10:27–29.

99. McGowan, "Food, Ritual, Power," 150.

100. Räisänen, *Rise of Christian Beliefs*, 279. Though Justin never spells out this distinction of laws, Räisänen believes that the distinction between "rational" and "irrational" parts is implicitly present in his writings. Justin, *Dialogue with Trypho*, 10–21 (ANF 1:199–204).

101. Räisänen, *Rise of Christian Beliefs*, 280.

102. Justin, *Dialogue with Trypho*, 20 (ANF 1:204).

103. Justin, *Dialogue with Trypho*, 20 (ANF 1:204).

104. Räisänen, *Rise of Christian Beliefs*, 281. He states that "the actual discontinuity" between Judaism and Christianity was "camouflaged with the use of language suggesting continuity."

During the periods of persecution those who were allowed to eat meat sacrificed to idols had an advantage of physical survival over those who avoided some kinds of meat.[105] During the persecutions, the Orthodox multitude of Christian believerscame to "imperial power and authority" and the discrete minorities were treated as heretics. The majority viewed the dietary laws of Torah as belonging to a group of the ritual laws of Torah. That presumed the viewing of those laws as ones of temporary validity or signs of a Jewish cult, replaced by the new covenant.

The Third Cause of Anti-Jewish Polemic

In many cases anti-Jewish polemic was a reaction to the observance of Jewish rituals by some Christian believers.[106] The premise for that was found in fact that the converts from God-fearers would continue to keep Jewish laws because "they know the Law *too* well and know that the requirements of food and calendar are not so easily disregarded."[107] During the first centuries CE Christianity still had some Jewish groups in minority. Some of them gave up their Jewish style of life and had been absorbed into the large Gentile Christianity, when others were "alienated from Gentile Christianity, which came to regard them as heretical."[108]

This process can be illustrated by the changes in the attitudes of the Fathers between Justin Martyr and Chrysostom. Justin Martyr expressed tolerance when stated that he "could regard Jewish believers as in order if they kept traditional Jewish customs."[109] Rodney Stark confirms that up to the third and fourth centuries some Jewish and Christian communities were interdependent and closely related.[110] At the end of the fourth century Chrysostom employs a rigorous tone toward some Christians in Antioch who venerated the synagogue to be a holy place, because of "the Law and the books of the prophets kept there," and who watched and participated in Jewish festivals.[111]

This shift in orthodox attitude toward Jewish customs can be explained by the parting of the ways "between mainstream Christianity and Jewish Christianity

---

105. McGowan, "Food, Ritual, Power," 150.

106. Fonrobert states that the parting of ways "is now viewed as having taken place much later and through a more gradual and varied process." He insists that Jewish Christians were claimed to be heretics "because church fathers or rabbis categorize them as such" and became a marginal movement. Fonrobert, "Jewish Christians," 235, 252–53.

107. Lieu, *Neither Jew Nor Greek*, 36–37, 45. She states that it is clear that some God-fearers observed Sabbath and kosher laws.

108. Ferguson, *Backgrounds of Early Christianity*, 614.

109. Chadwick, *From Apostolic Times*, 8.

110. Stark, *Triumph of Christianity*, 79.

111. This quotation of John Chrysostom, *Against the Jews*, 1.5.850 (TLG) was translated in English and mentioned by Fonrobert, "Jewish Christians," 239–41. Fonrobert stresses that Chrysostom's sermons called Christians to affirm their identity by rejection of involvement in Jewish practices. Thus Christians had to avoid even greetings with the Jews.

rather than simply between Christianity as a single whole and rabbinic Judaism."[112] Fergusson, Parkers and Wilken suppose that an assault in Antioch at Chrysostom's time was rather an issue of authority than the need of local society. They argued that the issue in Antioch had an ecclesiastical origin, gathering all religious practices and bending them in conformity to Orthodoxy.[113]

Stages of Forming a New Theological Pattern for the Content of the Decree

The three causes of anti-Jewish polemic mentioned above were forming a new theological and ritual pattern, which replaced the original Jewish Christianity. According to Metzger the patristic quotations can "serve to localize and date readings and types of text in Greek manuscripts and versions."[114] The process of altering the text of the Decree can be subdivided into four periods: the period of theological transition, the period of theological pre-shift, the period of theological shift and the period of variant readings.

The Period of Theological Transition (c. 75–225 CE)

The period of theological transition embraces the writings of the Apostolic Fathers and the Fathers of the late second century. The main tendencies of this period may be assumed to be self-defence in time of persecution, and polemic against heretical movements that were based on the Jewish inheritance of the early church and Jewish beliefs mixed with faith in Christ. At the same time the Jews triggered many persecutions against Christians with the help of Gentile authorities. Thus the church was involved in anti-Jewish polemic. The interpretation of the Decree was subjected to this struggle for self-definition.

This period had the following main features: 1) preservation of the Decree's original reading, 2) interpretation of the Decree in accordance with its origin in Jewish cult, 3) growth of anti-Jewish polemic and 4) avoiding mentioning the Decree in the polemic. There is enough data to say that the content of the Decree had been altered through the first four centuries. It becomes clear from references to the Decree by the church fathers. The direct quotations of the Decree will be summarized first, followed by the possible allusions and echoes.

---

112. Dunn, *Parting of the Ways*, 239. Fonrobert argues against Dunn, who following F. C. Baur pictures early Christianity as two competing blocks, namely, the Gentile Christianity led by Paul's radical freedom from the law and the primitive church headed by Peter with its conservative attitude to the law. Dunn also accepts the view of A. Ritschl, who included the group of Hellenistic Christianity, which was in-between Jewish and Gentile Christians and functioned as gapfiller between the major parties.

113. Fonrobert, "Jewish Christians," 241–42.

114. Metzger, *Text of New Testament*, 86.

The earliest direct quotations of the Decree appear in the works of Clement of Alexandria (150–215 CE). Clement quotes the Apostolic Decree in *Paedagogus* and *Stromata* following word order in Acts 15:29 of the Alexandrian reading and keeping its fourfold tradition.[115] Clement believes that one may buy things from markets asking no questions "with the exception of the things mentioned in the Catholic epistle of all the apostles . . . which is written in the Acts of the Apostles, and conveyed to the faithful by the hands of Paul himself."[116] According to that "Catholic epistle of all the apostles" Clement sees that Christians "must of necessity abstain from things offered to idols, and from blood, and from things strangled, and from fornication, from which keeping themselves they should do well."[117] This quotation lacks any form of the Golden Rule. Clement might have quoted either a Greek manuscript of Acts, or the copy of the apostolic letter which was carried by Paul and Barnabas.

Tertullian's (160–225 CE) *Apology* shed light on practices of some Christians in the end of the second century CE. He wrote, "for we do not include even animal's blood in our natural diet."[118] He also uses the word *abstinemus* (which corresponds with ἀπέχεσθαι of the Decree) to show that Christians abstain from things strangled or that die of themselves. He also explains the reason for abstaining from strangled things; "that we may not in any way be polluted by blood."[119] Here the use of the word *contaminemur*, "polluted," corresponds to τῶν ἀλισγημάτων of the Decree in Acts 15:20. The wording Tertullian provides in his *Apology* has strong similarities with the wording of the Decree.

Further, Tertullian explains the Christian view on diet and its rationale. For him the rationale is, "in any way not be polluted by blood, even if it is buried in the meat."[120] This means that Tertullian keeps the prohibition of blood consumption in mind when writing his Apology. He uses the word *contaminemur* to refer also to blood hidden in meat as also forbidden for Christians.[121] He describes Christian marriage as "guarded by chastity, supremely careful and faithful."[122] He declares it, "safe from random intercourse and from all excess after marriage."[123] Tertullian argues that πορνεία flourishes among his contemporary gentile citizens and cannot be found among the Christians. He has no other example of any group like Christians

---

115. Clement, *Instructor*, 7 (ANF 2:252). Clement, *Stromata*, 15 (ANF 2:427).
116. Clement, *Stromata*, 15 (ANF 2:427).
117. Clement, *Stromata*, 15 (ANF 2:427).
118. Tertullian, *Apology*, 51
119. Tertullian, *Apology*, 51
120. Tertullian, *Apology*, 51–53.
121. Tertullian, *Apology*, 53. Another Tertullian work keeps the word "contaminate" in connection to meats and lusts together and describes the Israelites who had by God been "fed forty years with manna, . . . and not contaminated with human passions, or fed on this world's meats, but fed on 'angel's loaves.'" Tertullian, *Answer to the Jews*, 3 (ANF 3:155).
122. Tertullian, *Apology*, 55.
123. Tertullian, *Apology*, 55.

who keep their moral standards high. These high moral standards were an important part of Christian teaching and not only a cultural issue; otherwise, Christians would not keep them inviolately under persecution.

However, a number of church fathers and martyrs before Clement and Tertullian echoed the Decree, including Ignatius of Antioch, Polycarp, Justun Martyr, and Ireneus of Lyon, though their works do not preserve any direct or indirect quotations of the Decree. Their sayings contain condemnation of those who join Jewish feasts and rites. From the beginning it was merely a prohibition of sacrifices, and soon it came to extreme rejection of any association with Jews, rejection of Jewish Scriptures, and denial of their culture. Horbury rightly notices that controversy between the Jews and Christians on the law was almost unavoidable.[124] As a result the law again became a subject of debate. In contrast to the Jerusalem Council's peaceful approach, the law in the works of church fathers seems to become an occasion for accusation against the Jews.

Ignatius (35 or 50–107 CE) teaches, "It is absurd to speak of Jesus Christ with the tongue, and to cherish in the mind a Judaism which has now come to an end. For where there is Christianity there cannot be Judaism."[125] He calls on Christians "to abstain" from schismatics and warns the Philadelphians not to listen to those who preach the Jewish law, and states that if someone "deems certain kinds of food abominable," he is led by the apostate dragon.[126] At the same time he invites the disciples to live according to Christian principles and advocates a careful attitude to the written laws.[127] His phrase παρανομίᾳ ῥυπανθῇ witnesses that he values the law, but his enmity against Judaism comes to a critical point when he says, "If anyone celebrates the passover alone with the Jews . . . he is partaker with those that killed the Lord and His apostles."[128]

Arguing with gnostic teaching, Ignatius refers to the Noachic law saying, "Do not altogether abstain from wine and flesh, for these things are not to be viewed with abhorrence, since [the Scripture] saith, 'Ye shall eat the good things of the earth.' And again, 'Ye shall eat flesh even as herbs.'"[129] It is noteworthy that in the second century Ignatius still applies to the Gentiles dietary rules known since Noah (Gen 9:3). He does not cite the rest of the text of Gen 9:4, which contains the prohibition of blood consumption. The quotation itself presumes that Ignatius does not doubt the validity of God's command

---

124. Horbury, *Jews and Christians*, 201.

125. Ignatius, *Epistle to the Magnesians*, 10 (ANF 1:63). According to Eusebius, Ignatius of Antioch in Syria was the second bishop of the church in Antioch after Euodius.

126. Ignatius, *Epistle to Philadelphians*, 6 (ANF 1:80, 82–83).

127. Ignatius, *Epistle to Hero*, 1 (ANF 1:113).

128. Ignatius, *Epistle to the Philippians*, 11, 14 (ANF 1:119).

129. Ignatius, *Epistle to Hero*, 1 (ANF 1:113). Here Ignatius undermined the polemic against Gnostics. He calls his readers to keep from the extremes in diet, as he says, "devote thyself to fasting and prayer, but not beyond measure, lest thou destroy thyself thereby."

given to Noah on account of food. This reveals that he understands the matters of the Decree linked to cult and to food, and not to ethical concepts alone.

Polycarp of Smyrna (69–150 CE) cites the formula of the Decree teaching to "abstain from covetousness, and that ye be chaste and truthful . . . If a man does not keep himself from covetousness, he shall be defiled by idolatry, and shall be judged as one of the heathen." [130] Further, Polycarp quotes 1 Thess 5:22, "Abstain from any form of evil."[131] The synonymous use of "idolatry" and "defilement" reveals that Christian writers of that time viewed Christian worship in terms of temple worship. The association of "defilement" with spiritual matters such as "covetousness" would presume worship in a spiritual temple. Spiritual idolatry was assumed to be the defilement of true worship. The spiritual approach to the temple was a result of common Christian practice not to sacrifice at all, "as the sacrifice of Christ on the cross had superseded all sacrifices."[132] Using wording similar to the Decree, Polycarp was trying to delineate spiritual idolatry. Thus the Apostolic Fathers might have introduced broadly an ethical explanation of the first prohibition of the Decree in responding to the main concern of that time, which was the issue of idolatry.

Justin Martyr (100–165 CE) taught that now a final law in Christ was given universally and it puts to an end and abrogates the previous law given solely to the Jews.[133] This view on the law reveals that the early church writers linked Christian conduct to the universal law of God instead of to Mosaic customs. The apostles likely did not place the dietary laws into a group of Mosaic customs, but fitted them into patterns of the universal law of God. Similar to Polycarp, Justin Martyr expresses particular concern about fornication. It might reveal the special need of the congregation to which Justin addressed his ms, "We who formerly delighted in fornication, but now embrace chastity alone."[134] This statement shows that in the days of Justin the things prohibited by the fourth regulation of the Decree had a literal application.

The author of the *Letter to Diognetus* combined numerous signs of Jewish identity, "But as to their scrupulosity concerning meats, and their superstition as respects the Sabbaths, and their boasting about circumcision, and their fancies about fasting and the new moons, which are utterly ridiculous and unworthy of notice,– I do not think that you require to learn anything from me."[135] The words reveal that Christians were still in disagreement about the role of some Jewish practices. This evidence from the patristic literature during the period of theological transition is silent in regards the text of the Decree because of its Jewish background.

130. Polycarp, *Epistle to the Philippians*, 11 (ANF 1:35).
131. Polycarp, *Epistle to the Philippians*, 11 (ANF 1:35).
132. Guy, *Introducing Early Christianity*, 74.
133. Justin, *Dialogue with Trypho*, 11 (ANF 1:200).
134. Justin, *First Apology*, 14 (ANF 1:167).
135. *Epistle to Diognetus*, 26.

The Period of Theological Pre-Shift (c. 225–320 CE)

The period of theological pre-shift is represented by the attitude toward the content of the Decree in the works of the church fathers of the third century. This period can be characterized by two features: 1) the church fathers understand the Jewish background of the Decree, 2) but at the same time build their theology on a different ground. The Fathers of this period appear to be influenced by a new anti-Jewish theological pattern. Content of the Decree, which was of the Jewish origin seems not to fit into the new anti-Jewish pattern and becomes a text with an unspecified meaning.

The process of the pattern replacement can be found in works of Origen (185–254 CE), who mentions πνικτῶν in two works.[136] In *Contra Celsus* he calls it "τροφῇ δαιμόνων" when he states, "Τὸ μὲν γὰρ εἰδωλόθυτον θύεται δαιμονίοις, καὶ οὐ χρὴ τὸν τοῦ θεοῦ ἄνθρωπον κοινωνὸν «τραπέζης δαιμονίων» γίνεσθαι."[137] The full citation of Origen in English translation reveals the context of his thought:

> . . . for that which is offered to idols is sacrificed to demons, and a man of God must not join the table of demons. As to things strangled, we are forbidden by Scripture to partake of them, because the blood is still in them; and blood, especially the odour arising from blood, is said to be the food of demons. Perhaps, then, if we were to eat of strangled animals, we might have such spirits feeding along with us. And the reason which forbids the use of strangled animals for food is also applicable to the use of blood.[138]

In addition, Origen recalls the saying of Sextus, "which is known to most Christians: 'The eating of animals, . . . is a matter of indifference; but to abstain from them is more agreeable to reason.'"[139]

Origen alludes to the Decree in Acts 15:29, ". . . μόνα τά, ὡς ὠνόμασαν, «ἐπάναγκες» ἀπαγορεύουσαν ἐσθίειν ταῦτα δ' ἐστὶ τὰ ἤτοι εἰδωλόθυτα ἢ τὰ πνικτὰ ἢ τὸ αἷμα."[140] This account of the Decree omits πορνείας. Fee describes Origen's

---

136. Greek text is found in Thesaurus Linguae Graecae (Origen of Alexandria, *Contra Celsus*, 8.30.3, 7, 8). English translation of this text appears in Origen, *Against Celsus*, 8:30 (ANF 4:650). Another text is found in Origen, *Comm. Matt.*, 11.12.58, TLG, translated in Origen, *Commentary on Matthew*, 11.12 (ANF 10:441).

137. Greek text is cited by Origen, *Contra Celsus*, 8.30, TLG. Note, that Clement of Rome provides the explanation of this term using the account of the Decree with some additional references: "«τραπέζης δαιμόνων» μὴ μεταλαμβάνειν (λέγω δὲ εἰδωλοθύτων, νεκρῶν, πνικτῶν, θηρια λώτων, αἵματος), μὴ ἀκαθάρτως βιοῦν, ἀπὸ κοίτης γυναικὸς λούεσθαι." The additional references link the Decree stronger to Leviticus. However, the link evidently has been made to dietary code rather than to holiness code. Clement of Rome, *Clem. Hom.*, 7.8.1.5, TLG.

138. Origen, *Against Celsus*, 8:30 (ANF 4:650).

139. Origen, *Against Celsus*, 8:30 (ANF 4:650). Here Origen cites the work of Sextus.

140. Greek text is cited by Origen, *Cels.*, 8.29.26, TLG. English translation reveals that Origen cites the Decree in the following wording, "They say it is necessary to abstain, namely, 'things offered to idols, things strangled, and blood.'" Origen, *Against Celsus*, 8:29 (ANF 4:650).

citing of Scripture as "precise."¹⁴¹ According to Metzger, Origen's comments were made according to 𝔓45 preserving the cultic form of the Decree.¹⁴² The fact of preferring of 𝔓45 cultic reading either may presume that it was the earliest form of the Decree, or that it was the form of the Decree preferred by Origen. It seems that for Origen the cultic form of the Decree is more reasonable, since it provides Jewish background of the Decree.

At the same time the works of Origen reveal the tincture of anti-Jewish polemic. In Origen's *Commentary on Matthew* he blames the Jews for their unbelieving hearts full of wickedness.¹⁴³ Origen sees that the Jews are defiled by their hostility, while the Christians are purified. He shows awareness that harm is not caused by the nature of the meat, but by the eater's defiled conscience. And he believes that a pure mind makes all things pure. Therefore Origen argues against Jewish kosher laws.

In addition to Jewish diet restriction to things accounted clean, Origen mentions that the Jews "do not use in their food the blood of an animal nor the flesh of an animal torn by wild beasts."¹⁴⁴ He believes that Jesus liberated Christians from "the imposition of a burdensome code of rules in regard to food."¹⁴⁵ Origen pictures Jesus "making all meats clean" according to Mark 7:19 and Matthew 15:11.¹⁴⁶ And from this perspective he treats the Decree in these words: "He then eats in faith who believes that that which is eaten has not been sacrificed in the temples of idols, and that it is not strangled nor blood; but he eats not of faith who is in doubt about any of these things."¹⁴⁷

However, Räisänen explains that the text Mark 7:15 cannot be assumed as the declaration made by Jesus that all foods are clean, otherwise it is "hard to understand why table-fellowship later became so controversial an issue (Gal 2:11–13)."¹⁴⁸ The arguing between Paul and Judaizers led to hot polemic during the Jerusalem Council that can be explained only from the viewpoint that Jesus did not teach a violation of Jewish dietary code.

---

141. Fee, "Use of the Greek Fathers," 192–93. He describes also the quotations by Eusebius as "moderately careful."

142. Metzger, *Textual Commentary on Greek NT*, 380.

143. Origen, *Commentary on Matthew*, 11–12 (*ANF* 10:440–41).

144. Origen, *Against Celsus*, 8:29 (*ANF* 4:650).

145. Origen, *Against Celsus*, 8:29 (*ANF* 4:650).

146. Origen, *Commentary on Matthew*, 12 (*ANF* 10:440).

147. Origen, *Commentary on Matthew*, 12 (*ANF* 10:441). Here Origen explains the list of chosen prohibitions pointing to a weakness of conscience. According to him one who knows that meat was sacrificed to idols pollutes his conscience when he eats it. Origen thus considers the pollution not to be connected to the nature of meat, but to opinions and beliefs.

148. Räisänen, *Rise of Christian Beliefs*, 252–53. He also believes that Jesus did not attack the temple cult, otherwise his disciples would not continue to attend the temple (Acts 2:46, 3:1, Matt 23–24) and observe Torah as they did.

Eusebius (260–340 CE) describes the beliefs of the martyrs of the early church, including Biblis who confessed Christians practices in the following manner: "How . . . could those eat children who do not think it lawful to taste the blood even of irrational animals?"[149] This citation is valuable as it stays out of anti-Jewish polemic. The purpose of this citation from its origin was to defend Christian lifestyle before Gentile extreme depravity. Thus the citation may serve as a balance for the opposite extreme, built up by Christian anti-Judaism. So, the citation of Eusebius is independent of this polemic, as it was not produced under pressure of dogma. From this one can assume that the citation reveals the real situation in the church, with a strong and deliberate conviction of the Christians to avoid blood consumption.

The data reveal that during the period of theological pre-shift the preservation of the original wording of the Decree made its fitting into the new theological pattern doubtful. As a result the text lost its original meaning and became difficult to interpret. The following period reveals attempts to explain the content of the Decree according to the new theological pattern.

The Period of Theological Shift (c. 320–380 CE)

This period is reflected in the works of the church fathers of the fourth century. It has two important features: 1) the church fathers quote the Decree with minor alterations in its wording and 2) they provide the interpretation of it under the strong influence of anti-Jewish polemic. At this time the alteration does not appear in the manuscripts of Acts, but in commentaries and periphrastic quotations of the Decree.

Ephrem the Syrian (306–373 CE) in his commentary uses the content of the Decree to recommend a wide range of dietary prohibitions.[150] Only after this preamble does he cite the four prohibitions, beginning with εἰδωλοθύτων, followed by αἵματος and πνικτοῦ. Then, instead of πορνείας, the quotation ends with θνησιμαίου.[151] Another time he lists the four prohibitions in an allusion to Acts 15:28, 29. After listing them, he adds "τὴν πολλὴν τῶν ἐντολῶν."[152] The facts of his deliberate use of the content of the Decree and his paraphrasing of it show an attempt to interpret the Decree in light of the changed theological pattern. Presuming the Jewish cultic pattern behind the content of the Decree, Ephrem fits it into the pattern of Christian ethics.

---

149. Eusebius, *Church History*, 5:1:26 (*NPNF* 1:214).

150. Ephrem the Syrian, *Sermo in secundum adventum domini nostri Iesu Christi*, 17.12, TLG, and *Interrogationes et responsiones*, 81.1, TLG.

151. The meaning of θνησιμαίων is "carcass of an animal, dead body." The prohibition of eating θνησιμαίων is written in Lev 7:24 and linked in vv. 26, 27 to the prohibition of blood consumption. Both prohibitions belong to the dietary law code.

152. Ephrem the Syrian, *Institutio ad monachos*, 358.12, TLG.

Another church father of that time, Cyril, bishop of Jerusalem (313–386 CE), notes that many Christians "stumble" in regard to meat.[153] He admonishes them, "neither condemn the men as sinners, nor abhor the flesh as strangled food." He justifies his order by the teaching of Paul in 1 Tim 4:1–5. However, nothing about "strangled" is stated there. Further, Cyril cites the Decree according to its cultic form: Καὶ γράφουσιν οἱ ἀπόστολοι καὶ οἱ πρεσβύτεροι πᾶσι τοῖς ἔθνεσι καθολικὴν ἐπιστολὴν, προηγουμένως τῶν εἰδωλοθύτων ἀπέχεσθαι, ἔπειτα δὲ καὶ αἵματος, καὶ πνικτοῦ.

One can notice that the Decree here appears in the form of indirect quotation. Moreover, it was introduced as καθολικὴν ἐπιστολὴν, written to all nations. This emphasis reveals a group of believers who associate themselves with apostolic authority. After the authority was established the word προηγουμένως "previously" appeared. Cyril here might express his belief that the Decree had temporary nature, but was still significant in his time. Then three prohibitions were casually recounted in a manner making αἵματος and πνικτοῦ look like additional restrictions to τῶν εἰδωλοθύτων of less importance.[154] With this Cyril condemned "the men of savage nature who, living like dogs, both lap up blood, in imitation of the manner of the fiercest beasts, and greedily devour things strangled."[155]

Later Cyril cites the Decree verbatim: ἀπέχεσθαι εἰδωλοθύτων καὶ αἵματος καὶ πνικτοῦ καὶ πορνείας, in fourfold tradition in the order preserved by Alexandrian text type (𝔓74, ℵ2, Ac, E, L, Ψ).[156] Cyril accompanies his quotation by the explanation:

> This Holy Spirit, who in unison with Father and Son has established a New Covenant in the Church Catholic, has set us free from the burdens of the law grievous to be borne, - those I mean, concerning things common and unclean, and meats, and Sabbaths, and new moon, and circumcision, and sprinklings, and sacrifices; which were given for a season and *had a shadow of the good things to come.*[157]

Cyril proves that the cancellation of the dietary laws refers to nothing other than the Decree in Acts 15:28, 29. He explains it as God's new covenant with the Catholic Church which frees Christians from unwanted practices. With all this Cyril assumes the authority of the apostolic letter and believes that "the Decree is universal from the

---

153. Cyril, *Catechetical Lectures*, 4.27–28 (NPNF 7:25–26). Cyril notes the diversity of opinions among the Christians of his time, when some of them eat meat offered to idols and some condemn those who do so.

154. Here Cyril notes that practice to abstain from things strangled and blood has continued to the present day in the Eastern Church, but was disregarded by the Latins. Cyril, *Catechetical Lectures*, 4.27 (NPNF 7:25).

155. Cyril, *Catechetical Lectures*, 4.27–28 (NPNF 7:25–26).

156. Cyril, *Catechetical Lectures*, 17.29 (NPNF 7:131). See Greek text in Cyril, *Catecheses ad illuminandos*, 17.29.17, TLG.

157. Cyril, *Catechetical Lectures*, 17.29 (NPNF 7:131). Here Cyril refers to Heb 10:1, which announces the end of the sacrificial system. Yet he does not provide any evidences for the canceling of dietary law from the OT.

Holy Ghost." The interpretation given by Cyril reveals that though the Decree is well known in its original form, its meaning was already influenced by the theological shift. The shift had a purely anti-Jewish nature, and appeared to demarcate the teaching of the Catholic Church from the Jewish background of Christianity, while preserving still a connection to apostolic authority.

With this one may note that John Chrysostom, bishop of Alexandria (347–407 CE), still quotes Acts 15:20, 21 according to the Alexandrian text type (preserved in ℵ 01, C 04, E 06, L).[158] He also quotes Acts 15:29 with minor changes using καὶ πνικτοῦ instead of plural πνικτῶν and omitting the article before the word according to the Alexandrian text type (in tradition found in 𝔓74, ℵ2, Ac, E 06, L, Ψ).[159] At the same time Chrysostom views consuming blood and what was strangled to be still under the curse of God, along with the flesh of beasts and birds which died in a trap.[160] Alluding to Gen 9:4 and Lev 17:11, 12, 14 he explains the rationale for the prohibition of blood consumption, stating that "the soul dwells in the blood" and πνικτῶν is the meat with its blood, thus he believes that those who eat the blood consume the souls.[161]

Finally, Chrysostom paraphrases Acts 21:25 with the insertion of his comments into the wording: "As touching the Gentiles which believe, we have written and concluded that they observe no such thing, save only that they keep themselves from things offered to idols, and from blood, and from strangled, and from fornication."[162] Although he cites the Decree with minor changes of articles and provides the full list of prohibitions which follow the order in the Alexandrian text type (𝔓74, ℵ, A, B, C, Ψ) his introduction to the list of prohibitions influences the meaning. Together with citing the original version of the Decree, Chrysostom upholds the polemic against the Judaizers in Antioch.[163] He fought against Christians who were regular members of the Antiochene congregation and were keeping Sabbath and observing Jewish rites and customs.[164]

---

158. John Chrysostom, *Hom. Act.*, 60.239.44–46, TLG. John cites in the first order the prohibitions of idolatry and fornication. He uses the wording "to abstain from pollutions of idols, and from fornication" to show his own interpretation of εἰδωλοθύτων. He refers these two prohibitions to the law of the apostles, not of Moses. He views that James divided the one legal prohibition of blood into two, "and from things strangled, and from blood" in purpose "to make the commandments many." Chrysostom views them as "necessary to be observed, because (these things) caused great evils." Yet he upheld that even the Jews "need observe no more (than these necessary things)." John Chrysostom, *Homilies on Acts*, 33 (*NPNF* 11:208). It is evident that alongside with quoting of the Decree John Chrysostom had given commentary on its four matters in full view of anti-Jewish polemic.

159. John Chrysostom, *Hom. Act.*, 60.240.29–30, TLG.

160. John Chrysostom, *De nativitate*, 92, 93, TLG. The list Chrysostom uses here seems to be more expanded then just four prohibitions of the Decree in Acts 15. It can be suggested that in the time of Chrysostom the four prohibitions of the Decree were not simply narrowed to be rudimentary practices of kashrut.

161. John Chrysostom, *Serm. Gen.*, 53.246.11, TLG.

162. John Chrysostom, *Homilies on Acts*, 46 (*NPNF* 11:278).

163. John Chrysostom, *Adv. Jud.*, 1.5, TLG.

164. Lieu, *Neither Jew Nor Greek*, 128. Lieu notes Chrysostom's attitude to the Jews as the destroyers

The same minor changes can be found in the works of other church fathers of the fourth century. Thus Didymus the Blind,[165] Diodorus of Tarsus,[166] Epiphanius, bishop of Salamis,[167] Cyril of Jerusalem,[168] Amphilochius, bishop of Iconium,[169] Severian, bishop of Gabala [170] and authors of the *Apostolic Constitution* used the fourfold list of prohibitions.[171] Those sources quoted the Decree of Acts 15:29 using καὶ πνικτοῦ instead of plural πνικτῶν and omitting the article before the word without any additions to the list of prohibitions. They also provided a variety of explanatory material and attempted to fit the Decree into the patterns of the newly formed theological shift. Ehrman believes that scribes of the third and fourth centuries altered words of Scripture "in order to make them more serviceable for the polemical task."[172]

The period of theological shift reveals the minor alterations of the text in patristic quotations which always coincide with developing anti-Jewish tendencies.[173] It is noteworthy that after Constantine's conversion, Christians began to persecute the Jews. The legislation against Jews prohibited the circumcision of Christian slaves, the intermarriages between Jews and Christians, and excluded Jews from all civil and political rights in Christian states.[174] Controversy was fierce and the emperor's edicts were called for to regulate the relationship of Jews and Christians in the empire. Those laws sometimes protected the welfare of Jews even more than that of some Christian sects that were perceived as heresies and which, in different ways, kept some Jewish religious practices.[175]

The indicators of the shift in theological patterns are contained in various documents. The *Gospel of Thomas*, dated around 340 CE, pictures Jesus teaching that "there

---

of the Christian flock (in *Adv. Jud.*, 4.3.6).

165. Didymus the Blind, *Trin.*, 39.624.2, TLG.

166. Diodorus of Tarsus, *Fr. in epistulam ad Romanos*, 100.18, 25, TLG. Diodorus changes the order of words and sometimes places separately.

167. Epiphanius, bishop of Salamis, *Pan.*, 1.331.19, TLG.

168. Cyril of Jerusalem, *Catech. ad illuminandos,* 17.29.18, TLG.

169. Amphilochius of Iconium, *Contra haereticos*, 769, 778, TLG.

170. Severian of Gabala, *Fr. in epistulam ad Galatas (in catenis)*, 298.18, TLG.

171. "Constitutions of the Holy Apostles" (*ANF*, 7:455). For Greek text see *Const. ap.*, 6.12.85, 109, TLG.

172. Ehrman, *Orthodox Corruption of Scripture*, 4.

173. It was asserted by J. Royse and E. Epp that the Western text in Acts "is anti-Judaic in several respects." Royse, "Scribal Tendencies in the Transmission of the Text, 240–41.

174. Stevenson, ed., *Creeds, Councils and Controversies*, 157. According to chronology the first was the law which prohibited the marriages of Christians and Jews of 388 CE. The laws ordered to consider such marriages as the equivalent of adultery. Another law of 415 CE allowed Jews to have a Christian slave but abolished their conversion to Judaism.

175. Stevenson, ed. *Creeds, Councils, Controversies*, 154–55. The edict from 423 CE commanded Christians do no harm to Jews and pagans who live quietly doing nothing contrary to law, but ordered to punish Manichaeans, Montanists, Novatianists, Protopaschites, and Sabbatians "with proscription of their goods and exile."

is no need to pray, fast . . . or obey any dietary or purity regulations (6; 14; 27; 104); the author thus rejects the Jewish identity altogether."[176] The anti-Jewish polemic amazingly influences the decision of the first church council, that of Acts 15 which becomes evident from three documents produced by the church in the period between the first and the fourth centuries.

The *Didache* composed in the late first century lacks anti-Jewish polemic. It pictures the custom of presenting the firstfruits in the early church (Πᾶσαν οὖν ἀπαρχὴν γεννημάτων ληνοῦ καὶ ἅλωνος, βοῶν τε καὶ προβάτων . . . τὴν ἀπαρχὴν λαβὼν δὸς κατὰ τὴν ἐντολήν).[177] Yet, instead of bringing the firstfruits to the temple or its altar, *Didache* suggests giving them to the priests and prophets (λαβὼν δώσεις τοῖς προφήταις· αὐτοὶ γάρ εἰσιν οἱ ἀρχιερεῖς ὑμῶν). It mentions Christians assembling on the [day] of the Lord (Κατὰ κυριακὴν δὲ Κυρίου συναχθέντες) and describes communion as "pure sacrifice" (ὅπως καθαρὰ ἡ θυσία ὑμῶν ἦ).[178] The purity of the sacrifice was highlighted by the words ἵνα μὴ κοινωθῇ ἡ θυσία ὑμῶν and referred to the law of Torah, Psalms and Prophets (starting with Exod 20:24, adding Ps 30:2, and Mal 1:11): Ἐν παντὶ τόπῳ καὶ χρόνῳ προσφέρειν μοι θυσίαν καθαράν· ὅτι βασιλεὺς μέγας εἰμί, λέγει Κύριος, καὶ τὸ ὄνομά μου θαυμαστὸν ἐν τοῖς ἔθνεσι.

By mentioning clean and unclean (καθαρὰ and μὴ κοινωθῇ) in relation to ἡ θυσία, the document suggests knowledge of the Jewish ritual law. In addition, *Didache* 6:3 states: Περὶ δὲ τῆς βρώσεως, ὃ δύνασαι βάστασον· ἀπὸ δὲ τοῦ εἰδωλοθύτου λίαν πρόσεχε· λατρεία γάρ ἐστι Θεῶν νεκρῶν "concerning food, bear what thou art able; but against that which is sacrificed to idols be exceedingly on thy guard; for it is the service of dead gods."[179] This was the only food prohibition mentioned in the document. In 5:1 πορνεῖαι and εἰδωλολατρίαι are described as deadly sins, while πνικτῶν and αἵματος do not occur. Their omission can be explained by the fact that the earliest preserved ms of *Didache* is dated to 1056 CE so its content could have been influenced by the ethical form of the Western reading of Acts 15.

The *Didascalia Apostolorum* (circa 230 CE) was modeled on the earlier *Didache* and wrongly attributed to apostolic authority at the time of the Jerusalem Council of Acts 15. *Didascalia* states that the apostles worked out and ratified the ordinances, confession and creed of the church.[180] However, the differences between these two documents are significant and reveal the crucial points of the anti-Jewish polemic which influenced writings after the first century CE. *Didascalia* attacks the laws of the "second legislation" in which Sabbath observance, body purification rituals and

---

176. Räisänen, *Rise of Christian Beliefs*, 277.
177. *Didache*, 13:3–5 (ANF 7:381).
178. *Didache*, 14.1, 2 (ANF 7:381).
179. *Didache*, 6:3 (ANF 7:379).
180. Fonrobert, "Jewish Christians," 243.

"distinction of meats" were considered as matters of purely Jewish identity.[181] Keeping those laws is made equal to idolatry.

Didascalia does not cite or discuss the prohibitions of the Decree. Issues connected to them appear displayed in an unusual manner. To say the names of idols was considered idolatry. Adornment of a man or a woman which might awaken someone's desire was made equal to adultery, which deserves "sore and bitter fire" (ch. 2). The food laws were replaced by fasting during Passion week, when one was allowed to sustain oneself with bread, salt and water only, and eat nothing for the whole Sabbath. *Didascalia* lists all types of heretical behavior, including the custom according to which "one was bound to withhold from swine only, but might eat those things which the Law pronounces clean."[182]

Thus, *Didascalia* differs from *Didache*, but harmonizes with the apocryphal fourth-century *Apostolic* Constitutions, which states:

> "But do ye abstain from things offered to idols; for they offer them honour of demons, that is, to the dishonor of the one God, that ye may not become partners with demons."[183]

Here the apostolic prohibition of εἰδωλοθύτων in Acts 15:29 was linked to the Pauline warning in 1 Cor 10:20. In another place the document seems to provide commentary on the term τῶν ἀλισγημάτων τῶν εἰδώλων in Acts 15:20:

> Endeavour therefore never to leave the Church of God; but if any one overlooks it, and goes either into a polluted temple of the heathens, or into a synagogue of the Jews or heretics, what apology will such one make to God in the day of judgment, who has forsaken the oracles of the living God . . . and has gone into an house of demons, or into a synagogue of the murderers of Christ, or the congregation of the wicked?[184]

The content of the Decree was also recalled in the debates about Easter observance. This was also a part of anti-Jewish policy when the Orthodox party attempted to replace the Jewish Passover with an Easter feast of Gentile origin. It is seen in Socrates,

---

181. This is a technical term of patristic writers derived by them from Mishnah. The authors of *Didascalia* insisted that some regulations of the law became a burden for Christians and consequently they have to be set apart as the laws of the second legislation. According to *Didascalia*, Christians no longer observe them. The *Didascalia* convicts everyone to know "what in the Law is the Law, and what are the bonds that are in the second legislation." Fonrobert, "Jewish Christians," 244, 253.

182. Fonrobert, "Jewish Christians," 244. The authors of *Didascalia* consider the ascetic teachings of Gnostics, simple abstaining from flesh and wine and specific rules based on the law of Torah, to be heretical altogether.

183. *Apostolic Constitutions*, 7.21 (ANF 7:469). The context (7.20, 21) reveals that the prohibition was placed by the writers of polemic against asceticism.

184. *Apostolic Constitutions*, 2.61 (ANF 7:423).

who "judged a single date for Easter to be among the unnecessary things mentioned in the Apostolic Decree of Acts 15:28."[185]

In general, this period pictures the process of fitting the Decree into new theological patterns. The patristic quotations provide insight into the interpretation of the Decree's content from different perspectives. Some of those interpretations deny its Jewish origin and others, which admit it, insist on temporary application of the Decree. The works of the fourth century Fathers show that in the days of Origen and Chrysostom the church had already defined the signs of Jewish identity and stepped aside from them. As a result the theological understanding of the text of the Decree had been changed, even though the written text in the manuscripts was not yet altered. It took another century of transmission of the text before the first variant readings appeared.

The Period of the Dominance of D05 among Several Variant Readings (c. 380 CE)

The period of the dominance of D05 among several variant readings embraces the works of church fathers from the last decades of the fourth century to the fifth century and can be defined by alternate wording of the Decree preserved in its quotations by the authoritative writers. During this period some church fathers cite the threefold list of prohibitions, while others kept πνικτῶν in the list.

Augustine of Hippo (354–430 CE), discussing the Jerusalem Council, usually avoids mentioning the Decree itself or commenting on it. He links the decision of the council to the teaching of the apostle Paul about things sacrificed to idols.[186] Once he mentions the content of the Decree, explaining what the "observance of pouring of the blood" means.[187] Augustine links this prohibition to the covenant with Noah described in Gen 9:6. He contrasts his view to the belief of his time, "to abstain from blood means not to be polluted with the crime of murder," and admits that the apostles taught the Christians "to abstain from the blood of animals, and not to eat of things strangled."[188] Thus Augustine understands that the prohibitions of the Decree had a cultic background and represented dietary law.

Although Augustine understands the cultic origin of the prohibitions he insists that the apostles on the council imposed those dietary restrictions in order to build a common and not burdensome basic law for both Jews and Gentiles. Thus his interpretation

185. Chadwick, *From Apostolic Times*, 9.

186. Augustine views "sacrificed to idols" in light of Rom 14; 15:1–3; 1 Cor 8:4; 10:19–25 and 28; 1 Tim 4:3–5. He shows the three reasons to abstain from flesh and wine in diet: to avoid becoming intoxicated, to avoid things sacrificed to idols, and "not to offend the weakness of those more feeble than ourselves." Augustine, *On the Morals of Manichaeans*, 14.31–35; 15.36–37 (*NPNF* 4:77–79). See also Augustine, *Reply to Faustus*, 19.17–18; 30.5–6 (*NPNF* 4:245–246, 330).

187. Augustine, *Reply to Faustus*, 32.13 (*NPNF* 4:336).

188. Augustine, *Reply to Faustus*, 32.13 (*NPNF* 4:336).

tends to be ethical, especially when he cites the ethical form of the Decree, showing this knowledge of the full list of prohibitions. Moreover, Augustine believes that the Decree had a temporary application until the day when the church would become "so entirely Gentile that none who are outwardly Israelites are to be found in it."[189] At this time he sees Christians as no longer under those restrictions when he notes, "any who still are afraid to touch these things are laughed at by the rest."[190]

Continuing his debate with Manichaeans he answered Faustus' question: "Why a Christian does not observe the distinction in food as enjoined in the law, if Christ came not to destroy the law, but to fulfill it"? According to Augustine it happened because "what was thus prefigured is now fulfilled in Christ, who admits into his body, which in his saints he has predestined to eternal life, nothing which in human conduct corresponds to the characteristic of forbidden animals."[191]

Augustine required "the priestly class to abstain from animal food; for we limit the prohibition to the priesthood."[192] He described the attitude of Christians of his time toward meats:

> Many do not eat flesh, and yet do not superstitiously regard it as unclean. And so the same people who abstain when in health take it when unwell without any fear, if it is required as a cure. Those then who are able, and they are without number, abstain both from flesh and from wine for two reasons: either for the weakness of their brethren, or for their own liberty.[193]

Here Augustine exalts their ascetic attitude in choice of diet. He clarifies that "all their endeavors are concerned not about the rejection of kinds of food as polluted, but about the subjugation of inordinate desire."[194] He calls the abstinence from certain kinds of food superstition, and accuses the Jews of being defiled in their mind when they avoided eating "Gentile food, especially that of sacrifices . . . when they were closing their mouth against blood and idol-feasts."[195]

John Cassian (360–435 CE) recalls the Decree in polemic about renunciation and covetousness in the church. He divides Christians into two groups according to their devotion to Christ. Then he exalts those who keep nothing from their property above those who hold on to their goods. He compares rich Christians to the Gentile converts who, "being unable to climb to the heights of the perfection of the gospel, clung to their own property, in whose case it was considered a great thing by the Apostle if at

---

189. Augustine, *Reply to Faustus*, 32.13 (*NPNF* 4:336). This work of Augustine is dated 400 CE.

190. Augustine, *Reply to Faustus*, 32.13 (*NPNF* 4:336).

191. Augustine, *Reply to Faustus*, 19.10 (*NPNF* 4:243).

192. Augustine, *Reply to Faustus*, 30.1 (*NPNF* 4:328). Here Augustine insists that the abstaining from meat in the diet is not connected to the issue of uncleanness, but was chosen to humble the flesh of the believer and strengthen his soul.

193. Augustine, *Morals of Catholic Church*, 33.72 (*NPNF* 4:61).

194. Augustine, *Morals of Catholic Church*, 33.71 (*NPNF* 4:61).

195. Augustine, *Reply to Faustus*, 31.1 (*NPNF* 4:331).

least they were restrained from the worship of idols, and from fornication, and from things strangled, and from blood."[196] Cassian's paraphrasing of the Decree places its four prohibitions in the context of ethical Christian behaviour.

Cyril of Alexandria (376–444 CE) referring to Acts 21:25 enumerates only the three prohibitions πορνείας, πνικτοῦ, αἵματος and omits εἰδωλοθύτων.[197] The same three regulations appear in his quotation of Acts 15:28–29.[198] Only once did he cite the full list of prohibitions, in a different order.[199] Metzger noted that in the fourth century some church fathers checked the variant readings according to the Latin version against Greek manuscripts.[200] This period of variant readings represents the attempts of the church to insert the varying interpretations of the Decree into its wording. Probably at this time, or later, the text of the manuscripts was influenced.

The well-known pseudepigraph of the fourth century, *Apostolic Constitutions* (circa 380 CE), provides its own account of the Jerusalem Council and paraphrases the Apostolic Decree in the following manner:

> ... we do not trouble those who from among the Gentiles turn unto God: but to charge them that they abstain from the pollutions of the Gentiles, and from what is sacrificed to idols, and from blood, and from things strangled, and from fornication; which laws were given to the ancients who lived before the law, under the law of nature, Enos, Enoch, Noah, Melchizedek, Job and if there be any other of the same sort.[201]

Further the document repeats the content of the Decree following the order in Acts 15:28, 29. After this the author states, "... we exhort you in the Lord to abstain from your old conversation, vain bonds, separations, observances, distinction of meats..."[202] This liberating approach, however, includes two restrictions. One of them insists, "But do ye abstain from things offered to idols; for they offer them in honor of demons, that is, to the dishonor of the one God, that ye may not become partners with demons."[203] The second implies the requirement that the blood has to be poured out.[204] It is known

---

196. Á, *Twelve Books*, 7:17 (ANF 11:254).

197. Cyril of Alexandria, *Commentarius in xii prophetas minoris*, 1.362.6, TLG.

198. Cyril of Alexandria, *De adoratione et cultu in spiritu et veritate*, vol. 68, 377.36, TLG.

199. Cyril of Alexandria, *Collectio dictorum veteris testamenti*, vol. 77, 1241.2, TLG.

200. Metzger, *Text of New Testament*, 201. Here he uses the opinion of Ambrosiaster as an example of work of this kind.

201. *Apostolic Constitutions*, 6.12 (ANF 7:455).

202. *Apostolic Constitutions*, 6.18.4 (ANF 7:458).

203. *Apostolic Constitutions*, 7:21 (ANF 7:469).

204. *Apostolic Constitutions*, 7:20 (ANF 7:469). Here the source allows believers to partake of any sort of food under condition that the blood was poured out. The explanation was built on the basis of Isa 1:19; Gen 9:3; Deut 15:23; Matt 15:11; Mark 7:22; Zech 9:17; Eccl 2:25 LXX; Neh 8:10. Surprisingly, these verses, written by Moses, Nehemiah, Solomon, Zechariah, Jesus and the apostles, who were Jews by birth and spoke and wrote in accord with their historical background, were taken as evidence for the abolishing of the dietary laws of Torah.

that *Apostolic Constitutions* was falsely attributed to apostolic origin and contained the apostles' address written in the first person for the purpose of gaining apostolic authority.

A similar attempt a century earlier was made in *Didascalia* (dated by 230 CE), a document produced under the influence of third-century orthodoxy. The church attributed the teaching of the *Didascalia* not simply to the apostles who were believed to have written this document, but to God himself. It gave the reader the idea of the equality of the apostolic decisions to those of heaven and of the holy church.[205] Without any doubt the document was composed to establish and expand Orthodox teaching as well as its authority by tying it to the Apostolic Council.

A document produced by the Orthodox branch of the church in 391 CE, called *The Effective Prohibition of Paganism*, which treats idolatry, shows the alteration of meaning of the Decree. It paraphrases the words of the Decree in a new manner: "No person shall pollute himself with sacrificial animals; no person shall slaughter an innocent victim; no person shall approach the shrines, shall wonder through the temples, or revere images formed by mortal labour, lest he become guilty by divine and human laws."[206] This edict treats only one prohibition out of the four, things sacrificed to idols. Some may detect the prohibition of blood hidden behind the words "slaughter an innocent victim." The prohibition of *pniktos* and *porneia* were not mentioned. If the church originally viewed the Decree as the way to reconcile Jewish and Gentile converts in common table fellowships, as some suggest, the edict would treat the issue of food in connection with idolatry more than the issue of sacrifices.

However, the wording of the edict does not address the consumption of what had been sacrificed. The edict looks more like the prohibition of Jewish or pagan sacrifices rather than requirements for common table fellowship. The theme of worship, there, is stressed more than ethical issues, or any attempt at reconciliation between Jewish and Gentile parties in the church. Thus, the church in the fourth century depicted any sacrificial system as equal to idolatry and did not call for keeping dietary laws at all.

If the original form of the Decree was ethical rather than cultic, then the prohibition of πορνεία should have appeared in an edict which opposed paganism. It is evident that in the fourth century πορνεία was regarded inappropriate behaviour which differentiated Christians from pagans. The mentioning of πορνεία in the edict would condemn unethical behaviour connected to pagan worship. This observation suggests that the church by that time did not understand the matters of the Decree in an ethical way. The fact that the church used the reference to the Decree in connection with the sacrificial system points to the cultic understanding. Based on this evidence, S. G. Wilson argues for the originally cultic form of the Decree and believes that there

---

205. Fonrobert, "Jewish Christians," 243.

206. Stevenson, ed. *Creeds, Councils, Controversies*, 27, 151. This edict was legislated by Theodorus I. *Codex Theodosianus*, 16.10.10. Also there were edicts of 341 CE and 356 CE which abolished sacrifices, destroyed temples, and ordered "all men shall abstain from sacrifices."

was a "shift from a 'cultic' to an 'ethical' form of the Decree."[207] According to him it was unnecessary to promulgate ethical standards by the Decree, because they had been self-evident to all Christians.[208]

At the same time, the link between idolatry and food sacrificed to idols, which is obvious in the New Testament and the Greco-Roman world, seems to disappear from the sight of the church, when the ethical interpretation of the Decree was suggested.[209] It seems that the ethical interpretation of the Decree does not treat any connection of pagan worship to food, though it took place, and does not presume that any food can be used in worship. The disconnect between food and the way of worship led to a theological disconnect between the prohibitions of the Decree and the dietary laws of Torah.

Following this disconnect the church fathers began to use two out of the four prohibitions, τῶν εἰδώλων and τῆς πορνείας, which were taken as prohibiting idolatry and fornication respectively, without any connotation of food. The anti-Jewish polemic of that time seemed to set aside the other two prohibitions, τοῦ πνικτοῦ/ῶν καὶ τοῦ αἵματος, as the signs of Jewish identity. They were blotted out along with the group of temporary laws of "second legislation." When the church gained the status of imperial approval, the dietary laws were treated radically negatively. As a result the wording of the Decree, with its previous cultic meaning, became a text with obscure meaning which needed a new interpretation, which would remove the Jewish elements from it.

That is why the wording of the Decree in some later manuscripts were subjected to intentional theological changes. Scribes altered the text in attempts to give it appropriate application. Ehrman notes that the "proto-orthodox Christians used literature in their early struggles for dominance, as they produced polemical treatises, forged supporting documents under the names of earlier authorities, collected apostolic works into an authoritative canon, and insisted on certain hermeneutical principles for the interpretation of these works."[210] This led to the alteration of the text of the Decree into its ethical form. The earliest witness to the ethical form is the Western

---

207. Wilson, *Luke and the Law*, 79. The omission of πνικτός and addition of the Golden Rule in the Western text makes it more ethical.

208. Wilson, *Luke and Law*, 80. He favours the cultic Decree (Alexandrian) for Jewish-Christians and considers that there was not any "law-free" Gentile mission.

209. McGowan, "Food, Ritual, Power," 145–46, 149. Also the link of idol worship to an idol meal is seen in 1 Cor 8:7; Rev 2:14, 20.

210. Ehrman, *Orthodox Corruption of Scripture*, xii. He dates the generation of variant readings up to the fourth century. The recent trends in textual criticism suggest that greater changes to manuscripts were made earlier due to less professionalism in the copying of NT manuscripts, while the church by the fourth century was wealthy enough to employ highly competent professional copyists. However, the type of the text alteration, namely, the addition of the negative form of the Golden Rule to the D05, can hardly be viewed as a copyist's mistake of hearing or of sight. That was an intentional alteration, made due to a theological presupposition to interpret the Decree in the ethical way. The absence of a word, or changes to declensions in variant readings, can be accepted as unintentional text corruptions that took place somewhere earlier than 200 CE due to errors of the unprofessional copyists.

text D 05; its reading became widely spread and supported by church authorities. Despite the ethical form's prominent role in the fifth century church, some witnesses still preserve the fourfold tradition.[211]

The quotation of the Decree by Jerome (347–420 CE) supports the view that the church fathers of this period fitted prohibitions in various patterns, trying to interpret them according to the needs of the contemporary church. He states, "they should keep themselves from idolatry, and from fornication, and from things strangled. As though they were providing for infant children, they gave them milk to drink, not solid food."[212] His last sentence, at first sight, looks like it was added to explain the meaning of "strangled" in a very innovative manner. However Jerome's intention was to show that the apostles imposed on the Gentiles the spiritual milk of their teaching, expressed in necessary regulations, not the whole Mosaic law.

As seen from his quotation, Jerome avoids mentioning "blood." This omission might show that either he quotes the Decree using one of the variant readings known to him, or that he makes an intentional change to its wording. One should note that Jerome's quotation is not a witness in favour of the ethical reading. He uses it in the context of anti-Jewish polemic. That is why he has no need to paraphrase or alter the wording of the reading which he had at hand.

The historian Socrates (380–439 CE) in his *Ecclesiastical History* mentions the diversity of beliefs in the Christian church. He explains that diversity was caused "by the bishops who in their respective eras governed the churches; and those who received these several rites and usages, transmitted them as laws to their posterity."[213] Here he recalls that even in the apostolic age many different views existed, as is seen in Acts 15.

Socrates quotes the Decree as follows: "that ye abstain from meats offered to idols, and from blood, and from things strangled, and from fornication."[214] This account of the Decree still seems to preserve the original fourfold tradition. He believes that Christ observed the law in the Jewish manner.[215] However, the Jewish customs and feasts, according to his opinion, needed an allegorical interpretation and presumed the obedience of the heart. He suggests the spiritual bearing of the Mosaic law instead of formal observance of it, since its rituals were the shadows of the events fulfilled in Christ.[216]

---

211. *Catena in Acts*, 250.29, TLG. This document is dated fifth century.

212. Jerome, *Dialogue Against Jovinianus*, 1.34 (*NPNF* 6:371).

213. Socrates, *Church History*, 5.22 (*NPNF* 2:133). Here Socrates states that at the Nicene Synod the bishops "convened earnestly labored to reduce the first dissenting minority to uniformity of practice with the rest of the people."

214. Socrates, *Church History*, 5.22 (*NPNF* 2:133). Here Socrates mentions those who viewed "all fornication to be an indifferent matter; but contend about holy-days" (Easter celebration was under discussion).

215. Socrates, *Church History*, 5.22 (*NPNF* 2:133).

216. Socrates, *Church History*, 5.22 (*NPNF* 2:134). As the topic concerns predominantly the day

Important evidence shedding light on alteration of manuscripts comes from the *Apology* of Rufinus, dated 400 CE. This document reveals polemic between Rufinus and Jerome concerning the translation of Greek OT texts to Latin.[217] It is likely that Jerome, in cases of uncertain meaning, checked Hebrew originals. Rufinus states that, earlier, Origen checked the Hebrew originals of Scripture and put marks on those manuscript readings which he considered to differ from his version.[218] However, he notices that Origen did this in order to disprove the validity of the Jewish sources, unlike Jerome. This fact reveals that at the time of Origen there were motives to explain the appearance of the variant readings, though the Greek text had been largely preserved without major changes.

In his discourse, Rufinus states that Christians have no need to clarify the meaning of texts according to Hebrew scriptures, because the law of God was rendered to Christians "from the first in the churches of God . . . that of Jerusalem" by the apostles, whom he assumes are the highest authority. Rufinus argues that the apostles, who "being born Jews, have become Christians; and their perfect acquaintance with both languages and their sufficient knowledge of the law is shewn by their administration of the pontifical office."[219] The attempts to produce a better text during its translation from Greek into Latin called for a better knowledge of Jewish backgrounds. This polemic reveals that Jewish identity was removed from the biblical text known to Orthodox Christians, and the authority was re-assigned to the "pontifical office."

Thus, the polemic between Rufinus and Jerome shows that Greek manuscripts at that time already carried some alterations of wording, which caused arguing over the preference of one reading over another. Here the tendency to abolish any attempts to clarify the meaning of the text appears.[220] Rufinus directs condemnation at those who "put forth some strange opinions in the interpretation of the law of God," and those who tried "to pervert the law itself and make it different from that which the Apostles

---

of Easter, his attitude to the prohibitions of the Decree is not clear. More likely he cited them to show that the observance of certain days was outside of the apostolic concern or considered by them as unnecessary. If so, one can assume that even in the end of the fourth century CE the original form of the Decree was in use.

217. Rufinus argues against Jerome's attempt to clarify the meaning of some texts taking into consideration their Jewish cultural background. They both refer to Origen's prior attempt to check the Greek biblical texts according to Jewish sources in order to disprove the false accusation made by the Jews that the Christian scriptures had been corrupted.

218. Rufinus, *Apology*, 2.36 (*NPNF* 3:477). According to Rufinus, Origen demonstrated that the Jewish claims were overestimated. This method also helped Origen to found out which word in translations had been "killed by the other translators and those which had been superfluously introduced."

219. Rufinus, *Apology*, 2:33 (*NPNF* 3:475).

220. Rufinus, *Apology*, 2.31–36 (*NPNF* 3:475–77). Rufinus argues with Jerome about translations of Holy Scriptures from Greek to Latin. He defends the Catholic anti-Jewish manuscripts of the Church and opposes any attempt to clarify the original reading, believing that the apostles had divine inspiration, while Jews wrote fables. The polemic reveals existence of variant readings in Greek manuscripts which some translators tried to correct while translating them to Latin.

handed down to us."²²¹ He argues against attempts to correct the meaning of a text: "For what can we call it but havoc, when some parts of it are transformed, and this is called the correction of an error?"²²² He believes that the attempt to correct or clarify the meaning of texts in the reading accepted by the Catholic Church would give heathens the right to reject the apostolic authority of the church: "It is not evident, how greatly the grounds for the heathens' unbelief have been increased by this proceeding? ... They know that our law has been amended, or at least changed."²²³ This polemic makes evident that manuscript changes were undertaken due to Jewish-Christian controversy prior to the time of Rufinus and Jerome.

Several scholars have attempted to explain this theological shift. According to Bart Erhman the text was corrupted by the work of scribes who "altered the words of their sacred texts to make them more patently Orthodox and to prevent their misuse by Christians who espoused aberrant views."²²⁴ He called them the "proponents of fourth-century Orthodoxy."²²⁵ Harry Maier argued that the early Christians could not regulate their diversity, since the churches were connected to different households, but when Christianity became "the empire's official and solely sanctioned cult" between 312 and 395 CE, it attempted to regulate the diversity of beliefs by anti-heretical legislation.²²⁶ The fact that changes in wording become part of the dominant text shows that the theological shift had been accepted by the majority of the church or by the ruling and dominant party.²²⁷

Metzger suggests viewing intentional alterations as attempts to clarify the meaning rather than speculative attempt to make the Scripture say what it should say according to theological understanding. "Since monks usually knew by heart extensive portions of the Scriptures . . . , the temptation to harmonize discordant parallels or quotations would be strong."²²⁸ He states that "the manuscripts of the New Testament preserve traces of two kinds of dogmatic alterations: those which involve the elimination or alteration of what was regarded as doctrinally unacceptable or

---

221. Rufinus, *Apology*, 2.32 (*NPNF* 3:475–77).

222. Rufinus, *Apology*, 2.33 (*NPNF* 3:475).

223. Rufinus, *Apology*, 2.35 (*NPNF* 3:476).

224. Ehrman, *Orthodox Corruption of Scripture*, xi.

225. Ehrman, *Orthodox Corruption of Scripture*, xii.

226. Maier, "Heresy, Households, and the Disciplining of Diversity," 221, 213. He shows the Christianity of those days as "a complex network of diverse communities representing competing perspectives."

227. Here Maier defines the Christianity under the reigns of Constantine and Theodosius as a struggle of Orthodoxy against heterodoxy, where the unity of orthodoxy finally overcame by the power of imperial forces. This unity of ideas, however, does not mean that victory was attained in continuity with apostolic truth. Maier, "Heresy, Households," 233.

228. Metzger, *Text of New Testament*, 197.

inconvenient, and those which introduce into the Scriptures 'proof' for a favourite theological tenet or practice."[229]

Summary

The period of variant readings reveals the alteration of the text of the Decree in manuscripts under influence of the theological shift from the Decree's cultic to its ethical form reflected in D 05, dated fifth century. This process took hundreds of years, proceeding from one variant meaning to another. Evidence in patristic literature indicates that the shift happened somewhere between the second half of the third and the fourth century, when anti-Jewish polemic reached its high point. The argument, presented so far in this chapter, can be summed up by the following five statements:

1. The alteration of the text of the Apostolic Decree was a result of anti-Jewish tendency from the side of an increasing Orthodoxy in the church.

2. The alteration of the text was influenced by the theological shift from Jewishness to Orthodoxy taking place somewhere between the third and the fourth centuries.

3. The theological shift was driven by groups in the church who gained imperial authority.

4. It took centuries for alterations to appear in manuscripts after the official position of the church was established and doctrine was formed.

5. The theological shift influenced the readings of the Decree during the process of transmission.

The Dominance of the Ethical Form of the Apostolic Decree

The Medieval Interpretation of the Ethical Form of the Decree

The medieval church period leaves an impression of being a non-productive period for exegetical work on the Lukan writings. "Very little information has come down to us concerning the study of the book of acts during the fifteen centuries prior to the Reformation."[230] This period preserves and repeats the ethical form of the Decree taken over from patristic literature. Moreover, the text of the Decree was employed by the Mediaeval church as a proof of its right to create and to cancel laws of Torah, since the church had come to view them as temporary regulations,

---

229. Metzger, *Text of New Testament*, 201.
230. Gasque, *History of Criticism of Acts*, 7.

and since it was commonly accepted that the apostles on the Jerusalem Council had done away with those Jewish laws.[231]

The Ethical Form of the Decree in the Works of the Protestant Reformers

The Protestant Reformers debated the mediaeval interpretation of the book of Acts.[232] Thus, John Calvin's (1509–64) interpretation of the Decree concentrates on the issue of whether the church can create laws and demand that they be kept "under pain of mortal sin."[233] His work shows that the Mediaeval church viewed the Decree as a document of temporary significance and of changeable matters.

While the main focus of the mediaeval interpreters was on anti-Jewish polemic, the Reformers approached Acts from the angle of anti-papal polemic. Calvin believed that the Decree's purpose was to avoid offence between the Jews and the Gentile converts in the church.[234] He accepted its temporary significance when he stated, "this law was foredone by Paul so soon as the tumult and contention was once ended."[235] Calvin, however, believed contrary to Papal teaching, that the apostles "pass not the bounds of the word of God when they set down an external law, as time requireth, whereby they may reconcile the Churches among themselves."[236]

Thus, theology contemporary to Calvin considered the prohibitions of Acts 15 to be: 1) regulations of external (or accidental) necessity, 2) of temporary significance, and 3) given because of some political issues in the church.[237] The only disagreement between Calvin's view and that of the papists is whether to accept those regulations as the will of God or as laws established by the church's own authority and exceeding the word of God.

---

231. This mediaeval approach to the text of the Decree was reflected and criticized in the work of the Reformer John Calvin, *Commentary upon Acts*, 77–79.

232. Gasque, *History of Criticism of Acts*, 8. He notices raised interest in Acts after the Mediaeval period among the Protestant scholars.

233. Calvin, *Commentary upon Acts*, 78. John Calvin did not discuss the date, the authorship and historical-cultural background; he searched for a main theme of Lukan work, which he defined as "sacred histories."

234. Gasque, *History of Criticism of Acts*, 15. The same view was later upheld by John Lightfoot (1602–75). He viewed Acts as "the story of only two apostles, Peter and Paul," and Christianity as divided between two leaders and two ways of hermeneutic, where the Pauline one was finally prevailing. As a result, the Decree was still viewed as the victory of Paul over the Jewishness of the Jerusalem congregation.

235. Calvin, *Commentary upon Acts*, 79, 80. Calvin believed that the Apostolic Decree represented the "political law" and had as its purpose to nourish the brotherly love between the Jewish and the Gentile converts.

236. Calvin, *Commentary upon Acts*, 80. Under the expression "external law" Calvin views the prohibitions of the Decree.

237. Gasque notes that Calvin's prime concern was in the practical application of the message of Acts to his contemporary church. Gasque, *History of Criticism of Acts*, 10.

The Reformers also viewed the Decree in terms of anti-Jewish polemic, providing temporary regulations of an ethical nature. Since the historical context of early Christianity had not been recovered at that time, the original theological key of interpretation of the Decree could not be found. As a result, the period of critical study of Acts which followed the Reformation ended with doubts not only about the originality of the Decree, the authorship and the sources, but also the possibility of reconstructing the original situation.

The Critical Study of Acts

In the nineteenth century Lukan writings came under the critical study of the "Tübingen school," which questioned not only the sources of Acts, but also its date, authorship and motives. This led to a careful reading of Acts. The views of the "Tübingen school" were summarized by Ward Gasque. According to him, the Tübingen school founder Ferdinand Christian Baur (1792–1860) "brings forward the hypothesis that Acts was written by a 'Paulinist' to defend the mission of Paul to the Gentiles against the criticism of the Jewish-Christian party."[238]

The Tübingen school's approach to Acts attributed to the Pauline writings greater authority than those of Luke. As a result, evidence from Luke-Acts was made secondary to Paul's, despite the differences which make Lukan work unique and independent of Paul's. Eduard Zeller viewed the events of Acts 15 in connection with those of Gal 2:1–10.[239] He argued against the Jewishness of Paul and his participation in cultic rituals. For him, Paul's final trip to Jerusalem in Acts 21 was for the collection of alms from the Gentile churches, rather than for observing Pentecost.[240]

The post-Tübingen school critical study of Acts 15 and 21 produced some significant positive results. Wilhelm Meyer (1800–73), comparing Gal 2 and Acts 15, sees, "Paul does not contrast himself with the primitive apostles in regard to doctrine, but in reference to the sphere of activity in the ministry of the same Gospel."[241] He "detects a combination of both oral and written traditions behind the narrative" of Acts 15.[242] Meyer believes that the purpose of the Decree was to build brotherly fel-

---

238. Gasque, *History of Criticism of Acts*, 30. Baur expressed his opinion on Acts in a series of essays. He used the method of "tendency criticism" to discover the special theological reasons for writing Acts. Baur saw the conflict of two groups in primitive Christianity. He believed that Luke wrote Acts to defend the theology of Paul.

239. Zeller's view was refuted by Ramsay, who argued against linking Gal 2 to Acts 15 and insisted on its link to Acts 11:30. According to Ramsay the letter to the Galatians was written before the events in Acts 15 had taken place. According to Gasque, Ramsay's view has become "very influential among British New Testament critics." Gasque, *History of Criticism of Acts*, 141–42.

240. Gasque, *History of Criticism of Acts*, 47. Zeller also defines Paul's participation in a vow as "unthinkable" and contradicting his theology.

241. Gasque, *History of Criticism of Acts*, 59.

242. Gasque, *History of Criticism of Acts*, 59. He states that although Luke arranged the tradition in his own literary style, the scholars still can recognize the Semitic and Hellenistic character of those

lowship in mixed communities, which does not contradict Paul's own approach.[243] Karl Schrader (1834–1913) also notes that Paul, in Acts, is pictured as a law obedient Jew, who demonstrates his respect to the authority of the apostles in Jerusalem.[244] Matthias Schneckenburger (1804–48) believes that Paul argued "against the law as the basis for salvation . . . not the act of piety."[245] Adolf Harnack (1851–1930) supports this view, assuming that Paul had never taught the freedom of all Christians from the law, but rather the freedom of the Gentile converts from it.[246]

Albrecht Ritschl (1822–1889) argued against Baur's view, "Early Christianity is far too complex to be understood in terms of a conflict between two monolithic parties."[247] Ritschl noted "the differences between the primitive apostles and the Judaizers, as well as between Pauline Christianity and that part of Gentile Christianity which was essentially independent of his influence."[248] Discussing the issue of Acts 15 he believes that the apostles imposed on the Gentile converts, "certain parts of the Jewish proselyte law."[249] Finally, Burton S. Easton stated, "the Christians themselves considered themselves to be Jews."[250] This observation further led the scholars of the twentieth century to search for the connections between the four prohibitions of the Decree and Lev17–18, as well as with the covenant with Noah in Gen 6. These searches served as precursors for the new search of the pre-Mosaic rationale of the Decree.

Martin Dibelius (1883–1947) developed the method of form criticism and wrote essays on the historical credibility of speeches in Acts.[251] The goal of Dibelius was to find grounds for historical credibility of Acts. He was led to the conclusion that Acts has no historical value for recovering original early church experience.[252] He stated

---

sources.

243. Gasque, *History of Criticism of Acts*, 59. Meyer explains the absence of reference to the Decree in Galatians "by the interim purpose of the recommendation."

244. Gasque, *History of Criticism of Acts*, 34–35. It was also noted that Paul makes vows, preaches the Gospel to the Jews first and, only then, turns to the Gentiles.

245. Gasque, *History of Criticism of Acts*, 37. From Paul's letters, Schneckenburger notes Paul's concern and arguing against the attempts to impute the law on the believing Gentiles. He found that Paul's belief described in Acts also agrees on this point.

246. Gasque, *History of Criticism of Acts*, 154.

247. Gasque, *History of Criticism of Acts*, 62. Albrecht Ritschl states the fact that "not all Jewish Christians were Judaizers or opponents of Paul; not all Gentile Christians were Paulinist."

248. Gasque, *History of Criticism of Acts*, 62–63.

249. Gasque, *History of Criticism of Acts*, 63–64. Ritschl stated that the sociological aspect of the debate in Acts 15 was important to create peace in mixed communities.

250. Gasque, *History of Criticism of Acts*, 196–97. Burton Scott Easton (1877–1950) views the historical score of Gentile Christianity predominantly under the supervision of the Jerusalem church. The Colossian church, independent from Jewish origin, was assumed by him as an exclusive example. He also defines the theology in Acts as of Jewish nature.

251. Dibelius, *Studies in Acts*, 96.

252. Gasque, *History of Criticism of Acts*, 207, 210–11, 217. He shows that Dibelius considered the speeches of Acts as the author's invention which stand in contrast to the theology of the Old and New Testaments. He also notes that in Acts the reader hears only one side of the story, which lacks

the impossibility of distinguishing between the information taken from the original sources and Luke's own theological interpretation of information.[253]

Dibelius believes that Peter's speech on the council existed prior to Luke in the form of a simple story of Cornelius' conversion, and was adjusted by Luke to fit his own theological design.[254] Dibelius assumes that the Decree existed in the form of a document available to Luke.[255] He considers the list of prohibitions were written in their ethical form. He concludes that the Apostolic Decree did not originate at the Jerusalem Council, and that Luke later found this document in Antioch.[256] If one accepts that the ethical form of the Decree was elaborated by scribes during the fourth century and preserved by D 05, then Debelius' conclusion makes sense. His presumption that the Decree (viewed by him in its ethical form) was a late elaboration of beliefs of the following generations of Christianity seems to be correct, in accord with the Western reading.

In the twentieth century Jürgen Wehnert followed Dibelius' approach.[257] He focused on what he understood to be the editorial "evolution" of the accounts of the Apostolic Decree in Acts chapters 15 and 21, arguing that Luke subjected these accounts to increasing redactional modification in order to achieve an integrated account of the deliberations of church leaders, and of the transmission of the resulting content of the Decree.[258] He concluded from his study that Luke, in Acts 15, has reworked two original independent traditions in composing the present form of chapter 15. Luke's goal was to merge into a united whole the various components of the decisions of leaders in Antioch and Jerusalem about what Jewish regulations would be required of Gentile believers.[259] His goal in doing this was to present a united response of church leaders to the Jew-Gentile conflict among early believers.[260]

---

independent verification.

253. Dibelius, *Studies in Acts*, 99–100. This fact, however, may show the problems of his methodology, which treated the validity of sources according to hypothetical reconstructions of Early Christian history. Acts was viewed from the perspective of the commonly accepted fact that Paul was fighting against the Jewishness of Christianity and law obedience. This placed Pauline theology in contrast to that appearing in Luke's writings.

254. Dibelius, *Studies in Acts*, 95. According to Gasque, Dibelius admired Lukan literary and artistic ability. Gasque, *History of Criticism of Acts*, 219.

255. Dibelius, *Studies in Acts*, 99.

256. Dibelius, *Studies in Acts*, 100.

257. Wehnert, *Die Reinheit des "christlichen Gottesvolkes"*, 65–71.

258. Wehnert, *Die Reinheit des "christlichen Gottesvolkes"*, 65.

259. Wehnert follows Dibelius, doubting the historical credibility of Luke's account of Acts 15, and follows Jervell arguing for the link between Acts 15:20 and Lev 17–18. He views the Apostolic Decree as Luke's redactional creation to explain the reaction of the Jerusalem church on Peter's mission to the Gentiles in Caesarea (Acts 10) and Luke's attempt to reconcile it with Paul's mission in Antioch (Gal 2). Wehnert, *Die Reinheit des "christlichen Gottesvolkes"*, 65.

260. Wehnert, *Die Reinheit des "christlichen Gottesvolkes"*, 71.

The critical study of Acts took two significantly different approaches. On one hand, form criticism disproved the validity of D 05 for the reconstruction of the historical context. The unoriginality of the ethical form of the Decree, thus, was argued. On the other hand, criticism laid the foundation for investigation of the theological design of Luke, and the Jewish background of the Apostolic Decree. The turning point in studies of the Decree in its ethical form to its Jewish roots will be discussed next, in section 3.

Turning from the Ethical Form of the Apostolic Decree to Its Jewish Roots

A great amount of scholarly work has been done to find a proto-text and traditions lying behind Acts as well as its theological, historical and literary values and applicability. Centuries of research have resulted in a number of ways to interpret the Apostolic Decree. This section focuses on work which contributed to the understanding of the Decree in Acts 15. It will be arranged in two main categories: 1) ethical rationale and 2) cultic rationale.[261] The cultic rationale rests on one of three bases for the Decree: (A) Leviticus 17–18, (B) Noachic laws, and (C) halakhic regulations.

Ethical Explanation of the Decree of Acts 15

The first rationale for the four prohibitions of the Decree assumes their ethical origin and application.[262] This was influenced by the dominant Western reading, which views the prohibition of εἰδωλοθύτων as an abrogation of idolatry and a prohibition of blood as a ban on murder. Omission of πνικτός removed all cultic associations and the addition of the negative form of the Golden Rule affirmed the tone of the Decree in an ethical form.

Commentators supporting the ethical form believe that main concern of early Christians was for unity and peace in mixed communities, rather than observing of Jewish customs.[263] Consequently, the ethical teaching of Jesus was exalted, at the expense of any Jewish tradition. Supporters viewed the ethical form of the Decree as a solution to the problem of common table fellowship and success of the Gentile mission, to which finally the cult was surrendered.

---

261. Dickinson noted two theological implications of the Decree: ethical and cultic. He viewed the ethical understanding of the Decree as an attempt to incorporate the Gentiles as the Gentiles into the people of God (which he sees from the reference to Moses in v. 21). According to him the cultic form of the Decree refers to Lev 17–18. Dickinson, "Theology of the Jerusalem Conference," 80.

262. Ajith, *Acts*, 421.

263. Haenchen and the supporters of the "ethical view" F. Bruce, D. Bock, and C. Blomberg.

Ernest Haenchen

The work of Haenchen on Acts was outstanding among exegetical studies of the twentieth century. As a follower of form criticism, he suggested studying Acts 15 from the position of its structure, rather than sources or their historical validity.[264] At the same time he disputed the dating and Lukan authorship of Acts.[265] Following the theory of invented speeches, he saw James' speech as a composition by Luke.[266]

Haenchen viewed the law from the perspective of Judaism and saw, "everything in the Law of Moses which is connected with the Temple cult has been rendered useless."[267] He noticed according to D (05) that the demand of the Judaizers at the Jerusalem Council was not simply for circumcision, but for observing the ritual law of Moses.[268] In contrast to this demand, the Gentiles viewed the law "as a mass of commandments and prohibitions which no man could fulfill."[269] Acts 10 and 11 allow Haenchen to make some conclusions prior to Acts 15. He argued that God sanctioned the mission to the Gentiles apart from the law and bestowed on Gentiles the necessary purity.[270] As a result, he includes the prohibition of πνικτός in the original content of the Decree, but still believes that its meaning has to be governed by the Golden Rule in the ethical way.[271]

---

264. Haenchen, *Die Apostelgeschichte*, 457–60.

265. Haenchen considered the author of Acts to be an unknown Christian "of the sub-apostolic age" (which likely corresponds to the second century CE), who described the realities of the church of the first century in the way they have reached him: "here we have no collaborator of Paul telling his story, but someone of a later generation trying in his own way to give an account of things that can no longer be viewed in their true perspective." Haenchen, *Apostelgeschichte*, 95–97, 124 (*Acts*, 83–85, 116).

266. "It is not James but Luke who is speaking here." Haenchen, *Acts*, 448.

267. Haenchen, *Apostelgeschichte*, 664 (*Acts*, 694). He distinguishes two aspects of the law: the ethical, which remains and ritual, which was revoked. He believes that the Gentile Church of Justin's day no longer understood the Jewish Christian "'ritual' commandments." As a result, the Western text provides necessary "transposition of the ritual into *moral* requirements" which removes tensions and contradictions in Acts. Haenchen, *Acts*, 470.

268. Haenchen, *Apostelgeschichte*, 425 n. 3 (*Acts*, 443 n. 2). He suggested to look at the topic more widely and to see a ban of the law of Moses as a whole.

269. Haenchen, *Apostelgeschichte*, 429 n. 1 (*Acts*, 446 n. 3). Haenchen finds it emphasized by the phrase ζυγὸν ἐπὶ τὸν τράχηλον in Acts 15:10.

270. Haenchen, *Apostelgeschichte*, 429–30 (*Acts*, 446–47). At this point his position raises the discussion with Bauernfeind concerning the possibility of employment of Pauline theology by Luke.

271. Haenchen, *Apostelgeschichte*, 431 n. 4, 455–56 (*Acts*, 449–50 n. 6, 471–72). He explains that the understanding of the Decree in a "moral" sense (idolatry, fornication, murder) was defended as original by Harnack, A. C. Clark, and Feine-Behm, when they took the Western text for the basis of the Decree. Zahn "buried" Harnack's explanation. Those who understood that "the prohibitions were originally of a ritual nature" were P. Wendland, Wendt, Diehl, Preuschen, J. Weiss, Goguel, Loisy, E. Meyer, Ropes, Lietzmann, Beyer, H. Waitz, Bauernfeind, Cerfaux, Dibelius, K. Schäfer, and W. G. Kümmel. Haenchen, however, believes that the Christians in the second century "no longer had any appreciation for 'ritual' prescriptions" and understood the prohibitions of the Decree in a moral sense. This led to understanding of the prohibitions "independently of the association with Jewish

According to Haenchen, the Decree was imposed on Gentile converts due to ethical requirements prescribed in the law about aliens who lived among the Jews, which led to the unanimity of the council decision.[272] Despite the cultic background of the Decree presumed by its association with Lev 17–20, Haenchen continues to interpret the Decree in the ethical sense. He makes this assumption influenced by his conception of Gentile freedom from the law. Later his view was developed by F. F. Bruce.[273]

F. F. Bruce

In contrast to Haenchen, Bruce accepts there is sufficient evidence for Lukan authorship of Acts.[274] He suggests that the council was appointed in response to the suggestion that Gentiles be adopted into the church by first making them proselytes before their baptism.[275] He assumes that the commandments of Torah were called ζυγὸς "in the sense of an intolerable weight."[276] At the same time he finds the idea of Judaizing by Peter to be "a figment of the Tübingen critics with no basis in history."[277]

Bruce rightly pictured James taking a cue from Peter's speech, and reverting to it in Acts 15:19. This finding supports the idea of the present study. Moreover, Bruce notes that in all cases where Paul deals with the issue of sacrifice to idols and fornication, he never refers it to the Apostolic Decree, but "argues from the order of creation and the ethical implication of the gospel."[278] This observation sheds light on connections between the Genesis creation narrative and Paul's use of prohibitions of εἰδωλοθύτων and πορνεία.

Viewing the variant readings of the Decree, Bruce recognizes the Western reading as secondary to the Alexandrian, which he accepts as original.[279] Despite this, he insists on the ethical rationale for the Decree, taking a cue from the difficulties in communication between Jewish and Gentile believers.

Christianity." From this Haenchen assumes that the practice reached Luke in its ethical context.

272. Haenchen, *Apostelgeschichte*, 432 nn. 3, 4; 433 n. 1; 453 (*Acts*, 449 nn. 4, 5; 450–51 n. 1; 469). Here he refers to the laws in Lev 17–18.

273. Bruce, *Acts*, 1–18.

274. Bruce, *Acts*, 1–18. Bruce dates Acts between the late 70s and early 80s of the first century. This provides an eye witness account of the life of the early Christian church, justifying the historicity of the council.

275. Bruce, *Acts*, 329, 333. He notices that circumcision was embodied in the Mosaic law (Lev 12:3).

276. Matt 23:4; Luke 11:46; Gal 5:1.

277. Bruce, *Acts*, 335, citing Lake, *Earlier Epistles of St. Paul* (London: Rivingtons, 1911), 116.

278. Bruce, *Acts*, 331.

279. Bruce, *Acts*, 342.

Darrel Bock

The ethical explanation of the Decree also was accepted by Darrel Bock.[280] Bock views the law of Moses as a purely Jewish custom rooted in the covenant with Abraham and irrelevant for salvation.[281] He rejects not only circumcision but also the food laws. He links Acts 10 and Acts 15 together as the key passages for the discussion of law observance.[282] According to Bock, Peter's vision declares all foods and all people clean.[283]

At the same time he notices that according to the Torah, to visit a Gentile home meant the same as to eat unclean food.[284] Combining the food laws and the Jewish attitude towards the Gentiles, Bock concludes that all laws were cancelled for the success of the mission. He states that after the vision Peter "could eat whatever might be set before him" and abide at any house for the sharing of Christ.[285] He suggests that the "law of Christ" liberates Christians from scrupulous observance of the Mosaic law.[286]

According to Bock the elders at the council attempted to impose food restrictions and the content of the Decree was a compromise.[287] He finds the rationale for their imposition in the fact that Moses is read in the synagogues (15:21).[288] He argues for the ethical form of the Decree, explaining that by keeping it, the new converts could avoid, the food of pagan rituals, eating meat from strangled animals, eating blood, and pagan temple prostitution.

From God's revelation that "circumcision is not to be a concern for Gentiles," Bock sees the end of the laws of Torah.[289] Through his commentary Bock shows that,

---

280. Bock, *Acts*, 15. Bock viewed Luke as "a second-generation convert, a sometime companion of Paul." This might mean that the description of events and all speeches in Acts 15 would be real.

281. Bock, *Acts*, 494. He repeats the thought of Bruce, connecting circumcision to Gen 17:10–14.

282. Bock, *Acts*, 39.

283. Bock, *Acts*, 39, 390. He states "God uses the picture of unclean food now made clean to portray unclean Gentiles now made clean."

284. Bock, *Acts*, 394. Defending this meaning of the law of cleansing and its historical context, Bock refers to Jubilee 22:16. In addition to that, the question about the contact of Jews with the Gentiles was debated by scholars. Jordan Rosenblum argues that in the Hasmonean period (pre-tannaitic) "some groups may have considered all table fellowship with Gentiles abominable while other groups had a more open attitude." Rosenblum, *Food and Identity in Early Rabbinic Judaism*, 36, 42–43, citing Zetterholm, *Formation of Christianity in Antioch*, 155. Here he notes that in tannaitic tradition the commensality between Jews and Gentiles was understood as potentially "idolatrous."

285. Bock, *Acts*, 390. This idea was earlier expressed by Marshall, *Acts*, 186;and Bruce, *Acts*, 256.

286. Bock, *Acts*, 497. Here Bock sees the "law of Christ" as the "royal law" (1 Cor 9:21; Gal 6:2; Jas 2:8). He connects the "requirements of the law of Moses" to the covenant of circumcision.

287. Bock, *Acts*, 37, 508. He insists that "Jewish believers are free to practice the faith in their way, just as Gentiles are not required to come under the law." However it puts believers in the situation of facing double standards. They were obliged now to keep some law in mixed meals, and different laws in separated meals. This new way according to Bock represents a realization of the law.

288. Bock, *Acts*, 390. Jervell challenges this thought, viewing that the decree was only about people, not food.

289. Bock, *Acts*, 38. Bock supports this thought with the opinions of Wilson, Blomberg, and Barrett. Wilson quarrels that Luke favored law observance. However Bock debates the position of

generally, Acts emphasized "the evangelism and God-honoring life as making up the central character" of the new people of God, while also supporting the preaching of freedom from the law. [290]

Craig L. Blomberg

The interpretation of the Decree suggested by Blomberg reflects an antinomian approach to Luke's theology in general.[291] He sees the Mosaic law playing a minor and background role in Luke's two-volume work.[292] He concludes that Luke pictures a shift from the law-observance age to the law-free age of Christianity.[293] He argues that all of the Hebrew Scriptures (Moses, Prophets, and Psalms) were fulfilled in the life, teaching and death of Jesus and are unnecessary for keeping by the church.[294] Thus he pictures the law and Jesus as two equivalent themes and assumes all laws to end in Christ.[295]

Peter's vision in Acts 10 was explained as "not only a cancellation of dietary laws but also the abolition of the barriers banning table-fellowship between Jews and Gentiles."[296] At the same time Blomberg interprets the list of prohibitions as practices offensive to the Jewish Christians during table fellowship, revealing the discrepancies in his approach to the table fellowship issue.[297] His view fails to explain why, having accepted the ban on dietary laws shown in Peter's vision, the church was still discussing the issue of food from the Jewish perspective. Finally, his connection of Acts

---

Blomberg, who showed the more complex picture.

290. Bock, *Acts*, 40.

291. Blomberg, "Law in Luke-Acts."

292. Blomberg, "Law in Luke-Acts," 70. Downing saw the early church continuing to observe the Jewish rites right to the end of Acts. Downing shows with quotations of Cicero, Philo, Dionysius of Halicarnassus, Josephus, and Plutarch that it was natural for ancient societies to respect and to observe their ancestral customs. Moreover he finds Luke, from the start, presenting the Christians "as evincing a true and joyful traditional piety." Downing, "Freedom from the Law in Luke-Acts," 49–52.

293. Blomberg, "Law in Luke-Acts," 72.

294. Blomberg, "Law in Luke-Acts," 71, 69. Blomberg also follows S. G. Wilson, who emphasizes that Luke's use of terms "law," "Moses," and "custom" is interchangeable.

295. Blomberg, "Law in Luke-Acts," 70. The idea of a liberal approach to the issue of the law is supported by Jon C. Olson. He argues for the acceptance of homosexuality on the basis of the Apostolic Decree, which becomes for him an example of charity toward marginals. He uses analogy between the Gentiles and homosexual persons and argues for a liberal position of the Church toward the Gentiles .Olson comes to this conclusion from the point that the church accepted the Gentiles as Gentiles, burdening them with a minimum of law. His position turns out to be the best argument against the idea of non-observing Torah Gentiles. Olson, "Jerusalem Decree," 380.

296. Blomberg, "Law in Luke-Acts," 64.

297. Blomberg, "Law in Luke-Acts," 66. If Peter was given an order to declare all unclean food as clean, the prohibitions of the decree seem to be a backward step. Also, it would seem impossible to apply the few dietary rules to non-kosher foods.

10 and 15 leads his readers to the idea of "freedom from the Law."[298] Avoiding this one-sided antinomian approach has prompted scholars to look for a more balanced interpretation of the Apostolic Decree.

I. Howard Marshall

I. Howard Marshall adopts the ethical view of the Decree, emphasizing that faith is the only ground for salvation of Jewish as well as Gentile converts.[299] He describes Luke as the author who used history in the service of his theology, and who was closely related to his sources.[300] Marshall sees the church trying to expresses its identity with the language of the ancient Jewish hopes.[301] That is why he stresses the wish of Luke to place value on piety by recalling the theme of Jewish ritual law.[302]

Marshall assumes that applying the term "yoke" to the law, reflects Luke's own attitude to the Mosaic Law.[303] He views it as a protest against overburdening, and sees the regulations of the Decree as the way to harmonize mixed communities. He believes that Luke in his work showed the demand of circumcision as a real threat to the Gospel and prepared the way for overcoming it.[304] Marshall insists on the ethical interpretation of the content of the Decree, though the issue of table fellowship between Jewish and Gentile converts was not simply of an ethical nature, and included some matters more unfitting than those reflected by the content of the Decree.

Cultic Explanation of the Apostolic Decree of Acts 15

Insofar as the Western reading of the decree was assumed to be secondary to the Alexandrian fourfold tradition, voices were heard arguing for the cultic form of the Apostolic Decree. Lisa Maguire Hess assumed the connections of three out of the four prohibitions to kashrut.[305] So they started to treat those three prohibitions as if they

---

298. Blomberg, "Law in Luke-Acts," 70. Jervell argued against it when he supports freedom from circumcision, but not from the law itself. Jervell, "Law in Luke-Acts," 33.

299. Marshall, *Luke*, 186, 192.

300. Marshall, *Luke*, 19.

301. Marshall, *Luke*, 186.

302. Marshall, *Luke*, 190. Here Marshall sees the pious life as a preparation for faith.

303. Marshall, *Luke*, 191. At this point his view agrees with that of Bruce, *Acts*, 336–37.

304. Marshall, *Luke*, 211. Here, Marshall definitely views the account of Acts through the concepts of the apostle Paul's theology.

305. Hess defines kashrut as "an ancient set of obligations (*mitzvot*), a practice of attentiveness or separation, and a way of eating and attending to all matters with respect to food while sensitized to what is defined as sacred, set apart." She identifies this Hebrew term with two meanings: "complying with the dietary laws" or "fit for ritual consumption." Hess, "Encountering Habits of Mind at Table," 329. Thus, not everything in kashrut has to be viewed as connected to cult.

fitted into the pattern of the dietary laws of Torah.[306] At the same time the prohibition of πορνεία in the Western reading could not be assumed to belong to the dietary laws, and called for a different pattern.[307] The attempts to reconcile the problem of the Decree were narrowed to the search for its cultic rationale. Thus the majority of writers prefer to see, in the content of the Apostolic Decree, the allusion to the law about strangers in the midst of Israel, which was included in Leviticus and known as the Holiness Code.[308] The common basis for the four prohibitions was suggested as a call for holiness in contrast to the immoralities of pagan worship.

Connection of the Decree to Leviticus 17-18

JACOB JERVELL

Jacob Jervell suggested a law-centered approach to the Decree and refuted Haenchen's ethical interpretation.[309] Jervell did not understand the church as "the New Israel" with the new form of covenant, but contrastingly, sees the church as a continuation of old Israel with the same law given on Sinai.[310] He shows that the split of the early church from Judaism took place when the Jews themselves separated from the true people of God that received the promise through Moses and the prophets.[311]

Jervell noticed that though Luke "freed" the Gentiles from circumcision, he insisted on a circumcised Messiah.[312] He viewed the Apostolic Decree as "neither an abrogation nor any new interpretation of the law."[313] However, the phrase by James in Acts 21:25, μηδὲν τοιοῦτον τηρεῖν αὐτούς leaves an impression of the

---

306. Suggit, "'Holy Spirit and We Resolved,'" 47. See also Tomson "Jewish Food," 208.

307. David Whitlock, following John B. Pohill, argued that the issue of fellowship was the main idea of the Decree, which presumes differences in cultic background, not in ethical. The ethical explanation of the Decree requires a "strict following of the Western text." Whitlock, "Exposition of Acts 15:1-29," 377-78.

308. Lev 17:8-14 is a discussion about cultic slaughtering and in Lev 18 continues with prohibited sexual relationships, which also applied to strangers (18:26).

309. Jervell, "Law in Luke-Acts." Jervell did not develop the "cultic" view on the Decree, but turned the attention of the scholars to the Jewish tradition, grounded in the laws of Torah and assigned it as the rationale for the Decree. After his work was published this idea triggered the search to discover the cultic background of the Decree. Jervell viewed the validity of the laws of Torah for the church as applying until our day. Despite this, the majority of theologians accepted the cultic view as the chance to converge the Decree and the Jewish ethos, and propose their temporary significance. Jervell's position remains unchanged in *Die Apostelgeschichte*, 388-400.

310. Jervell, "Law in Luke-Acts," 23. Dickinson agrees with Jervell on the point about one and only Israel. He also understands the history of Israel as a story of failure to keep the law. Dickinson, "Theology of Jerusalem Conference," 70, 77.

311. Jervell, "Law in Luke-Acts," 23. He argues that the people of God still remain as one Israel and notices that the term "the New Israel" is not found in the New Testament.

312. Jervell, "Law in Luke-Acts," 27. The Lukan Messiah lived in all faithfulness to the law since childhood and died in accordance with it.

313. Jervell, "Law in Luke-Acts," 32-33.

cancellation of the wider scope of the laws (including the purification laws), at least regarding their practical use.

He viewed the true Israel as people of the law, who stood as the foundation of the church, and the Gentiles as joining them.[314] Jervell linked the four prohibitions to the law about aliens associated with Israel (Leviticus 17–18).[315] His law-centered approach to the Apostolic Decree sheds light on the historical context of Acts. One intertextuality attracted the attention of NT scholars; this interpretation of the Decree became known as "cultic."[316]

Joseph Fitzmyer

Fitzmyer notices that Luke pictured the messiahship of Jesus according to the scriptural tradition, without altering the law.[317] He believes that the church became heir of the previous covenant and all its laws.[318] However, he believes that the church does not continue to practice the Mosaic law, which is unable to save people, who receive salvation by faith in Jesus. At this point the church still refers to the law with its normative function, and provides four rules for the Gentiles from the precise passage in Leviticus.[319]

As a result, he considers all references to the law in Acts which use the word νόμος to refer to the law given on Sinai.[320] Scrutinizing the speeches from the Jerusalem Council, he shows James asking the Gentile Christians to adopt the same lifestyle practiced by the Jewish Christians "as the law itself demands of pagan sojourners

---

314. Jervell, "Law in Luke-Acts," 32.

315. Jervell, "Law in Luke-Acts," 33.

316. Wilson, Fitzmyer, Pao, Sandt, Glenny, Dickinson link the four prohibitions of the Decree to the laws of Torah.

317. Fitzmyer, *Luke the Theologian*, 40–50. Fitzmyer treats the infancy narrative to show Jesus' christological identification. He mentions the purification according to the law of Moses in Luke 2:22. Following the law of purification, a firstborn son had to be "redeemed" (Exod 13:1–2; Num 3:47–48). Since Luke grouped all references to the Mosaic law under the heading of purification, it seemed that Jesus needed purification too. For that reason Fitzmyer explains the phrase "their purification" in Luke 2:22 as Luke's lack of detailed knowledge of Jewish customs.

318. Fitzmyer, *Luke the Theologian*, 191–93. Fitzmyer shows the necessity for the Jewish Christians to receive salvation "through grace," just as the Gentile Christians. He explains the new approach by Israel's failure to keep the covenantal relationships. Later he states, "Peter as a Jewish Christian recognizes the impossibility of human beings ever being able to carry out (*bastazein*) all the demands of the Mosaic law." Fitzmyer, *Acts of the Apostles*, 547–48.

319. Fitzmyer, *Luke the Theologian*, 194. See also Fitzmyer, *Acts*, 556–58.

320. Fitzmyer, *Luke the Theologian*, 186. See also Fitzmyer, *Acts*, 557.

S. G. Wilson

Investigating terminology, νόμος, ἐντολή, and ἔθος in Luke's writings, Wilson notices a parallel between the "customs of Moses" in Acts 15:1 and the "law of Moses" in Acts 15:5.[323] He shows the Lukan tendency to reveal that the minority raised the demand for circumcision of the Gentiles.[324] He emphasizes the close relation between the accounts in Acts 10 and 15. Treating Peter's vision as a sort of parable, he explains that the part of the law concerning clean and unclean persons was overturned, cancelling the social segregation of Jews from Gentiles.

Wilson further insists that the Apostolic Decree was circulated widely "in both oral and written form."[325] He viewed the regulations of the Decree as the things from which God-fearers normally abstained.[326] According to him the problem was solved by posing certain Levitical obligations.[327] Wilson shows from patristic literature that the libertine Gnostics practiced eating food offered to idols and participating in pagan cults. Thus, the Decree could be viewed as prevention of that deviation. He understands the rationale for the Decree in terms of expressing piety.[328]

H. Sandt

Sandt suggests viewing Acts 15 from the perspective of intertextuality. He notices a link between the events in Acts and the Exodus story and the Sinaitic covenant,

---

321. Fitzmyer, *Luke the Theologian*, 194. Fitzmyer connected the four prohibitions to the law of the strangers in Lev 17–18. This view however does not explain why churches in Antioch, Syria and Cilicia, consisting predominantly of the Gentile converts, had to keep the law about the "aliens who live in your midst," which related to those who lived among the Jews.

322. This view was supported by Jervell, Wilson, Pao, Sandt and Glenny.

323. Wilson, *Luke and Law*, 4. Wilson considers ἔθος and νόμος as interchangeable words for Luke. He assumes "customs" in Acts 15:1 in two ways: as specified customs, and the Jewish way of life in general sense. The group of a specified customs includes the customs of priesthood (Luke 1:9), circumcision (Acts 15:1), and Passover (Luke 2:42).

324. Wilson, *Luke and Law*, 73.

325. Wilson, *Luke and Law*, 78. Wilson suggests treating both readings (Western and proto-Alexandrian) as potentially original.

326. Wilson, *Luke and Law*, 74. Wilson doesn't see God-fearers as the proselytes, who had to be circumcised and fully become Jews.

327. Wilson, *Luke and Law*, 76. He refers to Lev 17–18, which was understood as the rules for strangers.

328. Wilson, *Luke and Law*, 61, 102. His attempt to explain the link of the Decree to the Holiness Code.

which suggests the re-establishment of the law.³²⁹ He assumes that the theophany in Acts 2 and 10 shared similar features with that on Sinai, and expects the repetition of the same law.³³⁰ Then he states, that "the law of Moses remains valid also for the Gentile believers" for they have to keep the law of strangers (Lev 17–18) in the midst of Israel (Acts15:20).³³¹

Sandt notes that speeches in Acts 15 by both Peter and of James share a similar structure.³³² His observation supports one thesis of this present study, that James uses some Peter's thoughts to create midrash. James' conclusion "with a reference to the authority of Moses (v 21)" suggests viewing Moses still as an authoritative source, rather than a burdensome one.³³³ Additionally, he rightly notes that the reasoning of Barnabas and Paul did not play any role in James' speech.

Sandt concludes his study by linking some prohibitions to the cultic context of Deut 4:23 and to the Exodus story. With this he seems to connect the four prohibitions to Lev17–18, viewing them as moral obligations. This uncertainty about a common background for all four prohibitions of the Decree reveals and highlights the need for a differentiation of purposes of the laws of Torah, and their validity at the time of the early church.

David W. Pao

Another attempt to explain the Decree with the help of intertextuality was that of David Pao, who finds patterns of a New Exodus "developed and transformed through the Isaianic corpus" behind Luke-Acts.³³⁴ He believes Luke structured his work according to the Exodus paradigm, which was also the central theological motif for Isaiah.³³⁵ According to Pao, this helped Luke to complete the redefinition of the people of God for his community.³³⁶ This redefinition allowed Gentile converts to be viewed

---

329. Sandt, "Explanation of Acts 15:6–21," 86–87. Sandt supports his view by linking Acts 15:7 to Acts 10:33b; Acts 2:1–13; and Deut 4:33. He relates the fiery theophany on Sinai (Deut 4:33) to the tongues, "as of fire," at Pentecost. Sandt believes that the Gentiles in Cornelius' home experienced Pentecost (Acts 10:44–48), and by that Sinai-like revelation were integrated into the "people of God."

330. Sandt, "Explanation of Acts 15:6–21," 89. Thus the word ἔθνος from Deut 4:34 had been replaced by λαὸν in Acts 15:14 which was usually reserved in Luke-Acts for the people of God, and "for himself" turned into "for his name," revealing the new status of the Gentiles.

331. Sandt, "Explanation of Acts 15:6–21," 93.

332. Sandt, "Explanation of Acts 15:6–21," 73.

333. Sandt, "Explanation of Acts 15:6–21," 74.

334. Pao, *Acts and the Isaianic New Exodus*, 5 n. 17. Pao notes that the idea of the Exodus typology in Isaiah had been discussed by Anderson and Harelson, eds., *Israel's Prophetic Heritage*, 177–95; E. John Hamlin, Deutero-Isaiah's Reinterpretation of Exodus"; and SLoewenstamm, *Evolution of the Exodus Tradition*, 2.1.66–105.

335. Pao, *Acts and the Isaianic New Exodus*, 249. He argues for the one hermeneutical key for both volumes of Luke's work.

336. Pao, *Acts and the Isaianic New Exodus*, 58, 239 n. 71. Pao discusses the equality of the Jews

as a part of the people of God. The phrase μεταξὺ ἡμῶν τε καὶ αὐτῶν in Peter's speech means the equality of Gentile converts with the Jewish believers.[337]

Pao notes that the demand of circumcision in Acts 15:1 received a negative response in 15:24. He concludes that this rite was thus no longer required for the Gentile believers as a condition for salvation.[338] The Mosaic law was not to be imposed on them.[339] Thus, Pao did not view the Decree in terms of regulations of the Mosaic law. For him the Exodus typology was a framework for the anti-idol polemic at the Jerusalem Council. So, the Decree has to be understood in the context of "the polemic against pagan worship."[340]

He argues against linking the Decree to the law about "strangers in the land" (Lev 17–18), pointing out that the recipients of the Decree were outside of the land of Israel and Levitical laws thus could not refer to them.[341] However, Pao's anti-idol polemic seems not to be a sufficient explanation for the list of prohibitions. This can be seen from the fact that the preaching of Moses in diaspora synagogues was not limited to the proclamation of the one God instead of many, but also provided for religious teaching about this one God. Despite these contradictions, Pao's work takes a fresh look at the content of the Decree from the perspective of intertextuality.

Concluding this section on the cultic interpretation of the Decree, linking its content to Lev 17–18, the following points need to be clarified. The link to Lev 17–18 presumes also a connection of the Decree to the Mosaic law. Many scholars view the Mosaic law as not applicable to Gentile converts. Since the Mosaic law was commonly understood as "done away with," as a requirement for Gentile converts during the council, the imposing of "the law about strangers" on the converts in Asia Minor has no solid justification. Scholars who take this position believe that the four prohibitions were only temporary requirements for the peace of the mixed communities.

Connection of the Decree to the Jewish Halakhah

The search for the background rationale of the cultic form of the decree has led scholars to consider the influence of Jewish *halakah* on the early Christian community in Jerusalem. The main work on this approach has been done by John Perry.

---

and Gentiles in their participation in the messianic kingdom; he also questions the evaluation of the law for the new Christian community due to "redefinition of the status of the people of God."

337. Pao, *Acts and the Isaianic New Exodus*, 238.

338. Pao, *Acts and the Isaianic New Exodus*, 239–41 nn. 74, 75. Pao recognies "the limitations of the salvific significance of the law." The distinction between ecclesiological and soteriological functions of the law was discussed by F. Bovon, J. Nolland, Jervell, and Wilson.

339. Pao, *Acts and the Isaianic New Exodus*, 241–42 n. 85.

340. Pao, *Acts and the Isaianic New Exodus*, 241.

341. Pao, *Acts and the Isaianic New Exodus*, 241 n. 80. He points out that recipients of the Decree were outside the land of Israel, so Levitical laws could not be applied to them.

John Perry

Perry reveals the presence of internal distinctions between the universal versus the particular laws in Acts, and in Torah itself.[342] Starting with the belief that Torah was not only about rituals, but it is also deeply moral, he emphasizes that "the early church's moral theology had its roots firmly planted in Jewish halakah."[343] He states that the church in Acts "consistently employed distinctions internal to Torah" namely halakhic categories of Leviticus, as well as Noachic laws.[344]

According to him the Gentiles could find salvation only in Torah's shadow, for "there is no salvation outside Torah."[345] Perry concludes that "the Mosaic law continued to shape the moral vision of the early church and it incorporated Gentiles by understanding them as aliens welcomed into the midst of a holy people."[346] However, Perry sees the moral influence of Torah in two different ways: universal and non-universal.[347] Here he places kashrut together with circumcision in a group of particular laws assigned to the descendants of Abraham.[348] He considers Torah's influence in Acts 15 as an imposition of non-universal ethics on Gentile Christians.[349] Thus scholars who hold the cultic view of the Decree have come to the conclusion that its prohibitions are temporary requirements, essential for the common meals in the early church, and later done away with as Jewish ethnic customs.

Charles H. Savelle

The idea of relating the four prohibitions to pre-Mosaic Torah ethos has been expressed by Charles Savelle.[350] Noticing the differences between the wording in Acts 15:20 and Acts 15:29 and the identical wording of Acts 15:29 and Acts 21:25, he considers that

---

342. Perry, "Are Christians the 'Aliens,'" 159.

343. Perry, "Ethics in Acts 10–15," 157, 159. He believes that Jews according to Jewish halakah understood "the ethical duties of Gentiles are either as *geirei toshav* (aliens who live in the midst of people) or as *bnai Noach* (children of Noah, bound by the minimum standards of law that oblige all humans as such)."

344. Perry, "Ethics in Acts 10–15," 159. He refers to Lev17–18 including the law of aliens who live in the midst. Moreover Perry suggests the connection of the Decree to the pre-Mosaic tradition.

345. Perry, "Ethics in Acts 10–15," 164. Thus, Paula Fredriksen viewed God-fearers as Sabbath keepers, observers of food laws and Jewish holidays. Paula Fredriksen, "Torah Observance and Christianity," 197.

346. Perry, "Ethics in Acts 10–15," 165–70. Here Perry describes the Gentile converts as pseudo-converts and at the same time as full-fledged members of the new community.

347. Perry, "Ethics in Acts 10–15," 161. According to him the distinction between moral and ritual laws of Torah was revealed as "legally unworkable or practically awkward."

348. Perry, "Ethics in Acts 10–15," 163.

349. Perry, "Ethics in Acts 10–15," 171. Perry does not accept the prohibitions literally.

350. Savelle, "Reexamination of Prohibitions," 458.

the Decree is presented in Acts 15:29 and 21:25 in its written form.³⁵¹ Savelle further examines the variant readings in Greek manuscripts.

He explains the omission of καὶ τῆς πορνείας in Acts 15:20 in 𝔓45 and some Ethiopian manuscripts as an intentional omission made by a scribe "since this phrase is the only explicit moral stipulation in the decree."³⁵² The omission of καὶ τοῦ πνικτοῦ in D (05) gig Ir lat is understood as a harmonization made in support of the ethical interpretation of the Decree, as well as an addition of the Golden Rule in Western manuscripts.³⁵³ He believes that the Alexandrian tradition preserves the original version of the Decree.

Discussing the prohibitions of the Decree, Savelle interprets εἰδωλοθύτων as "something offered to a cultic image/idol."³⁵⁴ According to literary, biblical and historical contexts, Savelle views the prohibition of πορνεία linked to the rest of the Decree not only in an ethical way, but also in a cultic way of true worship.³⁵⁵ He tends to interpret αἵμα in connection with the OT food laws.³⁵⁶ The term πνικτός and the verb πνίγω in the NT metaphorically refers to "strangled, or choked."³⁵⁷ He links πνικτός to the OT food law (Lev 17:13–14; Deut 12:16, 23) understanding that it refers to an animal killed improperly without draining its blood.³⁵⁸

In Savelle's view the four regulations fit the cultic form of the Decree, completed by the influence of Lev 17–18 and enriched by Noachic precepts and rabbinic teachings,³⁵⁹ which he also regards "as contributing something to the origins of the

---

351. Savelle, "Reexamination of Prohibitions," 449–51. Savelle compares the list of the prohibitions in all three passages (15:20, 29; 21:25). He notes that the differences between πορνείας/ πορνείαν and αἵματος/αἵμα are not significant, but he calls the change from "τῶν ἀλισγημάτων τῶν εἰδώλων" in Acts 15:20, to εἰδωλοθύτων, "a deliberate attempt to clarify" the meaning of the phrase.

352. Savelle, "Reexamination of Prohibitions," 450.

353. Savelle, "Reexamination of Prohibitions," 450, citing Barrett, *Critical Commentary on Acts*, 735–36.

354. Savelle, "Reexamination of Prohibitions," 452–53. He mentions that in the New Testament this word is used five times in Paul's epistles (1 Cor 8:1, 4, 7, 10; 10:19) and two times in Revelation (2:14, 20) in connection with the eating of meats sacrificed to idols. However, 4 Macc 5:1–2 ties consuming of unclean meat and things offered to idols together.

355. Savelle, "Reexamination of Prohibitions," 453–54. The term πορνεία in the NT refers to sexual immorality of various kinds and in the writings of John (John 8:41; Rev 2:21; 17:2, 4; 18:3; 19:2) connects with Babylon's spiritual harlotry. The "true worship" has to be understood as the worship of one God according to the way he had chosen and ascribed in the Torah.

356. Savelle, "Reexamination of Prohibitions," 454–55. See Gen 9:4; Lev 3:17; 7:26–27; 17:10–14; 19:26; Deut 12:16; 23–25, 27; 15:23; 1 Sam 14:32–34; Ezek 33:25; Zech 9:7. For him αἵμα has three basic meanings: 1. The basic component of the body; 2. Life, seat of life, or expiatory sacrifice; 3. Disaster in apocalyptic literature and a metonym for murder.

357. Savelle, "Reexamination of Prohibitions," 456.

358. Savelle, "Reexamination of Prohibitions," 456. Savelle refers to Philo's description of using strangled meat in sacrifices of pagan cults.

359. Savelle, "Reexamination of Prohibitions," 457–58, 461. Savelle explains "Moses" in Acts15:21 as a summary of the OT in one word. Lierman presents the many-faceted portrait of Moses in Torah and the NT, which suggests that Moses was seen as prophet, priest, apostle and law-giver. Lierman,

prohibitions."[360] As a result, he relates the prohibitions to "Jewish ethos," but not to "one specifically identifiable origin."[361] Savelle's concludes his study with the words, "keeping the prohibitions would be spiritually and relationally beneficial."[362] Assuming a temporary validity of the Decree, he sees its purpose to keep new converts from associating with pagan cults, and as the re-introduction of dietary rules appropriate for the common meals in the early church.[363]

Connection of the Decree to the Noachic Laws

Some scholars argue a pre-Mosaic origin of the four prohibitions of the Decree in Acts by linking them to the Noachic laws.[364] They have recognized a renewed creation order established with Noah after the flood according to Gen 9:1–7, which includes the prohibition of blood consumption. This allows the application of these prohibitions to Gentile as well as to Hebrew descendants of Noah. This has resulted in placing the Noachic laws as background of the Decree.[365] This view tries to fix the gap between the prohibitions and Lev 17–18, and the need for rules to regulate the behavior of aliens in Israel.[366]

JUSTIN TAYLOR

Justin Taylor searches for the rationale of the Decree in the seven Noachide commandments.[367] He supports both the view that links the Decree to proto-Noachide commandments, and the view that links it to Lev 17:7–9.

Justification for imposing the Noachic laws on Gentiles is found in the rabbinical teaching preserved in the Tosefta: "all human communities are expected to uphold"

"New Testament Moses," 317–20.

360. Savelle, "Reexamination of Prohibitions," 461. Savelle views the Noachic laws as one possible "mindset behind the prohibitions" together with unidentified ethos.

361. Savelle, "Reexamination of Prohibitions," 468.

362. Savelle, "Reexamination of Prohibitions," 467.

363. Savelle, "Reexamination of Prohibitions," 467.

364. This view has support from Taylor, Bockmuehl, and is partially accepted by Savelle. Also, the Noachic covenant was assumed as of decisive importance for it "establishes the basis or foundation for the story (God's commitment to creation, and in particular, the preservation of life on earth) . . . and provides an anticipation of the conclusion of the story of redemption (God's judgments on sin, salvation of the righteous, and renewal of creation)." Chalmers, "Importance of the Noahic Covenant," 207.

365. This interpretation of the Decree in connection to Noachic laws has one weak point: the Decree is linked to pre-Mosaic laws on the basis of Gen 9:1–11, while the Noachic laws are the product of rabbinical teachings in the Tosefta.

366. The view of the Decree connecting it to the Noachic laws also overlooks the fact that the division of fauna into clean and unclean comes in the midst of the flood narrative. Thus the flood narrative seems to be linked to Lev 11 as well as Lev 17–18.

367. Schwartz, "Noahide Laws, Christian Covenants," 768.

these seven Noachide commandments.³⁶⁸ Rabbis viewed the Gentiles as the sons of Noah standing outside of the covenant with Abraham.³⁶⁹ This presupposes a shared background and the presence of common beliefs shared by Jews and non-Jews.

Here, Taylor notes that the Jerusalem Council discussed the status of Gentile converts and their relation to the ritual law.³⁷⁰ He states that James at the council did not refer to the Decalogue at all. From this point Taylor concludes that the apostles did not bind the Gentile converts to the Mosaic law.³⁷¹ He thus rejects the connection of the four prohibitions to Mosaic law established by the Sinaitic covenant, and looks for their pre-Sinaitic origin.

Taylor links the prohibition of πορνεία to the curse of Ham, who uncovered the nakedness of his father Noah.³⁷² Further, he sees the τῶν ἀλισγημάτων τῶν εἰδωλοθύτων as a call to avoid pagan rites. The prohibitions of πνικτός together with αἷμα he connects to Genesis 9:4 and accepts "in the sense of meat that has not been killed correctly."³⁷³ This, however, does not lead him to discover the link between the prohibitions and the food laws of Torah.

Markus Bockmuehl

Marcus Bockmuehl understands the Noachide commandments "as a key formulation of Jewish ethics for Gentiles."³⁷⁴ Noting that Luke recalls the *halakhah* "with great accuracy," he shows Luke treating Gentiles as Noachides.³⁷⁵ Bockmuehl emphasizes

---

368. Novak, "Jewish Mission," 42. Novak relates these seven Noachic laws to the Tosefta of the second century CE. In this document the second commandment abolished idolatry, the fourth prohibited sexual immorality, the fifth was written against shedding of blood, and the seventh prohibited the consumption of meat torn from a live animal.

369. Hirsh, "Beyond the Noahide Laws," 28.

370. Taylor, "Jerusalem Decrees," 375.

371. Taylor, "Jerusalem Decrees," 376. However, it seems that the Decalogue represents the moral law of God rather than Mosaic law.

372. Here Taylor recalls the phrase "uncover the nakedness" referring it to all sexual immorality prohibited in Lev 18:6–25. Taylor, "Jerusalem Decrees," 376.

373. Taylor, "Jerusalem Decrees," 376. Taylor also considers the term αἵματος in both senses as eating the blood of animals and as shedding of human blood. He also recalls the way of cooking meat by "suffocation" in pagan offerings. He is ready to see the meaning of the word πνικτός as "torment" and harmonize it with the negative form of the Golden Rule in the Western reading. His view is supported by Instone-Brewer explaining πνικτός as the prohibition of infanticide in the Gentile world. Instone-Brewer, "Infanticide and the Apostolic Decree," 313–16, 320, 321.

374. Bockmuehl, *Jewish Law in Gentile Churches*, 146, 172. Here Bockmuehl sees the Noachide commandments as a "rabbinic development of the biblical laws about resident aliens." He believes that *halakhah* in the first century AD influenced the forming of the Apostolic Decree.

375. Bockmuehl, *Jewish Law in Gentile Churches*, 53, 57, 164. Bockmuehl provides the evidences for the presence of Jewish settlement in Antioch in the 170s BCE. By this fact he shows the patency of the God-fearers from the Gentiles in Antioch to be familiar with the Jewish *halakhah*. He also states that many of them enjoined a social integration with the Jewish population. This means that Jews had a common ground to accept those Gentiles not only on the basis of making them proselytes.

that the Decree deals with "three carefully defined forbidden foods: food sacrificed to idols, meat with blood still in it (*nebelah*, i.e. probably including that which died by itself), and meat from an animal that was not properly slaughtered (i.e. 'strangled' or possibly also 'torn,' *terefah*)."[376]

Treating the four prohibitions in Acts 15, Bockmuehl takes αἵματος "as a dietary injunction with broader implication" and sees in it the abrogation of homicide.[377] The term πορνεία is interpreted by him as extramarital sex, because in the NT this term applies to "neither specifically adultery nor illicit degrees of kinship, but (like זנות) any kind of unlawful sexual relationship."[378] He insists that the prohibitions of idolatry, bloodshed and sexual immorality could form the triplet of Jewish capital crimes. As those crimes were mentioned in the Noachide laws, Bockmuehl sees them as suitable to account for the content of the Apostolic Decree.

The clear allusions of the Apostolic Decree to Deut 12:16, 23–25; 4:29–35, Lev 17–18 and Gen 9:4 indicate that their rationale is rooted in the laws of Torah, and not simply in Jewish *halakhah* or sacral ancestral tradition referred to by ἔθος. The attempts to represent the Noachic *laws* as the background of the four prohibitions in Acts 15:20 appear to be inadequate because of a lack of adequate scriptural ground.[379] The flood narrative and the covenant with Noah are, however, intermediate sources for apostolic ethics and prohibitions of the Decree.

Significant Premises for the Present Study

The trends that have been revealed by the analysis of recent research reflect a widening of the search for the Old Testament basis for concepts of the Decree and a willingness to consider including the Genesis flood narrative. The present study is an attempt to discover in Gen 1–3 the basis for the four prohibitions of the Apostolic Decree. The creation-fall account in Gen 1–3 is the most important composition prior to the flood narrative. This has support from three recently developed Old Testament theological concepts echoed in the NT. These are the creation–fall–re-creation paradigm, the concept of natural/universal law, and false versus true worship motifs.[380] These three

376. Bockmuehl, *Jewish Law in Gentile Churches*, 166.

377. Bockmuehl, *Jewish Law in Gentile Churches*, 166. Contrastingly Wedderburn notes the connection of τοῦ πνικτοῦ to τοῦ αἵματος and explains τοῦ πνικτοῦ as food which contains blood. Wedderburn, "'Apostolic Decree,'" 371.

378. Bockmuehl, *Jewish Law in Gentile Churches*, 21. However, Wedderburn sees the term πορνεία in the New Testament as taken in a broader sense and commonly associated with idolatry (Rev 2:14, 20; 1 Cor 5:11, 6:9, 10:7–8). Wedderburn, "Apostolic Decree," 364.

379. As Callan notes, the content of the Noachic laws differs from that of the Apostolic Decree. He states: "Many different lists of the Noachic laws are found (e.g., *Jub.* 7:20; *b. Sanh.* 56b), but none corresponds exactly to the laws underlying the Apostolic Decree." Callan, "Background of the Apostolic Decree," 293.

380. According to Block, the temple theology is rooted in creation theology and temple motifs in the OT and the NT prefigured the world's re-creation. The temple also denoted the role of Christ "as

concepts, in what follows, will together provide the platform to support the prohibitions of the Apostolic Decree.

Roland Deines, in his recent work, argues that the lasting significance of the four prohibitions "lies in the component that relates them to natural law."[381] He views that "the Decree obliges Gentile Christians to live a life according to the most basic elements of God's order of creation (cf. the references to Luke's creation theology in Acts 14:15–17; 17:24–7."[382] This view of Deines is supported by Bettina Rost.[383] Identification of the creation theology in the writings of Luke suggests that the early church understood the universal significance of the creation motifs and could employ them in forming a decree of universal significance, which regulated the life of Christians in non-Jewish cultural contexts.

This thesis will argue that the apostles during the Jerusalem Council crystallized the four prohibitions from the mass of theological principles of the law, with the help of what is known as the creation–fall–re-creation paradigm. During the process of reviewing the law, the apostles came to understand the temple motifs of the OT to be fulfilled in Christ. As a result, the parts of the law such as those governing temple cult were assumed unnecessary for salvation. At the same time the apostles recognized the validity of the natural law of God rooted in the Genesis creation-fall account. For them, the four prohibitions of the Apostolic Decree fitted into the pattern of the natural law of God as reflected in Gen 1–3. As will emerge later in this thesis these three concepts, working together, reveal the rationale of the Apostolic Decree.

The Definition of the "Natural Law of God"

The natural law of God as used in this thesis is to be understood as an adaptation of the universal law of creation, as impacted by the consequences of the fall. The existence of this natural law established by God is evident; "the serpent's lie is a lie about nature: idolatry denies the natural ordinance that God is God and man is man."[384] This universal law as the divinely ordained order of the whole universe, established at and valid since its origin, seems to be reflected in the creation account of Gen 1–2.[385] True worship, dietary regulations and marriage order were

---

the link between a fallen world and a heavenly court." Block, "Eden: A Temple?," 26–27.

381. Deines, *Acts of God in History*, 187.

382. Deines, *Acts of God in History*, 186.

383. Rost, "Das Aposteldekret im Verhältnis zur Mosetora," 575–76.

384. Bockmuehl argues for "the idea of law according to nature." He derives this idea from selected prophetic and wisdom passages "which argue for moral propositions from a natural state of affairs." Thus, he notes that God's order in creation is fundamentally related to the order expressed in Torah. He shows they "are not the independent edicts of autonomos nature, but the direct response to God's sending forth his word to the earth." Bockmuehl, "Natural Law in Second Temple Judaism," 17, 19–20, 43.

385. According to VanDrunen, the natural law is for preservation of life after the fall. Though he views the Noachic covenant in Gen 8–9 as the starting point for natural law, he believes that it

established at creation. After the fall, universal law experienced changes and was adjusted to fit the consequences of life under the curses of the fall.[386] This extension of the universal law will be referred to as the "natural law of God," since God made those adjustments to fit natural law to fallen human nature living after the fall.[387] As a result, the worship system, the dietary regulations and the marital order were also adjusted to the new conditions of life after the fall.

The history of humankind reveals attempts of humans themselves to adjust the natural law of God to the life conditions of fallen humanity. This adjustment will be labelled "natural laws of nations." These culturally conditioned laws reveal diverse attitudes toward worship, marital and dietary regulations among the nations of the world. Violation of the biblical order led to the appearance of alternative cultic systems among the nations. The cultic laws of the Gentiles were more immoral than their civil laws, due to the close association of Gentile cults with demonic worship.[388] The concepts of true worship, marital relationships and diet were corrupted by pagan cults.

As will emerge later in this thesis, the discussion on the Jerusalem Council was aimed finding a theological core which would redirect the Gentile converts from worshiping in pagan cults, back to true worship. To make this reversal possible, the apostles invited Gentile converts to live according to the light of the natural law of

---

represents a repetition of the covenant with Adam from Gen 1:28–30, adjusted to new life conditions. VanDrunen, "Natural Law in Noachic Accent," 137. John Wood and Fowler White propose the theory of the Adamic covenant. See Wood, "Merit in the Midst of Grace," 144–48. See also White, "Last Adam and His Seed," 67, 72.

386. The universal law of creation in Gen 1–2 predicated: 1) the true worship affirming holiness, blessings, covenant keeping; 2) an ideal diet (1:29); 3) immortality; 4) ideal marriage; 5) procreation; 6) dominion over the Earth; 6) innocence of people. The natural law of God appeared after the fall in Gen 3 reflects some changes: 1) restoration of the true worship due to repentance, confession of sin and redemption (God's call to Adam in 3:9–13); 2) change of diet (3:17–19); 3) natural law of death (3:19); 4) woman's desire for a husband and her submissive role (3:16); 5) pains in bearing and delivering of children (3:16); 6) antagonism in the animal kingdom (3:15); 7) shame of "nakedness" (3:10). All these consequences of the fall can be assumed as natural at the present stage of life.

387. David Novak defines the "natural law" in terms of "the universally valid and rationally discernible norms of human conduct." Novak, "Law of Moses, Law of Nature," 45. He also additionally describes the "natural law" as the basic moral norms "accessible to human reason independent of divine revelation." Hughes, "David Novak," 5–6. The present study finds it necessary to differentiate the "natural law of God," which is divinely ordained order (in Gen 1–2; 3:9–19 and 9:1–4) from the "natural law of nations," which fits better Novak's concept of "natural law."

388. Gen 20:9 repeats the words of the Gentile king Abimelech to Abraham, who called his wife "a sister" and allowed her to be engaged in relationship with another man, "You have done things to me that should never be done." The phrase reveals that even in Canaan culture it was unlawfull to commit sexual intercourse with someone else's wife. Gen 26:11 refers to the civil law protecting marital union. At the same time pagan religious practices allowed more than the violation of the marital union (Gen 38:12–26; Lev 18:3–24, where the forms of cultic prostitution, and incestuous relationships are described). Exod 34:15–16 links cultic prostitution of Canaanites to their religion. Deut 18:9–14 demonstrates that such practice, like human sacrifices and necromancy, were linked to pagan idolatry, divination and witchcraft.

God. This law "from ancient generations" was preached and "read in the synagogues every Sabbath" (Acts 15:21). According to apostolic advice, the Gentile converts were not to be subjected to the Mosaic ritual system, but to the natural law of God, which would unite all nations to God on the grounds of Gen 1–3.

In order to make Gentile conversion possible, the apostles prescribed a reversal in Gentiles' lives of three main practices: worship, diet and marriage. The prohibition of εἰδωλοθύτων can be understood as a reversal of the core of worship. It seems also to coincide with dietary law. The connection of the prohibitions of αἵματος and πνικτῶν to a pattern of dietary law is clear. Moskala suggests that the prohibitions of the Decree are linked to the dietary laws, "in light of Lev 17:10–14 . . . apostolic prohibitions implicitly include the clean and unclean food distinction."[389] Moreover, the connection of the prohibitions to Lev 17–18, commonly known as the Holiness Code, implies that they include a call to holiness.[390] The dietary laws in general were daily reminders leading the believer "into patterns of ethical behavior."[391]

It is hard to define which part of the dietary laws belong to natural law and which to universal law. Some scholars assume that the dietary laws of Torah reflect the process of rational separation, programmed in Gen 1 as a part of the universal law of creation.[392] However, the present study views the dietary system of Leviticus (11 and 17) as part of the "natural law of God" developed after the fall, though the primordial dietary regulations existed since creation as a part of the universal law. The detailed exegesis of Gen 1–3, in chapter 3, argues that the prohibitions of εἰδωλοθύτων, αἵματος and πνικτῶν originated after the fall and fit into the pattern of the natural law of God.

The prohibition of πορνείας to be linked to the marital laws of Torah, developed out of Gen 1–3. The ground for this prohibition in the Holiness Code has also been noted by scholars. On one hand, this presumes the association of the marital laws with the true worship, and on the other hand defines πορνεία as an activity associated with fornication in pagan cults. The detailed explanation which fits the prohibition of πορνεία into the patterns of the natural law, will be provided in chapter 3.

The Role of the Worship Motifs in the Apostolic Decree

According to Roy Gane, all OT laws were traditionally divided in four categories: 1) *moral laws* including the Ten Commandments, which "express timeless and universal principles"; 2) *ritual laws* which "served as 'types' and 'shadows' until they met

---

389. Moskala, *Laws of Clean and Unclean*, 377.

390. Milgrom, *Leviticus 1–16*, 730–31.

391. Milgrom, *Leviticus 1–16*, 736.

392. The term "rational separation" was used by J. Moskala in order to show that some separations were made by God during the process of creation, including separation of the animals into groups of clean and unclean. Moskala, *Laws of Clean and Unclean*, 150, 212, 365. Leon R. Kass also links the dietary system to an eternal universal law. Kass, "Why the Dietary Laws," 42, 43.

their fulfillment at the cross"; 3) *civil laws* "applicable only under Israel's theocratic government"; and 4) *health laws* "which have ongoing value because human bodies function the same today as they did in ancient times."[393]

The worship motifs in Torah are explicitly associated with the temple cult. This cult was designed to deal with the consequences of the fall. True worship before the fall presumes people's roles as priests and guardians of the temple-garden. This stage of worship is implicitly present in the narratives of Gen 1–2. Gen 3 presents the motif of redemption, which is also implicit at that stage. Hope for redemption becomes a basis for the ritual system.

The role of rituals was rightly understood to project the image and hope for the Messiah, who would make atonement possible. For the apostles, Christ's atoning sacrifice accomplished redemption. The ritual law accomplished its purpose, and was then canceled and therefore has to be assumed as no longer necessary for salvation. This assumption found agreement among the apostles on the Jerusalem Council. As a result, no ritual law was included in the content of the Decree. The apostles did not impose the ritual law upon Gentile converts, since they recognized its temporary validity.[394] Moreover, the apostles found this new way of salvation in Christ more appropriate than requiring Gentile converts to become Jews first. The four prohibitions of the Decree were in no way associated with the temple cult and are to be understood as practical observations of key aspects of the natural law of God.[395] By observing these rules the converts were called on to experience a reversal from their former paganism to the true worship of God.

The Creation–Fall–Re-creation Paradigm

With help of the creation–fall–re-creation paradigm, the eternal validity of the universal laws of creation can be brought into view. On the other hand, natural law originating after the fall, has temporary validity which, according to the creation–fall–re-creation paradigm anticipates the reversal of natural law and the restoring of creation to its pristine state. Douglas J. Moo sees "new creation" as the act of restoring this original state of creation, which presupposes the inner renewal of individual hearts and the

---

393. Gane, ed., *Leviticus, Numbers*, 306.

394. Milgrom sees a connection between the dietary laws (precisely blood prohibition) and Acts 15. He argues for the abolition of the dietary system by the Jerusalem Council, except for the prohibition of blood, because "it is incumbent on mankind." He links the dietary laws to a pre-Mosaic tradition originating in the flood narrative. Milgrom, *Leviticus 1–16*, 726. However, this study reveals that 1) the premises for the distinction between clean and unclean creatures appear in the Gen 1–3 account (discussed in chapter 3); 2) Luke reflects the inclination of demons to associate with unclean creatures (discussed in chapter 4); 3) pagan worship included sacrificing unclean creatures.

395. Idol sacrifices, things strangled and fornication were never prescribed in the temple cult of Israel. The rituals performed with blood did not presume its consumption. They were divided into cultic slaughtering and non-cultic slaughtering. Both types of slaughtering required the blood to be drained out of the body.

restoration of the whole community.[396] VanDrunen believes that eschatologically the new creation will provide "liberation from life under the natural law."[397] The hope for the restoration of all creation to its initial state found expression in the Old Testament.[398] The Old Testament reveals "not the hope of the creator God's annihilation of his good creation, but of its ultimate restoration, fulfillment, and renewal."[399] This hope is also reflected in the Jewish writings contemporary with Luke.[400] The Lukan hope for restoration is linked to the Genesis account.[401]

Continuing validity of the dietary laws, up to the time of the re-creation, is determined by their association with the natural law.[402] Since the prohibitions of the Decree are associated with the dietary laws, marital laws and the core of true worship, they were understood by the apostles as necessary things up to the time of re-creation. Moreover, the unbroken validity of the dietary laws for New Testament believers until the time of the re-creation has support from the wider biblical context.[403]

The literature summary provided in this chapter reveals that the search for a unified rationale for the four prohibitions of the Apostolic Decree which eluded scholars through the Christian era now can be reopened with the help of new theological concepts and methods which suggest a possible connection between the Apostolic Decree and the universal/natural laws grounded in the creation account of Gen 1–3. They also have to be understood as a call for a reversal out of the false worship to the true worship which is fitted into the creation–fall–re-creation paradigm. Temple motifs reveal that the role of the ritual law was to shape the mission of Christ and point to its fulfillment. They presume the restoration of true worship on a deeper spiritual level, and hope for

---

396. Moo, "Creation and New Creation," 39, 42–47, 60.

397. VanDrunen, "Natural Law in Noachic Accent," 146.

398. Enns also finds the motifs of the creation and re-creation in Ps 95 and Heb 3:1—4:13. He states that even Exodus and the return from Babylon were understood as an act of God's new creation. Enns sees the fulfilling of hope for the "new creation" in the time of eschatological rest. This will be the same rest that "God has enjoyed since the completion of his creative work" as expressed in Gen 2:2. Enns, "Creation and Re-Creation," 259, 278.

399. Ware, "Paul's Hope and Ours," 130.

400. Wright, *Jesus and the Victory of God*, 444–46.

401. Pilgrim, "Luke-Acts and a Theology of Creation," 51–52, 58. Here Pilgrim argues that "Luke links creation and redemption." He states that "in the theology of Luke the whole created order bears testimony to the goodness of the Creator." He also notes that images of the new heaven and new earth in Rev 21–22 "correspond to Luke's own view of God's ultimate plan for creation." The connections of Lukan thoughts to the creation account were also expressed by Minear and Heyler. See Minear, *Christians and the New Creation*, 53–55; and Helyer, "Luke and the Restoration of Israel," 321.

402. The health laws, which Gane discusses here, are the natural laws. Thus, he views the dietary laws of Lev 11 and 17:10–14 as part of the health laws. He describes them as the laws of eternal validity (after the fall) since the human body functions after the fall similarly in all periods of human history. Gane, ed., *Leviticus, Numbers*, 309–10.

403. Moskala, *Laws of Clean and Unclean*, 371. He takes a number of texts as the larger New Testament context of the dietary laws of Torah: Matt 15:11, 17–20; Mark 7:19; Acts 10:15; 15:19–21, 28–29; Rom 14:14; 1 Cor 8:8; 10:23–27; Eph 2:15; Col 2:14–16; 1 Tim 4:1–5; Titus 1:15; Heb 9:10; 13:9.

Methodology of the Present Study

Intertextuality

This study employs intertextuality, a method that maps the memory associations "evoked in one's mind, between one text and another."[404] This method shares similarities with classical biblical exegesis, which presupposes the investigation of the linguistic context of Acts 15 in relation to Luke-Acts and its wider biblical context, literary structures, genres, cultural context and textual commentaries. Since the aim of this research is to discover the background rationale of the Apostolic Decree, the need for intertextual investigation of motifs, formulas, type-scenes and parallel accounts of Acts 15 is self-evident.[405]

Intertextuality as a method was first proposed by Julia Kristeva in 1969,[406] and then, employed by Richard Hays in 1989 for the study of Old Testament echoes in Pauline letters. Hays defines his method as "imbedding of fragments of an earlier text within a later one."[407] David I. Yoon argues that originally intertextuality was a secular term "applied to works of literature, such as novels and epics, as well as works of art, not authoritative writings as the Scriptures."[408] For him intertextuality "does not categorically apply to biblical studies unless one wants to study it simply as literature and not as authoritative writings designed to convey truth propositions regarding God and his gospel."[409]

However, Hays did not introduce a new method, but a new term in order to identify the old rabbinic method of interpretation of the biblical texts.[410] As a method of critical study, intertextuality was not invented to destroy the authority of Scriptures, but to recognize the Jewish thoughts or theological concepts of the Old Testament known prior to the particular text in the New Testament, concepts which apostles found worthy to be used as a basis of their theology.

Intertextuality will be used to disclose explicit and implicit echoes and allusions in the Decree of passages of the Hebrew Bible. It is anticipated that linguistic data will be helpful to find word-markers or catch-words employed to combine complex Old Testament quotations. These markers will be identified to assist in reconstructing the

---

404. Edenburg, "Intertextuality," 137.
405. Edenburg, "Intertextuality," 137.
406. Reynolds, "Echoes of Daniel," 5–6.
407. Hays, *Echoes of Scriptur*, 14.
408. Yoon, "Ideological Inception of Intertextuality," 73.
409. Yoon, "Ideological Inception of Intertextuality," 73.
410. Hays, *Echoes of Scripture*, 14.

original context of those Hebrew Bible quotations, in order that their original contextual meaning can be recovered and rightly understood.

Diagrams

Semantic diagramming of passages in Acts 15 and 21 has been employed to better reveal the structure of the Greek text. This type of diagraming has been developed in order to reveal semantic structures such as narrative links, dialogues and speeches, elements of Jewish tradition, temporal indicators, comparisons, contrasts, plus Luke's conclusions. The peculiarities of Luke's composition, developed to help the original audience comprehend and remember the narrative, will reveal the theological purposes of his work. It is likely that Acts narratives employed well-known literary patterns to enhance audience understanding.

Midrash

The discovery of midrashic tradition in Acts 15 will be another main feature of the present research. Midrash represents a "process by which one 'searches out' the meaning of scripture," which presumes the interpretation of the texts in halakhic, haggadic and homiletic interests by verbal expansion (as in Targums), and by the transformation of words, phrases and clauses (as in LXX).[411] At this stage, for the discovery of patterns behind the Decree, we will look for the key ideas of Gen 1–3. Analysis of the structure of Acts 15 will show the influence of midrash.[412] The goal will be to find all correlations between the speeches in Acts 15 and the creation–fall–re-creation paradigm through which the reconstitution of the new people of God would occur. To achieve this, we will explore relevant methods of Jewish rabbinical exegesis and their use in biblical writings, contemporary to the New Testament era.

Historical Reconstruction and the Concept of "Law" in Luke-Acts

This research will involve exploration of the historical context of Acts 15 in connection with its theological issues. The most important step here is the search for Luke's understanding of the law as a complex of various blocks, fitted into different patterns, rather than a single entity. This thesis also explores selected texts in Luke-Acts that mention law (explicitly or implicitly), and investigate the literary structure and rationale for evidence of different types of uncleanness. The aim will be to find traces of the

---

411. Chilton, "Varieties and Tendencies of Midrash," 9–10, 24.

412. Midrashic elements found in the NT differ from the classical midrash known in Targums. R. T. France suggests the use, in cases of NT midrashic tradition, of the term "creative midrash." He suggests that this kind of midrash has to be studied from the relation between the scripture and history in the actual text of the gospels. France, "Jewish Historiography," 99, 124.

so-called natural law of God, that is, an extension of the eternal principles of creation made by God in order to maintain life after the fall.

Chapter Summary

This chapter reviewed the history of interpretation of the Apostolic Decree in Acts 15. The history can be summarized in the following points:

1. The fourfold tradition of the Alexandrian (ambivalent) reading of the Apostolic Decree preserved by 𝔓74, ℵ 01, A 02, B 03, E 06, L and Ψ should be accepted as original.

2. The threefold Western (ethical) form of the Decree preserved by D 05 represents the fourth-century alteration of its text, which preserves attempts to introduce an ethical interpretation of its provisions as a result of anti-Jewish polemic in the church between the first and the fourth centuries.

3. The cultic form of the Decree preserved by 𝔓45 is a variation of the threefold tradition not influenced by the ethical interpretation. It preserves a tendency to interpret the Decree in association with Jewish cultic law.

4. The dominance of the Western text of Acts 15 above the others was a result of anti-Jewish policy due to increasing Orthodoxy in the church.

5. The alteration of the text into the form found in D 05 was the result of a process that included four stages: theological transition, theological pre-shift, theological shift and the period of variant readings. This alteration of the text was caused by the theological shift from Jewishness to Orthodoxy, taking place in mainstream Christianity during the third and fourth centuries.

6. This theological shift influenced the transmission of the text of Acts 15.

7. During the Mediaeval period, the text of the Apostolic Decree preserved the ethical form, plus alterations made during its transmission in previous centuries. The period of the Protestant Reformation, and the period of the critical study of Acts continued to deal with the same alterations. The critical study of Acts which investigated the possible sources of Acts, preserved in D 05, revealed that those sources cannot be identified and their trustworthiness cannot be proved.

8. Contemporary studies reflect various attempts to find a unified rationale for the four prohibitions of the Apostolic Decree. They represent a search for the original form of the Decree, and led the attention of scholars from the ethical form of the Decree back to its Jewish roots.

9. The unsatisfactory results of the approaches surveyed in this chapter call for new research: to find a connection between the Alexandrian form of the Apostolic Decree and the universal/natural laws grounded in the creation account

of Gen 1–3. The argument of this thesis is that the Genesis creation-fall account provides a common basis for the four prohibitions of the Alexandrian (ambivalent) form of the Apostolic Decree, rooted in the controversy between true and false worship.

2

Exegetical Study of the Apostolic Decree in Its Narrative Context

THIS CHAPTER INVESTIGATES THE three accounts of the Apostolic Decree found in Acts 15:19, 20, Acts 15:29 and Acts 21:25. Each account is fitted into its literary context. The aim of this chapter is to show Luke's purpose in preserving the Apostolic Decree in triple tradition. The first two accounts are fitted into the structure of Acts 15, and follow one another in logical sequence. The third Lukan account of the Decree is fitted into a different literary context of Acts 21:17–26.

The Exegetical Study of The First Account of the Apostolic Decree in Acts 15:1–21

General Structure of Acts 15:1–35

The text of Acts 15 represents Luke's report of the Jerusalem Council. It consists of five units of information linked by narrative. The units reveal the main stages of the council polemic: 1) the original issue in the Antiochene church, 2) the opinions of parties in Antioch, Phoenicia, Samaria and Jerusalem congregations, 3) the speech of Peter, 4) the speech of James 5) the apostolic letter.[1]

    Each unit is constructed with the help of a narrative frame around the "nucleus of authentic information."[2] By "nucleus of authentic information" is meant the factual data preserved by Luke which he placed either in direct quotation or in letter form. The nuclei report the factual data of the council, which most likely existed in Luke's source and were chosen by him for their credibility. Thus, Luke could use the collec-

---

1. F. F. Bruce divides the units of Acts 15 into eight parts, however the semantic organization of the units is similar to the present study with some exceptions. Thus, he treats Acts 15:1–2 and 15:3–5 as separate units. V. 6 according to Bruce seems to be separated from v. 5 and forms a new unit by itself. This subdivision, however, does not help to identify the unit formed by a single verse and the purpose of this unit. Bruce, *Acts*, 332–48.

2. The term "authentic information" indicates information reaching Luke, which he found trustworthy, approved by trusted eyewitnesses, and derived from the apostolic letter. He places it in the nucleus of his structure. It is accepted in this thesis that Luke leaves the authentic information with a minimum of his redactional work, while in the narrative frames Luke, likely, was more flexible.

tive memory of the Antiochene and Jerusalem congregations which were preserved in the form of sayings, outlines of the polemic written down by various people.[3]

The "narrative frame" provides Luke's personal explanation of the polemic. The narrative preserves in several places Luke's personal judgment of the opinions of the parties, his exaltation of mission work, his rendering of the apostolic decision as wise and beneficial, and his account of the unanimity, gladness and peace in the churches. The aim of the narrative was to link the nucliei of information in a logical way and to show the progress of the polemic. It was later woven according to Lukan design in between the nucliei of information. Thus the introductory words, current explanations, and consequent actions furnish the narrative frame for the exact nucliei.

The nuclei of information and their narrative frame, together, form one unit. In accord with the subdivision taken for units of information, the narrative frame also has to be divided into groups. There are seven groups of narrative frame in 15:1–35. Five are related to their units and two have a special purpose. The units will be described in sequence.

Unit one (15:1, 2) reveals the original matter of the debates in Antioch: the relation between the Mosaic law and the salvation of men. The nucleus of information here is provided by the direct quotation of the words of the opposition. The narrative frame designed for this unit describes the origin of contradiction, the growth of polemic, and the manner of its treatment in Antioch.

Unit two (15:3–5) represents two different attitudes toward the conversion of the Gentiles: those who accepted Paul's report with gladness and those who found the work unaccomplished without circumcising the converts and binding the Mosaic law on them. The nucleus of information here is represented by a direct quotation of the Pharisaic party. The narrative frame describes the trip of delegates to Jerusalem, their promotion of the mission for the Gentiles, the reaction of churches in Phoenicia and Samaria, and the reaction of converts from the Pharisees in the Jerusalem congregations.

Unit three (15:6–11) is constructed with the help of a short narrative frame around the large nucleus of information. The information here is presented in the form of a direct quotation of Peter's speech. In order to highlight it, Luke writes the speech of Peter in the first person. The narrative frame here pictures the assembling of the council, the long arguing of the parties, the introduction to Peter's speech, and then, the response to it.

Also, *Unit three* lays the foundation for a more spacious structure, namely, the theological core of the council's debate, expressed in the form of midrash.[4] Thus the narrative

---

3. Dibelius, *Studies in Acts*, 3, see also n. 4. Dibelius regards the speeches in Acts to be an "older formula of a kerygmatic or liturgical nature." The text's structure, thus, may reveal the kerygmatic core of the Jerusalem Council.

4. Midrash means "searching, enquiring, investigating." "Midrash entails searching the text for clarification beyond the obvious." Evans, "Old Testament in the New," 131–32.

frame of *Unit three* provides discussion about the νόμος Μωϋσέως as a base clue to the presence of midrash. Following that, *Unit three* includes Peter's speech, which builds a bridge between νῦν and ἡμερῶν ἀρχαίων and connects the midrash to creation.[5] Following the narrative link (C), in 15:12, and *Unit four* (15:13–21) will provide the links to creation, a complex quotation of prophets and a final text of midrash.[6]

The following narrative link was placed by Luke between two main speeches of Peter and James. This fourth narrative was not connected to any unit of information, as it was designed to designate the crucial point of the council. Luke uses the fourth narrative while mentioning Paul's and Barnabas' speech, which was written from the third person not only to preserve the order of speeches, but also to stress the most positive aspect of their God-approved ministry. Thus the work of Paul and Barnabas, which was placed in the middle of the council proceedings, between the two main speeches, appears as the fulfilment of God's salvific plan for the Gentiles. Consequently this fourth narrative link represents the turning point of the council and has to be recognized as the central narrative link (C) in 15:12.

Unit four (15:13–21) contains in its nucleus the speech of James written in first person. This emphasizes the authenticity of the information. The narrative frame gives a short introduction, possibly designed to show that James' opinion provided explanation of and support for both Peter's and Paul's experiences in their mission field. This unit smoothly transitions to the final decision of the council. The whole of Acts 15:13–21 reveals the main features of midrash: the summary of previous statements, the complex-quotation from the prophets with an explanatory formula, the reverse-element linked to creation, and the final text which is linked to Moses as well. The unit also provides a well proposed decision based on the midrashic tradition and set for the council's approval.

Unit five (15:22–19) reveals a new source of information, which is the Apostolic Decree, which becomes the nucleus of this unit. Its narrative frame serves a special purpose. It pictures the unanimity of the assembly, the decision to choose representative messengers, and an agreement to write the decision in the form of a letter.

Finally, the concluding (C') narrative (15:30–35) is not based on any source that Luke quotes. It was added by Luke to his factual data to show the positive impact of the Decree on the Antiochene congregation. The narrative shows that the interpretation and ratification of the Decree in the church in Antioch was undertaken by the prophets-messengers sent from Jerusalem. It also describes the church as glad and encouraged by the content of the Apostolic Decree.

---

5. This connection to creation will be demonstrated in section 1.4 of this chapter. The midrash (*Unit four*) will be described in 1.6.

6. Fernandez Perez notes that NT midrash "often had been fitted by evangelists into the narrative for the theatrical representation of the Old Testament text and Jesus' teaching." Perez, "Midrash and the New Testament," 367–69.

THE FOUR PROHIBITIONS OF ACTS 15

Exegesis of *Unit one*, Acts 15:1, 2

Unit one which includes the first two verses shows the origin of the problem. For convenience of study this unit is divided into three chronological parts.

Figure 1: Unit one—Acts 15:1, 2

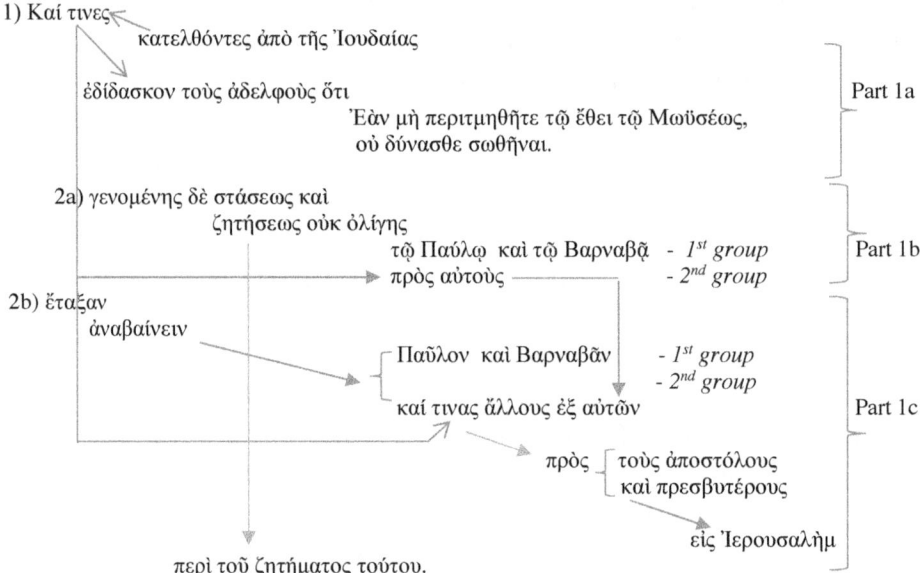

Part 1a reveals that the issue appeared after some men from Judea started to teach in Antioch.[7] The issue was not about cultural differences, but about differences in teachings, as it arose when those men started to teach. This suggests that from the beginning the church in Antioch accepted those Gentiles as brothers in Christ without cultural discrimination. It might suggest that the congregation did not view the Mosaic custom as a divisive issue.[8] This also suggests that Paul and Barnabas, who were Jews by origin, did not create a problem by imposing circumcision and purity laws on the Gentiles as necessary for their fellowship.[9]

The teaching of men from Judea contradicted that of Paul and Barnabas. Luke clarifies what led to disagreement in v. 1: Ἐὰν μὴ περιτμηθῆτε τῷ ἔθει τῷ Μωϋσέως,

---

7. Bruce suggests to identify them with "messangers from James in Gal 2:12, who exceeded their rights," or optionally with "false brothers secretly brought in" Gal 2:24. He also connects those men to "zealots for the law" in Acts 21:20. Bruce, *Acts*, 333.

8. Bruce pictures the church in Antioch as holding a liberal attitude toward Jewish customs from its origin. He attributes this attitude to the liberal theology of Paul. Bruce, *Acts*, 329.

9. Bruce notes that some Jews at that time thought "the physical rite of circumcision might be neglected" and explained the significance of this rite in a spiritual sense. He observes this fact from the polemic in Philo and Josephus. Bruce, *Acts*, 329.

οὐ δύνασθε σωθῆναι. Here, Luke uses a sentence expressing a more probable future condition. The conjunction ἐὰν, together with the negative particle μὴ, translates "unless, except." The meaning of the first clause thus becomes, "unless you are circumcised..."

The subjunctive mood is used in regards to events that are possible if certain prior conditions are met. The construction ἐὰν+subjunctive points to the more probable future condition, which is οὐ δύνασθε σωθῆναι. Consequently, the prior condition which makes salvation possible is circumcision.[10] In addition to it, the negative particle μὴ indicates that the expected answer is "no." Thus the construction is formed in a way which denies the possibility of salvation if the rite of circumcision is omitted. Thus, the reason for the sharp dispute appears to be the demand for circumcision. From this point Paul and Barnabas were likely arguing against the specific issue: the necessity of circumcision for one's salvation.[11]

The mentioning of the sharp dispute in part 1b (v. 2a) is placed by Luke as consistent with the teaching preached by the men from Judea, at the end of part 1a (v. 1). Thus the dispute might be triggered not only by the demand to follow the custom of Moses, but also by an attempt to make salvation conditional, and make it dependent on the custom of Moses. Describing the circumcision party, Bruce notes that "a Pharisee could add acceptance of Jesus as Messiah to his existing beliefs without ceasing to be a Pharisee."[12] The rite of circumcision had always been embodied in Mosaic customs.[13] There was nothing surprisingly new about it. The new claim was made in regards to salvation. Thus, one may assume that the reason for the dispute was making circumcision a requirement for salvation.[14]

The phrase, περιτμηθῆτε τῷ ἔθει τῷ Μωϋσέως employs a dative of reference and is translated "unless you are circumcised with reference to the custom of Moses." This would make the custom of Moses into an additional demand along with circumcision.[15] Alternatively, the phrase can be viewed as a dative of cause and translated, "unless you

---

10. Here, the statement of the men from Judea "takes the form of a conditional sentence, in which circumcision forms the condition for salvation itself." Johnson, *Acts of the Apostles*, 259.

11. Fitzmyer suggests understanding of "salvation" here in its eschatological sense. Fitzmyer, *Acts*, 541, see note on 15:1.

12. Bruce, *Acts*, 334.

13. Jervell, *Apostelgeschichte*, 389. Although Bruce views the law of circumcision known since Abraham (Gen 17:10–14), he assumes it to be embodied in the Mosaic law (Lev 12:3). Bruce, *Acts*, 333. Johnson also sees the long history of the development of this rite in Gen 17:10–14, 23–27; 21:4; 34:15–24; Exod 12:44, 48; Lev 12:3; Josh 5:2–8. Johnson, *Acts*, 259.

14. See Jervell, *Apostelgeschichte*, 389.

15. According to some views, the demand of circumcision here makes reference to the law or custom by which it was presupposed. Lake and Cadbury, *English Translation and Commentary*, 170. It is noteworthy, that *Didache* at this point adds the phrase "except you are circumcised, and walk in the custom of Moses, and are purified from foods and all other things." With the help of this additional phrase *Didache* identifies the parts of the Mosaic law that are supposed to be cancelled. These specified customs are represented as connected to wrong beliefs of men from Judea and negatively viewed by the apostles.

are circumcised because of the custom of Moses . . ."[16] There is also the instrumental dative option. The "instrumental dative" makes the custom to be an instrument of salvation. The first option makes the men from Judea refer to Mosaic custom in order to base the need of circumcision on an authoritative source. The second option makes the Mosaic custom the reason for circumcision. Yet, it is unlikely that those men would represent the custom of Moses as a duty for the Gentiles. The third explanation seems more adequate as it clarifies the matter of the following debate.

Although there was a connection of circumcision to Mosaic custom, this rite was a sign of the covenant made with Abraham. However, Abraham was saved according to his faith. Paul and Barnabas, thus, could argue against the use of the rite as an instrument of salvation. They could argue not against the Mosaic custom itself, but against the presupposition which makes salvation dependent on any custom. Also they could see no applicability of the covenant made with Abraham to the Gentile converts. Finally, they could see no need to keep the covenant of Abraham in the time when Jesus Christ became its fulfillment.

Moreover, the wording suggests that the issue was about customs, not laws. Here Luke uses the phrase τῷ ἔθει τῷ Μωϋσέως, but not κατὰ τὸν νόμον Μωϋσέως which he uses in Luke 2:22 and not κατὰ τὸν νόμον κυρίου which he uses in Luke 2:39. These phrases might have similar and interchangeable ideas, if Luke used them in a similar context.[17] However, Luke refers to the law of Moses and to the law of God in passages taken to approve someone's actions. He used the wording "custom of Moses" for the contrary, in order to show the insignificance of the issue. When circumcision was declared by "some men" as the condition necessary for salvation, Luke chose this wording for the purpose of minimising its role. Thus, Luke contrasted salvation by faith in Christ to the demands of the covenant with Abraham, which anticipated messianic salvation. This difference in beliefs led to sharp dispute between Paul and "some men."

The translation of ἔταξαν causes some difficulties. The phrase, Καί τινες κατελθόντες ἀπὸ τῆς Ἰουδαίας ἐδίδασκον τοὺς ἀδελφοὺς (Act 15:1), reveals that the Judaizers are τινες κατελθόντες ἀπὸ τῆς Ἰουδαίας, while the members of the church in Antioch are identified as τοὺς ἀδελφοὺς. The phrase, ἔταξαν ἀναβαίνειν Παῦλον καὶ Βαρναβᾶν καί τινας ἄλλους ἐξ αὐτῶν πρὸς τοὺς ἀποστόλους (Act 15:2), does not reveal who those were who sent Paul and τινας ἄλλους ἐξ αὐτῶν. The phrase τινας ἄλλους ἐξ αὐτῶν identifies those who were sent with Paul to Jerusalem.

The Western reviser in D 05 assumed from vv.1–2, that the men from Judea become the subject of the second sentence.[18] Most modern commentators, how-

---

16. Bock, *Acts*, 494. He sees here a dative of cause or rule, referring to Moulton, Turner and Wallace. Under τῷ ἔθει τῷ Μωϋσέως he sees the Jewish traditional law rooted in the covenant with Abraham. He follows Bruce placing the ground for the circumcision in Gen 17:10–14.

17. Contrary to Jervell, *Apostelgeschichte*, 389.

18. Lake and Cadbury, *English Translation and Commentary*, 169. They suggested that "the grammar of this sentence is defective" and support the idea that Paul obeyed the order of men from Judea.

ever, suppose that τοὺς ἀδελφοὺς is the subject of ἔταξαν.[19] This view understands that the members of the church in Antioch sent Paul and Barnabas to Jerusalem.[20] This is supported by comparing Acts 15:2 with 11:30, where τοὺς ἀδελφοὺς of the church in Antioch sent Paul on a mission. Also they sent their gifts to Jerusalem with Paul in Acts 13:1–3.[21] The wording of Acts 15:24 also clarifies that the men from Judea did not represent the authority of the Jerusalem church and thus could not be understood as authoritative figures to send Paul and Barnabas to be judged in Jerusalem. Taking in account these observations, the view that τοὺς ἀδελφοὺς as the subject of ἔταξαν is preferable.

Part 1c (v. 2b) pictures the church in Antioch looking for an authoritative opinion. They delegated Paul and Barnabas and some of those men from Judea to seek the judgment of the Jerusalem congregation. The word στάσις is translated in BDAG as "lack of agreement respecting policy, *strife, discord, disunion.*"[22] The word ζήτησις means "engagement in a controversial discussion, *discussion, debate, argument.*"[23]

The phrase γενομένης δὲ στάσεως καὶ ζητήσεως οὐκ ὀλίγης . . . πρὸς αὐτοὺς with a temporal clause, adverbial participle γενομένης and two nouns, the genitive case reflects the genitive absolute construction.[24] It should be translated, "When dissension and no small debate arose . . . with them," then Paul and Barnabas were appointed by the church to go up to Jerusalem.[25] The cause for Paul and Barnabas' journey to Jerusalem was "no small dissention," which stopped the progress of the Gospel mission reported in Acts 14:26–28.

The issue which arose in Antioch presupposed deep knowledge of the laws of Torah and their purpose. Both sides of the dispute, Paul and Barnabas and those from Judea, were Jews. Therefore they had to examine their views in the presence of the Jewish congregation of the Jerusalem church. That is why v. 2b pictures the church of Antioch in subordination to Jerusalem, in teaching.[26] As one can assume from this point that both the Antioch and Jerusalem churches had the same teaching, although they might treat the ritual issues differently in practice.[27]

---

19. Lake and Cadbury, *English Translation and Commentary*, 170.

20. Bruce rightly notes that although there is no explicit subject for ἔταξαν, it is evident from v. 3 that it was the Antiochene congregation that made this decision. Bruce, *Acts*, 333.

21. Lake and Cadbury, *English Translation and Commentary*, 170.

22. BDAG, στάσις, 3. Luke uses this word also in Acts 23:7, 10 and 24:5.

23. BDAG, ζήτησις, 3. In John 3:25 ζήτησις describes a debate of John's disciples with the Pharisees also on purification.

24. McLean, *New Testament Greek*, 172–73. See also Wallace, *Greek Grammar*, 654–55.

25. Ehrhardt, *Acts of the Apostles*, 73. He believes that Luke in Acts 15:2, 23 and 21:18 acknowledged the unique status of the Jerusalem church "as the Sanhedrin of the new Israel of God."

26. Bruce here notes that although it is hard to decide whether the primacy of Jerusalem had a formal status or not, the opinion of its authorities was unquestionably of more weight in theological disputes. Bruce, *Acts*, 333.

27. Bruce, *Acts*, 333. Bruce states, that "the church in Antioch would have felt it wiser to keep in step with Jerusalem."

THE FOUR PROHIBITIONS OF ACTS 15

Exegesis of *Unit two*, Acts 15:3–5

Unit two describes the trip of delegates to Jerusalem. The unit can be devided into two parts. The first (15:3–4) represents the positive account of the trip to Jerusalem, including reports about the success of their mission, given on the way and in Jerusalem, to the congregations. The second (15:5) reveals the opposition group in the Jerusalem church and their demands.

Figure 2: Unit two—Acts 15:3–5

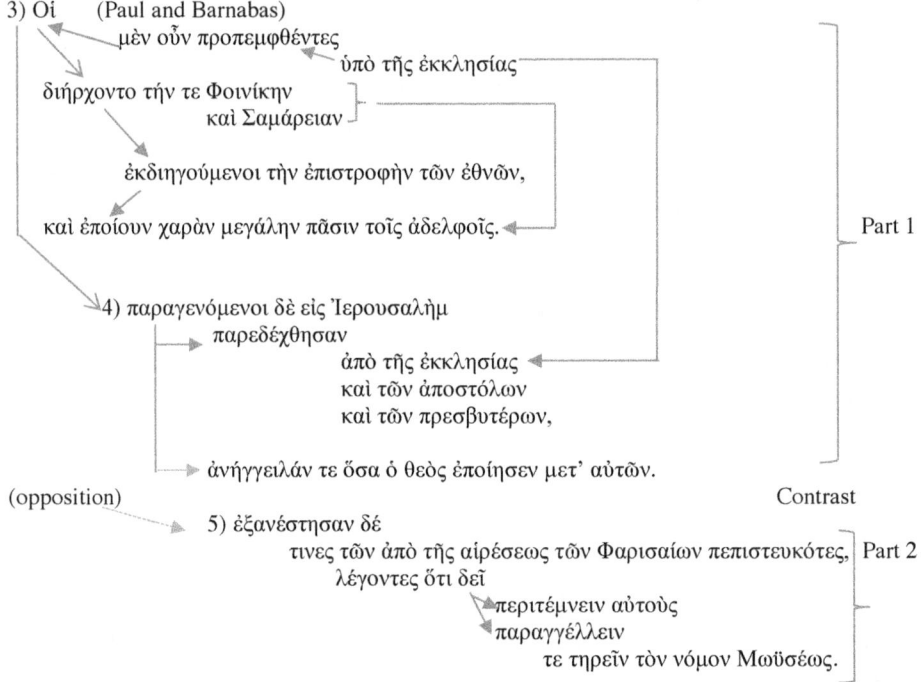

Part 1 (15:3–4) describes the trip to Jerusalem: προπεμφθέντες ὑπὸ τῆς ἐκκλησίας. This phrase establishes that the Antioch church "helped the delegates on their way."[28] This might include financial support as well as prayer and recommendations. In the center of Part 1, Paul and Barnabas report to the churches on their way to Jerusalem.[29] This part ends with their arrival in Jerusalem and warm reception by the church.[30]

---

28. BDAG, προπέμπω, 2, "to assist someone in making a journey, *send on one's way* with food, money, by arranging for companions."

29. Fitzmyer notes that their report on the way to Jerusalem refers to the report mentioned in Acts 14:27. He also sees that Paul's reports in Acts 15:3, 4, 12 have the same connection to the previous missionary jorney described in Acts 14. Fitzmyer, *Acts*, 545, see note on 15:4.

30. Arrington notes that "such a warm welcome would not have been possible if the church had sympathized with the Judaizers." Arrington, *Acts*, 151. Also Jervell, *Apostelgeschichte*, 390.

The adverbial participle ἐκδιηγούμενοι shows Paul and Barnabas "providing detailed information" about the conversion of the Gentiles.[31] It may also picture them connecting their separate stories into one strategically chosen apologetic line. As a modal participle, ἐκδιηγούμενοι describes an accompanying mode of the action of διήρχοντο, indicating that Paul and Barnabas intentionally visited all those brothers aiming to share the news.[32]

The phrase ἐποίουν χαρὰν μεγάλην shows the response to the report: great joy for all the brothers.[33] Luke emphasizes that all churches gladly accepted the conversion of the Gentiles. This additional feature of their trip was important for Luke, because it described Paul's ministry to the Gentiles as not creating conflict, and as good news in the eyes of the majority of believers.[34] Luke thus implies that the debate in Antioch was caused by an opposing minority.

Luke refers to the conversion of the Gentiles, described in Acts 13:1–14:28. Antioch was the starting point of Paul's missionary trip, and on their return Paul reported the mighty deeds of God among the Gentiles during that journey.[35] The church, according to Acts 11:19–26, was of mixed Jewish and Gentile background since its origin.[36] The message initially was preached by Jews, and for Jews. At that time some Jews from the diaspora (originally from Cyprus and Cyrene) started to preach the good news about the Lord Jesus to Greeks. As a result, the Antioch congregation was filled with Gentile converts, as suggested by Acts 14:20, 21: "the Lord's hand was with those [who preached to Greeks] and a great number of people [possibly, Greeks] believed and turned to the Lord." It can be assumed that the majority were Gentile converts.

The passage also indicates that the church in Antioch maintained a theological connection to Jerusalem, regarding teaching. One may assume that the Jews would teach the good news in line with their cultural inheritance, using scriptural proofs and picturing salvation in Jesus as a fulfillment of Israel's national hope, rather than teaching the Gospel disconnected from its Jewish background. Thus, the Gentile mission without the law seems at that stage to be doubtful.

Sometime later, Barnabas who belonged to Jerusalem church, Paul who was educated in Jerusalem, and also some prophets from that city built the doctrinal basis of the Antioch church. Luke records nothing about relations between their teaching and the issue of the law. It may be assumed that all those teachers from Jerusalem shared

---

31. BDAG, ἐκδιηγέομαι.
32. Bruce, *Acts*, 334.
33. Johnson, *Acts*, 260. He views this phrase as one of Luke's indicators of a positive decision.
34. So does Haenchen, *Apostelgeschichte*, 426.
35. Johnson also connects the report of Paul and Barnabas which they did in churches on the way to Jerusalem with their report in the Antiochene church described earlier in Acts 14:27. Johnson, *Acts*, 260 n. 4.
36. Peterson, *Acts of the Apostles*, 419–20.

the same view concerning the issue of the law for Gentile converts. That view had to be traditional and commonly accepted by the disciples of Jesus, since Luke did not introduce any new approach.

The phrase παρεδέχθησαν ἀπὸ τῆς ἐκκλησίας καὶ τῶν ἀποστόλων καὶ τῶν πρεσβυτέρων, in Part 1 opens with παρεδέχθησαν (third-person passive aorist of παραδέχομαι) "they were accepted/welcomed" by the church as a whole, and by all its key figures.[37] Luke does not mention whether delegates from the opposition travelled with them. It is likely they did not, since Luke gave them no voice on the journey. Luke's reason for leaving them voiceless might also be due to the fact that they did nothing important excepting the disturbance in Antioch, where Paul and Barnabas had positive testimony to their work, and used this testimony to convince their audiences.

The last phrase of Part 1 (v. 4), ἀνήγγειλάν τε ὅσα ὁ θεὸς ἐποίησεν μετ' αὐτῶν, reveals to the Jerusalem congregation what God had accomplished through Paul and Barnabas.[38] The phrase μετ' αὐτῶν should be translated "with them." Thus, ὁ θεὸς becomes the subject, who acts (ἐποίησεν). Paul and Barnabas here become agents of God, who acts. Here it is likely that Luke stresses their subordination and makes them the agents of God's will, to show God's prime concern for the salvation of the Gentiles.

Part 2 (15:5) reveals that some of the Jerusalem congregation "stood up" (ἐξανέστησαν) to confront Paul's report.[39] The situation changes from positive to negative as Luke shows by the particle δέ. Those, who ἐξανέστησαν, were defined by Luke with τινες, which shows them to be a minority.[40] Further Luke explains that τινες . . . πεπιστευκότες employing the adverbial perfect tense participle to describe those who come to believe in Christ after following the Pharisaic movement.[41] They are the subject of an entire sentence.

The phrase τῆς αἱρέσεως τῶν Φαρισαίων might be understood as a negative expression toward Pharisaic teaching, not the τινες.[42] The problem rose because some of them, even after they had become Christians, upheld strong Pharisaic beliefs.[43] Their

---

37. BDAG, παραδέχομαι, 2, "to accept the presence of someone in a hospitable manner, *receive, accept*." Also Fitzmyer views the reaction of the Jerusalem church as a "welcoming reception." Fitzmyer, *Acts*, 545, see note on 15:5.

38. BDAG, ἀναγγέλλω, 1, "to carry back information, *to report*."

39. BDAG, ἐξανίστημι, 3a, "to come to the fore, *stand up . . . to speak*."

40. Fitzmyer notes here that it was not said that the Jewish Christians "stood up" to argue against Paul. He sees that τινες as the small group of Jewish Christians of Pharisaic background. Fitzmyer, *Acts*, 545, see note on 15:5. This point had already appeared in Haenchen, *Apostelgeschichte*, 427.

41. Lake and Cadbury translate τινες . . . πεπιστευκότες as "converts." Lake and Cadbury, *English Translation and Commentary*, 171–72.

42. Johnson, *Acts*, 260 n. 5. Johnson states that Luke in his two-volume book always pictures the Pharisees as "opposing God's plans."

43. Dibelius calls them "Christian Pharisees from Judea." Dibelius, *Studies in Acts*, 93–94. See also Maddox, *Purpose of Luke-Acts*, 67. Bruce links τῆς αἱρέσεως τῶν Φαρισαίων πεπιστευκότες to μυριάδες . . . τῶν πεπιστευκότων in Acts 21:20. This however lacks sense, because in both cases Luke himself clarifies which πεπιστευκότες he assumes. Thus, Luke represents the group in Acts 15:5 as

beliefs were expressed in following words: ὅτι δεῖ περιτέμνειν αὐτοὺς παραγγέλλειν τε τηρεῖν τὸν νόμον Μωϋσέως "that it is needful to circumcise them and to command them to keep the law of Moses." Fitzmyer notes that Pharisaic demands, here, were "based on the way they interpreted God's words to Abraham in Gen 17:10–14 (cf. Josh 5:2–9) and to Moses in Deut 5:28–33."[44]

The particle of necessity, δεῖ, here has a sense of ultimate demand, "must."[45] The language of necessity presumes a reference to God's will.[46] The words περιτέμνειν, παραγγέλλειν and τηρεῖν are infinitives which are governed by δεῖ. The word τηρεῖν (infinitive from τηρέω) means "to persist in obedience, *keep, observe, fulfill, pay attention to.*"[47] The believers from the Pharisees insisted on persisting in obedience to the whole law of Torah including its ritual parts for all Christian believers. The ritual law was, in their view, behind their demand to circumcise Gentile converts in order to initiate them for the temple cult and the ritual law connected with this cult. The τῷ ἔθει τῷ Μωϋσέως in v. 1 changes here into τὸν νόμον Μωϋσέως, possibly to show that the Pharisaic demands related to the teaching of Torah and not only to Jewish customs. This feature also reveals that the issue before the council concerned the various parts of the law of Torah. With help of the change from ἔθει to νόμον Luke clarifies that the council had to review all Mosaic laws to decide whether or not those laws must be observed for salvation.[48]

Thus, the first two units of information form the council agenda: 1) to define whether the Mosaic laws are necessary for salvation. 2) to find out whether the Mosaic laws are still necessary to be observed. 3) to clarify whether or not the Gentile converts have to keep some points out of the Mosaic law, and for which purpose. As soon as the question raised by the Pharisaic party appealed to the will of God expressed in Torah, the appologists for the Gentile mission also had to provide the scriptural proofs in support of their understanding of the will of God.[49]

---

the πεπιστευκότες from the Pharisees in ἐκκλησία. Another group of πεπιστευκότες in Acts 21:20 is represented by Luke as μυριάδες . . . τῶν πεπιστευκότων, which existed outside the ἐκκλησία (εἰσὶν ἐν τοῖς Ἰουδαίοις is taken in the sense of *ethnos*) and was ζηλωταὶ τοῦ νόμου. Bruce, *Acts*, 334.

44. Fitzmyer, *Acts*, 546, see note on 15:5. Their understanding of eschatological salvation could be influenced by the phrase εἰς διαθήκην αἰώνιον in Gen 17:13 and the promises of eternal blessings in Deut 5:29.

45. Here "the compulsion of law or custom" is intended. BDAG, δεῖ, 1 b.

46. Peterson, *Acts*, 423. The Parisaic party probably tried to show their demands in accord with God's will expressed in the laws of Torah.

47. BDAG, τηρέω, 3

48. This can be inferred from the use of σωθῆναι in 15:1.

49. Peterson notes that the crucial point has been passed when the council recognized the theological evidences of the God's will in support to the mission to the Gentiles. Peterson, *Acts*, 423.

Exegesis of *Unit three*, Acts 15:6–11

Unit three provides the narrative link which fits the speech of Peter into the council debates. It shows that Peter's speech was not a part of the debates in the Jerusalem congregation, but part of the specially appointed "elder's meeting" (15:6). The infinitive of purpose ἰδεῖν shows that the council was summoned to work out a common solution.[50]

Figure 3: Unit three—Acts 15:6–11

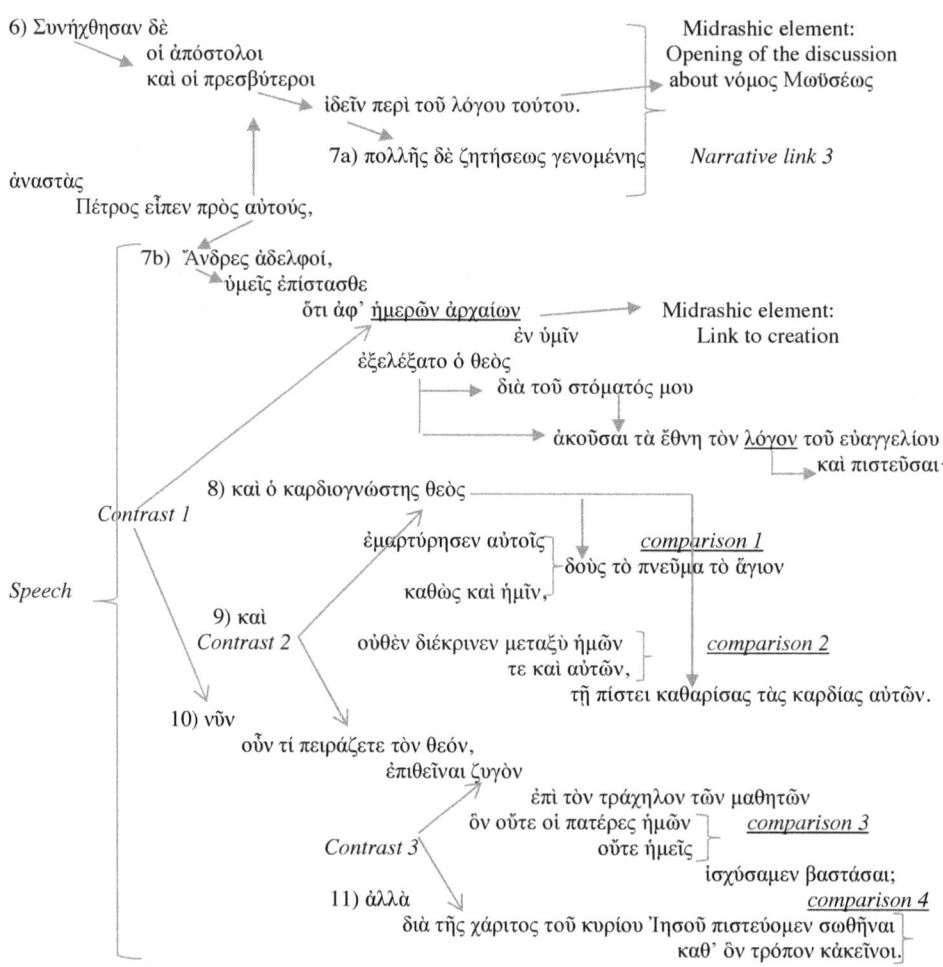

According to the narrative, Peter took courage to express his thoughts after a long discussion.[51] The phrase πολλῆς δὲ ζητήσεως γενομένης (15:7a) is a genitive

---

50. Bruce notes that the phrase ἰδεῖν περὶ can be "a coinage on the analogy of Lat. *uidere de*," used to show the purpose of the meeting. Bruce, *Acts*, 335.

51. Fernando shows that v. 7 placed before Peter's speech were added by Luke to emphasize that "the Judaizers had a chance to say what they wanted to say." Ajith, *Acts*, 421.

absolute construction describing the timing of Peter's speech.⁵² The construction can be translated "during or after a big dispute." Peter's speech (15:7b-11) was purposely positioned in Luke's record of the big dispute. The discussion was "drowning" in a multitude of opinions prior to the juncture when Peter stated his decisive resolution to the dispute.

The structure of *Unit three* shows Peter using four comparisons between ἡμῖν/ἡμῶν (us) and αὐτοῖς/αὐτῶν (them). Comparison 1 (v. 8) reflects the equality of the status of those who are saved from the Gentiles to those who are saved from the Jews. Then he uses aorist ἐμαρτύρησεν to state God's past action referring most probably to his experience in Caesarea, at Cornelius' household. There, God poured out the gift of the Holy Spirit on uncircumcised Gentile believers who experienced a Pentecostal speaking in tongues and praising God (Acts 10:45, 46).⁵³

This event was understood by Peter as a sign of God's benevolence in deciding to baptize Gentiles without making them Jews first. He said, "Can anyone keep these people from being baptized with water? They have received the Holy Spirit just as we have" (Acts 10:47). This Gentile Pentecost was referred to by Peter at the council: ἐμαρτύρησεν αὐτοῖς δοὺς τὸ πνεῦμα τὸ ἅγιον καθὼς καὶ ἡμῖν. The modal adverbial participle, δοὺς (from δίδωμι), describes the manner by which God witnessed to the faith of the Gentile converts. He gave them the Holy Spirit equally to those from the Jews. Appealing to God's authority and provision, Peter finds the status of Gentile and Jewish converts equal, and witnessed by presence of the Holy Spirit. They had no need to become Jews first.

In comparison 2 (v. 9), Peter even puts stress on the words οὐθὲν διέκρινεν μεταξὺ ἡμῶν τε καὶ αὐτῶν ("*God* made no distinction between us and them"), clarifying that God himself has chosen to remove previously-existing distinctions.⁵⁴ According to Pao the phrase μεταξὺ ἡμῶν τε καὶ αὐτῶν, in Peter's speech, means that the Gentiles become an equal party.⁵⁵ Luke uses καθαρίσας (modal participle of καθαρίζω), which refers to "moral and cultic cleansing."⁵⁶ The aorist participle presumes that the ac-

---

52. McIver, *Intermediate NT Greek*, 20, 169. See also Wallace, *Greek Grammar*, 654–55.

53. Peterson, *Acts*, 425. He shows the parallel between Cornelius' story and Pentecost.

54. The Apostolic Decree is connected to Rev 2:23, which contains two out of four prohibitions (εἰδωλοθύτων and πορνεία), and partially preserves the wording of Acts 15:8–9. The phrase ὅτι ἐγώ εἰμι ὁ ἐραυνῶν νεφροὺς καὶ καρδίας (Rev 2:23) describes God in characteristics similar to Peter's ὁ καρδιογνώστης θεὸς (Acts 15:8). Peter reflected God's ability to see the inner thoughts of a believer. He proved that God has shown no partiality between the believers from the Jews and those from the Gentiles. God himself establishes distinction or removes distinction (see the use of διακρίνω in Acts 15:9). The removal of the distinction reveals the unity of the believers in true worship. Contrastingly, in Revelation the ability of God to know the inner thoughts of the believers establishes the distinction again (δώσω ὑμῖν ἑκάστῳ κατὰ τὰ ἔργα ὑμῶν). Here, God puts a distinction between those Christians who eat εἰδωλοθύτων, worshiping idols in their hearts and those who practice true worship, though publicity all of them profess one faith.

55. Pao, *Acts and the Isaianic New Exodus*, 238.

56. BDAG, καθαρίζω 3, b α, "to purify through ritual cleansing, *make clean, declare clean* . . . of

tion takes place before the action of the main verb διακρίνω, "[God] did not make a distinction." The association of καθαρίσας and οὐθὲν διέκρινεν suggests the removal of distinction by purification. According to Luke, Peter says that God now makes no distinction because the purification took its place.

Here Luke declares the inward purity of the people by faith in the lordship of Jesus.[57] The phrase τῇ πίστει καθαρίσας τὰς καρδίας αὐτῶν, "for he purified their hearts by faith," reveals that the distinction was removed by inner purification of those who turned to God from among the Gentiles.[58] According to Bruce, the only other occurences of διακρίνω in Acts are 10:20 and 11:2, 12, in connection with the Cornelius story. Occurences of ἐκαθάρισεν are in Acts 10:15; 11:9.[59]

Mentioning of purification might shed light on the main issue which blocked the communication between Jews and Gentiles. As Gentiles did not practice ritual purification according to Mosaic law, they were viewed by Jews as ritually unclean. Association with a Gentile, thus, might profane a Jew and made him temporarily unable to participate in the temple cult. This issue of ritual uncleanness was viewed as temporary and reversible for both Jews and Gentiles. The issue was invoked by the ritual law, which was to prevent the defilement of the temple by bringing ritually unclean things/humans/animals into a ritually holy place. The phrase τῷ ἔθει τῷ Μωϋσέωv (Acts 15:1; 6:14; 21:21; 28:17) referes to Mosaic custom connected to the temple cult.[60]

The temple cult was pictured in Stephen's apology (Acts 7:44–50) as narrowed by tradition to a number of ritualistic actions performed in a special place.[61] Because of their superficial attitude, the temple cult lost its ability to influence minds and renew the heart long before the coming of Messiah (Acts 7:51, 52). Since Jesus fulfilled the purpose of the ritual law of Moses, the need for the temple cult was set aside

---

moral and cultic cleansing." Here καθαρίζω refers to the aspect of purification by ritual cleansing. Thus, Peter explained to the audience that the Gentile converts have been already ritually cleansed by faith in Jesus, which is evident from the presence of the Holy Spirit in them.

57. Pao, *Acts and the Isaianic New Exodus*, 236–37 n. 64. This concept of inward purity has always been used to support the redefinition of the law in the new era, especially for the rejection of food laws. However it seems inadequate to support the rejection of food laws for the Christian community.

58. Peterson, *Acts*, 425. He notes that καθαρίζω was used in Acts 10:15, 28 describing the cleansing of the Gentiles. He sees that the Gentiles lacked the "purifying benefits of the law" and were considered to be unclean. From this observation one may assume that the vision in Acts 10 with its following application to the issue of the Gentiles was concerning the Gentile converts and not the distinction of meats.

59. Bruce, *Acts*, 336. Bruce sees Acts 10 and 15 linked by the same idea. He argues that Ps 24:4; 51:12 and Matt 5:8 also express the concept of purity of heart.

60. Jervell notes that "the connection between temple and law is demonstrated in Acts 6–7." Jervell, "Law in Luke-Acts," 24. See also Jervell, *Apostelgeschichte*, 226–27. Also Braulik views the rites as "entrance liturgy" as one approaches the sanctuary. Braulik, "Law as Gospel," 7–8.

61. Johnson shows that the phrase τοῖς ἔργοις τῶν χειρῶν αὐτῶν in Acts 7:41 was used in LXX for idols (Isa 16:12). Luke uses similar language: χειροποιήτοις κατοικεῖ in Acts 7:48 is appealing to the Jewish audience by the lips of Stephen, and χειροποιήτοις ναοῖς in Acts 17:24 is appealing to a Gentile audience by the lips of Paul. Johnson, *Acts*, 133 n. 48.

(Rom 10:4; Gal 3:19, 24, Heb 7:19). Jesus predicted the replacement of the temple cult with worship in Spirit and truth (John 4:23, 24; Rom 8:4, see also Luke 3:16).

Comparison 3 (v. 10) is intended to show no difference between the Jews and the Gentiles in relation to the ritual law (Heb 10:1). It is seen from the point that the Israelites also failed to reach the standards of the law. Peter's expression for the law is ζυγός "a yoke."[62] Arrington, Jackson and Lake suggest that Peter's ζυγός was the allusion to Jesus' words in Matt 11:29 with the parallel sayings: ὁ γὰρ ζυγός μου χρηστὸς καὶ τὸ φορτίον μου ἐλαφρόν ἐστιν.[63] Thus, Jesus showed his mission to be one of liberation from a heavy yoke, to be exchanged for a lighter one.

Since a possible allusion to ζυγός in Matt 11:29–30 was recognized, the second allusion to ζυγός in Matt 21:5 must also be noted. It echoes Zech 9:9. The image in Zechariah's prophecy presents the Messiah coming "on a donkey, and the colt an offspring of a yoked donkey," ἐπὶ ὄνον καὶ πῶλον υἱὸν ὑποζυγίου. Jesus sent his disciples to untie the donkey and bring her with her colt. This prophetic image of a donkey depicts Israel tied by bonds of the ritual law, followed by her colt which had never been under its yoke. Jesus possibly employed these OT prophetic images when he entered Jerusalem as royal Messiah to demonstrate his will to lead all people in his kingdom unbound, liberated.

Peter, impressed by Jesus' action, might have kept in mind the fact that the donkey bore the yoke, and that it had to pass it on to her colt as an inheritance. That is why Peter exclaims during the council, "Why do you tempt God trying to pass the yoke from Israel on to the Gentile converts? You inherited it from your fathers, but could not bear it! " So, the yoke of ritual law should not pass from the Jews to the Gentile converts. This picture reveals a deeper meaning of the prophecy: the conversion of the Gentiles will follow the initial release of Israel.

Peterson sees the depiction of the law by the image of a yoke to be a common tradition shared by Matthew and Luke.[64] Also Paul mentioned ζυγῶν δουλείας when he gave a negative description of Jewish circumcision in Gal 5:1–2.[65] These passages signal liberation of the people of God from keeping the rite of circumcision, and consequently, from the burden of the ritual law.

Echoing the image of the OT, Peter pictured the ritual law as a yoke. He then exclaimed, νῦν οὖν τί πειράζετε τὸν θεόν ἐπιθεῖναι ζυγὸν ἐπὶ τὸν τράχηλον τῶν μαθητῶν. This phrase has prompted scholarly discussion. Thus, Bruce views ζυγὸς as the yoke of the commandments of Torah, "in the sense of an intolerable weight" and

---

62. BDAG, ζυγός, 1, "in the case of humans, to expedite the bearing of burdens, *yoke*."

63. Lake and Cadbury, *English Translation and Commentary*, 174. The same thought appears in Arrington's work. Arrington, *Acts*, 152.

64. Peterson, *Acts*, 427. He notes that Luke 11:46 repeats Matt 23:4, where he changes Matthew's φορτία βαρέα to the φορτία δυσβάστακτα, intensifying the negative impression of the ritual law.

65. Lake and Cadbury, *English Translation and Commentary*, 174.

THE FOUR PROHIBITIONS OF ACTS 15

connects it to "burden" in v. 28.[66] Marshall believes that when Peter calls the Law a "yoke," one needs to understand Luke expressing his own attitude to the law.[67] Johnson mentions the literal meaning of ζυγὸς in Deut 21:3 and as a figurative metaphor of political or social oppression.[68] The context of the chapter, however, suggests viewing ζυγὸς in light of Matt 11:29–30 and Gal 5:1, where ζυγὸς can be explained in terms of the Jewish ritual law.

According to Peter, God liberated Israel from the demands of ritual law and if someone now tries to impose it on the Gentiles, this tests the grace of the Lord. The phrase πειράζετε τὸν θεόν ἐπιθεῖναι ζυγὸν translates as, "*you* test God to impose the yoke . . ." Here, θεόν is the direct object of πειράζετε and the aorist infinitive ἐπιθεῖναι subordinated to πειράζετε forms a prepositional phrase describing a tempting action by some Jewish believers.[69] Here, Lake and Cadbury suggest that πειράζετε was chosen in view of Exod 17:2 and Deut 6:16, where it describes one "acting against the declared will of God, and so tempting him to inflict punishment."[70] Bruce rightly showed that in the LXX πειράζω can mean "to stretch the patience *of God* or invite his judgment," imposing conditions "over and above those which God has required."[71] From Sandt's point of view the word πειράζω in Acts 15:10 means "to try" or "to put to the test" and he sees that "imposing the law upon the Gentiles delays the realization of God's design."[72] Here, Peter emphasizes the senselessness of ritual law keeping by repetition ὃν οὔτε οἱ πατέρες ἡμῶν οὔτε ἡμεῖς ἰσχύσαμεν βαστάσαι "[the yoke] which neither our fathers nor ourselves were able to carry" since no one is made better by serving it.[73]

Comparison 4 (v. 11) provides the solution of the problem. The ritual law revealed the predestination of all people to disobedience, after which God predestined

---

66. Bruce, *Acts*, 337. Bruce cites the words of Jesus in Matt 23:4; Luke 11:46; Gal 5:1; Matt 11:29, linking his yoke to the yoke of the Jewish law.

67. Marshall, *Luke*, 191.

68. Johnson, *Acts*, 262–63 n. 10. The word is used in this sense in 2 Chr 10:10; 1 Macc 8:31; LXX Ps 2:3; 1 Tim 6:1.

69. BDAG, ἐπιτίθημι, 1a α, to "*lay/put upon*," and BDAG, πειράζω 2 c, "to endeavor, to discover the nature or character of something by testing, *try, make a trial of, put to the test*," speaks of "a trial of God by humans."

70. Lake and Cadbury, *English Translation and Commentary*, 173. See also Arrington, *Acts*, 152.

71. Bruce, *Acts*, 336. It is evident from Exod 17:2; Ps 77:41. Bruce saw the matter of temptation in imposing of additional rules on the converts whom God has already approved by pouring out the Spirit on them.

72. Sandt, "Explanation of Acts 15:6–21," 89 n. 1. The meaning "put to test" or "to tempt" in connection to the "yoke" of the law suggests that the law is considered not only as the yoke but also as the temptation. This should be another view of tempting God by treating the law improperly, namely, using it as means of salvation. Thus, Dickinson understands πειράζω as acting against the declared will of God, tempting Him to inflict punishment. Dickinson, "Theology of Jerusalem Conference," 69.

73. Dibelius translates these words to mean that "the law has always been unbearable, even for Jews." He, however, believes that the law was cancelled not for this reason, but because Christ fulfilled it. Dibelius, *Studies in Acts*, 95.

them all to receive mercy (Rom 11:32). From this perspective Peter states: ἀλλὰ διὰ τῆς χάριτος τοῦ κυρίου Ἰησοῦ πιστεύομεν σωθῆναι καθ' ὃν τρόπον κἀκεῖνοι. He uses διὰ instrumentally, revealing that God's grace is the instrument of salvation.[74] The infinitive σωθῆναι is the direct object of πιστεύομεν, and the phrase is in indirect speech.[75] The phrase, thus, can be translated literally as "but through the grace of the Lord Jesus, we believe to be saved, in the same manner with them."

Here, Peter uses three contrasts as well. The first contrast (vv. 7b, 10) is between the days of old and the situation at present, and it is expressed by contrasting ἀφ' ἡμερῶν ἀρχαίων with νῦν οὖν between the two parts of his speech.[76] The apostle explains that in God's provision the plan of salvation was chosen from the days of old (ἀφ' ἡμερῶν ἀρχαίων).

There are three possible ways to explain contrast between ἀφ' ἡμερῶν ἀρχαίων and νῦν οὖν. The first way is to view ἀφ' ἡμερῶν ἀρχαίων as a reference to the Cornelius' story in Acts 10 and νῦν οὖν as the time of Jerusalem Council. According to Dibelius, ἀρχαίων might remind hearers of the event in Caesarea.[77] Pao also believes that both speeches of Peter and James in Acts 15 have a connection to the Cornelius story in Acts 10.[78] The Cornelius story may be assumed to be a "classic prototype" of Gentile conversion.[79] These scholarly observations suggest that the Cornelius story can be taken as one of many backgrounds of the discussion in Acts 15. Its purpose was to demonstrate the acceptance of the Gentile converts into the "people of God."

---

74. BDAG, διὰ, 3.

75. Bruce identifies three ways of translation of πιστεύομεν σωθῆναι: 1) "we believe we shall be saved" (for the aor. infin. in the future sense), 2) "we believe we have been saved," or 3) "we believe (so as) to be saved" (epexegetc infin.). He prefers the last interpretation. Bruce, *Acts*, 337. However, the infinitive σωθῆναι (in passive voice, the direct object of πιστεύομεν) appears in indirect speech. Thus, "σωθῆναι expresses the content of what is believed" and the phrase πιστεύομεν σωθῆναι has to be translated "we believe to be saved." McIver, *Intermediate NT Greek*, 22–23, 26, 61, 190. For the use of the infinitive as a direct object of a verb in indirect discourse see Wallace, *Greek Grammar*, 603–5.

76. Dickinson also notes in Peter's speech two temporal indicators: "in the early days" (Acts 15:7) and "now" (Acts 15:10). Dickinson, "Theology of the Jerusalem Conference," 68. According to Sandt, in Acts 15:7–9 Peter relates God's provision for the Gentiles to Cornelius' story and in Acts 15:10–11 he shifts to his day (νῦν οὖν). However, he mentions that G. Zuntz and B Prete view these temporal indicators as a reference not to the Cornelius' story, but to a distant past, since LXX in Pss 43:2; 76:6; 142:5; Isa 37:26; Lam 2:17 and in Luke 9:8, 19 uses these indicators as a terminology referring to a distant past. Sandt, "Explanation of Acts 15:6–21," 73, 74 n. 1.

77. Dibelius links the words ἀφ' ἡμερῶν ἀρχαίων to Cornelius' story assuming that the words of Peter, διὰ τοῦ στόματός μου ἀκοῦσαι τὰ ἔθνη τὸν λόγον τοῦ εὐαγγελίου, could refer only to the account of Acts 10. He believes that by the phrase ἀφ' ἡμερῶν ἀρχαίων Luke gave to Cornelius' story a fundamental significance. Dibelius, however, notes that Peter's reference to Cornelius' story "is quite vague," and could not be understood by Peter's hearers. He states, that only Lukan readers could see this parallel. Further, he links Peter's ἀφ' ἡμερῶν ἀρχαίων to the words of James, καθὼς πρῶτον ὁ θεὸς ἐπεσκέψατο. Dibelius, *Studies in Acts*, 94–95, 118.

78. Pao, *Acts and the Isaianic New Exodus*, 237–38 n. 65. Here he argues that the context represents Cornelius as a Gentile rather than God-fearer.

79. Fitzmyer, *Acts*, 547, see note on 15:7.

The second way to explain Peter's use of ἀρχαίων, and later James' use of πρῶτον, is to referring these time indicators to the time of the Exodus.[80] Though Pao links Acts 15 to Acts 10, he also traces it back to the Exodus narrative and notes that the Exodus has connections to the creation story. Lake and Cadbury accept the meaning of ἀρχαίων here in terms of "ancient."[81] They agree that "Luke recognized that the history of the church had covered a longer time than his relatively few and rapid narratives might suggest."[82]

However, Luke's choice of ἀρχαίων, the adjective of ἀρχή, is not accidental, but deliberate. It becomes obvious in comparison with Acts 21:16, "where ἀρχαῖος μαθητής surely means 'an original disciple.'"[83] Moreover, in Acts 15:7 ἡμερῶν ἀρχαίων is connected to τὸν λόγον τοῦ εὐαγγελίου. This link shows God making the new conversion (indicated by νῦν) in a way similar to the creation of the world (indicated by ἀρχαίων). The midrashic keyword λόγος here makes a reference to creation.[84] Thus, the meaning of ἡμερῶν ἀρχαίων in Luke's writings can also be taken to mean "the days of origin," which represents the third way of explanation of the contrast between ἀφ' ἡμερῶν ἀρχαίων and νῦν οὖν.

In addition to Luke's use of ἀρχαίων to designate "the days of origin," ἀρχαίων can also mean "what was in former times, *long ago, ancient*."[85] The use of ἀρχή and ἀρχαίων attributed to Peter elsewhere deserves special attention. In 2 Pet 3:4 the phrase, ἀπ ἀρχῆς κτίσεως fits perfectly the creation account.[86] "This is an allusion to the Creation account in Genesis 1."[87]

---

80. Pao, *Acts and the Isaianic New Exodus*, 56–57. Sandt also develops the link of Acts 15:7 and 14 to Deut 4:32. He argues that temporal indicators are echoing creation, and states that Luke also first of all had the purpose "to prove that the conversion and salvation of the gentiles was known from the beginning of the world." Sandt, "Explanation of Acts 15:6–21," 74–75, 84.

81. Lake and Cadbury, *English Translation and Commentary*, 172.

82. Lake and Cadbury, *English Translation and Commentary*, 172. The Exodus narrative shows the people of a particular nation. They were taken out of nations to be "the people of God." To belong to the "people of God" meant to be circumcised and keep the law of Moses. If we are to assume the Exodus in the background of Peter's ἡμερῶν ἀρχαίων, than it means that the law of Moses is still valid. However, Peter identifies the ritual law of Moses as a "yoke" and states that circumcision is not necessary for salvation. Consequently, he has to find more appropriate background than the Exodus story.

83. Lake and Cadbury, *English Translation and Commentary*, 172.

84. Robinson describes the same connection of the "logos" with an allusion to creation in the prologue of the Gospel of John constructed in the form of midrash. Marilynne Robinson, "Wisdom and Light," 11. In addition MacLeod connects the "logos" to the Creator of the universe and to redemptive work of Christ. MacLeod, "Creation of the Universe," 189.

85. BDAG, ἀρχαῖος, 2. Peterson connects this term to "from former days," by which he clarifies that the salvation of the Gentiles is the action of God and is in accord with his will. Peterson, *Acts*, 424–25.

86. Gene L. Green notes that ἀπ ἀρχῆς κτίσεως is a common expression in Mark 10:6; 13:19; 1 En 15.9; Barn 15:3, which refers to the time of Creation. Green, *Jude and 2 Peter*, 318.

87. Rees, *2 Peter and Jude*, 165.

In 2 Pet 2:5 the apostle describes the world before the flood as ἀρχαίου κόσμου. Though many scholars translate ἀρχαίου κόσμου as "the ancient world" referring it only to the flood narrative, the flood itself "implies that the destruction resulted from God's undoing of the work of creation."[88] The wording in Acts 15:7 ἀφ' ἡμερῶν ἀρχαίων, thus, most likely refers to the creation narrative.

The creation narrative depicts a world without the necessity of circumcision undivided into clean and unclean groups from its origin, until the fall. The church in Acts 10:15, 28 and 11:5–18 is also called to remove this distinction between people. Thus, the phrase ἡμερῶν ἀρχαίων and πρῶτον in Peter's speech can refer to the creation narrative. This meaning becomes possible if one assumes that the apostle Peter viewed the church's origin in terms of re-creation and restoration of the eternal plan of God for his creation.

Some NT passages suggest Jesus, the Twelve and the early church could understand ἡμερῶν ἀρχαίων in light of the creation–fall paradigm.[89] Thus, Pao finds that the Isaianic scheme of judgment—salvation has been reversed in the writtings of Luke.[90] Marshall states that both quotations from Amos 5 and Amos 9, which Luke uses in Acts 15:16, 17, represent the judgment and following restoration.[91] In 1 Pet 1:20, the apostle compares his contemporary time with the time before foundation of the world when he states that at the very beginning Jesus was foreordained to be an atoning sacrifice, in terms of ritual law. Further, Peter shows that the decision made before the foundation of the world was manifested in his time, when Jesus accomplished the task of the ritual law, redeemed people and removed all their sins.

In a similar manner, Jesus pictured his kingdom as prepared for his people before the foundation of the world. It is noteworthy that Jesus in Matt 25:34 and Peter in 1 Pet 1:20 refer to time ἀπὸ καταβολῆς κόσμου and not to ἀφ' ἡμερῶν ἀρχαίων, as Peter does in Acts 15:7. However, both expressions might share a common meaning as they represent the starting point in time when the salvific plan was designed; awaiting future fulfillment. This thought is clearly expressed by Paul in Eph 1:4 when he states that God ἐξελέξατο ἡμᾶς ἐν αὐτῷ [in Christ] πρὸ καταβολῆς

---

88. Davids and Bauckham view 2 Pet 2:5 only in light of the flood narrative, Davids, *Letters of 2 Peter and Jude*, 226–27. See also Osborne, "2 Peter," 315. However, the link between 2 Pet 2:5 and 3:4 was noticed by scholars, who argue for the context of creation (Gen 1:2, 6–9) behind both passages. Callan, "Rhetography and Rhetology," 82. Also Green notes that 2 Pet 2:2–8 has "broad interpretive tradition that connects the angelic fall, human sin, and divine judgment." Green, *Jude and 2 Peter*, 252.

89. Johnson rightly shows that the restoration of the Twelve in Acts 1:16–26 plays an important role. The eleven had made their decision by "lot." The "lot" could mean symbolically "inheritance" associated with the land and preserve the picture of when the tribes in the days of Exodus divided the land into portions "by lot" (Num 16:14; 26:55; 33:35). Johnson, *Acts*, 35 n. 17. This allusion to the inheritance of the Promised Land views the Creation in the background. Moreover the Twelve apostles represent the twelve tribes in the heavenly kingdom. This idea was kept in mind by the disciples of Jesus.

90. Pao, *Acts and the Isaianic New Exodus*, 108.

91. Marshall, "Acts," 593.

κόσμου. This corresponds with Peter's words at the council: ἀφ' ἡμερῶν ἀρχαίων ἐν ὑμῖν ἐξελέξατο ὁ θεὸς διὰ τοῦ στόματός μου ἀκοῦσαι τὰ ἔθνη τὸν λόγον (Act 15:7). Peter might view his task to be an apostle serving both Jews and Gentiles, as the part of the ancient plan of God. The choice of ἀρχαίων ties in better with the concept of "ancient plan" than it does with an account of recent events in Caesarea. The creation–fall–re-creation paradigm in Peter's speech serves as a core, to show God bringing his eternal plan to fulfillment.

The second contrast (vv. 8, 10) Peter uses, is between the salvific work of God and men's misuse of his laws. Here καρδιογνώστης θεὸς contrasts to τί πειράζετε τὸν θεόν and reveals that God knows the inner world of the heart, while some are unable to recognize his ways. Since the Holy Spirit dwells in the hearts of believers, there is no need to demonstrate faith by keeping rites. From this point demands to enslave the Gentiles under the yoke of the ritual law become an intervention in God's plan of salvation, and look harmful in light of the new Exodus inaugurated by Christ. Peter thus calls on his audience to use the laws according to their purpose.

In addition one can note that καρδιογνώστης is a unique term of Luke's and is found only in Acts 1:24 and 15:8 in the NT.[92] The first occurrence, Acts 1:24, describes God choosing which one of two disciples would become an apostle and restore the Twelve. This restoration signified the restoration of Israel.[93] Moreover, a new person is called to replace Judas who betrayed Jesus and thus "fell away" from God. By comparison with another occurrence of καρδιογνώστης in Acts 15:8, it is clear that Gentile converts are called to replace those Jews who "fell away" from God. By this action God restores Israel, the people chosen in his name.

The third contrast in Peter's speech (vv. 10, 11) represents the failure of salvation by works and the triumph of salvation by faith.[94] Pao notes that the "yoke" contrasts with "grace" by the adversative conjunction ἀλλά.[95] Peter firmly states that salvation of all people, without distinction, is possible only in Christ, by grace. No law serves as an instrument of salvation, however much it may feature in the zealous "dreams" of Israel. The wording, διὰ τῆς χάριτος τοῦ κυρίου Ἰησοῦ employing διὰ + genitive, clearly means "through the grace of Jesus," thus declaring grace to be the channel of salvation. The phrase, διὰ τῆς χάριτος . . . πιστεύομεν σωθῆναι, can be translated then as "through grace . . . we believe to be saved." One reaches salvation due to the grace of Christ and through a decision to believe.

---

92. Petersen finds a link of this Lukan term to 1 Sam 16:7 and Ps 139:1–12. Peterson, *Acts*, 425.

93. Pao, *Acts and the Isaianic New Exodus*, 58, 124–25, 239. Here Pao shows the parallels between Jesus' selection of the Twelve in Luke 6:12–16 and Acts 1:15–26. It can be interpreted as the actions for the restoration of Israel. That is why the narrative of Acts begins with the reconstruction of the Twelve and continues with the inclusion of the Gentiles into the people of God.

94. Klinghardt states: "the Torah for Jews is insufficient as criteria of belonging to the people of God, unless conversion is added to it." Klinghardt, *Gesetz und Volk Gottes*, 114.

95. Pao, *Acts and the Isaianic New Exodus*, 239-2\40.

When Peter recalls some laws, he does not view them as an instrument of salvation. At the same time Peter's speech hints at the kind of laws under discussion during the council. Peter uses the word καθαρίσας which indicates that the apostles revised the laws of purification. It has to be viewed together with the emphasis by Luke, in *Units one* and *two* on issues of Mosaic law, customs and circumcision. The fact that the opposing view was supported by Pharisees, who interpreted the law in restrictive ways, shows Peter arguing against a suppressive use of law and against overstating its role in salvation. When Peter declares the end of the ritual law, he does not mean the end of all laws of Torah. It can be assumed that he himself, the other apostles, and the elders who were present at the council, lived in accordance with Torah moral teaching.

Exegesis of the Central (C) Narrative Link in Acts 15:12

Figure 4: Central (C) Narrative Link—Acts 15:12

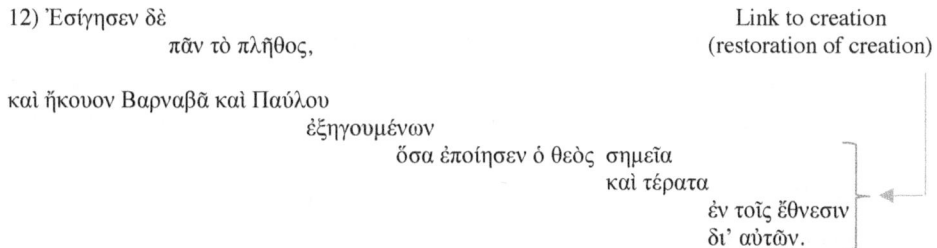

The first phrase can be translated "then the multitude became silent." The adversative conjunction δὲ and shift from πολλῆς δὲ ζητήσεως in v. 7 to ἐσίγησεν δὲ πᾶν τὸ πλῆθος in v. 12 denote the turning point of the debate. The shift after Peter's speech means that the audience agreed with his arguments or at least took them into consideration. It suggests that the arguing declined and the first steps toward unanimity were taken.

The verb ἀκούω followed by a participle ἐξηγουμένων "to relate in detail, *tell, report, describe, to set forth in great detail*," reveals that the attention of the audience was drawn to Paul's and Barnabas' explanation of God's mighty deeds.[96] They were explaining ὅσα ἐποίησεν ὁ θεὸς σημεῖα καὶ τέρατα ἐν τοῖς ἔθνεσιν. This phrase shows God as acting subject. The addition δι' αὐτῶν represents Paul and Barnabas as agents of God's actions directed to the Gentiles.[97]

96. BDAG, ἐξηγέομαι, 1, 2. Fitzmyer notes the inactivity of Paul in the process of the making of the decision. This decision is made with assumption that Luke gives Paul the minor role and scarcely mentions his report from the third person. Fitzmyer, *Acts*, 546, see note on 15:6. However, the opposite view on the role of Paul can be assumed if one takes into account that Paul's report is placed by Luke in the central, crucial point of the council and shows the support of Paul's mission from God.

97. BDAG, διά, 4a, "marker of pers. agency, *through, by . . . by human agency*."

The central narrative link thus shows God to be the invisible motivator and conductor of all salvific work in Israel and among the nations as well.[98] Here, God becomes the main initiator of mission to the Gentiles. This explains why Luke provides Paul's report in the third person at this crucial moment. He wants the reader to switch and listen to God. Although God does not speak during the council, Luke represents God's intention by the success of the Gentile mission. Luke does not refer to the success of the Gentile mission to strengthen Paul's authority, but to show mission was in the hands of God the Savior, who called workers and equipped them by miracles and wonders for this unique purpose.

Exegesis of *Unit four* with the First Lukan Account of the Decree

Unit four contains the speech of James in Acts 15:13–21. The narrative frame of this unit appears in v. 13a. The nucleus of information is vv. 13b-21. The passage contains several rare words: ἀνοικοδομήσω, κατάλοιποι, παρενοχλεῖν, ἀλισγημάτων and πνικτοῦ.[99]

Although the narrative frame of *Unit four* is very short, it plays an important role in the whole narrative. The phrase, μετὰ δὲ τὸ σιγῆσαι αὐτοὺς more likely relates to Paul's and Barnabas' report in v. 12. The construction (μετὰ δὲ τὸ + articular infinitive σιγῆσαι) reflects subsequent time and should be translated "after they stopped speaking."[100] This helps to put the speeches of Peter, Paul and James in chronological order, showing the progress of thought, and the developing of a logical pattern for the coming decision. The order of speeches shows the ability of the council to turn an unproductive debate into a logically arranged pattern. That pattern begins in *Unit three*, follows into the central narrative link and, finally, crystallizes in *Unit four* in form of midrashic tradition. The wording, ἀπεκρίθη Ἰάκωβος λέγων marks James' speech as an answer to all debate.

---

98. Dibelius rightly argues that the aim of this "colourless transitional statement" was to show that "God had associated himself with this kind of mission" and supports it with the signs and wonders. Dibelius, *Studies in Acts* 95–96.

99. Kubo, *Reader's Greek-English Lexicon*, 116. These words appear rarely in the writings of Luke and are absent from the rest of the NT. If one assumes that these words are Lukan special terms, then it is hard to explain that he does not use them anywhere else, but attributes them to someone's speech. Thus, it is likely, Luke here quotes from James' speech, either written in Greek by an amanuensis during the council or translated by Luke from the source in Aramaic.

100. McIver, *Intermediate NT Greek*, 24, 208.

Figure 5: Unit four—Acts 15:13–21

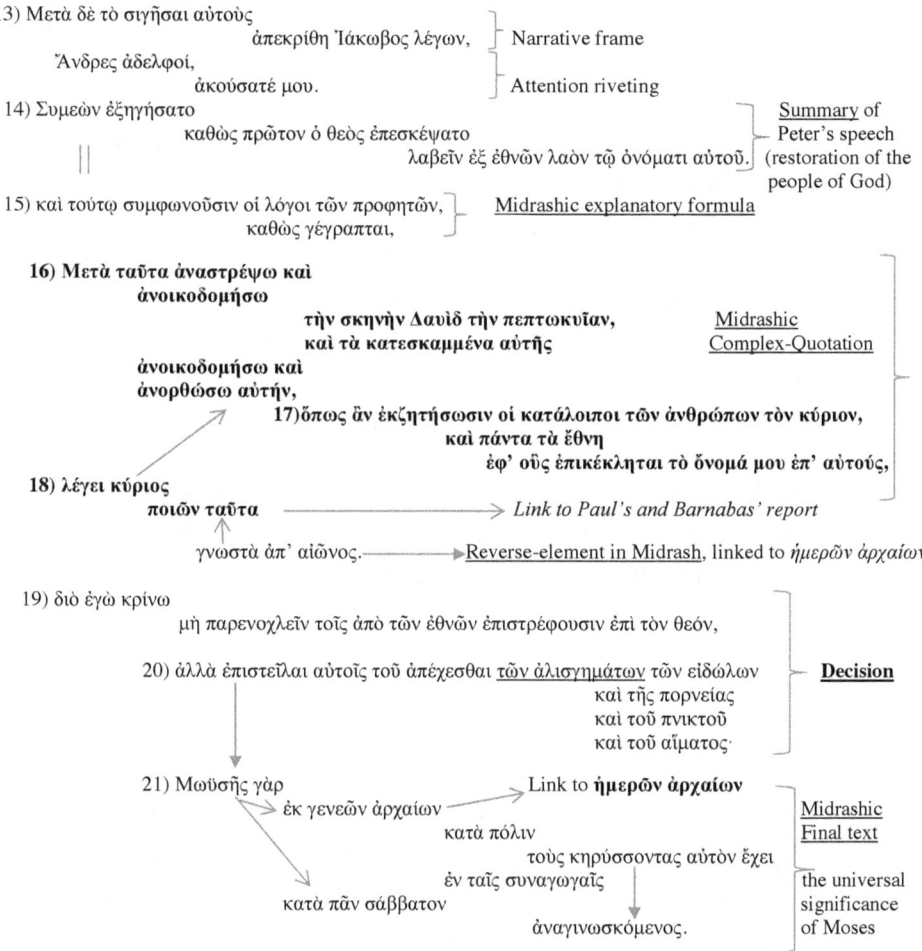

James started his answer with an imperative of request, ἀκούσατέ μου. This feature reflects a common way to start a speech and could be omitted with no harm to the idea. Luke, however, keeps the wording in order to call the reader to attention, because the following exposition by James provides the answer to all discussion and convinces the council. The way in which James has chosen to arrange his arguments reflects midrashic tradition. This type of Torah explanation allowed James to summarize previous opinions and bring them into accordance with the teaching of Torah. The midrashic explanation was always employed when the inner meaning of Torah was needed. Because the Pharisaic party stated that the will of God, according Torah, demands making Gentile converts into proselytes, the opponents had to disprove those statements, and supplant them by providing stronger Torah-based arguments.

James chose to start with Συμεὼν ἐξηγήσατο, introducing a summary of Peter's arguments. This shows that James agreed with Peter's opinion and took it as a starting point for his own explanation.[101] Sandt notices that the two speeches in Acts 15, those of Peter and of James, have a similar structure.[102] Bruce rightly pictured James taking his cue from Peter's speech and reverting to it in v. 19.[103] He makes one remarkable statement: in all cases where Paul deals with the issue of sacrifice to idols and fornication, he never refers to the Apostolic Decree, but "argues from the order of creation and the ethical implication of the gospel."[104] Thus, using Peter's link between νῦν and ἡμερῶν ἀρχαίων, which links the present time to the time of creation, James fits the creation-re-creation pattern into the basis of his midrash.[105]

Moreover, the rabbinic midrashic tradition in *Genesis Rabbah* (final editing 400 CE) assumes ἀπ' ἀρχῆς related to the time of, or even prior to creation. Thus, six matters were described as preceeding the creation of the world: Torah (Prov 8:22), throne of Glory (Ps 93:2), heavenly sanctuary (Jer 17:12), Israel as the people of God (Ps 74:2), the name of the Messiah (Ps 72:17), repentance (Ps 90:2, 3).[106] In Ps 74:2 (73:2 LXX) it was said about Israel: μνήσθητι τῆς συναγωγῆς σου ἧς ἐκτήσω ἀπ' ἀρχῆς. Here, the temporal indicator ἀπ' ἀρχῆς corresponds to Hebrew *kedem* which means, "before the creation of the world."[107] Also ἀρχὴν in Prov 8:22 is assumed by rabbis as a reference to the time of creation. In Ps 72:17 the name of the Messiah is said

---

101. Dibelius rightly notes that James uses the Semitic form of Peter's name. Dibelius, *Studies in Acts*, 96. From this point, one can assume that James was ready to use linguistic forms appropriate for Jewish mentality.

102. Sandt, "Explanation of Acts 15:6–21," 74 n. 1, 76. He argues for the influence of the LXX version of Deut 4:29–35 on Acts 15:6–21. According to him, "the quotation of Amos 9:11–12 (LXX) with its universal significance, replaces Deut 4:29–31 in Acts 15:16–17. The allusion to Isa 45:21 in Acts 15:18 accounts for the temporal indications in Acts 15:7, 14." E. Richard found similarities between the quotation from Amos in Acts 15:16, 17 and that one in Acts 7:42–43, including three key words: "tent," "David," and "Build/rebuild." Richard, "Creative Use of Amos," 49–50.

103. Bruce, *Acts*, 337–44.

104. Bruce, *Acts*, 331.

105. The frequent use of several keywords linked to creation in different texts of the NT suggests the tradition of midrash, known to the apostles. Thus, the more explicit creation motif can be seen in Jas 1:18, where the word ἀπαρχήν (firstfruit) and the same root with Acts 15:7(ἀρχαίων) appears in connection with λόγῳ ἀληθείας and τῶν κτισμάτων. R. Martin notes that ἀπαρχήν, here, "has a wide range of meanings," and "could refer to the old creation but more likely is used in regard to believers as the eschatological creation of God." Martin, *James*, 40. Except James' use of ἀπαρχήν in Jas 1:18 has the same root ἀρχ as used by Luke in Acts 15:7 (ἀρχαίων) and by John in John 1:1 (ἀρχῇ). The word ἀπαρχήν may mean "in beginning" (in 2 Thess 2:13) and is used in Rom 16:5 as analogue of one's conversion. It was noticed that "in the NT, firstfruits represent the beginning of God's redemption of all creation." McCartney, *James*, 110–11. In Jas 1:18 ἀπαρχήν is contrasted with πειράζομαι in v. 13. The reversed order of this contrast can be observed in Acts 15. Here, Peter's ἀφ' ἡμερῶν ἀρχαίων in Acts 15:7 is contrasted with πειράζετε in Acts 15:10. The pointing to the prime will of God by ὁ θεὸς ἐξελέξατο, and the fulfillment of God's will by τὸν λόγον τοῦ εὐαγγελίου both suggest the presence of the creation motif in Peter's and James' speeches at the council.

106. Shuchat, *Creation According to the Midrash Rabbah*, 15–17.

107. Shuchat, *Creation According to the Midrash Rabbah*, 16.

to be present before the creation of the Sun, and εἰς τοὺς αἰῶνας, which corresponds to the time before the creation of the world.[108]

Such connections of the apostolic age with the "primeval" part of Genesis might seem strange at first glance. However, the frequent telling of the ancestral stories by the characters of Acts in their speeches opens up the possibility of such a connection.[109] Genesis was assumed as "the fundamental text of the Bible."[110] Pao emphasizes that "most of the quotations that Luke uses, come from the Pentateuch."[111] There are six direct quotations and 33 allusions to Genesis in Acts itself. In addition to this, Genesis was cited five times and alluded to 28 times in the Gospel of Luke.[112]

The rabbinic tradition supports the idea that James' midrash in Acts 15 represents a reference to the creation of the world, and not merely to the Exodus story. As the apostles during the Jerusalem Council, were rethinking the laws of Torah, and the new community of believers as the "people of God," and also the role of the Messiah, it is likely they viewed these concepts as linked to the time of creation and eternity preceeding it, which is similar to rabbinic tradition.[113] Consequently, the link to creation was reflected in Peter's speech in the phrase, ἀφ' ἡμερῶν ἀρχαίων (Act 15:7) and the link to the eternity was shown by James in the phrase, γνωστὰ ἀπ' αἰῶνος (Acts 15:17).

James further paraphrases Peter's words using καθὼς πρῶτον ὁ θεὸς ἐπεσκέψατο λαβεῖν ἐξ ἐθνῶν λαὸν τῷ ὀνόματι αὐτοῦ.[114] Translation of πρῶτον depends on the context. Here, the adverb of time, πρῶτον, is not to be translated "for the first time," which in Hellenistic Greek would be expressed by πρώτως (Acts 11:26).[115] Instead, the meaning of James' πρῶτον, likely, has reference to Peter's ἡμερῶν ἀρχαίων, and, thus, to the creation account.[116] This thought has support from M. Rich, who sees the Lukan "beginning" of Jesus only in Luke 3:23–32, when Jesus appears to be the son of Adam,

---

108. Shuchat, *Creation According to the Midrash Rabbah*, 17.

109. Havrelock, *Reception History of Genesis*, 11. Downing, "Freedom from Law," 49.

110. Havrelock, *Reception History of Genesis*, 11.

111. Pao, *Commentary on the New Testament Use*, 252.

112. Aland and Aland, eds., *Greek New Testament*, 887–91.

113. In the classical form of midrash the text usually was taken from the Sabbath texts of the synagogue lectionary cycle. However, New Testament writers didn't employ them and used simple allusions to Pentateuch stories. Despite the tradition, Christians often didn't use this secondary text and their final text might not correspond or allude to the initial text. Ellis, "How the New Testament Uses the Old," 206.

114. Peterson views the meaning of πρῶτον in the sense, "at first," which refers to the action of God sending the Messiah to Israel. Peterson, *Acts*, 429.

115. Lake and Cadbury, *English Translation and Commentary*, 175. Here the adverb πρῶτος is used, which means "*the first, the earliest.*" BDAG, πρῶτος, 1 a α. The difference in meaning can be seen from the comparison in Acts 11:26, where the word πρώτως is used. BDAG, πρώτως "*for the first tme.*"

116. Jeannine Brown notes a NT tradition to associate ἐν ἀρχῇ with creation and views creation and renewal inaugurated in Jesus, explicit in the Gospel of John and implicitly present in all Gospels. Brown, "Creation's Renewal," 275, 277, 290.

who is the Son of God.[117] Here, πρῶτον seems to mean "the earliest."[118] Thus, Luke's design represents one uniting background for all the nations in one forefather, Adam.

Pao notes the transfer from "ἐθνῶν" to "λαὸν τῷ ὀνόματι αὐτοῦ" in James' speech (15:14) as the acceptance of the Gentiles into the framework of the New Exodus of Acts as the Gentiles.[119] Peterson explains that James' use of ἐπεσκέψατο is comparable to LXX use of this word to describe God's visitation of Israel in Exodus narrative of Exod 3:16.[120] Dickinson argues that the conjunction, καὶ, in Acts 15:17 should be considered epexegetically, and the redeemed Gentiles are the remnant, and not included in the remnant.[121] Indeed the wording λαβεῖν ἐξ ἐθνῶν λαὸν τῷ ὀνόματι αὐτοῦ (15:14) echoes God calling the Israelites out of Egyptian bondage to be the people of God.

The Exodus event, however, might preserve a meaning deeper than just liberation from bondage, but also a new status.[122] Gathering of people under the name of God may also signify the process of establishing the kingdom of God. Simon Butticaz states,

> From time immemorial, in effect, God had envisaged the universalisation of his elect movement, the outcome of which came with the accomplishment of the reconstruction of the booth of David. On reaching this point in the narrative of Acts, the Lukan reader/listener discovers the wideness of the ecclesial journey up to this moment. The entire saved community, born at Pentecost, now constitutes the *ekklēsia* of God. Not only Israel restored, the kingdom of David raised up from the ruins, but also pagans, converted solely to the Lord Jesus.[123]

Moreover, the infinitive of purpose, λαβεῖν, reveals that the purpose of God has not come to an end with liberation from slavery, even from slavery to sin, but it presupposes future restoration of the world to the state known from creation. Thus, the theme of the restoration of creation resides in the background thought of James' speech, together with the Exodus theme.

The theme of re-creation becomes more evident from the following complex quotation of the biblical prophets. Glenny understands Acts 15:15–17 as a conflation of passages from several prophets. For him the opening words, "Μετὰ ταῦτα ἀναστρέψω," and the last words, "γνωστὰ ἀπ' αἰῶνος," of the quotation were taken

---

117. Rich sees the different use of the "beginning" by evangelists. Thus, for Mark "in the beginning" linked to the beginning of Jesus' public ministry; Matthew connects "beginning" to genealogy from Abraham; John traces it back to God. Luke gives Jesus' beginning only after infancy narratives in Luke 3:23–38, and pictures Jesus' origin from Adam, son of God. Rich, "In the Beginning," 25.

118. BDAG, πρῶτον, 1 a β, "*first, in the first place, before, earlier, to begin with.*"

119. Pao, *Acts and the Isaianic New Exodus*, 239, see also n. 71.

120. Peterson, *Acts*, 429 n. 39.

121. Dickinson, "Theology of Jerusalem Conference," 77.

122. Sandt, "Explanation of Acts 15:6–21," 89. Thus the word ἔθνος from Deut 4:34 had been replaced by the λαὸν in Acts 15:14 which was usually reserved in Luke-Acts for the people of God, and "for himself" turned into "for his name" revealing the new status of the Gentiles.

123. Butticaz, *L'identité de l'Eglise*, 330.

from Hos 3:45.¹²⁴ At the same time the Lord's promise of ἀναστρέψω can relate to Zech 8:3 or Jer 12:15.¹²⁵ The last allusion was added to the quotation from Isa 45:21, which declares the things known from the beginning.¹²⁶ In addition, James introduced his quotation as "the words of prophets" which actually reveals the fact that he develops the complex quotation from a combination of passages.

Further, James uses repetitions of ἀνοικοδομήσω, to "*build up again*,"¹²⁷ and ἀνορθώσω "to rebuild, restore."¹²⁸ These show that restoration is the prominent theme of his speech.¹²⁹ This finding is important, because James makes a parallel comparison between his summary of Peter, and his complex quotation of prophets with the help of a midrashic explanatory formula, καὶ τούτῳ συμφωνοῦσιν οἱ λόγοι τῶν προφητῶν. This explanatory formula demonstrates that these two parallel sayings uphold the same idea, namely, the restoration of the people of God in expectation of the re-creation of the world, rather than a new Exodus.

The phrase πρῶτον ὁ θεὸς ἐπεσκέψατο echoes Luke 1:68–70, ὅτι ἐπεσκέψατο καὶ ἐποίησεν λύτρωσιν . . . καθὼς ἐλάλησεν διὰ στόματος τῶν ἁγίων ἀπ αἰῶνος τῶν προφητῶν αὐτοῦ, where ἐπεσκέψατο is connected with ἀπ αἰῶνος and might suggest a reference to the earliest prophecies of Genesis and the very beginning of salvation history.¹³⁰ The adverb of time, πρῶτον, can also emphasize Peter's assurance that success of the mission among the Gentiles was due to God's prime concern and his leading role in salvation history.¹³¹ Although ἐπισκέπτομαι plainly means "to visit," it appears in Luke's writings to imply the redemptive act of God (Luke 1:68, 78; 7:16; 7:23, 19:44) or an act of care for people's physical wellbeing and spiritual growth (Acts 6:3; 15:36).¹³² The word usually applied to the people of God, now is applied to Gentile converts.¹³³

124. Glenny, "Septuagint and Apostolic Hermeneutics," 11. However, Dickinson notes that Peter's speech had two temporal indicators: "in the early days" (Acts 15:7) and "now" (Acts 15:10). Dickinson, "Theology of Jerusalem Conference," 68.

125. Glenny, "Septuagint and Apostolic Hermeneutics," 12–13 n. 52.

126. Glenny, "Septuagint and Apostolic Hermeneutics," 14.

127. BDAG, ἀνοικοδομέω.

128. BDAG, ἀνορθόω, 1, "to build smth up again after it has fallen, *rebuild, restore*."

129. Soards, *Speeches in Acts*, 94. He notes that the restoration described in Acts 15:16 might bring to mind the promise in Jer 12:15, where the restoration is shown in its eschatological meaning.

130. BDAG, αἰῶνος, 1 a, "a long period of time, without ref. to beginning or end, *the past, earliest times*."

131. William Mounce notes the use of πρῶτον in the NT; meanings include "first in time" in Mark 4:28; 16:9; "at the first, formerly" in John 12:16; 19:39; and "before all things" in Matt 6:33. The Marcan use seems to be closer to Peter's meaning. Mounce, *Analytical Lexicon*, 402–3.

132. BDAG, ἐπισκέπτομαι, 3. Here, the verb means "to exercise oversight in behalf of, *look after, make an appearance to help*."

133. Kaiser views the word ἀναστρέψω as indicator of the messianic era and salvation of the nations, and fits this salvation of nations into the blessings of the "seed of Abraham." With this he overlooks that the promised "seed" of Abraham presumes a root in the promise of the messianic "seed" in Gen 3:15. Kaiser, "Davidic Promise," 106–11.

It is noteworthy that τὴν πεπτωκυῖαν is a perfect active participle of the verb πίπτω.[134] This participle relates to τὴν σκηνὴν Δαυίδ and describes David's tent as "fallen." The phrase καὶ τὰ κατεσκαμμένα αὐτῆς also refers to "David's fallen tent."[135] The perfect tense might stress that the Israelite nation has already fallen and remains in ruins. The quotation from this point supports Peter's observation about the yoke that neither the Jews of their time nor of their fathers' have been able to bear (Acts 15:10). This states that all Jewish attempts to base their salvation on the cult of the earthly tabernacle have collapsed. Thus, James answers the first question of the council agenda: are the Mosaic laws necessary for salvation? According to him the Mosaic laws do not provide salvation even to those who keep them.

It is important to mention the connections between two quotations of Amos in Acts 7:42–43 and 15:16. The quotations in Stephen's apology and in James' speech are two out of twenty NT quotes introduced by the formula "καθὼς γέγραπται."[136] During his apology Stephen recalled the worship of the golden calf at the beginning of Israel's history and their constant idolatry, turning them back into exile. This picture of idolatry could explain the phrase, "David's fallen tent," in Amos 9:11 and Acts 15:16.[137]

However, the manner in which James quotes the prophets suggests that he refers not only to the Exodus event. Thus, James quotes Amos 9:11, according to the LXX, to the Jewish audience assembled in Jerusalem.[138] He could rather have used the original Hebrew wording, instead of the reading in the LXX. The difference is significant. The Hebrew reads "and I will build them as in the days of old, that they (the Israelites) may inherit (יירשו) what remains of Edom (את שארית אדום) and of the other nations over which my name is named."[139] The LXX reads יירשו as ידרשו (omitting את), and translates it ἐκζητήσωσι, "to seek." According to Glenny, the Hebrew "they may possess the remnant of Edom," appears in the LXX as "that the remnant of men may seek me."[140]

---

134. BDAG, πίπτω, 1 b β. The verb means *"fall, fall to pieces, collapse, go down."*

135. Fitzmyer notes that τὴν σκηνὴν Δαυίδ was interpreted by Essenes in the sense of "the books of the law" in CD 7:16. By its restoration, the renewal of the Mosaic law was envisaged. Fitzmyer, *Acts*, 556, see note on 15:18.

136. Sandt, "Explanation of Acts 15:6–21," 77 n. 2, referring to Paulo, *Le probleme ecclésial des Actes*, 29, 47.

137. Sandt, "Explanation of Acts 15:6–21," 78. Sandt believes that the origin of the quotation in Acts 15:16 is the story of the golden calf described in Exod 32:1–6. Later, the first allusion to this story moved through Deut 4:1–28 on to Amos 5:26–27. The second allusion reflects upon Deut 4:29–31 and Amos 9:11, "projecting" into Acts 15:16. This can be understood as a split of two pictures of the "day of the Lord" since Deuteronomy. As a result they come in different parts of Amos' prophetic book, despite both pictures being connected to doomsday.

138. Stamps, writing about different methods of interpretation of the OT in the NT, recognizes that the OT was not only quoted from MT. The NT writers used different recensions for the LXX. They also used Aramaic targumic traditions. Stamps stresses three major lines of interpretation: terminology, hermeneutics and theological issues. Stamps, "Use of the Old Testament," 10–16.

139. Lake and Cadbury, *English Translation and Commentary*, 176.

140. Glenny explains the contradiction by the translator's misreading of the second *yod* in the word יירשו ("possess"), which lead to the change to *dalet* and became ידרשו ("seek"). Glenny, "Septuagint

Moreover, LXX reads סודא as סדא, and takes סדא as the subject of the verb instead of the object. Thus, "men" becomes the subject of the sentence instead of "Edom."[141] As a result, the meaning of the whole phrase shifts from "a promise that Israel should posses their lands" to a promise of conversion of the Gentiles.[142]

According to Glenny's observation the LXX translation of Amos 9:11 contradicts the other passages in the Minor Prophets (Hos 9:6; Amos 2:10; Obad 17, 19, 20; Mic 1:15; Hab 1:6: Zech 9:4), where the Hebrew, *yāraš*, was translated with the Greek, κληρονομέω, "to inherit," and not "seek." Glenny accounts for it by the fact that LXX translators could have been influenced by the wording of Zechariah's prophecy.[143] Zech 14:2, 9, 16, similar to Amos 9:12, contain the phrase πάντα τά ἔθνη and καταλειφθῶσιν ἐκ πάντων τῶν ἐθνῶν. The wording of Zech 8:22 repeats in the following manner, καὶ ἔθνη πολλὰ ἐκζητῆσαι τὸ πρόσωπον κυρίου. Here, the aorist infinitive ἐκζητῆσαι means "to exert effort to find out or learn someth., *seek out, search for*."[144] The LXX translators most likely adjusted the wording of Amos to the similar text in Zechariah's prophecy.[145] If one accepts that the LXX was used by Jews living in the diaspora, and that they had access to the Greek translation of these Hebrew prophecies, it becomes clear that the reading, "that the rest of men may seek the Lord," appeared preferable.

However, one needs to enquire why James uses the LXX reading for his Jewish audience. There are three possible answers. The first is that James quotes the LXX because final judgment concerns the Gentile converts, not Jewish ones. This, however, is doubtful, because Greek secondary quotations make James' statement less convincing to his Jewish audience, who knew the original MT wording as well. The second is that James spoke Greek, or that Luke uses a Greek version of James' speech. This also is difficult to accept, since from the first words of his speech James uses the Aramaic version of Peter's name. Moreover, if Luke used the LXX version of the text which James pronounced according to MT, it is hard to see from which point James could have drawn the conclusion that the Gentiles have to be accepted into the people of God, instead of repeating the aggressive territorial message of MT.

The third explanation presents James preferring the meaning of LXX over the meaning of the MT. Here James clearly prefers the wording which presumes an inheritance achieved by way of conversion of the Gentiles to the wording which suggests the way of territorial expansion. His view on the restoration of the fallen tent appears in terms of the growth of the Gospel message, and not in terms of land possession. In contrast to the military tone of the Exodus narrative, the interpretation of

---

and Apostolic Hermeneutics," 6, 7.

141. Lake and Cadbury, *English Translation and Commentary*, 176.

142. Lake and Cadbury, *English Translation and Commentary*, 176.

143. Glenny, "Septuagint and Apostolic Hermeneutics," 8.

144. BDAG, ἐκζητέω, 1.

145. Glenny, "Septuagint and Apostolic Hermeneutics," 8.

the prophets, declared by James at the council, reveals a peaceful restoration of the kingdom (ἀνοικοδομήσω and ἀνορθώσω linked to the "booth of David"), where all nations are accepted (ὅπως ἂν ἐκζητήσωσιν . . . τὸν κύριον . . . πάντα τὰ ἔθνη). This contrasts the idea expressed by the Exodus narrative, and likely finds its meaning in terms of the final restoration of the whole creation. That is why James prefers the LXX reading to MT, as it helps him to go further back than the Exodus, and reach the time of creation and the foundation of the world in its undivided wholistic condition.

Moreover, the purpose of James' LXX citation was to link the promised restoration of the kingdom (ἀνοικοδομήσω and ἀνορθώσω) with Jesus' victory over death.[146] Glenny states that in v. 17 πάντα τὰ ἔθνη is connected by ὅπως + the aorist subjunctive ἐκζητήσωσιν to the previously mentioned "booth of David."[147] From this point he explains the restoration of the "booth of David" in terms of the resurrection of the Messiah, with the result that Gentiles may now seek the Lord.[148] Thus, at the council, James shifted the focus of discussion "from a proselyte model to an eschatological one."[149]

However, Marshall believes that here Luke uses ἀνοικοδομήσω and ἀνορθώσω, but not ἀνίστημι, which usually describes the resurrection of Jesus.[150] Luke uses the words which can be employed to describe building restoration. Dickinson interprets Luke's ὅπως ἂν + aorist subjunctive ἐκζητήσωσιν as a purpose clause which indicates that the mission to the Gentiles has as its purpose their restoration.[151] Their restoration can be understood as the global world restoration, not limited to the single event of Jesus' resurrection.[152] Thus, restoration started with the resurrection of Jesus and as a final goal includes all nations.

Sandt interprets the reason for the replacement of, "in the last days," in Joel's prophecy by "after these things" in Acts 15:16 as due to its connection to the Pentecost event.[153] Supporting this thought, Sandt argued that "γνωστὰ ἀπ' αἰῶνος" in Acts

---

146. Arrington, *Acts*, 154. He believes that this prophecy "was fulfilled in the resurrection of the crucified Son of David."

147. Glenny, "Septuagint and Apostolic Hermeneutics," 5–6.

148. Glenny, "Septuagint and Apostolic Hermeneutics," 6 n. 19, 18.

149. Longenecker, *Acts*, 446.

150. Marshall, "Acts," 592. Here, Marshall sees that Luke, by making an analogy with Jesus' resurrection, pictures the restoration of the eschatological temple.

151. Dickinson, "Theology of the Jerusalem Conference," 76.

152. The Jews in John 2:19–22 employ the term ἀνοικοδομήθη in relation to the temple's restoration. Jesus compares his body to be a temple of God and uses the term ἐγερῶ in order to emphasize the rapidity of its restoration. This may suggest that Jesus viewed his resurrection as the dawn of the restoration of his church in a global sense, which is a spiritual temple in the NT era and Jesus' spiritual body. In the OT era this was understood and represented as the restoration of σκηνὴν Δαυὶδ.

153. Sandt, "Explanation of Acts 15:6–21," 79–80. In Acts 2:17 Peter quotes Joel on the Pentecost. The next quotation of Joel in Acts 15 turns to be the consequence of "that day" or "these things." This means that disputants of the council understood their days as last days or days of the judgment for rebels and restoration of the true Israel from all nations.

15:18, taken from Isa 45:18–25, reveals the Gentiles' search for God and the end of their exile.[154] As James rightly noted, it was "foreknown from of old" or "from the beginning." Sandt understands the "beginning" as the echo of Israel's exodus out of slavery, connected to the kerygma of the Gentiles' emancipation.[155]

At the end of the complex quotation James refers no longer to prophets, but to God himself, saying λέγει κύριος. He adds, λέγει κύριος ποιῶν ταῦτα, assuming that God has begun to bring his promises to fulfillment. On one hand James applies the prophetic promises to the recent events among the Gentiles and their conversions, as reported by Paul and Barnabas. On the other hand he sets those events in connection to the will of God, who predicted through the prophets things known to him from the very beginning.[156]

After this, James states that the salvific work of God was γνωστὰ ἀπ'αἰῶνος, which means "known from eternity."[157] Here, γνωστὰ presumes "knowledge," which did not originate with James or one of prophets.[158] James refers here to the knowledge of God, who knows the end from the beginning. The addition γνωστὰ ἀπ'αἰῶνος inserted by James, just after the complex quotation, helps him 1) to present the meaning of the quotation grounded in the creation account and 2) to form the reverse-element of midrash.[159] With the help of this element, James points to the beginning in its perfect initial state, and shows God's purpose to restore his people to that perfect original condition. Barrett supports this idea when he states that "God has not suddenly thought of the inclusion of the Gentiles; it has always been his intention, and he has long made his intention known."[160] Consequently, on the council James demonstrates

154. Sandt, "Explanation of Acts 15:6–21," 82.

155. Sandt links the ἡμερῶν ἀρχαίων in Peter's speech in Acts 15:7 to the event of the Sinai revelation in Deut 4:32–34. He notices a peculiar terminology, when Peter in Acts 15:7 said "διὰ τοῦ στόματός μου ἀκοῦσαι τὰ ἔθνη τὸν λόγον τοῦ εὐαγγελίου" that, according to Sandt, refers to "ἀνοίξας δὲ Πέτρος τὸ στόμα εἶπεν" in Acts 10:34. Further, he connects the outpouring of the Spirit upon the Gentiles in Cornelius' household and that upon Jews in the Pentecost event. As everyone knows, the theophany at Pentecost had been expressed in the miracle of "tongues as fire." From this point Sandt argues that the Pentecost and Sinai were associated events. Later he connects all four events described in Deut 4:32–34; Acts 2:1–13; 10:33–48 with 11:15–18 and 15:7 by the same pattern of God's revelation to the "people of God," chosen from the nations. Sandt, "Explanation of Acts 15:6–21," 74 n. 1, 87.

156. Butticaz describes the Decree as "God's accomplishment of a decree from time immemorial, rendered public by the prophets of ancient Israel." Butticaz, L'identité de l'Eglise, 345.

157. Arrington, Acts, 154.

158. Jackson, however, attributes this additional phrase γνωστὰ ἀπ'αἰῶνος to a confused memory of the καθὼς αἱ ἡμέραι τοῦ αἰῶνος in Amos 9:11. He assumes that Luke might transfer the one part of the quotation to another. He states "the Hebrew parallelism lent itself to such transfer of phrases." The phrase also could reflect a tendency to round out the quotation in biblical style. Lake and Cadbury, English Translation and Commentary, 176–77.

159. Ellis, "New Testament Uses the Old," 207. Ellis describes the Christian practice of midrash using an eschatological exegesis, when all prophecies and promises of the Old Testament had been seen as finding their fulfillment at the time of the writer's community, as if writer was looking back for the promises to the current event.

160. Here, Barrett states that choosing ἀπ'αἰῶνος instead of ἀπ'ἀρχῆς James speaks more forcefully,

that 1) salvation is the supreme will of God, 2) the cult has been rescinded, and 3) God fulfilled the task of the cult.

At this point James comes to his conclusion in which he needs to propose a solution. As is known, the council was triggered by the difference in attitudes to the role of the Mosaic law. Most likely, James proposes his solution in view of the main concern of the council. Thus one expects him to answer three main questions: 1) whether the Mosaic laws are necessary for salvation? 2) whether the Mosaic laws are still necessary to be observed? 3) whether or not the Gentile converts have to keep some points of the Mosaic law, and if so, for which purpose?

Here James shifts to his personal judgment of the Mosaic law. The shift seems to be appropriate, since James proposes his own opinion. Before it is accepted by the unanimous decision of the council it cannot be presented as the will of God. He uses the inferential conjunction διὸ to link his decision by inference to all that was previously spoken, then he declares, ἐγὼ κρίνω, "I judge/decide/consider."[161] James then formulates the consequences of the divine initiative in the four requirements for Gentile converts.[162]

The discussion now turns to answering the second question of the council agenda: are the Mosaic laws still necessary to be observed? At this point James states his judgment: μὴ παρενοχλεῖν . . . ἀλλὰ.[163] This phrase states the practical consequences of James' (ἐγὼ κρίνω) decision: μὴ παρενοχλεῖν (present infinitive meaning "to cause unnecessary trouble, *cause difficulty . . . annoy*").[164] Here "the tense of the infinitive indicates the *aspect* of the action, not the time of the action."[165] Thus, μὴ παρενοχλεῖν prohibits ongoing action, the attempt to impose the ritual law on the Gentiles. Haenchen views μὴ παρενοχλεῖν as an infinitive expressing the present imperative, and translates it as "stop overburdening."[166] He links the meaning of μὴ παρενοχλεῖν to Peter's ζυγὸν in Acts 15:10. This understanding was rejected by Jervell and Fitzmyer.[167] Johnson, who views μὴ παρενοχλεῖν in the sense of "to stop troubling," seems to be right.[168]

---

revealing that the Gentiles were part of God's eternal plan. Barrett, *Critical Commentary on Acts*, 728.

161. Jackson believes that here James is acting by his personal authority. Lake and Cadbury, *English Translation and Commentary*, 177.

162. Sandt, "Explanation of Acts 15:6–21," 73–74.

163. Jackson shows the discussion to be about whether the παρά in παρενοχλεῖν implies the sense of "extra" and controls the meaning of the phrase, in the sense, "to put additional burdens." Here the scholars reject the translation of παρενοχλεῖν as "extra burdens" and suggest translation of the whole phrase μὴ παρενοχλεῖν in meaning "stop annoying" rather than "do not annoy." Lake and Cadbury, *English Translation and Commentary*, 177.

164. BDAG, παρενοχλέω.

165. McLean, *New Testament Greek*, 200–201.

166. Haenchen, *Acts*, 448 n. 6, citing Lake and Cadbury, *English Translation and Commentary*, 177.

167. Jervell, *Luke and the People of God*, 143–44; repeated in Jervell, *Apostelgeschichte*, 392–93; 396. Jervell's view also had support from Fitzmyer, *Luke the Theologian*, 176.

168. Johnson, *Acts*, 266 n. 19.

The conjunction ἀλλὰ can be viewed as adversative, coordinating or emphatic. The sentence should not be interpreted in such a way that the principal decision is μὴ παρενοχλεῖν, with an added subordinate clause starting with ἀλλά.[169] Some scholars view it as a set of temporal regulations in respect of common table fellowship between the Jewish and Gentile converts.[170] Thus, Blomberg accepts that both chapters, Acts 10 and 15, had the purpose of leading readers to the idea of "freedom from the Law."[171] He takes Peter's vision in Acts 10 as "not only cancellation of dietary laws but also the abolition of the barriers banning table fellowship between Jews and Gentiles."[172] Supporting his view Glenny states: "James's quotations from Amos 9 in Acts 15:16–18 are the scriptural basis for not imposing the Law on the Gentile converts at the Jerusalem Council."[173]

The opposing view was expressed by Jervell, Marshall, and Fitzmyer. First of all, Jervell states that the Decree presumed the freedom from circumcision and not from the law itself.[174] According to Marshall, Luke had no intention of cancelling all of the Law, but only the ritual law.[175] Fitzmyer demonstrates that for Luke the Mosaic law continues "to be a valid norm of human conduct . . . and also a means of identifying God's people."[176] Supporting this idea, Fitzmyer shows the linguistic heterogeneity of the words νόμος, ἐντολή, and ἔθος.[177] These terms tell us about the law from different perspectives, and have different meanings. The issue of the laws of Torah was disputed

---

169. Pao argues for the connection in functioning of ἀλλὰ in Peter's and James' speeches. He states that in Acts 15:10–11 by ἀλλὰ, the "yoke," is explicitly contrasted with "grace." In 15:19–20 Poa indicates the same function of the adversative conjunction ἀλλὰ translated, "but." Pao, *Acts and the Isaianic New Exodus*, 239–41. The present thesis suggests that the conjunction ἀλλὰ here reveals the phrase contrasted with μὴ παρενοχλεῖν due to a different reason. It does not contrast "grace" of v. 19 with "yoke" of v. 20, but reveals that the content of v. 20 (related to the matters of natural law) stays separate from the content of v. 19 (matters of ritual law). Thus, ἀλλὰ joins two parallel phrases, contrasting to one another in meaning.

170. This view has support in the work of Blomberg. Blomberg, "Law in Luke-Acts," 64. Perry also argues for the temporal significance of the four prohibitions. Perry, "Ethics in Acts 10–15," 171. Barrett states that a better explanation for the prohibitions is "the desire to make it easier for Jewish and Gentile Christians to eat together." Barrett, *Critical Commentary on Acts*, 734 (d).

171. Blomberg, "Law in Luke-Acts," 70. This view was maintained by Seifrid, "Jesus and the Law in Acts," 51–53.

172. Blomberg, "Law in Luke-Acts," 64. Darrel Bock also views Acts 10 and 15 together and then concludes that "Jewish believers are free to practice the faith in their way, just as Gentiles are not required to come under the law." Bock, *Acts*, 37, 508. However, it puts believers in the situation of double standards. They had been obliged now to keep one law in mixed meals and a different law in separated meals.

173. Glenny, "Apostolic Hermeneutics," 20–21. Here Glenny insists that the four prohibitions were driven from Lev 17–18.

174. Jervell, "Law in Luke-Acts," 33, repeated in *Apostelgeschichte*, 397.

175. Marshall, *Luke*, 20, 185. Marshall considers that only the Jewish ritual Law became unnecessary to keep. He asserts that all aspects of the Mosaic law were fulfilled in Christ.

176. Fitzmyer, *Luke the Theologian*, 176.

177. Fitzmyer, *Luke the Theologian*, 177.

also by Mattheus Klinghardt who argues that the law, even after Christ's death and resurrection, remains valid in its modified form (the form which has been crystallized in the Apostolic Decree) for the ecclessia consisting of Jews and Gentiles.[178]

Secondly, it is less likely that Peter in the vision of Acts 10 was given an order to declare all unclean food as clean. If so, then the prohibitions of the Decree seem to be a step back. Also, it would seem impossible to apply the few dietary prohibitions to non-kosher foods. The cancellation of the dietary laws in Acts 10 cannot explain the reason to keep practicing one part of dietary system, while rejecting another. What kind of table fellowship could be possible between Jewish Christians and those from the Gentiles if the table is full of unclean meat, even though the blood had been drained out? Moreover, in Acts 10:19, 28; 11:10–12 Peter clarifies that his vision had a clear application to the issue of Gentile converts. He never mentioned any application of his vision to dietary law.

Thirdly, explaining the prohibitions of the Decree in terms of temporary significance also seems doubtful. Goppelt states that the Decree was written in order to regulate common life in mixed communities and was of a temporary and incomplete character.[179] However, Dibelius emphasized that the four prohibitions were given without saying that "these conditions will be necessary, especially if Jewish and Gentile Christians are to associate with one another."[180] Additionally, the temporary application of the prohibitions would require the subordinate clause to be written as a temporal clause. There are, however, no markers of a temporal sense.

The phrase μὴ παρενοχλεῖν . . . ἀλλὰ can be better interpreted by understanding it as the connection of two clauses with a paratactic relationship, indicating two clauses of equal importance. It can then be interpreted as a judgment about the Mosaic law, and a judgment concerning different laws, which are tied in a list of exclusions. Thus, the adversative conjunction ἀλλὰ serves to introduce matters which readers should not mix together with the Mosaic laws. It is evident from the fact that the infinitive, ἐπιστεῖλαι, is the direct object of a verb κρίνω in v. 19. This supports the view that ἀλλὰ joins two paratactic clauses.

The following clause, ἐπιστεῖλαι αὐτοῖς τοῦ ἀπέχεσθαι, is constructed with two infinitives. The first, ἐπιστεῖλαι, describes the decision of James to send the answer, when the pronoun's antecedent identifies the recipients as the believers in Antioch (15:1).[181] The genitive articular infinitive, τοῦ ἀπέχεσθαι, expresses purpose, to warn the reader about necessary things: "I judge . . . to write to them in order that they avoid . . ."[182] Thus, v. 19 has to be structured as follows:

178. Klinghardt, *Gesetz*, 306–10.

179. Leonhard Goppelt, *Apostolic and Post-Apostolic Times*, 70. He bases his view of the Decree on the law of aliens, written in Lev 17–18.

180. Dibelius, *Studies in Acts* 97.

181. BDAG, "to send someth. to, *inform/ instruct by letter.*"

182. Wallace, *Greek Grammar*, 591–93. Johnson mentions here that the word ἀπέχεσθαι occurs in

Figure 6: Additional Diagram 1—Acts 15:19, 20

19) διὸ ἐγὼ κρίνω

    μὴ παρενοχλεῖν τοῖς ἀπὸ τῶν ἐθνῶν ἐπιστρέφουσιν ἐπὶ τὸν θεόν,

20) ἀλλὰ ἐπιστεῖλαι αὐτοῖς τοῦ ἀπέχεσθαι
                              τῶν ἀλισγημάτων τῶν εἰδώλων
                              καὶ τῆς πορνείας
                              καὶ τοῦ πνικτοῦ
                              καὶ τοῦ αἵματος·

The next important point is to interpret the list of prohibitions. The list belongs to purpose the clause starting with τοῦ ἀπέχεσθαι, meaning "to keep away/ to abstain."[183] Consequently, the phrase τῶν ἀλισγημάτων τῶν εἰδώλων can be translated as "of the pollutions of idols."[184] Haenchen states, εἰδωλοθύτων is the prohibition of "not only a participation in pagan cultic meals but buying sacrificed meat in the market."[185] Bock and Savelle note that the verbal form of ἀλίσγημα appears in Dan 1:8 and Mal 1:7, 12, "where it concerns the eating of food and suggests a kind of desecration."[186] Bock interprets the prohibition of τῶν ἀλισγημάτων τῶν εἰδώλων as participation in pagan idolatry. He also notes that the omission of πορνεία in 𝔓45 makes the Decree "exclusively ritualistic."[187]

Citing Acts 15:20, Pao gives an interesting translation of the Greek phrase "τοῦ ἀπέχεσθαι τῶν ἀλισγημάτων" as "to abstain only from things polluted."[188] He sees the key to the understanding of the Decree in "context of the polemic against pagan worship," which matches the anti-idol polemic of Isaiah and Luke-Acts as a whole.[189]

LXX Job 28:28; Prov 9:18; Isa 54:14; 1 Thess 4:3; 1 Tim 4:3; 1 Pet 2:11 all of which should be understood as literal prohibitions. Johnson, *Acts*, 266 n. 20.

183. BDAG, ἀπέχω, 5, "to avoid contact w. or use of someth., *keep away, abstain, refrain from*."

184. BDAG, ἀλίσγημα, "*pollution*," from ἀλισγέω "make ceremonially impure" LXX.

185. Haenchen, *Acts*, 449 n. 3, repeated in *Apostelgeschichte*, 432 n. 2. However, the word εἰδωλοθύτων was used in 1 Cor 8:7 in a ritual manner: "Some people are still so accustomed to idols that when they eat such food they think of it as having been sacrificed to an idol, and since their conscience is weak, it is defiled." This text shows that pollution comes not by buying sacrificed meat, but when the worship to idols is taking place.

186. Bock, *Acts*, 505. Savelle shows that the meaning of "ἀλίσγημα" is confirmed by the fifth-century CE lexicographer Hesychius defining this word as "the taking as food of defiling sacrifices." Savelle, "Reexamination of Prohibitions," 452 n. 9. Savelle quotes from E.A. Sophocles, *Greek Lexicon of the Roman and Byzantine Periods*, 1:114. The desecration was presumed by the laws of Lev 17:7 and Exod 20:4, which link the Decree to the food laws. Otherwise it seems incomprehensible to repeat the prohibition of idolatry three times in different forms at one resolution of the Decree.

187. Bock, *Acts*, 509. Bock views the Alexandrian text as the closest to the original.

188. Pao, *Acts and the Isaianic New Exodus*, 240–41. It is clear that the word "only" is absent in the original text. Such an enthusiastic approach might betray his presupposition concerning the four prohibitions of the Decree.

189. Pao, *Acts and the Isaianic New Exodus*, 241–42. Developing the idea of the anti-idol polemic

Also, εἰδωλοθύτων in v. 29 clarifies the meaning of τῶν ἀλισγημάτων τῶν εἰδώλων in v. 20.[190] The word τῶν ἀλισγημάτων less likely relates to each of four prohibitions, as their cases do not correspond. Furthermore, Jackson and Lake refer ἀλισγημάτων to ritual dietary defilement, rather than moral pollution.[191]

While εἰδωλοθύτων means "meat offered to idols," without negative connotation, ἀλισγημάτων seems to put stress on defilement that idols cause.[192] Thus, τοῦ ἀπέχεσθαι τῶν ἀλισγημάτων could provide a rationale for the prohibition, namely, to prevent defilement from idols. Focus on the rationale could explain the fact that Luke preserved these two different wordings. The following prohibitions, καὶ τῆς πορνείας καὶ τοῦ πνικτοῦ καὶ τοῦ αἵματος are expressed with nouns, which serve as the direct objects of ἀπέχεσθαι.

Looking for an explanation of τοῦ πνικτοῦ as "strangled," Haenchen held it was influenced by the Golden Rule in an ethical sense.[193] However, he mentioned the evidence "that abhorrence of blood and strangled meat had survived into the second century, independently of consideration for the Jewish Christians."[194] Also Gager mentions that Christian polemic against Judaizers discussed the issue of the distinction among foods even in the fourth century CE.[195] Johnson notes that τοῦ πνικτοῦ, "strangled/choked," could echo the meaning of πνίγω in Mark 5:13, and Matt 13:7; 18:28.[196] Also, ἀπέπνιξαν in Luke 8:7 (aorist of αποπνίγω) has the same root, πνίγω, and is translated as "choked." Another form of αποπνίγω in Luke 8:33 (ἀπεπνίγη) means "drown."[197] These occurances

---

Pao believes that the Decree was invoked to call God-fearers from the Gentiles to worship the one true God. He rejects the thought that the Decree could be a compromise between the Jewish and Gentile parties in the church and points to the challenge of worshipping the true God instead of idols. However it seems to be a useless interpretation of the Decree, for it represents the discussion about evident matters. If this Decree could not suit the demand of the Antioch church members, then their joy after its reception becomes surprising.

190. McIver, *Intermediate NT Greek*, 62.

191. Lake and Cadbury, *English Translation and Commentary*, 177. They note that συναλισγο(ύ)μενοι appears in a manuscript of Aristeas 142 in a context which presupposes ritual dietary defilement.

192. Johnson relates this prohibition specifically to "food offered at the shrines of idols." Johnson, *Acts*, 266 n. 20.

193. Haenchen, *Acts*, 449–50 n. 6. He supports this with the opinions of Resch, Harnack, Clark, and Feine-Behm, who viewed the prohibitions in a moral sense. At the same time he acknowledged that Zahn, Wendland, Deihe, Preuschen, Weiss, Goguel, Loisy, Meyer, Ropes, Leitzmann, Beyer, Waitz, Bauernfeind, Cerfaux, Dibelius, Schafer, and Kummel argue for the ritual nature of the prohibitions. Repeated in Haenchen, *Apostelgeschichte*, 432 n. 5.

194. Haenchen, *Acts*, 472; and *Apostelgeschichte*, 456. He refers to the witnesses such as Justin, *Dialogue wih Trypho*, 34.8; Minucius Felix, 36.6; Eusebius, *Hist. eccl.* 5.1.26; and Tertullian, *Apol*, 9.13.

195. Gager, *Origins of Anti-Semitism*, 122.

196. Johnson, *Acts*, 267 n. 20. Johnson states that "strangled" was mentioned in the meaning of "meat with its blood." The word πνικτοῦ, meaning "strangled, choked to death," appears only in the text of the Decree in Acts 15:20, 29; 21:25. BDAG, πνίγω, 1, 2 a b c. In Matt 13:7; 18:28 it means "to be stifled, choke" and "drown" in Mark 5:13.

197. BDAG, αποπνίγω, a b, "to check normal breathing," "choke," "drown."

of πνίγω were mentioned to illustrate spiritual lessons. Together with the ethical aspect, they involve a cultic aspect referring to the laws of Torah.

Pao also suggests that τοῦ πνικτοῦ and αἵματος may point to pagan religious practices.[198] Wilson refers to the historical context of four prohibitions.[199] He argues that αἵματος in Luke-Acts, always meant "kill" or "murder" and never referred to eating.[200] However, Johnson points out that, in Torah, αἷμα had frequent connection to animal sacrifice. If Luke took the four prohibitions from the authentic apostolic letter and did not invent the main themes of the speeches, then one may assume that he preserved the actual account of James' argument. As a Jewish leader, James had to refer to the meaning of αἷμα, found in Torah. His use of αἷμα would not depend on meaning of this term in the entire context of Luke-Acts, but would rather depend on the meaning that αἷμα had in Torah.

The order in which the prohibitions are listed in variant readings most likely reflects three main concepts: idol worship, fornication and dietary rules. This is seen from the fact that τοῦ πνικτοῦ καὶ τοῦ αἵματος are usually linked one to another.[201] Barrett states that the link of πνικτοῦ to αἵματος suggests one should view them as references to a ritual food law.[202] The cultic reading of 𝔓45, while it omits τῆς πορνείας still keeps a link between τοῦ πνικτοῦ καὶ τοῦ αἵματος. The ethical reading of D 05 might intentionally omit τοῦ πνικτοῦ in order to break the link and remove the reference to dietary law.

As both prohibitions refer to the same law, they could be understood as replaceable/interchangeable. Arrington supports this view arguing for the meaning of τοῦ πνικτοῦ in the sense of meat from the animal, killed without draining its blood.[203] That explains the fact that sometimes only one of them was retained, as is evident in cases where τοῦ αἵματος was retained and τοῦ πνικτοῦ omitted. This, however, might point to the situation when the manuscripts with the threefold tradition, where τοῦ πνικτοῦ and τοῦ αἵματος were disconnected, reflected the loss of the original meaning of the prohibitions.

---

198. Pao, *Acts and the Isaianic New Exodus*, 241. If so, this approach doesn't explain the addition of the negative form of the Golden Rule and omission of πνικτός in Western reading.

199. Wilson, *Luke and Law*, 92. Wilson sees that meat was not a major dietary item in the ancient world. That's why the four requirements were not a burden for the readers of the Decree.

200. Wilson, *Luke and Law*, 100. See also Luke 11:50–55, 13:1; Acts 5:28, 22:20. Moreover, Wilson cites Weiss, who sees here the distinction between unclean meat from forbidden animals (Lev 11) and unclean meat because of the way (Lev 17) of its preparation. Wilson, *Luke and Law*, 75.

201. Arrington supports the observation of the close relation between τοῦ πνικτοῦ καὶ τοῦ αἵματος and suggests treating them together. Arrington, *Acts*, 155.

202. Barrett, *Critical Commentary on Acts*, 735 (b). The phrase "ritual food laws" seems to be here out of sense. The word "ritual" does not fit the concept of the food laws of Torah which prohibit blood consumption. The ritual food laws presume ritual cleansing before the meal.

203. Arrington, *Acts*, 155. He sees a clear theological connection between τοῦ πνικτοῦ and τοῦ αἵματος and relates both prohibitions to "certain laws" in Lev 17:10–15; Deut 12:16, 23.

The meaning of πορνεία also needs clarification. Fitzmyer provides detailed study of the word πορνεία in Jewish literature of pre-Christian Palestine.[204] He notes that the Hebrew analogue of πορνεία in the LXX, the noun זנות, is found in Num 14:33; Hos 6:10; Jer 3:2 and reflects the symbolic meaning of "idolatry."[205] While Jürgen Wehnert views the term πορνεία to be underpinned by regulations of the so-called Holiness Code (Lev 18:6–30),[206] Fitzmyer argues that this term does not occur in Lev 17–18. Instead, he notes the rabbinic explanation of זנות in the sense of marriage within prohibited degrees of kinship (the contravention of Lev 18:13), and polygamy or divorce (the contravention of Gen 1:27; 7:9; Deut 17:17).[207] Pao considers the term πορνεία in the sense of sacred prostitution, or even in terms of "a general criticism of the morality of the Gentiles."[208] Johnson adds that the meaning of πορνεία, most discussed in the New Testament, is sexual immorality.[209] Although commentators argue which of these meanings of זנות was intended by πορνεία in the Decree, one still needs to keep in mind the contravention of Gen 1:27 as its background.[210]

This finding is important because it explains the use of Gen 1:27 in Jesus' commentary on divorce in Matt 19:3–9; Mark 10:2–12.[211] His teaching is in agreement with Qumran *halakhic* tradition.[212] Moreover, both these passages discuss the link between divorce and πορνεία. Jesus viewed πορνεία as contrary to God's original purpose for marriage. Mark 10:2–12 reflects midrash, which Jesus created during his discussion with Pharisees.[213] With help of midrash, he appealed to the authority of

---

204. Fitzmyer, *Acts*, 557–58.

205. Johnson supports this view and adds Ezek 16:15–46 to the list of scriptural evidences. Johnson, *Acts*, 266.

206. Wehnert links all four prohibitions of the Decree to Lev 17–18, emphasising the primacy of the idolatry ban among the four prohibitions. He makes James the author of the so-called "abstention rules" by observing the connection between the three appearances of James in Acts and the treefold repetition of the Decree (15:20, 29, and 21:25). Wehnert, *Die Reinheit des "christlichen Gottesvolkes"*, 65–67.

207. Fitzmyer, *Acts*, 558.

208. Pao, *Acts and the Isaianic New Exodus*, 241.

209. Johnson recalls different forms of πορνεία in NT (1 Cor 6:18; 7:2; 2 Cor 12:21; Gal 5:19; Eph 5:3; Col 3:5; 1 Thess 4:3; Heb 13:4) and connected to divorce (Matt 5:32; 19:9). Johnson, *Acts*, 267.

210. Fitzmyer refers to CD 4:20–21 arguing that the rabbis of that time understood זנות as the contravention of Gen 1:27. Fitzmyer, *Acts*, 557–558, see note on 15:20.

211. Regarding marriage (Mark 10:2–5), Jesus alluded in his answer to the creation story (Mark 10:6–9).
Elledge, "'From the Beginning,'" 374.

212. Some scholars recognize the similarities of the "principle of creation" in Mark 10:2–9 and the Damascus Document of Qumran literature. Frierich, "Jesus and Purity," 255. The same thought appears in Thompson, "Divorce Halakhah," 322.

213. M. D. Goulder sees that "Matthew wrote a commentary on Mark" and was "eager to see the midrashic matrices of apparently invented materials." Goulder, "Midrash in Matthew," 207.

natural/universal law of pre-Mosaic Torah, which was above that of Mosaic law written later "to a post-creation period 'hardened' humanity."[214]

Luke 16:18 repeats this saying of Jesus about πορνεία, omitting the link to Gen 1:27.[215] This may be explained by the fact, that Luke wrote his Gospel for a predominantly Gentile audience, unfamiliar with this hermeneutical method. Matthew's community, though it had a substantial Gentile component, was formed mainly by Christians of Jewish descend that predetermined "the interest of the Gospel in issues relating to Jews."[216] Matthew's account addressed to a reader who is familiar with Jewish Scriptures, repeats the link between marriage and creation and shows πορνεία as contrary to God's plan appointed at creation. Thus, one can argue that the creation account provides the background of the prohibition of πορνεία in Acts 15:20.

Finally, James recalls the writings of Moses: Μωϋσῆς γὰρ . . . ἀναγινωσκόμενος. He does not specify which part of those writings he views here and, thus, he likely implies the sum of Mosaic writings, the Torah. The reason James did not to use the word "Torah," but replaced it with "Moses," is his need to include the final statement of his midrash, in which the final text has to recall the initial issue. The initial issue of the council was the discussion about νόμος Μωϋσέως, so James had to refer to Μωϋσῆς in the final text.[217]

Some scholars understand the reference to Moses in v. 21 differently. Dibelius translates v. 21 as "Moses also is proclaimed to the world without our assistance."[218] Haenchen applies "Moses" from v. 21 to the immediately preceding v. 20. As a result he sees the necessity of the four prohibitions in the understanding that the law is preached everywhere.[219] Bruce agrees that the need for keeping of the four prohibitions is because Moses is taught in every synagogue, and Christians should bear in mind that many people were aware of Torah, or practiced it.[220] This view, however, would impose the four prohibitions on Gentile converts as a negative result of the universal preaching of Moses. The word ἀναγινωσκόμενος means "*read aloud* for public hearing."[221] If one assumed

---

214. Moyise notes that in Mark 10:2–9 Jesus valued the will of God more than the command of Moses and linked marriage to a weighty law—the natural law of creation. Moyise, *Evoking Scripture*, 24–25.

215. Craign Evans notes that the pericope of Mark 10:1–12 was expanded by Matthew and abbreviated by Luke. Evans, *Mark 8:27—16:20*, 79.

216. McIver, *Mainstream or Marginal?*, 209.

217. Dibelius mentions here the possibility of "a little Midrash" connected to the quotation from the prophets. He saw the midrash lying somewhere between vv. 17 and 21. Dibelius, *Studies in Acts*, 98. Similar interpretation was suggested by James Hardy Ropes, "Acts XV.21," and later taken up by Lake and Cadbury, *English Translation and Commentary*, 177f.

218. Dibelius, *Studies in Acts*, 97 n. 9. Dibelius believes, that the prohibitions were given because of the dispersion of the Mosaic law in the world.

219. Haenchen, *Acts*, 450 n. 1; and *Apostelgeschichte*, 433 n. 1. Haenchen's view was supported by Bock, *Acts*, 390.

220. Bruce, *Acts*, 344.

221. BDAG, ἀναγινώσκω, 1 b. Similar reference to the "old covenant" (τῆς παλαιᾶς διαθήκης) in

THE FOUR PROHIBITIONS OF ACTS 15

that the spread of Mosaic law made the set of prohibitions an unavoidable fact, then the judgment of James, stated with μὴ παρενοχλεῖν . . . ἀλλὰ, has to provide connections to Μωϋσῆς γὰρ. Thus, v. 21 has to be linked in meaning to v. 19 and not to v. 20. Also with this assumption it would have been better for James to rearrange the phrase in the following manner: διὸ ἐγὼ κρίνω μὴ παρενοχλεῖν τοῖς ἀπὸ τῶν ἐθνῶν ἐπιστρέφουσιν ἐπὶ τὸν θεόν. Ἐπιστεῖλαι δε αὐτοῖς τοῦ ἀπέχεσθαι . . . Μωϋσῆς γὰρ . . . ἀναγινωσκόμενος. Thus, the structure of the phrase would suggest that the prohibitions be imposed on the Gentiles because of the spread of Mosaic law.

However, James forms his phrase differently and refers to Moses with a different purpose. His reference to Moses in v. 21 could imply more than the law of Moses.²²² The word Μωϋσῆς, in the New Testament, implies a many-faceted portrait of Moses.²²³ It suggests that Moses was seen as a prophet (Deut 18:15, 18; 34:10), and a lawgiver (Exod 24:4, 12; 34:28, 29; Deut 4:14; 31:9, 24–26). Thus, "Moses" could simply refer to Torah. The phraseology we have in Acts 15:19–21 suggests that μὴ παρενοχλεῖν . . . ἀλλὰ both are governed by κρίνω. Thus, Μωϋσῆς γὰρ has to be an object of μὴ παρενοχλεῖν as well as of ἀλλὰ ἐπιστεῖλαι. Jackson and Lake survey several opinions on the meaning of the reference to Moses, where the conjunction γὰρ provides the reason for the previouse statement, κρίνω μὴ παρενοχλεῖν, or for the "decrees" themselves.²²⁴

The positive role of reference to Moses in v. 21 was demonstrated by Jervell, who represented his role as a witness of the Decree from the angle of the books of the law.²²⁵ Wilson noticed that the connection of v. 21 with v. 20 is more natural, for he sees the preaching of Moses in the synagogues as justification for the four prohibitions.²²⁶ Sandt emphasized that James concludes his words "with a reference to the authority of Moses (v. 21)."²²⁷ Sandt stresses James' reference to Moses in v. 21 as "the law associated explicitly with Moses," representing the highest authority of his books for an adequate view of God's will toward the Gentiles.²²⁸ Finally, Pao insists that the preaching of Moses, to which James refers, is important because it means the proclamation

---

terms of "Moses" is found in 2 Cor 3:14, 15. The term "old covenant" here may refer to the ritual law of Torah.

222. Jervell, "Law in Luke-Acts," 24–25. See also Jervell, *Apostelgeschichte*, 399. Jervell notices the unique use of παρανομῶν in 23:5, in the words "only Luke talks about 'Moses being preached.'" This nuance suggests that the phrase might have a special purpose. Jervell states that here Luke represents the "law" by the name "Moses."

223. Lierman, "New Testament Moses," 317–20.

224. Lake and Cadbury, *English Translation and Commentary*, 177.

225. Jervell, "Law in Luke-Acts," 33.

226. Wilson, *Luke and Law*, 83–85. Wilson views these four demands as matters with Mosaic connection and states that they were preached by Diaspora Jews in the synagogues to the Gentiles.

227. Sandt, "Explanation of Acts 15:6–21," 74.

228. Linking Acts 15 and Deuteronomy 4, Sandt states that "the law of Moses remains in force also for the Gentile believers." Sandt, "Explanation of Acts 15:6–21," 93.

of the one true God among all the nations.²²⁹ In light of these suggestions, one may assume that the final mention of Moses in James' speech does not carry a negative judgment. Instead, it seems to be a simple assertion that the preaching and reading of Torah is spread universally.

James Hardy Ropes suggests that James first gave the quotation from Amos, which speaks about the kingdom of David, and then had to show that the restoration includes not only Israel, but all nations of the world. To support this thought, James used another argument and referred to the fact that the synagogues are present in every town and that Moses is widely preached. Thus, according to Ropes, James tried to show that the inclusion of nations was also presumed by Amos' prophecy.²³⁰ This explanation, however, needs support from textual links from vv. 16–17 to v. 21, which are not evident.

This thesis takes into account that James uses a midrashic structure. His reference to Mosaic writings at the end of the midrash is its final element.²³¹ On one hand James might refer to Moses in order to show the spread of the Mosaic law around the world and to confirm the global meaning of Amos' quotation. On the other hand James could intend to show that the Mosaic law is well known and people can see the difference between its parts, whether they are ritual, or whether they refer to the natural law for all humanity.

The question now is, whether James made the final reference to Moses assuming Mosaic law (the original matter of the debate), or assuming Mosaic writings (the Torah).²³² If the first assumption is right, then James referred to Moses in the sense of Mosaic ritual law and the rite of circumcision, which were the original issues of the debate. If the second is right, than James made the reference to Mosaic writings in general, the wide distribution of which enabled the content of the Decree to be understood.²³³ Thus, James' decision can be represented in the following diagram as 1) a rule, 2) an exception from the rule, and 3) an explanation of the rule:

---

229. Pao, *Acts and the Isaianic New Exodus*, 242 n. 85.

230. Lake and Cadbury, *English Translation and Commentary*, 177–78. However here they could not provide any sufficient explanation for κηρύσσοντας αὐτὸν ἔχει, where the word κηρύσσειν presupposes the proclamation of previously unknown teaching. According to Jackson and Lake the proclamation of the Mosaic law for the God-fearers among the Gentiles was the exact application of v. 21.

231. Ellis, "New Testament Uses the Old," 203–5.

232. Johnson views reference to Moses in v. 21 as the reference to Torah. He states: "Undoubtedly ... Luke regards these conditions as rooted in Torah." Johnson, *Acts*, 267.

233. T. E. Fretheim believes that the apostolic letter was written in a "law-giving context." He shows that one basis for the moral law established on "those laws that are directly commanded by God," while the second basis is rooted in "natural law, a basic moral sense that God has built into the very stuctures of the created order." The food laws are associated by him to this natural law. Fretheim, *God and World*, 140–41.

THE FOUR PROHIBITIONS OF ACTS 15

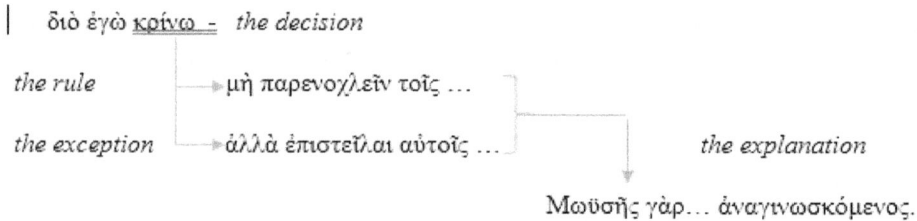

Here, Μωϋσῆς γὰρ becomes the explanation of the previously made decision.[234] When James chose not to cause difficulty to those who are turning to God, and decided not to impose the ritual law of Moses on them, he stressed the concepts were of pre-Mosaic origin. Doing this, James had to be sure that people could see a clear difference between ritual Mosaic laws and the laws of pre-Mosaic origin.[235] As James stated, it was easy even for those who lived in the Diaspora because it is said: Μωϋσῆς γὰρ . . . κατὰ πόλιν τοὺς κηρύσσοντας αὐτὸν ἔχει.[236] Thus, the reason for mentioning Moses is viewed by the present study as an affirmation of the knowledge of Moses across the civilized world.

Figure 7: Additional Diagram 2—Acts 15:21

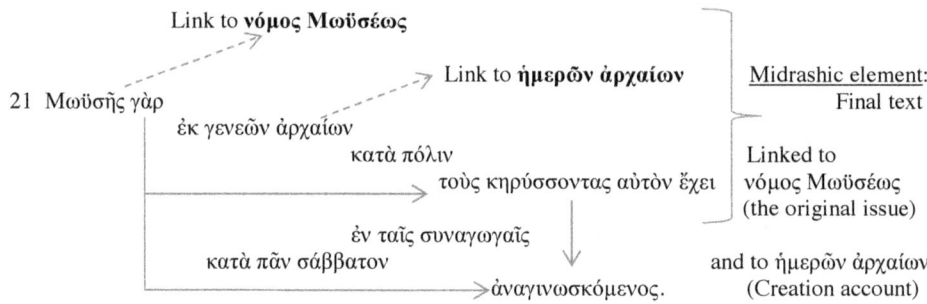

It is noteworthy that Μωϋσῆς here is a subject of the verb ἔχει.[237] The τοὺς κηρύσσοντας is the direct object: "Moses . . . has those who preach him." The modal adverbial participle ἀναγινωσκόμενος also relates to Μωϋσῆς and further explains the manner in which Moses is preached. The phrase can be translated, "Moses . . . has those who preach him, being read in synagogues every Sabbath." The prepositional phrases also

---

234. Peterson also finds the link of "Moses" in v. 21 to v. 20 alone as the most obvious link. Peterson, *Acts*, 435–36.

235. Arrington supports this idea: "therefore, the Gentile Christians ought to have known the law as a standard of conduct and the requirements demanded on them." Arrington, *Acts*, 155.

236. Fitzmyer also sees that the reference to Moses in v. 21 as the affirmation of the fact that the Gentile converts have access to the Pentateuch and can recognize the rationale behind the four prohibitions of the Decree. Fitzmyer, *Acts*, 558.

237. McIver, *Intermediate NT Greek*, 62.

have an important role in this sentence. Luke puts the prepositional phrases before verbs to show that the frequency of preaching and reading of Moses is what he wanted to stress.[238] The construction thus helps James to show, not the fact that Moses is preached and read, but that he is preached and read every Sabbath in every town where a synagogue exists.

It is interesting that Moses is the subject of the sentence. The sentence reveals no concern regarding the Jews or tensions in table fellowship. If he were concerned about the problem with the Jews, James might have said, ". . . for the Jews preach Moses every Sabbath in every town." However, he chooses to shift from νόμος Μωϋσέως to Μωϋσῆς and personify the law. This shift was mentioned by Jervell who noted that only Luke writes about "Moses being preached."[239] According to Jervell the phrase Μωϋσῆς . . . τοὺς κηρύσσοντας . . . ἔχει demonstrates that Moses is still a powerful witness and grants him authority.[240] This shift from νόμος Μωϋσέως to Μωϋσῆς was likely designed to emphasize that Torah provides sufficient knowledge to determine the pattern in which the Decree has to be understood. This pattern also was shown by James in the same sentence with help of γενεῶν ἀρχαίων.[241]

At the same time, the phrase ἐκ γενεῶν ἀρχαίων is a verbal link to ἡμερῶν ἀρχαίων, which in turn links to the creation account.[242] The question might arise whether the law of Moses was preached or read from creation. The link, nevertheless, can be viewed between creation and the natural law, rooted in the creation narrative of the Mosaic writings. This natural law is reflected in the creation-fall narratives of Genesis, and is further explained in Leviticus and Deuteronomy together with ritual law, but not mixed with it.[243] The reason for recalling the natural law in books designed for the ritual law made sense. The technique of midrash helped to recall the rationale for keeping the

---

238. Johnson also stresses that this statement of James reflects "the long-standing," "widespread," and "regular" practice of preaching Torah in synagogues of the Diaspora. Johnson, *Acts*, 267 n. 21.

239. Jervell, "Law in Luke-Acts," 24–25. The Mosaic law was also personified by Jesus (John 5:45), where the law/Moses took the role of an accuser. Cf. Jervell, *Apostelgeschichte*, 399.

240. Jervell, "Law in Luke-Acts," 24–25.

241. Bruce notes that Judaism in general traces the whole system of preaching of Moses to the time of Moses himself. Thus, the meaning of γενεῶν ἀρχαίων can be viewed as a link to the origin of Torah. Bruce, *Acts*, 344. Cf. Jervell, *Apostelgeschichte*, 399.

242. These temporal indicators (ἐκ γενεῶν ἀρχαίων and ἡμερῶν ἀρχαίων) were linked by Enns to creation. He argues that the return from Babylon and the Exodus story always alluded to creation and presupposed re-creation. He rightly stresses that "there is a tradition in Scripture that understands both the Exodus and the return from Babylon to be antitypes of creation." Enns, "Creation and Re-Creation," 261.

243. The dietary prohibitions listed in the Decree have natural law of God in their background (examples Gen 6:19, 20; 7:2, 3; 9:3, 4; Lev 3:17; 7:22–27; 11:1–27, 17:10–14; Deut 12:21–25). They have to be viewed separately from the dietary restrictions rooted in the ritual law and tied to the religious feasts, holy place, ritual slaughter, involvement of priesthood, and permition of consumption only to a ritually clean person; (examples Exod 12:3–11, 15; 13:6, 7; Lev 6:14–18, 26–30; 7:15–21; 11:32–35, 40; 17:15).

natural law. Now the apostles separated the ritual system, which was built to deal with consequences of transgressions against the natural law, from the natural law itself.

At this point, the present study suggests that some laws of Torah were viewed by the apostles as natural law. They were not understood to be a part of the ritual law, even though placed in Torah in proximity to it. The writings of Moses, thus, reveal the eternal universal law of God, known from the origin of the world, and its extension in the fallen world in the form of natural law. So, the writings of Moses provide an explanation of the creation–fall–re-creation paradigm, which is important for the proper understanding of salvation. The detailed explanation for this pattern will be provided in chapter 3 of the present study. In general, the apostles probably viewed salvation as fitting into the creation–fall–re-creation pattern preserved in the writings of Moses. When discussing the role of the Mosaic law in salvific history, the apostles had to differentiate the ritual law, written for the Israelites, from the natural law known from the very beginning and embracing all nations of the world. The rationale for reference to Moses in James' speech, thus, becomes clear, especially when it is placed together with the reference to creation.

Exegesis of the Second Lukan Account of the Apostolic Decree, Acts 15:22–35

Exegesis of *Unit five*, Acts 15:22–29

Unit five starts with the narrative frame, which brings the reader back into the council hall. Luke describes the way in which the unanimous decision was made. The semantic diagram of this unit, has the narrative frame first.

The Narrative Frame of Unit five, Acts 15:22–23a

Figure 8: Unit five Narrative Frame—Acts 15:22–23a

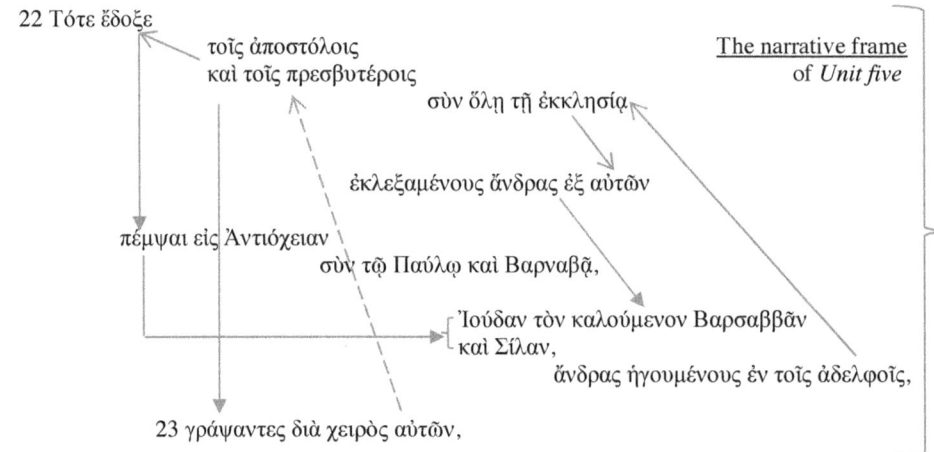

EXEGETICAL STUDY OF THE APOSTOLIC DECREE IN ITS NARRATIVE CONTEXT

The structure of the narrative frame in this unit deserves detailed attention. The personal pronouns (ἐξ αὐτῶν and διὰ χειρὸς αὐτῶν), at first sight, seem to belong to the same group of people.[244] If so, the congregation in Jerusalem becomes responsible for the content of the Decree.

The personal pronouns (ἐξ αὐτῶν and διὰ χειρὸς αὐτῶν), however, can describe two different groups, one of which was the ἐκκλησία of Jerusalem, the other was the audience of the council.[245] As it is evident from v. 6, although the debate arose in ἐκκλησία (v. 5), the council consisted only of the apostles and the elders of that ἐκκλησία. Thus, two groups were temporarily separated, although finally they appeared to be unanimous in this decision. The preposition σὺν in v. 22, followed by dative ὅλῃ τῇ ἐκκλησίᾳ, should be translated, "with." In this sentence, Luke combines one group with the help of καὶ, as it is seen in the phrase τοῖς ἀποστόλοις καὶ τοῖς πρεσβυτέροις, and conjoins the other group by σὺν in the following phrase: σὺν ὅλῃ τῇ ἐκκλησίᾳ. Thus, Luke uses two different ways to join people together, demonstrating that two groups are present in one audience, but the temporary separation has not yet been cancelled.

One can then assume that the decision, ἐκλεξαμένους ἄνδρας, was taken by the council, but ἐξ αὐτῶν likely refers to the previously-mentioned σὺν ὅλῃ τῇ ἐκκλησίᾳ. It is likely that the council made the decisions when the ἐκκλησία chose the delegates. This has support from the observation that the phrase ἐκλεξαμένους . . . ἄνδρας ἡγουμένους ἐν τοῖς ἀδελφοῖς cannot connect τοῖς ἀδελφοῖς to the council assembly, because this would make Silas and Judas the leaders of the council.[246] It is evident that the delegates had to be chosen from the leading brothers of the ἐκκλησία, but not from the apostles.

The same issue appears in reference to διὰ χειρὸς αὐτῶν.[247] The task of the council was to make a decision and to write it. The letter was then written by the hands of the apostles and those of the "council group."[248] It follows that αὐτῶν refers to the apostles

---

244. Fitzmyer brings the idea of two independent Jerusalem assemblies and decisions joined by Luke together as one "Council Decree." He states that the decision, with the four prohibitions, was made by the elders during the whole church assembly. Fitzmyer, *Acts*, 563. Bruce supports this idea, trying to remove a contradiction between Acts 15 and Gal 2. Bruce, *Acts*, 331. Haenchen shows that the overwhelming majority of Protestant scholars followed the Tübingen school and see the Decree as drafted later in Antioch, without Paul's collaboration. However, Overbeck and Jacquier, Wendt, Schlatter, Lyder Brun, Zahn, Michaelis view the Decree as related to the Apostolic Council. Haenchen, *Acts*, 468.

245. The group, consisting of the apostles, elders and the church, can be understood as one, in the sense they all belong to the ἐκκλησία of Jerusalem. The apostles and the elders belonged also to a smaller group of members of the council, as is seen in v. 6. Thus, the apostles and the elders were the members of two groups at the same time, namely, the large group, which is ἐκκλησία in Jerusalem and a smaller group, which is the council body.

246. Barrett still notes with uncertainty that "one may guess that Judas and Silas were among the πρεσβυτέροι." Barrett, *Critical Commentary on Acts*, 739 (v. 22).

247. Johnson connects διὰ χειρὸς αὐτῶν to Judas and Silas. Johnson, *Acts*, 275 n. 23.

248. Barrett, following Blass-Debrunner, notes the anacoluthon ἔδοξε . . . πέμψαι . . . γράψαντες

and the elders, not to Judas and Silas and not to the other members. Less likely, the council made its decision in verbal form and then passed the responsibility to write it to the members of the congregation, who had not attended the council. It seems more plausible to accept that the apostles and the elders wrote the letter.

In Acts 15:1–35, Luke uses ἐπιστεῖλαι (ἐπιστέλλω) and πέμψαι (πέμπω), both meaning "to send." The word πέμψαι in v. 22 echoes προπεμφθέντες ὑπὸ τῆς ἐκκλησίας about Paul and Barnabas in v. 3. The word can also mean "to commission, appoint." This would closely tie the letter to the mission for which Judas and Silas were chosen and sent. Accordingly, their mission consisted carrying the letter, confirming its authenticity, and interpreting it for the Antiochene congregation.

Consequently, the main need for choosing the brothers was not to guide Paul and Barnabas, but to carry and authenticate the apostolic letter. Because it contained a judgment in favour of Paul's and Barnabas' view on the Mosaic law and the issue of salvation, Luke places the preposition σὺν before τῷ Παύλῳ καὶ Βαρναβᾷ, showing that Judas and Silas were commissioned by the Jerusalem Church with Paul and Barnabas in response to Antioch's request.

As it is seen from v. 3, not only Paul and Barnabas were delegated by the Antiochene church. There were also τινας ἄλλους ἐξ αὐτῶν, where αὐτῶν refers to τινες κατελθόντες ἀπὸ τῆς Ἰουδαίας. To clarify that the apostles did not support their view, but judged in favour of Paul and Barnabas, Luke pictures Judas and Silas joining Paul and Barnabas. With the help of σὺν Luke confirms that the council took the side of Paul and Barnabas.

The nucleus of *Unit five* is based on the apostolic letter. The source which Luke quotes was apparently either the original document, or a copy made by Luke himself from the original.[249] One can suggest also that Luke inherited the content of the letter from Paul, who, likely, had a copy himself.[250]

διὰ χειρὸς αὐτῶν. Barrett, *Critical Commentary on Acts*, 739 (v. 23).

249. Fitzmyer attributes Luke's sources of information about the Jerusalem Council to the written tradition of the Antiochene church. Fitzmyer, *Acts*, 540–41.

250. Narrative in Acts 16:4 reveals that Paul delivered the decisions of the council to the churches in Asia Minor. It would be unacceptable to rely on memory to recall the Decree, instead of reading the apostolic letter.

The Nucleus of Unit five

Figure 9: Unit five—Acts 15:23b–29

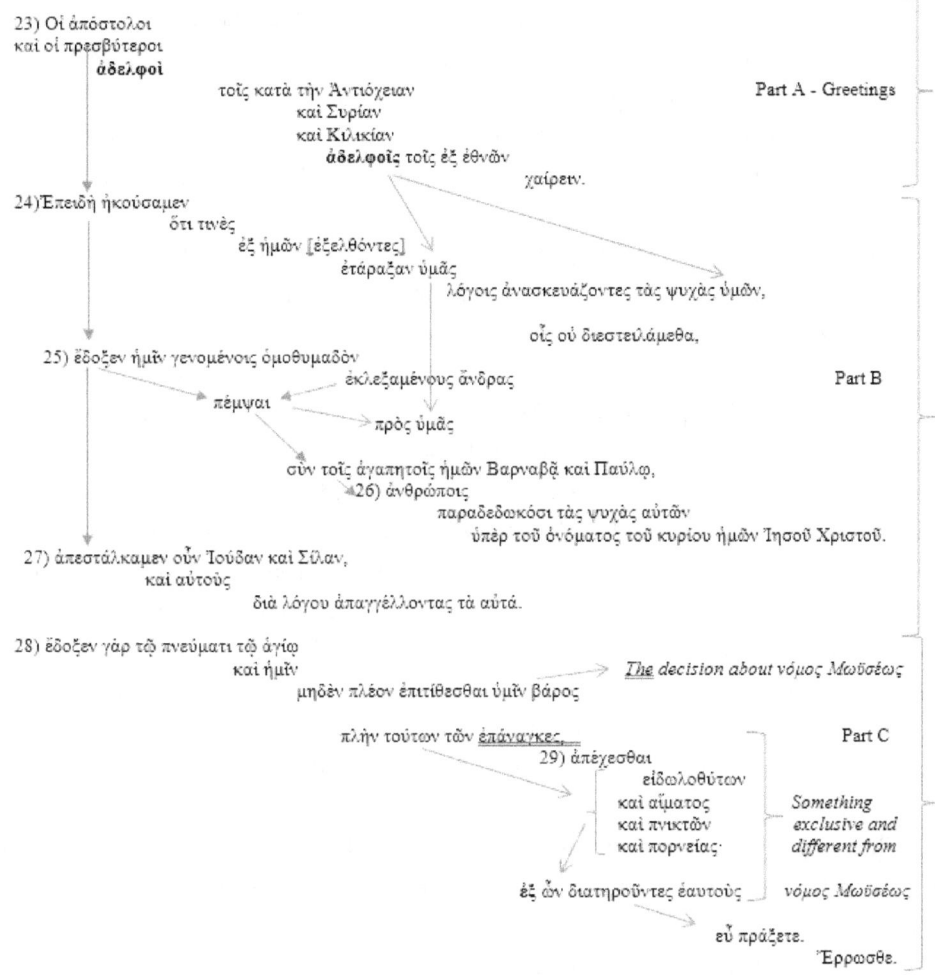

The letter can be divided into three parts. Part A (v. 23) in Figure 9 reveals the common pattern of an introduction and contains the apostolic autograph, the recipients of the letter and greetings (χαίρειν) in an epistolary genre.[251] It demonstrates a friendly approach as it designates members of the council with simple ἀδελφοί, and the recipients with ἀδελφοῖς τοῖς ἐξ ἐθνῶν.[252]

Part B (vv. 24–27) is organized around two verbs: ἠκούσαμεν . . . ἔδοξεν "we heard . . . we decided." The causal conjunction ἐπειδὴ with ἠκούσαμεν means "since"

---

251. Bruce, *Acts*, 345.

252. Barrett shows that the letter made "brothers" of both the apostles and those ἐξ ἐθνῶν on a common basis of Christian belief. Barrett, *Critical Commentary on Acts*, 740.

or "because we heard" and gives the grounds for the action.²⁵³ The following subordinate clause starts with the conjunction ὅτι, introducing the content of what was heard, using an object clause τινὲς ... ἐτάραξαν ὑμᾶς.²⁵⁴ This subordinate clause has two supplementary clauses, constructed with adverbial participles ἐξελθόντες and ἀνασκευάζοντες. The first clause, ἐξ ἡμῶν [ἐξελθόντες], clarifies where τινὲς came from. The second supplementary clause, ἀνασκευάζοντες τὰς ψυχὰς ὑμῶν "upsetting, unsettling," describes the manner in which τινὲς disturbed the church in Antioch. ²⁵⁵ The letter adds that the church was disturbed by λόγοις of τινὲς, namely, by their teaching.

After mentioning τινὲς as the source of wrong teaching, the letter comes back to the apostles with the words: οἷς οὐ διεστειλάμεθα (from διαστέλλω, "to define or express in no uncertain terms what one must do, *order, give orders*"),²⁵⁶ meaning "we did not delegate them to teach" and thus relates to λόγοις.²⁵⁷ Thus, the letter emphasizes that although the apostles and the elders were countrymen of τινὲς, they did not associate themselves with their wrong teaching.

The first occurrence of ἔδοξεν (v. 25) indicated that the decision is taken. Moreover, the decision was taken ὁμοθυμαδὸν, "*with one mind/purpose/impulse, ... unanimously.*"²⁵⁸ The aorist participle γενομένοις shows that the decision was made at the stage when the council came to one mind, revealing that the council decision was not the opinion of a dominant party. The letter describes two decisions. The first was to choose the delegates (the participle ἐκλεξαμένους).²⁵⁹ The second was to send (πέμψαι) the delegates (the chosen ἄνδρας) to the recipients of the letter (πρὸς ὑμᾶς). The perfect ἀπεστάλκαμεν shows that the apostles fulfilled the first part of the council's decision.

Choosing and sending the delegates was not the council's main decision, but rather an additional (or preparatory) step.²⁶⁰ This step was taken to ratify the Decree in Antioch (15:30–32), to guarantee its authenticity, and to interpret its wording in oral form. This perception has support from καὶ αὐτοὺς διὰ λόγου ἀπαγγέλλοντας τὰ

---

253. Wallace, *Greek Grammar*, 674.

254. Wallace, *Greek Grammar*, 678.

255. Bruce suggests the meaning "subverting," which can be understood as "a military metaphor for plundering a town." Bruce, *Acts*, 345.

256. BDAG, διαστέλλω.

257. Barrett, *Critical Commentary on Acts*, 741. He states that "the troble-makers are emphatically disowned. They had no official backing." See also Fitzmyer, *Acts*, 565.

258. BDAG, ὁμοθυμαδὸν. Citing Acts 15:25, Barret views ὁμοθυμαδὸν in the sense of "reached a common mind," so "even the extremists agreed." Barrett, *Critical Commentary on Acts*, 742. Bruce notes it as the favourite adverb of Luke. Bruce, *Acts*, 106.

259. Arrington, *Acts*, 157. He notes that two delegates from the Jerusalem church were sent "with strict orders ... to relate by words of mouth the content of the letter." He explains the need of additional oral explanation of the letter because its content was written briefly.

260. The main decision has to provide a solution to the original issue in Antioch. It was organized by the members of the council in the form of the Decree which is interpreted below in part C.

αὐτά. The meaning of the pronoun αὐτά is determined by the coordinate conjunction γὰρ in v. 28, which links the idea of v. 28 to the previous idea, expressed by αὐτά. The verb ἀπαγγέλλοντας indicates future action. The construction of διὰ+gen shows the λόγος to be an agent, by which the proclamation of αὐτά will be taken.

Part C (vv. 28–29) contains the second (main) decision is introduced by the repetition of ἔδοξεν (v. 28) and expressed in the form of the Decree.[261] Here, ἔδοξεν is used impersonaly, though the decision is attributed to τῷ πνεύματι τῷ ἁγίῳ καὶ ἡμῖν. Writing the letter and approaching the part when the main decision was to be stated, the apostles shifted from "we decided" to "the Holy Spirit and we decided." They acknowledged God's priority in making the decision.[262] Furthermore, they demonstrated assurance that the following Decree was inspired and approved by God. Thus, the content of the Decree constitutes the revealed will of God.

It is evident that the account of the Decree in v. 28 is formed into two lines. The first line μηδὲν πλέον ἐπιτίθεσθαι ὑμῖν βάρος, where βάρος likely refers to Peter's ζυγὸν in verse 10.[263] Goppelt believes that according to Acts the only difference between Jewish and Gentile Christians was in the observance of the ritual laws.[264] It becomes clear from the fact that the phrase ἐπιτίθεσθαι...βάρος is similar to ἐπιθεῖναι ζυγὸν, sharing the same root of verb ἐπιτίθημι. The βάρος and ζυγὸς seem to refer to νόμος Μωϋσέως, the original issue of the debate, and describes it as a burden.[265] The word πλέον, here, is used as a comparative, meaning "more/greater."[266] The meaning of the first part of the Decree seems to be: "It was decided by the Holy Spirit and us to lay upon you no greater burden *except* . . ."

The second line (v. 28) appears to be a parallel saying and starts with the conjunction πλὴν, which can be subordinate or adversative.[267] Here, πλὴν is likely used in a subordinate way, different to the manner expressed by the adversative conjunction ἀλλὰ in v. 20.[268] Then, πλὴν subordinates the following phrase, τούτων τῶν ἐπάναγκες,

---

261. BDAG, δοκέω, 2 bβ, "*it seems best to me, I decide, I resolve*" and expresses subjective opinion.

262. Peterson notes that the council "came to affirm what the Spirit had already shown." Peterson, *Acts*, 439. Bruce, *Acts*, 346.

263. Barret observes the connection of βάρος here to v. 10 and also rightly notes that βάρος here also is similar to οὐ βάλλω ἐφ ὑμᾶς ἄλλο βάρος in Rev 2:24, which also is linked to εἰδωλοθύτων and πορνεία in Rev 2:20. Barrett, *Critical Commentary on Acts*, 744.

264. Goppelt, *Apostolic Times*, 64, 67. He views the life of the early church through the issues reflected in Galatians and other Pauline writings. He also believes that the church in Antioch followed Paul's theology. For Goppelt, the Decree in Acts 15 provided the grounds for the common table fellowship.

265. BDAG, βάρος, 1, "experience of someth. that is particulary oppressive, *burden*."

266. Johnson sees this statement as similar to James' μὴ παρενοχλεῖν in v. 19. Johnson, *Acts*, 277 n. 28. In 1 Tim 5:16 Paul uses a similar prohibition in relation to βάρος saying: μὴ βαρείσθω ἡ ἐκκλησία.

267. Barret notes that here πλὴν is used as animproper preposition, taking the genitive and translates as "*except.*" Barrett, *Critical Commentary on Acts*, 744.

268. Peterson also notes that the whole phrase, μηδὲν πλέον ἐπιτίθεσθαι ὑμῖν βάρος πλὴν τούτων τῶν ἐπάναγκες, although it reflected lexic of vv. 10, 19 and 29, was based on v. 20. Peterson, *Acts*, 439.

to the previous sentence and by this shows the exception/limitations of the previous statement μηδὲν πλέον ἐπιτίθεσθαι ὑμῖν βάρος.²⁶⁹ Then the four necessary limitations appear: ἀπέχεσθαι εἰδωλοθύτων καὶ αἵματος καὶ πνικτῶν καὶ πορνείας (v. 29). The word ἀπέχεσθαι means "to avoid contact with or use of someth., *keep away, abstain*."²⁷⁰ The meaning of the Decree, then, is that the πλέον βάρος, the ritual part of the νόμος Μωϋσέως, was taken away, and is not to be imposed on Gentile converts.²⁷¹

The original issue in Antioch was viewed from the the perspective of salvation. Thus, keeping those four prohibitions was declared to be ἐπάναγκες ("necessary"). The context of Peter's speech makes it clear that διὰ τῆς χάριτος τοῦ κυρίου Ἰησοῦ πιστεύομεν σωθῆναι. Thus, the prohibitions cannot be viewed as necessary conditions for salvation.²⁷² They were necessary, but not for salvation. If to take into account that the main object of the sentence is the Holy Spirit, it might be assumed that the prohibitions are necessary for τῷ πνεύματι τῷ ἁγίῳ. This idea will be examined in chapter 3.

The four prohibitions in v. 29 are similar to v. 20. The only significant change is that τῶν ἀλισγημάτων τῶν εἰδώλων is replaced, and clarified by εἰδωλοθύτων, meaning "*something offered to a cultic image/idol, food sacrificed to idols.*"²⁷³ The other changes, namely, the different order of words (εἰδωλοθύτων, αἵματος, πνικτῶν and πορνείας instead of τοῦ ἀπέχεσθαι τῶν ἀλισγημάτων τῶν εἰδώλων, πορνείας, πνικτοῦ and αἵματος) and use of plural πνικτῶν instead of singular, are minor and insignificant changes. The last phrase, ἐξ ὧν διατηροῦντες ἑαυτοὺς εὖ πράξετε, represents the concluding exortation expressed in covenant form. Wilson thus assumes that the Decree was so decisive for Luke that "its authority is not challenged from that point on."²⁷⁴

Summary of the Interpretations of the Decree

In general, interpretations of the content of the Decree, in this research study, have taken three main directions: the "ethical," the "cultic" and "pre-Mosaic." The ethical interpretation of the content of the Decree employed by Haenchen carried the features of the earlier (mediaeval) exegesis. A similar position was taken by Bruce, Bock, and Blomberg. They argue that the function of the four prohibitions was to regulate the life

---

269. Barret suggests τούτων τῶν ἐπάναγκες to represent the corresponding adverb. He also notes that ἐπάναγκες may indicate things "necessary" for salvation if to assume that Judaizers sounded the necessity of Mosaic custom in relation to salvation in v. 1 and in v. 5. Barrett, *Critical Commentary on Acts*, 745.

270. BDAG, ἀπέχω, 5.

271. Here Johnson compares πλέον βάρος with its use in Matt 20:12; 2 Cor 4:17; Gal 6:2; and Rev 2:24. Johnson, *Acts*, 277 n. 28.

272. Barrett observes "necessary" in v. 28 with reference to the salvation issue in vv. 1, 5. Barrett, *Critical Commentary on Acts*, 745.

273. BDAG, εἰδωλόθυτο. Johnson puts stress on "idol," instead of the nature of meat. Johnson, *Acts*, 277 n. 29.

274. Wilson, *Luke and Law*, 107. This means Luke agreed with such a form of the Decree.

in mixed communities and to enable common table fellowship, as well as to support the success of the Gentile mission.[275]

The cultic interpretation suggests that the content of the Decree represents an allusion to the law about strangers in the midst of Israel in the Holiness Code.[276] It is noteworthy that despite his espousal of the ethical approach, Haenchen viewed the rationale for the four prohibitions of the Decree linked to this law about aliens. Jervell agrees with this point of view.[277] Later this view was adopted by Fitzmyer, Wilson, Sandt and Glenny.[278] Pao, however, argues against the connection between the four requirements and the law about "strangers in the land" in Lev 17–18.[279] Dickinson, moreover, notes that if the cultic implication is linked to Lev 17–18, one may suggest that a distinction between clean and unclean still makes sense.[280]

Another explanation of the "cultic" interpretation views the content of the Decree as an allusion to Jewish halakhah. Thus, Perry and Savelle link the prohibitions to the "Jewish ethos" and not to "one specifically identifiable origin."[281] This inability to identify the background of the Decree in Jewish tradition makes their explanation uncertain. The benefit of this approach is that it helps in the discovery of the pre-Mosaic origin of the rationale for the Apostolic Decree.

A third group of scholars connect the Decree to the Noachic laws.[282] Following this approach Taylor makes proto-Noachide laws of first importance and satisfactory rationales for the content of the Decree. According to him these laws "assign a status to Gentiles which in no way compromises the separate position of Jews."[283] Instone-Brewer considers πνικτός to be "an additional sin" to the three "mortal" sins known

---

275. Schnabel argues that the prohibition of idolatry was necessary for conversion of the Gentiles rather than for common table fellowship. At the same time the Decree allowed the Gentile converts to remain uncircumcised. Schnabel, *Acts*, 644.

276. Lev 17:8–14, the discussion is about cultic slaughtering and in Lev 18 shifts to prohibited sexual relationships which were imposed also on strangers (18:26). Schnabel notes that the law about aliens does not fit the rationale for the Decree either: it does not explain why the dietary prohibitions appear in the Decree when Sabbath keeping is not mentioned. He notes that the Sabbath was also imposed on aliens. Schnabel, *Acts*, 645 n. 73.

277. Jervell, "Law in Luke-Acts," 33.

278. Wilson, *Luke and Law*, 76.

279. Pao sees the differences in a social context and details of the Decree and Lev 17–18, such as application of these rules, only relevant to people residing in the land of Israel. Pao notes a lack of evidence if these Levitical commandments were applied to proselytes in the first century. He points out that the recipients of the Decree were outside of the land of Israel and Levitical laws could not be applied to them. Pao, *Acts and the Isaianic New Exodus*, 241 n. 80.

280. Dickinson, "Theology of Jerusalem Conference," 80.

281. Savelle, "Reexamination of Prohibitions," 468.

282. Novak relates these seven Noachic laws (Noachian commands) to the rabbinic text of Tosefta of the second century CE. In this document the second commandment prohibited idolatry; the fourth prohibited sexual immorality, the fifth was written against shedding of blood and the seventh prohibited the practice of eating meat torn from a live animal. Novak, "Jewish Mission," 42.

283. Taylor, "Jerusalem Decrees," 374.

THE FOUR PROHIBITIONS OF ACTS 15

from rabbinic literature. At this point, he links πνικτός not only to halakhah, but also to Noachian commands.[284] Bockmuehl explains the content of the Decree in Acts 15 in connection to the pre-Sinaitic/pre-Mosaic covenant. He also sees the background of this covenant older than the covenant made with Abraham. For him the Noachic commands, developed later in the second century CE by rabbis, become now those legal constructs, which "provide an essential clue to the specific *rationale and content of early Christian ethics.*"[285]

From the discussion above, it becomes evident that the search for the rationale of the content of the apostolic letter reveals a move from arguing its Mosaic context to a search for a pre-Mosaic origin. The interpretation of the prohibitions also moved its focus from an ethical rationale to a cultic one. Yet, there is a possibility that the rationale includes both (cultic and ethical) aspects.

Exegesis of the Concluding (C') Narrative Link

Figure 10: Concluding (C') Narrative Link—Acts 15:30–35

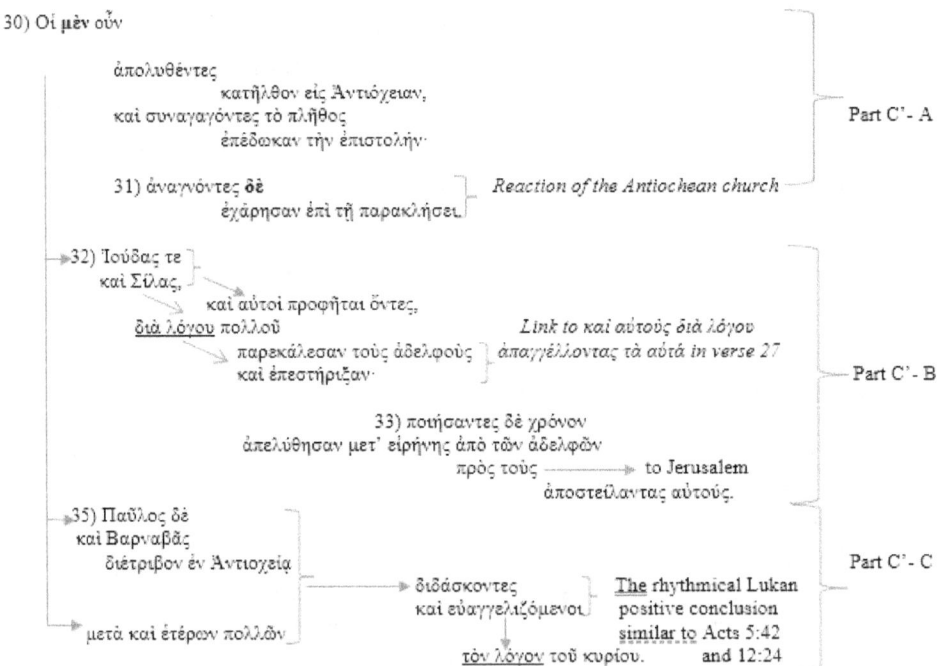

---

284. Instone-Brewer, "Infanticide and Apostolic Decree," 312–13.

285. Bockmuehl, *Jewish Law in Gentile Churches*, 173. Bockmuehl believes that the law of resident aliens "established the hermeneutical parameters" for Christian ethics. It helped early Christians to appropriate "the moral teaching and example of Jesus for a worldwide church." It also had been reflected in the Noachic laws of the second century CE.

The concluding (C') narrative link was created by Luke for the purpose of showing the positive impact of the Decree on Gentile believers, and its practical significance. The structure of the narrative link C' can be subdivided into three parts, which are three steps designed by Luke to end the story. Part C'-A (15:30–31) represents the narrative of parts 1b, 1c of *Unit one* (15:2) and part 1 of *Unit two* (15:3–4) and is reversed in order and meaning. To remind the reader, part 1b (v. 2a) records the beginning of the debate in Antioch. Part 1c (v. 2b) shows the Antiochene church in strife and disunion, looking for an answer. Part 1 of *Unit two* (vv. 3–4) pictured the Antiochene church sending delegates to Jerusalem, their trip and arrival to Jerusalem, and their reception by that congregation.

Looking back, one finds the narrative of C'-A (vv. 30–31) arranged around the same three points. First of all, delegates Silas and Judas together with Paul and Barnabas were ἀπολυθέντες, "sent back" from the Jerusalem ἐκκλησία. The narrative does not state whether or not they preached to the brothers on the way. The possible explanation of that omission is that they hurried to deliver the letter and address the question that arose in Antioch. The cascade of the participles and verbs here suggests a dynamic scene: ἀπολυθέντες κατῆλθον . . . καὶ συναγαγόντες . . . ἐπέδωκαν τὴν ἐπιστολήν. The definite article οἱ (referring to the understood subjects Paul and Barnabas) functions here as subject whose actions are stated first by the participle ἀπολυθέντες. The following participial phrase, συναγαγόντες τὸ πλῆθος, prepares the scene for their main action, stated by the phrase ἐπέδωκαν τὴν ἐπιστολήν. So, verse 30 has to be translated: "They [Paul and Barnabas] being sent off, went down to Antioch and, gathering the assembly, delivered the letter."

The following phrase, ἀναγνόντες δὲ ἐχάρησαν ἐπὶ τῇ παρακλήσει, might represent either the reaction of the Antiochene congregation or the joy of the delegates, who read the letter to the people and were comforted, seeing gladness and union in the church.[286] The most probable solution is to accept the conjunction δὲ as correlative to μὲν. Then, the paired conjunction μὲν . . . δὲ designates two sides of the assembly.[287] On one hand, there were the delegates with the letter from Jerusalem, but on the other hand, there were the disciples in Antioch, who were reading and became joyful over the comforting news.

The word ἐπὶ τῇ παρακλήσει here might echo the work of the Holy Spirit, and demonstrate the final eschatological comfort awaiting in the kingdom of God.[288] It could anticipate the time of the re-creation of paradise. Luke often uses this word (Luke 2:25; 6:24; Acts 4:36; 9:31; 13:15). In Acts 9:31 the comfort in the church

---

286. Fitzmyer sees here the Lukan idyllic picture of the Church. Fitzmyer, *Acts*, 568, see note on 15:31. Johnson states that joy represents "a positive response to God's visitation" (cf with Acts. 13:48). Johnson, *Acts*, 278 n. 31. Barret interprets it as "they had got what they wanted." Barrett, *Critical Commentary on Acts*, 748 (v. 31).

287. Wallace, *Greek Grammar*, 672.

288. Johnson views παρακλήσει here as "consolation" in regard to eschatological salvation. Johnson, *Acts*, 278 n. 31.

THE FOUR PROHIBITIONS OF ACTS 15

is linked to the work of the Holy Spirit: εἶχεν εἰρηνην . . . καὶ τῇ παρακλήσει τοῦ ἁγίου πνεύματος ἐπληθύνετο. Similar results appear in Acts 15:31–32, expressed by ἐχάρησαν ἐπὶ τῇ παρακλήσει, and following the work of prophets παρεκάλεσαν . . . καὶ ἐπεστήριξαν . . . ἀπελύθησαν μετ' εἰρήνης.

The part C'-B (15:32–33) describes the ministry of the prophets Judas and Silas. They are designated αὐτοὶ προφῆται ὄντες "being prophets themselves."[289] The expression διὰ λόγου πολλοῦ employs διὰ+gen, makes λόγος the agent by which the prophets encouraged (παρεκάλεσαν)[290] and strengthened (ἐπεστήριξαν) the church.[291] This phrase also recalls the purpose for which they were sent from Jerusalem (v. 27) expressed by: καὶ αὐτοὺς διὰ λόγου ἀπαγγέλλοντας τὰ αὐτά.[292] The pronoun τὰ αὐτά designates the content of the Decree, and describes Judas and Silas transmitting or interpreting its content. It is noteworthy that the message they preached is defined in v. 32 as "strengthening" and "encouraging." Here, the word ἐπεστήριξαν is specifically Lukan, found in Acts 14:22; 15:41 and 18:43 and used in the sense of "making of the disciples strong" in faith.

The phrase ποιήσαντες δὲ χρόνον ἀπελύθησαν μετ' εἰρήνης (v. 33) has one interesting feature. Here the work of Judas and Silas is described by ποιέω and not by its synonym πράσσω. Luke thus describes their ministry with ποιήσαντες, pointing at the same time to διὰ λόγου . . . παρεκάλεσαν.[293] This is a possible reference to the work of God in the process of creation, where the word was God's creative agent.[294] Moreover μετ' εἰρήνης describes their work as bringing peace, and could serve as an expression for the completed mission.[295]

The third part C'-C (15:35) shows the ministry of Paul and others in Antioch. Bruce views this transition of scenes as the forming of a generalizing sentence similar to Acts 14:28, showing that life in Antioch returned to the initial peaceful stage that existed before the debate.[296] Luke then shifts to the imperfect tense, describing that Paul and Barnabas διέτριβον ἐν Ἀντιοχείᾳ, which indicates a period of time. Men-

---

289. McIver, *Intermediate NT Greek*, 63.

290. BDAG, παρακαλέω, 2, "to urge strongly, *appeal to, urge, exhort, encourage.*"

291. BDAG, ἐπιστηρίζω, "to cause someone to become stronger or more firm, *strengthen.*" This would suggest that the messengers confirmed and made firm the original beliefs of the Antiochean church before the influence of Judaizers. It means that the Decree approved the mission to the Gentiles, freeing them from the ritual law.

292. Bruce, *Acts*, 346. Their purpose was to announce the apostolic letter and to "strengthen" the church.

293. Here Bruce notes the link "between prophecy and exhortation" as it is shown in 1 Cor 14:3. Bruce, *Acts*, 348.

294. It evident from the repetition καὶ εἶπεν ὁ θεός . . . καὶ ἐγένετο (Gen 1:3, 6, 9, 11, 14–15, 20, 24, 29–30) and καὶ εἶπεν ὁ θεός . . . καὶ ἐποίησεν ὁ θεός (Gen 1:26, 27). The same is confirmed by Ps 32:6–9.

295. Barret interprets μετ' εἰρήνης to be a "general situation of Christian well-being." Barrett, *Critical Commentary on Acts*, 749 (v. 33).

296. Bruce, *Acts*, 348.

tion of μετὰ καὶ ἑτέρων πολλῶν shows the number of ministers in the Antiochean congregation serving the growth of faith.²⁹⁷ The wording of Acts 15:35 echoes the rhythmical repetitions in Acts 5:42, 12:24, indicating the end of the passage.

Conclusion

Exegesis revealed that the apostolic decision was structured around two points: 1) the ritual Jewish law was found to be unnecessary for salvation, 2) four matters were noted as necessary for observing. It has been argued in this chapter so far, that the explanation for imposing these four prohibitions on Gentile converts was provided by the pesher-midrash in Acts 15:14–21, which was employed in order to give a firm foundation to the proposal of the Decree on the grounds of Torah.²⁹⁸ Thus, the literary form of the Decree in Acts 15 presumes the defense of the apostolic decision on basis of the law of Torah, and not a total cancelling of those laws, with the exception of the four specific matters.

The present research has concluded that the debate began with the issue of the validity of the ritual law for salvation. Moreover, during the Jerusalem Council the requirements of the ritual law were differentiated from those rooted in the natural law of God in the creation-fall account. As a result, the ritual law was viewed as fulfilled in Christ and not necessary for keeping. The content of the Decree was authorized with the help of midrash created from the creation account of Gen 1–3. The reversal element of the midrash suggests that a creation–fall–re-creation paradigm is involved in the background of the Decree. Finally, the motives for worship evoked in the Decree were stated by the word ἀλίσγημα, which in context suggests a kind of desecration in terms of worship. Also, the decision not to make the turning of the Gentiles to God difficult presumes changes in worship, yet made with the minimum of necessary regulations.

The Third Lukan Account of the Apostolic Decree, Acts 21:17–26

Luke returns to the account of the Decree once again in Acts 21:25. His third account of the Decree stresses the importance of the document and its significance for the life of the church. For the benefit of the current research a close look is needed at the context of Acts 21:25, especially vv. 17–26. The passage starts with a genitive absolute,

---

297. Barrett views them as prophets and teachers of Acts 13:1 and 11:19, namely, those who first preached in Antioch. Barrett, *Critical Commentary on Acts*, 750 (v. 35). Gager notes that "from the very beginning there are strong indications that Christianity from Antioch in the West to Mesopotamia in the East was strongly influenced by Judaism." Gager, *Origins of Anti-Semitism*, 124.

298. David Halivni states that the function of midrash is to be "intellectual endeavor that anchors the present in the past." David Halivni, *Midrash, Mishnah, and Gemara: The Jewish Predilection for Justified Law* (Cambridge: Harvard University Press, 1986), 16.

General Structure of Acts 21:17–26

This passage represents a union of the narrative frame (vv. 17–20a and 26) and the direct speech (vv. 20b-25). The structure of this passage consists of six parts: 1) Paul's arrival in Jerusalem (Acts 21:17, 18); 2) Paul's report (Acts 21:19, 20a); 3) the problem of Mosaic law (Acts 21:20b-22); 4) the offered solution (Acts 21:23, 24); 5) reference to the Decree (Acts 21:25); 6) Paul's consent (Acts 21:26).

Exegesis of part 1, Acts 21:17, 18

Figure 11: Part 1—Acts 21:17, 18

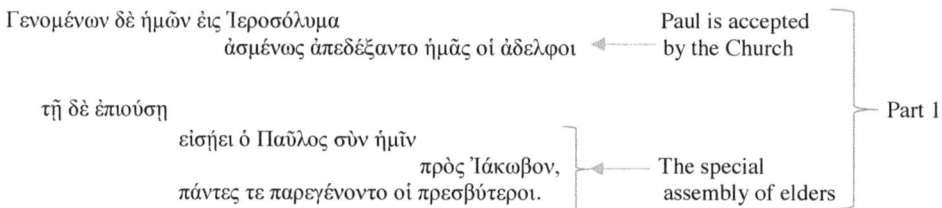

Part 1 describes Paul's coming to Jerusalem and to the assembly of elders. The passage starts in v. 17 with the genitive absolute construction γενομένων δὲ ἡμῶν, with temporal meaning.[299] The passage belongs to the so-called "we-sections," indicating that Luke at this time was a companion of Paul and an eye-witness of the events. Here, οἱ ἀδελφοί are the subject of the sentence and ημᾶς the direct object of aorist ἀπεδέξαντο. The word οἱ ἀδελφοί might designate the particular brothers, one of which was Mnason, a man from Cyprus and one of the early disciples.[300] However, mentioning οἱ ἀδελφοί separately from οἱ πρεσβύτεροι repeats the manner in which the elders were assembled in Acts 15:6 out of the whole Jerusalem congregation.[301] Thus, more likely, by the phrase ἀσμένως ἀπεδέξαντο οἱ ἀδελφοί, Luke demonstrates that the church from the beginning warmly received Paul.[302]

---

299. McIver, *Intermediate NT Greek*, 66.

300. Johnson notes the similar use of ἀρχή elsewhere in Luke (Luke 1:2; Acts 11:15; 15:7). He assumes Mnason to be among the first missioneres "from Cyrene and Cyprus" mentioned in Acts 11:20. Johnson, *Acts*, 373 n. 16. Therefore, it is likely, that Luke uses the word ἀρχή towards the events staying in the "very beginning," in origin of something, in the basis of following events.

301. Peterson suggests that was "a more formal scene" when the visitors appeared before the Jerusalem authorities. Peterson, *Acts*, 584. Johnson also sees the regularity in appearance of the board of elders here and in Acts 15:4, 6, 22–23. Johnson, *Acts*, 374 n. 18.

302. Fitzmyer also notes that the Jewish Christians of the Jerusalem church warmly welcomed

This observation presupposes that those whom James calls ἐν τοῖς Ἰουδαίοις τῶν πεπιστευκότων in Acts 21:20 were not the members of the Jerusalem congregation. They could be Jews who came to believe in Christ during his ministry. John in his Gospel states, καὶ πολλοὶ ἐπίστευσαν εἰς αὐτόν, in the area across the Jordan (John 10:42). With similar words, πολλοὶ οὖν ἐκ τῶν Ἰουδαίων . . . ἐπίστευσαν εἰς αὐτόν, John states that "many of the Jews" believed around Bethany (John 11:45). Although those people put their faith in Jesus, they did not join the εκκλησία. John reveals that "many even among the leaders believed in Jesus. But because of the Pharisees they would not confess their faith, for fear they would be put out of the synagogue" (John 12:42). Thus, all those Jews who had believed in Jesus' messiahship remained a great mission field.

The tradition of preaching at the feasts, when a large crowd was gathered in Jerusalem existed according to John 2:23; 12:11, 12. James and the elders likely expected those believers who had not yet joined the church, to arrive in multitudes in Jerusalem for the feast in Acts 21:20. It was known since Pentecost eve that the crowd which gathered in Jerusalem during feasts responded gladly to the Gospel message (Acts 2:5; 4:4). Thus, in Acts 21:17–26 Luke demonstrates the church preparing to witness once again on the day of Pentecost. Paul likely was in a hurry (Acts 20:16) to reach Jerusalem before Pentecost in order to preach to the crowd, as stated in Acts 21:22: πάντως ἀκούσονται ὅτι ἐλήλυθας.

Verse 22 has variant readings, one of which adds δεῖ συνελθεῖν πλῆθος· ἀκούσονται γάρ before ὅτι ἐλήλυθας (preserved in 𝔓74, ℵ2, A 02, E 06 and 33, 181, 945 etc). Another reading preserved by D 05, Ψ, L and P changes the order of words: δεῖ πλῆθος συνελθεῖν· ἀκούσονται γάρ before ὅτι ἐλήλυθας. They likely preserve a later reading in comparison to the one found in B 03 (fourth century CE).[303] The text of Acts 21 is absent from 𝔓45 (250 CE). So, the non-interpolation preserved in B 03, C*vid, 36, 307, 453, 614, 1175 seems to be the original reading.

However, the presence of the additional clause might be explained by the need for thought clarification. With help of the explanatory phrase, the copyist might have transmitted the oral tradition surviving until his time, which provided extra information and could have appeared in manuscript margins or between the columns, and later inserted into the text.[304] Although the addition in v. 22 can be viewed as a later addition, it did not change the doctrinal meaning. Its purpose was to clarify what kind of problem the elders viewed that the arrival of Paul could bring.

With its help one can see in what light the fifth-century oral tradition understood Paul's arrival in Jerusalem for Pentecost. Probably they expected him to preach. The Jerusalem church received Paul warmly, seen from the fact that Luke calls them οἱ

Paul. Fitzmyer, *Acts*, 692, see note on 21:17.

303. Dating of manuscript according to Metzger, *Text of New Testament*, 37, 41.

304. See the similar cases of the intentional text corruption described by Metzger, *Text of New Testament*, 258.

THE FOUR PROHIBITIONS OF ACTS 15

ἀδελφοι.³⁰⁵ He also adds ἀσμένως ἀπεδέξαντο, translated "gladly recognized."³⁰⁶ This pictures the church as friendly to Paul.

The next day, however, the problem appeared. Luke intentionally emphasizes the urgency of the situation by τῇ δὲ ἐπιούσῃ. "The next day" designates an event similar to the council, except for the absence of the apostles. The phrase, εἰσῄει ὁ Παῦλος σὺν ἡμῖν πρὸς Ἰάκωβον, could designate the specially appointed gathering in the home of the head elder of the church.³⁰⁷ Mentioning πάντες τε παρεγένοντο οἱ πρεσβύτεροι also shows the ultimate importance of that meeting. The elders were all assembled to look for the best solution to the issue caused by Paul's arrival.

Some scholars hold that the issue might result from a misunderstanding of Paul's mission to the Gentiles by the members of the Jerusalem church. However, the issue which the elders pose seems not to originate among the church members. As was shown above, they gladly recognized Paul and received him with brotherly warmth.

Exegesis of part 2, Acts 21:19, 20a

Figure 12: Part 2—Acts 21:19, 20a

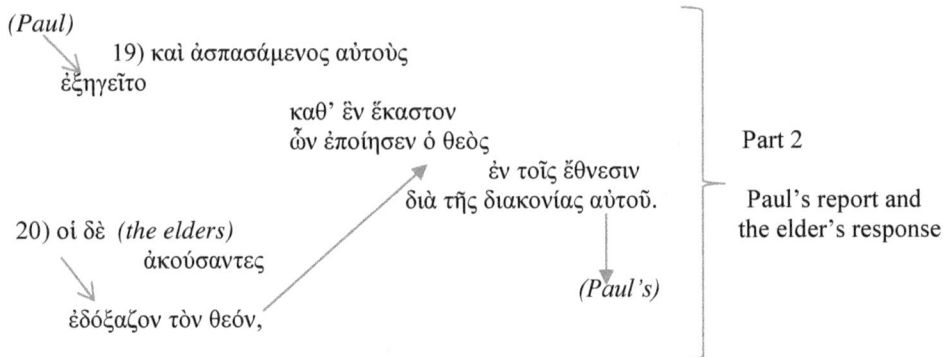

Part 2 reveals two important features of the discussion. First, Paul reported the success of his mission among the Gentiles, attributing it to God's providence. Secondly, Luke shows the attitude of the elders toward Paul's report.³⁰⁸ Luke writes ἀσπασάμενος αὐτούς, "Paul having greeted them," thus implying that the atmosphere of the meeting was friendly from the beginning.

---

305. Barrett shows that the warm welcoming of Paul proves that "there were no serious differences between him and the Jerusalem believers, only false rumors." Barrett, *Critical Commentary on Acts*, 1004–5.

306. Johnson translates ἀσμένως as "gladly" and notes that Lukan ἀσμένως is a NT *hapax legomenon*. Johnson, *Acts*, 374 n. 17.

307. Barrett, *Critical Commentary on Acts*, 1005.

308. Fitzmyer indicates that the elders and James "willingly praise God for Paul's ministry." Fitzmyer, *Acts*, 693, see note on 21:20.

EXEGETICAL STUDY OF THE APOSTOLIC DECREE IN ITS NARRATIVE CONTEXT

The mentioning of ἐξηγεῖτο καθ' ἓν ἕκαστον depicts Paul reporting and interpreting examples of conversions among the Gentiles.[309] The phrase, ὧν ἐποίησεν ὁ θεὸς ἐν τοῖς ἔθνεσιν διὰ τῆς διακονίας αὐτοῦ, reveals the leadership of God in the work of salvation.[310] Paul shows God acting through the work of men, and demonstrates his mission is subordinated to God. The phrase, οἱ δὲ ἀκούσαντες ἐδόξαζον τὸν θεόν, emphasizes that the elders "glorified God" and consequently received Paul's report gladly.[311] The glorifying of God suggests that the elders recognized Paul's ministry as guided and supported by God. This signifies that the church and the elders had nothing to say against Paul and his mission. What, then, was the source of the problem?

Exegesis of part 3, Acts 21:20b-22

Figure 13: Part 3—Acts 21:20b-22

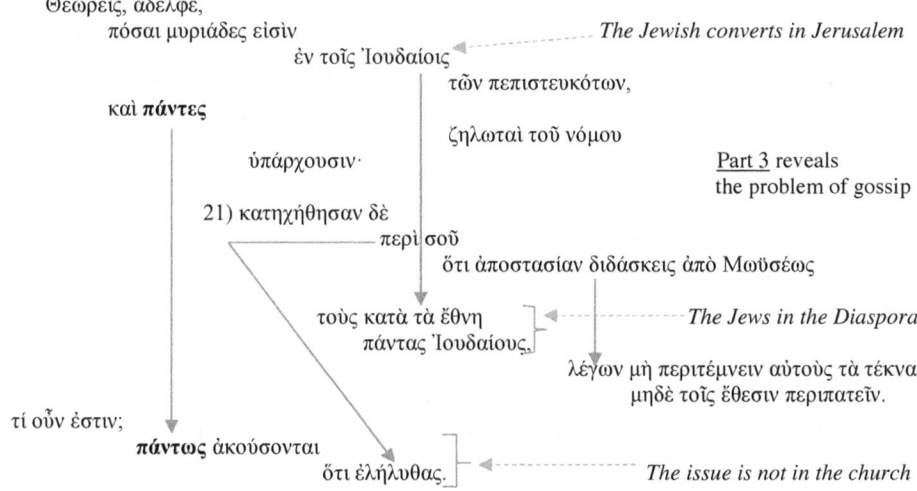

309. BDAG, ἐξηγέομαι, 1, "to relate in detail, *tell, report, describe*." Luke uses ἐξηγέομαι in 15:12 in connection to σημεῖα καὶ τέρατα and in 15:14 to Peter's experience of Cornelius' conversion. It seems that in 21:19 Paul based his report not on the miracles, but rather on experience of conversions. This idea is supported by Barrett, who notes that the following καθ' ἓν ἕκαστον refers to the conversion of the Gentiles, and "makes no clear reference to miracles at all." Barrett, *Critical Commentary on Acts*, 1006.

310. Here διὰ τῆς διακονίας (διὰ + gen) should be translated "through" and shows God as the one who works through that mission. Johnson, *Acts*, 374 n. 19. However, διακονία in 11:29 refers not to the collection, but to the purpose of that collection. Barrett also understands διακονία in terms of Paul's service to God converting the Gentiles. Barrett, *Critical Commentary on Acts*, 1006.

311. Johnson notes that ἐδόξαζον shows the recognition of a "God visiting people" experience (in Luke 2:20; 5:25–26; 7:16; 13:13; 17:15; 18:43; 23:47; Acts 4:21; 11:18). Johnson, *Acts*, 374 n. 20. The term "God visiting" has to be understood as having eschatological meaning. The frequency of this term in Luke's writings shows his acknowledgment that salvation of people was always in the eternal plan of God, known to Him from the beginning.

Part 3 reveals that the problem appeared outside the church. The phrase, πόσαι μυριάδες εἰσὶν ἐν τοῖς Ἰουδαίοις τῶν πεπιστευκότων, points to the gathering of the Jews for the feast.³¹² James uses the adjectival participle πεπιστευκότων to present them as believing Jews (ἐν τοῖς Ἰουδαίοις clarifies the meaning of πεπιστευκότων).³¹³ Literally the phrase reads "there are thousands among the Jews who have believed (and continue to believe)."³¹⁴ Perfect tense πεπιστευκότων describes Jews who experienced conversion.

Does this refer to the conversion of those Jews to Christian belief?³¹⁵ It could not indicate their conversion from simple Judaism to zealous Judaism, because such a division never existed. Thus, James could not refer to zealous Jews with πεπιστευκότων. It also would not refer to those who have become Christians and later were influenced by Pharisaic teaching. This becomes obvious from the fact that those πεπιστευκότων were ζηλωταὶ τοῦ νόμου and were taught (κατηχήθησαν) wrong things about Paul.

The term κατηχήω means "to share a communication that one receives, *report, inform*" in the context of indoctrination.³¹⁶ This kind of instruction hardly could be given in church meeting. From the beginning, it is put on record that church members welcomed Paul. Thus, the instruction had to have been given in synagogues, and points to groups of believers who attended the synagogues, and did not belong to the church.³¹⁷ From James' point of view the μυριάδες . . . τῶν πεπιστευκότων likely

---

312. Barrett shows that Baur, Munck, and Nock view μυριάδες . . . τῶν πεπιστευκότων to be not Christians. Barrett also notes that the perfect participle πεπιστευκότων shows those who have believed and continue to believe. He views them as Christians, who were influenced by the Pharisaic beliefs. Barrett, *Critical Commentary on Acts*, 1006–7. Bruce views them as strongly believing Jews (ἐν τοῖς Ἰουδαίοις). Bruce, *Acts*, 445. However, it seems odd that Luke would divide the Jews in two classes and define the more zealous of them as πεπιστευκότων.

313. Fitzmyer assumes those Jews to be Christians who still observe the Mosaic law. He believes that Luke uses hyperbole describing them as "myriads." Fitzmyer, *Acts*, 693, see note on 21:20. However, according to Acts 2:41 three thousand Jews in Jerusalem had been baptized on Pentecost. In comparison to crowd gathering on the Feast in Jerusalem this number could not be described as "myriads." After that, Acts 4:4 shows another five thousand of those who have believed, but it is not recorded whether they had been baptized or not. Also there were some who believed during Jesus' ministry. Thus, there were Jews in Jerusalem who believed, but not yet baptized. They had not joined the church but belonged to synagogues. This interpretation of "myriads" helps to present the Lukan picture as true and not a hyperbole.

314. Although Fitzmyer sees the "myriads" as "Jewish Christians," he assumes that πάντως in v. 22 refers to the Jews in Jerusalem in a general sense. Fitzmyer, *Acts*, 693–94, see notes on 21:20, 22. However, it has to be noted that πάντως in v. 22 and πάντες in v. 20 might refer to the same group. It supports the idea that the "myriads" does not refer to Christians, because the church warmly received Paul and provoked no threats to his safety.

315. Barret notes that those πεπιστευκότων could be Hellenist Jewish Christians. Barrett, *Critical Commentary on Acts*, 1006–7.

316. BDAG, κατηχέω, 1.

317. This might be assumed from the point that if they were the attendants of both at the same time, the church would influence and reduce their presupposition against Paul which was planted in the synagogue. However, the situation looks like the elders could not influence that group of πεπιστευκότων, because it had no connection with the church. The only opportunity to meet those

meant those among the Jews, who believed in Jesus, but had not joined the church.[318] Those Jews continued their membership in synagogues. Many of them, according to Acts 5:14, were able to experience conversion and join the church.

James notes the danger. The enmity of some Jews in the synagogues toward the church had already emerged, described by Luke in Acts 6:9. The martyrdom of Stephen had similar features to that about which the elders warn Paul (Acts 21:21).[319] Comparing the two stories, one can find that in both cases the enmity was caused by the spreading of gossip. The charges against Stephen were laid with support of false witnesses (Acts 6:13, 14), who mentioned τὰ ἔθη ἃ παρέδωκεν ἡμῖν Μωϋσῆς.[320] Some members of the synagogue "secretly persuaded some men to say, 'We have heard Stephen speak words of blasphemy against Moses and against God'" (Acts 6:11). Thus, the matters of Stephen's accusation were, ῥήματα βλάσφημα εἰς Μωϋσῆν καὶ τὸν θεον. The accusation was made clear later by the words, ῥήματα κατὰ τοῦ τόπου τοῦ ἁγίου καὶ τοῦ νόμου, where the blasphemy against Moses was clarified as sayings against τὰ ἔθη ἃ παρέδωκεν ἡμῖν Μωϋσῆς. Thus, the charges against Stephen seem similar to those against Paul.[321]

The elders warned Paul about the gathering of the Jews, who have been taught that Paul teaches "to turn away from Moses" (Acts 21:21). Instead of Paul preaching the Gospel, the situation at Pentecost appeared to lead to his martyrdom. Consequently, the elders of the church were assembled to look for a better solution and an opportunity to prevent the threat against Paul's life. That is why they met urgently on the day following Paul's arrival in Jerusalem.[322]

It is seen from the words, καὶ πάντες ζηλωταὶ τοῦ νόμου ὑπάρχουσιν, by which James describes those gathering Jews as, "all of them are zealous for the law," that their understanding of the role of the Mosaic law remained the same it was before Jesus' death and resurrection. This was a result of the lack of the Holy Spirit, who seems to be poured out only on those, who confessed the Lordship of Jesus and were baptized in

---

Jews was their gathering in the temple during the feast of Pentecost, but it was too late to protect Paul from their enmity.

318. In John 9:22, it is said that some did not confess their beliefs because they were afraid of the Jews, "for already the Jews had decided that anyone who acknowledged that Jesus was the Christ would be put out of the synagogue." A similar issue is described in Acts 6:9–11, where it is written that those who fell upon Stephen were the members of the Synagogue of the Freedmen.

319. J. C. O'Neill sees similarities in charges raised against Jesus (Mark 14:58), against Stephen (Acts 6:14) and also against Paul (Acts 21:28). He argues that those charges were false, because according to the Old Testament prophecies, "the Temple was not God's dwelling place." O'Neill, *Theology of Acts*, 73.

320. This term reappears in 15:1. Sandt, "Explanation of Acts 15:6–21," 77 n. 4.

321. Johnson agrees that the charges against Stephen have strong resemblance to those in Acts 21:21. Johnson, *Acts*, 375 n. 21.

322. Johnson notes εἶπόν (the plural form of εἶπάν) in v. 20, which means that the advice was a common opinion of a board of elders. Johnson, *Acts*, 374 n. 20.

his name. Thus, the μυριάδες ... τῶν πεπιστευκότων who potentially could be finally converted, remained still zealous for the temple cult.[323]

Viewing εκκλησία as a new temple was probably familiar to members of the Jerusalem church.[324] The words of Jesus, λύσατε τὸν ναὸν τοῦτον καὶ ἐν τρισὶν ἡμέραις ἐγερῶ αὐτόν in John 2:19, demonstrate the prophetic claim, the meaning of which is clarified by John in the words, ἐκεῖνος δὲ ἔλεγεν περὶ τοῦ ναοῦ τοῦ σώματος αὐτοῦ, in John 2:21. This comparison refers not only to Jesus' resurrection in bodily form.[325] Paul himself, in 1 Cor 12:27, writes: "Now you are the body of Christ, and each one of you is a part of it."[326] In Eph 1:22, 23 he states, "And God ... appointed him to be head over everything for the church, which is his body." Comparing the church to the body of Christ, Paul at the same time represents it as the temple of the Holy Spirit in 1 Cor 6:19, 20, when he states, τὸ σῶμα ὑμῶν ναὸς τοῦ ἐν ὑμῖν ἁγίου πνεύματός ἐστιν.[327] These references could mean that the "church" of those days was identified as the body of believers who together constituted the living body of Jesus in this world.[328] At the same time, this body of believers became the new spiritual temple of God.[329]

Moreover, the words of Peter to the council, "We believe it is through the grace of our Lord Jesus that we are saved" (Acts 15:11), were understood by the church. However, the Jews who upheld the temple cult would not understand Peter. The issue appeared as a result of the wrong understanding of the role of the temple cult, which the zealous Jews still maintained. The difficulty consisted in the fact that those Jews had a potential inclination to conversion, but they were injured by prejudices growing out of the gossip. The leaders of the church knew that preaching the cancellation of the ritual law to those who had not accepted Christ would end with denial of the message. That is why the elders suggested Paul show respect for the cultural issues of those who could potentially be saved from among the Jews.

---

323. Johnson notes that the meaning of ζηλωταὶ τοῦ νόμου here can be clarified by its use in Gal 1:14 by Paul, when he describes himself as ζηλωτὴς "for the traditions of his ancestors," which presupposes observance of rites and "honor to be paid to Torah." Johnson, *Acts*, 374 n. 20.

324. O'Neill, *Theology of Acts*, 76–77. He notes that despite the outwardly respectful attitude to the temple in the writings of Luke (Luke 2; 19:47—21:38; Acts 21:23; 22:17; 24:6, 17–19; 25:8) closer examination shows that Luke views the temple as "a house of prayer." Thus, Luke intentionally removes the last part of the quotation from Isa 56:7 found in Mark 11:17, and states in Luke 19:46: "My house will be a house of prayer."

325. O'Neill, *Theology of Acts*, 74. He shows similarities between Mark 14:58, Acts 6:14 and Acts 21:28. He states that "when Jesus dies, the Temple ceases to be God's dwelling place, and at his Resurrection his body becomes the new Temple."

326. See similar comparisons of the church to the body of Christ in 1 Cor 10:17; 12:12, 13, 20; Rom 12:55.

327. It was stated that the church community "is the physical presence of Christ in the world." Murphy-O'Connor, *Keys to First Corinthians*, 104.

328. Thompson observes that the temple was viewed by the church as the place of proclamation of Jesus "as the one who fulfils and replaces the temple." Thompson, "Acts of the Risen Lord Jesus," 91.

329. Marshall states that "the restored temple is in fact the Christian community." Marshall, "Acts," 592.

Here, James reveals the existence of the two groups of Ἰουδαῖοι. First of all he referred to those μυριάδες . . . τῶν πεπιστευκότων who εἰσὶν ἐν τοῖς Ἰουδαίοις. He also designated them by use of πάντες ζηλωταὶ τοῦ νόμου. They are those who live in Judea and attend the Jerusalem feasts.[330] Then, with the words τοὺς κατὰ τὰ ἔθνη πάντας Ἰουδαίους James indicates the second group of the Jews, namely, those who live in the diaspora.[331] The accusation against Paul, thus, was expressed as ὅτι ἀποστασίαν διδάσκεις ἀπὸ Μωϋσέως . . . λέγων μὴ περιτέμνειν αὐτοὺς τὰ τέκνα μηδὲ τοῖς ἔθεσιν περιπατεῖν.[332] The synagogue leaders in Judea informed the believers that Paul taught τοὺς κατὰ τὰ ἔθνη πάντας Ἰουδαίους (the Jews among the Gentiles) to apostatize from Mosaic law, namely, the rite of circumcision and other customs of a ritual nature.

While numerous scholars represent Paul establishing the theology of freedom from the law, there are those who view Paul as a pious Jew. Thus, Robert Maddox notes the opinion of Krister Stendahl:

> Paul . . . always remained a Jew: he did not see his experience on the Damascus road as a "conversion" from one "religion" called Judaism to another called Christianity, but rather as a call to a son of Abraham from the God of Abraham, to become his apostle to the nations, because of the new situation caused by the coming of the Messiah.[333]

The substance of the accusation lay in arguing about the need for Mosaic ritual law. For most Jews the Mosaic law was the sign of Jewish identity, involving doctrinal and cultural issues. According to the information given in chapter 15, the apostles did not view the Mosaic ritual law as the instrument of salvation. The temple cult for them was replaced by worship in spirit and truth. However, they had chosen to respect those who understood its role according to the old pattern.[334]

The issue in chapter 21 seems not to be a step back from the decision achieved by the council in Acts 15. The decision of the Jerusalem Council created a new foothold for salvation through Jesus only and, thus, made the Mosaic law rudimentary for salvation. Narrative in Acts 15 demonstrates an attempt made by the apostles to adjust the life of Gentile converts to the new understanding of salvation in Christ. Acts 21

---

330. Lake and Cadbury, *English Translation and Commentary*, 271. They suggest that those were the people of Judea. They were coming to feasts in Jerusalem. They rightly note that the term Ἰουδαίοις had a tendency to be used in scholarly research in a religious sense, where in the beginning it might mean ethnicity.

331. Johnson, *Acts*, 375 n. 21. He views this group as the Jews of the diaspora.

332. Johnson notes that ἔθεσιν περιπατεῖν can refer to "customs" of cultural identity without direct relation to the life of faith. He translates μὴ+infinitive here in the sense, "to stop circumcising/following." Johnson, *Acts*, 375 n. 21.

333. Maddox, *Purpose of Luke-Acts*, 31.

334. Johnson notes that Paul followed some rites: he has circumcised Timothy (16:3), has taken a Nasarite vow (18:18), has observed the feasts (20:5, 17). Moreover, in Paul's own letters "there is no suggestion that he ever advocated Jewish believers forsaking circumcision or their customs," but he argued against the necessity of tose rites for the Gentiles. Johnson, *Acts*, 375 n. 21.

shows that now the elders had to find a way to adjust their new understanding to the traditional Jewish background in which they lived. So they had to define their attitude toward the temple cult while the temple still existed.[335]

Taking into account the Jewish background of the Jerusalem church, it seems natural for them to approach the temple in a manner in which they would practice the rites of consecration.[336] The breaking of those rites could bring an extremely negative reaction from believing Jews outside the church. They honored the temple and rites of consecration according to the old pattern. The changes of this system seemed impossible for them. Their severe hostility toward the church threatened to destroy the missionary work among the Jewish converts.[337] For the sake of mission, James and the elders suggested to Paul a temporary submission to the demands of the Mosaic ritual law.[338]

This explanation agrees with Paul's statement in 1 Cor 9:20, "To the Jews I became like a Jew, to win the Jews. To those under the law I became like one under the law (though I myself am not under the law), so as to win those under the law." From this point one can conclude that James and the elders asked Paul for a temporary submission to the old pattern, at least in those things which could be viewed as necessary for one who enters the temple. Those thing were necessary, not for the salvation of someone, but for participating in temple worship.[339]

At this point the question arises, did Paul uphold the ritual system? From Acts 18:18 it is seen that Paul kept a vow. The visual manifestation of that vow consisted probably in growing hair, thus echoing the Nazirite vow. However, Paul did not cut his hair in the temple court and did not accompany the ceremony by bringing sacrifices. So, the manner in which Paul kept the Nazirite vow differed from that prescribed in Num 6:1–21. Some scholars insist that Paul kept his private vow. It is also possible that Paul kept not a private vow, but the Nazirite vow, through his new understanding of its role. Maddox notes that Paul "certainly was redirected in his theological perception of

---

335. Thompson, "Acts of Risen Jesus," 190–91. Thompson states that Paul's participation in the temple cult should not be observed as "another supposedly 'positive' example of continuing temple activity among the early Christians." On the contrary it has to be viewed as "respect to Jewish sensitivities as to what is deemed appropriate in the temple."

336. Braulik views the rites as "entrance liturgy" as one approaches the sanctuary. He shows the idea of redemption even in the Deuteronomy laws. Braulik, "Law as Gospel," 7–8.

337. Marshall considers that only the Jewish ritual law became unnecessary to keep. He asserts that all aspects of the Mosaic law were fulfilled in Christ. He believes that only the Jewish Christians in the early church were obliged to keep the ritual law, which is seen from Acts 16:3, 18:18, 21:26. In his opinion it remained important not for salvation, but for the prevention of any accusation from the Jews. Marshall, *Luke*, 185–86.

338. Johnson proposes that the reason for the elders' advice was to please the Jews "zealous for the law" by Paul's demonstration of piety. Johnson, *Acts*, 375 n. 22.

339. Jervell, "Law in Luke-Acts," 26. Jervell noticed Luke's concern with the problem of the ritual law: demands of ritual purity, connection between the temple and the law, acceptance of the God-fearers. Cf. Jervell, *Apostelgeschichte*, 527.

what it means to be a Jew."³⁴⁰ His understanding likely derived from his view of church as the new temple of God.

The text of Acts 16:3 surprisingly shows that Paul, after the decision by the council, submits to the law of Moses when he circumcises Timothy, καὶ λαβὼν περιέτεμεν αὐτὸν διὰ τοὺς Ἰουδαίους τοὺς ὄντας ἐν τοῖς τόποις ἐκείνοις. The use of διὰ τοὺς Ἰουδαίους includes the construction διά+acc, which demonstrates the cause of action. Thus it should be translated "because of the Jews" or "for the sake of the Jews." The presence of Jews in those places where Paul planned missions caused him to have recourse to Μωϋσῆς for the sake of those missions.

It is noteworthy that Paul did these things before the events of chapter 21. This means that the elders did not invent a new solution. Paul has already viewed the cultural limitations of the liberty from the law of Moses in the same way long before. The advice of the elders did not push Paul to practice strange rituals and betray his own advanced approach for the sake of the Jewishness of the Jerusalem congregation. Wilson states, "keeping the law is not an issue of salvation, but a matter of expressing piety."³⁴¹ Luke in Acts 16:3–5 pictures Paul's ambivalent approach, which made him keep the custom of Moses where it was necessary, for the sake of the Jews, and for liberating Gentile converts from its burden. Maddox believes "the leaders of the Christian movement are portrayed as consistently loyal and courteous toward the Hebrew traditions."³⁴² In addition, Goppelt notes that Paul strove for friendship between the Jerusalem church and the churches consisting of Gentile converts.³⁴³

From this point, one can see that the gossip about Paul spread in the synagogues was untrue. The Jewish leaders falsely declared that Paul taught the Jews who lived in the diaspora to apostasize from Mosaic law.³⁴⁴ However, this seems incorrect from two points: Paul kept the Mosaic law when it was needed for the sake of conversion of the Jews, and the decision of the council that was made concerning Gentile converts. Because the decision of the council was taken from a theological perspective in the presence of the apostles, it has to be assumed as the main decision of the church about the Mosaic law.

The issue of Acts 21 seems to be a secondary ad hoc regulation, suggested by the elders on account of a threat to Paul's life and to the church's mission. The temporary and ad hoc nature of this regulation becomes obvious from the phrase τοῦτο οὖν ποίησον which Luke constructs with help of the inferential postpositive conjunction

---

340. Maddox, *Purpose of Luke-Acts*, 31.

341. Wilson, *Luke and Law*, 61, 102. Wilson follows Jervell, who sees the church as the renewed Israel that had to keep the law.

342. Maddox, *Purpose of Luke-Acts*, 55–56.

343. Goppelt, *Apostolic Times*, 68.

344. The verse shows their verbal accusation, ὅτι ἀποστασίαν διδάσκεις ἀπὸ Μωϋσέως and reveals that they pictured Paul teaching τοὺς κατὰ τὰ ἔθνη πάντας Ἰουδαίους apostasy from the law of Moses. This apostasy was present in λέγων μὴ περιτέμνειν αὐτοὺς τὰ τέκνα μηδὲ τοῖς ἔθεσιν περιπατεῖν, when λέγων relates to διδάσκεις and reveals the manner in which Paul allegedly taught the Jews in diaspora.

οὖν followed by the imperative ποίησον. Thus, their suggestion appears to be dictated by present circumstances, which James has stated before in vv. 20–22.

Exegesis of part 4, Acts 21:23, 24

Figure 14: Part 4—Acts 21:23, 24

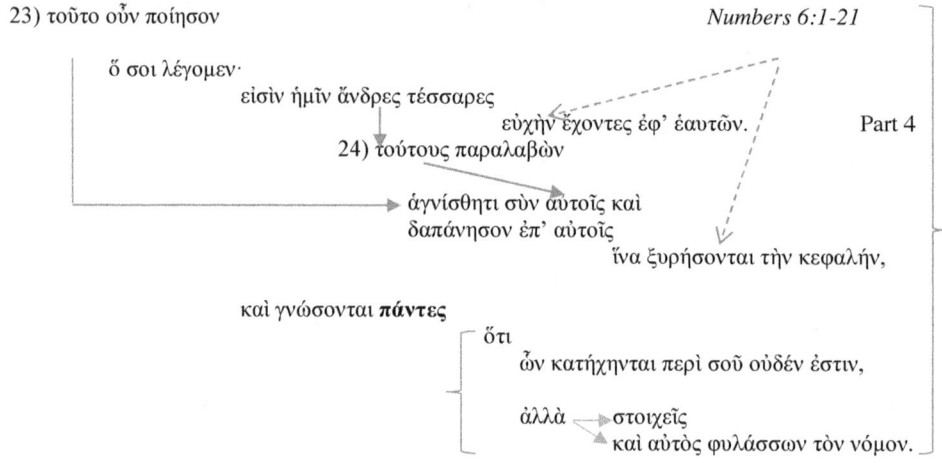

Part 4 contains the advice itself. James suggests a situation by which Paul can show his respect for Mosaic law and enter the temple, having been consecrated according to ritual.[345] James gives him four church members, "who are placing the vow on themselves."[346] Here εὐχὴν ἔχοντες describes the men currently under vow, indicated by the pronoun τούτους in the phrase τούτους παραλαβὼν describes Paul "joining these [men]." Paul is instructed to "become consecrated," by the aorist ἁγνίσθητι.[347] The instruction continues with the parallel imperative phrase καὶ δαπάνησον ἐπ᾽ αὐτοῖς ἵνα ξυρήσονται τὴν κεφαλήν and provides the condition, which Paul has to fulfill. It can be translated, "and pay for them [their expenses], so that they can cut the [hair of their] heads." Here, the result clause ἵνα ξυρήσονται expresses the desired result of Paul's participation. Thus, Luke demonstrates knowledge of the Nazirite ritual in which cutting the hair must follow the offering of the sacrifice.[348]

So, James invited Paul to join the Nazirite vow of those men and participate in ritual purification, consecration and bringing sacrifices to the temple.[349] James stated

345. Bruce views the need for purification in relation to a temple ceremony. Bruce, *Acts*, 447–48.

346. Bruce, *Acts*, 447.

347. BDAG, ἁγνίζω, 1 b. Here ἁγνίσθητι (singular passive imperative aorist of ἁγνίζω) means "be purified or cleansed and so made acceptable for cultic use."

348. Fitzmyer refers to this keeping of the Nazirite vow, which "was believed to make one 'holy' (Num. 6:5)." He believes that in Acts 18:18 Paul keeps the Nazirite vow. Fitzmyer, *Acts*, 694, see notes on 21:23, 24.

349. Bruce shows that once Paul had completed his vow, "he could help the four Nazirites to

the goal of his request with a second result clause, καὶ γνώσονται πάντες ὅτι ὧν κατήχηνται περὶ σοῦ οὐδέν ἐστιν ("that all may know that things taught about you are not *true*").[350] The word πάντες here, likely recalls πάντες ζηλωταὶ τοῦ νόμου of v. 20. They also are those μυριάδες . . . τῶν πεπιστευκότων, with whom James starts the description of the issue. Thus the Jews who have believed, but have not yet joined the church, were the main concern of James. For their sake he put the request before Paul to participate in Mosaic ritual law.

The purpose of this action was expressed further by ὅτι ὧν κατήχηνται περὶ σοῦ οὐδέν ἐστιν and ἀλλὰ στοιχεῖς καὶ αὐτὸς φυλάσσων τὸν νόμον ("but that you yourself live in observance of the law" Act 21:24).[351] The clause ὅτι ὧν κατήχηνται περὶ σοῦ οὐδέν ἐστιν expresses James' hope to refute the false information about Paul in general.[352] The clause following adversative ἀλλὰ states the desired positive picture of Paul (περὶ σοῦ), using στοιχεῖς Paul "*holds to, agrees with, follows*, conforms to"[353] and "*observes, follows*' (φυλάσσων) the law (τὸν νόμον).[354] This implied that the information spread by the synagogues was senseless gossip, and that Paul did not teach the diaspora Jews to abandon the Mosaic law. He taught Gentile converts that they are saved in Jesus, without becoming Jews first.[355]

Paul's personal understanding of the ritual law did not mean he abandoned it. On the contrary, Paul could rethink the role of the ritual law and keep it only for the purpose of self discipline. Once the gossip ceased, Paul presented his understanding of the Mosaic ritual system. James hoped to return Paul's reputation as a pious Jew in order to defend his mission. That is why James outwardly subjected Paul to the temple cult to solve a temporary issue.[356] At the same time, James repeated the council decision addressed to the Gentile converts.

---

complete theirs by paying their expenses." Bruce, *Acts*, 447.

350. This may be what Wallace terms a "purpose-result ἵνα clause." Wallace, *Greek Grammar*, 473.

351. Jackson and Lake note the discussion about the Nazirite vow in which James suggested to Paul to participate. The scholars believe that the "seven days" of purification may be interpreted as the accidental ritual defilement of those four men. They needed to purify themselves, shave their heads and start their vows over again. Thus, Paul had to pay the expences for their purification: eight pigeons and four lambs. A similar participation in the Nazirite vow was taken by Agrippa I and recorded by Josephus, *Antiq.*, 19.6.1. Lake and Cadbury, *English Translation and Commentary*, 272.

352. According to Fitzmyer this clause reveals the purpose of James' advice. Fitzmyer, *Acts*, 694, see note on 21:24.

353. BDAG, στοιχέω.

354. BDAG, φυλάσσω, 5 a.

355. Here scholars observe that when Acts was written (about 70 CE) Jewish Christianity "was still flourishing, and that the Pauline Christians were anxious to establish the compromise that the Jews should continue to practice circumcision, but Gentiles should not adopt it." Lake and Cadbury, *English Translation and Commentary*, 271.

356. Paul was asked to participate in a "seven-day" purification. Fitzmyer suggests that it is not to be viewed as a Nazirite vow, but rather as the ceremony "required of a Jew returning from a trip abroad (to pagan territories) to undergo a purification that would rid him of the defilement." Fitzmyer, *Acts*, 694.

Exegesis of part 5, Acts 21:25

Figure 15: Part 5—Acts 21:25

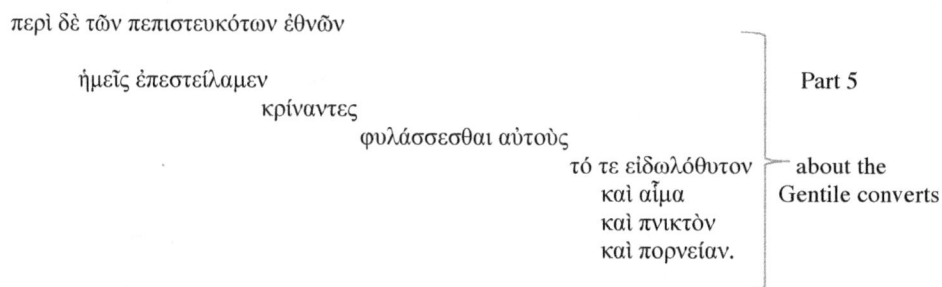

First of all, James refers here to τῶν πεπιστευκότων ἐθνῶν. This group differs from μυριάδες . . . τῶν πεπιστευκότων who, according to James, εἰσὶν ἐν τοῖς Ἰουδαίοις. Both groups have one common feature which is designated by the adjectival participle, πεπιστευκότων, those who have believed in Christ Jesus. However, the groups differ in a cultural sense. The first group in v. 20 are believing Jews, and the second group, mentioned in v. 25 are Gentile believers.

The phrase περὶ δὲ τῶν πεπιστευκότων ἐθνῶν, is best translated, "concerning those among the Gentiles who have believed..." With help of the adversative conjunction δὲ James shifts the current discussion from the Jewish converts to the Gentiles, presuming a shift in cultural background.[357] His quotation of the Decree follows this shift of backgrounds and thus appears in a non-Jewish cultural context. The shift from one cultural issue to another is significant, emphasizing that the apostles on the council supposed that both sides of the Church would grow, and therefore they adapted the basic principles of faith to different cultural issues. This became the origin of two different approaches. The Jewish one still maintained the practicing of the Mosaic law, at least in some special cases. The other, given to the Gentile converts, was linked to natural law and specified just four main regulations from it.[358]

James declared that Paul taught the Gentile converts not to keep the Mosaic law not because of his own frivolous approach, but following the unanimous apostolic decision taken by the council.[359] The phrase ἡμεῖς ἐπεστείλαμεν κρίναντες shows that James refers not to the current solution of elders, but to the apostolic decision.[360] James

---

357. Bruce understands it as a shift in the decisions, when the Jewish Christians were given one decision and those from a Gentile background were given the opposite decision. Bruce, *Acts*, 447–48.

358. O'Neill, *Theology of Acts*, 78–79. He insists that one has to distinguish the universal morality in the law of Moses from its customs. He believes that "all Christians should accept Moses as their moral guide."

359. Wilson, *Luke and Law*, 103. Wilson assumes following the Decree to be the manifestation of Gentile piety which is necessary for the witnessing of the Gospel.

360. Fitzmyer argues that the council had two meetings and Paul did not present to the second

states that Paul acted in agreement with the Decree. The word ἡμεῖς is the subject of the phrase, focusing on ἡμεῖς ἐπεστείλαμεν, not on τῶν πεπιστευκότων ἐθνῶν. The phrase stresses the common agreement by the apostles and elders on the council about the ritual law.[361] That agreement was that the ritual law is not necessary for salvation. This was noted in the first account of the Decree. The Decree allowed Gentile converts to become Christians without becoming Jews first.[362] This was the main decision to which James refers now.

After ἐπεστείλαμεν κρίναντες, James quotes the Decree, repeating also the four prohibitions. The wording in Acts 21:25 differs from the account of Acts 15:29 in the following features: 1) replacement of ἀπέχεσθαι with φυλάσσεσθαι αὐτούς; 2) presence of τό τε εἰδωλόθυτον instead of εἰδωλοθύτων; 3) καὶ αἵματος replaced with καὶ αἷμα; 4) καὶ πνικτῶν replaced with καὶ πνικτόν; 5) πορνείας replaced with πορνείαν.[363] The manner of the Decree correlates with that in Acts 15:29 and contains two parts. The first part confirms the ban on imposing the ritual law on Gentile converts. The second part clarifies the four exclusive matters taken out of the ritual system. These changes consist mostly of variations of case, gender and number.[364] In Acts 15:29 the prohibited εἰδωλοθύτων is neutral plural genitive, while πνικτῶν, αἵματος and πορνείας are neutral

---

one, when the letter was written. Therefore, only here in Acts 21:25, talking with James, Paul learnt for the first time about that letter, which the elders had sent in Acts 15:22–29. Fitzmyer, *Acts*, 694, see note on 21:25. Thus, Fitzmyer asserts that Paul would argue against the additional four requirements imposed on the Gentiles. This interpretation, however, seems doubtful if we accept that Paul received James' advice about purification positively. He probably would not accept this advice and pretend to look pious, if he did not agree with the content of the letter and did not respect the ritual law of Torah. Otherwise, Paul would become a hypocrite.

361. Bruce states that this verse "has the nature of a footnote." He assumes that the elders were glad to know that Paul does not teach Jewish believers to give up the ritual law and confirmed their agreement about the Gentile converts not to submit to the ritual law. Bruce, *Acts*, 447–48. This view seems doubtful because it presupposes the double standards in the church, even among its spiritual leaders. It seems preferable to assume that the issue was outside the church and of cultural nature. Thus, James and the elders might ask Paul to disprove the false claims which arose because of misunderstanding the role of the ritual law. The church has shown that the ritual law is not necessary for salvation. This applied to Jews as well as Gentiles. Thus, the words of James in Acts 21:25 refer to the common agreement of the church leaders about the role of the ritual law for both parties, and not to the Gentiles only. The advice to participate in the vow has to be viewed as a concession to the cultural context of the particular church.

362. Barrett notes that the first person plural ἡμεῖς here might be assumed as "the elders and I (James)" or as "the elders, you (Paul) and I (James)." He shows the variety of views and assumes them in one sentence clarifying that James and the elders are saying, "We are not going back on our pledge to the Gentiles, you therefore may do what we ask." Barrett, *Critical Commentary on Acts*, 1015.

363. The wording of the Decree in Acts 21:25 differs also from Acts 15:19: 1) replacement of ἀπέχεσθαι with φυλάσσεσθαι αὐτούς; 2) avoiding ἀλισγημάτων; 3) James clarifies the meaning of τῶν ἀλισγημάτων τῶν εἰδώλων with words τό τε εἰδωλόθυτον; 4) τοῦ αἵματος replaced with καὶ αἷμα and shifted from last place to second. The word τοῦ πνικτοῦ is replaced with καὶ πνικτόν. The word τῆς πορνείας replaced with πορνείαν and shifted from second place to last place.

364. Lake and Cadbury, *English Translation and Commentary*, 273. They drew on the Western reading (D 05), which omits πνικτόν, and conclude that only the observance of certain matters from all ritual law was imposed on the Gentiles, while the Jews remain under the ritual law.

singular genitive. In Acts 21:25, the different cases and number of these words are employed. Thus, εἰδωλόθυτον and πνικτὸν appear as masculine singular accusative. The word αἷμα appears in feminine singular nominative and πορνείαν in feminine singular accusative. Moreover, the prohibitions in Acts 21 are stated by anarthrous nouns.

From these data one can note some common features: the prohibitions shift from plural in Acts 15:20 to singular in 21:25, in 15:29 they are uniformly in the genetive case, while in Acts 21:25 they are uniformly in the accusative case. The shift from plural to singular can depend on the article plus conjunction τό τε, which could be derived from an original τότε, meaning "then, next, after that." The text could be translated "to keep themselves away after that…" The conjunction τότε, here, makes the prohibitions more concrete, and presupposes the singular number of each.

Also, the shift to the accusative case could show that the prohibitions are direct objects of a verb, φυλάσσεσθαι.[365] The accusative helps to subordinate the prohibitions to φυλάσσεσθαι, which is an infinitive used in indirect speech. With the pronoun αὐτοὺς James refers to τῶν πεπιστευκότων ἐθνῶν. The Gentile converts were ordered "to guard themselves from" four matters. Thus, in Acts 21:25, James reminds the elders that the apostles sent the elders' decision to the converts, to guard themselves against what is expressed in four singular statements.

Exegesis of part 6, Acts 21:26

Figure 16: Part 6—Acts 21:26

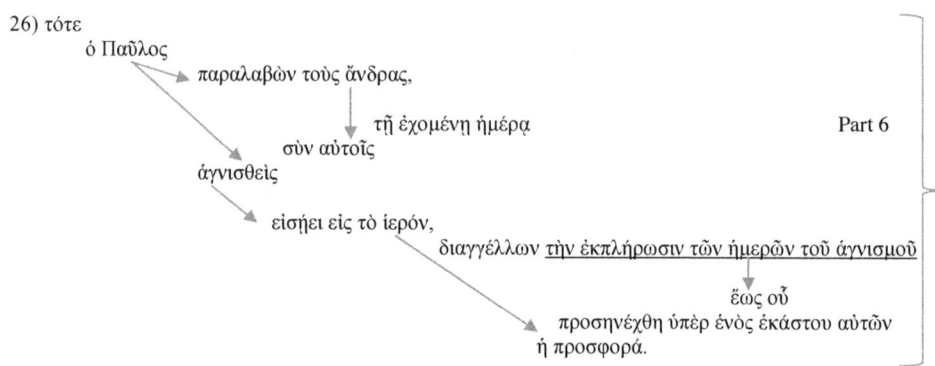

Part 6 pictures Paul following the advice of James. The word τότε, "then, next, after that" connects Paul's actions to the previously dispensed advice. The phrase παραλαβὼν τοὺς ἄνδρας, τῇ ἐχομένῃ ἡμέρᾳ σὺν αὐτοῖς ἁγνισθεὶς is a precursory phrase, where

---

365. Here, James, for the benefit of Gentile converts, repeats the verb φυλάσσω, with which he described Paul's way of life. The only difference is that the Gentile converts have to "guard themselves" on account of just four matters, while Paul "guards himself" according to the Mosaic law, when approaching the temple.

the participles παραλαβὼν and ἁγνισθεὶς describe the manner in which Paul entered the temple (εἰσῄει εἰς τὸ ἱερόν).³⁶⁶

The wording, also, can indirectly clarify the purpose of Paul's arrival in Jerusalem, as an attempt to preach in the temple. Here, the participles state the way Paul chose to enter the temple. As seen from the discussion above, Paul originally had no intention to participate in a Nazirite vow. The instruction of James and the elders made him a participant.³⁶⁷ That instruction was given on account of widely spread, wrong information about Paul. Then, Paul chooses the Nazirite vow to resolve two issues: his hope to be in the temple, and the need to refute false information.

The following participle, διαγγέλλων, again was used to describe the manner in which Paul entered the temple.³⁶⁸ Obviously, his main concern was not to enter the temple to anounce the accomplishment of the rite of purification, but to preach the Gospel. Participation in the Nazirite vow became a safe way to enter the temple.³⁶⁹ The participation in the vow made his coming to the temple, on the eighth day, necessary. Luke emphasizes that Paul entered the temple, thus giving every observer notice of the purification rite's completion, on the correct day for bringing sacrifices. The text says, ἕως οὗ προσηνέχθη ὑπὲρ ἑνὸς ἑκάστου αὐτῶν ἡ προσφορά. The sacrifice (ἡ προσφορά) could not be presented elsewhere, but in the temple; so Paul had to be there. In this manner Paul provided himself a good reason to enter the "holy place," but his chief reason from the beginning, was to preach of the Gospel.³⁷⁰

Conclusion

In retrospect, the Decree of the Jerusalem Council in Acts 15 appears in Acts 21 adapted to the Jewish cultural context. The council reverted to the previous pattern of the Mosaic ritual law; a shift that facilitated the salvation of Jews. As is evident in Acts 15, the

---

366. Barrett mentions a number of views, among which are the need of purification for entering the temple after travelling in Gentile regions and the need of completing the Nazirite vow (Acts 18:18). Barrett, *Critical Commentary on Acts*, 1011. The view that Paul needed to terminate his own Nazirite vow seems unlikely, for the hair has to be shaved (Luke uses ξυράω) in the temple court. It seems doubtfull that Paul would bring his hair, which he had cut (Luke uses κείρω) in Cenchrea and terminate the Nazirite vow. It is likely, that Paul participated in a simple rite of purification.

367. Johnson views that participation of Paul presumed an "announce" made "in the sense of "check off" with some priest each day of purification as it passed." Johnson, *Acts*, 377 n. 26.

368. BDAG, διαγγέλλω, 2, "to make a report, *announce*."

369. According to O'Neill, Luke "believes that Christian theology as a whole has repudiated the traditionlal Jewish view of the Temple." O'Neill, *Theology of Acts*, 83. He supports his view referring to Qumran literature and OT pseudepigrapha (Sib. Or. 4.8–12), early patristic literature (Justin, *Dialogue with Trypho*, 117.2) and NT apocripha (Barn. and Ps.-Clem.). These sources might be influenced by anti-Jewish polemic of that time and show an extreme point of view rather than a healthy one. The writings of Luke, however, do not reflect any hostility of Christians toward the temple. The Christians might review the role of the temple, but not reject its cultic significance.

370. Bruce states that Paul's participation in a temple ceremony "in no way compromised the gospel." Bruce, *Acts*, 447.

law of Moses was not viewed by the church as an instrument of salvation.[371] However, the law of Moses provided the rites of purification, which were understood as necessary to enter the temple. Because the temple was understood as a holy place by the majority of Jews, rules were needed to govern how one could approach the temple.

This issue could be understood as temporary and cultural, if one were to assume that the shift from the previous understanding of salvation to the new approach needed time. The elders knew that it was impossible to explain the new understanding of salvation to those who hardly believed in Jesus. That model of salvation, known by the Jews, was provided by the Mosaic ritual law and temple cult. James therefore suggested encasing the Gospel news within the pattern of the Mosaic law in order to make it easier for the Jews to accept. By this means, Paul and the church, probably intended to bring Jewish people to Christ.

Chapter Summary

The exegesis of the three Lukan accounts of the Apostolic Decree in their literary contexts revealed that:

1. the apostolic decision was structured around two points: the ritual Jewish law was found to be unnecessary for salvation, and the four prohibitions were denoted as necessary for keeping.

2. the explanation for imposing those four prohibitions on Gentile converts was provided by the pesher-midrash in Acts 15:14–21. This pesher-midrash was employed in order to give a firm foundation, in Torah, to the proposal of the Decree. Thus, the literary form of the Decree in Acts 15 presumes the defense of the apostolic decision on the basis of the law of Torah.

3. the debate on the Jerusalem Council began with the issue of the validity of the ritual law for salvation. During the debate regulations belonging to the ritual law were differentiated from those rooted in the natural law of God revealed in the Genesis creation-fall account.

4. the ritual law was viewed as fulfilled in Christ and not necessary to be kept, while the content of the Decree was supported with help of midrash created on the basis of the Genesis creation-fall account.

5. the reversal element within midrash suggests that the creation–fall–re-creation paradigm is involved as an aspect in the background of the Decree.

---

371. Arrington writes that the sacrificial death of Christ exposed the meaning of sacrifices and purification rites. He also shows by the number of texts of the NT that the early church understood that purity, in the sense of moral purity, is "demanded by God of all Christians (Jas 4:8; 1Pet 1:22, 1 John 3:3)." Arrington, *Acts*, 214.

6. worship motifs are reflected in the Decree. They are suggested by the word ἀλίσγημα, the context of which includes a motif of desecration of things accounted as holy. Also, the conversion of the Gentiles to God involves worship motifs, when the converts are invited to make changes from pagan worship to the true worship based on Torah. The decision not to make the turning of the Gentiles to God difficult results in imposing on them only necessary regulations of worship.

7. the Decree in Acts 21:25 reveals that salvation, independent of the patterns of the ritual law, was first adapted for the Gentile party in Acts 15:20, 29; 21:25 and later adapted to the Jewish cultural context in Acts 21:23, 24. The adaptation to the Jewish context was made by returning to the previous pattern of the Mosaic ritual law, authorising the rites of purification, which were understood by the Jewish majority as necessary to enter the temple.

8. the shift from the new pattern to the old one has to be understood as temporary and cultural. In Acts 21:23–25 James did not display a double standard (imposing the ritual law on the Jews while liberating the Gentile converts from it), but suggested that for the purpose of reaching the Jews, the Gospel be encased in the pattern of the Mosaic law in order to make it easier for the Jews to accept. By this means Paul and the church probably hoped to bring people to Christ.

3

Biblical and Theological Context of the Apostolic Decree

Basic Theological Concepts Developed on the Basis of Genesis 1:24—3:24

THIS CHAPTER ARGUES THAT the rationale behind the four prohibitions of the Apostolic Decree in Acts 15 is found in the creation–fall–re-creation paradigm, as expressed in the narratives of Gen 1–3. In view of this, the research will rely on the diagrams of Gen 1–3 given in Appendix 2. In order to see possible allusions and echoes of Gen 1–3 in Acts 15, the diagrams of Genesis are made according to the Greek text of the LXX from which the apostles quoted at the council.

The use of LXX over MT Gen 1–3 can be justified by the following linguistic and literary reasons. Historically Greek had long been spoken in Jerusalem by Jewish immigrants from the Diaspora and their descendants, the Seven including Stephen (all of whom had Greek names, Acts 6:1–5).[1] Members of the "synagogue of the libertines" (6:9), who opposed Stephen, were part of that Greek-speaking population of Jerusalem. The city of Antioch, which became the support base for mission work by Barnabas and Paul (11:19–26; 14:26–28), was a significant Greek cultural centre for the region. Greek language would have dominated among its converts to Christianity, who provided generous support for the Greek-speaking Gentile mission by Barnabas and Paul. Some of those Greek-speaking Antioch believers joined Barnabas and Paul as participants in the Jerusalem Council (15:1–3). On the literary front, Luke preserved, in James' speech to the council, quotations of the prophets which correspond best to the LXX. Finally, as will be pointed out below, a number of allusions to and echoes of Gen 1–3 in Acts 15 reflect the LXX. Finally, Luke as an author targeted Greek readers, whose only access to the OT would have been by means of the LXX.

The four prohibitions of the Decree are connected to four aspects of worship. Thus, εἰδωλοθύτων presumes not only food involved in worship, but also the idols involved. The prohibition of αἷμα and πνικτὸς, although reflecting the dietary laws of Torah, also represents the returning of blood to the dust, and the breath of life to

---

1. The significant research on use of the LXX in Acts was done by Clarke, "Use of the Septuagint in Acts."

God (Gen 3:19). The role of these two concepts becomes significant for the sacrificial system of true worship as well as for non-cultic food consumption. The prohibition of πορνεία was associated with pagan ecstatic worship involving nakedness and sacral prostitution, in contrast to true worship, which demanded that worshipers wear garments before God, covering their nakedness. The worship aspect behind the four prohibitions of the Apostolic Decree has to be viewed as foundational, already expressed in Gen 1–3. They are fitted in the creation–fall–re-creation paradigm because they not only explain the mechanisms of the fall, but also reveal the way of true worship and subsequent restoration.

The narrative in Gen 1–3 pictures the following three steps of the creation–fall–re-creation paradigm: 1) Gen 1:1–2:3 describes a brief sketch of the creation of the world;[2] 2) Gen 2:4–25 provides an enlarged account of creation with an accent placed on the sixth day and the creation of human beings;[3] 3) Gen 3:1–24 contains the fall narrative and promise of restoration. Each of these three units in the narrative in Gen 1–3 contains one theological concept, which later through divine revelation, is developed to become the theological basis of the entire Hebrew Bible.

The present study focuses on the creation narrative beginning with the appearance of humans, labelled as *Unit one* of passage (1)."[4] This unit includes the text of Gen 1:24–30 which provides a short description of the origin of earthly creatures, including humans. The account of the seventh day forms *Unit two* of passage (1). Passage (1) has one narrative link which provides a summary of the previous account of creation connecting two units and is denoted "link A." Passage (2) contains the text of Gen 2:4–25 which has the precursory link B and four units of narrative. The patterns in passage (3) are designed to show the origin of sin and its consequences.

Gen 1:24–3:24 present a field for the development of three pairs of contrasts: true worship versus idolatry; life versus death; the modest cult conduct versus cultic fornication.[5] The last contrast is the reason for the Torah's prescription of a cultic

---

2. Gordon Wenham and Allen Ross view the passage in Gen 1:1–2:3 as the first part of Genesis, which "stands apart from the narratives" and is called "an overture to the whole work." The opposite opinion, upheld by the majority of modern scholars, insists that "the opening section of Genesis ends with 2:4a, not with 2:3." However, Wenham shows two arguments against this view: 1) it is unusual for the phrase, "this is the story of," to conclude a section, while elsewhere in Genesis it introduces a development of a new passage; 2) it is unlikely that the source splits up in the middle of the verse. Wenham's view is supported by J. Cross and Tengström. Wenham, *Genesis 1–15*, 5–6. Ross, "Genesis," 42.

3. Allen Ross states that everything created before was "prepared for the final creation of human beings." Ross, "Genesis," 39.

4. The reason for marking units by 1' and 2' is that they are the last two units of the passage (1). However, as the previous units are not relevant to the present study, it seems appropriate to omit them and make the sixth day of creation form *Unit one'*.

5. M. Bockmuehl notes that midrash created by rabbis shows that Genesis 2.16–17 is a basis for "six commandments given to Adam," which include "the prohibition of idolatry, blasphemy, adjudication, homicide, illicit sex, theft" (*Gen. Rab.* 16.6; 24.5; *Deut. Rab.* 2.25; *Cant. Rab.*1.16; *b. Sanh.* 56b; *Pesiq. Rab Kah.* 12.1). The rabbis believed that those commandments were relevant to all human beings. Bockmuehl, *Jewish Law in Gentile Churches*, 150–51.

service tending to remove sexuality from the cultic practices (wearing of the cultic long dress, concentration of the priestly service in the hands of one sex, and sexual abstinence before the great feasts). At the same time the pagan cults employed sexuality in the cultic practices in the form of cultic fornication (demonstrative nakedness, temple prostitution, orgies).[6] This contrast suggests that the ban on cultic fornication in Torah is the background for the apostolic prohibition of πορνεία.[7]

True Worship versus Idolatry in Genesis 1–3 and the Apostolic Prohibition of εἰδωλοθύτων

The narrative in Gen 1–3 describes the creation (1:1–3:1) and the fall (3:2–24). The creation story opens with the theme of true, undivided worship. This true undivided worship was maintained until the fall. The fall passage narrates the first act of idolatry. The period pictured in Gen 1:24–3:1 reflects some features of the true worship. According to the diagram, it correlates to passages 1 and 2.[8] Passage 3 (Gen 3:2–24) by contrast narrates the entry of idolatry.

True Worship Established at the Creation

The first aspect of true worship in the creation narrative is the holiness of God. *Unit two* for the first time refers to the holiness of the Creator God. His holiness is assumed from the fact that he makes things holy. His sanctification of time plays also a significant role.[9] Main verbs of this unit describe God as an acting subject. Here, ἡμέραν τὴν ἑβδόμην becomes the object of his action. God ηὐλόγησεν "blessed" the seventh day and ἡγίασεν αὐτήν "made it holy."[10] Thus, God designates the special "holy time' for worship.[11]

6. Brian S. Rosser notes that "the link between sexual immorality and idolatry may point to the practice of prostitution occurring in the context of pagan worship." Rosser, "Temple Prostitution in 1 Corinthians 6:12–20," 344.

7. The equation of πορνεία with cultic fornication will be argued in section 2 of this chapter.

8. Passages 1 and 2 are represented by diagrams in Appendix 2. They include the text of Gen 1:1—3:1 (LXX) and describe the story of creation before the fall. The passages are divided into units and narrative links. Passage 1 contains three parts, which are designated *Unit one*' (Gen 1:24–31), the narrative link A (Gen 2:1), and *Unit two*' (Gen 2:2, 3). Passage 2 contains five parts, which are the narrative link B (Gen 2:4–6), *Unit one* (Gen 2:7), *Unit two* (Gen 2:8–15), *Unit three* (Gen 2:16–17), *Unit four* (Gen 2:18–3:1).

9. *Unit two*' reflects the sanctification of the seventh day.

10. According to Ross, "make holy" means "setting apart to the worship and service of the Lord." Ross, "Genesis," 41. Waltke states that the seventh day "is the first thing in the Torah to which God imparts his holiness." Waltke, *Genesis*, 68.

11. Waltke notices that the word ἡγίασεν presumes the separation of the seventh day from other days and pictures it as "the first thing in the Torah to which God imparts his holiness and so sets apart to himself (Exod 20:11)." He believs that on the Sabbath day God summons humanity "to confess God's lordship and their consecration to him." Waltke, *Genesis*, 67–68.

The second aspect of worship is human accessibility to God. *Unit one* part 2 (Gen 1:26–31) describes the close relationship between God and humans.[12] Here, the impersonal cohortative command, "let there be," of the previous days changes to the personal "let us," which reflects the personal involvement of God. Humans are described as created κατ'εἰκόνα of God and καθ' ὁμοίωσιν of God.[13] This makes people "God's image-bearers on earth."[14] The ability to reflect God's likeness spiritually also leads people into worship relationships. According to Ross, the place of worship was a temple-garden.[15] All these features suggest the context of true worship in Eden from creation.[16]

The third aspect of worship is contained in the pronouncement of blessings (Gen 1:27–30). Blessings in the OT are often linked with true worship. The wording of the part 2 in *Unit one* reveals the extensive character of blessings. The blessings include four main aspects (αὐξάνεσθε, πληθύνεσθε, πληρώσατε τὴν γῆν, κατακυριεύσατε αὐτῆς).[17] Three of these four blessings relate to marital relationships. The fourth blessing (κατακυριεύσατε) presupposes dominion over all the earth. Dominion is expressed further by ἄρχετε over all living creatures. At this point the prominent role of people within the entire creation appears.[18] The humans' task was to be priests in the created world.[19] The thought that Eden can be understood as the first temple-garden

---

12. Its diagram is provided in Appendix 2.

13. Ross believes that "image" means that humans share with God abilities of "intelligence, knowledge, spiritual standing, creativity, wisdom, love, compassion, holiness, justice . . ." He considers that "all these capacities were given by the inbreathing of the breath of life." Ross, "Genesis," 39–40.

14. The term εἰκών, translated "likeness, image," is attributed in OT to both humans and idols. Also ὅμοιος means "similar, resembling." Muraoka, *Greek-English Lexicon*, 192, 496.

15. Here the description of the garden with trees, river, the pure gold and precious gems pictures special symbols of the garden sanctuary. Later, many of these features will be imitated in the earthly sanctuary. Finally, the heavenly sanctuary in a new creation will keep the same details (Rev 21:10–11, 21; 22:1–2). Ross, "Genesis," 45.

16. Waltke, *Genesis*, 86. He viewes not only the fellowship between humans and God, but also the context of a worship.

17. Waltke mentions only two, which are procreation and dominion. Waltke, *Genesis*, 67. However, three first orders are not homogenous. The order "be fruitful" likely represents procreation ability, while "increase in number" shows the growth of humankind, and the phrase "fill the earth" relates to territorial domain.

18. Humans became "the apex of the created order: the whole narrative moves toward the creation of man." Wenham, *Genesis*, 38.

19. Thus, Gary Anderson demonstrates that "not only is Eden modeled on the Temple—a common topos in Jewish and Christian literature—but the very sin of Adam is understood as a violation of the laws of Temple-purity." Anderson, "Celibacy or Consummation," 143. Also, Ross notes here that the "service to the Lord" is presumed rather than just simply "working of land." The word "serve" in 2:15 is used frequently in Torah in meaning "serving the Lord" (Deut 28:47) and described Levitical service (Num 3:7–8; 4:23–24, 26). Also, "keep" would reflect the Levitical duties (Num 3:7–8; 8:26; 18:5–6). So, it can be assumed now that man was placed in the garden for both purposes: serving God and keeping the created world. Ross, "Genesis," 46–47.

has been expressed by Waltke, Wenham and Ross.[20] This makes humans key figures in earthly worship.[21] Their theomorphic nature presumes global (for the whole world) and personal (for themselves) components of worship.

The assignation of food for humans (v. 29) and animals (v. 30) can be assumed as primordial table fellowship at the close of worship.[22] Here the phrase πᾶν ξύλον in v. 29 is taken in a general sense, while later two special trees are appointed for a different purpose.[23] The presence of God in Eden at this time can be linked to true worship and table fellowship.[24] The images of trees, fruit and table fellowship often appear in Israel's sanctuary. The table fellowship in the presence of God prefigures the imagery of the banquet in the heavenly kingdom (this biblical motif appears in Matt 22:2–10; 25:10; Luke 5:34; 12:36, 37; 13:29; Rev 19:9).

The fourth aspect of true worship consisted of keeping the covenant that is described in *Unit three* (Gen 2:16–17). It shows humans' responsibility for true worship.[25] It is interesting that two special trees represented two opposite conditions. In taking from one, humans automatically were refusing the other. After people took from the fruit of the tree of knowledge, they lost access to the garden-temple, the tree of life and the holy presence of God.[26] Consequently, unfaithfulness to the covenant dramatically affected their worship. This thought will be explained by the diagram for *Unit three*.

Unit three continues the theme of the trees of the garden described in *Unit two* (Gen 2:8–15). The only tree mentioned separately from the group of trees designed for food was the tree of knowledge.[27] This tree represented the possibility of annihilation,

---

20. Wenham sees the garden as not only a home, but also "an archetypal sanctuary, prefiguring the later tabernacle and temples." He views it to be the place where God dwells. Wenham, *Genesis*, 61. Ross supports this view and states that the work of man was appointed in a context of a sanctuary service, rather than merely working the ground. After the fall, the work of man "became focused on serving the ground to survive, while the work of keeping the way to the tree of life was given over to the angels (3:24)." Ross, "Genesis," 47.

21. The role of man on the earth is to be a priest in the garden temple, which was separated from the rest of creation. Waltke, *Genesis*, 81.

22. The garden at this moment is pictured as a "banqueting table." Waltke, *Genesis*, 86.

23. Waltke sets two trees separately from the "all kind of trees." He believes that the tree of knowledge served as a possibility of "ethical awareness." Waltke, *Genesis*, 86.

24. Wenham notes that "paradise in Eden and the later tabernacle share a common symbolism . . . of the presence of God." He assumes it from the fact that the great river is a symbol of the "life-giving presence of God." This assumption was made on the basis of links between Gen 2 and Ps 46:5 and Ezek 47:1–12. Wenham, *Genesis*, 65.

25. The diagram for the *Unit three* of passage 2 is given in Appendix 2.

26. The supporting data can be found in the work of Michael Morales, who believes that "Creation in Genesis . . . is described as a temple." Morales, *Tabernacle Pre-Figured*, 88. See also Anderson, "Biblical Origins," 19–21, 28–29.

27. At this time the narrative in chapter 2 "forms the basis for the account of the temptation" described in chapter 3. Ross, "Genesis," 43.

which is the reverse condition of creation.[28] The tree of life is not mentioned in *Unit three*, while it was mentioned in *Unit two*. This omission may presume the association of the tree of life with the other good trees in the temple garden. After the fall the picture changes radically and the tree of life becomes separated from all other trees, set apart for the Lord and protected from fallen humans.[29] Later in the sanctuary, the tree of life becomes associated with the things made "holy."[30] The reversal seems to be pictured by contrast between two special trees of the garden.

In text of *Unit three* (2:16, 17) the tree of knowledge was separated from others through the use of the contrasting particle δὲ. The structure of the covenant thus was built between two parallel clauses, which both start with ἀπὸ. The first clause appears as a main rule, ἀπὸ παντὸς ξύλου τοῦ ἐν τῷ παραδείσῳ βρώσει φάγῃ, and the second clause as an exception to the main rule, ἀπὸ δὲ τοῦ ξύλου τοῦ γινώσκειν καλὸν καὶ πονηρόν, οὐ φάγεσθε ἀπ' αὐτοῦ.[31] The exception is strengthened by the double reference "from the tree" (ἀπὸ δὲ in the beginning of the phrase and ἀπ'αὐτοῦ at the end).[32]

The explanation given after the covenant formula starts with ᾗ δ' and then clearly states, θανάτῳ ἀποθανεῖσθε.[33] The inevitability of death is stressed by the indicator ἂν ἡμέρᾳ. Thus the conditional clause shows that ἂν ἡμέρᾳ φάγητε ἀπ' αὐτοῦ (in the day in which you eat from it) the result follows θανάτῳ ἀποθανεῖσθε (you will die by death).[34] Thus, the structure of *Unit three* then creates a core of the covenant with only two possible ways: life or death.[35] The phrase θανάτῳ ἀποθανεῖσθε presumes the reversal of life by death.

---

28. Ross, "Genesis," 45. This tree was a potential disaster for people. To eat its fruit meant to decide who will control their lives.

29. According to Waltke, though the tree of life is mentioned first in the narrative, people focus on the second one, likely because of prime concern for power, and not life. Waltke, *Genesis*, 86.

30. The tree of life was not only the symbol of fullness of life, but also was associated with holy things. After the fall, people are separated from this tree. Later, the menorah of the sanctuary "was a stylized tree of life." Morales, *Tabernacle Pre-Figured*, 89.

31. The prohibitions of the Apostolic Decree were designed similarly: the first line of the Decree provided the main rule, while the second listed the necessary exceptions.

32. The structure of this sentence in Hebrew reveals a perfect balance established between the two poles, "you shall" and "you shall not" with help of the coordinating conjunction *vav*, "and/but." Korsak, "Fresh Look," 141. The similar construction of the Apostolic Decree in Acts 15:19, 20 and 28, 29 also reflects a permission in the first part of the phrase and the prohibition in the second part, connected by the adversative conjunction ἀλλὰ in 15:20 and πλὴν in 15:28.

33. According to Speiser the phrase can be better translated "you shall be doomed to death." This shows death as the result of separation from a source of life. Speiser, *Genesis*, 17.

34. Here, not only physical, but also a spiritual death is in view. Waltke, *Genesis*, 87. The capacity of death locked in the tree of knowledge suggests viewing it as opposite to holiness (since death is unclean in the Torah).

35. Wenham notes that this first prohibition "resembles in its form the Ten Commandments: לֹא 'not' followed by the imperfect." According to Wenham, this form of command "is used for long standing prohibitions." Wenham, *Genesis*, 67.

Thus, the first covenant linked obedience with fullness of life and disobedience with death.[36] At the same time both options were connected to food. Thus the first prohibition is given in connection to food.[37] This fact presupposes that the prohibition "is the paradigm for the future Torah legislation relating to dietary laws."[38] Moreover, the contrast between holy and common was later brought forth in the ritual system of Israel. Yet, the origin of the distinction between holy and common is rooted in creation-fall narrative of Gen 1–3.[39]

The way in which the first prohibition was introduced is: καὶ ἐνετείλατο κύριος ὁ θεὸς τῷ Αδαμ λέγων. This emphasis on "Yahweh God" defines the first humans as "people of God."[40] The selection of humans by God for his image-bearing and keeping of the temple-garden required keeping the first covenant as well.[41] God's purpose was to reveal himself to human beings with the help of the covenant relationship.[42] Keeping the first covenant, people could share with God the knowledge of faithfulness. The knowledge of a faithful God would let people worship him in truth. That is why the keeping the covenant has to be assumed as part of true worship.

The First Idolatry Described in the Fall Narrative

Terje Stordalen notes that "in Genesis 2–3 a human attempt to copy divinity occurs, only as a hidden conflict."[43] The diagram in Appendix 2 helps to reveal this hidden controversy between true worship and idolatry.[44] Thus passage 3 pictures the fall. This picture begins with *Unit five* (3:1–5) and describes the temptation.[45] Unit starts with the representation of a new personage.[46] The alternative conjunction δὲ in the

---

36. Russell Reno shows that "the divine legislation at Sinai frames a choice that recapitulates the original situation in Eden." This is revealed in the call of Moses, in Deut 30:15–18, to choose between life and good or death and evil. He states that although "the larger New Testament judgment that Gentile Christians are not subject to the full scope of Mosaic law, we cannot imagine that new life in Christ transcends the basic pattern of commandment and obedience." Reno, *Genesis*, 71.

37. Stephen Reed observing documents of the Qumran community notes that food plays an important role in their covenant relationship with God. Food represented God's blessings, because the divine provision of food was known since Gen 1–2. Festive food also signified immortality of the future messianic banquet. Reed, "Role of Food," 138, 159.

38. Sarna, *Genesis*, 21.

39. Gen 1–3 "provides essential background to the primeval history, which provides background for the patriarchal, exodus, and tabernacle narratives." Block, "Eden," 21.

40. Ross, "Genesis," 43. It shows that the Gen 1–3 narrative was fundamental for the following Exodus story. That is why the motifs of Exodus always can be traced back in time to the time of creation-fall.

41. Walton, *Genesis*, 52.

42. Walton, *Genesis*, 52.

43. Stordalen, *Echoes of Eden*, 289.

44. Passage 3 is represented in a diagram in Appendix 2.

45. The diagram in *Unit five* of the passage 3 is in Appendix 2.

46. Ross notes that the curse pronouncement on the serpent in Gen 3:14–15 presumes a reference

phrase ὁ δὲ ὄφις is employed to make a contrast with the previously stated harmony of the world and unity of the first pair. The serpent is described with the help of the adjective φρονιμώτατος, which is derived from φρόνιμος "wise, sensible, thoughtful, shrewder."[47] His craftiness was defined in superlative degree as excelling all other animals (ἦν φρονιμώτατος πάντων τῶν θηρίων τῶν ἐπὶ τῆς γῆς).[48] It is described as wiser than all land animals, yet it was not wiser than humans and God the Creator. That is why part 1 (3:1) stresses that the serpent represents the animal kingdom, was made by God (ὧν ἐποίησεν κύριος ὁ θεός), and belonged to God.

The serpent started to talk in human language and delivered a logically constructed speech. Its words appear to be motivated by sympathy and care for the humans. The serpent's question Τί ὅτι εἶπεν ὁ θεός οὐ μὴ φάγητε ἀπὸ παντὸς ξύλου τοῦ ἐν τῷ παραδείσῳ ("Is that what God said: do not eat from any trees in the garden?") implies a harsh degree of limitations.[49] The reference to God in the epexegetical clause ὅτι εἶπεν ὁ θεός implied that the limitation was caused by God's commandment.[50] The question insinuates that nobody in the world cares for the humans' wellbeing except the serpent.[51]

The words of the dialogue here represent an archetypal way of temptation.[52] The serpent initiates the dialogue with the human couple. Answering, the woman repeats the same structure of the commandment preserved in *Unit three* (2:16, 17), when the covenant was given in two parallel statements, both starting with ἀπὸ and linked by the adversative conjunction δὲ. She, however, does not call the tree ξύλον τόν γινώσκειν καλὸν καὶ πονηρόν.[53] Instead, she puts stress on its location, saying, ξύλον, ὅ ἐστιν ἐν μέσῳ τοῦ παραδείσου.

To the words of the command οὐ φάγεσθε ἀπ' αὐτοῦ ("do not eat of it") found in *Unit three*, the woman adds οὐδὲ μὴ ἅψησθε αὐτοῦ ("do not touch it").[54] This double

---

to it as to a reptile (3:14) as well as to a spiritual force behind it (3:15). That spiritual force in 3:1 "used the form of an actual reptile," which agrees with Rev 12:7; 20:2. Ross, "Genesis," 49–50.

47. Muraoka, *Greek-English Lexicon*, 720. He suggests meaning "shrewd in judgment."

48. It is noteworthy that "early Jewish and Christian commentators identified the snake with Satan." Wenham, *Genesis*, 72.

49. Waltke shows that the serpent "subverts obedience and distorts perspective by emphasizing God's prohibition, not his provision, reducing God's command to a question, doubting his sincerity, defaming his motives, and denying the truthfulness of his threat." Waltke, *Genesis*, 91.

50. Wallace, *Greek Grammar*, 661–62, 678. The way in which the serpent uses simply a title "God" instead of "the Lord God" (which is how God is usually called in Gen 2–3) pictures the serpent's distance from God. Wenham, *Genesis*, 73.

51. Sarna notes that the serpent pretends to be the woman's friend, "solicitous of her interests." Sarna, *Genesis*, 27.

52. Ross, "Genesis," 50. He notes that the temptation of Jesus, described in Matt 4:1–11, becomes a counterpart of the temptation in the garden.

53. Here, "knowing" can mean "distinguishing between" as in 2 Sam 19:35 and 1 Kgs 3:9 and reflects moral or physical matters, and not a process of divination. Speiser, *Genesis*, 26.

54. Wallace, *Greek Grammar*, 667, 669. The coordinating conjunction οὐδὲ creates a paratactic

denial strengthens the prohibition.⁵⁵ The subordinate phrase following, reveals the purpose of the prohibition by the purpose conjunction ἵνα: ἵνα μὴ ἀποθάνητε ("in order that you will not die").⁵⁶ Thus, the woman states that the prohibition was given only about one particular tree in order to prevent death.

Part 3 of *Unit five* (3:4, 5) provides the final and convincing statement of the serpent, after which the woman stops to argue, and starts to act. The words of the serpent, οὐ θανάτῳ ἀποθανεῖσθε, include the negative adverb οὐ appearing with the future indicative ἀποθανεῖσθε.⁵⁷ The Greek phrase can be translated, "you will not die." Walton notices that the serpent's statement can be paraphrased, "Don't think that death is such an immediate threat."⁵⁸

When the serpent provides his own explanation of the prohibition, he again refers to God, though not to what God has said. The serpent refers to what God thinks (this is obvious in the phrase ᾔδει γὰρ ὁ θεὸς).⁵⁹ Then the serpent tells what God knows and hides from people: ὅτι . . . διανοιχθήσονται ὑμῶν οἱ ὀφθαλμοί, καὶ ἔσεσθε ὡς θεοὶ γινώσκοντες καλὸν καὶ πονηρόν.⁶⁰ The result conjunction, ὅτι, shows the result of the knowledge obtained: "you will be like God."⁶¹

The serpent links the knowledge of good and evil to the ability to obtain the divine status. The comparative conjunction ὡς points to the equality of status.⁶² The two other promises expressed with the help of participles can be viewed as parallel sayings: διανοιχθήσονται ὑμῶν οἱ ὀφθαλμοί (your eyes will be opened) and γινώσκοντες καλὸν καὶ πονηρόν (you will be knowing good and evil). The process, called the "opening" of eyes, was presented in terms of enlightenment, in order to emphasize the limits of human eyes, which cannot see the hidden meanings of things.⁶³ Here, the serpent also reveals the good knowledge of the commandment, quoting the part of its

---

connection linking equal elements together. Here, it links two denial phrases, οὐ φάγεσθε ἀπ' αὐτοῦ ("do not eat of it") and μὴ ἅψησθε αὐτοῦ ("do not touch").

55. Here, μὴ introduces an emphatic negation subjunctive, the "strongest way to negate something in Greek." The coordinating conjunction οὐδὲ has the meaning "and not," plus the negative conjunction μὴ with the second-person plural future indicative ἅψησθε. Wallace, *Greek Grammar*, 468–69.

56. Wallace, *Greek Grammar*, 676.

57. This construction is unusual with the negative particle placed in front of the words of penalty. Ross, "Genesis," 51–52. Thus, the serpent puts "not" before the cited words of God, "you will certainly die" and adds different divine motivation. Wenham, *Genesis*, 74.

58. Walton, *Genesis*, 205.

59. Here, the serpent pictures itself as "able to probe God's mind and intent." Sarna, *Genesis*, 24.

60. Here, the serpent promises divinity which was wrongly and jealously reserved by God from the people. It was stated that the full potential of people is "to be gods." Ross, "Genesis," 52.

61. Wallace, *Greek Grammar*, 677.

62. Wallace, *Greek Grammar*, 675.

63. At this point Gen 3:5 has a link to 2:25, where it was stated that all creation was "very good" even though the couple was naked. After eating of fruit, the vision of people became different, in the sense of a letdown. Wenham, *Genesis*, 76.

wording, ἐν ᾗ ἂν ἡμέρᾳ φάγητε ἀπ' αὐτοῦ, which the woman has omitted. However, the serpent uses the quotation in the opposite way and states that the immediate result of the action will be not death, but divination.[64]

At this point the serpent claims the particular food can make someone like God. The serpent claims to have his personal knowledge, separate from God's knowledge.[65] His knowledge was not based on the word of God, but rather on the serpent's own experience of enlightenment. This, and the ability of the serpent to speak human language, could create an illusion of supernatural abilities, which accompany special knowledge. Thus people were told that the commandment of God instead of protecting them from death, hinders them from getting the advantages of the special knowledge.[66] The knowledge of good and evil was said to help to become gods and judges.[67] The idea of the plurality of gods (θεοί) comes forward at this time.[68]

This idea of a plurality of gods stands in contrast to monotheism and thus appears first in Gen 1 and 2. Even the serpent is described as ὦν ἐποίησεν κύριος ὁ θεός ("which God made"). The tree of knowledge was also planted by God (ἐξανέτειλεν ὁ θεὸς . . . τὸ ξύλον τοῦ εἰδέναι γνωστὸν καλοῦ καὶ πονηροῦ). Despite the fact that God was the Creator of the universe, the serpent suggested that created beings also may become gods. The serpent called people to use the forbidden fruit as food for the purpose of obtaining divine status. Acting like this, people would accept the possibility of the existence of many gods and commit idolatry. In addition to idolatry, the serpent invited humans to use the forbidden fruit as the first εἰδωλοθύτων. They are convinced that the divination depends on the particular food. The eating of this fruit, prompted by the belief in its supernatural power, makes humans participants in the first sacrifice to false gods, created beings; later are reflected in the form of idols.

Unit six of passage 3 (3:6–8) depicts sin as the force reversing the process of creation.[69] Part A shows the mechanism of the transgression, which also can be subdivided into two stages. The first stage reveals the change of mind, when the understanding of the protective role of a prohibition is replaced by the view of it as something rigorously suppressing desires. It is evident from the development of the woman's thought which goes from ὅτι καλὸν . . . εἰς βρῶσιν (the aspect of physical need) to ὅτι ἀρεστὸν

---

64 Here, Duane Smith shows the possibility of play in Hebrew, between "snake" and "practice divination" along with its nominal forms. Also the phrase "you will be like gods knowing good and evil" could presume the context of divination, in terms of "fortune" or "misfortune." The phrase could mean "those who know the results of divination." Smith, "Divine Snake," 36, 42.

65. Thus, the serpent calls humans to use "moral autonomy, deciding what is right without reference to God's revealed will." Wenham, *Genesis*, 64.

66. Waltke sees that the knowledge which people were seeking is not a need for "more information, but hunger for power." Waltke, *Genesis*, 91–92.

67. The new knowledge is pictured in terms of "new mental powers, with the capacity for reflection that allows one to make decisions independently of God." Sarna, *Genesis*, 25.

68. Waltke, *Genesis*, 91.

69. The diagram for the *Unit six* of the passage 3 is provided in Appendix 2.

τοῖς ὀφθαλμοῖς ἰδεῖν (the aesthetic aspect) and then to ὡραῖόν ἐστιν τοῦ κατανοῆσαι, meaning, "is attractive to consider/contemplate" (the aspect of a desire and changes on the mental level).[70] The word τοῦ κατανοῆσαι here may reflect a human interest not only in the physical phenomenon of the forbidden fruit. It also presumes a desire for intellectual meditation on forbidden things, which brings mental changes. In this manner, desire becomes strengthened by the imagination which, influenced by desire, results in making the wrong decision.[71]

Although God made the trustworthiness of his word evident to humans in creation, they decided to rely upon the words of the serpent. The serpent's words, in contrast, were confirmed only by his own testimony and the supernatural ability to speak human language. This should not be enough to prove the statements pronounced against God to be false. However, Adam and Eve accepted the serpent's words and personal experience of enlightenment as a trustworthy source of knowledge. It led to the situation in which the interest in divine knowledge was overestimated, while the consequences were overlooked.

As a result, the woman makes her decision to eat the fruit and break the commandment. The actions of the woman are described by a participle, λαβοῦσα, followed by the chain of aorists ἔφαγεν . . . ἔδωκεν. Aorist ἔφαγον describes Adam's action and concludes the chain of aorists in v. 6.[72] The emphasis put on τῷ ἀνδρὶ αὐτῆς μετ' αὐτῆς reveals that Adam was present at the dialogue with the serpent, however his role remained passive.[73] Adam seems to follow the decision of his wife, who was a created being, and who followed the persuasion of another created being.

Acting in this manner, Adam neglected relying on the word of the Creator himself. That is why throughout the whole biblical revelation, an ability to trust the word of God becomes central to true worship.[74] On the contrary, attempts to serve mystical sources of knowledge, which claim to exist apart from God, become the subject of

---

70. Sarna, *Genesis*, 25.

71. Ross also notes the removal of punishment and doubts in God's goodness as the elements supporting transgression. Ross, "Genesis," 52.

72. Wenham notes that the scene in vv. 6–8 comes to a central point "and he ate." Before this the expectations are mentioned, and after, the actual consequences are shown. Wenham, *Genesis*, 75.

73. The role of Adam in the fall narrative was recently discussed by David Stein. Jewish tradition uses the term "Adam's sin" pointing to him as the participant of the drama. Although Eve was denoted as the leader in making the decision, Adam was accused "not for failing to stop Eve but for eating the fruit (v. 17)." Stein, "Rejoinder Concerning Genesis 3:6," 51–52. Also, Sarna believes that Adam was "a full participant in the sin." Speaking to the woman the serpent uses a plural form, φάγητε and ἔσεσθε ὡς θεοί, and refers to them both in the phrase οἱ ὀφθαλμοί (Gen 3:5). Sarna concludes that "the man was all the time within ear's reach of the conversation and was equally seduced by its persuasiveness." Sarna, *Genesis*, 25.

74. This has support from Matt 4:1–10, which describes the testing of Jesus by Satan. There, Satan began his temptation with a question concerning bread, but finished with questions about the center of true worship. Jesus, unlike Adam, withstood Satan by relying on the word of God. Also, Jesus' call for faith addressed to his contemporaries when he miraculously saves one, becomes explicable in view of the original lack of faith of that led to the fall.

idolatry. Food eaten for the purpose of becoming like θεοὶ could be considered the first εἰδωλοθύτων.

Part B of *Unit six* (3:7–8) reveals those consequences that were overlooked by people at the time of their idolatry. The first result of sin was guilt, expressed by shame (or feeling of self-abhorrence) and fear of God. This part of the narrative pictures the ineffective attempts of people to deal with their guilt, at the level of removal of its external signs.

The second statment reveals the spiritual, rather than physical nature of the event, when it says, ἔγνωσαν ὅτι γυμνοὶ ἦσαν, meaning, "they perceived that they were naked," which presumed their acquiring of knowledge.[75] Here, the subordinated clause shows what kind of knowledge the people received.[76] Their perception of themselves as γυμνοὶ reflects the negative experience of shame caused by a defiled nature.[77] Although people covered their nakedness by leaves (ἐποίησαν ἑαυτοῖς περιζώματα), they could not remove the internal/spiritual consequences of the fall.[78] Their guilt resulted also in realization of spiritual imperfection and took the form of fear.

Thus, when they heard the voice of the Lord in the garden, they hid themselves from the face of the Lord God. The phrase, ἐκρύβησαν ὅ τε Αδαμ καὶ ἡ γυνὴ αὐτοῦ ἀπὸ προσώπου κυρίου τοῦ θεοῦ, reflects the tendency of a fallen (defiled) nature to flee from the presence of the Holy God.[79] "Hiding among the trees of the garden" (ἐν μέσῳ τοῦ ξύλου τοῦ παραδείσου), denotes in people an attempt to isolate themselves from holy things. The attempt to become θεοὶ turned to be an apostasy from God. Consequently, the "opening" of eyes and "knowing of good and evil" became synonymous with "defilement" that was a result of the first idol worship.

Units five and *six* of Gen 3 show that food became an instrument by which a sin was committed. The food was believed to activate human divination. In addition, *Genesis Rabbah* (Parashah 18:6.2) reveals the rabbinic assumption that sexual relationship was involved in the first temptation and transgression.[80] This thesis argues that instead of sexual intercource, to which *Genesis Rabbah* attributes the shame of nakedness,

---

75. Waltke believes that not only physical nakedness is presumed here, but also "describes someone in terms of being defenseless, weak, or humiliated (Deut 28:48; Job 1:21; Isa 58:7)." Waltke, *Genesis*, 92.

76. Russell Reno supposes the situation when the eye "becomes carnal, taking the physical and finite as the measure of all things." Reno, *Genesis*, 92.

77. Youngblood, *Book of Genesis*, 54. He shows that the shameful perception revealed a spiritual harm, which was lack of faith.

78. In the OT nakedness "is commonly employed as a symbol of guilt" and humiliation. Kulikovsky, *Creation, Fall, Restoration*, 201.

79. The word which describes God walking in the garden has special etymology. The participle "walking" περιπατοῦντος (Gen 3:8) from περιπατέω, which forms are used "of God's presence in Israelite tent sanctuary (Lev 26:12; Deut 23:15[14]; 2 Sam 7:6–7)." This fact stresses the typological association between the garden and later tabernacle and temples. Wenham, *Genesis*, 76.

80. Neusner, *Genesis Rabbah*, 196. The final editing of Genesis Rabbah is dated around 400 CE (according to Neusner).

there the implicit fornication, taken in a spiritual sense emerged. The indicator of that implicit fornication is the shame of nakedness, which appeared immediately after the eating of the fruit. This represents an implicit form of πορνεία (the perverse perception of sexuality). The phrase, καὶ διηνοίχθησαν οἱ ὀφθαλμοὶ τῶν δύο, καὶ ἔγνωσαν ὅτι γυμνοὶ ἦσαν, indicates that the change of their understanding of sexuality had happened. The fornication likely took place in the mind, which led to a feeling of shame. This observation suggests that the first εἰδωλοθύτων was a part of idolatry and included hidden inclination to πορνεία.

The controversy between true worship and idolatry stood in the background of the consumption of the first εἰδωλοθύτων. The apostolic prohibition of εἰδωλοθύτων presumed its connection to idol worship, which hindered the Gentiles from a complete conversion to Christ.[81] Moreover, the εἰδωλοθύτων in the Apostolic Decree is placed in line with two other dietary prohibitions and the prohibition of πορνεία. The New Testament reflection of this idea appears in Pauline anti-idol polemic. His view of εἰδωλοθύτων and its association with πορνεία will be sketched below in paragraph 3.

The discussion so far reveals that Genesis 1–3 establishes two patterns of worship: true worship of God, and idolatry. Controversy between holy and common as well as the reversal of life and death are rooted in Gen 1–3, and have to be viewed in light of the creation–fall–re-creation paradigm. While the fallen condition dominates humans, their theomorphic nature enables them to experience spiritual birth in terms of a re-creation process.[82] This spiritual birth of someone in response to the word of God is the repetition in miniature the process of the first creation. This allows placing the creation–fall–re-creation as part of the background to apostolic speeches in Acts 15.

Restoration of True Worship

Units seven (3:9–13) and *nine* (3:21–24) of passage 3 describe the restoration of true worship attempted by God. According to the structure of Genesis 3, the restoration includes confession of sin, dealing with the consequences of sin, and the process of redemption. The most significant feature of these units is the need for spiritual conversion (which is evident from the necessity of deep confession of sin) at the beginning of true worship. The units also reveal the need for faith in the saving power of God, establishment of the new style of worship, including bringing a sacrifice, and honouring the permitted and prohibited approaches to the holy place of God's presence. These ideas are explained below.

---

81. In Rev 2:14 εἰδωλοθύτων and πορνεία become the masks under which idol worship is veiled. The idolatry there is shown as "a significant threat to the churches." Beale, *John's Use of the Old Testament*, 97.

82. Waltke, *Genesis*, 70–71.

Unit seven (3:9–13) describes the confession of sin, reflecting God's deliberate choice to take the first step toward reconciliation.[83] This is evident from the words καὶ ἐκάλεσεν κύριος ὁ θεὸς τὸν Αδαμ: Αδαμ, ποῦ εἶ? God's deliberate action to save his fallen creatures would later provide a firm foundation for apostolic thought, expressed in the words of Peter in Acts 15:7 ἀφ' ἡμερῶν ἀρχαίων ἐν ὑμῖν ἐξελέξατο ὁ θεὸς.[84] Peter's election by God may refer not to the time of Peter's conversion, but to the time of the very beginning (Gen 1–3) and the salvation planned by God in his foresight since the fall. The phrase ἡμερῶν ἀρχαίων is the indicator of God's actions undertaken in the Genesis creation-fall narrative.

Peter's concluding statement, ἀλλὰ διὰ τῆς χάριτος τοῦ κυρίου Ἰησοῦ πιστεύομεν σωθῆναι, in Acts 15:11, also recalls the fall narrative of Gen 3. Here, salvation becomes possible only due to the grace of God who first comes to help. Similar thoughts form a core of James' speech, when he states, καθὼς πρῶτον ὁ θεὸς ἐπεσκέψατο, in Acts 15:14, where he expresses that the first step to reconciliation always is made by God. In Acts 15:17, 18 James stresses this idea even more in the phrase, λέγει κύριος ποιῶν ταῦτα γνωστὰ ἀπ' αἰῶνος.

While the first step of the worship restoration is made by God, the second requires confession of sin by humans. *Unit seven* represents a typical confession of sin. The man answers two times. In his first confession Adam concentrates on the external signs of his transgression, when he says καὶ ἐφοβήθην, ὅτι γυμνός εἰμι, καὶ ἐκρύβην.[85] However, God wants Adam to reconstruct the chain of events in the way which could explain the changes which happened to them. God needs Adam to realize that fear and shame become the emotional consequences of sin. God calls the man to deep self-examination, when he asks again: μὴ ἀπὸ τοῦ ξύλου . . . ἔφαγες; ("did you not eat from that tree?").

This question allowed Adam to focus on the internal issue which was the breaking of the covenant, expressed by οὗ ἐνετειλάμην σοι τούτου μόνου. The double reference to the tree (μὴ ἀπὸ τοῦ ξύλου . . . μὴ φαγεῖν ἀπ' αὐτοῦ) makes a frame for ἐνετειλάμην ("commanded"). The commandment then becomes the emphatic center of the question. This construction shows that the real reason for the fear and shame was the breaking of the commandment. This presumes the confession of sin on a deeper level and treats the core of the transgression, which is disobedience to God. The two levels of repentance are important for the Lukan account. The motif of inward obedience/

---

83. It was noted that here reverting to the term κύριος ὁ θεὸς takes place after a temporary shift in Gen 3:1–5 to simply ὁ θεὸς. Wenham emphasizes that "the narrator hints that God can still be man's covenant partner as well as his creator and judge." Wenham, *Genesis*, 76.

84. The detailed exegesis of the text of Acts 15 is provided in chapter 2. Chapter 3 reveals the connections between Acts 15 and Gen 3, and the thoughts in the background of the apostolic prohibitions.

85. God created humans in a condition which is identified by the phrase καλὰ λίαν. Now they describe their feeling as ἐφοβήθην and γυμνός. The "fear of God" and the perception of themselves as "naked" are connected. Though the nakedness was claimed to be a reason of the fear, it seems to be a projection of fear and shame on the physical condition of humans.

disobedience to God is often employed by Luke.[86] He contrasts the significance of inner spiritual conversion to God with the superficial performance of rites.

In *Unit seven* (3:9–13) each individual confesses their own sins. The serpent, however, stops speaking as soon as God appears, remaining speechless to the end of passage 3 and refusing confession.[87] Here the serpent becomes the type for unrepentant beings.[88] The serpent's punishment in *Unit eight* (3:14–20) appears to be the most harsh and leads ultimately to complete destruction (αὐτός σου τηρήσει κεφαλήν "he/it will crush your head"). The irreversible nature of demon uncleanness is demonstrated in Luke 8:26–40. The permanent uncleanness of demons can be figuratively compared to the permanent uncleanness of some creatures in Torah.[89] Those creatures illustrate a deep spiritual lesson.[90]

Concluding the study of *Unit seven*, one can suggest several links between Gen 1–3 and Acts 15, which were developed in chapter 2. The first link can be found in that the word of God was an instrument of creation at the beginning. *Unit one* (1:24—2:3) shows the structure of the creation process, which always turns around three main verbs εἶπεν, ἐποίησεν, εἶδεν . . . ὅτι καλά.[91] Here, creation is described as the deliberate act of God made by the power of his word.[92] In addition to this, *Unit seven* (3:9–13) pictures restoration of the relationship as a deliberate choice of God and also linked to the power of God's word.

The deliberate choice of God to start the re-creation lies in background of the wording, ἀφ' ἡμερῶν ἀρχαίων and ἐξελέξατο ὁ θεὸς διὰ τοῦ στόματός μου ἀκοῦσαι

---

86. Luke 1:6, 20; 2:25; 3:2–3, 8; 4:1–14; 5:27–32; 6:45; 7:30, 47; 8:11–15, 21; 11:24–26; 12:10, 16:15; 17:21; 18:9–14; 20:45–47; Acts 3:19; 5:3, 9; 7:51; 8:21; 10:44–47; 11:23–24; 15:8, 9; 16:14, 15; 28:27.

87. Wenham believes that the serpent was not given a chance to explain his sin. Wenham, *Genesis*, 78. This treatment of the serpent confirms its possession by a demon. When the demon disappeared, the serpent stopped talking. Then it became impossible to ask it for an explanation.

88. J. Beale links the serpent to the issue of the first uncleanness. He compares the garden of Eden to the first temple of God, which was defiled by the uncleanness of the serpent, the instrument of deceit. Beale, "Eden, the Temple," 8–10.

89. Lance Hawley notes that the uncleanness of animals is associated to their anatomic features (Lev 11:1–31), and this type of uncleanness has to be viewed as permanent (irreversible). Hawley, "Agenda of Priestly Taxonomy." Also Moskala states: "Unclean animals are unclean from birth to death, because this type of uncleanness is innate, hereditary, or natural. Nothing can change that—time, isolation, sacrifices, purification rites, killing, or cooking." Moskala, *Laws of Clean and Unclean*, 170.

90. The law of Lev 11:1–31 speaks only about animals, and nothing about demons. However, since the permanent uncleanness relates only to animals and to demons, the animals (visible beings) can be assumed as the illustration of uncleanness of the invisible spiritual beings. The example of the illustrative role of the unclean animals is reflected in Luke 8:26–40 which will be studied in chapter 4.

91. Wenham denotes a number of recurrent formulae in Gen1: 1) announcement of the commandment; 2) order; 3) fulfillment formula; 4) execution formula; 5) approval formula; 6) blessing; 7) mention of the days. Wenham, *Genesis*, 6.

92. It was noted that Gen 1 is linked to Pss 8, 136, 148, then to Prov 8:22–31 and Job 38. All these passages, together with Gen 1, exalt God the Creator. Moreover, although Gen 1 does not describe cultic concepts, it serves "to reinforce the significance and privilege of worship." Wenham, *Genesis*, 10.

τὰ ἔθνη τὸν λόγον τοῦ εὐαγγελίου, of Peter's speech in Acts 15:7. Here, the word of God becomes the instrument of re-creation. For Peter, λόγον τοῦ εὐαγγελίου, which reaches the nations signifies the time of a new beginning (in terms of the restoration of the world to its ideal state). The preaching of the Gospel to the Gentiles becomes the recreative instrument by which God begins a re-creation among them. It makes them καλὰ λίαν, sanctifies and unites them by the one true worship.

Unit nine (3:21–24) is important in view of the controversy between true worship and idolatry, because it reveals the redemption process.[93] The unit pictures the new style of worship established after the fall. The first part of the unit describes χιτῶνας δερματίνους "garments of skin." The Greek word χιτῶνας describes the kind of a dress which covers the whole body, except hands and legs.[94] The Hebrew term in MT for a "long dress" presumes garments appropriate in a worship context.[95] This contrasts with περιζώματα ("wrapped around/apron" in Greek and "gird/encircle" in Hebrew).[96] This can be viewed as the primitive variant of dress.[97] This contrast plays an important role in understanding of the third controversy between Israel's non-sexualized cult and the fornication of the pagan cults.[98] On a personal level this controversy can be stated as undefiled marriage versus pagan fornication.

The word δερματίνους, "leather," shows that the garment was made of animal skin.[99] This feature may indicate the bringing of the first sacrificial animals for the sins

93. The diagram for *Unit nine* of passage 3 is in Appendix 2.

94. Muraoka, *Greek-English Lexicon*, 733. The word χιτών means "garment worn next to the skin." The phrase χιτῶνας δερματίνους in Gen 3:21 refers to "leather garments." These garments were made to cover the body, not legs and hands. The long garment of a priest is also called χιτών in Exod 28:4 and is described as καὶ τὸν ποδήρη καὶ χιτῶνα κοσυμβωτόν; in Exod 29:5 it is called τὸν χιτῶνα τὸν ποδήρη that denotes a garment "so long as to reach down to the feet"; and in Lev 16:4 it is called χιτῶνα λινοῦν ἡγιασμένον.

95. Ross observes the fact of sacrifice here. He states that an "Israelite reader would think of sacrifice, as well, because in the Tabernacle the skins of the animals went to the priests for clothing." The clothing also became the symbol of God's "gracious provision." Ross, "Genesis," 57.

96. Muraoka, *Greek-English Lexicon*, 548. Here περίζωμα means "loin-cloth."

97. This Hebrew word elsewhere is used for a belt (1 Kgs 2:5; 2 Kgs 3:21; Isa 3:24), while the usual term for loincloth is אזור. Here the "skimpiness of their clothing is being emphasized." Wenham, *Genesis*, 76.

98. This contrast can be assumed at least from the fact that the Adamic myth in Ugaritic texts contains the explicit descriptions of sexuality emphasizing the importance of procreation, while the Hebrew narrative in Gen 3:7, 10 contrastingly is a lack of it, and reveals that nakedness became shameful. Korpel and Moor, *Adam, Eve, and the Devil*, 119.

99. Walton denies that the sacrifices of animals took place there. He views this clothing in garments of skin as an act of investiture (ceremony of installation of kings and priests in OT context). He views this as merely "an act of grace" of God, who prepared people for the more difficult environment outside the garden. Walton, *Genesis*, 230. The weakness of this view can be seen at three points: 1) In OT context the investiture of priests and kings was followed or even preceded by sacrifices (cf. Lev 8–9). 2) The removal of painful feeling of shame, guilt and frustration of Adam and Eve in that situation were more important than the preparation for a difficult environment. The redeeming sacrifice could be viewed as a remedy from it. 3) Sacrificial practice in Gen 4 needs to be attached to the time of initial sacrifice. This archetypal sacrifice dealing with the removal of sin has to be placed

of the people.[100] Garments made thus seem to be necessary for cultic purposes.[101] The fact that God made the garments for the first couple can be understood as the promise of a "new skin" (in terms of "new life"), and a new nature, which can be viewed as a restoration of bodies to the condition which they had before the fall.[102] God's action also demonstrated the cost of the restoration, which required a sacrifice, which should be viewed in terms of redemption.[103] Redemption shows that the consequences of the fall are not yet irreversible.

God then acted to prevent people from touching the tree of life.[104] The tree of life was to enable people ζήσεται εἰς τὸν αἰῶνα ("to live for a very long stretch of time ahead, for ever").[105] Eating of this fruit might make the fallen human condition irreversible. Human disobedience in regards to the forbidden fruit indicated that they would easily do the same with the fruit of another tree (this is clear from καὶ νῦν). It is expressed in the phrase, μήποτε ἐκτείνῃ τὴν καὶ λάβῃ τοῦ ξύλου τῆς ζωῆς καὶ φάγῃ, "lest [Adam] stretch forth [his hand] and take of the tree of life and eat"). Here the conjunction μήποτε has meaning "lest/ in order that . . . not."[106] This construction expresses the prevention of a possible action, and describes the need to prevent humans eating from the tree of life, which would make their condition irreversible.[107] The idea

---

somewhere before chapter 4, namely in Gen 3.

100. Wenham stresses that God "clothed them," which can refer either to honoring of kings or to "the dressing of priests in their sacred vestments, usually put on by Moses." The last variant is mentioned in Exod 28:41; 29:8; 40:14; Lev 8:13. He sees here the story in the garden associated with worship in the tabernacle. Wenham, *Genesis*, 84. Moreover, Richard Belcher believes that the fact that God uses animal skin to cover people's nakedness "foreshadows the importance of substitutionary sacrifice," which later appears in the OT. Belcher, *Genesis*, 76. See also Firmage, *Biblical Dietary*, 185–95. He argues that the sacrificial system preceded the dietary laws and the domestic animals were understood as the food for God. Though the present study does not view the sacrifices as God's food, it accepts the possibility of the first sacrifice in Eden, after the fall, in terms of the restoration of true worship.

101. Waltke also views those garments made from skins of "sacrificed'animals. The sacrifice was needed to remove the shame of sin and restore people to fellowship with God. Waltke, *Genesis*, 95.

102. According to the Georgian version of *Vita*, clothing with skin might mean the transformation of the body when one becomes covered with mortal human skin. Anderson, *Garments of Skin*, 140–43. The covering of human mortal skin with the new garments of skin in 3:21 were both an act of grace and a reassertion of the Creator's rights. Wenham, *Genesis*, 75.

103. Midrash in *Numbers Rabbah* 4.8 presumes that this first mention of garments of skin referred to the first sacrifice done by God, when people were still in the garden. Rubin and Kosman, "Clothing of the Primordial Adam," 172. Also, Reno views the garments of skin in terms of redemption. He finds the echoing of this verse in the NT (Rom 13:14; Col 2:9, 11; 2 Cor 5:1–2, 4; with reinforcement of the Genesis story by Job 19:26 and Isa 52:1). Reno, *Genesis*, 96.

104. The expulsion of sinful humans from the garden sanctuary was done in order to prevent the irreversible consequences of eating of the fruit of the tree of life. Instead, death should now "take its decreed course and end the life of toil and trouble." Ross, "Genesis," 58.

105. Muraoka, *Greek-English Lexicon*, 18–19. In Gen 3:22 αἰών means "forever."

106. McIver, *Intermediate NT Greek*, 211. For the meaning of μήποτε see Muraoka, *Greek-English Lexicon*, 460.

107. Here, "God forestalls man's next step towards self-divinization by his own preemptive first strike." Wenham, *Genesis*, 85.

of the transition of reversible sinfulness to an irreversible state finds its reflection in the writings of Luke and will be developed in chapter 4.

Gen 3:22–24 pictures the life of Adam and Eve only in its physical aspect (ἐργάζεσθαι τὴν γῆν, ἐξ ἧς ἐλήμφθη). Their life reflects a tendency to narrow their interests to the material world, not the spiritual. The aorists ἐξαπέστειλεν ("they were expelled, driven out"), ἐξέβαλεν ("they were made to move out") describe God's actions.[108] These actions can be viewed as a cleansing of the temple-garden (cf. John 2:12–17; Rev 21:27) from all κοινὸν things, namely, from defilement.[109] The idea of defilement, caused by touching and eating of the forbidden fruit, that divided the world into the holy and common things, has support in the OT pseudepigraph *The Books of Adam and Eve*, 6.1: "we are unworthy to address the Lord, for our lips are unclean from the unlawful and forbidden tree."[110] Here, the contrast between holy and common first appears. This act of expulsion suggests the dividing of the world into holy and common categories.[111]

The meaning of κατῴκισεν (aorist of κατοικίζω "cause to dwell") and ἀπέναντι ("opposite, before, in full view of") τοῦ παραδείσου τῆς τρυφῆς suggests that God did not oust them from his presence, but that God remained near people as well as people being in full view of God.[112] If so, people who were unable to live in the holy place or see a holy God, still could participate in true worship.[113] Two cherubs were appointed by God to guard the garden (ἔταξεν τὰ χερουβιμ "appointed/designated cherubs").[114] This may signify the continuity of true worship of God after the fall in a way similar to Exod 25:22: καὶ γνωσθήσομαί σοι ἐκεῖθεν καὶ λαλήσω σοι ἄνωθεν τοῦ ἱλαστηρίου ἀνὰ μέσον τῶν δύο χερουβιμ ("And there I will meet with you, and I will speak with you from above the mercy seat, from between the two cherubim").

---

108. Muraoka, *Greek-English Lexicon*, 204, 247

109. Waltke, *Genesis*, 96. It was noted that καινός "new," which appears in Rev 21:1, 2 in relation to a new heaven, new earth and new Jerusalem, presumes "renewal." Toenges, "'See I Am Making All Things New,'" 139. The theme of renewal in terms of cleansing is presumed in Rev 21:27, where the new city is pictured as free from the "unclean" matters.

110. The source dated by 388 CE. Wells, "Books of Adam and Eve," 126, 135.

111. Morales views Eden in the Gen 2–3 account as an archetypal holy of holies. He rightly notes that in Pentateuch the theme of worship is of the greatest importance. Morales, *Tabernacle Pre-Figured*, 88–89.

112. The fact that the divinely originated redemption of God takes place before the expulsion of humans from Eden shows that the eviction from Eden does not mean the elimination from the presence of God. Nixon, *Redemption in Genesis*, 45. The word "caused to camp" is associated "with God's camping in the tabernacle among people" (Exod 25:8). The cultic overtones, here, are "reinforced by the presence of cherubims . . . the traditional guardians of holy places." Wenham, *Genesis*, 86.

113. The motif of a true worship, here, can be assumed on basis of parallels with Exod 25:22 and Num 7:89 when two cherubs are mentioned over the ark in the tabernacle. Also, Jer 7:3–7 was noted as the corresponding reading. Raanan, "When God Abandoned the Garden of Eden," 23.

114. The cherubs were traditionally viewed as the guardian of the sanctuary. Morales, *Tabernacle Pre-Figured*, 88.

The phrase might link the cherubs to the sword τὴν φλογίνην ῥομφαίαν, "the fiery sword that turns around" by the conjunction καὶ. Both cherubs and sword protect/keep the way to the tree of life (τὴν φυλάσσειν τὴν ὁδὸν τοῦ ξύλου τῆς ζωῆς). However, the plural of τὰ χερουβιμ does not match the singular τὴν φλογίνην ῥομφαίαν. The cherubs seem not to be given enough swords.[115] The one sword, nevertheless, appears sufficient for protection of the tree. In rabbinic tradition the image of the fiery sword is linked to the time of judgment.[116] The fiery sword could represent condemnation.[117] If so, the role of cherubs here is not to obstruct the way to eternity, but to guard of it for people, namely, in continuation of true worship. Later, two cherubs were crafted on the cover of the ark of the testimony. From this point, one can argue that the only way into the holy presence of God is by true worship.[118] This worship includes calling upon the mercy and grace of God. Thus, true worship appears to be re-established on the basis of God's grace.

While the Old Testament links salvation to the sanctuary cult, the New Testament makes salvation possible in Christ alone. In the Lukan view, Christ becomes the fulfillment of the sanctuary cult and the ritual system.[119] Since the fulfillment of the Jewish temple cult, the early followers of Jesus inherit the restored true worship. If the physical aspect of the true worship was revealed and fulfilled in the messiahship of Jesus, his followers, according to Luke, practice the spiritual aspect of true worship. This explains the prominent role of the Holy Spirit in the writings of Luke.

---

115. Sarna also notices that the sword is "not said to be in the hands of the cherubim." The sword in MT and in Greek has the definite article τὴν φλογίνην ῥομφαίαν (Gen 3:24) and likely represents something well known to Israelites. Sarna, *Genesis*, 30.

116. Neusner, *Genesis Rabbah*, 237–38. Here, rabbis view the fiery sword as reference to final judgment, to Torah (Ps 149:6), and to circumcision.

117. The term "turning," here, can recall God's judgment in Midianite camp in Judg 7:13. The description of the divine sword as "flame" and "lightning" appears in Ezek 21:14–15. Lichtenstein, "Fearsome Sword of Genesis 3:24," 54. Also, Wenham states that "fire is a regular symbol of the presence of God, especially in judgment (e.g., Exod 19:18; Ps 104:4). The word τὴν στρεφομένην here means "to turn itself." This expression is used in description "of the cake, which 'rolled' into the camp of Midian in Judg 7:13." Wenham, *Genesis*, 86.

118. After the fall, the life of people turns around two concepts: holiness is related to life, while ṭāmē' "impurity" stands for the forces of death. Milgrom, *Leviticus 1–16*, 733.

119. Robert Badenas discusses the use of Lev 18:5 by Paul in Rom 10:5. He shows that τέλος νόμου (τέλος + genitive) indicates the result, purpose, fulfillment and object of the law, and not its abrogation or termination. He states that "Paul equated 'the righteousness taught by the law' with 'righteousness by faith' in a clearly new way, meaning . . . that doing the righteousness taught by the law is coming to Christ for salvation." Badenas, *Christ the End of the Law*, 79, 125, 145. In addition, Peter Scaer notes that the ritual law plays a significant role up to the end of the book of Acts, "but it begins to take on the character of pious religious custom," when the purity laws are no longer necessary things, and when "decisions on keeping the Law begin to have more to do with tradition, diplomacy, and strategy." Scaer, "Luke, Jesus, 106–7. It seems that the "fulfillment of the law" in Christ means that the ritual law of Torah reached its highest purpose in Christ.

Life versus Death and the Apostolic Prohibition of αἷμα

The controversy between life and death forms the second antithesis of Gen 1–3.[120] This antithesis provides a deep spiritual meaning for humans, whose actions inflicted the curse of death on the whole creation. Humans alone are intelligent enough to weigh the consequences of sin, although animals also are included in the life and death controversy, they serve only as an illustration of the spiritual concept for humans.[121] That is why Torah views the life-death antithesis from a human perspective, namely, repeating the pattern of the creation of humans.[122] For this reason, the patterns of human and animal creation need to be explored.

Creation of ψυχὴν ζῶσαν as a Basis for the Pattern of Life

Unit one contains a brief sketch of the sixth day of creation.[123] Part 1 of *Unit one* (vv. 24, 25) pictures the creation of land animals. Here, the animals are called ψυχὴν ζῶσαν. For the first time this term appears in Gen 1:20–21 in relation to the water animals created on the fifth day. The term ψυχὴν ζῶσαν is associated with ἑρπετά.[124] This word reflects an ability of living creatures to move and is used in the meaning, "to swarm, to teem," as in Ps 104:25 [103:25 LXX].[125]

Gen 2:7 narrates the creation of humans differently to the creation of animals, for God breathed πνοὴν ζωῆς into their face and ἐγένετο ὁ ἄνθρωπος εἰς ψυχὴν ζῶσαν. Despite differences in the creation all three, the wateranimals, those on land, and humans, they are united by the common term ψυχὴν ζῶσαν. Consequently, the phrase ψυχὴν ζῶσαν, used here, indicates life itself. This becomes more evident in the phrase

---

120. Tryggve Mettinger notes the controversy of death and immortality in Gen 1–3. Mettinger, *Eden Narrative*, 47–48. The importance of this controversy can be assumed from the stressed fact of "God's absence from death" and that contact with dead bodies excluded one from the contact with the holy things. In Mishnah, "death and its defilement stand outside the cult, outside of life, and ultimately outside of God." Feldman, *Biblical and Post-Biblical Defilement*, 14–15, 17.

121. Belcher and Waltke view the rationale for the prohibition of blood consumption written in Gen 9:4 as "reverence for life" and in prevention of carnivorous behavior. Belcher, *Genesis*, 99. Waltke, *Genesis*, 144–45. However, it seems illogical to assume that respect for life can be formally exercised by draining blood, while the slaughtering of animals has divine approval. This assumption reveals the need for a different rationale.

122. See the diagram for *Unit one* of passage 2, in 1.2.2 of Appendix 2. Here, the process of the creation of man reveals two main features: the forming of man out of dust/soil and the breathing of the breath of life into the nostrils of a formed body.

123. Its diagram is in Appendix 2.

124. Here, ἑρπετά represent the common features of the living creatures: to move following their desires, and appetite. Human "soul" is distinguished from an animal's "soul" by the unique ability of craving for God. Waltke, *Genesis*, 63.

125. Muraoka, *Greek-English Lexicon*, 292. The word ἕρπω means "move slowly," consequently ἑρπετόν designates "creeping animal."

ψυχὴν ζῶσαν, where the accent is put on the word "living," because the ability to live is their common feature.

The Pattern for the Creation of Humans

The role of *Unit one* (Gen 2:7) is to show two special components of human life: dust, and breath of God.[126] Here πλάσσω "to form, fashion, and mould" is used instead of ἐποίησεν.[127] This feature separates humans from animals as unique creatures.[128] However, the connection of the human body to the ground reveals dependence for life on the πνοὴν ζωῆς of God.[129]

Figure 17: Gen 2:7

7 καὶ ἔπλασεν ὁ θεὸς τὸν ἄνθρωπον χοῦν ἀπὸ τῆς γῆς
καὶ ἐνεφύσησεν εἰς τὸ πρόσωπον αὐτοῦ πνοὴν ζωῆς,

καὶ ἐγένετο ὁ ἄνθρωπος εἰς ψυχὴν ζῶσαν.

The fall and separation from God ends with the pronouncement: "... for dust you are and to dust you will return" Gen 3:19. This possibility for human life to return into dust sustains the basis of the controversy between life and death. The controversy presumes a reversal of life by death.[130]

The reversal itself can be found in Gen 1–3 when the units seven and eight are taken together. In *Unit seven* (3:9–13) the man is the first to confess his sin. Then the woman gets the right to speak. The serpent appears last on the scene, only mentioned by the woman. In *Unit eight* (3:14–20) the order in which the characters appear in God's pronouncements is the opposite: the serpent reseives the curse first, then the woman, and the man last. *Units seven* and *eight*, taken together, locate the serpent in the midst of God's judgment and condemnation.

---

126. The diagram for *Unit one* of passage 2 is in Appendix 2.

127. Muraoka, *Greek-English Lexicon*, 561.

128. The uniqueness of humans is shown in "that man alone receives the breath of God directly." Wenham, *Genesis*, 61.

129. Ross believes that the dignity of humans was due to the "breath of life" from God, which made them living spiritual beings (with capacity of communing with God). This makes re-creation very important for the restoration of relationships with God. Ross, "Genesis," 43–44.

130. Gilbert notes that "the act of disobedience tragically locked humanity into a sphere of existence that came to be characterized by death (Gen 2:17). The text describes the outcome of this act in terms of alienation: (1) from God (Gen 3:8–10); (2) from other humans and human nature itself (Gen 3:11–19); and (3) from the natural enviroment (Gen 3:11–19)." Gilbert, "He Never Meant for Us to Die," 50.

From the discussion above one can conclude: 1) The reversal of Gen 3 presumes that life and death now are interchangeable matters and that both conditions are reversible; 2) The controversy is linked to food (the forbidden fruit in Gen 2:16, 17; the tree of life in Gen 3:22 in terms of eternal life; and the food from the land in Gen 3:17–19 in terms of temporal living); 3) The serpent is placed in the centre of God's judgment and condemnation, which represents the irreversible degree of apostasy; 4) the strife of evil forces for dominion over humans forms a transition of the reversible stage of uncleanness into an irreversible stage; 5) prohibitions of both αἷμα and of πνικτός consumption are linked together in a single pattern of the life-death controversy.

The first point of the controversy relates to a reversal. *Unit eight* in vv. 18–20 shows that curses are limited by the death of a human being: ἕως ἀποστρέψαι σε εἰς τὴν γῆν ἐξ ἧς ἐλήμφθης.[131] Here the word ἀποστρέψαι is used to express the fall in terms of a turning point or a reversal in order to return human life to its original components. The concept of ἀποστρέψαι . . . εἰς τὴν γῆν "the returning of life to the ground" plays an important role in the Torah.[132] Thus, Milgrom explains the connection between prohibition of blood consumption and the concept of life: "Man has no right to put an animal to death except by God's sanction. Hence, he must eschew the blood, drain it, and return it, as it were, to the Creator."[133] He argues for the presence of a rationale in an ancient taboo of blood consumption with the words:

> Since Israel alone among its neighbors enjoined a blood prohibition that was universal and absolute—for both Jew and non-Jew, for both sacrificial animals and the ordinary kind—we may conclude that this blood prohibition was no vestigial leftover of an ancient taboo; it must have been the result of a rational, deliberate opposition to the prevalent practice of the environment.[134]

In cases when the life of an animal is taken for the purpose of sacrifice or for food, the blood, which represents life, has to be poured on the ground. If the life of a man is taken by murder, his blood "cries out from the ground" for justice (Gen 4:10). Here the actions, which can no longer be attributed to life, since it is taken away, are attributed to the blood. Thus, the blood is a synonym for life. Note the phrase in the Holiness Code about one who commits a deadly sin and rejects repentance: "their blood will be on their own heads" (Lev 20:11–13, 16, and 27).

In this case, the blood also might be viewed in terms of life. It shows symbolically that wrong decisions might cost someone his life. These passages confirm that

---

131. Waltke also shows that death "delivers mortals from eternal consignment to the curse." Waltke, *Genesis*, 95.

132. Gen 2–3 is "both paradigmatic and protohistorical." It provides a model of the great theological tradition of the OT. This becomes also a basis for the covenant theology, which shows that disobedience to God's commandments inevitably brings death. Wenham, *Genesis*, 90–91.

133. Milgrom, "Biblical Diet Laws," 289.

134. Milgrom, "Biblical Diet Laws," 289.

the blood is significant in Torah, functioning as a synonym for life.[135] While blood flows in blood vessels, the living being is alive; when it stops, the living being dies.[136] That is why blood plays a key role in the covenant and becomes an important element of the ritual law.[137]

The ritual of pouring blood on the ground reflects the belief that God is able to re-create the world. In contrast to the first unbelief, God calls people to reveal faith in his intention and ability to restore the life of someone even from the dust.[138] This belief is represented in the words: "I, am he, and there is no god beside me; I kill and I make alive," in Deut 32:39.[139] Reed believes that the number of OT texts "indicate that God has control over life and death."[140] Anthony Petterson, discussing belief in resurrection in Torah, also concludes that "the resurrection hope which is found there is grounded in creation, in the belief that the God who created life from the dust of the earth, is able to bring life out of death."[141]

"Manipulations with blood were included in the vast majority of private and public sacrificial offerings . . . made by Israelites."[142] According to Torah, the cultic use of blood (in sanctuary rituals) included its tossing on the top, placing on sides, or pouring at the base of the altar. The non-cultic use of blood (draining prior to non-cultic meat consumption) required only that it be poured on the ground and covered with soil (Lev 17:13). Thus, both ways of blood disposal included the returning of blood: 1) to dust, or 2) to God. These two ways of blood disposal later formed two most prominent patterns of the Sinaitic law. These patterns are: the natural (non-cultic) law and the ritual (cultic) law. According to these patterns the law of God was to be understood and carried out by humans (see Deut 12:10–28, which represents the cultic pattern in 12:10–19 and the non-cultic pattern in 12:20–28).

---

135. Baker notices the biological and theological concepts connected with blood. He shows that biologically, "flowing blood keeps flesh alive" and "its loss leads to death." Theologically, blood purifies the altar from sins, "which could lead to separation and death." The ceremony with blood brings the person "back to God, the source of all life Baker, "Leviticus," 126.

136. The same observation that "a beating heart and strong pulsation are the clearest evidence of life" is mentioned by Wenham. He also sees the rationale for the prohibition of blood consumption in respect for life and the giver of life. Wenham, *Genesis*, 193.

137. Wenham, *Genesis*, 193.

138. This hope of resurrection was described in 2 Macc 7:23 and expressed with help of creation motifs. Ollenburger, "If Mortals Die," 30–31.

139. Petterson, "Antecedents of the Christian Hope," 5. Moreover, this text was used by rabbis, according to Tannaite sources, to prove resurrection. Neusner and Chilton, *Jewish and Christian Doctrines*, 160.

140. Reed, "Imagining Resurrection in the Old Testament," 10–12. He links Gen 2:7 to Ezek 37. He also shows the hope for a resurrection in 1 Sam 2:6; Isa 26:19; Dan 12:1–3, also resurrection language in Pss 16:10–11; 23:6.

141. Petterson, "Hope of Resurrection," 3–5, 15.

142. Meshel, "Form and Function," 289. He discusses several explanation of the ritual with blood, which are purgation, withholding from human consumption, belief that blood belongs prior to God. With this he believes that P "remains silent regarding the precise meaning of this particular ritual."

These patterns were established by God in such order that people would maintain a belief in the future restoration of life and re-creation of the world. It is noteworthy that in Genesis and Leviticus the units related to the natural (non-cultic) law appear in close proximity to the units that relate to the cultic system. As a result it caused difficulties for differenciation. This can explain why the apostles during the Jerusalem Council pointed out precisely the four prohibitions among many others. These four were difficult to demarcate, differenciate from the cultic regulations, which were now assumed as unnecessary things. The apostles were to make sure that the converts from the Gentiles would not confuse these four with the regulations of the cultic system, when they refered them to Moses.

The proximity of two patterns of the law in the narratives of Genesis and Leviticus suggests the early stage of religion, when the cultic system was not yet been developed. Even at that early stage in Gen 9:4 the blood represented life. According to Gen 3:19, life shall be returned to dust. The idea "blood represents life" later appears in Lev 17:14 among cultic regulations and then in Deut 12:10–28 where cultic and non-cultic patterns seem to be finally developed and separated. This suggests that rituals with blood originally represented the life-death controversy. This, in its turn, suggests that once in human history the reversal of the fall is to be expected. The connection of rituals with blood to the Mosaic ritual law in Leviticus and Deuteronomy points to the role of the Savior in the ratification of the life-death controversy.

If one accepts that death has no need for special symbolical representation, then the practical application of the belief of its reversal by renewed life could be the purpose of the rituals with the blood.[143] Hebrew 9:22 explains the typology of the rituals with the blood in terms of the redemption fulfilled in Christ: "Under the law almost everything is purified with blood, and without the shedding of blood there is no forgiveness of sins." The ritual law was thus linked to the redemptive mission of Christ, which includes his death and resurrection. The rituals with blood in the sanctuary, pouring blood on the ground, and prohibiting the eating of blood, were linked to each other in meaning and demonstrate, on a practical level, the belief in the possibility of the reversal of death back to life.

The second point shows that the issue of food is involved in the controversy between life and death. The shift in diet that took place between the fall and the flood has to be investigated. This is important because the covenant of Gen 2:16, 17 and that two prohibitions of the Decree are dietary prohibitions. It is seen from *Unit one* (1:24–31), placed immediately after creation and blessings, that the dominion over animals did not include eating them.[144] The diet of the first humans in Gen 1:29 differs

---

143. The creation-fall narrative in Gen 1–3 seems to be left as an uncompleted pattern. The expectation of the re-creation makes the pattern built according to rules of chiastic structure. Thus, the A-B-A' pattern could lie behind the creation–fall–re-creation paradigm.

144. Nahum Sarna assumes that the human race had been created originally vegetarian. Sarna, *Genesis*, 21.

from that of Gen 9:3. This change includes an extension into the animal kingdom as a result of the fall and the flood. [145]

Allusions to the resurrection of the dead in the flood narrative were noted by Byron Wheaton, who states that "the primeval state of the pre-creation situation is returned" and Noah "enters into a pristine, newly re-formed world to originate a new humanity."[146] It is noteworthy that the story of Enoch in Gen 5:22 is placed in between two major themes: the fall and the flood. The idea of escaping death, thus, is contrasted with the sentence of death in the fall narrative and the picture of death in a global sense in the flood narrative. Wendell Frerichs states that "since two persons, Enoch and Elijah, were reported to have been translated directly into the heavenly world, the idea of escaping death altogether was at least known."[147] The Talmud expresses Jewish understanding that belief in resurrection was implicitly present in Torah.[148] This is seen in Mishnah tractate *Sanhedrin* 11:1–2 composed before 400 CE: "And these are the ones who have no portion in the world to come: he who says, the resurrection of the dead is a teaching which does not derive from the Torah."[149]

Thus Gen 9:3 can be viewed as a reversal of the diet of Gen 1:29, 30. This reversal appears in Gen 9:1–7.[150] Conceptually Gen 1:24, 25 becomes linked to Gen 9:1–7, which for the first time mentions the prohibition of blood consumption. Here, the phrase ἐν αἵματι ψυχῆς can be translated "with blood of life."[151] This concept will be explained later in this chapter in connection with Lev 17:10–14 and Deut 12:23–27.

The third point of the controversy between life and death relates to the matter of the irreversible condition of apostasy from God. The sentence of the serpent was

---

145. Natural law here needs to be viewed as an extension of the universal law of creation as a consequence of the fall. This natural law was now called to regulate life in the fallen world, when the thorns appeared and the fertility of the land was reduced. Also the flood influenced diet, since the crops and trees perished. Instead the animals were increasing in number and became a danger for people. In this situation God permitted the use of meat as food.

146. Wheaton, "As It Is Written," 248–49. He notes in the flood narrative features common for the resurrection motifs: "the sentence of death is delivered, the process of destruction gets under way, there is no human solution that can lead to deliverance, there is a miraculous intervention, and the regained life issues in a new order of things." He also believes that story of Abraham sacrificing Isaac in Gen 22:5–18 also represents a death-resurrection ordeal.

147. Frerichs, "Death and Resurrection," 20.

148. Martin McNamara discusses the resurrection belief in the tradition of rabbinic midrash and in the NT. He states that the rabbis of the second and third centuries CE found resurrection deducible from the Torah. He also notes that in 4 Macc 7:19; 16:25 the belief was based on the hopes of the patriarchs. McNamara, *Palestinian Judaism and the New Testament*, 180–83

149. Neusner and Chilton, *Jewish and Christian Doctrines*, 152.

150. The diagram is in Appendix 2.

151. Sarna believes that here the prohibition concerns: 1) the consumption of limbs of a living animal; 2) and "of the blood that oozes out of the animal's dying body"; 3) the meat in which blood remains. He states that "these laws are here made incumbent on all humanity." Later the draining of blood formed the basis of the Jewish dietary laws. Its purpose was to ensure the maximum extraction of blood from the flesh before cooking. Sarna, *Genesis*, 60–61.

executed by the removal of its limbs.¹⁵² This action symbolized the serpents' extreme closeness to death (it was doomed to crawl in the dust), as well as its association with chthonic forces and irreversible degree of apostasy from God. The serpent was symbolicaly made a type of the unclean forces. The depiction of some animal in the group of permanently unclean creatures was formed according to the same principle (the means of locomotion and the means of food consumption, stated in Deut 14:6). All reptiles were associated with the pole of unclean forces (Lev 11:42–43). They were made lower in status to cattle and beasts, as shown in Gen 3:14 by the phrase ἐπικατάρατος σὺ ἀπὸ πάντων τῶν κτηνῶν καὶ ἀπὸ πάντων τῶν θηρίων τῆς γῆς.¹⁵³ The preposition ἀπὸ + genitive πάντων here means "from all, away from all . . ." and is used to stress the separation of serpents from the other animals of the land.¹⁵⁴

Thus, serpents form the pole at one end of a continuum from evil to holy.¹⁵⁵ The curse was imposed on the serpent's means of locomotion and food consumption.¹⁵⁶ It was noted that "partial absence of life, such as torn limbs" was associated in Jewish belief with death.¹⁵⁷ That is why serpent became a prototype of desacralisation. Along with serpents, all permanently unclean animals symbolize the irreversible degree of apostasy from God.¹⁵⁸ This apostasy is not to be understood literally of these animals; they are an illustration for people and point to spiritual reality. The animals, whom people can see, represent the irreversible demons.¹⁵⁹ In Luke 8:33

---

152. It was said ἐπὶ τῷ στήθει σου καὶ τῇ κοιλίᾳ πορεύσῃ. This phrase emphasises two parts of the body, στήθει and κοιλίᾳ. Because it is difficult to decide where serpents have their breast or belly, the phrase seems to have a special meaning. Unlike the other quadrupeds who walk on the limbs fitted to chest and pelvis (legs of the pectoral arch and legs of the pelvic arch), the serpents were deprived of both. It is also said καὶ γῆν φάγῃ πάσας which shows the serpent's diet as unclean, associated with death.

153. Here, the curse of the serpent presumes eschatological condemnation. God uses this formula "Cursed you are" only here and in Gen 4:11. Elswhere, afterwards "some third person pronounces the curse" and not God. Wenham, *Genesis*, 78.

154. Wallace, *Greek Grammar*, 107–8. This separation might be assumed from the fact of recalling, in the curse of the serpent, his initial distinctiveness from all the beasts. The phrase "more cursed" echoes "more shrewd" in 3:1. Here also the curse is assumed in the sense of separation from other animals. Wenham, *Genesis*.

155. Wenham supports this view stating, "according to classification of animals found in Lev 11 and Deut 14, the snake must count as an archetypal unclean animal. Its swarming, writhing locomotion puts it at the farthest point from those pure animals that can be offered in sacrifice." Thus the serpent becomes an anti-God symbol, which is associated with God's enemies. Wenham, *Genesis*, 73.

156. See Douglas, *Purity and Danger*, 55. Sarna mentions that "the transgression involved eating, and so does the punishment." Sarna, *Genesis*, 27. According to Genesis Rabbah R. Hoshaiah believes that the serpent from the beginning "stood erect like a reed and had feet." In Genesis Rabbah Parashah 20:5 the phrase "upon your belly you shall go" is interpreted as "the angel came down and cut off the serpent's hands and feet." Neusner, *Genesis Rabbah*, 200, 217.

157. Feldman, *Defilement and Mourning*, 47.

158. Wenham notes that the only parallel to the serpent's diet and its way of locomotion is Lev 11:42, "which brands all such creatures as unclean." Wenham, *Genesis*, 79.

159. This point will be developed in chapter 4.

demons are associated with unclean animals. In Luke and Acts, demons are pictured as irreversibly unclean.

The fourth point of the controversy between life and death in Genesis 1–3, is strife for dominion.[160] The chain of parallel sayings in Gen 3:16 reveals that the battle is happening not just between the first woman and her tempter. Waltke states that the judgment of God "refers to both the serpent and Satan."[161] New Testament belief identifies the promised "seed" with Christ.[162] Early Christians also could identify "the seed" with Christ and his mission. Thus, in Gal 3:16 Paul states: οὐ λέγει· καὶ τοῖς σπέρμασιν, ὡς ἐπὶ πολλῶν ἀλλ᾽ ὡς ἐφ᾽ ἑνός· καὶ τῷ σπέρματί σου, ὅς ἐστιν Χριστός, referring to the "seed of Abraham" in Gen 17:7. The only promise of "the seed" before Gen 17:7 is Gen 3:15. In 2 Tim 2:8 Paul calls Jesus "the seed of David" (ἐκ σπέρματος Δαυίδ), while Luke 3:23–38 unites David, Abraham and Adam in one geneology, that of Jesus.

The battle predicted in the phrase αὐτός σου τηρήσει κεφαλήν, καὶ σὺ τηρήσεις αὐτοῦ πτέρναν, "he shall watch against your head and you shall watch against his heel," shows a need to avoid being bitten and a need to destroy the head of the serpent as the most poisonous part of the reptile's body.[163] Early Christians viewed it as an enduring battle between Satan and Christ in the heart of each person. The battle explains why the spiritual uncleanness of a person from the beginning is reversible, but may revert to an irreversible condition.

The last point of the controversy between life and death shows the prohibitions of αἷμα and πνικτὸς linked in the one pattern. This is apparent for a number of reasons: 1) both, life returning to dust and the breath of life returning to God, reflect the reversal of the process of the creation of humans; 2) both occurences of αἷμα and πνικτὸς are illustrated by dietary prohibitions on account of proper slaughtering, which presume the returning of life to dust (the draining of the blood) and the returning of the breath of life to God (by a prohibition of strangling);[164] 3) both prohibitions of αἷμα and πνικτὸς are linked in the one pattern of the life-death controversy; 4) the spiritual meaning of both dietary prohibitions reveals the belief in God's power to restore

---

160. Here "the curse envisages a long struggle between good and evil." Wenham refers to the early church fathers, who saw 3:15 as "the first messianic prophecy in the OT." Wenham, *Genesis*, 80–81.

161. Waltke, *Genesis*, 93.

162. There is an opinion that the "seed of the woman" could refer to: 1) to Cain, but he failed in a struggle with evil; 2) the whole human race, because Eve, "life," became the mother of all living, but humanity in general did no better than Cain; 3) it was noted by the apostles that Jesus Christ was the promised "seed" (Gal 3:16; 4:4). Ross, "Genesis," 55.

163. This can be supported by the following symbolical mentioning of sin in the image of a snake in 4:7, where sin is eager to control a man, but he is called to master it. Ross, "Genesis," 56.

164. It is known that "hebraic anthropology locates a person's life both in breath (Gen 2:7) and in the blood." Hartley, *Leviticus*, 274.

creation and life to its original state;¹⁶⁵ 5) the ignorance of both dietary prohibitions, of αἷμα and πνικτός, represents the lack of such a belief.¹⁶⁶

The beliefs of the apostles at the Jerusalem Council predetermined their interpretation of Torah in the way which made the role of Jesus for future re-creation prominent.¹⁶⁷ This agrees with the concept of a life-death controversy rooted in the Gen 1–3 account.¹⁶⁸ That is why the apostolic letter includes the prohibitions of αἷμα and πνικτός. This definitely reveals the apostles' hopes for a renewal of creation. In the apostolic view of Christianity uniting all the nations, the event of renewal has already taken place in the outpouring of the Holy Spirit and the purification of hearts. Wright shows that the presence of the Spirit in the church recalls "the real return from exile, the exile in which Adam and Eve found themselves expelled from a free, deathless Eden."¹⁶⁹ This view supports the main argument that the apostolic view of the life-death controversy was rooted in the creation story, which gave the apostles the belief in re-creation.

Thus, the prelimennary conclusion for this discussion would view the prohibition of αἷμα as the illustration of "belief in restoration of the world," implicitly present in Torah. In contrast, the consumption of αἷμα or πνικτός presents the opposite to a belief in restoration of life. Deliberate participation in the destruction of this natural circle (by strangling of an animal for pagan sacrifices or by eating its meat) would express an extreme point of unbelief in God's control over life and death.¹⁷⁰

---

165. This is clear from the fact that the animal itself does not represent any beliefs, when it dies naturally. Only when humans slaughter an animal can they impute that belief to their actions. Here the text of Leviticus is "the only text in the OT that comes close to giving a reason why blood effects atonement." Hartley, *Leviticus*, 273.

166. It is asserted that "throughout the ancient world it was a common practice to consume animal blood in a variety of forms" by Hartley, *Leviticus*, 273.

167. An intertextual reading of Acts 1–7 and Gen 1–12 reveals that both passages "share three themes in common (creation, sin and its curse, and the creation of a people)." Phillips, "Creation, Sin and Its Curse," 147.

168. Hartley shows that the prohibitions of αἷμα and πνικτός were imposed on the Gentile converts because of the importance of "blood" in salvific work of God. They assumed that Jesus' blood "was central to his atoning work on the cross." He also explains πνικτός as a condition, when blood remains hidden in flesh. Hartley, *Leviticus*, 279. The πνικτός, however, more likely refers to "breath" than "blood" symbolism and needs explanation in a wider concept than salvation in terms of cultic law. This concept is a "life-death controversy," where Jesus's death is a key role too.

169. Wright, *Paul*, 149. Thus the Exodus is traced back to the creation-fall narrative in terms of Jewish Second Temple eschatology. Wright states that "Paul's vision of the end of all things is derived from the Old Testament, ultimately from the story of creation itself; note the way in which Genesis 1–3 lies near the heart of both of Romans 8 and 1 Corinthians 15."

170. Savelle refers to Philo's description of using strangled meat in sacrifices of pagan cults. Savelle, "Reexamination of Prohibitions," 456.

THE FOUR PROHIBITIONS OF ACTS 15

The Uniting Role of Gen 9:1–7 and the Prohibition of αἷμα

The role of Gen 9:1–7 is to unite concepts of ψυχὴν ζῶσαν (נפש חיה) of Gen 1:24, 25 and "life returning to dust" (ἀποστρέψαι . . . εἰς τὴν γῆν) of Gen 3:19. First of all, Gen 9:1–7 reveals close associations with Gen 1:24–30. The blessings to Noah recall the blessings to Adam in Gen 1:28.[171] Adam was given dominion over the animals as one of the blessings.[172] Adam's dominion included ruling and governing the animals, expressed by ἄρχετε. After the pronouncement of the dominion, the next blessing is diet.[173]

In Gen 9:2 the dominion reflects that the animals are ὁ τρόμος and ὁ φόβος of people and are given into the hands of people.[174] From this point, the dominion of people over animals dramatically extends human diet, which here is inserted in the account of blessings. The blessings αὐξάνεσθε and πληρώσατε are repeated two times, πληθύνεσθε is repeated three times, and κατακυριεύσατε appears once. At the same time, κατακυριεύσατε is extended by the inclusion of meat in human diet, limitations of the new diet, and responsibilities of humans and beasts in relation to blood.[175] The order of animals here differs from Gen 1:28 and does not follow the order of creation. Instead, water animals and the beasts appear in reverse order.

Verse 3 shows that the new diet permits the use of animal flesh (κρέας) as a food for people. However, the new diet has limitations. The first limitation is hidden in the phrase καὶ πᾶν ἑρπετόν, ὅ ἐστιν ζῶν, which often is viewed with the stress on πᾶν, meaning "all." However, it is clarified by the subordinate clause ὅ ἐστιν ζῶν, and the accent is placed on ἑρπετόν, rather than πᾶν. The ἑρπετόν, meaning "creeping, teeming, moving," represents a main feature of living things: locomotion.[176] The double reference to the presence of life in the animal plays a significant role here, as it prevents consumption of carrion flesh (the dead animal has no ability to move).[177]

---

171. Wenham, *Genesis*, 192.

172. Ross sees the dominion of humans over the earth in light of their ability to bear in themselves the "image of God." Thus a human being was representative of God for all the animal kingdom and was responsible for carrying out God's love to creation. Ross, "Genesis," 40.

173. Human diet consisted of every seed-bearing plant and every tree that has fruit with seed in it (Gen 1:29), while animals were given every green plant for food. (Gen 1:30). Animals eating one another, and the consumption of meat of animals by humans at that state is unlikely.

174. Here, the military terminology appears similar to Deut 1:21; 11:25; 31:8. Wenham, *Genesis*, 192.

175. Reno assumes that the prohibition of blood "serves as a bridge to the commandment to punish murder with the death of the murderer." Thus, he sees the prohibition of blood consumption here, in Gen 9, presuming an ethical aspect. Reno, *Genesis*, 125.

176. Muraoka, *Greek-English Lexicon*, 292. The verb ἕρπω, "move slowly," indicates that the main feature of ἑρπετόν is their ability to move, creep.

177. Wenham, *Genesis*, 192. Moreover, Walton states that the permission to eat meat in Gen 9:3 provided the qualification "that the animal is living" and Gen 9:4 provided the qualification "that the meat cannot be eaten with the lifeblood in it." Walton, *Genesis*, 342–43.

The second limitation is presented clearly by the prohibition of blood consumption.¹⁷⁸ A detailed view of the life-death antithesis links Gen 1:24–30 with 2:7 describing the creation of life, to Gen 3:19 and describing the inevitable reality of death, which appears as the reverse process of the creation of life. The term ψυχὴν ζῶσαν of Gen 1:24, 25 later appears linked to a prohibition of blood consumption in Gen 9:1–7 (πλὴν κρέας ἐν αἵματι ψυχῆς οὐ φάγεσθε). Here the concept, "blood represents life," is present implicitly in the phrase ἐν αἵματι ψυχῆς.¹⁷⁹ The same concept, "blood represents life" (γὰρ ψυχὴ πάσης σαρκὸς αἷμα αὐτοῦ ἐστιν), is found in Lev 17:11.¹⁸⁰ Gen 9:1–7, Lev 17–10–14 and Deut 12:20–28 appear to be linked by the concept "blood represents life."¹⁸¹ At this point the connection between ψυχὴν ζῶσαν (חיה נפש) of Gen 1:24, 25 and "life returning to dust" (ἀποστρέψαι . . . εἰς τὴν γῆν) of Gen 3:19 can be stated.¹⁸² It is reflected in the ritual of draining the blood of slaughtered animals and covering it with soil. For the detailed examination of this connection the exegetical study of Lev 17–10–14 and Deut 12:20–28 is needed.

The Prohibition of αἷμα in Lev 17:10–14

Lev 17:10–14 sheds light on the prohibition of blood consumption.¹⁸³ Its structure reveals two forms of the same law.¹⁸⁴ Part 1 describes the unlawful behavior, which includes eating meat with its blood.¹⁸⁵ This starts with καὶ ἄνθρωπος . . . ὃς ἂν φάγῃ πᾶν αἷμα, a conditional clause describing the deviation from normal behavior and

---

178. Wenham stresses that "Genesis is interesting in tracing back the fundamental principles of ethics and worship to earliest times, so it is likely that it is here prohibiting any consumption of blood." Wenham, *Genesis*, 193.

179. Waltke confirms that "blood is equated with life in the Old Testament." Waltke, *Genesis*, 144.

180. Hartley states that for ancient people, blood served "as the tangible center of an animal's life force," which expiates the guilt of sins and gives a cost of expiation. Hartley, *Leviticus*, 274–75.

181. Peter Vogt notes that Lev 17:13 and Deut 12:16, 24 are linked by the blood ritual. He shows that while Leviticus obliges covering blood with earth, Deuteronomy implies to pour it out "like water." He views the Deuteronomic legislation as an attempt to remove any sacral quality from the blood and to show it as having "no more a sacral value than water has." Vogt, *Deuteronomic Theology*, 165. So, one can conclude that in cases of noncultic slaughtering, the blood was not viewed in terms of a redemptive agent and had no sacral symbolism except its role in general life-death controversy, where the blood represents life.

182. This thought has the support of Philip Jenson, who states: "Both life and death are probably associated with the most powerful means of purification, the sprinkling or application of the blood of a sacrificed animal. Although blood does not cleanse physically, it is essential to life (like water) and its loss leads to death." Jenson, *Graded Holiness*, 166.

183. Lester Grabbe states that "blood itself is a central element in this chapter." Grabbe, *Leviticus*, 78.

184. It was noticed that the passage Lev 17:1–16 has two parts (vv. 2–7 and 8–16). The first section describes the laws about sacrifices, while the second focuses on the prohibition of blood. Hartley, *Leviticus*, 264. However, it becomes clear from the diagram that these two sections reveal two different laws about slaughtering (cultic and noncultic).

185. The diagram of this passage is in Appendix 2.

indicating God's resulting punishment: καὶ ἐπιστήσω τὸ πρόσωπόν μου . . . καὶ ἀπολῶ αὐτὴν ἐκ τοῦ λαοῦ αὐτῆς. This kind of introduction suggests that the prohibition of blood is well known to Israel.[186] That is why the introduction focuses first on unlawful behaviour, assuming a clear knowledge of lawful behaviour.

The explanation given for punishment appears in part 1 in two variants. First, the text provides the general explanation of the concept "blood represents life," repeated in part 2. Part 1 then has an additional explanation which follows the general one, where God explains the concept "blood redeems life."[187] This additional "blood redeems life" concept works only in relation to the sanctuary. The phrase states: καὶ ἐγὼ δέδωκα αὐτὸ ὑμῖν ἐπὶ τοῦ θυσιαστηρίου ἐξιλάσκεσθαι περὶ τῶν ψυχῶν ὑμῶν· τὸ γὰρ αἷμα αὐτοῦ ἀντὶ τῆς ψυχῆς ἐξιλάσεται. The blood here is conceptually involved in the redemptive ministry of God.[188]

Both explanations of part 1 clarify two main concepts: "blood represents life" and "blood redeems life."[189] The first shows that blood is viewed as an element identical to life. The returning of life to dust, thus, demands the same action taken when returning blood.[190] This action seems to be imposed on humankind as a demonstration of the belief that life must return to dust, and can be raised again out of dust by the power of God. In the case of sacrifices the concept offers a special clue, involving the element of redemption and the hope of forgiveness of sins and future restoration of the world. That is why in relation to sacrifices in the sanctuary this concept is expressed as "blood redeems life."

Part 2 starts with regulating consumption of the meat of a non-sacrificial animal: καὶ ἄνθρωπος . . . ὃς ἂν θηρεύσῃ θήρευμα. Here no redemptive aspect is involved.[191] However, if people eat meat of an animal which was not sacrificed, they still have to pour its blood out and cover it with dust.[192] Thus, the law accents only the general concept, "blood represents life."[193] This is evident from the fact that part 2 provides

---

186. Moreover, here, the introductory phrase "if any person . . ." in vv. 3, 8, 10 and 13 suggests the universal scope of the law "applying to everyone living in Israel at all times." Hartley, *Leviticus*, 265. This view stresses the universal application of the law for both residents and aliens in Israel.

187. Gane, ed., *Leviticus, Numbers*, 304. He notices the "ransom" effect of blood in Lev 17:11.

188. Hartley, *Leviticus*, 267. "The interplay of the terms נפש, "life" (3x), and דם, "blood" (3x), and כפר, "expiate" (2x), creates a great rhetorical force."

189. Hartley notices that the concept "blood redeems life" echoes the principle "life for life" (24:20). In Deut 19:21 it has the meaning of "blood in place of life." Hartley, *Leviticus*, 276.

190. There is an idea that "the consummation of blood results in the destruction of the means of propitiation." Kiuchi, ed. *Leviticus*, 323.

191. Milgrom shows the lack of a "ransom" aspect in non-sacrificial slaughter in Lev 17:13-14. He stresses that in the prevention of chthonic worship, the blood has to be "buried" and links Gen 9:4 to Lev 17:13-14 and to Deut 12:23. Milgrom, *Leviticus 17-22*, 1480-84.

192. Here in v. 7 the law was described as "a perpetual decree to coming generations." The rationale for the prohibition of εἰδωλοθύτων in the Holiness Code lies beyond the cultic reasons and seems to be tied to the issue of true worship. Hartley, *Leviticus*, 267-68.

193. Gane, ed., *Leviticus, Numbers*, 309. He confirms the presence of the nonsacrificial part of the

only a general explanation, by repetition of the same phrase, ὅτι ἡ ψυχὴ πάσης σαρκὸς αἷμα αὐτοῦ ἐστιν, while the redemptive concept is omitted.

The Prohibition of αἷμα in Deut 12:20–28

Rules regulating meat consumption also appear in Deut 12:20–28.[194] The previous passage, Deut 12:10–19 describes the consumption of the meat of sacrificed animals.[195] According to the law, all sacrifices must be brought to the sanctuary.[196] Deut 12:20–28 takes into discussion the issue of meat from an animal slaughtered for food, without sacrificing it.[197] The structure of the law contains sets of conditions, permissions and blessings. The passage can be divided into three parts.

Part 1 describes the regulations of meat consumption in a situation when people live far from the sanctuary.[198] Condition 1, Ἐὰν δὲ ἐμπλατύνῃ κύριος ὁ θεός σου τὰ ὅριά σου, presumes that people are scattered across territory, and distance does not allow them to bring animals to the sanctuary every time they want to eat them. Permission 1, allows people to eat meat when they wish. The following pair, condition 2 and permission 2, clarify the practical aspects of home slaughtering. Although condition 2 uses different wording than condition 1 (ἐὰν δὲ μακρότερον ἀπέχῃ σου ὁ τόπος), circumstance remains the same: the distance between home and the sanctuary.

The phrase ὁ τόπος ὃν ἂν ἐκλέξηται κύριος ὁ θεός σου ἐπικληθῆναι τὸ ὄνομα αὐτοῦ ἐκεῖ relates to the sanctuary. From this point one should keep in mind that the law following deals with non-ritual slaughtering of an animal. In this case, the concept "blood redeems life" will not apply. However, the concept "blood represents

---

law, where the blood simply represents life.

194. The diagram of this passage is in Appendix 2.

195. Deut 12:10–19 belongs to the first section of laws, which focuses on the sanctuary. These laws describe the cultic slaughtering. Tigay, ed., *Deuteronomy*, 118. The cultic slaughtering has to be done in a single sanctuary, where people were gathered on feasts. They could eat the meat of the sacrifice of well-being. The blood of a sacrifice had to be drained completely out and dashed on the altar. Ritually unclean people could not participate. Christensen, *Deuteronomy 1:1—21:9*, 254–55.

196. The order not to sacrifice elsewhere except the single sanctuary was made on purpose to prohibit the Canaanites' religious practices. Tigay, ed., *Deuteronomy*, 120. Here, it becomes evident that the double worship cannot please the Lord. Moreover, Vogt adds that Deut 12 is linked to Exod 20:24, 25, where the focus was on true "Yahweh worship in contrast to idols, not on the number of altars." Vogt, *Deuteronomy Theology*, 169. Thus, the link between true worship and the concept "blood redeems life" is evident.

197. This nonsacrificial slaughtering was not linked to a ritual or the sanctuary and could take place in local assemblies, anytime, by ritually clean and unclean people, without dashing of blood on the altar. However, this kind also presumed the pouring of blood, out on the ground like water (vv. 23–25). Christensen, *Deuteronomy 1:1—21:9*, 257–58.

198. The temple scroll "defines the distance as three days' journey," while the rabbinic halakhah "permits secular slaughter anywehere outside the Temple Court." According to v.15 the non-cultic slaughter might be done in any of Israel's settlements. Tigay, ed., *Deuteronomy*, 125.

THE FOUR PROHIBITIONS OF ACTS 15

life" will apply.[199] This latter concept is not connected to the ritual law in the sanctuary, but assumes the presence of natural law.[200] Natural law, here, reflects the regulations imposed on nature since the fall.[201]

According to natural law, meat consumption is permitted, if governed by particular regulations. The first mentioned source of meat specified: ἀπὸ τῶν βοῶν σου καὶ ἀπὸ τῶν προβάτων σου. Another source appears in the phrase ἡ δορκὰς καὶ ἡ ἔλαφος, which presumes that people could hunt some game animals. The notification that the cattle from the flock have to be eaten in the same manner as game animals would emphasize that it is not to be connected to religious rituals.[202] This thought is further clarified by the following statement: ὁ ἀκάθαρτος ἐν σοὶ καὶ ὁ καθαρὸς ὡσαύτως, which made this type of meat consumption a non-ritual and non-cultic matter.

However, even non-sacrificial slaughtering required draining of blood.[203] Part 1 states this prohibition of blood consumption in the phrase πρόσεχε ἰσχυρῶς τοῦ μὴ φαγεῖν αἷμα. Here, πρόσεχε ἰσχυρῶς poses the prohibition itself, which is further explained in terms of the general concept, "blood represents life": ὅτι τὸ αἷμα αὐτοῦ ψυχή.[204] This shows again that meat consumption, not connected to cult, involved no redemptive element, but still involved the prohibition of blood consumption on the basis of natural law of God.[205] The following parallel sayings: οὐ βρωθήσεται ἡ ψυχὴ

---

199. Tigay, ed., *Deuteronomy*, 126. Tigay notes here the connection of the prohibition of blood consumption to two passages of Torah, Gen 1:29–30 and Gen 9:2–4. He states that originally all creatures were given a vegetarian diet. When, after the flood, the eating of meat was permitted it was immediately limited by the prohibition of blood consumption. According to the thesis of the present study, the link between Gen 1:29–30 and Gen 9:2–4 can be assumed as an illustration of the life-death controversy. The rituals with blood then have to be understood as the visible demonstration of this controversy.

200. See the definition of the concept "natural law" in chapter 1 section 4.3.1, while the difference between "universal" and "natural" laws is explained in footnote 144 of chapter 3 of the present study.

201. Christensen notes that according to some Jewish beliefs "demons were thought to take delight in the blood." Thus, those who eat blood were assumed as being in communion with demons." Christensen, *Deuteronomy 1:1—21:9*, 260-261. He believes that this view was present in the first century CE. The apostles at the Jerusalem Council could keep it in mind as a secondary reason. The main rationale for the prohibition was placed in terms of a natural law of God, not Jewish halakhah, which appeared centuries after the first prohibitions of blood in Gen 9:1–7.

202. Tigay, ed., *Deuteronomy*, 124. Tigay states that "only game animals could be slaughtered nonsacrificially," while "domestic cattle could only be slaughtered on altars." However, this statement contradicts v. 21, where nonsacrificial slaughtering includes game animals and domestic cattle in the common prohibition to eat blood from both types of animals. This observation does not allow the prohibition of blood consumption to be tied to the Jewish cult. Instead, it presumes the rationale lies beyond cultic matters.

203. According to Edward Woods, vv. 13–19 create a chiastic structure where the prohibition of blood consumption stays as the central thought of the chiasm. He states that "the principle of not eating blood lies deeper than sacrifice." He views the rationale for the prohibition in terms of: the pouring of the blood out on the ground presumes a belief that the blood belongs to God alone who gives life. Woods, *Deuteronomy*, 191–92.

204. Here the "blood is the life force in living creatures." Tigay, ed., *Deuteronomy*, 126.

205. Christensen sees the "reverence for life" as the rationale for the prohibition. He states that

μετὰ τῶν κρεῶν and οὐ φάγεσθε ἐπὶ τὴν γῆν ἐκχεεῖτε αὐτὸ ὡς ὕδωρ make clear the significance of the two concepts, "blood represents life" and "life returns to dust." The third repetition of the prohibition οὐ φάγῃ αὐτό is connected to blessings for law obedience.[206] The whole wording of the law in Deut 12:20–28 is positive, like a father reminding a son of the benefits of good behavior.

Following the law of non-cultic meat consumption, part 2 repeats and summarizes the law of Deut 12:10–19, discussing matters connected to cult. These relate to meat which has to be slaughtered and eaten in the sanctuary.[207] The text in part 2 makes clear that πλὴν τὰ ἅγιά σου, ἐὰν γένηταί σοι, καὶ τὰς εὐχάς σου which one would celebrate with consumption of meat, belong to cultic law. This meat must be consumed in the sanctuary: λαβὼν ἥξεις εἰς τὸν τόπον ὃν ἂν ἐκλέξηται κύριος ὁ θεός σου. The connection to the sanctuary switches to a different set of laws which are of cultic origin, summarized in the following phrases: καὶ ποιήσεις τὰ ὁλοκαυτώματά σου· τὰ κρέα ἀνοίσεις ἐπὶ τὸ θυσιαστήριον κυρίου τοῦ θεοῦ σου, τὸ δὲ αἷμα τῶν θυσιῶν σου προσχεεῖς πρὸς τὴν βάσιν τοῦ θυσιαστηρίου κυρίου τοῦ θεοῦ σου, τὰ δὲ κρέα φάγῃ. Here the ritual is controlled by cultic regulations, which involve an element of redemption.

Part 3 is written as a summary of both kinds of laws, cultic and natural, which regulate the preparation of meat for consumption. The structure of part 3 is covenantal in form. The first sentence, φυλάσσου καὶ ἄκουε καὶ ποιήσεις πάντας τοὺς λόγους οὓς ἐγὼ ἐντέλλομαί σοι (Deut 12:28) is a covenant command. This becomes clear not only by the use of imperative φυλάσσου but also by use of ἐγὼ ἐντέλλομαί, which echoes the wording of the fall narrative (Gen 3:11, 17), where ἐνετειλάμην was also used in relation to food.

Moreover, the command ἄκουε (listen) in addition to φυλάσσου and ποιήσεις would also reflect Adam's sin, when he listened to his wife instead of God's command.[208] The word φυλάσσου often introduces covenant commands in the LXX. This can explain the change of ἀπέχεσθαι in Acts 15:20 to φυλάσσεσθαι in Acts 21:25 and the appearance of an apostolic variant account of the Decree. The shift in wording could suggest

---

people were commanded to pour the blood out on ground to show their belief that the blood belongs to God and not to them. Christensen, *Deuteronomy 1:1—21:9*, 258. This assumption comes closer to the idea proposed by the present study. However, the returning of blood to the ground has to be associated with the returning of "dust to dust" (Gen 3:19).

206. Here, the blessings (ἵνα εὖ σοι γένηται) which follow the obedience to natural law include τοῖς υἱοῖς σου μετὰ σέ (include the descendants). At the same time, the blessings in v. 28 concluding the laws of both sacrificial and nonsacrificial slaughtering presume the promise of eternal life: καὶ τοῖς υἱοῖς σου δι' αἰῶνος. The eternal dimension of the conclusive blessing is explained in the main text below.

207. Merrill states that cultic meat consumption was possible during three annual religious festivals; they "included fellowship meals in which Yahweh and Israel broke bread together." Merrill, "Deuteronomy," 554.

208. This becomes clear from the phrase of Gen 3:17, Ὅτι ἤκουσας τῆς φωνῆς τῆς γυναικός . . .

that the apostles accepted the four prohibitions of the Decree as commandments, not just temporal regulations of table-fellowship in mixed communities.

After this general commandment, part 3 also contains general blessings. Those of v. 28 and those of v. 25 differ in only one feature, the addition of δι' αἰῶνος "through the ages," in v. 28.[209] This addition provides the eternal dimension of the blessings. If one assumes that the summary of laws in v. 28 includes cultic laws as well as natural ones, then it helps to show the involvement of the redemptive element in the life-death controversy of nature.

Life versus Death andt the Apostolic Prohibition of πνικτὸς

The discussion above connects the apostolic prohibition of πνικτὸς to the term πνοὴν ζωῆς, which appears in Gen 2:7 and later in Gen 7:21, 22. Several scholars consider that πνικτὸς implies leaving the blood in the flesh of a dead animal.[210] However, the present study will argue that πνικτὸς (suffocated) relates not to the failure to drain blood, but to the returning of πνοὴν ζωῆς (breath of life) to God. It is evident that the New Testament use of πνίγω (from the same root as πνικτός) metaphorically describes choking out a plant (Matt 13:7), or choking a debtor (18:28) and swine drowning in the Sea of Galillee (Mark 5:13).[211] Here, in two out of three cases the cessation of breathing is presumed.

Gen 2:7 puts emphasis on πνοὴν ζωῆς at the time of the creation of humans. Note that πνοὴν ζωῆς does not appear in Gen 1:24, 25, where the creation of animals is described. There the term ψυχὴν ζῶσαν is used, which means "living being." Despite this, the presence of πνοὴν ζωῆς is presumed in relation to all living beings of the land, as becomes clear from the flood narrative.

The flood narrative (Gen 7–9) is a panoramic picture of the death of living creatures, which is a reversal of their creation.[212] Gen 7:21–22 contains a parallel structure. In the first line σὰρξ κινουμένη describes animals. The parallel line includes humans

---

209. The blessings in v. 28, written for both parts of the law, refer to multiple generations: καὶ τοῖς υἱοῖς σου δι' αἰῶνος. The phrase presumes the eternal dimension of the blessing. It also presupposes the involvement of the redemption process by sacrificial slaughtering, which is linked to the concept "blood redeems life." Because both concepts, "blood redeems life" and "blood represents life," are united in v. 28 under common blessings, the eternal dimension appears there also.

210. Savelle associates "strangled" with improperly killed animals without draining of blood and, thus, suggests the common basis for two different prohibitions. He links πνικτὸς in Acts to the Old Testament's food law (Lev 17:13–14; Deut 12:16, 23), suggesting that strangled animals retain blood in their carcasses. Savelle, "Reexamination of Prohibitions," 456. It seems right to view the prohibition of "strangled" consumption as part of Torah food laws. However, the link between πνοὴν ζωῆς, in Gen 2:7 and Gen 7:21, 22 would suggest the context of cessation of breath, rather than draining of blood. That is why the prohibitions of "blood" and "strangled" would have different background concepts, although they are united by a common context of life-death antithesis.

211. Savelle, "Reexamination of Prohibitions," 456. In a parallel passage, Luke uses a compound form of ἀποπνίγω.

212. An echo of 2:7 in reversed order. Wenham, *Genesis*, 183.

in the phrase καὶ πᾶς ἄνθρωπος. After that, humans and animals seem to be viewed together in the phrase πάντα, ὅσα ἔχει πνοὴν ζωῆς, which presumes the presence of "wind in their nostrils."²¹³ The commonality of humans and animals, here, is that they breathe air. Drowning stops their ability to breathe air, which is shown by πάντα ὅσα ἔχει πνοὴν ζωῆς ("all that had the breath of life") in v. 22.²¹⁴ From this point the drowned creatures can be described by the term πνικτὸς, which comes to mean the blocking of πνοὴν ζωῆς.²¹⁵

People who drowned during the flood were condemned to death by God because of their unbelief, so πνικτὸς became symbolically associated with the kind of death resulting from condemnation. Suffocation breaks the natural return of the breath of life to God. It destroys the life-death circle appointed by God. Returning the breath of life to God by contrast suggests belief in the restoration of life, namely, resurrection.²¹⁶ Hubbard notes the connection between "spirit" and "life" in Gen 1:2; 2:7; and 6:17.²¹⁷ In LXX: Ps 103:29, 30 (Ps 104:29, 30) πνοὴν ζωῆς seems to be pictured in terms of reversal of death by life.

Figure 18: Ps 103:29, 30

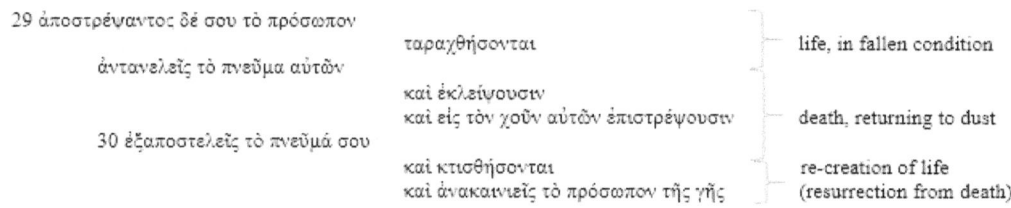

Here, the adverbial participle κτισθήσονται describes the process of creation. In this instance, creation likely implies re-creation of life in terms of resurrection. This is confirmed in the parallel phrase καὶ ἀνακαινιεῖς, which pictures a renewal of a life which previously existed and was reversed by death. This passage reflects the creation–fall–re-creation paradigm explicitly present in Gen 1–3. Wright

---

213. The word πνοὴν relates to their common ability to inhale and exhale breath.

214. According to Sarna a blend of Gen 2:7 and 6:17 takes place here in vv. 21–22. Sarna, *Genesis*, 56.

215. Hartley says that "breath, being invisible and intangible, symbolizes the fleeting, mysterious aspect of human existence." Hartley, *Leviticus*, 274.

216. This study will argue that the hope of resurrection was implicitly present in the teaching of Torah. Thus,

2 Kgs 4:18–37; 13:20–21 describes the reality of the resurrection in the time of the Old Testament. Jesus, in Luke 20:38, states that the idea of resurrection was present even in Exod 3:6, 15 and was revealed to Moses. In Heb 11:19, Paul shows that Abraham believed in the resurrection. In Job 19:25, 26, the resurrection is pictured as the hope of future restoration of the body (ὁ ἐκλύειν με μέλλων ἐπὶ γῆς ἀναστῆσαι τὸ δέρμα μου τὸ ἀνατλῶν ταῦτα). The levirate law of Deut 25:6, 7 was also called on to illustrate the hope of the resurrection, presumed by "establishing of the name."

217. Hubbard, *New Creation in Paul's Letters and Thought*, 116–17.

acknowledges the significance of this paradigm for the church, when he argues that the new creation presupposes the reversal of the Gen 3 narrative, when "God's word comes from heaven to recreate the earth."[218] The Genesis creation–fall–re-creation paradigm was also understood by the apostles, who in Acts 15 looked for the common, basic principles of true worship.

The discussion above supports the conclusion that the pulsation of blood and the moving of the breath in the nostrils become signs of the presence of life in living creatures. Thus, both features, blood and breathing, symbolize life. If animal meat is used for food, part of it still has to be returned to the dust. This is why the blood must be poured out on the ground, because blood represents life.[219] Also the breath has to depart without being blocked, since breath also represents life. Faith in the resurrection was based on the word of God, but demonstrated in the act of the pouring out of blood. From this point, the prohibition of blood consumption, as well as the consumption of meat of a strangled animal, had as its purpose to uphold hope in the restoration of humanity and their world.

Cultic Fornication and the Apostolic Prohibition of πορνεία

The stark contrast between undefiled marriage (including non-sexualized cult) rooted in Gen 1–3 and pagan cultic fornication, sheds light on the prohibition of πορνεία.[220] *Unit four* (Gen 2:18–3:1) describes the creation of woman and of the first pair.[221] Detailed exegesis of the unit reveals three significant points: 1) the first pair were created out of one flesh; 2) the first marriage is viewed in terms "two become one flesh;" 3) people were created with the shameless condition of self perception and perception of each other. These points describe the first marriage in agreement with "the divinely ordained natural order."[222] All three conditions create an environment in which the first pair could naturally conduct true worship.[223]

---

218. Wright, *Paul*, 131.

219. Walton comes close to the idea of this thesis when he concludes that "ritually speaking, the draining of the blood before eating the meat was a way of returning the life force of the animal to God who gave it." Walton, *Genesis*, 343. However, his assumption that the prohibition had a ritual manner seems doubtful, for in this passage it was not given particularly for the ritual slaughtering at a holy place, but to any slaughtering anywhere.

220. Ciampa views this first marriage as a prototypical one. He also shows that Paul in his Epistles often uses quotations, allusions and echoes to this first marriage (Eph 5:31; 1 Cor 6:13, 19; 7:4). Ciampa and Rosner, *First Letter to the Corinthians*, 259.

221. Wenham states that in this passage, "the Old Testament fundamental convictions about the nature and purpose of marriage" were shown. "Here the ideal of marriage as it was understood in ancient Israel is being portrayed, a relationship characterized by harmony and intimacy between the partners." Wenham, *Genesis*, 69.

222. Sarna, *Genesis*, 23.

223. Wenham states that marriage, established by God, presumed participation in true worship, which later stood in opposition to pagan fertility cults. That is why the participation in fertility cults or

The harmony of marital relationship of the first humans was modelled by God.[224] Their "holy and ideal state of marriage" reflected the holiness of God.[225] Later the Holiness Code of Lev 18–20 would reflect the principles of this model marriage. This account of marriage in Gen 2:18 - 3:1 reflected in the Holiness Code contains a link between the condition of marriage and the condition of worship.[226] The priests were to model ideal marriages.[227] In the anti-idolatry polemic of the Pauline letters, the issue of πορνεία often is supported by citation and argumentation from the Holiness Code.[228] These features of the model marriage will now be discussed.

The first feature of this ideal marriage was a "separation." The separation is reflected in *Unit four* in two ways: it is made by God (in part 3 . . . ᾠκοδόμησεν κύριος ὁ θεὸς τὴν πλευράν ἣν ἔλαβεν ἀπὸ τοῦ Αδαμ εἰς γυναῖκα) and it is affirmed by Adam (in part 4 ὀστοῦν ἐκ τῶν ὀστέων μου καὶ σὰρξ ἐκ τῆς σαρκός μου).[229] Adam's interpretation of God's action focuses beforehand on the need of separation from the "mother cell." It was stated in the phrase καταλείψει ἄνθρωπος τὸν πατέρα αὐτοῦ καὶ τὴν μητέρα αὐτοῦ. As a result, the marriage with a close relative (at least, mother and father) was pictured as unnatural from the beginning and later was prohibited in the Holiness Code (Lev 18:6–18).

The second feature was "unity." *Unit four* reflects this "unity" in two ways similar to a "separation." The first step toward unity in v. 22 was taken by God, when he brought the woman to Adam (ἤγαγεν αὐτὴν πρὸς τὸν Αδαμ). The second step was made by Adam when he accepted the woman as his own woman/wife (αὕτη κληθήσεται γυνή, ὅτι ἐκ τοῦ ἀνδρὸς αὐτῆς ἐλήμφθη αὕτη). The intention of "unity" was expressed by καὶ προσκολληθήσεται πρὸς τὴν γυναῖκα αὐτοῦ.[230] The unity of the first marriage was stated by ἔσονται οἱ δύο εἰς σάρκα μίαν.

This monogamous model of marriage would set the pattern for healthy marital relationships according to the principle in v. 24, προσκολληθήσεται (which

---

"use of other devices to secure fertility" was considered to be a mark of unbelief. Wenham, *Genesis*, 33. Hilary Lipka shows that "the sexual norms and mores of the Hebrew Bible are a part of a theological construction, a set of ideals that may or may not reflect the sexual attitudes of the ancient Israelite majority." Lipka, *Sexual Transgression*, 36.

224. Belcher, *Genesis*, 64.

225. Waltke, *Genesis*, 89. He states that the first marriage became the exact model to which Jesus compared any other marriage.

226. The context of Israel's covenant with God suggests that marriage in the Old Testament also was understood in terms of a covenant. Wenham, *Genesis*, 71.

227. The constant call for holiness in Lev 17–20, in terms of "be holy for I am holy," reveals the role of humans from the beginning, to bear the image of God. Hartley, *Leviticus*, 292. This call proves the validity of the concepts established in Gen 1–3 for the "people of God."

228. This link is present in Rom 1:26, 27; 1 Cor 5:1, 15; 6:9–20; 1 Tim 1:10; Gal 5:19–21; Heb 13:4.

229. The diagram for *Unit four* of passage 2 is in Appendix 2.

230. To become "one flesh" would mean that "separated elements seek one another for reunification." Sarna, *Genesis*, 23.

means "to attach firmly, to enter into close association").²³¹ The violation of this προσκολληθήσεται principle and the destruction of the "one flesh" concept would result in a perverted marital relationship, which would interfere with true worship. That is why a priest, according to Lev 21:6–8, 13–15, is to marry a virgin of his own people, avoiding widows, divorced women, or those profaned by harlotry.²³² By this, a priest was expected to reflect Genesis creation holiness in the marital union. The same idea was repeated in Ezek 44:22, with the only change to include the widow of another priest. These rigorous rules were imposed on ministers of the cult in order to stress their closeness to God and their role in preserving true worship.

The third feature was the "shameless" condition of a mind uncorrupted by sin. Gen 3:1 καὶ ἦσαν οἱ δύο γυμνοί, ὅ τε Αδαμ καὶ ἡ γυνὴ αὐτοῦ, καὶ οὐκ ᾐσχύνοντο can be interpreted in two ways.²³³ First, the "shameless condition" of Adam and his wife can be explained by accepting that they are relative parts of one another. This may explain their lack of shame before each other, but cannot explain the lack of shame of nakedness before God, angels and future generations of people. The second explanation would view their lack of shame as the condition of minds uncorrupted by lust and perverted thoughts.

Consequently their unique "unawareness of shame" witnessed the ultimate purity (uncorrupted state) of people's self perception, their view of each other, and of the world.²³⁴ This condition contrasts with the shamelessness of pagan cultic fornication, where the monogamous model of "union" was consciously distorted.²³⁵ There the natural feeling of shame was supressed by ecstasy or opiate substances (like those in Prov 23:30–33).²³⁶ The first mention of shame in Gen 3:7–10 reveals the real degree of anguish associated with this feeling. The suddenness of the consequences was expressed by the phrase καὶ διηνοίχθησαν οἱ ὀφθαλμοὶ τῶν δύο (when the διηνοίχθησαν

---

231. Muraoka, *Greek-English Lexicon*, 596. The verb in LXX expresses both aspects: προσκολλήσαι κύριος in Deut 28:21 and προσκολληθήσεται πρὸς τὴν γυναῖκα in Gen 2:24. The "unity," here, also echoes the language of covenant commitment, when marriage reflects the faithfulness of God to his people. Waltke, *Genesis*, 90.

232. Though a marriage with widow cannot be viewed as polygamy, it implicitly presumed the alteration of the concept "two become one flesh." In cases with divorced women and harlots, the concept "two become one flesh" could not be maintained.

233. Ross believes that nakedness here "stresses the fact that they were completely at ease with each other." He sees it as sign of purity and integrity. Ross, "Genesis," 49.

234. Sarna interprets shamelessness when he states that their "pristine innocence and dignity of sexuality was not dispoiled." Sarna, *Genesis*, 23.

235. Hartley, *Leviticus*, 293–94. He views Lev 18, 20 in connection to the Gen 2:24 concept "two become one flesh." The argumentation in the Holiness Code against incestuous marriages is defined as, שאר בשר "inner flesh of his flesh." Accordingly, the Holiness Code was given to prevent the perversions of unfaithfulness, when the marriage includes many partners. Incest, to the contrary, takes place when the couple cannot be identified as "two," but they are "one blood kinship."

236. The preceeding passage of Prov 23:27, 28 describes a harlot, and supposedly links together πορνεία and use of wine.

is the passive aorist of διανοιγω, "to lay open").²³⁷ It means that immediately after the fall, people realized in themselves the shame of nakedness (ἔγνωσαν ὅτι γυμνοὶ ἦσαν) and fear before God (ἐφοβήθην ὅτι γυμνός εἰμι).²³⁸ The word γυμνοί, "naked," also may connote "guilty" and "vulnerable," which emphasizes that not the nakedness itself, but that guilt was a reason for shame.²³⁹ The fact that they made (ἐποίησαν ἑαυτοῖς περιζώματα) reflects human self-abhorrence and an attempt to hide this shameful nakedness. Later it leads the couple to hide in the middle of the garden in darkness and separates them.²⁴⁰ The transfer of guilt and fear in vv. 10, 12, 13 becomes the last indicator of experiencing shame.²⁴¹

The situation in *Unit seven* (3:9–13) illustrates that people involved in shameful actions are not able to offer true worship. It seems that each of them had chosen their own code of ethics, so they could not reflect God's holiness.²⁴² Instead the couple fled and hid from his holy presence. They clung to the ways of separation, darkness and death. The first shame also designated a new condition of the human mind after the fall, which can be defined as constant inclination to sin. Later this inclination seems to be used and abused in the pagan fertility cults.

The prominence of fertility cults brought participants to experiences which often contradicted the natural law appointed by God, and challenged human natural feelings of shame.²⁴³ Licentiousness resulting from pagan cult practices was called in the LXX πορνεία ("to commit fornication, to prostitute, pursue adulterously, to act as a harlot").²⁴⁴ The Holiness Code uses πορνεία in relation to extreme sexual perversions.²⁴⁵ Lipka states that "the Holiness collection (as well as the Decalogue)

---

237. Muraoka, *Greek-English Lexicon*, 155–56. The verb διανοιγω in Gen 3:5, 7 describes the discerning "eyes of a resuscitated human."

238. This can be assumed from the diagram of *Unit six* of Appendix 2.

239. Ross, "Genesis," 52. According to Muraoka, γυμνός means "undressed, naked." One wearing only an undergarment or tunic "may still be described as γυμνοί." This word can describe "a defeated nation being taken into captivity" in Isa 20:4. Muraoka, *Greek-English Lexicon*, 137.

240. Waltke, *Genesis*, 92. He notes that the sewing of fig leaves symbolizes the building of barriers between people and reveals their alienation from one another.

241. Here, people try "to minimise their culpability by suggesting that something else is more to blame." Wenham, *Genesis*, 89.

242. Waltke, *Genesis*, 92. He states that the knowing of good and evil is not a neutral state, it reveals human's ethical autonomy and spiritual separation from God.

243. It is noteworthy that in the Holiness Code πορνεία and other marriages with prohibited degree of union, are formed around the terms "nakedness" (21x) and "uncover" (16x), reflecting the shame of "nakedness," described in Gen 3:7. Hartley, *Leviticus*, 291.

244. According to the Greek Lexicon, the LXX use of πορνεία would imply, first of all, the meaning of sexual immorality, and in second order, unfaithfulness and apostasy in relation to God. It also in general, may mean "activity and attitude indicative of lust and search for gratification." Muraoka, *Greek-English Lexicon*, 578.

245. Lev 17–20. This passage discusses three out of four prohibitions, namely, idolatry, blood consumption, and fornication, calling these practices "abominable customs" which defile the participant and cut him off.

characterizes adultery solely as a transgression against religious boundaries."²⁴⁶ Strong antipathy toward basic concepts of marriage was embedded in the practices of paganism.²⁴⁷ Thus, πορνεία was different to μοιχεία, which means "act of adultery" and refers primarily to unfaithfulness in marriage without cultic connotations.²⁴⁸

Torah regularly associates πορνεία with pagan cultic activity.²⁴⁹ Even in cases when πορνεία was practiced without explicit involvement in pagan cults, it was presumed implicitly.²⁵⁰ Thus "nakedness" became an instrument of divination and found application in making of nude male and female images of gods, male and female temple prostitution, and orgies which accompanied religious feasts.²⁵¹ It reversed not only God's original design of creation but also the idea of true worship, hence Torah employs the language of harsh accusation in relation to fornication, expressed by πορνεία.²⁵² In Deut 22:22, sexual transgression is blamed for polluting the land and the people.²⁵³

Finally units *seven*, *eight*, and *nine* reveal that the unity of the first couple was achieved again. This process of restoration starts in Gen 3:9, when God initiated reconciliation with Adam, and ends in 3:22–25 when true worship is restored. Making priestly garments from animal skins, and bringing the first sacrifices, become the

---

246. Lipka, *Sexual Transgression*, 62.

247. There was "an ideological connection between sexual offences and certain pagan rites." The defilement, which comes from following pagan customs is identified by three roots: "unclean" (vv. 24 [2x], 25, 27, 28, 30), "detestable things" (vv. 26, 27, 29, 30), and "vomit" (vv. 25, 28 [2x]). Hartley, *Leviticus*, 290.

248. Muraoka, *Greek-English Lexicon*, 466.

249. OT passages expressing this association include: Gen 38:15, 24; Exod 34:15, 16; Num 25:1, 2; Deut 31:16; Judg 2:17; 8:27, 33; 2 Kgs 9:22; 1 Chr 5:25; 2 Chr 21:11; Jer 2:20; 3:6; 5:7; Ezek 6:9; 16:16, 17; 23:49; Hos 4:12–15; Mic 1:7; Nah 3:4. Rosser notes that "the link between apostasy or idolatry and πορνεία which can be found in the OT is strengthened in early Jewish teaching. Both idolatry and sexual immorality are associated with demons." He suppots this statement with several texts in the Testaments of the Twelve Patriarchs. He notes that CD and 1QS associate porneia with demons: "Sexual immorality in such texts is surrounded by demonic dangers and threats." Rosser, "Temple Prostitution," 344.

250. The story of Judah and Tamar would illustrate this thought. Although Tamar was not associated with temple prostitution, her actions copied the fertility cult pattern.

251. Stordalen notes that pagan cults included "sacred marriage" drama, which traditionally took place in the gardens (in order to imitate Eden) or dedicated chambers and included the banquets. Stordalen, *Echoes of Eden*, 107–9. Archeological evidences of Canaanite culture reveal images of crowned nude goddess found in Lachish and Taanach from the tenth to eleventh centuries BCE. Those images belonged to Asherah and were used in cults. Kitchen, *On the Reliability*, 408–10. Similar practices are recordered in Hos 4:11–15; Isa 57:3–13; Jer 2:20; 3:6.

252. The Holiness Code in Lev 18:19–23 describes the prohibitions of "polluting sexual unions" which includes moral and cultic defilement: sexual intercourse with a wife during menses or with a neighbor's wife, the sacrifice of children to Molech, unnatural sexual activities, homosexuality, and bestiality. The defiling nature of these practices was emphasised by the words "it is a detestable act" (v. 22), "it is a perversion" (v. 23), or "it is a lewd act" (v. 17). Hartley, *Leviticus*, 289.

253. Lipka, *Sexual Transgression*, 75.

precursors of the sanctuary cult.[254] Here, the cult is not yet developed, but only outlined in worship symbolism. The cherubs and the sword became the first symbols of the pattern of true worship at the gates of the garden.

At this point the hypothesis that the term πορνεία employed by the apostles in Acts 15:20, 29; 21:25 is linked to the Holiness Code can be postulated.[255] With that the rationale of the prohibition of πορνεία has to be viewed as rooted in Genesis 1–3. This is affirmed by Jesus' teaching about πορνεία.[256] The difference between πορνεία and μοιχεία is stressed in Matt 5:31, 32; 19:1–12; Mark 10:1–12 and Luke 16:18.[257] Here, Matt 19:1–12 and Mark 10:1–12 employ a midrashic form, the special feature of which is the direct quotation of Gen 2:23, 24.[258] Thus, the quotation clearly represents the basis on which the original concept rests, namely the account of Gen 1–3.[259]

The prohibition of πορνεία in Acts 15 is an attempt by the apostles to help the Gentile converts "reverse" their fallen condition to the state of a new creation.[260] Consequently, the rationale for the prohibition can be viewed as the restoration of true worship, which was made in order: 1) to prevent idolatry and practicing of fertility cults, 2) to prevent adultery and destruction of marriages, 3) to teach principles of God's universal law revealed in Torah, 4) to teach the new converts the holiness of God and the necessity of bearing God's image. Redirecting the converts from paganism toward the moral precepts of Torah would become the process of reversing the

---

254. The meaning of "garments of skin" is treated differently in rabbinic tradition: R. Eleazar states that the garments were made of goat-skin, while R. Yose bar Hanina pictures them as of skin with wool, and another source H. says that the name "garments of skin" is given to them because they were made from skin. Neusner, *Genesis Rabbah*, 2:227.

255. Klinghardt, *Gesetz*, 201. He states that the use of the term πορνεία in Acts 15:20 "was determined not by social but by cultic motives."

256. This term was used by Jesus in Matt 5:32. Also, in Matt 19:4–9, Jesus links the term πορνεία to the destruction of the original plan of God given at creation and consisting in unity of a human couple. It could also be a synonym for μοιχεία which is clear from Mark 7:21, when both terms are used together. In Luke 16:18, which parallels Matt 19:9, Jesus uses μοιχεία, similar to the tradition preserved in Mark 10:11, 12.

257. McIver argues, "the key word in Matt 5:32 and 19:9, πορνεία, has a wide variety of meanings in the rest of the NT, all associated with sexual impropriety. It is used to mean incest (1 Cor 5:1), prostitution (1 Cor 6:13), and probably with regard to prohibited degrees of marriage (Acts 15:20). It appears to be a more generic word than μοιχεία, which is specific to adultery." McIver, *Mainstream or Marginal*, 159.

258. The detailed description of this midrash is provided by Ellis, *Prophecy and Hermeneutic*, 159. The significant feature of this midrash is the concluding allusion to the initial text with help of the temporal indicator ἀπ' ἀρχῆς.

259. The allusion to Gen 2:24 is "used within the OT to prohibit divorce, as in Mal 2:15–16." Also, this text was usually quoted in the discussion of marriage (e.g. in Philo). Ciampa and Rosner, *First Letter to the Corinthians*, 259.

260. The pollution from πορνεία in the apostolic command τοῦ ἀπέχεσθαι τῶν ἀλισγημάτων . . . τῆς πορνείας can be explained from the perspective of Torah that viewed this practice as polluting. Hartley rightly shows that "ironically the very fertility rites the people engage in to increase the fertility of their land will pollute the land." Hartley, *Leviticus*, 298.

fall, and would support the healing of the believers from previous apostasy and habitual idolatry.[261]

New Testament Extra-Lukan Echoes of the Content of the Apostolic Decree

Echoes of the Decree in 1 Corinthians

There are similarities between Paul's theology in his epistles and the Lukan account of apostolic speeches in Acts 15.[262] His polemic against εἰδωλοθύτων and πορνεία supports the necessity to clarify the meaning of these two prohibitions of the Decree.[263] Evidence that the two prohibitions were found in his letters, led Bruce to conclude that Paul gladly received the resolutions of the Apostolic Decree.[264]

If one accepts Paul's connecting εἰδωλοθύτων and πορνεία to the two prohibitions of the Decree, how does one explain the absence of the other two prohibitions? Bruce suggests that Paul omitted the dietary prohibitions in all these passages because he offered no objection to food itself.[265] Moreover, Tomson shows that Paul seems to prohibit εἰδωλόθυτον in one part of the letter and permit it in another part.[266] Another issue is the nature of the food which is described as οὐδὲν κοινὸν δι' ἑαυτοῦ and πάντα μὲν καθαρά. How is it related to the "weakness" of the believer and the attitude to εἰδωλόθυτον in the different epistles?

Paul uses Jewish arguments, since many of them are similar to second temple Judaism halakhah.[267] This presumes that Paul would not view the prohibitions in a way contrary to that familiar to other Jews. Hays states that Paul in 1 Corinthians provides two different stages of typology, where the first is the antithetical correlation between Adam and Christ, and the second is the positive correlation between Israel

---

261. It has to be clarified that the changes in lifestyle, here, are not viewed as conditions for salvation. The redirecting of converts toward the moral law of Torah can be seen in James' reference to Moses in Acts 15:21.

262. Aageson, "Typology, Correspondence," 67–68. Thus, he sees the similarities between Gal 2:7–9 and Acts 15:7, where it is said that God chose to whom to entrust the Gospel to the Gentiles; also similarities between Gal 2:6 and Acts 15:9 where it is said that God "shows no partiality"; and similarity in belief that salvation is by faith in Gal 2:16 and Acts 15:11. Finally, the thought that the law was given "through the instrumentality" of angels in Gal 3:19–20 and Acts 7:53. Thus, it seems that the Twelve in Jerusalem and Paul shared similar beliefs.

263. Bruce explains εἰδωλοθύτων and πορνεία in Pauline letters in connection to the Apostolic Decree. He sees the references to the Decree in 1 Cor 6:18; 8:7–13; 10:25—11:1 and Rom 14:1—15:6.

264. Bruce, *Acts*, 331. The hypothetic antipathy between Paul and Peter (and James) seems to be a single case of Gal 2. In 1 Corinthians "Cephas is mentioned without any trace of hostility (1:12; 3:22; 9:5; 15:5); and the same is true of James (15:7; cf. 9:5)." Watson, *Paul, Judaism, and the Gentiles*, 151.

265. Bruce, *Acts*, 331.

266. Tomson, *Paul and the Jewish Law*, 207–8.

267. Tomson, *Paul and Jewish Law*, 202.

and the church.²⁶⁸ The link between creation and covenant "remains at the heart of Judaism and . . . was always central for Paul."²⁶⁹ For this reason one can expect the rationale to be rooted in the creation account which lies behind Pauline prohibitions of εἰδωλοθύτων and πορνεία.

The Reference to πόρνοι and εἰδωλολάτραι in 1 Cor 6:9–20

1 Cor 6:9–20 mentions both prohibitions and needs detailed exegesis.²⁷⁰ First, the main theme of this letter was polemic against idolatry. Paul probably wrote this Epistle from Ephesus.²⁷¹ His audience would be Gentile converts rather than pious Jews.²⁷² It is unlikely that Paul argues against Judaizers in the Corinthian congregation, because the issue in 1 Corinthians reflects the danger of a reversion to pagan idolatry rather than the danger of Jewish influence.²⁷³ Fee clarifies that in 1 Corinthians Paul argues against Corinthian γνῶσις, which they use to justify their right to attend idol feasts, since an idol is not a real god.²⁷⁴ Finally, Hays shows that typology, here, presumes that Christians in Corinth were "tempted to participate in pagan temple feasts."²⁷⁵

The diagram of this passage reveals Paul's theology.²⁷⁶ Part 1 (6:9–11) contains two specific matters, πόρνοι and εἰδωλολάτραι, listed under ἄδικοι.²⁷⁷ Here, πόρνοι echoes πορνείας (Acts 15:20, 29). The word εἰδωλολάτραι designates the cultic sacrifice brought to an idol shrine and is synonymous with εἰδωλοθύτων (Acts 15:29). Paul

---

268. Hays, *Echoes of Scripture*, 101. He shows an allusion in 1 Cor 10:20 to Deut 32:17 and denotes demons as the real subject of worship in idolatry. Then he also states the imagery correlation between Christian baptism and following Moses in the cloud and in the sea. Then, he shows an allusion of a "spiritual rock" to Christ. This typology helps Paul to demonstrate a contrast between idolatry and true worship. Thus, meat sacrificed to idols was defiling. The nature of meat is not under discussion here at all. The passage does not discuss the dietary laws and their role in the life of community.

269. Wright, *Paul*, 21, 23. He states, that "the book of Genesis demands to be read in this way: the promises to Abraham echo the commands to Adam." Moreover, Wright notes that the passage of Deut 27–30 "brings together creation and covenant in terms of the Land" and the passage of Isa 40–55 brings together creation and covenant in terms of restoration of Israel.

270. The diagram for this passage is in Appendix 2.

271. Watson, *Paul, Judaism, and the Gentiles*, 150–51. Roy Ciampa adds that 1 Corinthians was sent from Ephesus (1 Cor 16:8) during Paul's third missionary journey in 54–55 CE. Ciampa and Rosner, *First Letter to the Corinthians*, 3.

272. It is evident from 1 Cor 12:2, where the church members are pictured as the Gentile converts in the words, "when you were pagans . . ." Ciampa and Rosner, *First Letter to the Corinthians*, 3.

273. Watson, *Paul, Judaism, Gentiles*, 152.

274. Fee, *Pauline Christology*, 84. Concurrently, Fee believes that Paul's main argumentation deals with Corinthians' behavior, rather than theology. He finds the future bodily resurrection as only a theological issue of the letter. However, the present study will argue that Paul uses some specifically Jewish methods of interpretation of Scripture: midrash, typology, and complex quotations.

275. Hays, *Echoes of Scripture*, 97–98.

276. The diagram is in 2.1 in Appendix 2.

277. BDAG, ἄδικος, 1, "acting in a way that is contrary to what is right, *unjust, crooked*."

THE FOUR PROHIBITIONS OF ACTS 15

speaks in terms of hope to inherit θεοῦ βασιλείαν. He describes all types of ἀδικία in terms οὐ κληρονομήσουσιν, "will not inherit," and rejects the opportunity for them to be saved.[278] It seems that for Paul, God has nothing in common with all those matters, including πόρνοι and εἰδωλολάτραι.

The study of Genesis 1–3 makes it clear that idolatry, from the very beginning, stood in opposition to true worship. Some Jewish tradition of the first century assumed "a fusion of the Adam story and the story of the giving of the Law on Mount Sinai."[279] That is the reason for all transgressions being typologically compared not only to the sins of Israelites in the wilderness, but also to the primordial sin of Adam.[280] Wright rightly notes that when covenant promises "seem to have come crashing to the ground," the Israelites would recall Genesis 1 and the Exodus narrative in pleading for the power of God the Creator.[281] Paul's concern for the spiritual wellbeing of the Corinthian church, thus, would remind him not only of the history of his ancestors (sons of Abraham), but also of Adam's story, which unites all nations under a single obligation of true worship.

The appearance of μοιχοὶ (from μοιχός "adulterer, one who is unfaithful to a spouse/ to God") in the list may indicate that it is different in meaning from πόρνοι.[282] The presense of πόρνοι, μοιχοί, μαλακοὶ (from μαλακός "soft, effeminate" in a same-sex relationship), ἀρσενοκοῖται (from ἀρσενοκοίτης, "male homosexual, sodomite") together in the same list may look like a particularization of sexual perversions.[283] It is noteworthy, that εἰδωλολάτραι appears among the four sexual matters, while κλέπται follows. The list of Corinthian vices in 5:9 contains only four of those matters (πόρνοι, εἰδωλολάτραι, πλεονέκται, and ἅρπαγες), while 5:11 adds to it μέθυσοι "drunkards" and λοίδοροι "revilers, abusive persons." Thus, the sexual perversions (μοιχοὶ,

---

278. Craig Blomberg views the twofold affirmation that the wicked will not inherit the kingdom of God in connection with the rebellious nature of the Corinthians (not a few particular sins, but a lifestyle). He states, "persistent rebellion . . . calls into question any prior profession of faith." Blomberg, *1 Corinthians*, 121. This persistent rebellion reveals the Corinthians as copying Israel's behavior in the wilderness and finally sharing the same damnation.

279. Ziesler, "Role of the Tenth Commandment," 144, 145. Targum Neofiti on Gen 2:15 states that Adam "was put into the Garden to observe the Law" and on Gen 3:24 states that "the tree of life is the Law."

280. In rabbinic midrash, the story of Adam in the garden of Eden is compared in tiny details to the story of Israel in the Land. The commandment in Gen 2:16 is linked to one in Exod 27:20 and Lev 24:2. Then Dan 9:11 is taken to describe a violation of the commandments by Israelites, while Jer 15:1 and Hos 9:15 picture the expulsion from the Land in a similar way to the expulsion from Paradise. Neusner, *Genesis Rabbah*, 2:201, 208–9.

281. Wright, *Paul*, 24, 38. He notes in Paul's letters the frequent allusions to creation: Col 1:15–20; 1 Cor 15; and Rom 1–11. Also, Paul mentions creation in Acts 17:22–31, in his preaching to the Gentiles. Wright states that in Paul's theology of creation and covenant all the nations can share a new creation on equal terms.

282. BDAG, μοίχος, 1, 2.

283. BDAG, μαλακός, 1, 2; ἀρσενοκοίτης. Also μοιχοὶ (from μοίχος "adulterer"), μαλακοὶ (from μαλακός "soft, effeminate"), ἀρσενοκοῖται (from ἀρσενοκοίτης, "male homosexual, sodomite").

μαλακοὶ, ἀρσενοκοῖται), followed by κλέπται, are mentioned only in 6:9.[284] The order can suggest that in 6:9, 10 Paul views the vices in terms of the Decalogue, and provides a full list of offences in relation to the seventh commandment, Exod 20:14 "you shall not commit adultery," before turning to the eighth. So, the first six vices reflect the Decalogue prohibitions.

It is also noteworthy, that while the seventh commandment (against adultery) has this fourfold expansion in 1 Cor, the first two commandments were summed up in one word: εἰδωλολάτραι. Placing εἰδωλολάτραι between πόρνοι and μοιχοὶ, and not before those matters, may indicate that sexual perversions in Corinth had been stimulated and promoted by pagan cults. The last five κλέπται, πλεονέκται, μέθυσοι, λοίδοροι, ἅρπαγες seem to reflect aspects of social life, and have no direct support from cults. It is hard to accept that any society would ideologically support the success of thieves, the greedy, drunkards, slanderers and swindlers. These vices were likely the indirect result of demon possession associated with pagan cults. From a spiritual perspective, they are to be viewed as self-destructive.[285]

In v. 11 Paul shows that those ten perversions were the practice of some members before their conversion to Christ: καὶ ταῦτά τινες ἦτε. Their previous condition could include possession by demons. Their present state presupposes their association with the Spirit of God and the name of Jesus. Paul calls for rejection of demon worship in the following phrase: ἀλλὰ ἀπελούσασθε, ἀλλὰ ἡγιάσθητε, ἀλλὰ ἐδικαιώθητε.[286] The word ἀπελούσασθε likely refers to baptism rite, while sanctification and righteousness become matters credited to believers: ἐν τῷ ὀνόματι τοῦ κυρίου Ἰησοῦ Χριστοῦ καὶ ἐν τῷ πνεύματι τοῦ θεοῦ ἡμῶν. Moreover, the way in which Paul describes conversion, progressing from "cleansed" to "made holy" suggests that the converts are prepared for true worship.[287]

Part 2 (6:12–14) starts with the repetition significant for Pauline writings "πάντα . . . ἀλλὰ."[288] This construction appears in 1 Cor 6:12 in the form of dialogue:

---

284. Ciampa and Rosner, *First Letter to the Corinthians*, 241–42. He states that Paul's denial of the homosexual relations seems to be derived from Lev 18:22 and 20:13 and built on a basis of creation theology.

285. Blomberg, *1 Corinthians*, 121.

286. Here, passive aorists ἀπελούσασθε from ἀπολούω, ἡγιάσθητε from ἁγιάζω and ἐδικαιώθητε from δικαιόω follow one another. BDAG, ἀπολούω, "wash someth. away, *wash oneself.*" BDAG, ἁγιάζω, 2, "*consecrate, dedicate, sanctify*" in both a cultic and moral sense. BDAG, δικαιόω, 3, "*make free/pure,*" the word "refers to a radical inner change." These three words "stress the transformation that has been effected by God." All three verbs are metaphors of conversion, which "refer to a break with the old life . . . and the beginning of a new life." Ciampa and Rosner, *First Letter to the Corinthians*, 244.

287. Ciampa notes that Paul, here, recalls the temple motif prominent in the letter. Ciampa and Rosner, *First Letter to the Corinthians*, 244.

288. Ciampa states that "much of Paul's language here is clipped and elliptical." Ciampa and Rosner, *First Letter to the Corinthians*, 245.

Πάντα μοι ἔξεστιν,
        ἀλλ' οὐ πάντα συμφέρει.
Πάντα μοι ἔξεστιν,
        ἀλλ' οὐκ ἐγὼ ἐξουσιασθήσομαι ὑπό τινος.

Similar rythmic repetition can be found in 1 Cor 10:23, 24, where Paul also discusses πορνεύωμεν (10:8), εἰδωλολατρίας (10:14), εἰδωλόθυτόν (10:19) and ἱερόθυτόν (10:28). Comparing these two passages, one can see that the first lines are repeated without change. The second line of 1 Cor 10:23 has different wording; the third line contains an addition, μηδεὶς τὸ ἑαυτοῦ ... ἀλλὰ τὸ τοῦ ἑτέρου.

Figure 19: 1 Cor 10:23b

Πάντα ἔξεστιν,
        ἀλλ' οὐ πάντα συμφέρει.
Πάντα ἔξεστιν,
        ἀλλ' οὐ πάντα οἰκοδομεῖ.
Μηδεὶς τὸ ἑαυτοῦ ζητείτω
        ἀλλὰ τὸ τοῦ ἑτέρου.

The first two lines keep the form of a dialogue, while the third becomes its turning point. All statements introduced by πάντα seem to be the claims of the Corinthians themselves, which reached Paul.[289] The phrase πάντα ἔξεστιν looks like permission of unlimited freedom of actions. The ἀλλ' οὐ reflects Paul's own opinion concerning πάντα ἔξεστιν, which presumes prudent limitations of that freedom. However, the third line does not begin with an unconditional declaration, πάντα ἔξεστιν.[290] It continues to deal with Paul's limitations, seen from the negative tone of μηδεὶς τὸ ἑαυτοῦ ζητείτω, "let no man seek his own," by which Paul brings a reader to the logical conclusion, ἀλλὰ τὸ τοῦ ἑτέρου. The phrase, here, reports not what the Corinthians said, but what they overlooked when saying, πάντα ἔξεστιν: rejection of self-centeredness and a beneficial other-centered life among Christians. Whether πάντα ἔξεστιν represents the belief of the congregation in unconditional, unlimited freedom of lifestyle is not clear, but Paul's view opposes a selfish approach and underscores the needs of others.

---

289. Blomberg views this phrase as a Pauline quotation of a Corinthian slogan. The scholar notes that Paul gives a limited endorsement of Corinthian thoughts and substantially qualifies them. Blomberg, *1 Corinthians*, 125.

290. It was noticed that even in the Gentile world, the uncontrolled desires were viewed in a negative sense. Thus Plato (*Republic*, 4.439d) and Demosthenes (*Funeral Speech*, 60.2) criticized the desire for the pleasures of sex and food and called citizens to control those matters by "reason." Malcolm, *World of 1 Corinthians*, 48.

It is noteworthy that a similar structure appears in Rom 14:20. Here, again, the first clause of the sentence, which is πάντα μὲν καθαρά, would represent the beginning of the dialogue in which the opinion of another side is summarized or repeated.

πάντα μὲν καθαρά,

ἀλλὰ κακὸν τῷ ἀνθρώπῳ τῷ διὰ προσκόμματος ἐσθίοντι.

This observation supports the assumption that the statement, πάντα μὲν καθαρά, was not Paul's own belief. On the contrary, this was the belief, which Paul questioned, discussed and brought into harmony with the teaching of Christ. The understanding that πάντα μὲν καθαρά is Paul's own opinion, could proceed from the phrase οἶδα καὶ πέπεισμαι ἐν κυρίῳ Ἰησοῦ ὅτι οὐδὲν κοινὸν δι' ἑαυτοῦ, which appears in Rom 14:14. Although the phrase reflects Paul's belief, written in the first person, it uses κοινὸν, not καθαρά, where the word κοινὸν usually refers to the ritual uncleanness. Paul's statement here could echo the teaching of Jesus in Matt 15:17–20 (Mark 7:19) involving the issue of ritual food uncleanness connected to eating with unwashed hands. Both Matthew and Paul use κοινὸν in relation to ritual uncleanness.

The phrase, πάντα μὲν καθαρά, appears only in Rom 14:20 and not in first person singular. It also does not maintain the structure of v. 14, where clauses are connected by the conjunction ὅτι. In v. 20 the clauses are connected by πάντα . . . ἀλλά. Futhermore, the phrase ἀλλὰ κακὸν τῷ ἀνθρώπῳ τῷ διὰ προσκόμματος ἐσθίοντι accents the needs of others, in contrast to a selfish attitude.[291] The rejection of selfish desires, in order not to harm anyone, is clearly stated in the following additional clause καλὸν τὸ μὴ φαγεῖν κρέα μηδὲ πιεῖν οἶνον μηδὲ ἐν ᾧ ὁ ἀδελφός σου προσκόπτει.[292] This additional clause is used to contrast κακὸν and καλὸν. Paul's purpose is to show good (καλὸν) behavior. Thus, his own view appears here, not earlier. At this time it becomes evident that πάντα μὲν καθαρά in Rom 14:20 reflects the opinion of Paul's listeners, with which he notably disagrees.

After two πάντα . . . ἀλλά statements in 1 Cor 6:12, Paul in v. 13 takes up the discussion of two matters: food and πορνεία. First, he states that the stomach and food are designed for one another: τὰ βρώματα τῇ κοιλίᾳ, καὶ ἡ κοιλία τοῖς βρώμασιν.[293] This belief could be employed by Paul to echo sayings known in Corinth. However, more likely, here Paul expresses his own observation of the hopeless condition of the person whose life is only a constant filling of the stomach. This constant care for physical needs of the stomach echoes Gen 3:18, 19, where God said to Adam: ἐν λύπαις φάγῃ αὐτὴν πάσας τὰς ἡμέρας τῆς ζωῆς σου. After pronouncing Adam's

---

291. The meaning ". . . but it is wrong for a man to eat anything that causes someone else to stumble" (Rom 14:20).

292. The meaning "It is better not to eat meat or drink wine or to do anything else that will cause your brother to fall" (Rom 14:21).

293. Blomberg views this Pauline statement as the specific reference to freedom from Jewish dietary laws. Blomberg, *1 Corinthians*, 126.

curse, God announced its temporal limitations: ἕως τοῦ ἀποστρέψαι σε εἰς τὴν γῆν, ἐξ ἧς ἐλήμφθης. This life-long curse of man to work for the needs of the stomach could be in the background of Paul's statement in 1 Cor 6:13. This is supported by Paul's statement which has two parts. In the first, the phrase τὰ βρώματα τῇ κοιλίᾳ, καὶ ἡ κοιλία τοῖς βρώμασιν emphasizes care for the stomach. The second part presents life-long limitations: ὁ δὲ θεὸς καὶ ταύτην καὶ ταῦτα καταργήσει.[294] The phrase ταῦτα [κοιλία] καταργήσει, "destroy the stomach," could have been understood to refer to death.[295] It could also reflect the Genesis statement of God: ὅτι γῆ εἶ καὶ εἰς γῆν ἀπελεύσῃ. Thus, the living person whose value is reduced to a constant filling of the stomach has no eternal hope. This statement contrasts with permission to eat food: ἡ κοιλία τοῖς βρώμασιν.

The situation with πορνεία is pictured by Paul as even worse. He states: τὸ δὲ σῶμα οὐ τῇ πορνείᾳ.[296] Thus, for Paul, πορνεία is the perversion of human behavior, and becomes a violation of natural law. Paul stresses his thought with the help of an additional clause, which defines the purpose for which the physical body has been made: ἀλλὰ τῷ κυρίῳ, καὶ ὁ κύριος τῷ σώματι.[297] The belief that the body belongs to God also reflects Gen 2:7. This is a reversal of a fallen condition in which life is viewed as given over only to physical needs of the stomach, in contrast to God who gives true meaning to life and brings hope.

This reversal suggests that the Genesis account is the background to Paul's thought. The consequences of Adam's sin were stated as, "by the sweat of your brow you will eat your food until you return to the ground" (Gen 3:19). This pronouncement narrowed the meaning of human life to a constant care for filling the stomach. Despite that the fact that the consequences of the fall are still present in the world, Paul calls Christians to revert from a focus on physical matters predicted in Gen 3:19, to the original unity with God described in Gen 2:7. Paul expresses this hope of reversion in verse 14: ὁ δὲ θεὸς καὶ τὸν κύριον ἤγειρεν καὶ ἡμᾶς ἐξεγερεῖ διὰ τῆς δυνάμεως

---

294. The meaning ". . . but God will destroy them both" (1 Cor 6:13).

295. It was suggested that this phrase shows that both matters (eating and sexuality) are limited to this life. Blomberg, *1 Corinthians*, 126.

296. Here the several aspects of πορνεία were suggested: 1) sexual immorality in general; 2) the incest mentioned in 5:1; 3) sacred prostitution; 4) temple prostitution; 5) secular prostitution. The cultic aspect of πορνεία, here, seems to be most preferable since Paul in vv. 12–20 uses sacral language. This cultic aspect presumes both sacred prostitution (belonging to the fertility cult in a sanctuary) and temple prostitution (taking place during pagan feasts). Thus, the participation in πορνεία has to be viewed not only as immorality, but also as unfaithfulness to God. Ciampa and Rosner, *First Letter to the Corinthians*, 246–49.

297. Ciampa detects an echo of Gen 2:24 in the Pauline statement, which emphasizes the mutuality of the relationship between human beings and their God which copies mutuality between a man and a woman. Ciampa and Rosner, *First Letter to the Corinthians*, 255. However it seems that Paul echoes Gen 2:7 here, rather than 2:24.

αὐτοῦ.²⁹⁸ The word δυνάμεως, becoming an agent of re-creation, brings about the echoing of creation in this passage.

Part 3 (6:15–20) is most likely an explanation of the previously stated concept, God's ownership of the body. This part clearly shows that Genesis 1–3 is in the background of Pauline ideas. This is shown by a direct quotation of Gen 2:24 in 1 Cor 6:16: Ἔσονται γάρ, φησίν, οἱ δύο εἰς σάρκα μίαν. Thus, for Paul, πορνεία becomes the violation of the law given at creation. Paul's three times repeated οὐκ οἴδατε indicates the presence of particular knowledge in the Corinthian church. It seems that the believers in Corinth were aware of the Genesis account of creation. Paul builds his arguments on the basis of natural law, known from Genesis. This demonstrates the validity of natural law for Christians in Paul's day. The assumption that Paul keeps the law in mind when he writes about πορνεία can be explained by his use of the word ἁμάρτημα, which reflects action against a commandment of the law, and not just wrong behavior.²⁹⁹

Paul employs two contrasts: πόρνη with Χριστοῦ, and σῶμά with πνεῦμά. For him, the Christians belong to Christ, because their σώματα, "bodies," have already become members of Christ's body. Further, in v. 17 the apostle shows that unity of many in the one body of Christ is achieved by the presence of the Holy Spirit in the believers. It is expressed by the phrase ὁ δὲ κολλώμενος τῷ κυρίῳ ἓν πνεῦμά ἐστιν, "but he who unites himself with the Lord becomes one in spirit" (1 Cor 6:17).³⁰⁰ This unity with God may be destroyed by sinning. Paul cursorily mentions πᾶν ἁμάρτημα, but focuses on πορνεία. He explains his emphasis in the phrase, ὁ δὲ πορνεύων εἰς τὸ ἴδιον σῶμα ἁμαρτάνει.³⁰¹ The contrast between sins "outside the body" and sin "against one's own body" may assume the element of defilement. Defilement of the body, for Paul is equal, to defilement of the temple.³⁰²

In v. 19 Paul asks again, ἢ οὐκ οἴδατε ὅτι τὸ σῶμα ὑμῶν ναὸς τοῦ ἐν ὑμῖν ἁγίου πνεύματός ἐστιν? This question, with reference to common knowledge, reveals that Corinthians had an earlier opportunity to hear this teaching. On this occasion Paul designates the reason: one's body is to be dedicated to God. His words, καὶ οὐκ ἐστὲ ἑαυτῶν and ἠγοράσθητε γὰρ τιμῆς, reveal that those who are redeemed from slavery

---

298. Here, Pauline eschatology corrects Corinthian beliefs that the body is insignificant and transitory. Paul states that body will be raised. Ciampa and Rosner, *First Letter to the Corinthians*, 255.

299. BDAG, ἁμάρτημα, "*sin, transgression.*"

300. The phrase may be interpreted in a way that "Paul corrects the Corinthians' misapplication of Christian freedom and asserts that believers' bodies come under the lordship of the risen Christ." Ciampa and Rosner, *First Letter to the Corinthians*, 251.

301. It seems that even the converts who had no Jewish background could understand Paul. In the Greco-Roman world philosophers viewed sexual purity as the order "to preserve the purpose or nobility of the marriage relationship." Moreover, "Roman moralists praised self-control and sexual morality." In art, "the noble enjoyment of bodily beauty was related to an appreciation of the beauty of the soul." Malcolm, *World of 1 Corinthians*, 70–74.

302. Blomberg notes that in vv. 19–20 Paul reapplies the temple imagery. He also states that τὸ σῶμα ὑμῶν may reflect the "distributive singular" construction, which allows Paul to speak about the individual bodies. Blomberg, *1 Corinthians*, 127.

to sin now belong to God.³⁰³ Although Paul states Christians are not their own, but servants of God, their service is different to the service of slaves and reflects priestly service. Their priestly (even prophetic) call is made obvious in the phrase δοξάσατε δὴ τὸν θεὸν ἐν τῷ σώματι ὑμῶν.³⁰⁴ This also correlates with the images of ναὸς and ἁγίου πνεύματός, whom the Christians have received from God.³⁰⁵

The idea of one's body belonging to God and his ναὸς may provide the common basis for all four prohibitions of the Apostolic Decree. It includes both cultic and ethical aspects of the Decree. These aspects of the Decree help: 1) to unite believers by renewed worship into a spiritual sanctuary of God; 2) to rethink the purpose of living in the world and not associating with its sinfulness; 3) to emphasize the holiness of believers in both spirit and body for the purpose of glorifying God. The integration of the cultic and ethical aspects of the Decree is grounded in Gen 1–3 and the principles of the natural law of God. The prohibitions can be united only on a basis of the eternal law of God known from the beginning of creation. This eternal law reflects the unity of body and spirit.

The Reference to εἰδωλοθύτων and πορνεία in 1 Cor 5:1, 9–11

This passage combines prohibitions of πορνεία and of εἰδωλοθύτων when dealing with a problem in the congregation itself. It also clarifies the meaning of πορνεία.

Figure 20: 1 Cor 5:1

Ὅλως ἀκούεται ἐν ὑμῖν πορνεία,
    → καὶ τοιαύτη πορνεία ἥτις οὐδὲ ἐν τοῖς ἔθνεσιν,
        → ὥστε γυναῖκά τινα τοῦ πατρὸς ἔχειν.

According to verse 1, the kind of πορνεία in the Corinthian church would not occur even among pagans.³⁰⁶ Here, Paul likely refers to natural law which, according to Rom 2:14, is known even to the Gentiles. It calls for uniting people in marriages which are in accord with the order in Gen 2:23, 24. The situation after the fall deformed mar-

---

303. The meaning, "you are not your own . . . you were bought at a price" (1 Cor 6:20)

304. This statement was assumed as concluding the previous discussion and positively pointing to the purpose of Christian bodily life. Ciampa and Rosner, *First Letter to the Corinthians*, 259.

305. The picture of bodies as temples filled with the Spirit of God reflects the idea of the constant presence of God with his people, which is known from creation.

306. Blomberg states that the marriage of a man to his stepmother was prohibited not only in Jewish law (Lev 18:8), but also was widely condemned in the Greco-Roman world. The negative attitude of the Gentile world to incestuous marriages can be found in Cicero's documents. Blomberg, *1 Corinthians*, 104.

riage life; divorce and polygamy appeared. Gentiles pacticed sacral prostitution linked to their idols' cults. These actions would be understood by Paul as πορνεία, which occurs among pagans. The case in the Corinthian congregation is treated by Paul in a very serious manner, because it violates the very heart of the marital law.

Here, the apostle again refers not only to Leviticus 18, but also to Gen 2:24, where it is stated: καταλείψει ἄνθρωπος τὸν πατέρα αὐτοῦ καὶ τὴν μητέρα αὐτοῦ. The necessity to leave parents is behind the law in Lev 18:8, when the wife of someone's father is understood as "his own nakedness," according to the principle ἔσονται οἱ δύο εἰς σάρκα μίαν. That is why uniting (προσκολληθήσεται) with one's father's wife would be viewed by Paul as an exceptional perversion. In relation to this matter, Paul suggests disfellowshipping.[307] In addition, vv. 7–8 use Passover imagery as the background to the discussion. Immorality, there, is compared to the "old leaven." The comparison metaphorically shows "the dynamic process by which a little evil spreads throughout the wider entity, until the whole becomes infected."[308]

The following passage, 1 Cor 5:9–11, continues the practical application of teaching about πορνεία. A reference to the previous letter (sent to him from the Corinthian church and not preserved) is behind the words, Ἔγραψα ὑμῖν ἐν τῇ ἐπιστολῇ. There, Paul was suggesting μὴ συναναμίγνυσθαι πόρνοις "not to associate with sexually immoral people" (1 Cor 5:9).[309] However, his further correction of a view suggests that the church had difficulties understanding it. Paul's corrected explanation contains two parts. The first speaks about πάντως τοῖς πόρνοις τοῦ κόσμου τούτου. In the previous letter (not preserved) the apostle suggested the church avoid connections with the adulterers of the world. That was suggested at the beginning of their Christian conversion, when many had a tendency to follow their old pagan habits. Now (νῦν δὲ) Paul sees another danger from those who bear the name of Christ (ἐάν τις ἀδελφὸς ὀνομαζόμενος) and at the same time remain ἢ πόρνος. It is noteworthy that here only six matters appear out of those ten which Paul mentions later in 6:9, 10. Hays rightly notes, "the implicit claim of 1 Cor 5:13 is made explicit in the metaphorical structure of the typology in 1 Cor 10:1–22."[310]

The matters μοιχοί, μαλακοί, ἀρσενοκοῖται, κλέπται, which Paul represents as sins of converts' previous pagan lives, are omitted in chapter 5, where Paul writes about the sins in this particular church. Omitting μοιχοί, μαλακοί, ἀρσενοκοῖται could be explained by the fact that those sins were parts of pagan idol worship, and that, having no support from the doctrinal teaching of the church, they vanished.

---

307. The meaning of v. 5 can be clarified by the Deuteronomic expulsion formula used in v. 13. Here the vv. 5, 7, 8 and 11 are the metaphorical expression of that expulsion, and not envisioning of a physical death. Ciampa and Rosner, *First Letter to the Corinthians*, 197.

308. Meyer, *End of the Law*, 49.

309. This prohibition could include dining with sexually immoral people in pagan temples. However, in 1 Corinthians Paul does not view the same matters. He likely speaks about simple social contact with non-believers. Ciampa and Rosner, *First Letter to the Corinthians*, 216.

310. Hays, *Echoes of Scripture*, 97.

Although the problem with εἰδωλολάτρης was still present, members of the Christian community would not practice it as part of the new service. If they did, they did it occasionaly, being involved in idolatry outside their Christian worship. However, πορνεία was still an unsolved issue of the congregation. To solve it Paul demands: τῷ τοιούτῳ μηδὲ συνεσθίειν.[311]

Here, Paul calls for the church to break table fellowship with those Christians who, by their way of life, are πόρνος, εἰδωλολάτρης etc. From this point the issue of common table fellowship in the church is raised.[312] However, Paul uses table fellowship not to unite the church, but to separate some from the church. The separation here is demanded in order to reject ἄδικοι.[313] The actions of Paul here recall those described in Ps 101:5–7. The Psalm provides a clue for table fellowship disciplining, when "the presence of God in the temple and evil are said to be incompatible."[314] Now it is evident that Paul views the situation in the church in terms of controversy between true worship and idolatry. The controversy itself echoes the fall narrative, where Adam was invited to share food that he should have rejected, in order to sustain true worship (Gen 3:6).

The kind of table fellowship regulations used by Paul may support the thought that the apostles on the council would not allow table fellowship as permission to mix with blatant sinners. Table fellowship was used to build unity in the church around a model of righteous behavior, not in order to permit a violation of the law. Participation in the Lord's Table presumed that all members are equally accepted in the kingdom of God. The common table fellowship was practiced to stress equality among the members, in terms of salvation, not in terms of the similarity of their diet.

This suggests that the four prohibitions of the Decree should not be understood as the regulations for common table fellowship in mixed communities. Otherwise they would become necessary for salvation.[315] The four prohibitions, contrastingly, were necessary not for salvation, but for the prevention of idolatry and defilement (or

---

311. Meaning "with such a man do not even eat" (1 Cor 5:11). BDAG, συνεσθίω, "*eat with someone.*"

312. The Passover context of this passage suggests that the sinning church members were to be rejected from communion (Lord's Table) first of all. The expulsion from the common meals also could be presumed. Ciampa and Rosner, *First Letter to the Corinthians*, 215.

313. Ciampa suggests that those sinners had to be excluded from the Lord's Table as well as other meals of church fellowship. This was viewed as a disciplining action, for the withdrawal from table fellowship that was commonly understood as a dishonoring action. Ciampa and Rosner, *First Letter to the Corinthians*, 218.

314. Ciampa and Rosner, *First Letter to the Corinthians*, 219.

315. The four prohibitions of the Decree were given to Gentile converts, in respect to the natural law of God known from the creation-fall narrative. This narrative built the common basis for all four prohibitions and pointed to God's ordained plan for all humankind: worshiping the one true God. This reversal from idolatry to the one true God was presupposed in the apostolic application of the natural law to the Gentiles. As long as the common meals in the church conformed to the practicing of true worship, they could be viewed in association with the four prohibitions of the Decree.

pollution) inflicted by a violation of the key points of the natural law of God.³¹⁶ The defilement, in turn, would separate one from true worship and God.

The sins described by Paul in chapter 5 (as issues in the church) and in chapter 6 (in the world) have nothing in common with the kingdom of God, as stated: μὴ πλανᾶσθε• οὔτε πόρνοι οὔτε εἰδωλολάτραι . . . βασιλείαν θεοῦ κληρονομήσουσιν. Hence Paul calls for a break of table fellowship with sinners in the church, not those in the world: οὐ πάντως τοῖς πόρνοις τοῦ κόσμου τούτου . . . ἢ εἰδωλολάτραις, ἐπεὶ ὠφείλετε ἄρα ἐκ τοῦ κόσμου ἐξελθεῖν. The prohibition of table fellowship, here, has a deep rationale.³¹⁷ It suggests that food in the days of the apostles had great illustrative power for spiritual matters. Banishment from the communion table or even from a common meal could be viewed as banishment from the kingdom of God.

From this point, the Apostolic Decree cannot be viewed as an indulgence for ἀδικία (for the freedom of the Gentile mission from the law). The apostles would not reduce the law to four senseless matters in order to equivocate the teaching of Torah for the sake of the Gentile party.³¹⁸ The prohibitions of the Decree were set in agreement with the teaching of Torah and that of the church where δικαιοσύνη was still of great value. Moreover, the regulation of table fellowship in the apostolic church was called for to support true worship and to reject idolatry.

The Reference to εἰδωλοθύτων in 1 Cor 8:1–13

1 Cor 8:1–13, according to internal logic, has to be divided into five parts. Part 1 (8:1–3) reveals the contrast between knowledge (γνῶσις), to which the Corinthian church has an inclination, and an ethical approach (ἀγάπη) for which Paul calls. At first sight it seems that Paul shows a preference for ethics above knowledge.³¹⁹ This unusual preference may suggest that the issue discussed here is not of doctrinal, but of ethical sense. However, this accent on ἀγάπη can be explained by the incompleteness,

---

316. The situation in 1 Cor 5:1–3 can be an illustration of how violating one of those four prohibitions "has defiled the holiness of God's temple, the church." Ciampa believes that Paul judging the sinner in the Corinthian church included the OT temple/holiness motif. According to his view, "the man must suffer 'destruction' because he has destroyed God's holy temple, the church." Ciampa and Rosner, *First Letter to the Corinthians*, 210.

317. Ciampa, with reference to Horbury, shows that "during the Second Temple period the scope of the laws of admission to the assembly, found in Deut 23:2–9 (1–8), were expanded beyond stipulations of physique and descent to include moral requirements." Josephus and Philo used Deut 23 to exclude "not only aliens and defective Jews, but also gravely-offending Jewish sinners." Ciampa and Rosner, *First Letter to the Corinthians*, 211.

318. On the contrary, the call of the Gentile converts to righteousness was to illustrate that "Christ died not just to cleanse them, but to transform them." Ciampa and Rosner, *First Letter to the Corinthians*, 215.

319. Blomberg suggests that "knowledge" here "must be interpreted, as in chapters 1–4, to refer to prideful human religious speculation." Also it is what "stresses freedom and human autonomy at the expense of concern of others." Blomberg, *1 Corinthians*, 161–64.

or even the unreliability of knowledge in the Corinthian church about εἰδωλοθύτων.[320] Their knowledge seemed to contradict the teaching of Christ on some points.[321]

This echoes the independent knowledge described in Genesis 3, where the forbidden fruit represents the first εἰδωλοθύτων. The serpent (independent from God) promised people they would become gods and judges of good and evil. The issue Paul discussed in 1 Cor 8:1–13 contains many allusions to Gen 3.[322] The reality of demons echoes the fall narrative, when the serpent revealed the cult of sacred knowledge. There the controversy between true worship and idolatry started. This can be compared to the double standard conscience of the "weak" in Corinth. The wish of the first humans to know good and evil can be assumed to be a desire for moral autonomy; the right to judge. This may find a parallel to the judgemental autonomy of the "strong" in Corinth.

Paul does not accept knowledge independent from the ἀγάπη of Christ. He warns that knowledge of this kind "puffs up, makes proud" (φυσιοῖ).[323] The adversative conjunction δὲ contrasts not only γνῶσις and ἀγάπη, but also φυσιοῖ and οἰκοδομεῖ. For the apostle the knowledge which puffs up is incomplete (οὔπω ἔγνω καθὼς δεῖ γνῶναι, "he does not yet know as he ought to know," in 1 Cor 8:2). The love which builds up (ἀγάπη οἰκοδομεῖ) is linked to true knowledge, which is at work through love for God (εἰ δέ τις ἀγαπᾷ τὸν θεόν). It is not disconnected from God (οὗτος ἔγνωσται ὑπ᾽ αὐτοῦ) and comes from God. Thus Paul started the discussion about εἰδωλοθύτων with a polemic about the sources and kinds of knowledge.

Part 2 (8:4–6) clarifies that in this passage Paul speaks about εἰδωλοθύτων in relation to food of different kinds (βρώσεως οὖν τῶν εἰδωλοθύτων).[324] Paul starts with the commonly accepted thought, οὐδὲν εἴδωλον ἐν κόσμῳ.[325] The phrase, εἰσὶν λεγόμενοι

---

320. Peter Gooch believes that the reference to knowledge in the Corinthian church would presume that Corinthians tended to teach their members that εἰδωλοθύτων is not harmful. Gooch, *Dangerous Food*, 73.

321. The interpretation of "knowledge" in the Corinthian church, in terms of Gnosticism, has support from many commentators. However, this term, though justified etymologically, is misleading. This term can be assumed as the "isolated traces of the beginnings of what later presented itself as 'Gnosticism.'" Murphy-O'Connor, *Keys to 1 Corinthians*, 88.

322. Discussing the terms "strong" and "weak" in 1 Corinthians, Murphy-O'Connor, Dupont and Pearson noticed Hellenistic-Jewish speculation on Gen 3:7, contemporary to Paul, according to which people were divided into two classes: those who are guided by divine spirit and those who live by pleasures of the flesh. Similar thoughts, with reference to Gen 3:7, appear in the works of Philo. Murphy-O'Connor, *Keys to 1 Corinthians*, 93.

323. BDAG, φυσιόω, "to have an exaggerated self-conception, *puff up, make proud*." See also for meaning, "arrogant" in Kohlenberg, *Greek-English Concordance*, 5889.

324. These could be not only of sacrifices of meat, but also wine, honey, figs and cakes. The meals with food sacrificed to gods were accompanied by songs and stories honouring those gods. Gooch, *Dangerous Food*, 22, 31.

325. In Jewish works (Ps 115:1–5; Jer 10:1–6; Bar 6:3–6; Wis 13:10) "the non-reality and folly of Gentile idols had become an important motif." Malcolm, *World of 1 Corinthians*, 86. Gooch believes that this phrase reveals "not Paul's view but a Corinthian slogan." Gooch, *Dangerous Food*, 51.

θεοὶ, refers to the polytheistic picture of the world in the minds of pagans. Their superstitious inclination to call every supernatural force "god" stands behind the meaning of λεγόμενοι. Paul compares those gods to earthly lords, diminishing their importance. In contrast to the Gentile pantheon of gods, Paul pronounces the Shema: οὐδεὶς θεὸς εἰ μὴ εἷς.[326] Then, by the adversative conjunction ἀλλ he contrasts those many false gods with εἷς θεὸς ὁ πατήρ and εἷς κύριος Ἰησοῦς Χριστός.

By these contrasts, Paul designates two alternative and mutually exclusive pictures of the creation. He describes the true creation as the result of the work of one God: εἷς θεὸς ὁ πατήρ, ἐξ οὗ τὰ πάντα καὶ ἡμεῖς εἰς αὐτόν, καὶ εἷς κύριος Ἰησοῦς Χριστός, δι' οὗ τὰ πάντα καὶ ἡμεῖς δι' αὐτοῦ. In 1 Cor 8:6 Christ is "both preexistent and the mediatorial agent of creation."[327] If so, one cannot believe in two alternative pictures of creation together, and simultaneously be a Christian and an idol worshipper. The issue of εἰδωλοθύτων becomes logically linked to the wrong apprehension of the creation account.

Part 3 (8:7, 8) reveals that though the two pictures of creation are mutually exclusive, some attempt to uphold both at the same time. Paul starts to write about Christians who try to keep both beliefs together with ἀλλ' οὐκ ἐν πᾶσιν ἡ γνῶσις. Then he explains the double standards of those people with the words, τινὲς δὲ τῇ συνηθείᾳ ἕως ἄρτι τοῦ εἰδώλου, "for some by habit until the present are idolators." This might mean that those Gentiles converted to Christ still believe that an idol is not simply a sculpture, but the incarnation of a deity. Those people eat food sacrificed to idols, assuming they are associated with supernatural forces (ὡς εἰδωλόθυτον ἐσθίουσιν), and that they somehow honour those deities whose food they consume.[328] Here the term εἰδωλοθύτων refers to the way by which meats could be secondarily defiled by being offered to idols in shrines. Thus, the issue posed for Paul by the situation in Corinth was concerning whether one is allowed to eat "meat offered to idols'" (8:1) and not the Jewish distinction between clean and unclean meats.[329]

This explains Paul's description of their conscience as "weak," καὶ ἡ συνείδησις αὐτῶν ἀσθενὴς.[330] The "weak" conscience is dedicated to Christ partially, not fully.

However, it seems that Paul agrees, in a general sense, with the assumption that an "idol is nothing" and uses it as a bridge to the following thought. Thus, according to Paul, although idols are nothing, the demons connected to their cults are real.

326. Young sees here Paul's reference to Shema (Deut 6:4, 5) in the context of anti-idol polemic. Young, *Paul, the Jewish Theologian*, 119–20.

327. Fee, *Pauline Christology*, 17. Moreover, Fee observes 1 Cor 8:6 as the reference to Shema and notes that the Wisdom literature, to which Paul might refer, here personifies Wisdom as an agent of creation.

328. Thus, a grave decoration from ancient Corinth pictured a person and gods reclining at a feast. Malcolm, *World of 1 Corinthians*, 88.

329. Meeks, "'And Rose Up to Play,'" 134–35. The issue treated here represents "the association of meat with pagan sacrifices."

330. Ciampa calls it "subjective idolatry," when one consciously participates in idol worship. He links this term to the "weak" members. The other term, "objective idolatry" describes the "strong"

When food sacrificed to any idol is placed before them, those who are "weak" associate it with that god. Giving thanks to that god, the "weak" participate in idol worship. Watson sees that the "weak" are those who continue to presume "the reality of the god in whose honour the sacred meal is held (8:7)."[331] This worship ends with a defilement of the conscience by the sin of idolatry. Paul states clearly, ἡ συνείδησις αὐτῶν ἀσθενὴς οὖσα μολύνεται, "their conscience (because it is weak; or being weak) is defiled" (1 Cor 8:7).[332]

The word μολύνεται, here, is the present indicative passive of μολύνω, "stain, be soiled, be defiled, be made unclean."[333] The passive form implies that the defiling agent (idol) remains outside and defiles the conscience in the same way something unclean can defile a holy place. Paul clearly shows that the source of danger is the "weak" conscience which is not dedicated to Christ completely, and not food itself. In v. 8, he admits that food is not the means by which believers are presented to God: βρῶμα δὲ ἡμᾶς οὐ παραστήσει τῷ θεῷ. Pagans believed that ritual practices with food brought them into contact with divine power. For Paul, food was just food, without any mystical meaning. The sentence, οὔτε ἐὰν μὴ φάγωμεν ὑστερούμεθα, οὔτε ἐὰν φάγωμεν περισσεύομεν, "we are no worse if we do not eat, and no better if we do" in 1 Cor 8:8, reveals that Paul has to deal with the belief that food can be an agent of divination.

Part 4 (8:9–12) puts emphasis on ἡ ἐξουσία ὑμῶν αὕτη. The pronoun αὕτη refers back to this liberty (ἡ ἐξουσία) of believers which is the knowledge described in part 2. It states that οὐδὲν εἴδωλον ἐν κόσμῳ. Although Paul agrees that an idol is nothing, he warns that the liberty should not become a trap for the "weak" (τοῖς ἀσθενέσιν). Here, Tomson believes that "weak" relates to a new convert, who formerly practiced idol worship.[334] Also, πρόσκομμα here means "*stumbling, cause for offence, cause for making a misstep.*"[335] According to the context, the reading "stumbling" becomes preferable.

---

members. They do not consider themselves idolaters because they do not believe in idols or other gods, however, they "participate in an activity . . . which in fact is idolatrous." Ciampa and Rosner, *First Letter to the Corinthians*, 369.

331. Watson, *Paul, Judaism, and the Gentiles*, 152. Thus, for Watson one's conscience becomes "defiled" when he participates in table fellowship and eats the meat sacrificed to idols, assuming the existence of those gods.

332. Here, ἡ συνείδησις is a noun, μολύνεται is a main verb, and οὖσα can be identified as a participle adjectively dependent on a noun. The subordinate phrase οὖσα ἀσθενὴς describes the noun ἡ συνείδησις.

333. BDAG, μολύνω, 2, "to be ritually impure, *defile.*" Also may mean "to become dirty or soiled." The "soiled garments" are considered as ritually unclean, while "unsoiled garments" represent "symbol of a spotless life"
(Rev 3:4). The ritual aspect is mentioned in Jer 23:11; 1 Cor 8:7; Rev 14:4 with the sense of a spiritual defilement.

334. Tomson, *Paul and Jewish Law*, 194–95.

335. BDAG, πρόσκομμα, 1 b, 2 b.

Thus, the freedom of some believers to eat meat sacrificed to an idol can cause stumbling in faith for the one who admits the existence of gods and Christ at the same time. Fee sees here a discussion about attendance at meals in pagan temples on feast days.[336] For the "weak," the freedom of "strong" believers becomes a trap for idolatry which defiles their conscience. The enclitic particle πως ("somehow") makes rejection of any case possible, where that liberty somehow becomes a trap.[337] This would mean that nobody should act in that way, which the "weak" would understand as permission for latent idolatry.

From this point, the apostle illustrates his prohibition by the simulation of a paradoxical situation, which appears when someone, τὸν ἔχοντα γνῶσιν, sits at the table in an idol shrine (ἐν εἰδωλείῳ κατακείμενον). The situation described by Paul seems exaggerated in order to create a paradoxical contrast. "Corinthian Christians could expect to receive many invitations to occasions where . . . the explicit identification of some food as offered to the Gods—would likely be met."[338] Paul intentionally creates a contrast between ἡ γνῶσις and ἡ ἀγάπη to reveal the real face of Corinthian "freedom," which originates in ἡ γνῶσις, which makes one arrogant (φυσιοῖ). This knowledge separated from ἡ ἀγάπη οἰκοδομεῖ would cause trouble, because Christians who dine in a shrine would tempt the "weak" to think that latent idol worship is permissible. Paul expresses it in the question, οὐχὶ ἡ συνείδησις αὐτοῦ ἀσθενοῦς ὄντος οἰκοδομηθήσεται εἰς τὸ τὰ εἰδωλόθυτα ἐσθίειν, "Will not one's weak conscience be emboldened to eat what is sacrificed to idols?" This question assumes the answer, "yes, it will embolden."

Paul also shows the consequences of this as ἀπόλλυται γὰρ ὁ ἀσθενῶν, the destruction of the spiritual experience of one who is "weak." Here Paul turns to the ἀγάπη concept and stresses that the "weak" one is ὁ ἀδελφὸς δι' ὃν Χριστὸς ἀπέθανεν. According to Paul's logic, the action of the "strong in faith," who does this, is a very cruel action toward the weak brother, and eventually Christ. It is expressed in a way that pictures the "strong" as destroying not only the "weak" brother, but hurting Christ himself. Thus, the "strong" brother would break the salvation bought at a great price, namely, the death of Jesus Christ (δι' ὃν Χριστὸς ἀπέθανεν).[339] Paul describes this action with the help of two participles ἁμαρτάνοντες and τύπτοντες (from τύπτω—"strike, beat, wound, assault") in terms of an assault on someone's conscience.[340] When the sin is commited against ἀδελφοὺς, it wounds Christ too. This thought is included in the phrase εἰς Χριστὸν ἁμαρτάνετε.

---

336. Fee, *Pauline Christology*, 88.

337. Wallace, *Greek Grammar*, 477. The construction of the sentence, "serves as a warning or suggests caution or anxiety."

338. Gooch, *Dangerous Food*, 46.

339. According to Fee, Paul viewed redemption connected to creation. Fee, *Pauline Christology*, 90.

340. BDAG, τύπτω, a, b.

Part 5 (8:13) was classified by Tomson as a "personal exclamation much like a vow of self-restraint."³⁴¹ Only here can one find Paul's personal view concerning εἰδωλοθύτων. With a conscience fully dedicated to Christ, and denying the significance of idols, he still commits himself to self-restraint. In Rom 14:21, Paul uses similar wording, but the tone of the phrase differs and sounds like "good advice."³⁴² His decision presumes both aspects (ethical and cultic), which points to a need for true worship.

For Paul the issue of worship is more important than the issue of food. With the help of a vow of self-restraint, he would prevent cases of double-standard worship and latent idolatry in the congregation.³⁴³ Paul thinks, "how much can I do to preserve the 'weak' from idolatry and defilement of conscience?" His exclamation of self-restraint is the vow of ultimate consecration to Christ, who is the only God of creation. This vow is not an ascetic choice of a diet with the hope to be closer to God (he denied this assumption in 8:8), but a call to true worship. This aspect links the discussion about εἰδωλοθύτων not only to the Genesis creation-fall account, but also presumes a reversion from the fall to re-creation.³⁴⁴

Creation and true worship, have for Paul, an eternal dimension.³⁴⁵ The εἰδωλοθύτων is linked to the fall, where false gods appeared. It is evident that Paul is ready to sacrifice his temporal personal freedom in order to make the "weak" become strong and practice only true worship. He states: οὐ μὴ φάγω κρέα εἰς τὸν αἰῶνα, ἵνα μὴ τὸν ἀδελφόν μου σκανδαλίσω. Here Paul's εἰς τὸν αἰῶνα reflects his belief in the eternal permanence of the true woship.

---

341. Tomson, *Paul and Jewish Law*, 191. Here, Tomson demonstrates the integrity of four units in passage 1 Cor 8–10. He states that "the restrictive tendency seems to be more prominent. It is enhanced by the rhetorical figure of 'all . . . but not all.'"

342. Ciampa notes that "since Rom 14 also deals with eating or abstaining from certain kinds of food and proper attitude toward 'weaker' believers, many read 1 Corinthians through a prism informed by that chapter." He believes that these two passages deal with two different issues. According to him, Rom 14 concerns Jewish food laws rooted in Lev 11:1–23, while 1 Cor 8–10 deals with idol food. Ciampa and Rosner, *First Letter to the Corinthians*, 371. This view will be debated in 3.1.5 of this chapter. Table 1 provides enough evidences that the issue in Rom 14 is the same as 1 Cor 8–10.

343. Gooch states, "Paul urges the Corinthians to beware of participation in the table of daimonia." He suspects "that Paul would not participate in meals of even a marginally religious character." Gooch, *Dangerous Food*, 107.

344. Ciampa states, "here both creation and eschatological restoration seems to be in mind." He shows that the OT provides a firm foundation for the thought that not only Israel, but also other nations would worship one true Lord (Isa 19:21; 49:26; Ezek 21:5; 25:11; 28:22–24; 29:6; 30:19; 25–26; 32:15; 35:4, 9, 12, 14–15; 36:23, 36; 37:28; 38:23; 39:6–7). Ciampa and Rosner, *First Letter to the Corinthians*, 374, 383.

345. When Paul alludes to creation, he does not reflect the idea of chaos, well known in the pagan ancient world and in Hellenistic Judaism, but stays close to the Gen 1 account. Gottfried Nebe, "Creation in Paul's Theology," in *Creation in Jewish and Christian Tradition*, ed. Henning Graf Reventlow and Hoffman Yair (Sheffield: Sheffield Academic, 2002), 116.

The Reference to εἰδωλοθύτων and πορνεία in 1 Cor 10:1–33

In 1 Cor 10 Paul "depended on Jewish aggadic traditions" and uses "interpretative techniques like those found in rabbinic midrash."[346] In order to view its structure, the passage can be divided into six parts: the first four are parts of midrash and last two are the practical applications of teaching. Thus midrash in 1 Cor 10:1–22, based on the episode of the golden calf, allows Paul to make a typological correlation between the church and Israel.[347] His purpose was to prohibit any contact with pagan cults.[348]

According to midrashic explanation of Scripture, Part 1 (10:1–5) opens the discourse with a text from the Pentateuch (in the current passage it is Exodus 32:6). Part 2 (10:6–14) contains a complex quotation (here, all texts of the quotation are taken from the Pentateuch) which illustrates the main thought. Part 3 (10:15–21) reveals the very cores of true and false worship, linking true worship to the salvific work of God, and false worship to the origin of demonic powers. True and false worship shadow the Exodus narrative and link to the creation-fall account.[349] Also, the "desire" motifs link the Genesis 2–3 narrative to Sinai and later to the post-Sinai history of Israel. As Watson notes, 1 Cor 10:6–10 with εἰδωλοθύτων and πορνεία becomes an echo not only of the Sinai narrative, but also of Genesis 2–3 with its primordial desires.[350]

Part 4 (10:22–23), concluding part of midrash, alludes to the initial Exodus text. Part 5 (10:24–30) of this passage represents the set of rules by which Paul applies the teaching about εἰδωλοθύτων to life's different circumstances. These elements of 1 Cor 10:1–4 suggest "Paul understood the wilderness narrative as speaking of the events that were to (re)occur in the final generation."[351] Part 6 (10:31–33) contains a general call, which becomes a summary of previous argumentation. This call is a repetition of 1 Cor 6:19, 20, which interprets it on a practical level. Finally, Paul applies the call to life by his personal example.

In details, Part 1 shows that an important element of 1 Corinthians is the connection of εἰδωλοθύτων to γνῶσις (8:1, 7, 10, 11; 10:1). However, Paul does not refer

346. Meeks, "Midrash in 1 Corinthians 10.1–22," 124. Tomson also recognises midrash in the passage of 1 Cor 10:1–22. Tomson, *Paul and Jewish Law*, 199.

347. Hays, *Echoes of Scripture*, 91. He notes the Israel/church typology used and developed by Paul. He also notes that the central concern of the Exodus quotation was "idolatry," not eating and drinking. Thus, Paul's use of "meat sacrificed to idols" is linked more to idolatry than the nature of meat.

348. Meeks, "Midrash in 1 Corinthians 10.1–22," 124–25. Here, Paul links Israel's idolatry in the Exodus narrative and the danger of pagan cults in Corinth.

349. Wenham notes the opinion of Wyatt, who "draws attention to points of contact in vocabulary between Gen 2–3 and exilic literature." Wenham, *Genesis*, 53. This observation helps to demonstrate that, even in the exilic period, people assumed that the call to a true worship is rooted in creation-fall account.

350. Watson, *Paul, Judaism, and the Gentiles*, 284.

351. DiMattei, "Biblical Narratives," 82. He states that the eschatological interpretation of this narrative was current in the Judaism contemporary to Paul. Paul's use of this narrative was also pedagogical.

to mystical knowledge, but uses knowledge from the Pentateuch. He links ὑμᾶς and ἡμῶν to the days of οἱ πατέρες, referring to the Exodus narrative. The uniting idea between the present and past generations is expressed in terms of baptism (πάντες . . . ἐβαπτίσαντο). He compares the present baptism in the early church to the ancient "baptism" ἐν τῇ νεφέλῃ καὶ ἐν τῇ θαλάσσῃ in Exodus.[352] Five times πάντες is repeated, relating to five main symbols of the Exodus narrative: cloud, sea, Moses, spiritual bread and spiritual drink.[353] This repetition of πάντες supports the idea that all fathers, without exception, had entered a covenant, which was similar to Christian baptism.[354] However, these five πάντες are contrasted with the adversative conjunction ἀλλ' and the phrase οὐκ ἐν τοῖς πλείοσιν αὐτῶν εὐδόκησεν ὁ θεός.[355] Paul shows that although "all" were engaged with God at the start of the Exodus, some could not pass the test of the wilderness: κατεστρώθησαν γὰρ ἐν τῇ ἐρήμῳ.

The passive aorist κατεστρώθησαν in 10:5 of καταστρώννυμι means "be laid low, be killed."[356] This word depicts many of those baptized into Moses, later being put to death in the desert as apostates from God. Thus, not "all" those who declared their faith at their "baptism" maintained it later. Here for the first time a contrast between πάντες and οὐκ ἐν τοῖς πλείοσιν appears. This contrast in part 1 is developed in part 4 (the final part of the midrash) into constructions πάντα . . . ἀλλ' οὐ πάντα.[357]

Avoiding mentioning the secondary text from the Pentateuch, Paul builds a complex-quotation in part 2 of the midrash. First, he does not quote the texts, but alludes to them, initially to the Exodus account in Numbers. His complex quotation also contains a *pesher* formula ὥσπερ γέγραπται. Moreover, from the beginning of part 2 he uses typology identified by τύπος in the opening and concluding phrases (vv. 6 and 11).

The opening phrase in v. 6 provides structure for the following five examples. The structure μὴ εἶναι ἡμᾶς . . . καθὼς κἀκεῖνοι builds a pattern for the comparisons between ἡμᾶς and κἀκεῖνος. The first comparison in v. 6, εἰς τὸ μὴ εἶναι ἡμᾶς ἐπιθυμητὰς

---

352. Meeks finds no analogy to this form of "baptism in Moses" in Jewish texts and accepts it as a "Christian construction by analogy with 'baptized in Christ.'" Meeks, "Midrash in 1 Corinthians 10.1–22," 126.

353. Meeks relates those πάντες of vv. 1–4 to the "some of them" in 6–10. Meeks, "Midrash in 1 Corinthians 10.1–22," 125.

354. Fee, *Pauline Christology*, 86, 94. Fee notes that to be "baptized" into Moses in the cloud and the sea might reflect the presence of Christ in Israel's story. For Paul, Jesus is co-creator from eternity, who also is present with Israel in the desert, which reveals the meaning of the phrase "call upon his name." The mentioning of manna and water from the rock as "spiritual food and drink" also presumes the reference to Christ and the Spirit. Thus, Paul pictures γνῶσις in Corinth in terms of Israel's idolatry.

355. Meaning ". . . but with many of them God was not well pleased" (1 Cor 10:5).

356. BDAG, καταστρώννυμι, 1, "lay low, kill."

357. In the 1 Cor 10:1–22 passage, there are five parallel clauses denoted by the repeated πάντες in vv. 1–4 which correspond to five statements about "some of them" in vv. 6–10. The five positive and five negative statements are linked to a conclusion in vv. 12–13.

κακῶν, καθὼς κἀκεῖνοι ἐπεθύμησαν, alludes to Num 11:4. Here Paul uses ἐπιθυμητὰς κακῶν, when LXX, in Numbers, uses ἐπιθύμησεν ἐπιθυμίαν, and stresses the evil nature of their desires. The change to κακῶν, by Paul, may reveal the core of the controversy between good and evil, and it may link the discussion about εἰδωλοθύτων to the ξύλου τοῦ γινώσκοντες καλὸν καὶ πονηρόν.

The second comparison μηδὲ εἰδωλολάτραι γίνεσθε, καθώς τινες αὐτῶν (v. 7) alludes to Exod 32:6. It becomes more evident from the following direct quotation from LXX, Ἐκάθισεν ὁ λαὸς φαγεῖν καὶ πεῖν, καὶ ἀνέστησαν παίζειν, precursored by the *pesher* formula ὥσπερ γέγραπται. Although εἰδωλολάτραι does not appear in the LXX, it is assumed in the phrase ἀνεβίβασεν ὁλοκαθώματα, καὶ προσήνεγκε θυσίαν σωτηρίου, where the "whole burnt-offering" and a "peace-offering" are mentioned. The shift from Numbers to Exodus and back to Numbers in the following comparison might accent the practice of idolatry as a reason for constant rebellion from the very beginning. The direct quotation of Exod 32:6 shows the connection between εἰδωλολάτραι and εἰδωλοθύτων, describing that after people offered sacrifices, they had a feast. This feast might also imply elements of πορνεία, hidden in the phrase ἀνέστησαν παίζειν ("dance, play," which elsewhere describes a "dallying married couple," cf Gen 26:8).[358]

While Paul's first statement, ἐπιθυμητὰς κακῶν, refers to the origin of the evil wishes, the second, εἰδωλολάτραι, alludes to the first εἰδωλοθύτων of Israel. Paul's third statement (v. 8) is concerning πορνεία. Alluding to Num 25:1, 9, the apostle writes, μηδὲ πορνεύωμεν, καθώς τινες αὐτῶν ἐπόρνευσαν, καὶ ἔπεσαν μιᾷ ἡμέρᾳ εἴκοσι τρεῖς χιλιάδες ("neither let us commit fornication, as some of them committed, and fell in one day three and twenty thousand," in 1 Cor 10:8).

It is noteworthy that Num 25:1, 2 again links πορνεία closely to εἰδωλοθύτων.[359] There, ὁ λαὸς ἐκπορνεῦσαι εἰς τὰς θυγατέρας Μωάβ, to which is added καὶ ἐκάλεσαν αὐτοὺς εἰς τὰς θυσίας τῶν εἰδώλων αὐτῶν· καὶ ἔφαγεν ὁ λαὸς τῶν θυσιῶν αὐτῶν ("and they called the people unto the sacrifices of their gods: and the people did eat, and bowed down to their gods") in Num 25:2. Thus, the narrative itself assumes that both πορνεία and εἰδωλοθύτων are linked to idolatry. The additional clause, καὶ ἔπεσαν μιᾷ ἡμέρᾳ εἴκοσι τρεῖς χιλιάδες, is quoted from Num 25:9 with an insignificant change, where it is said that those that died in the plague were twenty four thousand, while Paul writes twenty three thousand. His emphasis is placed not on number, but a

---

358. Muraoka, *Greek-English Lexicon*, παίζω.

359. Ciampa states that "idolatry and sexual immorality are tied together in both Num 25:1–2 and 1 Cor 10:7–8. He views πορνεία in terms of ritual prostitution with reference to the Num 25 narrative. The similarity between Corinthians' behavior and that of Israelites in the wilderness suggest that πορνεία in Corinth was also connected to pagan cults. Ciampa and Rosner, *First Letter to the Corinthians*, 459. The idolatry and sexual immorality are coinside because both matters represent a violation of the natural law. Thus, for the people who live in sexual immorality is naturally easier to participate in idolatry, than to uphold a true worship.

period of time, μιᾷ ἡμέρᾳ. The destruction of a multitude in one day evokes a picture of eschatological judgment.

The fourth statement (v. 9) is μηδὲ ἐκπειράζωμεν τὸν κύριον, καθώς τινες αὐτῶν ἐξεπείρασαν ("we should not test the Lord, as some of them did" in 1 Cor 10:9). The word πειράζω attracts an even more negative sense than idolatry or fornication, because it indicates an irreversible degree of rebellion.[360] Here, the rebellion was again associated with food preferences (cf. Num 21:5) and lack of faith. Pauline wording, καὶ ὑπὸ τῶν ὄφεων ἀπώλλυντο, ("and were killed by snakes" in 1 Cor 10:9) echoes Gen 3, where the serpent, first caused death. Paul's complex quotation conflates Num 21:6 ὄφεις τοὺς θανατοῦντας and Ps 106:14 ἐπείρασαν (aorist from πειράζω "tempt, test"), which offends God.[361] Punishment by serpents echoes the pronouncement of God: αὐτός σου τηρήσει κεφαλήν, καὶ σὺ τηρήσεις αὐτοῦ πτέρναν in Gen 3:16. People who died from serpents were those who, metaphorically, did not "strike" the sinful desires. They rebelled against God and put him to the test.

The last comparison of this passage, μηδὲ γογγύζετε, καθάπερ τινὲς αὐτῶν ἐγόγγυσαν ("do not grumble, as some of them did-and were killed by the destroying angel" 1 Cor 10:10) highlights the issue of murmuring and alludes to Num 14:36.[362] Although the story in Num 14 does not mention εἰδωλοθύτων, it reveals the problem of weakness of faith, which caused the Israelites to remain in the desert for forty years. This lack of faith contrasts with all the mighty deeds of God done for their sake. Num 14:33 calls their rebellion πορνεία, when the record states, ἀνοίσουσι τὴν πορνείαν ὑμῶν. Here, πορνεία is used in terms of spiritual unfaithfulness to God. If one assumes that Pauline thought proceeds chronologically from Sinai idolatry to the last temptation after the twelve spies explored the land, then the picture of constant rebellion becomes clear.

The constant holding on to idols is expressed by the words οὐκ ἐν τοῖς πλείοσιν αὐτῶν εὐδόκησεν ὁ θεός, κατεστρώθησαν γὰρ ἐν τῇ ἐρήμῳ ("but with many of them God was not well pleased: for they were overthrown in the wilderness") in 1 Cor 10:5. Here, a curse on an unbelieving generation corresponds to that put on the Egyptians. Paul concludes καὶ ἀπώλοντο ὑπὸ τοῦ ὀλοθρευτοῦ, which refers to Exod 12:23, where ὀλοθρεύοντα ("the destroyer") was also mentioned. In the Exodus story, blood of the Passover lamb protected believers from the destroyer. The story in Num 14 correlates with Exod 12 at the point where the Israelites turned back for Egypt. Their decision reveals preference for idol worship, instead of worshipping

---

360. Meeks notes that the verb πειράζω in v. 9 does not appear in the account of Num 21:4–9, but appears in a parallel narrative in Exod 17:1–7. Meeks, "Midrash in 1 Corinthians 10.1–22," 129.

361. Kohlenberg, *Greek-English Concordance*, 4273.

362. According to Meeks, the verb γογγύζειν has the meaning of "grumbling" and frequently occurs in the wilderness narratives. It is mentioned together with the plague in Num 11:33 and 16:49. Meeks views the Pauline reference as made to the last rebellion which is Korah's. Meeks, "Midrash in 1 Corinthians 10.1–22," 129.

of God. The wording ἀπώλοντο ὑπὸ τοῦ ὀλοθρευτοῦ, here, suggests the same curse as for the Egyptians, a condemnation.

These similarities echo not only the Exodus story, but also Gen 3. According to Jewish traditions, the Law (i.e., the Torah) was present in Eden.[363] The first command was given to Adam (2:17) and later repeated at Sinai.[364] Use of forbidden fruit for gaining occult knowledge can be assumed as identical to practicing of magic or divination.[365] This primordial idolatry, expressed by εἰδωλοθύτων, established a common pattern for similar practices later at Sinai and Corinth. Consequently, the fall narrative first provides the pattern of human reluctance to keep the covenant with the one true God.

The concluding phrase of part 2 (v. 11) again shows Pauline typology: ταῦτα δὲ τυπικῶς συνέβαινεν ἐκείνοις ("these things happened to them as examples" in 1 Cor 10:11). Although the events took place more than a thousand years before, Paul insists that the spiritual lessons hidden in them can apply again to each generation.[366] Practicing false worship leads to a hardening of heart and "provoking" God that makes people irreformable. This observation suggests that Paul recalled the prohibitions in order to prevent the harmful effects of idol worship.

The phrase, τὰ τέλη τῶν αἰώνων, can be translated as "fulfillment of the ages." The whole phrase ἐγράφη δὲ πρὸς νουθεσίαν ἡμῶν, εἰς οὓς τὰ τέλη τῶν αἰώνων κατήντηκεν ("were written down as warnings for us, on whom the fulfillment of the ages has come" in 1 Cor 10:11) reveals that typologically Christians, also, are fitted into the creation–fall–re-creation paradigm. Matters like εἰδωλοθύτων and πορνεία in the Exodus story become πρὸς νουθεσίαν (with meaning "instruction, warning") to those, who τὰ τέλη τῶν αἰώνων κατήντηκεν.[367] Because of this the prohibitions of εἰδωλοθύτων and πορνεία can be viewed as temporary prohibitions in force in this fallen world, until God's kingdom comes. The final call of this part, expressed as,

---

363. Vlachos, *Law and Knowledge*, 176.

364. Vlachos, *Law and Knowledge*, 178, 133–34. He views the Eden and Sinai narratives as paralleled in terms of law, presence of the Lord in Eden and later in tabernacle, temptation, motif of magic knowledge, and death. He states that צוה found in Gen 2:16–17 often appears in pentateuchal laws (Deuteronomy) and has to be applied only to prohibition of something. Thus, the command of God in Eden has to be seen as "a single prohibition that is set against the background of a bounteous provision." The similar contrast between provision and prohibition was noted in Gen 9:3–4, when the prohibition of blood consumption appears, as previously stated.

365. Vlachos, *Law and Knowledge*, 167–168.

366. Paul Barker believes that the issue of sin has to be viewed more broadly than the story of the golden calf. He states that the golden calf typifies continual sinfulness. Barker, *Triumph of Grace*, 89–90.

367. The ancient stories prepared a foundation for the theme of a new creation developed in the Second Temple Judaism. Isaianic reinterpretation of Exodus, in Isa 40–55, points to a new-creation theme in Isa 65 and 66. Hubbard shows the frequent occurrence in Isaiah 40–55 of principal verbs, which are used in the Genesis creation narrative. Also, the Pauline motif of new creation was taken from Second Temple Jewish eschatological expectations. The message of Isaiah 40–55 linked together the expectations of new exodus and new creation. Hubbard, *New Creation*, 11–16.

διόπερ, ἀγαπητοί μου, φεύγετε ἀπὸ τῆς εἰδωλολατρίας ("therefore, my dear friends, flee from idolatry" 1 Cor 10:14), was addressed to all Christians and represents the call to participate only in true worship.

Part 3 of Paul's midrash (10:15–21) concentrates on the symbols of God's covenant: altar, lamb, cup and bread. In this part Paul describes true worship in terms of the Passover night. He links the Last Supper and Christian communion to the Passover of Exodus. Thus, Paul touches the very core of true and false worship, differentiating the worship of God from a worship of demons. He brings readers to the point of decision. Midrash provokes deep thinking, and Paul challenges his listeners with, ὡς φρονίμοις λέγω• κρίνατε ὑμεῖς ὅ φημι, "I speak to sensible people; judge for yourselves what I say," (10:15).

Turning to the symbols of communion, Paul carefully interprets them in terms of the Passover covenant. The phrase, ποτήριον τῆς εὐλογίας ὃ εὐλογοῦμεν, "the cup of thanksgiving for which we give thanks," (10:16) is a symbol of the new covenant of Christ, established during the Last Supper.[368] Paul links it to αἵματος τοῦ Χριστοῦ, and alludes to Christ as the unique Passover lamb and atoning sacrifice.[369] The link reveals that the new covenant established in Christ's blood is not new to the believers, but the ancient "blood redeems life" concept of Torah. The concept "blood redeems life" was of cultic significance. It prescribed a ritual routine to be followed, with the sacrifice by the priests in the holy place of the tabernacle. This cultic concept linked any sacrificed meat to cult, and not simply to a festive table. As a result, all sacrificed food became a matter viewed under the shadow of cult, either Jewish or pagan.[370] Accordingly, Paul contrasts εἰδωλοθύτων with αἵματος τοῦ Χριστοῦ, as a matter of cultic significance.[371]

Discussing the issue of εἰδωλοθύτων in 1 Corinthians, Paul intentionally views it in light of the ritual law of Torah, in order to show the absurdity of idolatry. The wish to contrast εἰδωλοθύτων with ποτήριον τῆς εὐλογίας ὃ εὐλογοῦμεν allows Paul to look at the issue from different angles. It explains why he prohibited eating εἰδωλοθύτων in a pagan temple, while he did not ban eating what was bought in the market place.

Thus, the food bought in the market place was dissociated with pagan cult by its use in marketing.[372] Also, according to Torah, non-cultic slaughtering did not involve

---

368. Here, "Paul's language stresses the religious context that is established for Christians by "merely" saying a blessing over the cup and eating the bread as a spiritual life-giving gift from Christ." Ciampa and Rosner, *First Letter to the Corinthians*, 475.

369. Meeks notes that the change of aorist to the present tense supports the idea of linking Christians to Israelites. Meeks, "Midrash in 1 Corinthians 10.1–22," 134.

370. Another connotation is that in Deut 14 "blood represents life," which presumed no cultic actions with the blood. It was imposed by natural law and demanded only the pouring of blood on the ground.

371. The controversy between idol worship and true worship raises an eschatological contrast between those, who keep the "old ways," living in idolatry, and those who removed "old leaven," purifying themselves in the moral sense. Meyer, *End of Law*, 57.

372. Ciampa calls this food, "food with unknown history." Ciampa and Rosner, *First Letter to the*

the concept of redemption (Lev 17:13–14; Deut 12:15–25). Since it carried no cultic sense, it could be eaten on the ground of the natural law of God (Gen 9:1–4). Whenever the food was set on a table in a shrine, or someone said that it had been consecrated to an idol, the cultic aspect was activated, and the food had to be rejected. Consequently, in these two pieces of advice by Paul, the difference between the cultic aspect of food and its non-cultic aspect was clearly stated. Furthermore, the εἰδωλοθύτων was clearly connected to a cultic context, which stands in contrast to the redemption offered by God in Christ, which lays a foundation for the hope of a new creation.[373]

Another significant point here is the aspect of κοινωνία, which may be understood as "fellowhip" among the worshipers and as spiritual "close relationship" with God.[374] The word in v. 16 (in relation to the "cup of thanksgiving" and the blood of Christ) is to be viewed as an aspect of redemption. The Pauline phrase κοινωνία τοῦ σώματος τοῦ Χριστοῦ proceeds even further, describing the unity of believer with Christ, similarly to a hand belonging to a body. The phrase, τὸν ἄρτον ὃν κλῶμεν, οὐχὶ κοινωνία τοῦ σώματος τοῦ Χριστοῦ ἐστιν, "the bread that we break is a participation in the body of Christ" (10:16), illustrates that kind of deep spiritual association with God.[375]

In order to illustrate the spiritual meaning of κοινωνία, Paul turns to Israel's cult, formed around ritual law. As he shows by the phrase, οἱ ἐσθίοντες τὰς θυσίας κοινωνοὶ τοῦ θυσιαστηρίου εἰσίν, "those who eat the sacrifices participate in the altar?" (10:18), the ritual law views those who eat from a sacrifice to be worshippers. A sacrifice is associated with an altar. In the same way, the participants in the cultic feast are associated with the particular cult, becoming its worshippers. In terms of the ritual law, those who bring a sacrifice become integrated into the eternal salvific plan of God and inherit its blessings. In order to emphasize the importance of κοινωνία, Paul uses it four times, here, in part 3. It is used three times in a positive sense and the fourth time contrastingly (ἀλλ'), referring to κοινωνοὺς τῶν δαιμονίων.[376]

Corinthians, 492.

373. Meyer states that "Christ represents the dawning of the 'new creation.'" Meyer, *End of the Law*, 49.

374. BDAG, κοινωνία, 1, 4. This word in the context of 1 Cor 10:16 has the meaning, "*participation, sharing*" during communion. The main meaning of this word is "*association, communion, fellowship, close relationship.*"

375. Ciampa provides several views on the meaning of κοινωνία. It could mean partaking at God's altar, the renewal of our covenantal relationship with God, or as becoming companions of God and enjoying food and drink in the presence of the Lord. Ciampa and Rosner, *First Letter to the Corinthians*, 473–74.

376. Peter Gooch discusses the different aspects of food in 1 Corinthians and concludes that "Paul believes that diamonia are real" and that "the meal of diamonia infects those who share it, just as the Lord's meal immunizes the believer against death." If one can accept the first statement about the reality of demonic forces, then the second one, talking about the contagiousness of it, seems doubtful. Gooch, *Dangerous Food*, 58–59.

From the beginning of v. 19, Paul shows the way in which the shift between cultic and non-cultic interpretation of εἰδωλόθυτόν works.[377] To begin, he focuses on the non-cultic dimension when he asks τί οὖν φημι ὅτι εἰδωλόθυτόν τί ἐστιν; ἢ ὅτι εἴδωλόν τί ἐστιν; The answer is going to be "definitely not," because Christians do not believe in the power of idols or any magical powers associated with food offered to them.[378] When the cultic aspect is involved (feast in a pagan temple) the issue of sharing food would include joining in idol worship. Here, idolatry is "the central issue being debated between 'the weak' and 'the strong' at Corinth."[379] Paul clarifies it in v. 20, when he writes, ἀλλ' ὅτι ἃ θύουσιν [τὰ ἔθνη], δαιμονίοις καὶ οὐ θεῷ θύουσιν, "but the sacrifices of pagans are offered to demons, not to God" (10:20), declaring the problem of idol worship.

At this point, Paul again employs the construction οὐ θέλω δὲ which corresponds to οὐ θέλω γὰρ in v. 1. He repeats the wording from the beginning of the phrase οὐ θέλω γὰρ ὑμᾶς ἀγνοεῖν, ἀδελφοί. This gives the impression that he returns to the thought with which he started. His concern is the lack of knowledge, which he indicates by ἀγνοεῖν. With the help of two parallel sayings in 1 Cor 10:20, Paul points to the lack of knowledge about the spiritual association of εἰδωλόθυτόν with worship of demons:

οὐ θέλω γὰρ ὑμᾶς ἀγνοεῖν, ἀδελφοί

οὐ θέλω δὲ ὑμᾶς κοινωνοὺς τῶν δαιμονίων γίνεσθαι

The first person singular of the emotional θέλω indicates that Paul is personally concerned about the situation. Yet he does not insist or command, when he describes the two objects of worship (God or demons), but allows his readers to choose,

---

377. This split of the cultic and non-cultic aspect of εἰδωλόθυτόν in Pauline writings has been overlooked by scholars. After an extensive search of previous literature on Paul's reference to εἰδωλοθύτων and πορνεία in 1 Cor 8 and 10, Christoph Heil, in his detailed survey of scholarship, reaches a conclusion in line with traditional exegesis on the topic, that for Paul and his Corinthian readers, "monotheism and belief in creation [should] neutralise any saving relevance of food taboos." Heil then concludes that "[Paul] also places considerable stress in 1 Cor 8–10 on the soteriological indicative, which he sets out to establish in order to correct certain members of the Corinthian congregation. The imperative of love would then follow logically." Heil, Die Ablehnung der Speisegebote, 212–35. His conclusion reveals that Pauline soteriology was assumed by scholars in an ethical way, rather than in the way which Torah prescribes in Deut 12:10–28 (cultic and non-cultic food consumption). Yet, the distinction between cultic and non-cultic patterns known from Deuteronomy would influence Paul's soteriology more than the "imperative of love" invented by modern scholarship and disconnected from Torah.

378. Meeks calls this part of Pauline monologue a "diatribal question," which later allows Paul to show that although pagan gods are not real gods, they have some reality as demons. Meeks, "Midrash in 1 Corinthians 10.1–22," 136.

379. Meeks, "Midrash in 1 Corinthians 10.1–22," 133. In vv. 15–22 Paul prohibits any participation in pagan cults. In v. 20 Paul quotes Deut 32:17 directly.

concurrently expressing his own opinion, οὐ θέλω δὲ ὑμᾶς κοινωνοὺς τῶν δαιμονίων γίνεσθαι, "I do not want you to be participants with demons" (10:20).[380]

After this personal request, Paul makes a strong uncompromising statement in case some would hope to keep on with "double worship": οὐ δύνασθε ποτήριον κυρίου πίνειν καὶ ποτήριον δαιμονίων· οὐ δύνασθε τραπέζης κυρίου μετέχειν καὶ τραπέζης δαιμονίων, "you cannot drink the cup of the Lord and the cup of demons too; you cannot have a part in both the Lord's table and the table of demons" (10:21). Fee states that Paul agrees with Corinthian believers in their belief that idols are not gods. However, Paul shows that "they lack a truly *biblical* understanding of idolatry, that the idols and their temples are the habitation of demons."[381] Here, Paul contrasts pagan meals with the Lord's meal.[382]

The phrase ποτήριον κυρίου refers to blood, as is clear from v. 16: ποτήριον . . . ἐστὶν τοῦ αἵματος τοῦ Χριστοῦ. Thus, ποτήριον κυρίου becomes linked to the Passover and the Exodus. Passover participation presumes that people have come to true worship from idolatry, denying their idols. That is why τραπέζης κυρίου cannot be associated with τραπέζης δαιμονίων. Otherwise, Corinthian believers would end up in the same way as the Israelites, who κατεστρώθησαν γὰρ ἐν τῇ ἐρήμῳ. The word μετέχειν "share, participate" and describes sharing in both idol worship and true worship.[383] This leads to compromised worship. Paul rejects the possibility of such compromise on the grounds of Passover typology.

Part 4 (10:22, 23) is the concluding element of midrash that 1) alludes to the initial text; 2) binds all thoughts of midrash together, and 3) makes a summary statement. Part 4 corresponds to all three features "in sequence." First of all, in v. 22 Paul alludes to the initially mentioned story of Israel's dwelling in the desert. In two questions, ἢ παραζηλοῦμεν τὸν κύριον; μὴ ἰσχυρότεροι αὐτοῦ ἐσμεν, "Are we trying to arouse the Lord's jealousy? Are we stronger than he?," Paul seems to conclude that the consequence of compromised worship, is God's punishment.[384] The device of questioning was chosen by Paul in order to switch attention from the ancient Israelites to his contemporary readers. The question could imply: Are we going to follow evil desires, worship idols, commit adultery, and make God jealous?

---

380. The phrase makes it clear that pagans worshipping idols communicate with spiritual beings. Here, the quotation is taken from Deut 32:17. Ciampa and Rosner, *First Letter to the Corinthians*, 479. Another passage which supports this belief is Ps 106:37.

381. Fee, *Pauline Christology*, 132, 134. Here, Paul's main point concerns the lordship of Jesus. Paul prohibits participation in festive pagan meals because the food which is sacrificed to demons becomes polluted, since the demons are real forces. Thus, Paul does not treat the issue of the distinction of meats, here, but only the fact of their pollution by sacrificing them to demons.

382. Fee, *Pauline Christology*, 132–33.

383. BDAG, μετέχω, 1, 2. The first meaning is "*share, participate*," and the second is "*eat, drink, enjoy.*"

384. It was noted that here Paul evokes Deut 32:21 LXX, where the παραζηλοῦμεν τὸν κύριον was caused by people's persisting idolatry. Ciampa and Rosner, *First Letter to the Corinthians*, 483.

The two questions in v. 22 presuppose a negative answer. Moreover, the results of those actions are clearly stated: κατεστρώθησαν, ἔπεσαν, and ἀπώλλυντο. With the help of these verbs Paul binds the thoughts of midrash together. Moreover, his stress on the issue of power in μὴ ἰσχυρότεροι αὐτοῦ poses a question: What do we think of ourselves? Or, in other words: How do we hope to remain unpunished? The thought hidden behind this question links the readers to the first fall, when people thought to escape the possibility of God's judgment. False worship and εἰδωλοθύτων first appeared at that time, leading people to κοινωνοὺς τῶν δαιμονίων and separation from God. The fall narrative reveals that people's perception of themselves as gods was false. Consequently, they fell under the judgment of God. The apostle shows the same inevitability of judgment for Christians who compromise true worship.

The last feature of this concluding part of midrash is expressed in 1 Cor 10:23, in two parallel summary statements:

Πάντα ἔξεστιν, ἀλλ' οὐ πάντα συμφέρει.

Πάντα ἔξεστιν, ἀλλ' οὐ πάντα οἰκοδομεῖ.

These statements recall the controversy between πάντες and ἀλλ' οὐκ ἐν τοῖς πλείοσιν αὐτῶν εὐδόκησεν ὁ θεός in 1 Cor 10:5. This supports the harmonization of the views of the readers of his letter, on account of πάντα. Paul calls Christians to think about community-building matters instead of selfish exploitation of their freedom in Christ.[385]

Part 5 (10:24–30) describes the practical application of the midrash composed by Paul. The first sentence of this part repeats closely the parallelism of the previous two sentences. V. 24 states that Christians' freedom presupposes serving each other: μηδεὶς τὸ ἑαυτοῦ ζητείτω ἀλλὰ τὸ τοῦ ἑτέρου. The introduction, which views freedom in terms of service, has an ethical aspect as well as a cultic one.[386] The whole passage is linked to Passover typology, when God liberated Israel from bondage and gave them freedom. This divine example of true service provides the background for Christian freedom, and calls Christians to care for one another and to prevent the stumbling of those who are "weak."

The discussion about εἰδωλοθύτων again bifurcates: the non-cultic and the cultic. Non-cultic consumption is explained first. In v. 25 Paul shows the general solution for non-cultic consumption: πᾶν τὸ ἐν μακέλλῳ πωλούμενον ("anything sold in the meat market" 1 Cor 10:25). Here, meat or other food, even after being offered

---

385. Blomberg, *1 Corinthians*, 202. Here, Paul shows the real freedom in Christ, which calls believers to serve others above self.

386. Paul points to the model of ethics revealed by Christ. For him "the celebration of Christ's sacrifice . . . serves as a centerpiece for Christian worship as did the temple in the Old Testament." Ciampa and Rosner, *First Letter to the Corinthians*, 482. From this he suggests to the church members to view their behavior in terms of holy temple service. The temple service presumed that priests would serve not their own needs, but the needs of others.

to idols, cannot be associated with the particular idol worship, because it is sold at a price, while cultic food is viewed first as a gift to the gods. Tomson argues, "in 1 Cor 8:1–10:22 Paul gives a general prohibition of food consecrated to idols and prohibits participation in cult meals (cf. 8:10, 10:21), while in 10:25–28 he deals with food of unspecified nature, separated from an actual cult ceremony."[387] That is why Paul says: ἐσθίετε μηδὲν ἀνακρίνοντες διὰ τὴν συνείδησιν, "eat . . . without raising questions of conscience" in 1 Cor 10:25. Further in v. 26 Paul explains the command with the conjunction γὰρ followed by a quotation of Deut 10:14, conflated with Ps 24:1. According to these texts any food can be perceived as God's rightful possession by the act of creation, unless it is involved in a rival cult.

After this general statement, Paul explains in detail. The first particular situation discussed is when an unbeliever invites a Christian for a meal.[388] Here, the condition is stated first, then the order. The single explanation for this command is presupposed in v. 26, mentioned above, which views all food as belonging to God, a priori. Referring to Ps 24:1, Paul in 1 Cor 10:25–27 states that the food bought at the market can be eaten "without enquiring."[389] Even the structure of Paul's suggestion for εἰδωλοθύτων repeats the structure of the law given in Deut 14. There the differentiation between cultic and non-cultic is seen clearly. Paul also repeats the order, according to which the general law comes first, then the conditional matters appear and regulations are followed by the explanations.

The second particular situation discussed is when the unbeliever or a "weak" believer claims the food τοῦτο ἱερόθυτόν ἐστιν. Paul here uses ἱερόθυτόν to emphasize that food was offered in the temple of a particular cult, while εἰδωλοθύτων has a more general sense. Tomson considers εἰδωλόθυτον in Acts 15:29, 21:25 and Rev 2:14, 20 to be a synonym for ἱερόθυτον in 1 Cor 10:28.[390] He notes that the verb θύω has the meaning of "slaughtered and ritually offered food" which includes more food than just meat.[391]

In this situation Paul uses an imperative of prohibition, μὴ ἐσθίετε, and provides a double explanation. The first is δι' ἐκεῖνον τὸν μηνύσαντα, and the second is καὶ τὴν συνείδησιν ("for the sake of the man who told you" and "for conscience' sake," 1 Cor 10:28). Paul clarifies which conscience he keeps in view: συνείδησιν δὲ λέγω οὐχὶ τὴν

---

387. Tomson, *Paul and Jewish Law*, 207–8.

388. The meals in private homes, even if meat from sacrifices was used, were not focusing on religious rituals and solemn religious worship from participants, but rather were meals of social importance (weddings, birthdays, and visit of returning friends). The Christians could attend these meals "as long as no one explicitly identifies the fare as idol-food." Gooch, *Dangerous Food*, 31.

389. Tomson, *Paul and Jewish Law*, 206.

390. Tomson, *Paul and Jewish Law*, 189. See also BDAG, θύω, 1, 4. The word predominantly has the meaning of "cultic offering, *sacrifice*, to kill ceremonially, *slaughter sacrificially*." In other cases it may refer to non-cultic slaughtering.

391. Tomson, *Paul and Jewish Law*, 168, 189. Tomson rightly notes that the wine and any other food offered to demons were strongly prohibited for consumption and having profit from them.

ἑαυτοῦ ἀλλὰ τὴν τοῦ ἑτέρου. He is concerned for the sake of both the "weak" and the "unbelieving." If a Christian eats what is declared ἱερόθυτόν, he would tempt the "weak" to idol worship and withhold testimony from the "unbelieving."

Paul then poses a secondary explanation expressed in the form of two questions. The first question, ἱνατί γὰρ ἡ ἐλευθερία μου κρίνεται ὑπὸ ἄλλης συνειδήσεως, "for why should my freedom be judged by another's conscience?" in v. 29, reveals the situation when Christian freedom works improperly and tempts someone.[392] If a Christian eats ἱερόθυτόν relying on freedom from its god, his behavior can be judged by pagans as a denial of any gods. As a result, their superstitious judgment can lead to a conclusion that Christians are irreligious.

The second question, in v. 30, is εἰ ἐγὼ χάριτι μετέχω, τί βλασφημοῦμαι ὑπὲρ οὗ ἐγὼ εὐχαριστῶ, "If I take part in the meal with thankfulness, why am I denounced because of something I thank God for?" It reveals a problem, when an unbeliever and a Christian sit at the table with ἱερόθυτόν. The gratitude of a Christian given to Christ for the gift of food would be immediately blasphemed by the follower of a rival cult in the context of which the ἱερόθυτόν was offered. Thus, Christian faith is threatened by double standard worship; Christ is blasphemed and a "weak" brother is tempted. The preventive behavior follows in part 6 in the form of a general call, detailed and illustrated from Paul's personal example.

The general call of part 6 (10:31–33) becomes a summary of the previous argumentation. The wording of v. 31 starts with connective conjunctions εἴτε ... εἴτε ... which can be translated, "whether ... or." The phrase, εἴτε οὖν ἐσθίετε εἴτε πίνετε εἴτε τι ποιεῖτε, means "everywhere whether you eat, whether you drink, or whatever you do." Here again πάντα can be found in the passage after the fivefold πάντες in part 1 and summary statements of part 4. The way in which πάντα is used in part 6 seems to have a positive tone, which contrasts with previous occurences of πάντα and πάντες. Whether or not previous πάντα reflects the frivolous attitude of Christians to their freedom in Christ, the last πάντα shows a godly attitude. This attitude is reflected in the imperative: πάντα εἰς δόξαν θεοῦ ποιεῖτε.[393]

In the Pauline letters the hope of re-creation includes true, undivided worship. Expectation of re-creation was reflected in a number of Jewish documents contemporary with Paul.[394] Malcolm states that "the idea of future resurrection of bodies (or a

---

392. Ciampa notes that "if the Christian does not abstain, their pagan friends may decide the Christian is not consistent with their convictions, or is a hypocrite." Ciampa and Rosner, *First Letter to the Corinthians*, 493.

393. It was noticed that the phrase δόξαν θεοῦ in 1 Cor 10:31 echoes the Gen 1–3 account. This link is evident in Apoc. Mos. 20:1–2; 21:5–6. There, Adam and Eve were deprived of the glory of God, but "it was promised that this glory would be restored in the eschaton (39:2)." Murphy-O'Connor, *Keys to 1 Corinthians*, 110.

394. Malcolm shows that in Qumran tradition (1 QH, column 2, lines 20–30) God was expected "to act as the great Reverser." Moreover, the hope of restoration similar to resurrection appears in Pss. Sol. 3:11–12 and T. Jud. 25:4. In these texts one's dedication to God is a necessary condition of future reversal. Also, some texts of the OT can be viewed as precursoring a "resurrection" theme (Ps 22, 30,

future return to new bodies) was certainly prominent in early Judaism, probably arising from scriptural themes evident in Isa 26:19 and Dan 12:1–3.[395] Also, the necessity of full commitment to God was clear from the prophetic writtings. Thus, the promise in Jer 31:31–34 of a new covenant written *on the heart* demonstrates the "inwardness" of the new covenant.[396] Ezekiel, like Jeremiah, speaks of a future inner renewal of people's hearts from idolatry.[397] It is likely that the apostles on the Jerusalem Council kept the same matters in mind while viewing the issue of Gentile converts.

After a general statement, details follow in v. 32: ἀπρόσκοποι καὶ Ἰουδαίοις γίνεσθε καὶ Ἕλλησιν καὶ τῇ ἐκκλησίᾳ τοῦ θεοῦ, "do not cause anyone to stumble, whether Jews, Greeks or the church of God." This reveals three of the most vulnerable spheres of Christian life, when it comes to the intersection of three different religions (Christianity, Judaism, paganism). Here, Paul shifts to his personal experience of dealing with different cultural contexts: κἀγὼ πάντα πᾶσιν ἀρέσκω, "even as I please all men in all things," in 1 Cor 10:33. Here πάντα appears again in the positive sense with ἀρέσκω πᾶσιν ("give pleasure, satisfy all others").[398] Paul in v. 31 clarifies serving in the context of Christian freedom by the words μὴ ζητῶν τὸ ἐμαυτοῦ σύμφορον ἀλλὰ τὸ τῶν πολλῶν, "not seeking mine own profit, but the profit of many." His target is "that they may be saved" (ἵνα σωθῶσιν), which perfectly fits into the Passover typology of the wider passage.

Moreover, the typology of the passage presumes salvation in an eternal sense in a creation–fall–re-creation paradigm.[399] This is clearly shown by use of images from the fall narrative in all four parts of the midrash. The call for salvation in this passage can be summarized by the call to be fully dedicated to God. For the "weak" this means a ban of compromising worship, and for the "strong" this means Christ-like behavior. The final call μιμηταί μου γίνεσθε, καθὼς κἀγὼ Χριστοῦ elucidates this idea by Paul's own example of complete dedication to Christ.

Isa 53, Ezek 37; Job, Esther). Malcolm, *World of 1 Corinthians*, 132, 138, 152.

395. Malcolm, *World of 1 Corinthians*, 152–54. He shows that in some places in 1 Corinthians letter, Paul places Gen 1–3 in the background. He concludes that "God's work in resurrection is thus paralleled with God's work of creation." The view that resurrection is paralleled to creation was not new with Paul, but was expressed in Ps 104:27–30; Isa 44:2, 24; 2 Macc 7:28–29; and Esd 6:6.

396. Similar thoughts are present in Luke 22:20 and 1 Cor 11:25 with the same accent on renewal of "heart." Hubbard, *New Creation*, 18.

397. Ezek 6:9; 11:21; 20:16 reflect the idolatry of Israelites which takes place in their hearts. Ezek11:19–20; 14:7; 36:26–27 speak about the renewal of hearts from idolatry and infusion of a new Spirit. Hubbard, *New Creation*, 22, 25.

398. BDAG, ἀρέσκω, 1, 2. The meaning is *"win favor, please, flatter,* to give pleasure/satisfaction, *accommodate."*

399. Murphy-O'Connor supports the idea of Pauline expectation of a re-creation. He states, "Adam before the fall was the revelation of what God intended humanity to be." In Christ the believers have been recreated according to the eternal plan of God. Murphy-O'Connor, *Keys to 1 Corinthians*, 111.

The Possible Reference to εἰδωλοθύτων in Romans 14:1—15:13

Rom 14:1—15:6 reveals several debated issues in the Roman congregation. Although εἰδωλοθύτων is not mentioned, some scholars discuss the similarities of this passage with the lexemes in 1 Cor 8:1–13.[400] Rom 14 raises debates about who can be understood as "the weak" and who as "the strong," from Paul's perspective. Some scholars believe that the issue is to be viewed as a dispute between Gentile and Jewish converts.[401] Thus, Watson identifies the "weak" as "Jewish Christians, not as ascetics or syncretists."[402] Also, Fee believes that, for Paul, the Gentile converts should not force "Gentile freedom" on the Jews.[403]

However, Brendan Byrne softens the discussion when he identifies the "strong" as those who are more confident in salvation granted to them in Christ, while the "weak"are those who "do not lack sufficient measure of faith . . . but they have not as yet allowed it to permeate all areas of life."[404] According to Byrne, faith was viewed by Paul in terms of faith in God as Creator, an ability "to discern God acting creatively."[405] Thus, the connection between Rom 14 and 1 Cor 8 can be explained in two ways: if the issue in Roman church was of cultic origin, then this common cultic background

---

400. The similarities were observed and discussed by Tobit, Karris, and Hultgren. Tobin, *Paul's Rhetoric*, 408–9. Hultgren, *Paul's Letter to the Romans*, 498. Moreover, Byrne views the issues of Romans 14, 1 Corinthians 8 and the Apostolic Decree in Acts 15 together. As a result, the Decree is viewed as reflecting the position of the "weak in faith." Byrne, *Romans*, 405.

401. Many scholars have tried to explain the issue of "weak" and "strong" in light of the diverse community in Rome. Robert Karris shows the contrasting opinions of Rauer and Minear. According to Minear, "the weak" described Jewish Christians, who were legalists and the Gentile converts who accepted the yoke of the law. The "strong" were the antinomians. Rauer at the same time believes that the "weak" are the Gentile Christians "whose practice of abstinence from meat stems from their prior religious background in Gnostic, Hellenistic mystery religions." Karris, "Romans 14:1—15:13," 66–69.

402. Watson, *Paul, Judaism, and the Gentiles*, 176. Here, Watson notes the similarities in language in Rom 14:1—15:13, where in Rom 14:14 the weak avoided the κοινόν. He believes that this term is connected to the Jewish dietary laws. He finds then, that in Rom 14:20 the phrase πάντα μὲν καθαρά is equivalent to οὐδὲν κοινόν in v. 14. He sees here similarities with Acts 10:15 and 11:9 in the phrase ἃ ὁ θεὸς ἐκαθάρισεν, σὺ μὴ κοίνου. Thus, according to Watson the "weak" identifies the Jewish Christians who like Daniel in Dan 1:8–16 avoids eating of meat and drinking wine from the table of Gentiles in order not to be defiled. At the same time Watson identifies the Gentile converts as "strong."

403. Fee, *Pauline Christology*, 260–61. He views this polemic in terms of observance/nonobservance of Jewish dietary laws and days and suggests freedom from these issues in Christ. At the same time he notes that the passage primarily points to Christ who is the Lord of all. Then the question arises of how to fit the "liberal" approach to the Jewishness of Christ, His people and Paul himself. Moreover, Fee notes that v. 11 provides "a collage of two Isaianic passages," as they appear in LXX in Isa 45:23 and 49:18. The Isaianic context does not provide any ground for the liberal approach to Sabbath observance or dietary law.

404. Byrne, *Romans*, 408–9. He mentions the "day observance" as a possible allusion to "the continuing validity of Jewish celebration of the Sabbath and other festivals." He notices that this issue remains undeveloped and thus is "of secondary importance to the main question concerning food."

405. Byrne, *Romans*, 408.

would support linking of Rom 14 to 1 Cor 8; if the issue was of ethical nature, then Rom 14 and 1 Cor 8 discuss different matters though the wording is similar.

The debate in Rom 14:1—15:6 was about food and days. However, it is not said that the debate was raised about Sabbath, kashrut and any other signs of Jewish identity.[406] Paul discusses the topic widely, and raises ethical questions in addition to those concerning food and days. He shows to the church the problems caused by a judgmental attitude, separation into groups, strife among the groups, and lack of concession to those who are "weak" in faith.[407] The diagram of this passage is provided in Appendix 2.

The diagram shows that the passage can be divided into three parts. *Part one* (14:1–4) discusses the debates around the food issue. Here, Paul starts with the same reference to τὸν δὲ ἀσθενοῦντα τῇ πίστει. The participle, ἀσθενοῦντα, also occurs as ὁ ἀσθενῶν in 1 Cor 8:11. The passage 1 Cor 8:7–12 contains five occurrences of this word in different variations. *Part two* (14:5–13) concentrates mostly on the issue of day observance, including a direct quotation of scripture from Isa 49:18; 45:23 (LXX).[408] The quotation, however, does not answer the questions about day observance raised by the Roman church. Instead, Paul uses scripture in order to point to the coming of the Judgment day. The third part starts with Paul's own opinion about matters mentioned above (food and days). Here Paul also quotes Ps 69:9 (LXX 68:10).[409] The quotation reflects an ethical approach to the matters mentioned. *Part three* (14:14—15:6) clarifies the issue of food more than the previous two parts. As is clear from the Table 1, these passages have many similarities.

---

406. Arland Hultgren notes, "in regard to vegetarianism, there are no commands in the Torah that anyone should abstain from consuming meat, as long as it is classified as 'clean.'" Here Hultgren states that "it may be too simplistic to conclude that Paul is referring to the observance of Jewish traditions by Christians in Rome." Hultgren, *Paul's Letter to the Romans*, 499–500.

407. It was noticed that the passage contains "the inconclusive results concerning foods and days" and reaches the point when everyone "must accommodate the sensibilities of others on issues that arise." Hultgren, *Paul's Letter to the Romans*, 504.

408. Tobin, *Paul's Rethoric*, 410.

409. Ps 69:9 was "one of the texts most frequently cited in the early Christian tradition in regard to the passion of Jesus." The text also presumes that Christ, for love of others, submitted himself to suffer violence from sinners. Byrne, *Romans*, 425.

Table 1: Comparative Study of 1 Cor 8:1-13 and Rom 14:1—15:6

The common ideas:	Rom 14:1—15:6	1 Cor 8:1-13
"Weakness"	1 Τὸν δὲ ἀσθενοῦντα τῇ πίστει . . .	10 . . . οὐχὶ ἡ συνείδησις αὐτοῦ ἀσθενοῦς ὄντος οἰκοδομηθήσεται εἰς τὸ τὰ εἰδωλόθυτα ἐσθίειν;
The "weak" avoid several kinds of food	2 ὃς μὲν πιστεύει φαγεῖν πάντα, ὁ δὲ ἀσθενῶν λάχανα ἐσθίει.	τινὲς δὲ τῇ συνηθείᾳ ἕως ἄρτι τοῦ εἰδώλου ὡς εἰδωλόθυτον ἐσθίουσιν, καὶ ἡ συνείδησις αὐτῶν ἀσθενὴς οὖσα μολύνεται.
Some kinds of food are tempting items for the "weak"	13 τὸ μὴ τιθέναι πρόσκομμα τῷ ἀδελφῷ ἢ σκάνδαλον . . .	μή πως ἡ ἐξουσία ὑμῶν αὕτη πρόσκομμα γένηται τοῖς ἀσθενέσιν.
Food does not defile by itself, unless it tempts the "weak"	20 μὴ ἕνεκεν βρώματος κατάλυε τὸ ἔργον τοῦ θεοῦ. πάντα μὲν καθαρά, ἀλλὰ κακὸν τῷ ἀνθρώπῳ τῷ διὰ προσκόμματος ἐσθίοντι.	8 βρῶμα δὲ ἡμᾶς οὐ παραστήσει τῷ θεῷ· οὔτε ἐὰν μὴ φάγωμεν ὑστερούμεθα, οὔτε ἐὰν φάγωμεν περισσεύομεν.
Ethical admonition concerning food	15 εἰ γὰρ διὰ βρῶμα ὁ ἀδελφός σου λυπεῖται, οὐκέτι κατὰ ἀγάπην περιπατεῖς.	13 διόπερ εἰ βρῶμα σκανδαλίζει τὸν ἀδελφόν μου . . .
Contrast between the value of food and the value of salvation	μὴ τῷ βρώματί σου ἐκεῖνον ἀπόλλυε ὑπὲρ οὗ Χριστὸς ἀπέθανεν . . .	11 ἀπόλλυται γὰρ ὁ ἀσθενῶν ἐν τῇ σῇ γνώσει, ὁ ἀδελφὸς δι' ὃν Χριστὸς ἀπέθανεν.
Restriction of food preventing temptation for the "weak"	21 καλὸν τὸ μὴ φαγεῖν κρέα μηδὲ πιεῖν οἶνον μηδὲ ἐν ᾧ ὁ ἀδελφός σου προσκόπτει.	οὐ μὴ φάγω κρέα εἰς τὸν αἰῶνα ἵνα μὴ τὸν ἀδελφόν μου σκανδαλίσω.
Tempting of the "weak" is a sin.	22 σὺ πίστιν [ἣν] ἔχεις κατὰ σεαυτὸν . . . 23 ὁ δὲ διακρινόμενος ἐὰν φάγῃ κατακέκριται, ὅτι οὐκ ἐκ πίστεως· πᾶν δὲ ὃ οὐκ ἐκ πίστεως ἁμαρτία ἐστίν.	12 οὕτως δὲ ἁμαρτάνοντες εἰς τοὺς ἀδελφοὺς καὶ τύπτοντες αὐτῶν τὴν συνείδησιν ἀσθενοῦσαν εἰς Χριστὸν ἁμαρτάνετε.

From Table 1 one can conclude that Rom 14:1—15:6 discusses the issue of meat differently from that in 1 Cor 8:1-12, where the meat sacrificed to idols is in view. The terms "food sacrificed to idols," "knowledge," "freedom," "idols" and "conscience" appear in 1 Cor 8-10, but not in Rom 14:1—15:6.[410] The issue raised in the letter to the Romans is not of doctrinal (or cultic sense), but rather of ethical significance, which makes it very distinctive from the issues of the Corinthian church.[411] Hult-

---

410. Hultgren, *Paul's Letter to the Romans*, 498. Tobin, *Paul's Rethoric*, 412-14. Moreover, Tobin notes that despite similarities in wording these two passages have differences in the nature of the disputes. The letter to the Romans deals with a lack of tolerance of members toward one another, whereas in Corinth the letter reflects a very tolerant approach of the church to sinners.

411. These differences between 1 Cor 8-10 and Rom 14:1—15:6 were overlooked by Heil who states: "In Romans 14:1—15:7 Paul addresses concrete problems in the Roman congregation, including tension surrounding the issue of Jewish food regulations . . . The ritual-cultic distinction

gren states: "One cannot conclude . . . that the passages in the two letters are about the same thing."⁴¹² From this point, Paul's dealing with the issue of εἰδωλοθύτων in Rom 14:1—15:6 becomes less possible.

The major part of Paul's argument in Rom 14:1—15:6 is based on Jesus' ethical teaching, and does not discuss the law of Torah. Paul's first argument is: Τὸν δὲ ἀσθενοῦντα τῇ πίστει προσλαμβάνεσθε ("Accept the one who is weak in faith").⁴¹³ This command is ethically rooted in the actions of God, as it is said, ὁ θεὸς γὰρ αὐτὸν προσελάβετο (which is, "for God accepts him"). Thus, the attitude of the church is compared to the attitude of God. Paul suggests that the restrictive diet of the "weak" should not be criticized, as it is said, προσλαμβάνεσθε μὴ εἰς διακρίσεις διαλογισμῶν ("accept . . . without passing judgment on disputable matters," in Rom 14:1).⁴¹⁴ The actions of people are contrasted with those of God, again, when Paul poses a question, ὁ θεὸς γὰρ αὐτὸν προσελάβετο . . . σὺ τίς εἶ ὁ κρίνων ἀλλότριον οἰκέτην? (". . . for God has accepted him . . . Who are you to judge someone else's servant?" Rom 14:3, 4). Then Paul states the third contrast in v. 4, which differentiates between the destructive power of the critical approach of someone and the constructive power of God.⁴¹⁵ The phrase, δυνατεῖ γὰρ ὁ κύριος στῆσαι αὐτόν, adopts the perspective of the strengthening of "weak" faith until one would be able to avoid unnecessary restrictions.⁴¹⁶

Part two discusses the issue of the observance of days, which may be connected to the issue of food. This becomes clear from v. 6, where days are linked to food: ὁ φρονῶν τὴν ἡμέραν κυρίῳ φρονεῖ· καὶ ὁ ἐσθίων κυρίῳ ἐσθίει, καὶ ὁ μὴ ἐσθίων κυρίῳ οὐκ ἐσθίει ("He who regards one day as special, does so to the Lord. He who eats meat, eats to the Lord"). The connection between day and food suggests the presence of local traditions. The relation of this issue to "things sacrificed to idols" cannot be established since no markers of idolatry appear in Rom 14:1—15:6. Instead, those traditions could be linked to days of fasting.⁴¹⁷

(clean-unclean) as a paradigm of salvation has now been eliminated. Food regulations, and along with them the Torah, have become suspended in Christ and the Kingdom of God." Heil, *Die Ablehnung der Speisegebote*, 265.

412. Hultgren, *Paul's Letter to the Romans*, 498.

413. Here, "Paul's call is for tolerance." Byrne, *Romans*, 408. Karris also notes that Paul is concerned to find a way not to separate striving groups, but unite them, despite differences of opinions. Karris, "Romans 14:1—15:13," 79.

414. Tobin, *Paul's Rethoric*, 412.The word προσλαμβάνεσθε appears in the "opening words" in 14:1 and the "concluding summary words" of 15:7. This word creates a frame for the discussed matters and stresses the ethical nature of the discussion.

415. Here, the phrase δυνατεῖ γὰρ ὁ κύριος στῆσαι αὐτόν, is placed in contrast to the previously stated μὴ εἰς διακρίσεις διαλογισμῶν and to two following questions: σὺ δὲ τί κρίνεις τὸν ἀδελφόν σου; ἢ καὶ σὺ τί ἐξουθενεῖς τὸν ἀδελφόν σου.

416. Paul's opinion here can be associated with the one of the "strong." However, with the same probability, Paul's opinion can presume a third point of view and the phrase δυνατεῖ γὰρ ὁ κύριος στῆσαι αὐτόν could be chosen as a rhetorical invention revealing the power of prayer which could change the opponents.

417. Discussing the observance of days, Hultgren also shows that "by the end of the first century

Paul views every human tradition in light of Christ's lordship. At the beginning (v. 4), Paul poses the question of the justifiability of criticizing others: σὺ δὲ τί κρίνεις τὸν ἀδελφόν σου; ἢ καὶ σὺ τί ἐξουθενεῖς τὸν ἀδελφόν σου;[418] His answer points to τῷ βήματι τοῦ θεοῦ ("judgment of God").[419] The thought has support from Isa 45:23, according to which everyone's judge and savior is God. For Paul, "the Day of the Lord" denoted the end of the world, similar to Amos and Jeremiah.[420] Thus, the polemic of both parts *one* and *two* show Paul's fight against critics who create strife in church, and not against one's diet. It suggests that strife arose around traditions.

Part three (14:14—5:6) seems to provide some key terms on the food issue. The problem of this part is the mix of terms. Paul states in v. 14b, οὐδὲν κοινὸν δι' ἑαυτοῦ and πάντα μὲν καθαρά. The language here reflects the issue of clean/unclean food.[421] However, the term κοινός used by Paul here is different to ἀκάθαρτος, used in Leviticus 11 in relation to meat of an "unclean" animal.[422] The sentence reflects Paul's own opinion, when he states in v. 14a in the first person οἶδα καὶ πέπεισμαι ἐν κυρίῳ Ἰησοῦ ὅτι οὐδὲν κοινὸν δι' ἑαυτοῦ ("I know and am convinced in the Lord Jesus, that nothing is common in itself") and continues this thought in v. 20 with πάντα μὲν καθαρά. The question arises whether Paul himself did away with the distinction between foods prescribed in Torah; or what kind of local tradition does he argue with?

The assumption that Paul argues against the relevance of dietary laws for Christians is a result of conjoining the two views (that of Paul and that of the "strong").[423]

---

some Christians fasted on Wednesdays and Fridays." Their choice of days was in respect of the fact that on Wednesday the betrayal of Jesus was arranged, while on Friday Jesus was crucified. Hultgren, *Paul's Letter to the Romans*, 500.

418. Here, the word ἐξουθενεῖν has the meaning of "belittle" and can have "a strong sense of contemptuous rejection" and even reminds of Herod's treatment of the captive Jesus in Luke 23:11. The Greek word κρίνειν has the sense "judge negatively, condemn." Byrne, *Romans*, 411–12.

419. The word βῆμα is the term used for "judgment seat," which is the platform for seating of a civic officer. Paul used this term in relation to the judgment of Christ in 2 Cor 5:10. Hultgren, *Paul's Letter to the Romans*, 514.

420. Wright, *Paul*, 141. The wording of the quotation repeats the LXX with the tiny difference of placing "every tongue" prior to the verb. The same quotation appears in Phil 2:10–11. Hultgren, *Paul's Letter to the Romans*, 514–515.

421. Hultgren, *Paul's Letter to the Romans*, 517. This distinction is "traditional in Judaism, expressed in Torah (Lev 20:25)." However, he notes that Paul uses the word κοινός for "unclean," while Leviticus and Hos 9:3 use ἀκάθαρτος. In Acts 10:14 both adjectives (κοινός and ἀκάθαρτος) are used together.

422. Bacchiocchi, *Sabbath under Crossfire*, 215. This observation helped him to view the κοινός meat in Rom 14 as "sacrificed to idols." There are two arguments against this assumption: 1) there is more evidence that the letter was written to Jewish converts rather than Gentile converts; 2) the theme of idolatry, well described in 1 Corinthians, is not an issue in Romans. Thus, the only point which can be accepted is that κοινός used by Paul was used not in relation to meat of "unclean" animals, but rather in relation to any ritual kind of uncleanness.

423. The assumption that Paul had done away with kashrut is the result of joining Paul's opinion to the opinion of a "strong" brother against the presupposition of the "weak" brother, who avoids meat in his diet.

However, it is difficult to ascertain with whose view (the "weak" or the "strong") Paul identifies. It appears that the passage reflects three different opinions. The phrase ὁ δὲ ἀσθενῶν λάχανα ἐσθίει does not state for which reason the "weak" avoid eating meat. While it is stated that (πιστεύει φαγεῖν πάντα) the "strong" do not restrict their diet, it is not stated that they extend their diet.[424] The word πάντα, here, might indicate all food is appropriate for consumption and thus does not contradict the principles of the dietary laws. Finally, it is not said what kind of καθαρά Paul has in mind when he states, πάντα μὲν καθαρά.

When Paul writes πάντα μὲν καθαρά, he might reflect the teaching of Jesus about "uncleanness" of food stipulated by the ritual law.[425] In Matt 15:11, the verb form κοινόω, "to make unclean," is mentioned precisely in relation to food.[426] However, in that particular text the issue of clean meat was not under discussion. The text treated the uncleanness which can be transmitted by "clean food" when cleansing rituals were neglected. Cleansing rituals were the part of the ritual law, viewed by the apostolic church as associated with the temple cult, fulfilled in Christ and since then, unnecessary for keeping.

This is indicated by another occurrence of κοινός and ἀκάθαρτος in one passage that appears in Acts 10:14.[427] There, Peter receives a vision, and in Acts 10:15 God states: Ἃ ὁ θεὸς ἐκαθάρισεν, σὺ μὴ κοίνου ("Do not call anything impure that God has made clean"). There, the statement was made not about meats, but about the nations viewed by the Jews as ritually unclean.[428] Moreover, interpreting Paul's statement πάντα μὲν καθαρά, one needs to keep in mind the Jewishness of Paul. Thus, it is less likely to understand πάντα μὲν καθαρά as linked to kashrut. The Jewish view of Torah "was the foundation of early Christian theology."[429] The news that Paul had done away with kashrut would be striking for the Roman congregation and would need to be

---

424. The cancellation of kashrut meat distinction would be viewed as an extension of the diet, because kashrut was a typical diet of the first Christians, who were the converts from Judaism.

425. Here Paul may assume that all reversible uncleanness of food imposed by the ritual law is now cleansed by the blood of Christ. Thus, BDAG, καθαρός, 1, 2, 3 ab, 4. Here the word indicates a ritual, cultic and moral sense of cleanness and purity, while ἀκάθαρτος presumes the same sort of ritual and moral impurity. Both words in Scripture relate to the context of holy versus unholy controversy. This word is employed often to indicate impurity, or moral fornication, which cannot be brought in contact with divinity. BDAG, ἀκάθαρτος, 1, 2. Contrastingly, κοινός means "common, shared collectively, *ordinary, profane*" and may mean "ceremonially impure"; BDAG, κοινός, 1 a,b,c; 2 a, b.

426. Hultgren, *Paul's Letter to the Romans*, 517.

427. Hultgren, *Paul's Letter to the Romans*, 517–18. He also mentions the Pauline view of "clean" and "unclean" in Romans in agreement with Mark 7:19; Acts 10:15; 1 Tim 4:3–4; Tit 1:15). All these texts support the ethical dimension in which ritual uncleanness has to be viewed.

428. Albert Hogeterp states that Paul tried to "defy the idea that the levitical commandment which distinguishes between the holy and the common, and between the unclean and the clean (Lev 10:10) should entail a distinction between Jews and Gentiles." Hogeterp, *Paul and God's Temple*, 280.

429. Young, *Paul, the Jewish Theologian*, 62.

supported by teaching.⁴³⁰ From this point the phrase πάντα μὲν καθαρά likely would presume the cancellation of the ritual "uncleanness" of food, rather then the dietary prohibitions rooted in the natural law of God.⁴³¹

The reason for Paul's view of all food as οὐδὲν κοινὸν, becomes evident in v. 15, where he states, εἰ γὰρ διὰ βρῶμα ὁ ἀδελφός σου λυπεῖται, οὐκέτι κατὰ ἀγάπην περιπατεῖς ("If your brother is distressed because of what you eat, you are no longer acting in love"). Here λυπεῖται, passive of λυπέω, means "to experience sadness or distress, *be sad, be distressed, grieve*."⁴³² This word contains an emotional component, and differs from τύπτοντες and σκανδαλίζει of 1 Cor 8:1–13, which were used in the discussion about idolatry.⁴³³ The phrase is followed by a cascade of statements of similar manner: μὴ τῷ βρώματί σου ἐκεῖνον ἀπόλλυε ὑπὲρ οὗ Χριστὸς ἀπέθανεν in v. 15; μὴ βλασφημείσθω οὖν ὑμῶν τὸ ἀγαθόν in verse 16; μὴ ἕνεκεν βρώματος κατάλυε τὸ ἔργον τοῦ θεοῦ in v. 20. As noted above, λυπεῖται in Romans is contrasted by behavior, κατὰ ἀγάπην, which controls the solution in an ethical sense.⁴³⁴

The consequences of strife in the Roman church (described by ἀπόλλυε and ἁμαρτία) have similarities with those indicating idolatry in 1 Cor 8 (ἀπόλλυται and εἰς Χριστὸν ἁμαρτάνετε). Both cases show that "weak" members of the congregation can be disappointed by fighting in the church. Yet the problem in Rome is pictured in terms of πρόσκομμα and προσκόπτει, which are definitely softer then μολύνεται, σκανδαλίσω, ἁμαρτάνοντες in 1 Corinthians. This gives support to the view that the issue in Romans was of an ethical nature.

This helps to explain the similarities between Rom 14 and 1 Cor 8. The grieving of the "weak" as a result of discord in church could destroy their relationship with Christ.⁴³⁵ The "strong," who puts at risk the salvation of the brother, would be viewed

---

430. If Paul had done away with this distinction long ago, and now agrees with the "believers" party who eat all foods, then he would bring the scriptural evidences for his new "belief" and show the lack of ground for beliefs of the "weak" party. Otherwise, the grounds of the "weak," who continue the distinction of meat according to the teaching of Torah, seems to be stronger than the ethical approach of the "strong" brothers.

431. Byrne notes, that Torah "did not prescribe abstention from meat nor forbid the consumption of wine." Byrne, *Romans*, 404. It is noteworthy that for Paul the uncleanness of food could be possible in several ways. For example, the issue of cleanness/ uncleanness of food was involved in the situation when food was cooked by a Gentile. Although this meat would be assumed as "unclean" by pious Jews, Paul would view it as "clean." In addition, Paul views the cleanness of food in terms of κακὸν and καλὸν in relation to ἀνθρώπῳ. In contrast to it, the clean/unclean food in Torah was usually viewed in terms of holiness, which was required from men by God, and not by an ethical approach of one to another.

432. BDAG, λυπέω, 2 b.

433. BDAG, τύπτω, b β, "to inflict a blow, *strike, beat, wound*" and figuratively "*strike, assault*." BDAG, σκανδαλίζω, 1 a, "to cause to be brought to a downfall, *cause to sin*."

434. "'Walking in love' is central to Paul's ethical teaching." Hultgren, *Paul's Letter to the Romans*, 518.

435. It was noted that the clause ὑπὲρ οὗ Χριστὸς ἀπέθανεν in v. 15 "speaks of the saving work of Christ and makes use of the kerygmatic ὑπερ-formula." This can be understood as the prevention

as one who values his own opinion more than someone's salvation. For Paul, if the issue does not contradict the teaching of Christ, it should be accepted as possible. The fighting for one's own opinion at the cost of destruction of someone's faith was, for Paul, similar to idolatry.

Finally, Paul in Rom 15:1 brings all his arguments to one common solution: Ὀφείλομεν δὲ ἡμεῖς οἱ δυνατοὶ τὰ ἀσθενήματα τῶν ἀδυνάτων βαστάζειν καὶ μὴ ἑαυτοῖς ἀρέσκειν (which is, "We who are strong ought to bear with the failings of the weak and not to please ourselves").[436] He justifies this solution by the example of Christ, καὶ γὰρ ὁ Χριστὸς οὐχ ἑαυτῷ ἤρεσεν. The solution says nothing about the distinction between foods.[437] It deals with strife in the church and competing opinions. This choice of two quotations reveals that the passage deals with ethical issues. To reconcile the arguing parties, Paul supported the opinion of "weak," namely, to restrict the diet. This is evident in his decisive statement in 14:21: καλὸν τὸ μὴ φαγεῖν κρέα μηδὲ πιεῖν οἶνον μηδὲ ἐν ᾧ ὁ ἀδελφός σου προσκόπτει.[438] The call in 15:6 appeals for unity in God (ὁμοθυμαδὸν ἐν ἑνὶ στόματι) and for glorifying God.

It was noted that Paul's scriptural proofs reflect: 1) the quotation about judgement of God (14:11) by which Paul reminds readers that each one answers for himself; 2) the ethics of Jesus (15:3) which Paul calls his readers to follow; and 3) the purpose of God for the salvation of both Jews and Gentiles (Rom 15:8–9). This latter reference, Rom 15:9, quotes Ps 18:49 (LXX 17:50), and is followed by a complex quotation from Deut 32:43, Ps 117:1 and Isa 11:10. All quotations show the acceptance of Gentile converts into the "people of God." This final quotation shows that Paul's main concern in Rom 14:1—15:13 is the salvation of the nations.[439] For this purpose, Paul unites the Christians practicing Jewish laws and their opponents by the Christological orientation of their beliefs.[440]

---

of behavior, which destroys another person who is also precious to Christ. Hultgren, *Paul's Letter to the Romans*, 518.

436. Here the word Ὀφείλομεν, "obligation," reflects the "way of love." The clause μὴ ἑαυτοῖς ἀρέσκειν is similar to 1 Cor 13:5, when it is said, "love . . . is not self-seeking." Byrne, *Romans*, 424.

437. The reference to Christ in 14:9 makes evident that Paul's solution has nothing in common with cancellation of kashrut. Christ's life and death cannot be accepted as a reason to cancel the distinction of meats, because Christ lived and died in agreement with the teaching of Torah. Rather, the cancellation of the ritual law of Torah can be viewed here as possibly Paul's solution. The cancellation of the ritual law and appealing to the example of Christ can be fitted into one thought, because he fulfilled the ritual law, bringing the atoning sacrifice.

438. The meaning "It is better not to eat meat or drink wine or to do anything else that will cause your brother to fall" (Rom 14:21). Here, the Greek aorist infinitives φαγεῖν and πιεῖν suggests, "he is recommending abstention not by way of a permanent ban but as something applicable when the danger of providing a 'stumbling block' is present." Byrne, *Romans*, 422.

439. Hogeterp, *Paul and God's Temple*, 292. He shows that Paul "redefined the idea of Israel's cult in light of the faith in Christ to unite the Gentiles in God's covenant."

440. It was noticed by Karris that Rom 15:7–13 deals with Jews and Gentiles. Thus, the "weak" has to be identified with the Jewish convert, who still keeps the ritual law. Karris, "Romans 14:1—15:13," 79–80.

This sheds light on the issue of Romans 14. The most probable reason for the "weak" in the Roman church to avoid eating meat is the issue of the ritual law, presuming uncleanness transmitted in food by its association with ritually unclean people or substances. This view has support from Dan 1:8, 12, 16; Tob 1:11; Add Esth 14:17; Jdt 12:1–2; T. Reu. 1:9–10; 2 Macc 5:27.[441] The possible connection of temporary "uncleannes'and food can be viewed on the basis of Lev 11:31–40.[442] This reason would be viewed by Christ and the apostles as temporary uncleanness.[443] Since Christ's death on the cross, the temporary uncleanness was cleansed and the ritual law became unnecessary to observe.

The distinction of days (ὁ φρονῶν τὴν ἡμέραν) in 14:6 reflects the Jewish observance of religious feasts, when pious Jews had to carry out purification rites.[444] In those days, Christians in the Roman congregation who kept the ritual law, likely observed the rites of purification. Jews in Jerusalem could purify themselves in the temple by bringing sacrifices. The Diaspora Jews were deprived of this opportunity. Their way of purification might be similar to one described in Dan 1:8, 10 (Moreover, Rome, in the days of the apostles, was compared to Babylon, in 1 Pet 5:13.). The idea of purification during the feasts can be seen in Paul's statement, οὐ γάρ ἐστιν ἡ βασιλεία τοῦ θεοῦ βρῶσις καὶ πόσις. This phrase might reflect that some believers in Rome viewed belonging to "kingdom of God" as practicing the restrictions of diet, in order to be closer to God. At the same time, the Jewish way to be closer to a holy God was provided by purification rituals during religious feasts.[445] Thus, it seems right to

---

441. Byrne, *Romans*, 404–5. Hultgren, *Paul's Letter to the Romans*, 499, 500, 512. Hultgren also notes that Eusebius (quoting from Hegesippus ca. 110–80 CE) described that James, the head of the Jerusalem church, refrained from drinking wine and eating meat (Eusebius, *Ecclesiastical History*, 2.23.4–5). However, the reasons for James' fasting in Jerusalem were, likely, different from those of the Diaspora Jews. Another probable solution would be the distinction of days of fasting in the Roman congregation. This view has support from New Testament tradition in Mark 2:20; Matt 9:15; and Luke 5:33. Although this solution would explain the connection between days and restrictions of diet, is fails to explain the polemic about κοινός and ἀκάθαρτος in Rom 14.

442. Hultgren, *Paul's Letter to the Romans*, 499. He refers to Lev 11:1–47 not making a distinction between the issues of permanent uncleanness of "unclean" animals and temporal uncleanness of "unclean" people, or things associating with something that is "unclean." The matter of distinction between two types of uncleanness would be viewed in the possibility to cleanse it, presumed by the phrase "and he will be unclean till evening." The temporal uncleanness of the "clean" meat would be viewed as a result of its contamination from the "uncleanness" of the Gentiles.

443. The temporal uncleanness has to be viewed as a matter associated with the ritual law of Torah, which was connected to the temple cult and was done away with on the Jerusalem Council. Preceeding the Jerusalem Council, the teaching of Christ on account of temporal uncleanness, will be described in the chapter 4 of the present study.

444. The assumption of ὁ φρονῶν τὴν ἡμέραν, as the observance of the days of feasts, is made in respect to the fact that φρονέω has the meaning of "to think highly of." The custom of purification during the Jewish religious feasts is reflected in Acts 21:20–26 regarding those in Jerusalem, and in Col 2:16 regarding those of the Diaspora.

445. It was noted that the Jews in the Diaspora were involved in ritual and cultic matters "on a regular basis within the synagogual culture of Paul's time." Hogeterp, referring to Josephus, *Ant.* 14.261, who states that for the Jews in the Diaspora "purity laws probably regulated common meals in

assume that those who practiced Jewish purification rites in the Roman congregation abstained from meat and wine during the days of the feast.

All these findings support the view that the distinction of food which took place in the Roman church: 1) had a local character; 2) reflected an ethical issue; 3) dealt with the ritual uncleanness of food.[446] From this point the relationship of the discussion in Romans 14 to the apostolic council can be assumed as possible.[447] The apostolic view of the ritual law in Acts 15 does not contradict that of Paul in Romans 14. Instead, both passages show agreement on the view that ritual observance was not necessary for salvation. In this situation, when some "weak in faith" had difficulties accepting it, Paul suggested a concession for them. That is why Paul's approach to the issue puts forward an ethical solution.

Chapter Summary

The discussion developed in this chapter builds a firm foundation for the following satements:

1. Detailed exegesis of Gen 1–3 reveals that the four prohibitions of the Apostolic Decree in Acts 15 are rooted in the creation-fall narrative.

2. The rationale for all four prohibitions of the Apostolic Decree is the natural law of God, known from the fall.

3. The prohibitions can be viewed in an ethical and cultic sense together, and linked to the issue of true versus false worship.

4. The creation–fall–re-creation paradigm provides the framework for the matters of the Apostolic Decree.

5. The prohibitions of αἵματος and πνικτῶν reflect the controversy between life and death (known since Gen 3:19). It was given to illustrate the belief that only God has power over life and death.

6. The prohibition of αἵματος has to be understood to contain two concepts: "blood represents life" and "blood redeems life." The first is rooted in the natural law of God, while the second was developed later in the form of the ritual system. The

---

Jewish congregations, for one decree addresses the issue of 'suitable food.'" Hogeterp, *Paul and God's Temple*, 246.

446. The ritual uncleanness of food has to be viewed as an ethical matter here, since the doctrinal review on its account was made during the Jerusalem Council and took the form of the Decree. Pauline permission to accept the opinion of the "weak," which has no theological grounds anymore, has to be viewed as the ethical approach.

447. Byrne, *Romans*, 405. He comes to the conclusion that in Romans 14 Paul likely was seeking to project "the kind of tolerance that would find room for the range of concerns reflected later in the Decree."

concept, "blood redeems life," was fulfilled in Christ's death and made keeping the ritual law unnecessary.

7. There were places in Mosaic law where the converts from the Gentiles could have difficulties to differenciate between cultic and non-cultic regulations. For this reason the apostles pointed out to the four prohibitions of the Apostolic Decree.

8. The prohibition of πνικτῶν, also, is rooted in the controversy between life and death. It pictures death as the process that reversed creation (Gen 2:7) and is in accord with the belief that the breath returns to God (Eccl 12:7). Resurrection is the reverse process, from death to life, yet similar to the creation of man (Ps 104:30). The "strangled" things symbolically represent the destruction of this natural cycle. Violation of natural law and deliberate eating of πνικτῶν would indicate an extreme degree of unbelief in God the Creator.

9. The prohibition of πορνεία also has roots in the natural law of God. The principle of separating two people from "one flesh" and then uniting them into "one flesh," becomes the basic rationale for marriage ordained by God. Deviations from it are described by two terms, πορνεία and μοιχεία. Here, πορνεία becomes the denial/destruction of the concept "two become one flesh" because of the cultic practices of pagan worship. The violation of the natural law thus becomes designated as "idolatry."

10. Mentioning of εἰδωλοθύτων and πορνεία in the Pauline writings also reveal the typology and midrashic constructions built on the basis of the creation-fall narrative. There, the prohibition of πορνεία also has to be linked to the issue of worship. Pauline logic passes judgment on idolatry with eternal punishment, and thus also fits it into the creation–fall–re-creation paradigm.

11. The apostles on the Jerusalem Council reviewed all the laws of Torah. They imposed no matters of the ritual law on the Gentile converts. The ritual system was called a "yoke." However, the issues which Paul faced after the Council (Acts 21) and which he reflected in his letter to Romans 14 show that he was tolerant on account of those who continued in keeping the ritual law.

The case for the link between the four prohibitions of the Apostolic Decree and the Gen 1–3 account has been clearly demonstrated. The prohibitions are fitted into the creation–fall–re-creation paradigm, which provides a logical, temporal and conceptual frame for all four. The worship motifs behind the prohibitions, whose role is to support the reversal from pagan idolatry to a true worship, is now evident.

4

The Literary Context of the Apostolic Decree in Luke-Acts

The Roles of Ritual and Universal Law in Luke-Acts

THIS CHAPTER ARGUES THAT Luke viewed Jewish ritual law to have been fulfilled in Jesus' messiahship. With the help of narratives, Luke shows that since the cross the ritual law has become unnecessary for Christians. Luke often discusses this issue from different angles and fits it into the creation–fall–re-creation paradigm.[1] Luke uses the issue of the ritual law separately from the moral law rooted in the universal law of creation and separately from those dietary laws, which are rooted in natural law, known since the fall.

The creation–fall–re-creation paradigm allows Luke to define Jesus' mission in terms of the restoration of God's universal order in the world.[2] This paradigm pictures the reversal of temporary ritual uncleanness and the process of the restoration of God's creation to the stage it had before the fall.[3] The concept of natural law, which takes its origin in the creation-fall account of Gen 1–3, provides an explanation of permanent uncleanness present in the world until the time of re-creation.

---

1. The creation–fall–re-creation paradigm is important for Luke: it correlates with the Levitical Jubilee and its eschatological interpretation in Isa 61:1, 2. Gurtner, "Luke's Isaianic Jubilee," 135–36.

2. Kulikovsky rightly notes that Paul, in Rom 8:19 and Phil 3:20–21, shows "that it is Christ Himself who conducts the transformation of our bodies in order that they become just like His glorious body," and who "on the cross has paved the way for the full restoration of human beings." He states that the restoration starts when one acknowledge Christ as Lord. Kulikovsky, *Creation, Fall, Restoration*, 279.

3. An illustrative role of a cleansing ritual is focused on the removal of sins from the world. Christopher Beetham describes the pattern of creation–fall–re-creation and concludes: "as the destruction by flood is depicted as de-creation, so the post-diluvian renewal is depicted as re-creation, as new creation." Thus, the apocalyptic aspect of the flood narrative represents cleansing of all uncleanness from the world with help of waters and the following process of re-creation. Beetham, "From Creation to New Creation," 242.

Rethinking the Role of Ritual Uncleanness in Light of Christ's Messiahship

This section shows how Luke in his double-volume work reflects a knowledge of different groupings of the Law. While he retains norms of moral law, he argues that keeping the ritual law is no longer necessary. Luke widely discusses the issue of the temple cult and the ritual law connected to it. Striking, however, is the lack of discussion of the dietary laws in Luke-Acts. When Luke raises the issue of food, it is to indicate its ritual uncleanness after its association with unclean matters. He views food as free from demands of the ritual law, leaving it only under demands of the dietary laws rooted in natural law, and not under the ritual law of Torah.

The ritual law is a significant issue for Luke.[4] The rites of purification, temporal uncleanness connected to leprosy, death, flow of blood, demon possession receive his attention. He shows that all these types of uncleanness were healed and cleansed by Jesus.[5] The progress of narratives brings the reader closer to the issue of spiritual cleansing. Luke shows the way in which ritual cleansing was replaced with spiritual. For him, baptism was established to express publically this spiritual cleansing, which invisibly had already taken place in the inner world of a believer. Finally, Luke rethinks the meaning of feasts connected to temple cult and levitical service, proposing a fresh spiritual meaning of the Passover, Pentecost and the priesthood of all believers.

The issue of the Gentiles becomes prominent in Acts. Here the author reveals the importance of faith, inner cleansing of the heart, and the pouring out of the Holy Spirit, since the ritual law has become unnecessary for salvation. All these ideas finally prepare for the decision taken at the Jerusalem Council. The relationship dilemma between being a believing Jew versus a Gentile convert is resolved after any partiality in the Church (the body of Christ) is rejected. According to the Decree, the Gentile converts are accepted without obliging them to become Jews, keeping the ritual law and participating in temple cult. At this time the dietary prohibitions of the Decree still appear among the necessary things. These are the matters associated with the dietary laws of Torah, rooted in natural law.[6] Their appointed role in the creation–fall–

---

4. Daniel Marguerat on the basis of Luke's Gospel narratives argues that Luke does not ignore the ritual component of the law. For Luke "the Law in its integrity remains in force." Marguerat, *First Christian Historian*, 60.

5. In Luke's Gospel, all of Jesus' healing miracles "function as signposts" called to reveal how the kingdom of God will be in its eschatological consummation. Beetham, "From Creation to New Creation," 250–51.

6. The dietary prohibitions listed in the Decree are associated with natural law (examples Gen 6:19, 20; 7:2, 3; 9:3, 4; Lev 3:17; 7:22–27; 11:1–27; 17:10–14; Deut 12:21–25) and have to be viewed separately from the dietary restrictions rooted in the ritual law (examples Exod 12:3–11, 15; 13:6, 7; Lev 6:14–18, 26–30; 7:15–21; 11:32–35, 40; 17:15). The difference between the two types of dietary laws has to be viewed in two aspects: 1) The dietary laws rooted in natural law are not connected with any cultic issues, imposed on Israelites as on aliens, performed everywhere, every time and by everyone, while the dietary laws linked to the ritual law are linked to the religious feasts, holy places, and sacrifices. The latter can be eaten by the priesthood or by a ritually clean person. 2) Violation of the dietary laws rooted in the natural law does not presume cleansing rituals, while the violation of

re-creation paradigm is to illustrate the issue of spiritual uncleanness until the time of complete re-creation of the world.

Focus on the Priestly Service in Luke 2:21–24, 39

The Gospel of Luke begins with the special focus on righteousness from the priestly perspective.[7] Luke places the narrative, where an angel is foretelling Jesus' birth (Luke 1:26–38) in the midst of another story (Luke 1:5–25 and 1:39–80). It seems that the shift was made not only to keep events in chronological order, but also for theological reasons. Beginning with the miracle in the family of the priest Zacharias, Luke changes perspective and inserts between v. 26 and v. 38 an announcement of Jesus' birth. Then, from v. 39 to v. 56 he joins two stories in order to record the announcement of Jesus' birth by Zacharias' family. Luke returns to Zacharias' family in 1:57–80. The insertion, here, of Mary's response to an angel could serve as a positive example of unconditional faith in God.[8] In contrast, Zacharias' righteousness, in accord with all the demands of the Mosaic law, seems inadequate for salvation (1:19, 20), since it lacked faith.[9] Later, in Luke 11:16, 29 Pharisaic demands for a sign from heaven are compared to Zacharias' demand, given no approval, and contrasted with true faith.[10] The faith of Mary (1:38), in contrast, is pictured as the only appropriate response to God's salvific work.

The "narrative within narrative" technique of Luke is used to reveal the great difference between the works of the law and the work of faith.[11] In chapter 1 of Luke, the effect of "narrative within narrative" becomes strengthened by reason of both

---

the dietary laws linked to the ritual law presumes the cleansing rituals (temporal uncleanness until evening, cleansing of body or a jug by water).

7. Bock notices that Luke often employs the motif "of obedience to the law and faithfulness to the temple" in Luke 2:23–24, 27, 37, 39, 46; 16:17; 19:45, 47; 21:37–38; 23:56; 24:53. Bock, *Luke 1:1—9:50*, 77 n. 17. The importance of temple motifs for Lukan theology can be assumed from the fact noted by Robert Stein: "Luke began and closed his gospel with a scene taking place in the temple." Stein, *Luke*, 74.

8. With help of "positive and negative examples of people struggling with faith," Luke implicitly invites the reader to believe and be blessed (Luke 1:20; 1:45; 8:12, 50; 22:67; 24:25; Acts 4:4, 32; 5:14; 8:12; 9:14; 10:43; 11:17; 16:31, 34). Trites, "Gospel of Luke," 44.

9. Zachariah's family is pictured "walking blameless" in ἐντολαῖς καὶ δικαιώμασιν (Luke 1:6), where ἐντολαῖς and δικαιώμασιν appear in LXX together in Exod 15:26; Deut 4:40; 6:17; 10:13; 27:10 and express "complete conformity to the will of God. Esler, *Community and Gospel*, 112. However, "a punitive miracle," similar to Acts 5:1–10; 13:6–11 performed by an angel reveals that Zacharias' righteousness without faith lacks God's approval and is even condemned. Fitzmyer, *Gospel According to Luke (I-IX)*, 328.

10. This parallel was mentioned by Garland, *Luke*, 69.

11. Here, Mary's childlike faith is contrasted with priest Zacharias' unbelief. Later the same technique appears in Luke 8:40–54, where Jairus, the ruler of the synagogue, is compared to an unnamed woman. His faith becomes strengthened by the miraculous healing of the woman (vv. 43–46) in response to her faith. Thus, the power of faith becomes the main motif stressed by the "narrative within narrative" technique of Luke, in both cases.

narratives sharing the same motif, namely the miraculous conception of a child.[12] In Mary's case, pregnancy is absolutely incomprehensible to human logic, and Luke stresses the role of faith in terms of salvific history.[13] Law obedience without faith in God's every word, as seen from the narrative, does not bring the fulfillment of hopes. Thus, from the beginning of Luke's Gospel the role of faith surpasses the role of works of the law.

When the narrative comes to Jesus' birth, Luke emphasizes the following important features: the birth took place in the city of David; the lineage of Joseph was from David, the announcement of Jesus' messianic role by the angels; the image of the Lamb of God hinted at by the manger, shepherds, and flocks against the background of the main theme. Soon after, Luke reverts to the ritual law theme, picturing Jesus's parents in Luke 2:21–24, 39–40 performing "all things according to the law of the Lord."[14] At the same time Luke inserts two personages into the narrative, Simeon and Anna, who prophesy about the messianic role of Jesus: φῶς εἰς ἀποκάλυψιν ἐθνῶν καὶ δόξαν λαοῦ σου Ἰσραήλ (Luke 2:32). At this point, it looks as if two themes, the messiahship of Jesus and that of the ritual system of Israel go "hand in hand."

Luke 2:21–24, 39 in the diagram in Appendix 3 is divided into three parts. Part 1 (v. 21) describes the circumcision of the infant Jesus. Circumcision was, supposedly, performed in or near Bethlehem, not in the Jerusalem temple, because Mary had to stay away from the temple during her temporary uncleanness after delivering the baby.[15] The possessive pronoun αὐτῶν in the phrase αἱ ἡμέραι τοῦ καθαρισμοῦ αὐτῶν (Luke 2:22) would likely indicate that the baby was considered unclean too, because of his close association with his mother.[16] Circumcision signified that a boy became a Jew and was consecrated to worship God according to the Jewish cultic system.[17]

---

12. Also Stein notices parallelism of the stories here. Stein, *Luke*, 69.

13. Garland, *Luke*, 81. He explains what makes Jesus' conception beyond extraordinary in comparison to John's extraordinary conception.

14. Bock shows the complex quotation of Laws here: the purification ceremony for a mother (Lev 12:2–4, 6) and the presentation of the first-born son (Exod 13:2, 12, 15; 34:19; Num 18:15–16). Bock, *Luke 1:1—9:50*, 234.

15. Here Luke refers to the law in Lev 12:1–4, which is viewed as the part of the ritual system. The first week after the delivery of a baby is compared with the ritual uncleanness of a woman during the time of her period: ". . . she shall be unclean seven days; as in the days of the impurity of her sickness shall she be unclean" (Lev 12:2). Then, the woman "shall continue in the blood of her purifying three and thirty days; she shall touch no hallowed thing, nor come into the sanctuary, until the days of her purifying be fulfilled" (Lev 12:4).

16. The temporary ritual uncleanness was viewed as contaminating according to Lev 15:3–12. However, the baby sharing the mother's uncleanness was not obliged to be purified by the bringing of sacrifices. His purification was made by cleansing the body with water. Bock notices that Joseph could be viewed as unclean, "because he aided in the delivery" (according to *m. Nid.* 5.1; 2.5; 1.3–5 contact with blood made one unclean). Bock, *Luke 1:1—9:50*, 236. Stein states that the temporal uncleanness of Joseph can be assumed on the basis of a "one flesh" concept of Gen 2:24. Stein, *Luke*, 113.

17. This rite was witnessed by friends and relatives and was a sign of the covenant in Gen 17:12, 21:4; Lev 12:3, the sign of election, which "marked off Jews from the heathen people around them."

Part 2 (vv. 22–24) describes the events in the Jerusalem temple, where sacrifices were required for the purification of the mother.[18] The child needed only to be cleansed by water. Another ritual was prescribed for firstborn sons, who had to be dedicated to the Lord, according to Exod 13:2, 12, 15 and Num 3:13, 8:17. The diagram of the passage presents these two rites separately (A and B). Both were described by Luke as κατὰ τὸν νόμον Μωϋσέως in v. 22.[19] The parallel, καὶ ὡς ἐτέλεσαν πάντα τὰ κατὰ τὸν νόμον κυρίου, is seen in v. 39. Either Luke had no idea how to classify these laws, or he viewed the ritual law as part of the Mosaic law. Moreover, the parallel statements suggest that Luke viewed the "law of Moses" as the "law of God," given through Moses.[20] Luke 2:41, 42 states that Jesus' parents attended the Jerusalem feasts annually.[21] The phrase κατὰ τὸ ἔθος in v. 42 does not refer to attending the sanctuary annually; that was a law obligation.[22] Rather, it explains why Jesus was included after he turned twelve.[23] Luke, even at this early stage of kerygma development, clarified the difference between κατὰ τὸν νόμον κυρίου and κατὰ τὸ ἔθος.

Part 3 (vv. 39–40) reports the covenant blessings: τὸ δὲ παιδίον ηὔξανεν καὶ ἐκραταιοῦτο πληρούμενον σοφίᾳ καὶ χάρις θεοῦ ἦν ἐπ'αὐτό describes blessings as spiritual, not material, wellbeing.[24] This would suggest that the spiritual growth of a child was not only the result of parents' obedience to the law of Torah, but also because of their faithfulness to God. Their faithfulness was in fulfillment of the covenant in a spiritual way, which pleased God, being more than just the formal keeping of a tradition. Thus, for Luke faith acquires an important role in the spiritual aspect of the covenant relationship.

Garland, *Luke*, 125.

18. Johnson, *Gospel of Luke*, 54 n. 22. See also Garland, *Luke*, 135.

19. Jervell notes that only Luke used phrases such as νόμῳ κυρίου (Luke 2:23, 24, 39) and τοῦ πατρῴου νόμου (Acts 22:3) in relation to the law of God, and the different phrase τῷ ἔθει τῷ Μωϋσέως (Acts 15:1; 6:14; 21:21; 28:17) when he was referring to Mosaic customs. Jervell, "Law in Luke-Acts," 24. See also Jervell, *Apostelgeschichte*, 389.

20. Fitzmyer, *Gospel According to Luke (I–IX)*, 426. He notices that the phrase "the Law of the Lord" is "Luke's way (see vv. 24, 39) of referring to the Mosaic Law (see v. 22)."

21. This shows that Jesus' parents "were utterly faithful to the law" given to Israel by Moses. Esler, *Community and Gospel*, 112.

22. The ritual system prescribed the bringing of sacrifices to the holy place, in single sanctuary (Exod 23:17; 34:23, 24; Lev 16:2; Deut 16:16). That was demanded by the law. The age when the child could join his parents was not stated by the law, but seems to be viewed individually. The tradition, derived from the Prophet Samuel's story in 1 Sam 1:20–24, viewed the readiness of a child to serve the Lord at approximately twelve years of age.

23. Johnson notes that Luke often presents pictures of "teaching in the temple" (Luke 2:46; 19:47; 20:1; 21:37; 22:53; Acts 4:2; 5:21, 25). Johnson, *Gospel of Luke*, 61. This may prefigure the role of Jesus' teaching, which supersedes the temple cult and sheds light on his reply "I must be in my Father's house" (2:49).

24. Here the phrase echoes Samuel's story, using the wording from 1 Sam 2:21c, 26. Fitzmyer, *Gospel According to Luke (I–IX)*, 432.

However, faith does not cancel the whole law. It seems that Luke shares James' idea: ἡ πίστις συνήργει τοῖς ἔργοις αὐτοῦ (James 2:22), at least, until the point in the Gospel when the messiahship of Jesus becomes clearly stated. From that point onward, faith dominates in the narratives, and takes on a key role in terms of salvation.[25] In some narratives the contrast between faith and law-keeping would allude to a cancellation of the law. In those cases the ritual law seems to be under discussion. Luke does not place the keeping of the moral law in opposition to faith.

Luke stresses Jesus' own loyalty to the moral law and to the high ethical principles of his teaching.[26] This observation leads to an assumption that Luke contrasts saving faith in the messiahship of Jesus with formal keeping of the ritual law. Johnson confirms, "Luke never connects circumcision to the issue of righteousness or salvation. It is for him a 'custom of people.'"[27] This aspect will be reviewed below in paragraph 1.1.2, in Luke 11:37–44, where ritual cleansing becomes a matter of dispute between Jesus and the Pharisees.

Luke 11:37–44

This passage raises the issue of ritual uncleanness and can be subdivided into six parts.[28] Part 1 (vv. 37, 38) pictures Jesus in the home of a Pharisee. The introductory phrase Ἐν δὲ τῷ λαλῆσαι suggests the importance of Jesus' words in vv. 34–36. Those words "ignited" imagery in the minds of listeners, which illustrated the difference between the pre(darkness) and post(light) condition of the human mind in relation to conversion.[29] This radical change effected by conversion links the prediction in Luke 1:79, "to shine upon those who sit in darkness and the shadow of death," to the final formulated purpose of the Gospel proclamation in Acts 26:18: "to open their eyes so that they may turn from darkness to light and from the dominion of Satan to God." The motif appears not only in Luke but also in other New Testament texts.[30]

---

25. Rebecca Harrocks noted that in Luke (as well as in the rest of the Synoptic tradition) the healing of the Gentiles by Jesus "are all carried out without bodily contact" (in Luke 7:1–10; 8:26–37; 17:11–19). She explains it by the fact that in all those cases "faith is put forward." Harrocks, "Jesus' Gentile Healings," 83–84, 98–100. Thus, faith is seen as a power which overcomes the ritual distinctions.

26. Esler notes that while Mark 12:28–34 simply represents Jesus' personal opinion to a scribe, Luke's Jesus refers to the law in these words: "What is written in the law?" Then the Deut 6:14 quotation follows. Esler, *Community and Gospel*, 115.

27. For the use of "ethos" in the writings of Luke, compare Luke 1:9; 2:42; 6:14 as well as Acts 16:21; 21:21; 26:3; 28:17). Johnson, *Acts*, 259 n. 1.

28. The diagram for this passage is given in Appendix 3.

29. Stein notices three proverbs here, linked by the word "light." The first saying links Jesus' ministry to light (2:32; 8:16, 11:33), the second saying pictures the recipients of the light (11:34, 35), while the third shows the influence of Jesus' light on the lives of those who receive him (11:36). Stein, *Luke*, 337.

30. Conversion, expressed by the turning from darkness to light, appears in 2 Cor 4:6; Eph 5:8; John 3:19; 1 Tim 5:5; 1 Pet 2:9.

This observation supports the expectation that in this passage Luke will view the ritual law from the perspective of one's personal conversion, which he contrasted with formal observance of the ritual law. Luke 11:37 sets the scene: ἐρωτᾷ αὐτὸν Φαρισαῖος ὅπως ἀριστήσῃ παρ' αὐτῷ "a Pharisee asked Him to have lunch with him." It can be assumed that the Pharisee had a positive attitude toward Jesus as he welcomed him to his home and share a meal. Jesus also had a positive attitude, accepting the invitation, εἰσελθὼν δὲ ἀνέπεσεν (he went in and reclined *at the table*).

The shift of the positive flow of the scene to the negative starts in v. 38. The indicator of the shift is the word ἐθαύμασεν (from θαυμάζω "wonder, marvel, be astonished").[31] It seems that the Pharisee perceived Jesus's actions as very unusual and inexplicable.[32] The subordinate clause ὅτι οὐ πρῶτον ἐβαπτίσθη πρὸ τοῦ ἀρίστου, "that He had not first ritually washed before the meal," clarifies that the matter was a violation of ritual cleansing. Here, ἐβαπτίσθη could indicate washing of the whole body by immersion in a basin, or just washing of hands.[33] The phrase πρῶτον πρὸ τοῦ ἀρίστου reveals the proper order of the ceremony: before a meal.[34]

The significance of this ritual was built upon the presupposition that in public places, one might acquire uncleanness from ritually unclean people.[35] According to Lev 15:7, "whoever touches the person with the discharge shall wash his clothes and bathe in water and be unclean until evening." Supposedly, since early morning Jesus had been surrounded by people who were looking for healing. Many of them had different kinds of uncleanness. The Pharisaic emphasis on washing before each meal reflected a belief that uncleanness itself can transfer with food from outside the body to the inside.[36] The Pharisee's astonishment can be explained by his doubt whether

---

31. BDAG, θαυμάζω, 1, a, αβγ.

32. In Exod 30:19–21; 40:12 only priests were commanded to wash hands before entering the holy place, yet Pharisaic oral tradition extended it to all people. Moreover, "a later rabbinic tradition likens eating bread without previously washing the hands to having intercourse with a harlot" (*b. Sotah* 4b). Garland, *Luke*, 493.

33. Johnson mentions Essenes' ritual bathing before meals, found in Josephus, *J.W.* 2:129. In m. *Yadaim*, esp. 4:6–8 the discussion on washing of hands is given. Johnson, *Gospel of Luke*, 188 n. 38. Garland speaks about the Pharisaic tradition of hand washing accompanied by the pronouncement: "Blessed is He who has sanctified us with his commandments and commanded us concerning the washing of hands" (*b. Ber.* 60b). Garland, *Luke*, 154 n. 9, 493.

34. Darrell Bock shows that this ritual was described, but not prescribed in the OT. The rabbis made it a custom. Bock, *Luke 9:51—24:53*, 1111, 1112 nn. 11, 12.

35. The ritual was developed in order to avoid the possibility of any contamination through "uncleanness" from people with ἡ ῥύσις αὐτοῦ ἀκάθαρτός ἐστιν (in Lev 15:2), which is "a discharge from someone's body." The source could be men or women, lepers, or demon possessed. The Gentiles were also considered to be unclean.

36. This belief was mentioned in Mark 7:2, 5 and Matt 15:20, where Jesus argues against this assumption. Moreover, it is said that the belief was not the teaching of Torah, but belonged to κατὰ τὴν παράδοσιν τῶν πρεσβυτέρων (Mark 7:5). Garland notes that according to Pharisaic beliefs, consuming unclean food would defile the inner parts of a body. Consequently, Pharisees believed that "the righteous could not be filled with Torah and prayer, if they were defiled." Garland, *Luke*, 493.

Jesus willingly violated τὴν παράδοσιν τῶν πρεσβυτέρων (the tradition of the elders) or because he was unaware?

In part 2 (v. 39) Jesus answers the Pharisee's doubts; εἶπεν δὲ ὁ κύριος πρὸς αὐτόν introduces a contrasting opinion by the conjunction δὲ. Jesus' words include several contrasts. The first is between the situation at present (described by the indicator of present time νῦν) and the future destiny of Pharisees (presumed in prediction ἀλλὰ οὐαὶ ὑμῖν . . .). The second contrast is between the ὑμεῖς οἱ Φαρισαῖοι (the pronoun shows to whom the speech was addressed) and Jesus himself.[37] The third contrast is between internal cleansing of the conscience and external cleansing of the body.

According to Jesus, the Pharisees were concerned about cleansing the outside of each cup and platter (τὸ ἔξωθεν τοῦ ποτηρίου καὶ τοῦ πίνακος καθαρίζετε). Jesus emphasizes the tendency of the Pharisees to focus on cleaning things which do not come in contact with food and look like an unnecessary precaution.[38] Jesus uses the opportunity to put the plate's outside alongside other things of secondary importance. Maximum attention is given by Jesus to the issues of people's hearts (τὸ δὲ ἔσωθεν ὑμῶν γέμει ἁρπαγῆς καὶ πονηρίας which means, "but inside you are full of robbery and wickedness").[39] The comparison between a cup and a heart reveals a dissonance: the cup is perfectly polished, while the heart remains dirty.[40] While the appearance of a cup merely impresses neighbors, the uncleanness of a heart attracts God's judgment.

The inevitability of judgment allows Jesus to make four exclamations. The first one appears in Part 3 (vv. 40, 41) and starts with the vocative adjective ἄφρονες, "foolish," addressed to listeners.[41] Their foolishness consists not only in negligence about the coming judgment, but also in a wrong assumption that one can separate the inner and outer natures of the person. Jesus asks: οὐχ ὁ ποιήσας τὸ ἔξωθεν καὶ τὸ ἔσωθεν ἐποίησεν; "did not He who made the outside make the inside also?" According to Jesus, one cannot be partially clean. For him, cleanness is total purification of heart and life before God and people. True cleansing is viewed by Jesus not as a merely formalistic ceremony, but as repentance and filling the heart with God's mercy.[42] Here,

---

37. Jesus' action revealed that "the oral law of the Pharisees is not given by God, and therefore had no authority over Jesus and his disciples." McIver, *Mainstream or Marginal?*, 157.

38. According to the rules of ritual purity the inside of the cup was primary. Cleansing the outside of the cup "does not affect the ritual status of the inside." Garland, *Luke*, 494.

39. Johnson notes that while the Pharisees accuse Jesus of not following their tradition, he accuses them as sinners against the laws of Torah (care of the needy in Deut 14:29). Johnson, *Gospel of Luke*, 192.

40. This notion is expressed in OT: 1 Sam 16:7; 1 Kgs 8:39; 1 Chr 28:9; 2 Chr 16:9; Ps 7:9; 139:2; Prov 15:11; 16:2; Jer 11:20. Also, the same thought appears in the NT, in Acts 1:24 and Rev 2:23. Trites, "Gospel of Luke," 184.

41. The word "fools" appears here and in Luke 12:20, in the story of the rich fool. Trites, "Gospel of Luke," 184–85. Lukan use of this word may presume the extreme foolishness of those who are considered to be spiritually rich, while they are unable to manage the treasures given to them by God.

42. Stein notes a Lukan link between appropriate cleansing and repentance leading to generosity. Stein, *Luke*, 340. Lukan dependence on Deuteronomy was noted by Brodie, *Birthing of the New*

the theme of conversion again becomes woven into a narrative. Luke brings the reader to understand that the Pharisee also needs a conversion of heart.

Jesus suggests: πλὴν τὰ ἐνόντα δότε ἐλεημοσύνην, "but that which is within give as alms."[43] Instead of the tradition of the elders, Jesus focuses attention on the ethics of Torah.[44] He adds, καὶ ἰδοὺ πάντα καθαρὰ ὑμῖν ἐστιν, "and then all things are clean for you." The phrase presumes an assurance that God is merciful enough to forgive people their errors in secondary issues, while they themselves are merciful to one another. The stress on alms is made intentionally. Practicing of charity teaches one to know the very heart of God. One's admission that God is a merciful savior would signify the beginning of conversion.

The following three exclamations include the triple pronouncement of woes. They refer to parts 4, 5, and 6. Part 4 (v. 42) describes the first "woe," which should not be defined by the following phrase ὅτι ἀποδεκατοῦτε, "that you pay tithe." The adversative conjunction ἀλλὰ before οὐαὶ ὑμῖν suggests that the negative example lies deeper. The conjunction ἀλλὰ refers to καὶ παρέρχεσθε τὴν κρίσιν καὶ τὴν ἀγάπην τοῦ θεοῦ. The verb παρέρχομαι means "pass by, transgress, neglect, disobey."[45] Then, in part 4 (v. 42b) Jesus continues the theme of God's love and mercy (τὴν ἀγάπην τοῦ θεοῦ), which he started in part 3 (v. 39b). The charity mentioned above, thus, can be viewed as the first practical application of God's love. Mentioning of tithe of every kind of garden herb intensifies the image of severe formalism, while negligence flourished regarding the moral aspects of Torah, such as justice and love.[46]

The pronouncement of οὐαί, "woe," in v. 42 is linked to God's wrath.[47] The woe can be assumed to be the future result of a imbalance in the spiritual sphere, caused by focusing on rituals, customs and man-made traditions instead of knowing and serving God in truth. The final statement of Jesus, ταῦτα δὲ ἔδει ποιῆσαι κἀκεῖνα μὴ παρεῖναι, "these *are the things you* should to have done, without neglecting the others," makes the task of the Pharisees twice as hard. This hyperbole is designed to show the senselessness of overdoing the law, and the prominent need of total spiritual conversion.

Part 5 (v. 43) contains the second woe pronouncement. In the previous part Jesus showed that the Pharisees παρέρχεσθε τὴν ἀγάπην τοῦ θεοῦ ("pass over the love of God"). This lack of love was compensated by the Pharisees' love of

---

Testament, 270–73. He believes that Luke shows the law of how much the law in Deut 4–6 is abused by the Pharisees.

43. Here Jesus could suggest to "give the things inside the cup" as alms. Stein, *Luke*, 340.

44. See Deut 15:7 later strengthened by Pss 41:1; 112:9; Prov 19:17; 31:20; Eccl 11:1, 2; Isa 58:7.

45. BDAG, παρέρχομαι, 4. In general meaning "to ignore something in the interest of other matters."

46. Stein shows that Pharisaic oral tradition was much more "extensive than the OT with regard to what one was supposed to tithe" (see Lev 27:30–33; Deut 14:22–29; 2 Chr 31:5–12). The importance of love and justice was stressed in Mic 6:8. Stein, *Luke*, 340.

47. Here, the woe represents the prophet's powerful denunciation: it is "akin to a curse that warns against catastrophe." Garland, *Luke*, 494.

self-aggrandizement: ἀγαπᾶτε τὴν πρωτοκαθεδρίαν ἐν ταῖς συναγωγαῖς καὶ τοὺς ἀσπασμοὺς ἐν ταῖς ἀγοραῖς, "for you love the front seats in the synagogues, and the respectful greetings in the market places" (Luke 11:43). Choosing this application of Torah, the Pharisees increased their selfishness.[48] This deprived them of the ability to be filled with the love of God for people, and withheld from them the experience of conversion and receiving salvation. That is why the warning was pronounced in the form of a "woe-exclamation."

Part 6 (v. 44) expresses the third "woe" against Pharisaic formalism. The dispute in the Pharisee's home began over a cleansing ritual (which was a rabbinic extension of the ritual law), expressing one's external piety. It then proceeded to the inner sphere of spiritual uncleanness. Reaching this point, Jesus turned the thought about and linked it again to the issue of the ritual law. After revealing the heart's deepest issues, which are hidden selfishness and lack of spiritual unity with God, Jesus brings the topic back to the issue of cleansing rituals. His reference to tombs shows a terrifying degree of uncleanness.[49] He literally says that some are very close to the condition of being spiritually dead.[50] This striking thought is accompanied by the fact that the tombs are τὰ ἄδηλα (neuter plural adjective ἄδηλος "*not clear, latent, unseen*").[51] In other words those tombs represented the most dangerous kind of masked uncleanness. People who came in contact with this uncleanness do not even know it!

The discussion above shows Luke's view that the only way to cleanse spiritual uncleanness is a total conversion. External cleansing rituals are contrasted by Jesus with the spiritual realms. The rituals have become a shadow of true conversion, precursory, preliminary treatments of temporary uncleanness given to God's people in anticipation of Christ's mission. The narratives in Luke-Acts one after another show that Jesus cleanses various types of temporary uncleanness. Repentance and faith are pictured as detergents cleansing hearts. Gradually, the cleansing rites become secondary, while God's call to a cleansing of conscience becomes prominent.

Replacement of Ritual Cleansing by Baptism

Luke tends to replace ritual cleansing with baptism.[52] This tendency is tied by Luke to God's sovereign will, expressed from the beginning. Note that Luke opens his Gospel by mentioning the divinely appointed mission of John the Baptist, whose mission was

---

48. Trites notes here Jesus' critique of Pharisaic self-centeredness. Trites, "Gospel of Luke," 186.

49. According to Num 19:16 and Lev 21:1–4, 11 the uncleanness of a dead body caused uncleanness for a week. In a similar way the Pharisees' pseudo-spirituality led people to the grave. Bock, *Luke 9:51—24:53*, 1117, see also n. 20.

50. The comparison with the tombs either likens the Pharisees to the "living dead" or represents their teaching as death-giving. Stein, *Luke*, 341.

51. BDAG, ἄδηλος, 1.

52. In the OT, prophets have already connected repentance and renewal with washing (Isa 1:16–17; 4:4; Ezek 36:25–26; Zech 13:1). Garland, *Luke*, 154.

outlined before his birth by the words "ἐπιστρέψαι καρδίας" (Luke 1:17). His ministry stressed the importance of repentance for forgiveness of sins: κηρύσσων βάπτισμα μετανοίας εἰς ἄφεσιν ἁμαρτιῶν (Luke 3:3).[53] The phrase, βάπτισμα μετανοίας, here can mean a "cleansing of repentance."[54]

The spiritual meaning of "cleansing of repentance," preached by John the Baptist, is preserved in narrative form in Luke 3:7–9. Luke introduces the baptismal sermon of John by ἔλεγεν οὖν τοῖς ἐκπορευομένοις ὄχλοις βαπτισθῆναι ὑπ' αὐτοῦ. The first statement of John's sermon unmasks people's attempts to perform the ritual cleansing without carrying its spiritual significance. For some, the opportunity to demonstrate loyalty to God in public seemed attractive. However, John demanded inner conversion of the heart, and was not pleased with a ritualistic approach. His phrase in v. 7, τίς ὑπέδειξεν ὑμῖν φυγεῖν ἀπὸ τῆς μελλούσης ὀργῆς, "Who warned you to flee from the wrath to come?" reveals that the motives of some new converts were in reality rooted in hypocrisy. Performing a ritual without sincere spiritual conversion would lead one God's inevitable judgment.

At the same time John declares how to respond: ποιήσατε οὖν καρποὺς ἀξίους τῆς μετανοίας, "bring forth fruits worthy of repentance." The noun μετάνοια has the meaning of "a change of mind, *repentance, turning about, conversion*."[55] Invisible "turning about" of the heart to God has to become evident in a new convert's real life.[56] John declares what hinders people from "cleansing with repentance': an assumption rooted in a popular belief that all Jews live under the protection of the covenant of Abraham:[57] καὶ μὴ ἄρξησθε λέγειν ἐν ἑαυτοῖς Πατέρα ἔχομεν τὸν Ἀβραάμ (v. 8). Ethnic inclusion in the Abrahamic covenant without conversion is insufficient. The baptism which John preached was a sign of spiritual renewal, a step towards re-creation. That is why John, in his illustration employed stones as suitable material for creating spiritual children for Abraham (δύναται ὁ θεὸς ἐκ τῶν λίθων τούτων ἐγεῖραι τέκνα τῷ Ἀβραάμ).[58]

---

53. Here, "repentance" literally means "*a change of mind*" and "forgiveness of sins" represents "a present realization of the future eschatological forgiveness at the final judgment." Stein, *Luke*, 128.

54. Josephus (*Antiquities* 18.116–19) states that John the Baptist required ψυχῆς δικαιοσύνῃ. Josephus viewed John's baptism as more meaningful than the baptism-washing at Qumran. Stein, *Luke*, 128.

55. BDAG, μετάνοια.

56. Luke stresses the universal need for repentance (11:29; 13:1–5; 11:13) which is "confirmed by subsequent life." John Nolland, *Luke 1—9:20*, 148.

57. According to some Jewish writings such as *m. B. Mes.* 8:1; *m. Abot* 5:19; *b. B. Qam.* 32b; *Gen. Rab.* 53:12, the Jews understood themselves to be the "sons of Abraham." They believed that this ancestral connection shielded them from God's wrath. Garland, *Luke*, 156.

58. The comparison with stones keeps in focus their lifelessness and uselessness. It reveals the same spiritual condition of the descendants of Abraham before God. This means "no automatic radical superiority or alienable birthright." Nolland, *Luke 1—9:20*, 148. In Luke 3:8, γὰρ presumes contrast in John's speech: not between stones and sons, but between their inability to bear fruits of repentance and God's ability to re-create, or even create new creatures from the stones. Thus, Luke puts stress on God's ability to raise new sons. Moreover, the word ἐγείρω, here, was chosen by Luke, instead of

Moreover, the comparison between the hardened hearts and the stones (τῶν λίθων τούτων) illustrates why hearts cannot be changed by merely a ritual cleansing. A fruitless tree in v. 9 cannot change its nature. The need for the re-creative power of God is made evident. The images of an ax, fruitless tree and fire in v. 9 illustrate the fate of unrepentant people and reveal the urgent need for re-creation. Emphasis on δύναται ὁ θεὸς presents spiritual conversion as an act on a par with creation, which only God can perform.[59]

Acts 2:37–39 continues the Lukan theme of the replacement of ritual cleansing by baptism.[60] The response to Peter's sermon at Pentecost is an example of the conversion of listeners, followed by baptism. Here, baptism was different to the situation in Luke 3:17–19. People were first "pierced to the heart" (κατενύγησαν τὴν καρδίαν) by Peter's message.[61] They found themselves in a hopeless condition, incurable by any procedures of the ritual law. Their question, τί ποιήσωμεν, ἄνδρες ἀδελφοί; "Brethren, what shall we do?" reveals this.

Peter opens before them the way of spiritual re-creation by declaring, Μετανοήσατε καὶ βαπτισθήτω ἕκαστος ὑμῶν ἐπὶ τῷ ὀνόματι Ἰησοῦ Χριστοῦ, "Repent, and let each of you be baptized in the name of Jesus Christ," in v. 38. He calls people to a personal (ἕκαστος ὑμῶν) experience of spiritual birth, which comes in three steps. The first, μετανοήσατε, relates to renewal of the inner person. The second step, βαπτισθήτω, is the outward sign of inward cleansing from sin. Baptism in the name of Jesus (ἐπὶ τῷ ὀνόματι Ἰησοῦ Χριστοῦ) is a declaration of Jesus Christ's lordship, which makes the cleansing from sin possible due to forgiveness (εἰς ἄφεσιν τῶν ἁμαρτιῶν ὑμῶν).

The third step of spiritual birth is linked to a promise of the Holy Spirit (καὶ λήμψεσθε τὴν δωρεὰν τοῦ ἁγίου πνεύματος) and attracts special attention. Ritual cleansings and other rites of purification illustrated that the only way for a believer to associate with a holy God is an absolute physical and spiritual cleansing. The presence of the Holy Spirit with the new converts signified such an absolute cleansing. Thus, a spiritual birth indicates one's inspiration, which testifies that re-creation of the heart has been accomplished.

"ποιέω." It was made because Luke was focused on re-creation and not simply on a new creation. Compare ἐγείρω in Luke (9:7, Acts 3:15, 4:10; 5:30, 10:40, 13:30, 37) and Pauline writings (1 Cor 15:12, 15, Gal 1:1; Eph 5:14, 1Th 1:10) where it is used to describe the resurrection or the future re-creation, which begins with "repentance."

59. Ryan Jackson states that early Christian literature "did use creation language to speak about conversion." Jackson, *New Creation in Paul's Letters*, 7. Also, Luke uses creation motifs for the baptism rite, when "the same creative spirit" known from Gen 1:2 "comes in fullness at Jesus' baptism (3:21–22)." Pilgrim, "Luke-Acts and Creation," 53.

60. Bock notes, "John the Baptist preached a unique baptism, a washing of preparation for the coming of God's salvation," which "involved a change of thinking" and change of behavior. Bock, *Luke 1:1—9:50*, 296.

61. Here, the word κατενύσσομαι is the same as used in Isa 6:5 which presumes regret (in its spiritual sense), with the meaning, "I am ruined/lost." Larkin, "Acts," 395.

As soon as Peter announces these three steps of a spiritual birth, he also recalls the covenant on the basis of which the promises (ἡ ἐπαγγελία) of salvation can work. It is likely that Peter, here, refers to the covenant with Abraham, since he uses similar wording in relation to the Abrahamic covenant in Acts 3:25.[62] For Peter, this covenant presupposes not national exclusiveness, but national inclusiveness. The salvific act of God, here, is also viewed as a re-creation of hearts.[63] In terms of the re-creation process, all nations are viewed as equally accepted.

Accordingly, from John the Baptist until the time of Peter's sermon, the ritual of baptism in the writings of Luke pointed to a new spiritual birth: the first step of re-creation. During this time a transition of the ritual's form took place, revealing the shift from outward submission to the Jewish ritual law to the inner re-creation of a believer by the power of God, expressed by Christian baptism. The presence of the Holy Spirit in baptism testified divine approval. Thus, baptism replaced the practice of ritual cleansings and became a foundational practice of the early church.

Uncleanness of Leprosy in Narratives
of Luke 5:12–14 and Luke 17:11–19

In addition to the replacement of ritual cleansing by baptism, Luke raises the issue of the ritual law and shows its fulfillment in Christ's earthly ministry. This thought is supported by passages which deal with the different types of ritual uncleanness: leprosy, flow of blood, dead bodies.[64] All of the latter are sources of temporary uncleanness, which is reversible.[65] The role of the ritual law, here, is to provide an official confirmation of the reversal, which has already taken place in the person's body. Thus, purification from uncleanness caused by leprosy was possible only after one had recovered.[66] The sacrifices appointed for ritual cleansing were brought by the

---

62. Here Peter states: "It is you who are the sons of the prophets, and of the covenant which God made with your fathers, saying to Abraham, 'And in your seed all the families of the earth shall be blessed'" (Acts 3:25). Here Peter's Ὑμεῖς ἐστε υἱοὶ . . . τῆς διαθήκης ἧς διέθετο ὁ θεὸς πρὸς τοὺς πατέρας ἡμῶν recalls the phrase ὑμῖν γάρ ἐστιν ἡ ἐπαγγελία in Acts 2:39. Moreover, the phrase Καὶ ἐν τῷ σπέρματί σου ἐνευλογηθήσονται πᾶσαι αἱ πατριαὶ τῆς γῆς in Acts 3:25, which includes under the blessings of the covenant all humanity, seems to be similar to καὶ τοῖς τέκνοις ὑμῶν καὶ πᾶσιν τοῖς εἰς μακρὰν ὅσους ἂν προσκαλέσηται κύριος ὁ θεὸς ἡμῶν, which in different words shows that the promises belong equally to the descendants of Abraham and to all chosen from among the nations.

63. According to Larkin, Peter points to the gift of the Holy Spirit that "regenerates, indwells, and transforms lives." Larkin, "Acts," 396.

64. The uncleanness of leprosy (and the flow of blood) in rabbinic writings was connected to the uncleanness of death. Leprosy's similarity to death was shown in Num 12:12, "which indicates that leprosy eats live flesh." Feldman, *Defilement and Mourning*, 37.

65. This can be assumed from the fact that all these types of uncleanness were connected to the cleansing rituals. After purification the person was considered as ritually clean.

66. Garland, *Luke*, 240.

recovered one to enable them to participate in temple cult.⁶⁷ That is why the ritual law, from the beginning, played a secondary role to the healing hand of God, who alone made that reversal possible.

Luke 5:12–14 and 17:11–19 record Jesus healing leprosy. Also, Jesus employed positive examples of healing from leprosy illustrating his teaching, including Naaman the Syrian, in Luke 4:27, and healing lepers as a sign of the messianic kingdom in 7:22. Also, Lazarus the leper was made a hero of Jesus' parable in 16:19–31. There, Lazarus, who remained ritually unclean until death, is mentioned by name and pictured as a true son of Abraham and God's saint.

Luke 5:12–14 is placed at the beginning of Jesus' ministry.⁶⁸ The phrase καὶ ἐγένετο ἐν τῷ εἶναι αὐτὸν ἐν μιᾷ τῶν πόλεων provides no information about the place in which the miracle was performed. However, the context of the chapter reveals that the cleansing of leprosy likely took place in a Galilean town.⁶⁹ The description, ἀνὴρ πλήρης λέπρας, reveals the last stage of the disease, when the whole skin is affected. The leper comes to Jesus as a last resort and his actions, πεσὼν ἐπὶ πρόσωπον ἐδεήθη, reveal a desperate need of healing. His plea, Κύριε, ἐὰν θέλῃς δύνασαί με καθαρίσαι, shows the lack of assurance posed by the conditional tone of ἐὰν θέλῃς, "if you wish . . ." That man lacked faith in God's cleansing power.⁷⁰ His coming to Jesus presumed that he believed that God worked through Jesus. His lack of assurance could reveal a tendency to consider the disease as punishment from God. The leper simply entrusts his case to God's mercy acting in Jesus.

According to Luke, Jesus stretches his hand, ἐκτείνας τὴν χεῖρα, and touches the leper, ἥψατο, with the meaning "to make close contact, *cling to*."⁷¹ The reason for touching is disputable, since Jesus healed by the power of his word, not by touch.⁷² The stretching of a hand and touching would likely relate to the first spoken word Θέλω ("I am willing"). A combination of Jesus' actions and words suggests that he desperately wants to assure the man of God's compassion toward him. And this, despite the fact that the leper had of no healthy spot on his skin. Jesus then commands: καθαρίσθητι. In touching the leper, Jesus is not hurrying to pronounce, "be clean." Apart from Jesus perhaps acquiring the disease, in touching the leper, he immediately shared with him

---

67. Lepers were ritually unclean, "cut off from the house of God (2 Chr 26:21), forbidden to mingle with others (Num 5:2; 12:14–15)." The laws for diagnosis and treatment of leprosy are written in Lev 13, while Lev 14 provides the law of purification. Trites, "Gospel of Luke," 92. Only after the priest found a leper recovered, could he appoint a purification rite according to Lev 14.

68. The diagram for this passage is given in Appendix 3.

69. Also, Mark 1:39–40, from where Luke likely employed the narrative, links the story to the Galilean ministry of Christ. Moreover, the mentioning of the miraculous fishing on the Galilean sea, just before the passage of healing in the Gospel of Luke, suggests the continuation of the theme.

70. Fitzmyer believes that the phrase means, "Jesus can cure him by an act of his will alone." Fitzmyer, *Gospel According to Luke (I–IX)*, 574, see note on 5:12.

71. BDAG, ἅπτω, 2, b c, also "touching, which conveys blessing" and may express sympathy.

72. This "touching" is different from one in 4:4, which makes Jesus' movement to be a result of his compassion, rather than a healing "touch." Fitzmyer, *Gospel According to Luke (I–IX)*, 574.

his ritual uncleanness.[73] Yet, Jesus not only remained unaffected by the contagiousness of leprosy or its uncleanness, but was still able to heal and cleanse.

It is evident that a ritually unclean man cannot perform cleansing. However, after Jesus says καθαρίσθητι, the leprosy immediately disappeared (καὶ εὐθέως ἡ λέπρα ἀπῆλθεν ἀπ' αὐτοῦ). Now, the man was physically healed and cleansed.[74] Yet, he still needed the official pronouncement about his cleansing, which signified that he is also clean from a ritual perspective.[75] This pronouncement could be made by a priest and accompanied by the cleansing ritual, which required bringing offerings to the temple.[76] Healing and cleansing were given to the man freely by the mercy of God, but the confirmation of that healing required a few more actions to be taken. If the healing took place in Galilee, the man had to go to Jerusalem.[77] In addition, he was to give sacrifices at his own expense. The ceremony itself lasted a minimum of eight days.

All these actions could be viewed as unnecessary if one accepts that the healing was complete and the uncleanness was just conditional due to a common Jewish submission to the temple cult. Despite this, Jesus commands the leper to tell no one (μηδενὶ εἰπεῖν), and to perform the purification ritual according to the Mosaic law. While Luke, in Acts 15, shows that the ritual law is no longer necessary for salvation for the follower of Jesus, Luke 5:12–14 seems to lead the reader to the opposite conclusion. At the same time, in v. 14, it is clearly stated that the purification rite was viewed by Jesus not in order to add something to his action. Instead, a subordinate purpose clause, εἰς μαρτύριον αὐτοῖς, in v. 14 indicates that the main purpose for observing the ritual law was to witness to αὐτοῖς.

Here, αὐτοῖς could refer to the priests.[78] However, the word τῷ ἱερεῖ is dative singular, while the αὐτοῖς is dative plural. The construction of the phrase in v. 14 reveals two parallel commands joined by the adversative conjunction ἀλλά. The first command states, μηδενὶ εἰπεῖν and though μηδενὶ is singular, "no one," it implies the possibility of spreading news among many people. Jesus prohibits this sharing, because it potentially would provoke people to view his mission as independent from the Jerusalem temple cult. The Hellenistic surroundings of Galilee might provoke it.

Instead, Jesus wants everyone to know that his messianic ministry is rooted in the Mosaic law and approved by the Old Testament. Moreover, it is connected to the

---

73. A leper was viewed as a walking corpse and "his cure was likened to raising the dead (*b. Sanh.* 47a–b). Garland, *Luke*, 239.

74. The fact that he was cleansed, not only healed, is assumed from Jesus' command: "be clean."

75. Jesus' command seems "to underline Jesus' compliance with of the OT law." Nolland, *Luke 1—9:20*, 228.

76. Singular "priest" in v. 14 "refers to the one on duty in the Temple at the time." Fitzmyer, *Gospel According to Luke (I-IX)*, 575.

77. The cleansing ceremony is described in Lev 14:1–20 and v. 11 refers to the ceremony which can be performed only in the sanctuary.

78. Several meanings of Jesus' command are presented by Bock. He suggests that the testimony of the messianic times is to be given to the priests first. Bock, *Luke 1:1—9:50*, 476–77.

temple cult, and presupposes the fulfillment of it. That is why Jesus gives the second command in two parts 1) ἀπελθὼν δεῖξον σεαυτὸν τῷ ἱερεῖ, 2) προσένεγκε περὶ τοῦ καθαρισμοῦ σου, καθὼς προσέταξεν Μωϋσῆς. The first point means that the messiahship of Jesus has to be viewed in terms of the priestly ministry (the Aaronic covenant and levitical ministry).[79] The second point views Jesus' messiahship in terms of a sacrifice and the ritual law of the sanctuary. Only this cultic perspective allows one to understand Jesus's messianic role adequately. Hence εἰς μαρτύριον αὐτοῖς has to be interpreted as "in testimony to those, whom the news reaches."

The next passage describing the cleansing of leprosy is Luke 17:11–19. Here, the miracle took place διὰ μέσον Σαμαρείας καὶ Γαλιλαίας, as Jesus was going to Jerusalem (ἐν τῷ πορεύεσθαι εἰς Ἰερουσαλὴμ).[80] Ten lepers (ἀπήντησαν [αὐτῷ] δέκα λεπροὶ ἄνδρες) met Jesus, but stood at a distance (οἳ ἔστησαν πόρρωθεν). The distance was maintained by the lepers, not by Jesus. This feature differs from the previous story, where the leper came close and knelt before Jesus. The distance either would suggest that the lepers knew in general that Jesus respects the regulations of the Mosaic law, or that they believed in his ability to heal by word.[81]

The distance caused several problems: 1) It required lepers to cry out loudly (αὐτοὶ ἦραν φωνὴν λέγοντες). 2) It did not allow them to get in "emotional" contact with Jesus so he would feel compassion. 3) It did not allow them to see Jesus' attitude. People would prefer to see their deliverer, especially if he is a famous miracle-worker. In such a situation people naturally would look for the opportunity to come closer in order to see his personal response to them. They would not stay at a distance in order to demonstrate their faith. The distance was likely due to the ritual law, and not due to their strength of faith. This also has support from the fact that they called Jesus ἐπιστάτα, "master," instead of κύριε, "Lord."

Jesus does not come to touch them, but calls to them: Πορευθέντες ἐπιδείξατε ἑαυτοὺς τοῖς ἱερεῦσιν, "Go and show yourselves to the priests." Luke reported that the miracle happened as they went to the priests (ἐν τῷ ὑπάγειν αὐτοὺς ἐκαθαρίσθησαν). Here, unlike the previous story, the cleansing followed his command to show themselves to the priests.[82] It also took place on their way, namely, when they started to fulfill his command. The connection, between the act of their healing and Jesus' command to keep the ritual law, is clear.

---

79. Intertestamental Judaism knew two competing hopes: the hope of a Davidic kingly Messiah and hope for a Levitic kingly Messiah, based on the promise of the eternal priesthood in Num 25:10–13, in language similar to the promise to David in 2 Sam 7. The expectations of the Levitic Messiah appear also in Dead Sea Scrolls tradition. Scott, *Jewish Backgrounds*, 311.

80. Bock, *Luke 9:51—24:53*, 1400.

81. Bock interprets the lepers' decision to keep at a distance by "their dispised disease." Bock, *Luke 9:51—24:53*, 1401.

82. Jesus' response shows "a clear recognition of the Jewish laws of purification." Trites, "Gospel of Luke," 236. Also it seems that Jesus viewed the Jewish laws of purification related to the Jewish and Samaritan lepers alike.

However, the differences between the two ways of healing in these two Lukan accounts suggests different levels of faith. The less people's faith in Jesus, the more he let them view his role in terms of the ritual law and the temple cult. In contrast, when people expressed great faith in his Lordship, he did not demand keeping the ritual law, but concluded with the explanation ἡ πίστις σου σέσωκέν σε.[83] Garland states that the passage "radically subverts the significance of the temple's rituals and sacrifices, when offering praise to God and thanks to Jesus not only suffice for making the required offerings . . . but surpass it."[84]

This idea is clearly shown in the narrative itself from v. 15, where the contrasting behavior between the healed Samaritan and the other nine creates a turning point.[85] One of those ten men (εἷς δὲ ἐξ αὐτῶν), who were cleansed by the word of Jesus decided to turn back. He had not yet reached the priests: ἰδὼν ὅτι ἰάθη, ὑπέστρεψεν. This means he decided to turn to Jesus as soon as he had found himself healed. He returned glorifying God with a loud voice (μετὰ φωνῆς μεγάλης δοξάζων τὸν θεόν). The manner of the glorification repeats the way in which the request was posed, namely, crying with a loud voice.

This feature, following ὑπέστρεψεν, creates a clear reversal of a scene. Now the man does not stay at a distance, but comes close to Jesus and thanks him, falling at Jesus' feet (ἔπεσεν ἐπὶ πρόσωπον παρὰ τοὺς πόδας αὐτοῦ εὐχαριστῶν αὐτῷ).[86] His thanksgiving is described in a manner which suggests worshipping. His actions reveal that he has recognized Jesus as Lord (κύριος), and not only as ἐπιστάτης, "a master." The healing by the power of a spoken word would allow the Samaritan to view the situation from the perspective of a new creation. Thus, he would conclude that Jesus is the messianic figure, who with divine authority performs a re-creation. The verbal reversal of the narrative supports the idea of creation–fall–re-creation in the background of the scene.

In v. 17, Jesus clearly states the contrast between nine most likely Jews and one foreigner.[87] Here, the contrast appears not in the healing, which all received (οἱ δέκα ἐκαθαρίσθησαν). Before they came to the priests. However, the familiar pattern of the ritual law keeping made them spiritually blind. Consequently, the physical cleansing of the nine, though it revealed the mercy of God, did not reveal conversion of their hearts. The spiritual conversion of one Samaritan signified the re-creation process,

---

83. It was noted that all lepers "required some faith," yet the outsider was declared saved by faith. Johnson, *Gospel of Luke*, 261–62.

84. Garland, *Luke*, 691.

85. Bock shows salvation of the Samaritan as not anti-Jewish point, but as pro-faith illustration challenging the nine Jewish lepers. Bock, *Luke 9:51—24:53*, 1403.

86. Luke often employs this formula "to exemplify the essence of faith." Garland, *Luke*, 691, citing McCaughey, "Paradigms of Faith."

87. In v. 18 the word "foreigner" presumes that the Samaritan cannot enter the Jewish temple. Yet he is saved "apart from the temple." Garland, *Luke*, 691.

which took place in him. Noticing this, Jesus pronounced: Ἀναστὰς πορεύου• ἡ πίστις σου σέσωκέν σε. His statement can be understood as a re-creation blessing.

Moreover, this phrase shows that salvation had already come to this particular man. Jesus did not direct him to a priest a second time. It can be argued that Jesus takes the place of the ritual system of the Mosaic law and its cleansing rites. The cleansing and purification rituals here are those which treat reversible, temporary uncleanness. The issue of permanent uncleanness was not the focus of Luke in these passages.

Uncleanness of a Dead Body

The uncleanness contracted from touching a dead body was viewed as temporal, reversible.[88] Yet, the purification law prescribed a seven day period of cleansing and involved bringing a sacrifice.[89] The sacrifice (a red heifer, slaughtered outside the camp in the presence of the chief priest) was called a sacrifice for the purification from sin.[90] Although the heifer had to be slaughtered and burned outside camp, the ritual was linked to the sanctuary cultic system by the sprinkling of blood toward the front of the sanctuary. This purification was necessary for the further participation in the temple cult. Neglecting the purification rites led to the "cut off" penalty (Num 19:20) understood in an eschatological sense. This suggests that the dead body was viewed as the source of a severe kind of uncleanness.[91]

The teaching of Jesus concerning death was also expressed in the Gospel of Luke. He taught that death was a reversible condition, which can be turned back into life by the power of God's word. The word of God which worked in Jesus removed even the ritual uncleanness of death. This removal took place before any rituals were performed. To see this, one has to look at two significant resurrection narratives: Luke 7:11–15 and 8:40–42, 49–54.

Luke 7:11–15 locates the event in Galilee, in Nain. Luke wrote: καὶ συνεπορεύοντο αὐτῷ οἱ μαθηταὶ αὐτοῦ καὶ ὄχλος πολύς, a big crowd followed Jesus to Nain. Suddenly,

---

88. Death itself, as a permanent condition, was associated with permanent ritual uncleanness of a corpse. It seems that only resurrection to life could make the reversal of this uncleanness possible, since resurrection was viewed in terms of re-creation. However, people who came in contact with a dead body were considered temporarily unclean. Contamination by uncleanness of a dead body led to a very persistent uncleanness, which was to be cleansed not only with water, but also through observing the purification rite (Num 19:1–22; 31:19–24).

89. The ritual in Num 19:1–22 included the sacrifice of purification from sin. The ashes of the red heifer had to be mixed with running water, the water of impurity. The ritual included sprinkling the water of impurity on a ritually unclean person on the third and seventh day of purification.

90. Here a corpse-contamination is viewed as a severe form of impurity. The concept of the uncleanness of death is built on the basis of Lev 11:32 and the rites of purification are further developed in Num 19 and 31. Wright, "Purification from Corpse-Contamination," 223.

91. In the OT it was clearly stated that "death and holiness are not compatible." It was assumed from the fact that death is totally absent from a relationship with God, the source of life. Subsequently, death presumes the ultimate defilement. Feldman, *Defilement and Mourning*, 35.

at the gates this entering crowd met another crowd. The appearance of a crowd in those days signified something important. Luke tells the reason: καὶ ἰδοὺ ἐξεκομίζετο τεθνηκώς. The deceased being the "only" son of a widow (μονογενὴς υἱὸς τῇ μητρὶ αὐτοῦ καὶ αὐτὴ ἦν χήρα), called for public compassion, which brought the crowd of sympathizing people together (καὶ ὄχλος τῆς πόλεως ἱκανὸς ἦν σὺν αὐτῇ).

However, the issue of ritual uncleanness would likely make the burial an unpopular event. Ritual uncleanness required the difficult, week-long purification rite. Those who were with the widow might be more interested in following Jesus. The situation was definitely "at risk" if the burial crowd dissolved. At this moment the Lord came to the widow with the words: Μὴ κλαῖε.[92] However, he interrupted the burial ceremony not only in order to express his compassion (ἐσπλαγχνίσθη, "*have pity, feel sympathy*").[93] After speaking to the grieving mother, he came forward and touched the coffin (προσελθὼν, ἥψατο τῆς σοροῦ). This action would make him ritually unclean.[94] The bearers of the coffin might suppose that Jesus wanted to weep too, so they stood still. Instead, Jesus called out: Νεανίσκε, σοὶ λέγω, ἐγέρθητι.[95]

Luke describes the process of resurrection by using two phrases: the animation of the body (καὶ ἀνεκάθισεν ὁ νεκρὸς), which was accompanied by a returning of the "breath of life," so he could speak (καὶ ἤρξατο λαλεῖν). This sequence echoes the creation of man in Gen 1:27; 2:7. Though Jesus did not breathe his spirit into the face of the boy, he commanded him personally using direct address: Νεανίσκε, σοὶ λέγω, likely looking at the boy's face.[96] From the crowd's point of view, it was unlikely that the dead could hear anything. Why then did Jesus address the deceased? Consequently, the phrase can be viewed as the analogue of "breathing," which carried the power of God to restore life.

This significant action of Jesus served as an echo of the creation of humans, and built up hope for the future resurrection (re-creation). The association of the power of re-creation with the figure of Jesus amazed the witnesses (ἔλαβεν δὲ φόβος πάντας

---

92. As was noted here, Luke uses Jesus' post-resurrection title, "Lord." Stein, *Luke*, 222. This feature allows one to see him rather as God-Creator, than as a man, Jesus.

93. BDAG, σπλαγχνίζομαι. The noun σπλάγχνον, with the same root, has the meaning of "the inner parts of a body, including viscera," which metaphorically presumes that Jesus felt deep sympathy.

94. Stein notes that this was a bier or litter, and not a closed coffin. The action would make one ritually unclean (Num 19:11, 16). Stein, *Luke*, 223.

95. Bock shows that the Lukan account of resurrection contrasts with the OT examples. Elijah in 1 Kgs 17:21 stretched himself three times over the boy, while Jesus resurrects by a word. For him it means that Jesus is a great prophet. Bock, *Luke 1:1—9:50*, 652. Because it contrasts with the actions of prophets, it may presume that Jesus was more than a prophet. He acts as a Creator; he restores life by speaking, as in Gen 1:27 where God created by speaking.

96. Jesus resurrecting the only son of a widow that echoes 1 Kgs 17:23 (LXX) and 2 Kgs 4:36. However, Jesus raised the dead in a manner different to that of Elijah and Elisha. Jesus does not carry the boy upstairs, lay him on a bed, remonstrate with God, does not stretch himself across the body three times, but simply touches the bier and commands the boy to rise. This convinces Garland to conclude that Jesus raises the boy "by the power of his own authoritative word." Garland, *Luke*, 303–4.

καὶ ἐδόξαζον τὸν θεὸν).⁹⁷ The fear and glorification of God expressed in the words, Ἐπεσκέψατο ὁ θεὸς τὸν λαὸν αὐτοῦ revealed that people were touched by the spiritual significance of the event, and its extraordinariness. People associated Jesus' actions with God's plan to visit (ἐπεσκέψατο) his people known long ago.⁹⁸ The resurrection in Nain affirmed the messianic role of Jesus, when he revealed his authority to restore life and the removal of temporary uncleanness. Thus, Jesus' messiahship again is shown in terms of his purifying and saving mission.

Luke 8:40–54 reports the resurrection of Jairus' daughter. Here, Luke uses the technique "narrative within narrative," which usually highlights the aspect of faith.⁹⁹ Meanwhile, vv. 40–42 and 49–54 deal with the resurrection itself; the central vv. 43–48 treat the issue of ritual uncleanness. This passage follows the one that describes the cleansing from demons (8:22–39). The context shows different consequences of the fall (sickness, demon possession, contamination from a dead body) which are viewed in terms of the ritual law, as cases of reversible ritual uncleanness.

Vv. 40–42 create a narrative bridge between these three stories, while vv. 49–54 describe the resurrection itself. V. 42 states that the girl was dying (ἀπέθνῃσκεν), when Jairus came to Jesus as a last hope. V. 49 reveals that with the girl's death, his last hope was about to be destroyed. Further, in v. 53 Luke reveals people's "skepticism that anyone could be revived from death."¹⁰⁰ Skepticism is evident in two features: 1) the pessimistic words of the messenger (μηκέτι σκύλλε τὸν διδάσκαλον in v. 49) and 2) people's mockery in response to the encouraging words of Jesus. This reaction presupposes the common belief that the death cannot be cured (καὶ κατεγέλων αὐτοῦ, εἰδότες ὅτι ἀπέθανεν, in v. 53). The lack of faith becomes the thematic frame of the narrative.

Contrastingly, the words and actions of Jesus were a call to strengthen faith.¹⁰¹ The encouraging example of the woman healed from the flow of blood, (her long unsuccessful experience seemed to be an irreversible curse), was followed by Je-

---

97. Bock notes that Jesus' command, ἐγέρθητι, in Luke 7:14 is in passive voice, while in Luke 8:54 it is active voice ἔγειρε. Bock, *Luke 1:1—9:50*, 803. The passive voice of ἐγέρθητι may correlate with God's command γενηθήτω φῶς (Gen 1:3, passive voice), which shows God engaged in the process of creating life.

98. The theme of God's visitation of his people appears in Luke 19:44 and Acts 15:14. Trites, "Gospel of Luke," 119. The "visitation" theme in Luke 1:68, 78 presumes the hope of redemption; in 7:16 it appears in the context of resurrection; in Luke 19:44 Jesus describes those who reject God's visitation (which supposedly could bring them the gift of life) as ones who inflict their own death. This allows one to conclude that Luke generally views "visitation" of God in terms of eschatological restoration. The word ἐπεσκέπτομαι in Acts 15:14, thus, has to be viewed in terms of eschatological restoration too. This theme of the restoration of creation allows one to link Acts 15:14 to the Gen 1–3 account, and not only Exod 3:16.

99. Nolland calls this technique a "double miracle" which "provides a crescendo," moving the narrative from the healing of a body to life restoration. Nolland, *Luke 1—9:20*, 418.

100. Garland, *Luke*, 369.

101. In this passage, the theme of saving faith is "brought emphatically to an explicit point." Johnson, *Gospel of Luke*, 143.

sus' words: Θάρσει, θύγατερ, ἡ πίστις σου σέσωκέν σε· πορεύου εἰς εἰρήνην (Luke 8:48).[102] Jesus' decision to go to Jairus' house after the arrival of the messenger who announces the girl's death, reassures the father that his daughter's life will be restored. The words, Μὴ φοβοῦ, μόνον πίστευσον, καὶ σωθήσεται, put special emphasis on faith (μόνον πίστευσον).[103]

The manner in which Luke describes the resurrection again echoes the creation of the first human being, described in Gen 2:7. There, the narrative of creation is followed by a description of an environment ready to sustain human life, including food provision. Luke sees some parallels in Jesus' actions:

1. Jesus does not give orders from a distance (from the place where the messenger met them), but comes and takes the girl's hand, which makes the re-creation a personal, "hands-on" process, similar to Gen 2:7 where the forming of man took up God's personal attention;

2. Jesus addresses the command directly to the girl, Ἡ παῖς, ἔγειρε. (There is no reference to the power of God or the power of life that returns the breath of life. The phrase, καὶ ἐπέστρεψεν τὸ πνεῦμα αὐτῆς, reveals that Jesus gives the life force);[104]

3. The girl began to move (καὶ ἀνέστη παραχρῆμα), which echoes the creation narrative, when all "living beings" (described by ψυχὴν ζῶσαν) were given the ability to move (a main characteristic of being alive) after their creation.[105]

4. Jesus commanded that she be given something to eat (καὶ διέταξεν αὐτῇ δοθῆναι φαγεῖν), which reminds readers of the creation narrative of Gen 2:7–17.[106] There, the creation of humans (*Unit one*) is followed by mentioning the creation of trees (*Unit two*) and permission to eat of every tree, except one (*Unit three*). This contrasts with the order of creation described in Gen 1, according to which trees were created two days before humans. This rearrangement of the narrative in Gen 2 suggests a picture of food and abundant life, which brings worship

---

102. Stein, *Luke*, 262. Jesus accents that faith brings not only visible physical healing, but also invisible spiritual healing.

103. Thus, Jesus tells Jairus to ignore the sad news and continue to have faith. The word σωθήσεται appears here in the context of physical restoration, although in general, the Lukan context relates to spiritual salvation. Garland, *Luke*, 369.

104. The returning of πνεῦμα can presume here nothing more than the life force. This is assumed from an allusion to the story in 1 Kgs 17:21–22, where נֶפֶשׁ was returning. This term often represents life itself in Torah. Nolland, *Luke 1—9:20*, 422.

105. This thought was developed in chapter 3 section 1.2.1.

106. It is represented in Appendix 2, passage 2, *Units one, two, and three* of the present thesis.

aspects into focus for the reader.¹⁰⁷ In Luke 8:55, Jesus' command to feed the girl also points to true worship aspects.¹⁰⁸

Luke ends the narrative in v. 56 with ὁ δὲ παρήγγειλεν αὐτοῖς μηδενὶ εἰπεῖν τὸ γεγονός. The prohibition to tell about resurrection was employed by Luke from Mark 5:43 and fits in "with the pattern of the messianic secret," which creates a mystery around Jesus' identity and power.¹⁰⁹ The secret becomes open for those who believe and accept Jesus' messianic role, while it remains hidden from those who have no faith.¹¹⁰ The reversal of death into life and the cleansing of all uncleanness connected to death, reveals Jesus' messianic role and its impact on the practices of the ritual system. Moreover, in cases of restoring life, Jesus acts as a life-giver and shows authority over both life and death. Those who accept his messiahship become spiritually converted to God, and experience a re-creation of their hearts. That is why only they are taken by Jesus to see the miracle of physical resurrection. Viewing resurrection through the lens of creation–fall–re-creation paradigm allows Luke to reveal the role of the ritual system, which reaches fulfillment in Christ, and is replaced by faith in his messiahship.

Uncleanness of the Flow of Blood

The idea of the replacement of the ritual system by Jesus' messiahship finds support from Luke's "narrative within narrative." It links two different issues, the issue of death and the issue of uncleanness from the flow of blood. In rabbinic tradition defilement caused by a loss of vital physical fluids (including blood) was set in the framework of the life-death controversy.¹¹¹ Jesus reverses both death and uncleanness. He cleanses the uncleanness of any kind. Though the narrative in Luke 8:43–46 literally states cleansing by a touch, the dialogue reveals that Jesus' cleansing power is of a spiritual nature.¹¹²

---

107. It was stated in chapter 3 of the present study in paragraph *"True Worship Established at the Creation,"* on pp. 144–146.

108. It was noted that in Luke a shift appears from λέγων (8:54), "said," before the resurrection, to διέταξεν (8:56), "commanded," after the resurrection. Nolland, *Luke 1—9:20*, 422. The giving of an order to feed somebody, may correlate with the right of a king to assign food for his people ἄρτους διέταξεν αὐτῷ described in 1 Kgs 11:18. Similar use of διέταξεν appears in 1 Cor 9:14. Gen 1:29 pictures God as the King of creation assigning food for his people, though LXX uses καὶ εἶπεν ὁ θεός and not διέταξεν (however, the phrase itself represents an instruction).

109. Fitzmyer, *Gospel According to Luke (I-IX)*, 749–50.

110. Fitzmyer notes the shadow of Isa 6:10 behind the Lukan connection of "faith" and "salvation." In the Isaiah account, καὶ ἐπιστρέψωσιν καὶ ἰάσομαι αὐτούς denotes that people have to experience spiritual conversion to God to be cured and saved. Fitzmyer, *Gospel According to Luke (I-IX)*, 713–14 n. on 8:12; 747 n. on 8:48.

111. Feldman, *Defilement and Mourning*, 35. When one's life elements were lost it was assumed as a foreshadowing of death.

112. Stein notes the tie between power and the Holy Spirit in the writings of Luke, based on Luke

The phrase, ἥψατο τοῦ κρασπέδου τοῦ ἱματίου αὐτοῦ, καὶ παραχρῆμα ἔστη ἡ ῥύσις τοῦ αἵματος αὐτῆς in Luke 8:44, suggests that healing took place in response to a touch of Jesus' garment by a woman.[113] Yet, Jesus stopped and investigated the case for people's sake, in order to clarify the real agent of healing. His words, ἡ πίστις σου σέσωκέν σε (v. 48), leave the impression that faith was the hidden agent.[114] The woman expresses trust in God's benevolent acceptance of her and, according to it, God purifies her heart. The work of the Holy Spirit remained invisible to the people, until Jesus pointed to it in the phrase, ἐγὼ γὰρ ἔγνων δύναμιν ἐξεληλυθυῖαν ἀπ' ἐμοῦ (v. 46). The presence of the Holy Spirit becomes a sign of a complete purification of her heart.

From this perspective, the phrase ἐγὼ γὰρ ἔγνων δύναμιν ἐξεληλυθυῖαν ἀπ' ἐμοῦ (v. 46) should be paraphrased as, "I recognized someone's faith which took power out of me, in response to that faith." Two emphases can be denoted here. The emphasis on faith becomes more evident if one accepts that the touch by the woman differed from the pressing of a crowd, only by the fact of her faith.[115] Her faith reflected the process of re-creation, which already took place in her heart in response to Jesus' word of the Gospel.[116] The emphasis on the power which has gone out of him recalls Luke 6:19 and links it to Acts 10:38. Thus, the power of God working through Jesus reveals that God has anointed him, namely, it symbolizes the coming of the messianic age.

The miracle of healing and cleansing indicates re-creation, not only of a physical nature, but also of a spiritual conversion to God. The completeness of cleansing in this case did not require any rituals. Jesus simply says to the woman: ἡ πίστις σου σέσωκέν σε, πορεύου εἰς εἰρήνην (v. 48). The completeness of the re-creation in both terms (healing and cleansing) would presuppose that the messianic role of Jesus replaces the ritual system.

Uncleanness of Demon Possession

Another form of uncleanness was caused by demon possession. In Luke 4:33, a demon is called πνεῦμα δαιμονίου ἀκαθάρτου, in contrast to πνεῦμα ἅγιον that belongs to God. The Old Testament concept of "unclean" can be defined as something that has

---

1:17 and between this power and healing based on Luke 5:17. Stein, *Luke*, 262.

113. Garland, *Luke*, 367. This was probably a hem on one of four corners of Jesus' cloak, described in Num 15:38–41 and Deut 22:12. They could remind the woman of God's holiness and great power revealed at the time of Exodus.

114. Bock shows that "there is no magic here, only belief in the spiritual action and power of the Almighty God." Bock, *Luke 1:1—9:50*, 798.

115. This is demonstrated in Part 2, vv. 45–46 on the diagram of Luke 8:43–48 in Appendix 2.

116. Johnson notes that both the daughter of Jairus and the woman are called "daughter" (Luke 8:48). Johnson, *Gospel of Luke*, 143. Jesus' use of "daughter" toward the woman who is older reveals that God cares for his creation no less than the father, Jairus, cares for his only daughter. This accent on the compassionate heart of God was called on to strengthen Jairus' faith.

"evaded the control of the divine holiness."[117] This kind of uncleanness was not tied to any ritual of purification in Torah. Jesus shows that this condition is reversible, when the demon is cast out.[118] The removal of an evil spirit can therefore be understood as a process of spiritual cleansing.[119]

The lack of a ritual, and the invisible nature of the process of spiritual cleansing illustrate four aspects: 1) It shows that externally performed rituals have no impact when the mind is not converted to God. 2) All kinds of uncleanness result from the fall and relate to different spheres of life affected by evil spirits. 3) Though the demon possession often is shown as a reversible kind of uncleanness, there are also an exceptions. The hardening of hearts to the Gospel leads to permanent demon possession, which results in permanent spiritual uncleanness. 4) The lack of a ritual in cases of demon possession would show that only God can cast demons out, destroying the power of Satan. That is why Jesus removes this kind of uncleanness and shares this power with his disciples. These four aspects are based on the four narratives of Luke, which will be discussed further below (1.6.1 to 1.6.3).

The Creation-Fall-Re-creation Pattern behind the Messianic Role of Jesus in Luke 4:31–41

The first narrative in Luke 4:31–41 can be subdivided into three units. The first two units describe Jesus' miracles on Sabbath, before sunset (vv. 31–39). The third unit (vv. 40–41) describes the variety of miracles which took place after sunset. The two miracles, which Jesus performed before sunset, are described in detail, while those after sunset (ἅπαντες ὅσοι εἶχον ἀσθενοῦντας νόσοις ποικίλαις) are mentioned in general terms.[120] Here, the contrasts appear between two people and ἅπαντες. Though the number of miracles after sunset exceeded those during the Sabbath hours, Luke focuses readers' attention on just two which took place during the Sabbath. The immediate literary context reveals that Luke does this contrast the events in the synagogue in Nazareth with those in Capernaum (4:16–30 and 4:31–36 respectively).

---

117. Garland, *Luke*, 214. He also states that for Luke, "unclean spirit" becomes the "evil phenomena that attempts to corrupt God's good purposes in the world."

118. The uncleanness of a demon is permanent, but those possessed by such spirit may reflect different degrees of uncleanness. Thus, in cases, where the spirit does not reveal itself in action, the man is considered as ritually clean. When possession involves association with death (Luke 8:26–40), foaming (Mark 9:20), and fever (Luke 4:38–39), the ritual uncleanness is evident. In cases of blasphemy against the Holy Spirit, a possession by evil spirits assumed a degree of irreversible permanent uncleanness (Luke 12:10; Acts 7:51).

119. The phrase "unclean spirit" includes a moral aspect, since no personal habits of man or of spirit are described. Here, the cosmic confrontation of good and evil forces is revealed. Bock, *Luke 1:1—9:50*, 43031.

120. It was noted that Jesus' miracles on Sabbath revealed "that in his deeds God was truly visiting the people." Johnson, *Gospel of Luke*, 86.

Luke's purpose might be to place the main emphasis not on Sabbath keeping or not keeping, but on a community gathering for the reading of Torah.

The events in Capernaum are narrated to remind the reader of Jesus' announcement in the synagogue of Nazareth of the messianic age (vv. 17–19).[121] Here the evangelist creates a link between the announcement and its realization. He plainly shows that the lack of healings in Nazareth was due to the total unbelief of that community. Jesus' teaching in Capernaum is not mentioned because, likely, it was a repetition of his teaching in Nazareth. However, the reaction of the listeners was different (καὶ ἐξεπλήσσοντο ἐπὶ τῇ διδαχῇ αὐτοῦ, ὅτι ἐν ἐξουσίᾳ ἦν ὁ λόγος αὐτοῦ), which revealed their interest in the external side of his teaching, performing miracles.[122] The subordinated clause ἐν ἐξουσίᾳ ἦν ὁ λόγος reveals that the most important feature of his teaching was its power.[123]

Significantly, the accent on power (ἐξουσίᾳ) in relation to this word was expressed two times: in v. 32 of the *Narrative link 1* (Luke 4:31, 32) and in v. 36 of *Unit 1* (Luke 4:33–36). The first accent precedes the miracle and the second concludes it. Before the miracle took place, people in the synagogue had already recognized the power of Jesus' word (teaching). The aim of the miracle was not to illustrate that the teaching made sense, but to help reveal his identity.[124] This shifts the accent from the teaching to the messianic figure of Jesus. The second occurrence of ἐξουσίᾳ shows that people were amazed by the personality of Jesus τίς ὁ λόγος οὗτος, ὅτι ἐν ἐξουσίᾳ καὶ δυνάμει ἐπιτάσσει τοῖς ἀκαθάρτοις πνεύμασιν, καὶ ἐξέρχονται. They could no longer view him simply as a rabbi. It also posed a question about greater authority. This unit inaugurates Jesus as the Messiah and shows the coming of his messianic kingdom.

By performing the miracle, Jesus achieves a victory over the evil forces. Luke stresses that Jesus casts the demon out without injuring the man (μηδὲν βλάψαν αὐτόν).[125] Luke thus pictures the man left by a demon in the same condition as when he entered him. The reversal itself shows not only that the man was liberated from the evil forces and became free as before, but also it clarifies that the man was cleansed from his spiritual uncleanness and restored to the condition he had before. This feature hints that the world will be completely cleansed of demons, and restored to its condition at creation. Luke's narrative thus begins to reveal a creation–fall–re-creation pattern. Viewing the passage in terms of this pattern, one comes to the conclusion that

---

121. Trites, "Gospel of Luke," 82. This connection of Jesus Messianic role and the power of Holy Spirit, quoted from Isa 61:1–2, was also reflected by Luke in Acts 10:38.

122. Nolland, *Luke 1—9:20*, 205.

123. The theological significance of λόγος for Luke is seen from the number of passages: 1:2; 4:32; 5:1; 8:11, 21; 11:28; Acts 4:4; 6:2, 7; 8:4; 19:10. Johnson, *Gospel of Luke*, 28 n. 2; 83 n. 32.

124. The "power" of Jesus' word, here, presumes a kind of spiritual authority that portrays in him not simply as an exorcist, as he was known in the Talmud (*b. Sanh.* 107b), but the one who overthrows all the power of demons. Garland, *Luke*, 216.

125. With the help of this phrase Luke defeats the man's exclamation, "have you come to destroy us?" Jesus has no intention to harm people and casts the demon out without injuring the man.

the uncleanness of the world is to be completely cleansed by the mission of Jesus, who as the messianic figure fulfills the work of re-creation.

Just as the work of creation was finished with the Sabbath rest, the re-creation and cleansing of the world from the evil forces also logically precede the Sabbath of rest. Jesus' idea of performing some miracles on Sabbath supports this view of his messianic role from the creation perspective.[126] At the same time Jesus' actions would not undermine the significance of keeping the law, and they should not be defined as the cancellation of Sabbath keeping. Instead they clarify the role of Jesus as Creator, who established the law and the Sabbath in a world free of disease and uncleanness. Jesus' role as Creator does not destroy the design of the perfect, original creation, but only fights with the consequences of the possession of this world by evil forces. Ritual uncleanness becomes one consequence. That is why Jesus' messianic role would treat the issue of uncleanness precisely. This assumption would illuminate why Luke brings the Jerusalem Council, finally, to the idea of cancelling the ritual law. For him, this particular part of the law was fulfilled by Jesus' earthly mission.

Unit 2 (Luke 4:38, 39) continues the messianic theme with some peculiarities. Here, the Lukan account differs from Mark 1:29–31.[127] Synoptic relationships show that Luke's theological approach to the messianic role of Jesus was special. Table 2 below illustrates the differences between the Lukan and Markan accounts.

Table 2: Comparative Study of Passages in Mark 1:29–31 and Luke 4:38, 39

Mark 1:29–31	Luke 4:38, 39
Καὶ εὐθὺς ἐκ τῆς συναγωγῆς ἐξελθόντες ἦλθον εἰς τὴν οἰκίαν Σίμωνος καὶ Ἀνδρέου μετὰ Ἰακώβου καὶ Ἰωάννου.	Ἀναστὰς δὲ ἐκ τῆς συναγωγῆς, εἰσῆλθεν εἰς τὴν οἰκίαν Σίμωνος·
Ἡ δὲ πενθερὰ Σίμωνος κατέκειτο πυρέσσουσα, καὶ εὐθέως λέγουσιν αὐτῷ περὶ αὐτῆς·	πενθερὰ δὲ τοῦ Σίμωνος ἦν συνεχομένη πυρετῷ μεγάλῳ· καὶ ἠρώτησαν αὐτὸν περὶ αὐτῆς.
καὶ προσελθὼν ἤγειρεν αὐτήν, κρατήσας τῆς χειρὸς αὐτῆς· καὶ ἀφῆκεν αὐτὴν ὁ πυρετὸς εὐθέως, καὶ διηκόνει αὐτοῖς.	Καὶ ἐπιστὰς ἐπάνω αὐτῆς, ἐπετίμησεν τῷ πυρετῷ, καὶ ἀφῆκεν αὐτήν· παραχρῆμα δὲ ἀναστᾶσα διηκόνει αὐτοῖς.

* underlined words highlight differences in wording

** words in bold font reveal specific use of εὐθέως by Mark, and Luke's use of a single παραχρῆμα instead of Markan threefold εὐθέως

Table 2 reveals that Luke's account represents a shortened version of the same passage in Mark. While Mark places εὐθέως three times before the healing, creating a

---

126. People's amazement "underscores that this event was not a normal occurrence every Sabbath in the synagogue." Garland, *Luke*, 216.

127. Matthew (8:14, 15) describes the event with less significant changes.

sense of the urgency of the situation, Luke avoids this.[128] Instead, he places παραχρῆμα after the miracle had been performed, which shows the immediacy of the convalescence/healing.[129] This immediacy echoes the creation of the world made by the power of God's word.[130] Moreover, when the world was created everything started to move and serve God's appointed purpose.

Similarly, Luke's account, with the help of a single temporal indicator, puts emphasis on the fact that Simon's mother-in-law began to serve them immediately (παραχρῆμα δὲ ἀναστᾶσα διηκόνει αὐτοῖς). Instead of the urgency of the situation described in Mark, Luke puts emphasis on a contrast between the severity of the fever (πυρετῷ μεγάλῳ) and the speed of restoration (παραχρῆμα δὲ ἀναστᾶσα διηκόνει). In addition, Luke completely alters Mark's phrase καὶ προσελθὼν ἤγειρεν αὐτήν, κρατήσας τῆς χειρὸς αὐτῆς into καὶ ἐπιστὰς ἐπάνω αὐτῆς, ἐπετίμησεν τῷ πυρετῷ, which gives a significantly different picture.[131] Luke pictures Jesus acting by the power of the word in the same way as God in creation. Moreover the phrase, ἐπετίμησεν τῷ πυρετῷ, may attribute a fever to a sickness sent by evil intelligent forces.[132] In Jewish tradition, found in *T. Sol.* 18:20, 23, fever "could be caused by a demon."[133]

The following *Unit 3* (4:40, 41) also creates a contrast between two special miracles performed before Sabbath sunset and the great number and wide variety of healings performed after sunset (ἅπαντες ὅσοι εἶχον ἀσθενοῦντας νόσοις ποικίλαις). At this point Luke changes the wording and Jesus is pictured healing by the laying on of hands (ἑνὶ ἑκάστῳ αὐτῶν τὰς χεῖρας ἐπιτιθεὶς), while before sunset he was intentionally described as healing by word.[134] Thus, it seems that the phrase δύνοντος δὲ τοῦ ἡλίου creates a shift in pictures, from a focus on Jesus' role of Creator to a wider picture of Messianic figure. The messianic theme is continued by the testimony to his divine son-ship by demons (ἐξήρχετο δὲ καὶ δαιμόνια ἀπὸ πολλῶν ... λέγοντα ὅτι Σὺ εἶ ὁ υἱὸς τοῦ θεοῦ).

128. BDAG, εὐθέως. The meaning is "*at once, immediately.*"

129. BDAG, παραχρῆμα. This word relates to a point of time that is immediately subsequent to an action, and also means "*at once, immediately.*"

130. The indicators of immediacy in Gen 1:31 are καὶ ἐγένετο ἑσπέρα, καὶ ἐγένετο πρωΐ, ἡμέρα ἕκτη. In Lukan narrative, the healings also fit the day patterns (healing before and after sunset). Also, in Gen 1:24, 25 a reader gets the impression of immediacy of creative action from the chain of verbs εἶπεν ὁ θεός ... ἐποίησεν ὁ θεός ... εἶδεν ὁ θεός. Sometimes the action described is even shorter: εἶπεν ὁ θεός ... ἐγένετο οὕτως (Gen 1:24). The creation, thus, is pictured as appearing to be an immediate response to the word of God. This is displayed in a diagram of *Unit one'* part 1 and 2 (Gen 1:24–31) of Appendix 2.

131. The tradition of Matthew follows Mark, which makes the Lucan account outstanding.

132. The attribution of sicknesses to the actions of demons also appears in Luke 11:14.

133. Garland, *Luke*, 216–17 n. 20.

134. The "laying hands on" for healing is an unknown practice in the OT, though it is mentioned in Deut 34:9. Stein, *Luke*, 164. In Deut 34:9 the "laying hands on" someone signifies sharing the Holy Spirit. Jesus seems to employ this ancient ritual in order to help people to understand that the Holy Spirit is working. This could be Jesus' reaction the words of amazement in the synagogue, when people did not recognize the creative power of God's word and assumed this as a mystical power.

In general, Luke 4:31–41 shows the messiahship of Jesus in terms of the creation–fall–re-creation paradigm and presents his miracles in the language of the re-creation process.[135] The re-creation becomes possible because of the reversal of the fall curses in the messianic mission of Jesus. The ritual part of the law, which dealt with the curses of the fall, now is pointed by Luke toward its replacement by the ministry of Jesus. The law established at creation and known as universal, however, remains unchanged.[136] The expanding of the universal law, known as the natural law of creation, also remains without change until the accomplishment of the reversal and complete removal of any demonic power from the world.

Spiritual Meaning of Ritual Uncleanness in Luke 8:26–36

In Luke 8:26–36 the issue of ritual uncleanness which accompanies demon possession is viewed from a slightly different angle. Demons are permanently unclean. That is the reason for demon possession not being mentioned among the cases of temporary ritual uncleanness in Lev 12–15. As long as one's behavior did not reveal demon possession it could not be assumed because of the invisible nature of demons and unclean spirits. The behavior of a demon-possessed person would reveal itself through an unnatural inclination to uncleanness and lawlessness.

This unnatural inclination is revealed in Part 1 (Luke 8:26–29) picturing a demoniac who does not wear clothes (οὐκ ἐνεδύσατο ἱμάτιον), lives in tombs (ἐν οἰκίᾳ οὐκ ἔμενεν ἀλλ' ἐν τοῖς μνήμασιν) and shows asocial and dangerous behavior (διαρρήσσων τὰ δεσμὰ ἠλαύνετο ὑπὸ τοῦ δαιμονίου εἰς τὰς ἐρήμους). This last feature demonstrates the tendency of demons and unclean spirits to destroy life, which is the main gift of creation. The rejection of wearing garments would also be viewed as a rejection of shame, introduced in the fall narrative.[137] Inhabiting tombs instead of homes would indicate either the denial of the reality of death itself or the denial of the issue of uncleanness. All these features reveal demonic-inspired attempts to resist the "reversal" of curses brought in at the fall. However, the torments caused by demons (πολλοῖς γὰρ χρόνοις συνηρπάκει αὐτόν) were part of the miserable condition of life under those curses, which replaced some of the blessings given at creation.

---

135. Intertestamental Jewish sources pictured the age of the Messiah not only as a destruction of hostile powers, but also in terms of renewal of the world, restoration of Eden (according to Isa 11:6–9), and renovation of nature. Scott, *Jewish Backgrounds*, 285, 288–89.

136. Comparing the original creation in Gen 1–3 and "new heaven and the new earth" in Isa 65:17; 2 Pet 3:13; and Rev 21:1, Kulikovsky concludes that from the biblical perspective, re-creation presumes "transformation of nature back to the perfect state of the original creation." Kulikovsky, *Creation, Fall, Restoration*, 283–85. This presupposes the eternal validity of the original natural order established by God.

137. The rejection of garments could be interpreted as "a sign of his shame and loss of identity." The tombs "were known as haunts for demons (see *b. Ber.* 3b; *b. Sabb.* 67a; *b. Git.* 70a; *b. Sanh.* 65b)." Garland, *Luke*, 357.

Another significant feature of the passage is the dialogue between Jesus and the demons, since they controlled the speech of the man.[138] The conjunction γὰρ in v. 29 (παρήγγειλεν γὰρ... ἐξελθεῖν ἀπὸ τοῦ ἀνθρώπου) shows that Jesus was first to speak. The demonic plea, δέομαί σου, μή με βασανίσῃς, "I beg you, do not torment me," contrasts with the fact that demons "seized the man violently for a long time" (πολλοῖς γὰρ χρόνοις συνηρπάκει αὐτόν). Luke pictures Jesus asking the name of the demon (Τί σοι ὄνομά ἐστιν) in order to show that even λεγιών are scared to deal with him.[139] At the same time the demons testified to Jesus as υἱὲ τοῦ θεοῦ τοῦ ὑψίστου, "son of God," who is the highest authority over creation.[140]

The following turn of the narrative, in Part 2 (8:30–33), seems very unusual. It appears to show Jesus having mercy on demons and destroying a herd of pigs.[141] However, the permission of Jesus for the demons to possess the herd can be viewed not as mercy toward them, but as another significant demonstration that even though the demons plea for mercy, they would not change their nature. This presupposes their irreversible apostasy from God. In spiritual terms the demons are permanently unclean. Jesus in his foresight knows the nature of demons. They tend to inhabit the ἄβυσσος, and lead the possessed to their complete destruction.[142] Jesus' knowledge of the irreversible apostasy of demons stands in sharp contrast to the requests of the demons, who ask ἵνα μὴ ἐπιτάξῃ αὐτοῖς εἰς τὴν ἄβυσσον ἀπελθεῖν. In the following scene they bring the herd of pigs into τὴν λίμνην (which can be understood here as a synonym for the abyss).[143]

By allowing the demons to enter the pigs, Jesus shows what would happen to the man if he did not cast the demons out. The narrative suggests that the demons in their irreversible condition would lead any creature into "abyss." As previously mentioned, possession remains an invisible condition until behavior reveals it. Demons have a tendency to destroy creation, which they do not disclose.[144] Their malignity is

---

138. Bock, *Luke 1:1—9:50*, 766.

139. Garland shows the widespread view reflected in *T. Sol.* 18:23, that "knowing the name of powers gave one some power to manipulate them." Garland, *Luke*, 358. The way in which the demon immediately tells Jesus his name does not mean that Jesus needs it to manipulate. The dialogue begins with the demon's plea for mercy. The disclosure of the name, thus, would symbolize the demon's submission and Jesus' victory over a legion of demons.

140. BDAG, ὕψιστος, 2, "highest in a spatial sense" and "highest in status."

141. Nolland notes that "the account certainly does not suggest that this was the only way Jesus could get the demons out of the man." Here, the demons unleash destructive power upon the pigs leading them to go into the abyss. Nolland, *Luke 1—9:20*, 411.

142. BDAG, ἄβυσσος, 1, 2. This word denotes "an immensely deep space, *depth, abyss,*" and also can presume "a transcendent place associated with the dead and hostile powers, *netherworld, abyss.*"

143. BDAG, λίμνη, 1 a, 2 a. Here the word has two meanings: 1) the *lake* (the Lake of Gennesaret), and 2) the transcendent lake-like phenomenon, namely, the *lake of fire* in which the enemies of God are punished. Also Bock notes that the abyss in the OT originally may refer to the depth of the earth or of the sea (Gen 1:2; 7:11; Job 41:32; Ps 71:20). Bock, *Luke 1:1—9:50*, 775.

144. It was noted that demons "will destroy anything they inhabit." Garland, *Luke*, 359.

compared in Torah to the permanent uncleanness of swine.[145] That is why the herd of pigs was employed by Jesus as an illustration of the permanent uncleanness and irreversibility of evil forces. The deep spiritual meaning of the narrative uncovers the possibility that a person can be possessed to an irreversible degree, when the abyss becomes inevitable.

Part 3 (8:34–36) reports three reactions: that of the herdsmen, of the people of that town, and of the healed man. The latter is especially relevant for our research because it reveals the man restored to his condition before the demons entered him. He is described in v. 36 as ἱματισμένον καὶ σωφρονοῦντα παρὰ τοὺς πόδας τοῦ Ἰησοῦ, which may echo God making clothing for Adam and Eve in Gen 3:21.[146] The scene itself illustrates God's work of re-creation, where the evil is consigned to the abyss, and God restores creation in agreement with his divine order. Consequently the whole passage illustrates: 1) the possibility of an irreversible degree of spiritual uncleanness, 2) the permanent uncleanness in some members of the animal kingdom as an illustration of human spiritual matters.

The Shift of Uncleanness from Reversible to Irreversible Form in Luke 11:14–26

This passage also can be divided into four parts. The first part (Part 1) describes one miracle, and the three that follow represent Jesus' teaching about demonic forces. Part 2 discusses the issue of Jesus' messianic power and authority over evil forces. It pictures the issue of power in parabolic form (*parable* 1). Part 4 contains *parable* 3, which shows the possibility of the transition of reversible uncleanness to its irreversible form.[147]

Part 1 (Luke 11:14) reveals that the curses of the fall which appear in various forms of diseases are the result of demonic activity.[148] However, it is hard to see demon possession in every case of human sickness. A condition such as muteness, may be a visible result of the fallen condition of human nature. In Luke's narrative it was an additional issue to demon possession. The connection of the casting out of the demon to the healing of muteness, here, could demonstrate the possibility of the full reversal

---

145. Bock, *Luke 1:1—9:50*, 775. He noted that here, "the 'unclean' spirit seeks an 'unclean' animal."

146. The natural law, which is the divinely ordained extension of the universal law of creation which took place after the fall presumes that the wearing of clothes would protect one from the shame of nakedness. Thus, the re-creation by Jesus, in this case, would not make one a perfect immortal and innocent being as Adam was before the Fall, but would restore him to a condition of Adam after the Fall, when he repented and received God's forgiveness. That will be his condition of life until the final global re-creation of nature at the time of Jesus' parousia.

147. Bock states that a man possessed by an evil spirit "is potentially subject to destruction." Bock, *Luke 1:1—9:50*, 432.

148. When Jesus liberated the man from the evil spirit "he regained his voice and the power of communication was restored." Trites, "Gospel of Luke," 179.

of curses, which Jesus will accomplish in the future re-creation. At the same time, the narrative clearly places the responsibility for the human disorder on demons.

Part 2 (11:15–20) provides in vv. 15 and 16 two of the most striking opinions of people about the nature of Jesus' power over evil spirits.[149] These opinions stand in sharp contrast to Luke's view of Jesus' power. Then Luke arranges Jesus' speech in the form of dialectical questions. First, Jesus composes a parable (*parable 1* in vv. 17–20) to show that the basis of any power rests in the unity of forces. Jesus turns the crowd's assumption into two questions to demonstrate its illogical nature (ἐν δακτύλῳ θεοῦ ἐκβάλλω τὰ δαιμόνια). His last statement is logical. It answers the second demand concerning the sign from heaven (ἔφθασεν ἐφ' ὑμᾶς ἡ βασιλεία τοῦ θεοῦ) in v. 16.[150] Part 3 (11:21–23) contains *parable 2*, which reveals that the conquest happens because the power of God exceeds the power of demons.[151]

Part 4 (11:24–26) is important for the present study. It shows that, if taken in a spiritual sense, the uncleanness of any human being can reach the irreversible (permanent) degree. To explain this, one need only recall the issue of the uncleanness recorded in Torah. There, the ritual law viewed people's uncleanness only in temporary terms, while the permanent uncleanness was the animals' condition.[152] The ritual law dealt with the uncleanness of a body associated with certain conditions (sickness, leprosy, flow of blood, touching the dead and unclean creatures). This ritual uncleanness symbolically represented the visible results of the curses of the fall. This kind of uncleanness was viewed as reversible and required ritual cleansing and purification rites.[153] The transition of reversible uncleanness into irreversible was possible when one neglected the purification rites. In that case, "cut off," eschatological punishment was called for.[154]

---

149. These people were not convinced by a miracle and attributed Jesus' power to sorcery. Afterwards, they started to demand a sign from heaven. Stein, *Luke*, 331.

150. The sign from heaven is something "apocalyptic in tone, triumphalistic in character" similar to the mighty deeds of God known since the Exodus. Garland, *Luke*, 481. According to Exod 7:9, 11, 13, Pharaoh asked for a miracle, δότε ἡμῖν σημεῖον ἢ τέρας, after which he hardened his heart even more.

151. Stein notes that Luke links the term ὁ ἰσχυρότερος, "someone stronger," related to Jesus in 3:16, to the same title in 11:21, 22. The title ὁ ἰσχυρὸς when viewed in light of Luke 10:18 would relate to Satan's defeat from one who is ὁ ἰσχυρότερος, namely, Jesus. Stein, *Luke*, 332.

152. Hawley, "Agenda of Priestly Taxonomy," 231–32, 236.

153. The purification rites were designed to reverse the uncleanness of discharge from one's body (Lev 15:1–33), giving birth to a child (Lev 12:1–8), the touching of a human or animal corpse (Lev 11:31–40; Num 19:1–22), and leprosy (Lev 13:1–59; 14:1–56). These rites did not cure sickness, but prohibited association with the temple cult and the holy place, holy things and sacrifices. The temporary uncleanness did not make one guilty in a moral sense, but simply reflected the curses of the fall. The purification rites thus illustrated that the reversal of these curses is possible and provided for by the ritual law.

154. The transgressions which inflicted "cut off" punishment were assumed as a deliberate rejection of the circumcision rite (Gen 17:14); pouring of holy anointing oil on someone other than a priest (Exod 30:33); use of holy incense as perfume (Exod 30:38); eating of a sacrifice being ritually unclean

In Luke, the issue of ritual uncleanness undergoes some changes. The reversal of the fall made possible by Jesus' messianic role, removes ritual uncleanness and makes purification rites unnecessary. In the messianic age, physical uncleanness becomes a secondary issue, while the issue of a spiritual uncleanness becomes prominent. Conversion from sin to righteousness includes cleansing of the heart, which is testified by the presence of the Holy Spirit. However, the rejection of Christ indicates the rejection of purification. This attitude leads to a hardening of spiritual uncleanness, and finally its transition into a permanent condition.

Most likely, permanent uncleanness of certain animals represents the presence of irreversible uncleanness in the world. This kind of uncleanness relates to demons, who are irreversibly cursed and doomed. This thought was affirmed in Luke 8:32, 33, where the demons were not only associated with permanently unclean animals, but also returned to the abyss. Association of a human being with demons would bring about the transition of spiritual uncleanness to an irreversible stage.

Part 4 (11:24–26) contains *parable 3* that shows four stages of demon possession. The first stage in v. 24 is described as reversible: an unclean spirit goes out of a man (stage 1).[155] It may indicate the repetition of a conquest, when the man remains unfilled by the Spirit of God, after the demon's expulsion.[156] Jesus' parable also reveals that a demon tends to associate with human beings in the way that a person prefers to live in a home instead of a wilderness. This explains a high possibility of a demon's return to a man (stage 2).[157] The parable also shows that a demon tends to make possession increasingly stronger (stage 3), which tends to bring the situation to its irreversible stage.[158] According to Jesus in v. 26, the situation of demon possession itself has an inner tendency to become, at last, irreversible. The last point of this drama is described by τὰ ἔσχατα, which presumes someone reaching the eternal/irreversible consequences of their choice (stage 4).[159]

---

or other cases of defilement of holy things (Lev 7:20, 21, 25; 22:3); eating of blood (Lev 7:27; 17:14); violation of a command to humble himself during the Day of Atonement (Lev 23:27–29); deliberate escape from participation in the Passover (Num 9:13); when one defiantly transgresses the law of God (Num 15:30–31); when one who is ritually unclean neglected the purification rites (Num 19:13, 20). All these cases presume the transition of reversible temporal uncleanness to the irreversible because of someone's deliberate choice not to obey the Lord.

155. According to Lev 16:10 and Isa 34:13–15 a desert often was viewed as inhabited by demons. Stein, *Luke*, 333.

156. Trites, "Gospel of Luke," 180–81.

157. Garland, *Luke*, 484.

158. Disobedience to God leads to the hardening of a heart and a worse spiritual condition, which is reflected in a number of NT texts: John 5:14; 2 Pet 2:20; Heb 6:4–8; 10:26–27. Stein, *Luke*, 333.

159. BDAG, ἔσχατος, 1, 2. The word relates to time, "the farthest boundary of an era, *last*," or to the "final item in a series, *last* in time."

Uncleanness of the Gentiles

Spiritual Cleansing of the Gentile Converts (Acts 10)

Luke treats the issue of Gentile uncleanness in a special manner.[160] First, he omits the story of the Canaanite woman, which appears in the double synoptic tradition in Mark 7:26 and Matt 15:22. He does this intentionally, in order not to attribute the comparison between Gentiles and dogs to Jesus. Viewing Gentiles as unclean, by pious Jews, appears only in Acts.[161] It seems that, for Luke the Cross makes a difference in relation to the Gentiles. That is why, only in Acts, the issue of Gentile uncleanness in particular, as well as uncleanness in general, comes under discussion. The reasons behind the Lukan view of the ritual purification rites and the significance of the Cross, in relation to this issue, finally appear in Acts 10 and 11.

The significance of the narrative in Acts 10 is stressed by its repetition in chapter 11. While chapter 10 describes the sequence of events, chapter 11 focuses predominantly on Peter's apologetic arguments. His arguments reflect the main points of a spiritual lesson which one can draw out from the events described in the preceding chapter. Moreover, chapter 10 plays a key role in disputes about the issue of the ritual law, in light of the progress of the apostolic mission. The dispute, clearly stated here, reaches its culmination in Acts 15, when common agreement finally seems to be reached. After that, the dispute is never raised again among church leaders. The narrative then turns to the peculiarities of the applications of the agreement.

Acts 10:1–48 can be divided in six parts. Part 1 (Acts 10:1–8) represents the prophetic vision of Cornelius.[162] This vision has features of a literal prophecy, whose meaning is clearly apprehensible, without the need for interpretation. The narrative starts with portraying Cornelius. After ἀνήρ, the first account of him appears, describing him as living in Gentile territory (τις ἐν Καισαρείᾳ), having a Roman name (ὀνόματι Κορνήλιος), and serving in the Roman army (ἑκατοντάρχης ἐκ σπείρης τῆς καλουμένης Ἰταλικῆς). Also mentioned is that Cornelius is a commander over a cohort, which indicates his responsibility and authority. This first account represents the

---

160. Klawans believes that only the eighteen-edicts tradition placed ritual impurity on the Gentiles. According to rabbinical teaching, the Gentiles were ritually unclean, because they didn't practice the laws of ritual purity, ate impure food, touched impure substances, committed idolatry and defiling sexual acts. Jonathan Klawans notices that *Antiquities* 12:145 connects the exclusion of proselytes from the temple to the purity law and that Gentiles were excluded from the temple "just as the flesh of unclean beasts is excluded from Jerusalem." Klawans, "Notions of Gentile Impurity," 289, 298, 309–11.

161. The book of Acts frequently discusses the divine plan concerning the inclusion of the Gentiles in the messianic kingdom of God: Acts 8:4, 5; 10; 11; 13.42- 48; 14:1, 27; 15; 16:14–15; 18:4, 6; 22:21; 26:20; 28:28.

162. It was noted that Luke, beginning to describe the mission to the Gentiles, focuses on Cornelius' piety. It was suggested that the angelophany at Cornelius' home is paralleled by Luke to the same event experienced by Zechariah the priest in Luke 1:11–20. This view is supported by mentioning piety, according to the Jewish law, in both cases. Pervo, *Acts*, 267.

public characteristics of Cornelius. In the eyes of a pious Jew, however, these attributes could be viewed as religiously and culturally unacceptable.

His second description starts in v. 2 and reflects the inner world of his heart, as known to God. He is pictured as pious (εὐσεβὴς) and a God-fearer (φοβούμενος τὸν θεὸν σὺν παντὶ τῷ οἴκῳ αὐτοῦ). In addition, he is known for the giving of many alms (ποιῶν ἐλεημοσύνας πολλὰς) and praying to God at all times (δεόμενος τοῦ θεοῦ διὰ παντός). The phrase, ποιῶν ἐλεημοσύνας πολλὰς τῷ λαῷ, likely presupposes the alms given to the Jewish people, because the singular λαός with the definite article usually designates the "people of God." This characteristic could be specially emphasized by Luke, in order to compensate for the negative impression which the image of a soldier creates, by presenting him as merciful even toward a hostile ethnic group.

Verse 3 states that Cornelius saw a vision, which appeared to him "clearly, evidently" (φανερῶς). This may indicate that his vision had no hidden meaning, but could be clearly understood. The *time indicator 1* (ὡσεὶ περὶ ὥραν ἐνάτην τῆς ἡμέρας) is the first out of six time indicators in this chapter. Its role, appearing later, is to show that both visions, that of Cornelius and that of Peter, are linked semantically. Later part 4 (Acts 10:30–33), in v. 30, reveals that Cornelius was fasting for four days and received his vision during his fast. The reason for fasting is not stated, yet can be assumed from the words of an angel in v. 4 (αἱ προσευχαί σου . . . ἀνέβησαν εἰς μνημόσυνον ἔμπροσθεν τοῦ θεοῦ). If one assumes that God answered Cornelius' prayers by sending him an apostle, then the prayers were somehow related to his need to know the way of salvation.[163]

This assumption can be strengthened by the *time indicator 2* (νῦν) by an angel in v. 5, who clarifies the time of the vision as the starting point. This observation authorizes the reader to view both visions (literally of Cornelius and symbolically of Peter) as semantically linked.[164] The second νῦν is mentioned in v. 33 again in relation to the words of an angel. Its function is to complete the chain of events which the angel started. The second νῦν shows that Cornelius had fulfilled all orders of angel given three days earlier. Consequently, the *time indicator 2*, νῦν, does not correlate to the exact date, but rather signifies the coming of salvation to the Gentiles.

Also the double occurrence of νῦν links two visions as if they were two parts of one event. Another significant feature is that Cornelius, having no idea about the vision which soon is to be given to Peter, chose three men (φονήσας δύο τῶν οἰκετῶν καὶ στρατιώτην εὐσεβῆ) and sent them to Joppa (ἀπέστειλεν αὐτοὺς εἰς τὴν Ἰόππην). This feature credits God not only for originating the events, but also for managing all

---

163. Larkin shows that Cornelius' piety had not yet brought him to a saving relationship with God, but led to more revelation. Larkin, "Acts," 469.

164. The connection between the two visions was stressed, when the four chronological markers were noticed: 1) on the next day, after Cornelius had a vision; 2) during the time, as soldiers sent by Cornelius were on their way; 3) when they were approaching the city; 4) at noon. Schnabel, *Acts*, 487–88.

pending circumstances. In addition, the number of people sent by Cornelius provides a clue to the symbols of Peter's vision.

Part 2 (Acts 10:9–16) shifts the scene from the Gentile home in Caesarea to the Jewish home in Joppa, where Peter was staying. Here, the issue of ritual uncleanness appears for the first time. Luke mentions three times that Peter resides in the house of Simon the tanner. "The Mishnah and Talmud strongly criticize tanners, because of their ongoing ritual defilement" from association with skins of dead animals.[165] Peter's decision to live there reveals "that the apostle is receptive to Jews who are considered marginalized and unclean."[166]

Verse 9 contains the *time indicator 3* (τῇ δὲ ἐπαύριον ὁδοιπορούντων ἐκείνων . . . περὶ ὥραν ἕκτην) pointing that the following events took place next morning, about the sixth hour. The mention of ὁδοιπορούντων in connection to time indicators and mention of a location in the clause καὶ τῇ πόλει ἐγγιζόντων stresses that they hurried and travelled through the night. Here, the accent is on the progress of the three travellers. Mention of their location with the *time indicator 3* creates a narrative link synchronizing three men's arrival with Peter's vision. The emphasis on their progress shows that only at the time they came near the city did the perplexing vision appear to Peter.

When Peter went to the housetop to pray (vv. 9, 10), he was caught by a surprisingly strong desire to taste food (ἐγένετο δὲ πρόσπεινος καὶ ἤθελεν γεύσασθαι). His hunger was unusual at this time of day and Peter could not find an explanation for it. The presence of Peter's unusual hunger sends the reader's thoughts to Cornelius, who is still fasting. A Jew enriched by God's mercy now stands in sharp contrast to the God-fearing Gentile, who has not yet "tasted" the grace of God. However, Peter does not know about this contrast revealed to the reader. The answer to Peter's amazement comes in the following prophetic symbolic vision (ἐγένετο ἐπ' αὐτὸν ἔκστασις).

The vision starts in v. 11 with the image of heaven opened up (τὸν οὐρανὸν ἀνεῳγμένον). The second image is a vessel coming down (καταβαῖνον σκεῦός) from heaven and lowered to the ground (καθιέμενον ἐπὶ τῆς γῆς). The special feature of this vessel was its similarity to a big linen cloth (ὡς ὀθόνην μεγάλην). This could remind readers of the linen cloth/wrapping for swathing the dead as in Luke 24:12 and John 19:40, 20:5–7 (where the linen cloth is also mentioned in the singular). According to John, Peter saw the linen cloth/wrapping on the morning of the resurrection. Thus, the linen cloth in Peter's vision in Acts 10:11 can be understood as Jesus' burial linen wrapping.

Acts 10:11 appears in variant readings.[167] The addition δεδεμένον καὶ suggests that the linen cloth was bound at the four corners (τέσσαρσιν ἀρχαῖς δεδεμένον). The

---

165. Nguyen, "Dismantling Cultural Boundaries," 457.

166. Nguyen, "Dismantling Cultural Boundaries," 457.

167. Metzger notes that "the Western text here lacked καταβαῖνον and described the vessel as 'tied (δεδεμένον) at (the) four corner.'" In the text of the old uncials, which read καταβαῖνον, the vessel is

perfect participle δεδεμένον may suggest that the four corners were tied together, if the "tied" relates to corners only. At the same time, the whole phrase, τέσσαρσιν ἀρχαῖς δεδεμένον καὶ καθιέμενον ἐπὶ τῆς γῆς, contains two participles, one in perfect tense and the second in present tense which can be translated, "having been tied by the four corners and being lowered to the ground." It may presuppose another picture: the big linen cloth coming down from heaven, having been tied by the four corners to the earth, and having been lowered to the ground. If one accepts that the addition of δεδεμένον καὶ is a later conflation of readings, then τέσσαρσιν ἀρχαῖς καθιέμενον ἐπὶ τῆς γῆς can be translated "by the four corners [it] is lowered to the ground."[168]

This picture may raise the question whether the linen cloth tied to the ground and arched up could carry the animals. The picture of a concave object suggests the image of a vessel. The lifting up of the cloth's center, and the binding of the corners of the cloth to the ground may however remind readers of a shelter (σκηνὴ, or σκῆνος) instead of a vessel (σκεῦος).[169] Such a shelter would take the form of a pitched tent, which would explain the fastening of it to the ground, precisely at its four corners. This suggestion of a tent or tabernacle would make sense to Peter, the Jew, and for Luke, who in his narrative came close to the issue of the ritual law. If so, σκεῦός would be better translated as *"thing, object,"* rather than *"vessel."*[170]

The conjectural scribal emendation of the text was likely due to the presence of the variant readings and betrays an attempt to clarify the meaning of the text.[171] The corruption of text could be an unintentional mistake of reading, when in case of uncertain reading, the letter ν (N) was assumed as υ (Y).[172] This mistake later could influence the reading of ῆ into ε in σκῆνος. In case of σκηνήν, the ending could also be

---

said to be 'lowered (καθιέμενον) by (the) four corners.'" Metzger, *Textual Commentary*, 326.

168. Metzger states: "A majority of the Committee judged that witnesses that have all three participles are conflated, and preferred the reading supported by 𝔓74 ℵ A B (C2) ite vg geo." Metzger, *Textual Commentary*, 326–27.

169. BDAG, σκῆνος, "*tent, lodging*" appears in 2 Cor 5:1, 4 in the phrase, "the earthly tent we live in." BDAG, σκηνή, 1 ab, 2. This word means "tent, hut, lodging, dwelling" and relates to the tents of nomads, cultic tent (the Tent of Testimony), and describes "transcendent celestial tent." Luke uses the derived forms of the word σκηνὴ five times in Luke 9:33; 16:9; Acts 7:43, 44; 15:16. The author of the Epistle to the Hebrews represents heaven typologically as a tent, and employs the image of the tabernacle to signify "God's presence in the midst of the wilderness wandering." Keene, "Heaven Is a Tent," 432.

170. BDAG, σκεῦός, 1.

171. The term "conjectural emendentions" was suggested by Metzger, *Text of New Testament*, 226–31.

172. This kind of corruption can be attributed to "errors arising from faulty eyesight," when similar letters were confused. Metzger, *Text of New Testament*, 251–53. The original σκῆνος could be presumed due to the fact that the words σκεῦός and σκῆνος look and sound similarly. Also σκηνὴν (acusative from σκηνή) could be original due to the accusative case of the whole sentence and because feminine σκηνή always refers to the tabernacle. The phrase, thus, may be read as καὶ καταβαῖνον σκηνήν τι ὡς ὀθόνην μεγάλην τέσσαρσιν ἀρχαῖς δεδεμένον καθιέμενον ἐπὶ τῆς γῆς and translated as "and descending tabernacle, going down by four corners upon the earth" (Acts 10:11).

changed since the word in all three accounts appears on the edge of a column and the reading of the last letter/s is uncertain.[173]

The presupposition of the copyist that God, through a vision, directed Peter to eat meat of any kind, made him choose σκεῦός instead of σκηνὴν/ σκῆνος, especially if this variant reading had support from earlier copies, where the mistake was made.[174] The choice of the word may also correlate with the hunger of Peter and the following command, to kill and eat. Thus, the image of a vessel would fit a meal picture in a copyist's mind.[175]

However, Peter's hunger can be linked to the image of a meal only superficially. His hunger has a stronger link to Cornelius' fasting with his desire for salvation. This link is supported by the Lukan use of the time indicators, which create an impression of a timer switched on at Cornelius' vision in Caesarea until Peter's arrival in Caesarea. Moreover, the picture of a vessel influenced by the order to kill and eat the animals also has no firm ground, because the cooking of meat in the linen vessel seems impossible. In general, the symbol of the linen vessel, whose corners are tied together does not bring to mind any echoes of Scripture, but only an allusion to meals.

The image of the tabernacle would provide a better meaning.[176] There, the slaughtering (θύω) and eating (φάγω) in the court of the tabernacle was prescribed by ritual law.[177] The verb θύω has two meanings, "kill" or "slaughter" taken in the ritual sense.[178] The double imperatives θῦσον καὶ φάγε, in view of the tabernacle, would more readily relate to ritual slaughter.[179] This assumption can be supported

---

173. The uncial of א shows that in two out of three ocurances (in Acts 10:16 and 11:5) the word σκεῦός is divided between two lines: "CKEY" on one line and "OC" on the line below. Thus, the letter "Y" comes on the edge, where it looks "scraped." Only in Acts 10:11does the word comes first in the line of the column as undivided, but the previous word "KATABAIN" lacks the ending, "ON" and thus does not reveal the case of vessel/tent. The scribal choice of σκεῦός presumes the nominative case, while the phrase comes in the accusative.

174. The interchange of σκηνὴν by σκεῦός can be explained by the common use of these words in relation to the tabernacle and its staff (Exod 30:26–28; 35:11–14; 39:13; Lev 8:11; Num 1:50; 3:8, 36; 4:15; Heb 9:21).

175. Metzger notes that in numerous manuscripts of Acts 10:30 the phrase (νηστεύων, καὶ) was added to the text. The insertion of "fasting," here in connection to prayer, was attributed by Metzger to "alterations made because of doctrinal considerations." Metzger, *Text of New Testament*, 268.

176. The phrase σκηνή δερματίνη in P Cairo Zen I. 59013 (dated by 259 BCE) had the meaning of "tent." Moulton and Milligan, *Vocabulary of the Greek Testament*, 577. This image brings to mind the tabernacle covered by animal skins in Exod 26:14; 36:19; 39:34.

177. The law of Deut 12:7 states φάγεσθε ἐκεῖ ἐναντίον κυρίου which presumes the eating of the sacrifices.

178. Haenchen understands this as the command to Peter to "slaughter," not "sacrifice" or kill ritually. He assumes it from the fact that unclean animals cannot be ritually slaughtered and sees the translation of ἐκαθάρισεν as "to declare clean." Haenchen, *Acts*, 348 nn. 2, 4. However, God's declaration of them to be ἐκαθάρισεν shows them as appropriate spiritual sacrifice. Billebeck, contrary to Haenchen, views θύω (in Acts 10:13) corresponding to the Hebrew word meaning "kill ritually." Billerbeck, *Kommentar zum Neuen Testament*, 708 (as cited in Haenchen, 348).

179. This action was described in Lev 19:5–6; Deut 12:15–16; 2 Chr 29:22. Larkin, "Acts," 473. All

by three arguments. The first appears in Rom 15:16, the Pauline comparison between conversion of the Gentiles and the bringing of sacrifices (ἱερουργοῦντα τὸ εὐαγγέλιον τοῦ θεοῦ, ἵνα γένηται ἡ προσφορὰ τῶν ἐθνῶν εὐπρόσδεκτος, ἡγιασμένη ἐν πνεύματι ἁγίῳ). This also agrees with Peter's explanation of the symbolism of his vision in terms of God's will to send him to preach to the Gentiles.

The second argument is that when the divine voice ordered: Ἀναστάς, Πέτρε, θῦσον καὶ φάγε, he refused and made an excuse.[180] His excuse had to be rational, otherwise it would not make any sense. The rationale of Peter's excuse appears in the phrase ὅτι οὐδέποτε ἔφαγον πᾶν κοινὸν καὶ ἀκάθαρτον.[181] Here, two words are used, κοινὸν and ἀκάθαρτον, which likely indicate two different kinds of uncleanness. The animals in the "vessel" represented the full variety of the animal kingdom (πάντα τὰ τετράποδα, καὶ ἑρπετὰ τῆς γῆς, καὶ πετεινὰ τοῦ οὐρανοῦ).[182] The phrase may allude to Gen 1:24, 26, 28; 9:2, 10 omitting only the water animals.[183] The word πάντα means that some of the animals were clean and Peter could chose which to sacrifice. Yet, he sees none which is neither κοινὸν nor ἀκάθαρτον.

It is noteworthy that the term for unclean animals in Torah is טָמֵא (Lev 11:4) and translated in LXX as ἀκάθαρτον and not κοινὸν.[184] The word ἀκάθαρτος would

---

these texts presume a cultic context of slaughtering.

180. Here, Peter's strong resistance has two strong negatives in his reply: "By no means [μηδαμῶς], Lord; for I have never [ουδέποτε] eaten anything that is profane or unclean!" (10:14). "Peter's response recalls the strongly worded response of Ezekiel to a similar command to defile himself (μηδαμως, κύριε θεε του Ισραήλ." Ἰδοὺ ἡ ψυχή μου ου μεμίανται εν ακαθαρσία [4:14, LXX]). Peter has never eaten anything profane or unclean, and, like Ezekiel, he is not going to start now." Matson and Brown, "Tuning the Faith," 456. It is noteworthy, that Ezekiel in his answer to God refers to temporal type of uncleanness counting θνησιμαῖον, θηριάλωτον, πᾶν κρέας ἕωλον, but not what is called βδέλυγμα (Lev 11:42; Deut 14:3).

181. In Acts 11:8 the disjunctive ἤ does occur instead of the connective καὶ, which makes the phrase to state, "nothing common *or* unclean has ever entered my mouth." The change from the connective "defiled and unclean" to the disjunctive "defiled or unclean" could be specially designed by Luke to stress that κοινὸς and ἀκάθαρτος are not synonyms. Thus, κοινὸς presumes ritual temporal uncleanness by being mixed with unclean food (cf. 11:47), while ἀκάθαρτος refers to food, which by its very nature (permanently, irreversibly) is "unclean." Parsons, "'Nothing Defiled AND Unclean,'" 268.

182. Pervo believes that Peter's vision has to be viewed in light of Gen 1:24–25, which shows the intent of the Creator to restore the goodness of all creation to its original condition. Pervo, *Acts*, 269–71 n. 54.

183. Also, here the allusion to the flood narrative and Noah's ark can be presumed, where the water animals also were absent, Gen 7:21. The typology of the ark was the one of the important elements of the tabernacle service. The reference to the flood is possible because of "the widespread typological interpretation of the flood in the Second Temple period and the NT literature." Moreover, in Matt 24 Jesus compares a time of his coming to Noah's time; also in 2 Pet 2:1–9, Peter displays a developed flood typology. Streett, "As It Was,'" 34, 51.

184. Note that κοινὸς means "desecrated/polluted by association," while ακάθαρτος means "unclean" in terms of permanent uncleanness. Moskala, *Laws of Clean and Unclean*, 375. Moskala's work was reviewed from the positive side by Hawkins, "Laws of Clean and Unclean," 112–13. Jacob Milgrom reviewing Moskala's work agrees with him about "rooting the dietary laws in creation," but argues for the order of God in Gen.9:3 to use all animals for food. Milgrom, "Review of J. Moskala," 250–51.

designate the permanently unclean condition of an animal, which is determined by its nature. The word κοινός relates to a different kind of uncleanness, which is ritual and temporary.[185] The evidence of it can be found in Mark 7:2 where κοινὸς is chosen to describe the uncleanness of unwashed hands (κοιναῖς χερσίν, τοῦτ' ἔστιν ἀνίπτοις).[186] Thus, the animals in the "vessel"/"tent" were divided by Peter into those ἀκάθαρτον (unclean by nature), and those κοινὸν (ritually unclean from being in touch with ἀκάθαρτον).[187] Eating meat affected by ritual uncleanness would not be viewed as sin, as long as one did not participate in a temple cult.[188] Contrastingly, when the cultic context is involved, the ritual system must be followed.

The third argument is connected to the fact that the tabernacle (the tent of meeting) would signify God's dwelling among his people. The vision of a linen cloth tent with the animals would symbolize Jesus' death, which as the atoning sacrifice covered the whole world, all nations, and included them all in the salvific plan of God.[189] The use of the linen fabric is also significant, because the only thing in the tabernacle made from linen seems to be priests' garments. For Peter the linen cloth covering the whole earth, here, could signify that the priestly and levitical ministry is fulfilled in Christ. This also has support from the fact that God commanded Peter (who was not a Levite) to slaughter an animal. The assumption that Peter could draw these conclusions from a vision can be seen from his own view of the priesthood of all believers (1 Pet 2:9).

It seems that a similar vision was given to the disciple John, who saw a shelter/tabernacle coming down from heaven (Rev 21:2, 3), full of people, not animals. Here, καταβαίνουσαν ἐκ τοῦ οὐρανοῦ and ἡ σκηνή describes the image of a tent filled with people (ἡ σκηνὴ τοῦ θεοῦ μετὰ τῶν ἀνθρώπων).[190] This possible parallel vision suggests that in Acts 10:11–16 the vision was about people, not animals.[191] Consequently, the cleansing of any animals' uncleanness was not under consideration in Acts 10:11–16.

---

185. Walter Houston insists that "κοινὸν" in Acts 10:28 is equivalent to "unclean" and not a synonym of ἢ ἀκάθαρτον. On this basis he suggests a social rationale for the laws of unclean animals rather than a universal non-Jewish context linked to the Creation. Houston, "Laws of Clean and Unclean," 132–34.

186. If one accepts that Mark wrote the Gospel drawing on Peter's sermons, the interpretation of κοινὸς in relation to ritual uncleanness would be attributed to Peter himself.

187. Nguyen states that the "uncleanness" in this case can be explained by contamination of clean animals by unclean animals. Nguyen, "Dismantling Cultural Boundaries," 459.

188. According to Deut 12:15, the ritual uncleanness would not affect meat consumption, if the meat is not of a sacrifice brought to a holy place.

189. The word σκηνή was employed to describe the inhabited world in antiquity. These words are ascribed to Democritus, ὁ κόσμος σκηνή, ὁ βίος πάροδος· ἦλθες, εἶδες, ἀπῆλθες. See also *Anth. Pal.* 10.72. Moulton and Milligan, *Vocabulary of the Greek Testament*, 577.

190. For μετά serving as marker of attendant objects see BDAG, μετά 3c.

191. According to Dan 7:17, the beasts in the vision represent kingdoms. Craig S. Keener supports the view that in apocalyptic visions animals symbolize various nations. Keener, *Acts*, 1766 n. 375.

The word σκηνή appears in the writings of Luke three times. First, Jesus tells about an eternal dwelling place, τὰς αἰωνίους σκηνάς (Luke 16:9).[192] Jesus' words are addressed to believers to instruct them not to forget "the priority of values related to future life."[193] The two-age eschatological understanding of Jesus' parable would direct believers to patterns of true worship. The second occurrence is in Stephen's reference to the earthly tabernacle in the desert τὴν σκηνὴν τοῦ Μόλοχ (Acts 7:43), his point is that "Israel had been idolatrous in their worship of God in the past and was again idolatrous in the present," denying God's salvation revealed in Jesus.[194] Thomas Golding notes, "the idolatry at the Jerusalem temple in Acts is nowhere near as graphic as in a passage like Ezekiel 8."[195]

The third time σκηνή appears is in James' speech at the Jerusalem Council in his reference to τὴν σκηνὴν Δαυὶδ τὴν πεπτωκυῖαν (Acts 15:16). Here, the "fallen tent" should be understood to refer to idolatry in times of the Hebrew kings until the Babylonian exile.[196] All three occurences of σκηνή in Luke-Acts suggest that Luke views the issue of a Jewish cult in light of the irreconcilability of true worship and false worship. Peter's vision in Acts 10:11 also was employed by Luke to emphasize the aspects common to true worship shared by Jewish converts and Gentile converts, who are no longer divided by the ritual purity aspects of the Jewish cultic system.[197]

God's dialogue with Peter ends with Ἃ ὁ θεὸς ἐκαθάρισεν σὺ μὴ κοίνου. While Peter's previous statement relates to two groups, κοινὸν and ἀκάθαρτον, the divine voice answers only about the first matter (σὺ μὴ κοίνου) leaving ἀκάθαρτον without any instruction. It is also not said whether ἀκάθαρτον was cleansed, because the phrase ὁ θεὸς ἐκαθάρισεν relates only to κοινὸν, as it follows from the imperative μὴ κοίνου.[198] The divine order to kill and eat, thus, cannot be attributed to all kinds

---

192. Here, the disciples were told "to be taken into eternal tabernacles beyond this world." The phrase "reflects the image of God's tabernacling or sheltering his people in heaven (Rev 7:15; 21:3). Garland, *Luke*, 652.

193. Stein, *Luke*, 414, citing Sabourin, *Luke*, 293

194. Beginning with the golden calf at Sinai (Acts 7:39–41) Israelites continued to worship other deities throughout their time in the wilderness (vv. 42–43; cf. Amos 5:25–26). Golding, "Pagan Worship in Jerusalem?," 309.

195. Golding, "Pagan Worship in Jerusalem?," 316. He notes that "the temple itself was not idolatrous or filled with idolatrous articles. Rather, the (stereotypical) perspective of the Jews concerning the temple was. Continuing to worship at the temple and venerate the temple while rejecting God's work through Jesus dishonored God."

196. Thus, Schnabel suggests that the "tent of David" may refer to the Jerusalem temple or Jerusalem destroyed in 587 BCE, yet it may also metaphorically represent the "temple" of the messianic age, the church. Schnabel, *Acts*, 638–39.

197. It was noted that the three most significant missionary speeches in Acts 13:13–41; 14:8–18; and 17:16–31 (addressed to the Gentile audience) reflect the call to true worship "introducing the true living God over against false gods." Gendy, "Style, Content and Culture," 263.

198. M. Parsons noticed that in Luke's writings there are eight occurrences of ἀκάθαρτος. Beyond those found in 10:14, 10:28; 11:8 (with ambiguous meaning), the other instances show the reference is to "unclean spirits" (Luke 4:33, 46; 6:18; 8:29; 9:42; 11:24; Acts 5:16; 8:7). Thus, Luke uses ἀκάθαρτος

of animals, because of the previously mentioned κοινὸν and ἀκάθαρτον; only about κοινὸν it is said, ἃ ὁ θεὸς ἐκαθάρισεν σὺ μὴ κοίνου, which means "what God has cleansed, *that* no longer view as common." Pervo sees here a Lukan allusion to the words of Jesus, spoken in the house of the Pharisee (Luke 11:41).[199] The words "everything will be clean (πάντα καθαρά) for you" were spoken about things unclean in a ritual sense which were to be cleansed by water. So, God's announcement of cleansing the animals in the linen cloth by all means would indicate cleansing their ritual, temporary uncleanness.

This understanding gives the reader the idea that God cleanses things which before were viewed as "ritually unclean." Later Peter confirms this understanding three times: 1) in Acts 10:47, 48 where he sees the converts filled with the Holy Spirit; 2) Acts 11:15–17, where Peter before the Jewish believers interprets the filling of the Gentile converts with the Holy Spirit as "spiritual baptism," predicted by Christ and coming from God; and 3) Acts 15:8–9 where Peter interprets this event as the cleansing of hearts which removes any distinctions between the Jewish and Gentile converts. The lifting of the tabernacle up into heaven εὐθὺς ἀνελήμφθη τὸ σκεῦος εἰς τὸν οὐρανόν presupposes that what is treated as clean by God and accepted in heaven, should not be assumed as unclean by men.[200]

The voice from heaven in v. 15, ἃ ὁ θεὸς ἐκαθάρισεν σὺ μὴ κοίνου, drove Peter into perplexity, because he did not understand that the Gentiles with their ritual uncleanness are now made clean in God's sight.[201] According to v. 17, he was meditating upon its symbolism (ὡς δὲ ἐν ἑαυτῷ διηπόρει ὁ Πέτρος τί ἂν εἴη τὸ ὅραμα ὃ εἶδεν). However, Luke writes the narrative in such a way as to make the meaning clear to the reader, who is aware that the three men, who were sent to find Peter, are now near Joppa. V. 16 reads, τοῦτο δὲ ἐγένετο ἐπὶ τρίς, putting accent on the number three. While v. 17 pictures Peter in perplexity, v. 18 again shifts to the three men (ἰδοὺ οἱ ἄνδρες οἱ ἀπεσταλμένοι ὑπὸ τοῦ Κορνηλίου). In addition, Peter's speech in

---

in relation to permanent uncleanness. Yet the verb form καθαρίζω, which occurs in our texts at Acts 10:15; 11:9; and 15:9, would presume cleansing of temporal uncleanness (the term occurs also at Luke 4:27; 5:12, 13; 7:22; 11:39; 17:14, 17, mostly in reference to the physical and ritual cleansing of lepers). Parsons, "Nothing Defiled AND Unclean," 270.

199. Pervo, *Acts*, 269.

200. Nguyen notes that the vertical movement (the descent and ascent of the animals) between heaven and earth metaphorically and theologically implies, "for Luke, there is no longer a division between sacred space (heaven) and profane space (earth)." Nguyen, "Dismantling Cultural Boundaries," 456.

201. The verb "made clean" (ἐκαθάρισεν), according to LXX, was used "for pronouncements of the priests concerning persons who had been impure and who, after the appropriate purification, were then declared clean (cf. Lev 13:6, 13, 17)." Schnabel, *Acts*, 491. Though Schnabel believes that God's pronouncement in Acts 10:15 included cleansing of animals, there was no ritual of purification in the Torah attributed to animals cleansing their uncleanness (which is assumed as permanent), but only to people, cleansing them from temporary ritual uncleanness.

Acts 11:10–11 links the three voice pronouncements in the vision to the three men approaching Simon's home.

Part 3 (10:17–29) provides in v. 19 a direct revelation from God concerning the vision just at the time of Peter's perplexity. The present tense participle διενθυμουμένου is part of a genitive absolute with temporal meaning. Exactly at the time, "while Peter was pondering the vision" the explanation was provided.[202] The construction links Peter's wish to understand the vision with the explanation given by the Holy Spirit: ἰδοὺ ἄνδρες ζητοῦσίν σε. Here, the number of men varies: δύο to τρεῖς; the number is omitted in some manuscripts, but the reader knows that three men were sent by Cornelius (v. 7). By this Luke reveals that though Cornelius was the immediate agent sending those men, God was the initiator of this meeting (ἐγὼ ἀπέσταλκα αὐτούς) and ruled over the events, according to his divine purpose.

In v. 20, the participle διακρινόμενος means "to differentiate by separation, make a distinction."[203] The previous divine revelation in v. 15 stated, σὺ μὴ κοίνου, which is similar in meaning to μηδὲν διακρινόμενος, because in both cases the distinction between holy and common in terms of the ritual law is presumed. Now it is clearly stated that the prohibition of any distinction is not about food, but only about people.[204] Peter has to go with these men even though they are Gentiles.

This story in Acts echoes Jonah, where the prophet also was sent on a mission to the Gentiles.[205] Yet, when he came to Joppa, Jonah changed course and became disobedient to God's call. The conversion of the sailors in Jon 1:14–16 and the Ninevites in Jon 3:5–10 reveals that preaching to the Gentiles was also in God's plan, long before the time of the apostles. The deliberate choice of God to save rather than to destroy Ninevah illustrates his care and loving attitude toward the entire creation. Jonah's struggles in the depth of the sea symbolize the spiritual as well as physical uncleanness of the disobedient prophet and its result. The lesson of Jonah's story probably made Peter obey God immediately, without arguing. Here, the *time indicator 4*, τῇ δὲ ἐπαύριον, in v. 23 reveals that Peter started his way to Caesarea next morning.

Peter's words in v. 28 even better explain that the ritual uncleanness of Gentiles was an issue that now is solved by God.[206] Here, the phrase ἡμεῖς ἐπίστασθε presumes that Cornelius is a God-fearer and being friendly with the Jews knows that ἀθέμιτόν ἐστιν ἀνδρὶ Ἰουδαίῳ κολλᾶσθαι ἢ προσέρχεσθαι ἀλλοφύλῳ. The word ἀθέμιτος, "not

---

202. Wallace, *Greek Grammar*, 654–55.

203. BDAG, διακρίνω, 1, 2, 6. Here also it can mean "to be uncertain, *be in odds, doubt.*"

204. Schnabel states, "Peter sees clearly that the issue at stake was not just food, but people." Schnabel, *Acts*, 496.

205. S. Oxley shows a few parallels between the story of Jonah and Peter (Simon son of Jonah) in Cornelius' story. Oxley, "Certainties Transformed," 325.

206. Here and in vv. 34–35 "Luke was interested not in kashrut but in barriers based on ethnocentricity." Pervo, *Acts*, 278 n. 154. Charles Selengut notes that in its biblical form, Judaism represents a belief in "a universal God for all humankind but stresses the sanctity of religious particularity and ethnic diversity." Selengut, "Law and Ritual," 43.

allowed, forbidden," refers "not to what is forbidden by ordinance, but to a violation of tradition."[207] Thus, common recognition and not divine command was the reason for segregation here. Peter tells Cornelius that God reveals a different attitude than is in common practice (κἀμοὶ ὁ θεὸς ἔδειξεν).[208] The will of God is stated in μηδένα κοινὸν ἢ ἀκάθαρτον λέγειν ἄνθρωπον (v. 28).[209] This command implies no discrimination based on the ritual system linked to the temple cult.

Part 4 (10:30–33) records Cornelius' story. The *time indicator 5* appears from the beginning. Its function is to synchronize two events, one in Caesarea and one in Joppa. According to Cornelius he was fasting all the time until Peter arrived (ἀπὸ τετάρτης ἡμέρας μέχρι ταύτης τῆς ὥρας ἤμην νηστεύων). It is evident that Peter's hunger was linked by God to Cornelius fasting in order to synchronize not only the visions or events, but also to prepare Peter emotionally for a compassionate and accepting attitude. The choice of hunger, a basic human need, functions to link the situation in Acts to the creation-fall narrative. Cornelius' wish to know God is stronger and more basic than hunger. This contrasts with the fall narrative, where appetite was the prominent feeling ruling over human minds.

In v. 33 the *time indicator 6*, νῦν, appears for the second time. This νῦν in 10:33 is often linked to νῦν in Acts 15:10.[210] Peter's ἀφ' ἡμερῶν ἀρχαίων in Acts 15:7 was designated as a reference to an event in the past. His time indicator, νῦν, in Acts 15:10 was attributed to the time of his speech at the Jerusalem Council. Thus, the contrast of ἀφ' ἡμερῶν ἀρχαίων and νῦν in Acts 15 was explained as Peter's reference to the experience in Caesarea made at the time of the Jerusalem Council.

However, the Cornelius' story, with help of double νῦν, *time indicators 2 and 5*, (in vv. 5 and 33), reveals that the event of Cornelius' conversion cannot be viewed as ἀφ' ἡμερῶν ἀρχαίων. For Luke, who writes the narrative, the *time indicators* work according to his theological purpose. For him both events (one in Caesarea and the other at the Jerusalem Council) denote the present "time of the realization" of God's

---

207. BDAG, ἀθέμιτος, 1.

208. Eating with the Gentiles was not prohibited in Torah and restricted by Jewish texts like *Jub.* 22:16. Schnabel, *Acts*, 496–97. See also texts of rabbinic law (*m. Avodah Zarah* 5:5; *m. Teharot* 7:6). Larkin, "Acts," 475.

209. Here, Peter "attributes his visit solely to his (interpretation of the) vision, omitting any reference to the direction of the Spirit." Pervo, *Acts*, 275. Thus, Peter himself shows that the vision was about ritual uncleanness of the Gentiles, not of animals. However, if the vision in any way may be related to food, it would presume the cancellation of solely ritual (temporal) uncleanness of food (meat or vegetables) without any relation to the issue of permanent uncleanness of animals. This assumption is made because Gentile uncleanness was viewed by Torah as reversible, what was presumed by the possibility of their conversion. Permanent uncleanness was not associated with humans.

210. See Johnson, *Acts*, 261. Also see Bruce, *Acts*, 335. However, this thesis argues that the phrase, "God made a choice among you that by my mouth the Gentiles should hear the word," can be attributed to the events of Acts 10. God in his foresight made this choice "from the very beginning," namely from the beginning described in Gen 1–3. Thus, Peter would imply that the events in Caesarea were intended by God not just since the beginning of the Gentile mission, but long ago, at the very beginning. The evidence for this implication is that the plan of God was known to prophets (15:15).

plan. Luke knows that the apostolic decision about Gentiles was stipulated by a clear revelation of God's will. God in his foresight knows things from eternity.

The events in Caesarea and in Jerusalem now are described as taking place in present time, denoted by νῦν (Acts 10:5, 33 and 15:10). At the Jerusalem Council, Peter uses both ἀφ' ἡμερῶν ἀρχαίων and νῦν, contrasting the invisible stage of God's plan, which happened sometime in the old days with the visible stage of realization of God's plan in the present. Also, Peter's emphasis on διὰ τοῦ στόματός, when he declares at the Jerusalem Council: "ἐξελέξατο ὁ θεὸς διὰ τοῦ στόματός μου ἀκοῦσαι τὰ ἔθνη τὸν λόγον τοῦ εὐαγγελίου" (Acts 15:7), corresponds with the wording of Acts 10:34 ἀνοίξας δὲ Πέτρος τὸ στόμα εἶπεν.[211]

Part 5 (10:34–43) presents Peter's sermon in Cornelius' household.[212] It contains abundant allusions to Acts 15. The phrase οὐκ ἔστιν προσωπολήμπτης ὁ θεός is repeated in Acts 15:8, 9 when God is called ὁ καρδιογνώστης θεός and when God does not discriminate among people (οὐθὲν διέκρινεν μεταξὺ ἡμῶν τε καὶ αὐτῶν). The following phrase in v. 35, ἀλλ' ἐν παντὶ ἔθνει puts stress on παντί.[213] Thus παντί correlates with πάντα in v. 43 and brings Peter's sermon to a logical conclusion ἄφεσιν ἁμαρτιῶν λαβεῖν διὰ τοῦ ὀνόματος αὐτοῦ (Jesus) πάντα τὸν πιστεύοντα εἰς αὐτόν. This thought is repeated in Acts 15:11: ἀλλὰ διὰ τῆς χάριτος τοῦ κυρίου Ἰησοῦ πιστεύομεν σωθῆναι, καθ' ὃν τρόπον κἀκεῖνοι.

The similarities between chapter 10 and 15 show that Peter did not come to this idea later, at the Jerusalem Council. Instead, he has already articulated it in Cornelius' home, so his speech on the council does not express a different understanding. This allows a reader to view two events as one present realization of God's plan, marked by the time indicator νῦν. Moreover, Peter's opinion against placing a "yoke" (ἐπιθεῖναι ζυγὸν) on the Gentile converts has to be viewed in terms of chapter 10, namely in relation to the issue of the Jewish ritual system, which caused the Jews to discriminate against the Gentiles as κοινόν. The symbolic vision revealed to Peter that since Jesus' death fulfilled the ritual law. That is why believers are cleansed by faith in Jesus (τῇ πίστει καθαρίσας τὰς καρδίας αὐτῶν) in Acts 15:9.

Peter's comment in Acts 15:10 that Israel could not carry this "yoke" (ὃν οὔτε οἱ πατέρες ἡμῶν οὔτε ἡμεῖς ἰσχύσαμεν βαστάσαι) can relate only to the ritual law. First, because the image of the yoke would illustrate a constant carrying of some duties.

---

211. There is a connection between Acts 10:1–2, 24, 28–29, 45; 11:3 and Acts 15:7. Schnabel, *Acts*, 633. This connection presumes that Peter at the Jerusalem Council referred to the experience of conversion at Cornelius' home. Thus, the phrase ἀφ' ἡμερῶν ἀρχαίων ὁ θεὸς ἐν ἡμῖν ἐξελέξατο, διὰ τοῦ στόματός μου (Act 15:7) shows that Peter assumes that God has chosen him to be the first preacher to the Gentiles, though God had made this choice from the beginning of the world (ἀφ' ἡμερῶν ἀρχαίων).

212. Pervo characterizes this sermon as "a brief and symmetrical speech of a catechetical rather than missionary type... The content is that of the creed." Pervo, *Acts*, 276.

213. Here παντὶ in v. 35 correlates to πάντων κύριος in v. 36. The latter expression means, "God's fulfillment of his promice of salvation for all people through Jesus." Schnabel, *Acts*, 500.

Also, the double address to οἱ πατέρες ἡμῶν and ἡμεῖς according to the use of personal pronouns can relate only to Israelites. The moral law would not be viewed in terms of a "yoke" here.[214] The issue treated by Peter relates only to Israelites, while the moral law is universal for all creation. The formal keeping of purification rites, accompanied by spiritual uncleanness, was treated many times in the narratives of Luke's Gospel and shown to be rejected by God, when "the veil of the temple was torn in two" (Luke 23:45). Now it is evident that his view of the ritual law as a "yoke" in Acts 15 was prepared by the narratives of the third Gospel and by Cornelius' story in Acts 10, which revealed the equality of all people in terms of salvation.

The lines on the diagram of Part 5 link v. 36 to v. 42 and v. 35 to v. 43, denoting the role of faith in Christ in the salvific plan of God.[215] In v. 38, λόγος is connected to Ἰησοῦν τὸν ἀπὸ Ναζαρέθ. The role of Israel was defined as τὸν λόγον [ὃν] ἀπέστειλεν τοῖς υἱοῖς Ἰσραὴλ. By keeping the ritual law and practicing the temple cult, Israel demonstrated God's salvific plan, which found its fulfillment in Jesus. Although salvation in Christ was preached to all nations (εὐαγγελιζόμενος εἰρήνην διὰ Ἰησοῦ Χριστοῦ — οὗτός ἐστιν πάντων κύριος), Jews were the first to whom the Gospel was preached (ὑμεῖς οἴδατε, τὸ γενόμενον ῥῆμα καθ᾽ ὅλης τῆς Ἰουδαίας).[216]

From this time Peter clarifies that though all Israel had chance to listen ῥῆμα καθ᾽ ὅλης τῆς Ἰουδαίας, ἀρξάμενος ἀπὸ τῆς Γαλιλαίας, the cross divided people into those who believe and those who do not. According to Peter in v. 39, after the cross, the mission of proclamation of salvation was shifted from the whole Israelite nation to the witnesses to the Christ event (ἡμεῖς μάρτυρες). These people are now sent by God to witness to Jesus' life (ὧν ἐποίησεν ἔν τε τῇ χώρᾳ τῶν Ἰουδαίων καὶ Ἰερουσαλήμ) and death (ὃν καὶ ἀνεῖλαν κρεμάσαντες ἐπὶ ξύλου).[217]

Peter views the sign of their election in that Jesus appeared visibly to them after the resurrection (ἔδωκεν αὐτὸν ἐμφανῆ γενέσθαι). He stresses, in v. 41, οὐ

---

214. Bruce notes that Peter uses this term here "in the sense of an intolerable weight." He states, "Jews rejoiced in the 'weight' of the law," and Peter likely presumed not the commandments of God, but the ritual part of the law, which was incapable of being kept by Gentiles. Bruce, *Acts*, 337.

215. The diagram is provided in Appendix 3.

216. Use of the word ῥῆμα in Acts 10:37 alludes to Luke 2:15, 17, where the angelophany to the shepherds was described. That angelophany to the Jewish people is linked to Acts 10:3-6 (angelophany to Cornelius) and shows that "the story is beginning anew." Pervo, *Acts*, 277. Luke has 9 occurrences of ῥῆμα (out of 19 in the NT) and only 2 instances of λόγος in 1:5–2:52; in Acts, out of 14 instances of ῥῆμα, 11 cluster in chs. 2, 5f., 10f., and 13. Though the use of ῥῆμα by Luke can be explained by the influence of the LXX, Christoph Burchard reveals that Luke "wrote it where he had a particular interest to bring out that genuine Judaism is ready for Christianity and that Christianity is the genuine fulfilment of OT religion." Burchard, "Note on Rhēma," 281–82, 295.

217. The phrase "hanging him on a cross" refers to God's curse on those who were executed by hanging on a tree (Deut 21:22-23). Luke puts this allusion on the lips of Peter in Acts 5:30 and in 10:39, while in Acts 13:28-29 Paul uses the same quotation. These cases in Acts emphasize the "redemptive nature of Christ's death" when he took people's curse on himself. Wilson, "'Upon a Tree,'" 47–48. The fact that God raised Christ from the dead proves him to be holy. Thus, apostles witnessed the fulfillment of prophecy and removal of a curse.

παντὶ τῷ λαῷ ἀλλὰ μάρτυσιν, "not to all, but to witnesses." These witnesses not only saw him after the resurrection but also συνεφάγομεν and συνεπίομεν αὐτῷ.[218] The apostle describes witnesses as people chosen by God "beforehand" (τοῖς προκεχειροτονημένοις, perfect participle passive of προχειροτονέω).[219] This phrase, τοῖς προκεχειροτονημένοις ὑπὸ τοῦ θεοῦ of Acts 10:41, later will be repeated by Peter as ἀφ' ἡμερῶν ἀρχαίων ὁ θεὸς ἐν ἡμῖν ἐξελέξατο at the Jerusalem Council (Acts 15:7). This supports the idea that the contrast between ἀφ' ἡμερῶν ἀρχαίων (the time of election in the past, in the foresight of God) and νῦν, the time of realization, which has to be understood to include proclamation (παρήγγειλεν ἡμῖν κηρύξαι τῷ λαῷ) and martyrdom (καὶ διαμαρτύρασθαι).

The phrase οὗτός ἐστιν . . . κριτὴς ζώντων καὶ νεκρῶν is significant here, because it reveals a new distinction between holy and common, which is taken in a spiritual sense. Those who remain unbelieving are judged as νεκρῶν and, thus, spiritually unclean. Those who believe are considered as ζώντων and cleansed (τῇ πίστει καθαρίσας τὰς καρδίας αὐτῶν in Acts 15:9) by the outpouring of the Holy Spirit (Acts 11:16). The distinction between life and death here echoes the issues in Gen 3:19, 22, and 24. Genesis pictures death predominantly as a physical process, while in Acts the matters are viewed from a spiritual perspective. Here, faith plays a key role in the transformation from death to life, as it might well have happened in Gen 3 if humans had relied on the word of God instead of the serpent's lies.

The concluding statement of Peter's sermon in v. 43 alludes to the message revealed in the testimony of the prophets (τούτῳ πάντες οἱ προφῆται μαρτυροῦσιν).[220] This phrase again forms a connection to the Jerusalem Council; not to the speech of Peter, but to James' speech (15:15–17), suggesting Peter and James' words are linked. The midrash in Acts 15:14–21, contains James' reference to Peter's speech, something like a summary of his words (v. 14). From this point of view, the midrash appears to be combined from both speeches.

The account of the Acts 10 contains Peter's reference to the prophets without citing them. His summary of the prophets puts emphasis on πάντα, confirming that all believers, Jewish and Gentile, are saved (ἄφεσιν ἁμαρτιῶν λαβεῖν . . . αὐτοῦ πάντα τὸν πιστεύοντα εἰς αὐτόν). This recalls Acts 15:11, where πάντα τὸν πιστεύοντα is clarified as πιστεύομεν σωθῆναι καθ' ὃν τρόπον κἀκεῖνοι. Moreover, both phrases (διὰ τῆς χάριτος τοῦ κυρίου Ἰησοῦ in 15:11) and (διὰ τοῦ ὀνόματος αὐτοῦ in 10:43) stress that Jesus now becomes the only way of salvation for both Jews and Gentiles.

---

218. This phrase emphasizes the physical nature of Jesus' resurrection, which was experienced by human senses. This kind of resurrection "establishes Jesus as universal lord and judge" for all humankind. Larkin, "Acts," 478.

219. BDAG, προχειροτονέω, "*to choose/appoint beforehand.*"

220. This could be either a general reference to the OT or to texts such as Isa 33:17–24; Jer 31:34; Joel 2:32. Schnabel, *Acts*, 504. See also Dan 9:24.

It confirms that the messianic role of Jesus was to fulfill the temple cult and the connected ritual law.

Part 6 (10:44–48) describes the miracle of speaking in tongues (λαλούντων γλώσσαις) by which the outpouring of the Holy Spirit was manifested.[221] Here, Luke uses the technique of speech interruption, which shows the outpouring of the Spirit in connection with the message of his sermon.[222] The event echoes Pentecost and represents a reversal of the Tower of Babel curse. Thus, the miracles in Luke-Acts, one by one, remind the reader of the ideal condition of the world, close to the time of creation. Here, not the miracle itself, but the spiritual significance would reveal to a reader the reversal, a re-creation process, started in the hearts of new converts.

Several features indicate, here, the allusion to creation, as well as to the Tower of Babel.[223] The outpouring of the Holy Spirit took place when people listened to Peter's sermon (ἀκούοντας τὸν λόγον).[224] Here, τὸν λόγον (v. 44) replaces the usually employed ῥῆμα (vv. 22, 37 and 44) purposely to picture the creation narrative, where λόγος was God's agent.[225]

Here, Luke by use of ἐξέστησαν shows that the circumcised who had come with Peter "were amazed."[226] Their amazement can be explained by a common Jewish belief that the Gentiles are ritually unclean and should not be allowed to associate with holy things. To their amazement the Holy Spirit had chosen the uncircumcised believers to be the place of its dwelling. Moreover, the phrase ἐπέπεσεν τὸ πνεῦμα τὸ ἅγιον ἐπὶ πάντας would indicate that circumcised believers also received the Holy Spirit. It is also seen that they understood the tongues in which the uncircumcised converts were prophesying (ἤκουον γὰρ αὐτῶν λαλούντων γλώσσαις καὶ μεγαλυνόντων τὸν θεόν) in v. 46. This supports the idea that God created the one spiritual temple to include both groups.

Witnessing the outpouring of the Holy Spirit on the uncircumcised converts, Peter poses a question about the possibility of their inclusion in the church as they are.[227]

---

221. The "speaking of tongues" is a second Pentecost now for the Gentiles (cf. 2:1–4), which gives Peter a right to state, "the Gentiles should enjoy full fellowship in the Christian community with the Jews through baptism (10:44–48)." Scholz, "'Rise, Peter,'" 56.

222. Another opinion suggests that here the interruption of a speech was made in order to give a clear sign of the will of God to a reader. Smith, *Interrupted Speech*, 188.

223. Keener, *Acts*, 1:842–43 n. 559. He notices that the "confusion" of Peter's audience at Pentecost looks similar to those "confused" in Gen 11:9. The scattering of the nations at Babel is paralleled to Adam's revolt and expulsion from Eden in Gen 3:5, 22–23. Finally, Luke employed lexemes and images of Babel (and Eden background) to highlight the reversal, which took place at Pentecost in Acts 2.

224. This outpouring of the Holy Spirit is recalled by Peter in his speech in Acts 15:8.

225. Stated on pp. 156–157 of thesis.

226. BDAG, ἐξίστημι, 1, 2 b, "be in a state in which things seem to make little or no sense, *confuse, amaze, astound*."

227. Pouring out of the Holy Spirit on the people of God was predicted in Ezek 39:29, accomplishing the transformation of heart which enables them to keep God's commandments in Ezek 11:17–21; 36:25–27. Schnabel, *Acts*, 505.

He asks: Μήτι τὸ ὕδωρ δύναται κωλῦσαί τις τοῦ μὴ βαπτισθῆναι τούτους οἵτινες τὸ πνεῦμα τὸ ἅγιον ἔλαβον ὡς καὶ ἡμεῖς; "Can anyone forbid water, that these should not be baptized, which have received the Holy Spirit as well as we?" Here an interrogative particle μήτι in a question expects a negative answer. Thus, one can answer Peter's question "no, one cannot forbid them being baptized." For him this sign of spiritual cleansing is sufficient to authorize their baptism.[228] Uncircumcised converts now are to be accepted into the church on an equal footing with those who are circumcised.

Signs of God's Approval of the Gentile Mission (Acts 11)

This chapter repeats some of the account of the previous chapter. This repetition is a summary of the experience of conversions in Caesarea, which Peter employs for his apology to the Jerusalem congregation. Here, he explains why he violated the ritual law in Caesarea. By repeating the account of Acts 10 Luke creates the effect of a double tradition.[229] This places Acts 11:1–3 in the center of a double tradition, where Acts 10:1–48 provides the first account of the events in Caesarea and Acts 11:4–24 the second.

The central passage of a double tradition, Part 1' (Acts 11:1–3), reveals the main topic of both narratives: the ritual law. Luke shows this in three steps: 1) the issue was raised by οἱ ἐκ περιτομῆς toward ἄνδρας ἀκροβυστίαν ἔχοντας (vv. 2, 3); 2) the circumcised believers passed judgment (διεκρίνοντο πρὸς αὐτὸν) on Peter's mission to the Gentile converts; 3) the accusation was ὅτι εἰσῆλθες πρὸς ἄνδρας ἀκροβυστίαν ἔχοντας καὶ συνέφαγες αὐτοῖς that Peter entered and συνέφαγες "ate with." The word συνέφαγες shows by the prefix συν that the accusation was not against the kind of food that Peter ate, but against his table fellowship with uncircumcised men. Thus, Chris Miller states, "Reading the charge of 'eating with the uncircumcised', as if it meant 'Peter ate pork', is ill-advised and is a weak foundation for saying that the vision refers to food."[230] All these features relate to the issue of the ritual law and do not relate to any part of moral law or even dietary law.

Part 2' (Acts 11:4–11) repeats the account of Acts 10:11–16 (Part 2). The variant readings show attempts of copyists to clarify the meaning. The phrase ἐκ τοῦ οὐρανοῦ in v. 5 appears after καθιεμένην and creates a picture of a vessel lowered *from* heaven by the four corners. When in Acts 10:11 it was καθιέμενον ἐπὶ τῆς γῆς,

---

228. Keener, *Acts*, 2:1826.

229. Here, "the literary art of this one-and-a-half chapter narrative lays the strongest possible emphasis upon the Spirit's mind in the matter." The Lukan technique of narrative repetition creates a triple account of Cornelius' vision, double account of Peter's vision and double reference to the baptism of Gentile converts. Thus, the baptism becomes a fulfillment of will of the Holy Spirit. McIntosh, "'For It Seemed Good,'" 135–36.

230. Miller, "Did Peter's Vision," 316–17. He shows that the way in which Luke drives the reader to understand a vision reveals that Luke "wanted his readers to understand the visions clearly in terms of men" Moreover, "Luke went to 'great pains' to avoid references to food."

in Acts 11:5 the word δεδεμένον is omitted and καθιεμένην is linked to οὐρανοῦ, instead of γῆς (in the phrase καθιεμένην ἐκ τοῦ οὐρανοῦ). The punctuation makes the variant reading even more significant. The following diagram (Figure 21) shows two parallel phrases, which describe from where the vessel appeared and whom it approached. The phrase ἐκ τοῦ οὐρανοῦ (11:5) most likely relates to καταβαῖνον, and καὶ ἦλθεν relates to ἄχρι ἐμοῦ.

Figure 21: Acts 11:5

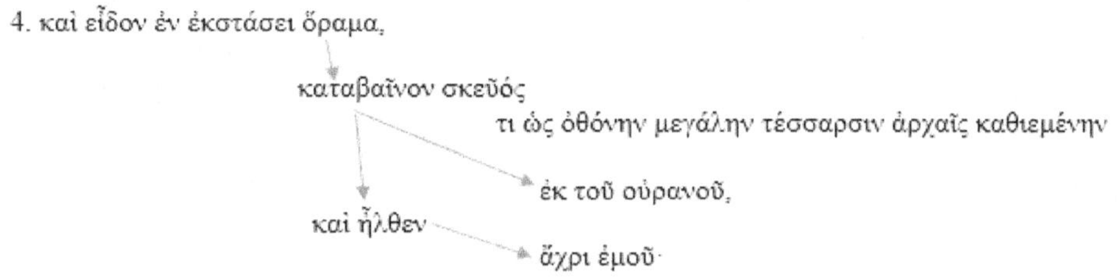

4. καὶ εἶδον ἐν ἐκστάσει ὅραμα,

    καταβαῖνον σκεῦός
              τι ὡς ὀθόνην μεγάλην τέσσαρσιν ἀρχαῖς καθιεμένην

              ἐκ τοῦ οὐρανοῦ,
    καὶ ἦλθεν
              ἄχρι ἐμοῦ·

Acts 11:10, 11 ties in closely τρίς (the number of pronouncements in the vision) to τρεῖς ἄνδρες who appeared at that time at Simon the tanner's gates.[231] Their arrival in Peter's apology is supported by the revelation given from the Holy Spirit. Three men sent by Cornelius are mentioned in Peter's speech exactly between the vision account and the words of the Holy Spirit. According to Luke's (or even Peter's) design, God's threefold pronouncement of cleansing was about humans.

God's order not to discriminate against people in Part 2' (11:4–11) is supported by the message of Part 3' (11:12–14), where in vv. 12, 13 Peter explains that he or his friends were not the first to enter the house of the Gentile (ἦλθον δὲ σὺν ἐμοὶ καὶ οἱ ἓξ ἀδελφοὶ οὗτοι). An angel entered before them (εἶδεν τὸν ἄγγελον ἐν τῷ οἴκῳ αὐτοῦ).[232] If the action was appropriate for a holy angel, why was it not for Peter?

One difficulty of Part 4' (11:15–17) is the *time indicators*. In v. 15 Peter refers to the day of Pentecost ὥσπερ καὶ ἐφ'ἡμᾶς ἐν ἀρχῇ ("at the beginning").[233] In the phrase ἐν δὲ τῷ ἄρξασθαί με λαλεῖν, he uses ἄρξασθαί (aorist infinitive of ἄρχω), which means "to initiate an action, process, or state of being, *begin*."[234] Peter states that Pentecost among the Gentiles took place when the sermon about Christ reached the listeners. It seems

---

231. It is not to be assumed that τρίς relates to the sheet with animals being three times lowing on the ground. The descending of the sheet was a single event, as is clear from the fact that the ascending sheet also was mentioned once. The word τρίς has to refer to three pronouncements in Peter's vision. Thus, three pronouncements of cleansing relate to tree men sent by Cornelius. So, it becomes clear that God cleanses humans, not animals.

232. Here, in Part 3' (11:12–14) Peter briefly repeats the account of both Part 3 (10:17–29) and Part 1 (10:1–6).

233. BDAG, ἀρχή, 1, ab, can also have meaning "*origin*."

234. BDAG, ἄρχω, 2.

that Peter, here, pictures two "beginnings': one for the Jews and one for the Gentiles.[235] Both events are to be assumed as new creations, evident in that both Pentecosts are linked to the word about Christ, signifying the reversal of the Tower of Babel curse and typologically linked to the beginning (ἀρχή), the time of creation.[236]

Peter understood the outpouring of the Holy Spirit as a sign of spiritual cleansing predicted by Christ (ἐμνήσθην δὲ τοῦ ῥήματος τοῦ κυρίου). He echoes the parallelism in Jesus' saying. The first line shows the baptism preached by John the Baptist (Ἰωάννης μὲν ἐβάπτισεν ὕδατι), while the second line completes it ὑμεῖς δὲ βαπτισθήσεσθε ἐν πνεύματι ἁγίῳ. Here, Peter shows that the spiritual point of baptism is a cleansing of the heart. While ritual cleansing and circumcision were physical signs of piety. Baptism, contrastingly, signified spiritual piety and faith in the Lordship of Jesus Christ.[237]

The baptism performed by Peter in Caesarea (v. 17) confirms the inner spiritual cleansing which has already taken place.[238] The cleansing of the Gentile converts and their equal acceptance by God is shown in Peter's comparison: τὴν ἴσην δωρεὰν ἔδωκεν αὐτοῖς . . . ὡς καὶ ἡμῖν. This comparison between αὐτοῖς and ἡμῖν also appears four times in Acts 15:8, 9, 10 and 11. The equality between αὐτοῖς and ἡμῖν (the Jewish and the Gentile converts) in Acts 11 and 15 is viewed only on a basis of a reversion to re-creation, which begins by faith in Jesus.

Part 5 (11:18) describes the Jerusalem Church in agreement with the will of God, concerning Gentile believers. Part 6 (11:19–21) pronounces God's favor of on those who preach the Gospel to Jews and Greeks without distinction. Part 7 (11:22–24) contains two important features: the choice of the missioner to Antioch, and the spiritual condition of the new converts in Antioch. The first feature reveals that, though there were some believers from the Pharisaic party, the members of the Jerusalem congregation did not choose them to work with Gentile converts. They elected Barnabas, a Levite (this presupposes knowledge of the Law) and at the same time ἀνὴρ ἀγαθὸς καὶ πλήρης πνεύματος ἁγίου καὶ πίστεως.[239]

---

235. Keener views here an allusion to the "prophetic empowerment of the seventy in Num 11:25." Keener, *Acts*, 2:1813. It is not said that the seventy had spoken in tongues, but only that God gave them the Spirit. The fact that they prophesied among Israelites reveals that the aim of the miracle was to renew Israelite faith by the power of the word of God. The miracle in Acts 10:44–48 also revealed the renewing power of the word.

236. Peter intentionaly uses λόγος in 10:36 (τὸν λόγον . . . εὐαγγελιζόμενος εἰρήνην διὰ Ἰησοῦ Χριστοῦ) and in 2:22 (ἀκούσατε τοὺς λόγους τούτους· Ἰησοῦν τὸν Ναζωραῖον . . .). Both events describe a spiritual conversion of listeners in response to the word about Christ, that establishes a "new" beginning.

237. Frank Matera notes that Peter's apology starts by describing the distinct differences between Jews and Gentiles and comes to the point which unites both parties in the church at the cross. According to Peter's sermon, "divine impartiality expresses itself through the Christ event. Universal salvation comes through the folly of the cross." Matera, "Acts 10:34–43," 65.

238. Since the Holy Spirit is "clean" in the strictest sense, his indwelling can be accepted as a proof of the inner cleansing of a believer. Evans, "Jesus and the Spirit," 33–36.

239. It was noted that Luke often pairs the Spirit and the gifts of the Spirit, such as "faith," "wisdom," and "power." Keener, *Acts*, 2:1845–46 n. 144. Thus, Barnabas can be understand as full of these

This choice shows that the Jerusalem Church from the beginning had no negativism toward the Antiochean congregation, but supported its spiritual growth in a most productive way (11:22, 23).[240] The condition of the new converts impressed Barnabas and he rejoiced (ἐχάρη) and began to encourage all believers (παρεκάλει πάντας). V. 23 pictures Barnabas' aim, παρεκάλει πάντας τῇ προθέσει τῇ καρδίας προσμένειν τῷ κυρίῳ.[241] The noun προθέσει "*setting forth, putting out, presentation*" echoes the presentation of the shewbread in the tabernacle.[242] In triple synoptic tradition (Matt 12:4, Mark 2:26, Luke 6:4), Jesus used this noun for "the loaves of presentation." Consequently, in Acts 11:23 the spiritual condition of the converts in the eyes of Barnabas was assumed to be as clean as the loaves of presentation before God. Luke's use of this term implies that Gentile converts are clean, holy and accepted by God. Moreover, their cleansing is achieved by faith in Jesus, without compliance with the temple cult.

The Dilemma: Believing Jew versus Believing Gentile

Chapters 10 and 11 prepare the reader for the decision made by Jerusalem Council (Acts 15) concerning the ritual law.[243] After chapter 15, the narratives reflect the application of the council decisions to practice. Here Luke's approach is ambivalent.[244] Despite the decision not to impose the ritual law on Gentile converts, Paul had Timothy circumcised (Acts 16:1–5) and Paul participated in purification rites (Acts 21:23–26). His custom was to preach first in synagogues (13:14; 17:10; 18:19; 19:8), and he made a private vow similar to the Nazarene vow (18:18).

---

qualities. Luke's phrase here shows the wisdom in accepting Gentile converts.

240. S. Jonathan Murphy emphasizes the role of Barnabas as a teacher of the Law, pointing to the fact that he spent a year teaching numerous people in Antioch. He also notes that this teacher had a combination of unique traits of character, as he was encourager, comforter, and Spirit-filled leader. Murphy, "Role of Barnabas," 326–27.

241. Martin Hengel states that Haenchen is in error when he pictures Barnabas as one of the "Hellenists." He explains that Barnabas was "one of the core community in Jerusalem directed by the 'Twelve' (Acts 4.36; 9.27), i.e. was one of the 'Hebrews.'" Hengel, *Acts and the History*, 101.

242. BDAG, πρόθεσις, 1. This noun also can be translated as "*purpose, resolve will*" and appears in Acts 27:13 and a number of Pauline letters (Rom 8:28; 9:11; Eph 1:11; 3:11; 2 Tim 1:9; 3:10). The meaning "resolute heart" describes the degree of deliberation of their decision.

243. Luke prepares the reader for the resolution of the Jerusalem Council. He shows receptive Gentiles on the Day of Pentecost (2:5–12), the Ethiopian eunuch (8:26–40), Paul's ministry to the Gentiles (9:15) and the detailed Cornelius story (10:1—11:18). Luke describes Paul's missionary tour and the Gentiles receiving the Gospel (13:1—14:28), which is followed by the statement "now we turn to the Gentiles" (13:46). In Acts 15 there are seven positive references to the Gentiles (Acts 15:3, 7, 12, 14, 17, 19, 23). Story, "Luke's Instructive Dynamics," 102. In all these cases the issue of the ritual law is involved implicitly.

244. Marguerat argues: "From a soteriological standpoint, the Christological event puts an end to the Law." However, he continues, "because the function of defining the people of God . . . remains attached to the Law, Luke, no more than Paul assumes the right to annul it. The law, therefore, continues to leave its imprint on Paul's actions (circumcision: 6.13; purification right: 21.20-6), certifying his irrevocable Jewishness." Marguerat, *First Christian Historian*, 61–62.

At the same time he communicated with Gentiles, entered the homes of Gentile converts (Acts 16:14-15), and ate with them (16:34; 27:33-35; 28:7). Paul not only regularly preached to Gentiles (Acts 16:14, 15, 27-34; 17:4, 12, 22-34; 18:4; 19:10; 20:20-21; 21:19; 21:29; 28:7-9, 30-31), but also refused to preach to unbelieving Jews (Acts 18:6; 22:17-21; 26:20-22; 28:26-30). Luke also reported a special instance of preaching God's creation according to Torah at the Areopagus. References of Paul communicating with Gentiles prevail.[245] In those cases, as the background to Paul's actions, Luke tries to emphasize God's leading role in making decisions.

These facts reveal that Paul had changed his attitude toward the ritual law and the Gentiles, although he honoured the patterns of ritual law for the sake of preaching the Gospel among Jews.[246] Providing evidences of Paul's ambiguous behavior, Luke pictures him acting cautiously in order not to become a provocateur of enmity between Jews and Christians. In those cases one can see Paul's flexibility, especially in cases of the ritual law, which took second place to the preaching of Christ.[247] This can be assumed from the fact that in Acts 16, following the decision of the Jerusalem Council, Luke notes that Paul circumcised Timothy. The diagram of this passage reveals that the reason for his decision had nothing in common with the Jewish party of the Jerusalem congregation.[248] The purpose clause of v. 3 denotes that Paul did so because of the Jews living in those places διὰ τοὺς Ἰουδαίους τοὺς ὄντας ἐν τοῖς τόποις ἐκείνοις, namely in Derbe and Lystra (v. 1).

Its purpose was either in order to keep Timothy safe from their jealousy, or to reach them by compliance with the law. The Jews of whom Luke writes here were not believing Jews. The context of Acts 14:6-22 shows that the Jews of Lystra and Derbe could be influenced by the suspicious attitude of the Jews of Antioch and Iconium, regarding Paul's mission.[249] Jews from Antioch and Iconium persuaded the people of Lystra and Derbe, and all their multitude, to stone Paul.

Though the word "multitude" likely refers to a mixed crowd (predominantly Gentile), Luke stresses that jealous Jews were the originators of the plot.[250] This can be also assumed from the fact that they had chosen capital punishment by stoning, which is one characteristic of Judaism. Moreover, the Gentiles of those places seem to

---

245. Concerning Paul's private vow in Acts 18:18, Bruce notes that while it is grammatically possible that Aquila's head was shorn, "the natural emphasis marks Paul as the subject here." Bruce, *Acts*, 397-98.

246. J. M. Heath believes that "Paul owed much to Jewish patterns of looking, albeit he focuses on new sights, interpreted through Christ." Heath, *Paul's Visual Piety*, 256.

247. Johnson notes the ambiguity of Paul's actions in Acts 16:1-4. He shows that the sentence structure points to a reason for Paul's action, which is to assure acceptability among the Jews. Johnson, *Acts*, 284 n. 3, 287.

248. The diagram is provided in Appendix 3 section 2.2.

249. The fact that the Jews from Antioch managed to get a hearing in Lystra presumes the existence of a Jewish community in the city. Schnabel, *Acts*, 612.

250. Johnson, *Acts*, 253 n. 19. According to him, Luke had in mind to minimize the rejection of the Gospel by the Gentiles, and to show that the opposition was raised by "a small band of fanatics."

be tolerant of the fact that Paul and Barnabas could be gods or their prophets. Only the Jews could become jealous about such matters as teaching about the risen Christ. Consequently, remembering what had happened with him in those places in the past, Paul wished to keep Timothy from the same danger.

While Timothy was Jewish through his mother, Paul decided to confirm Timothy's Jewish identity rather than that of Gentile.[251] A Gentile, preaching Jesus from Torah, would generate a negative resonance among the Jews toward Jesus.[252] The enmity toward Jesus would become even worse if Jews learned that Paul had made a descendant of Abraham into an "apostate." The flexibility of Paul in this case seems to reflect his wisdom: care for his friend and helper on one hand, and benefit of preaching the Gospel on the other.

Rethinking the Role of Priestly and Levitical Ministry

This section reviews the role of the ritual law in relation to priestly and levitical ministry in Luke-Acts. The main feasts of Passover and Pentecost (the Feast of Tabernacles), through Luke's two-volume work, lose their cultic orientation while assuming a spiritual significance for believers. The role of the levitical ministry after Jesus' death and resurrection focuses on preaching the word and making disciples. Also, the spiritual aspect of teaching becomes more prominent. The cleansing role of faith and the Holy Spirit's presence within converts becomes the first step of the reversal from the fall to re-creation.

Though Luke starts his Gospel by mentioning the righteous priest Zachariah, he reveals the priest's lack of faith (1:20) in contrast to ordinary people like Mary, Anna, and Simeon. Furthermore, at the beginning of the Gospel proclamation, Jesus sends lepers to a priest to witness the cleansing (5:12–14 and 17:11–19). However, by the Gospel's end Luke shows Jesus cleansing the temple (Luke 19:45, 46) and the priests plotting against Jesus (19:47; 20:19; 22:2), paying for his betrayal (Luke 22:3–5), accusing him vehemently before the Gentiles (Luke 23:10) and unjustly demanding

---

251. Shaye Cohen notes that according to rabbinical teaching, "a Jewish woman bears Jewish children, a Gentile woman bears Gentile children." *Mishna* declares the child of a Jewish mother and a Gentile father to be a *mamzēr* (*m. Yebam.* 7:5). "This ruling was disputed in the *Tosepta* and the *Talmudim*, since many rabbis felt that such offspring were Jews of blemished ancestry (and permitted to marry all Jews, except priests), not *mamzērîm*. This view ultimately prevailed. All rabbinic authorities, however, seem to agree that the child of a Jewish woman by a Gentile man was a Jew." Cohen, "Was Timothy Jewish," 265.

252. Craig S. Keener states that the Jews of that period had no universal standards concerning the offspring of intermarriages. He believes that "Timothy could hardly be accepted as properly Jewish without being circumcised first." Keener, "Interethnic Marriages," 38.

THE FOUR PROHIBITIONS OF ACTS 15

capital punishment (Luke 23:23).²⁵³ The scene ends with the tearing of the veil in the temple (Luke 23:45) at the time of Jesus' death.²⁵⁴

In Acts, priests are pictured persecuting the apostles (Acts 4:1–3), using plots and threats (4:15–21), being filled with jealousy (5:17–18), beating of the apostles and prohibiting the preaching of the Gospel (5:40). Moreover, Luke describes the priests variously: "being cut to the heart," but also "gnashing their teeth," "crying out with a loud voice," "covering their ears" and rushing to stone Stephen to death (7:54–58).²⁵⁵ The image of priests ruled by demonic forces dramatically increases in Acts. Acts 23:1–3 represents the hypocrisy of the priests on the Sanhedrin. The epithet τοῖχε κεκονιαμένε (meaning, "a white washed wall"), which Paul applied to the high priest, echoes Jesus' statement of τάφοις κεκονιαμένοις in Matt 23:27, revealing their hypocrisy. In Luke 11:44 the phrase is recorded as τὰ μνημεῖα τὰ ἄδηλα, which obviously evokes a sense of the danger of hidden spiritual uncleanness. The lies and plots of priests (23:12–15; 25:2, 3) are disproved and thwarted at the end of Acts (25:18–19, 25–27).

The narrative of Acts mentions only one positive example of a Levite, Barnabas. His faith in Jesus makes him different from the priestly elite. While the priests are described as ἐπλήσθησαν ζήλου (Acts 5:17), Barnabas is pictured as πλήρης πνεύματος ἁγίου καὶ πίστεως (Acts 11:24). When Barnabas first appears in Acts (4:36, 37) he is called by the apostles υἱὸς παρακλήσεως.²⁵⁶ It is said that Barnabas was a Levite (Λευΐτης, Κύπριος τῷ γένει) and belonged to privileged and rich group of society (ὑπάρχοντος αὐτῷ ἀγροῦ).²⁵⁷

However, he seemed to disregard the privileges of his levitical ministry when he became a believer. The act of having sold his land for the sake of poor members in the church (πωλήσας ἤνεγκεν τὸ χρῆμα) shows him accepting the church as his new family and new ministry (4:36–37).²⁵⁸ For him the ministry of preaching Christ

---

253. In the Markan account the plot to kill Jesus is provoked by his action of cleansing of the temple. In the Lukan account Jesus' teaching provoke the Pharisees to kill him. Stein, *Luke*, 483. It seems that for Luke Jesus' teaching works as a cleansing power.

254. Here the passive voice of ἐσχίσθη "was split" suggests that the action was of the divine nature. This was the second curtain which separated the holy place of the temple from the most holy place. Garland, *Luke*, 928. This events was assumed as the end of the ritual system of the old covenant. Stein, *Luke*, 595–96.

255. The phrase "grinding the teeth" relates in Luke 13:28 to those excluded from the kingdom. Johnson, *Acts*, 139 n. 54. This suggests that they are filled with demonic power rebelling against God.

256. The name given by apostles may emphasize the fact that he was filled with the Holy Spirit (ὁ παράκλητος in John 15:26). The characteristic given by Luke to Barnabas recalls the one given to Simeon in Luke 2:25, whose wish for consolation (προσδεχόμενος παράκλησιν τοῦ Ἰσραήλ) was connected to the presence of the Holy Spirit (καὶ πνεῦμα ἦν ἅγιον ἐπ' αὐτόν). Barnabas' name "fits the emphasis on the Holy Spirit." Schnabel, *Acts*, 273.

257. According to Num 18:20, 24 and Deut 10:9 priests and Levites could not own any land. However in Josephus, *Life* 68–83 and Jer 32:6–15 they held property. Bruce, *Acts*, 160.

258. It was noted that the phrase, "at the feet," was repeated three times (4:37; 5:2, 10). Barnabas receives a new name from the apostles and lays possessions at their feet. These actions were assumed

replaces his earlier involvement in the temple cult. The phrase, καὶ ἔθηκεν παρὰ τοὺς πόδας τῶν ἀποστόλων, emphasizes the readiness of Barnabas to accept that apostolic authority replaces the authority of a chief-priest. It seems that he understands and accepts the changes to the ritual system. He believed that the ritual law was fulfilled in the mission of Christ and he viewed all believers as priests.

Chapter Summary

The main goal of this chapter was to investigate the role of the ritual law in the creation–fall–re-creation framework of Luke. The results of this investigation can be summarized in the following statements:

1. The theme of the ritual law is crucial for the Lukan writings, together with the theme of Jesus' messiahship. The evangelist brings the reader to a recognition of Jesus' role through the pattern of the ritual law.

2. Luke widely discusses purification rites and temporary uncleanness connected to leprosy, dead bodies, flow of blood, and demon possession. He shows that all these types of uncleanness were healed and cleansed by Christ. Luke also shows that Christ is the only true fulfillment of the temple cult and its ritual law. This allows him to place the decision of the Jerusalem Council in its correct setting by not imposing the Mosaic law upon the Gentile converts. This is authorized by Jesus' messiahship.

3. Only a few passages in the Gospel of Luke treat the issue of Gentiles, whereas in Acts, after Jesus' death and resurrection, they become prominent. This fact emphasizes that Jesus supersedes the temple cult as the source of true cleansing. According to Luke, faith in Jesus cleanses the Gentile converts and makes them and Jewish believers equally acceptable to God. For this reason observing the Jewish ritual law and initiation into the temple cult become unnecessary for Gentile salvation.

4. Luke shows that many kinds of uncleanness relate to areas of life that are affected by evil spirits. He presents demon possession as a reversible kind of uncleanness, though the demons themselves are permanently unclean. The removal of the evil spirit has to be included in the process of spiritual cleansing. Luke pictures demons as associated with permanently unclean creatures. Demon possession is manifested in human behavior as an unnatural human inclination to uncleanness and lawlessness, namely, the violation of natural law.

---

as the double submission of Barnabas to the apostles that made him a model believer. Johnson, *Acts*, 87 n. 35. The two other occurances of the phrase show the curse of double-standard worship. Barnabas was a prophet, a teacher (13:1) and an apostle (1 Cor 9:6) Schnabel, *Acts*, 273. This fact reveals blessings of a full commitment to true worship.

5. The hardening of one's heart to the Gospel would lead a person to the condition of permanent uncleanness. That is the reason for the four prohibitions of the Decree dealing with matters based on natural law, thus establishing a necessary pattern for Gentile converts, leading them from previous idolatry to true worship.

6. Luke rethinks the meaning of the Jewish feasts and the levitical service. He proposes a fresh spiritual meaning for Passover, Pentecost and the priesthood of all believers. The ritual cleansing which depended heavily on the service of priests and Levites in the temple was replaced by the inner cleansing of a heart in response to faith and signified by the presence of the Holy Spirit.

7. The lack of discussion about the dietary laws in Luke-Acts suggests that Luke did not plan to inform the reader about any changes concerning these laws. The cases where Luke did raise the issue of food assume the ritual uncleanness of food, after its association with unclean matter. Luke shows that food has to be viewed as standing free from the demands of the ritual law. Thus, Luke views the dietary laws separately from the ritual law. For him, dietary laws are rooted in natural law known since the creation-fall narrative. Rejecting the ritual demands, he leaves food only under the control of dietary laws rooted in natural law, and not under the ritual law of Torah.

8. Finally, though the role of the ritual law is fulfilled in Christ, natural law is fitted into the creation–fall–re-creation paradigm and is valid until the time of the parousia. Its appointed role, in light of the creation–fall–re-creation paradigm, is to achieve the reversal from the unclean condition to clean, and from the fallen condition to that which was established at creation. The fulfillment of the ritual law in Jesus' messiahship allows one to experience this reversal on a spiritual level from the moment of conversion, while keeping natural law testifies to the believers' hope for the future reversal of their physical nature at the time of eschatological re-creation.

5

Summary and Conclusion

Achieving the Main Goals of the Study

THE PURPOSE OF THE present research has been to show that the four prohibitions of Acts 15 are based on the patterns of true worship established on the principles of the natural law of God in Gen 1–3. The necessity of the study was due to the unsolved theological issues raised by the decision of the Jerusalem Council in Acts 15. Those issues emerged as scholars tried to determine: 1) the kinds of laws which were under investigation by the apostles and elders during the Council; 2) the rationale according to which some laws were understood as no longer relevant; 3) the need to form the list of prohibitions; 4) the relevance of these prohibitions for early church practice after the cross; 5) the temporal limitations of the prohibitions.

In the present study, the four prohibitions of the Decree were viewed through the lens of a creation–fall–re-creation paradigm, the patterns of the natural law of God reflected in Gen 1–3 account, and the worship motifs of the New and the Old Testaments. Semantic diagrams supported the inductive derivation of information from the passages. The subdivision of the passages into units, nuclei of information, and their narrative links were made with the help of form criticism. Diagraming of the passages revealed the midrashic structure, contrasts, comparisons, complex-quotations, and other structural units.

Intertextuality, employed to discover the echoes and allusions of the large biblical context behind the four prohibitions revealed that the concepts forming the content of the Decree were rooted in Gen 1–3. Reconstruction of the historical context on the basis of data from the known Jewish sources was made in order to view the task through the eyes of Jewish Christianity contemporary to Luke.

The present study was organized around four goals. The first was to describe the history of interpretation of the Apostolic Decree, to find its original form, and to classify known views on the content of the Decree according to the rationale they propose. The second goal was to find the literary, linguistic and historical contexts of the Decree and the grammatical and semantic structures of all three Lukan accounts of the Decree in Acts 15:1–21; 15:22–35 and 21:17–26 by means of an exegetical study of these passages. The third goal was to describe the basic theological concepts developed on the basis of Genesis 1:24–3:24 and show their connections to the four prohibitions of the Decree. The fourth goal was to reveal and differentiate between the roles of ritual and natural law in the creation–fall–re-creation framework of Luke, as developed throughout his two-volume work.

The present research was based on inductive logic, where the semantic diagrams of the biblical passages were developed to make more accessible the fundamental ideas of the texts. This approach allowed the researcher to interpret the texts according to the inner logic reflected in their structures, and by their historical, linguistic and literary contexts. The four main goals of the study formed four steps which helped to identify these fundamental ideas, organize them systematically, and interpret the Apostolic Decree on the basis of Gen 1–3.

The First Goal: Describe the History of the Interpretation of the Apostolic Decree

The study first focused on the variant readings and different manuscript traditions of the Lukan accounts of the Decree. Their history of interpretation was outlined and their original form determined. At that point the following conclusions were reached:

1. The fourfold tradition of the Alexandrian (ambivalent) reading of the Apostolic Decree preserved by $\mathfrak{P}$74, ℵ 01, A 02, B 03, E 06, L and Ψ should be accepted as original.

2. The threefold Western (ethical) form of the Decree preserved by D 05 represents the fourth-century alteration of its text, which reveals an attempt to introduce an ethical interpretation of its provisions, the result of anti-Jewish polemic in the church between the first and fourth centuries CE.

3. The cultic form of the Decree preserved by $\mathfrak{P}$45 is a variation of the threefold tradition not influenced by the ethical interpretation. It reveals a tendency to interpret the Decree in association with Jewish cultic law.

The next step focused on the variant readings of the Decree and its interpretation preserved in the writings of the church fathers. That data revealed four stages of interpretation of the Decree's content, which led to the alteration of its text. Findings can be summarized in the following points:

1. The alteration of the text into the form found in D 05 was the result of a process that covered the following four periods: theological transition, theological pre-shift, theological shift and the period of variant readings.

2. This alteration of the text was caused by the theological shift from Jewishness to Orthodoxy taking place in mainstream Christianity during the third and fourth centuries CE.

3. The dominance of the Western text of Acts 15 was a result of anti-Jewish policy because of increasing Orthodoxy in the church.
4. The theological shift influenced the transmission of the text of Acts 15 during the process of copying.
5. The mediaeval period of interpretation of the text of the Apostolic Decree reflects the dominance of its ethical form, from among the alterations made during its transmission in the previous centuries.
6. The writings of the Reformers and the period of the critical study of Acts deal with the same alterations.
7. The investigation of D 05, as part of the critical study of Acts, revealed that its sources cannot be identified, and their trustworthiness cannot be attested.

The shift from the Alexandrian ambivalent reading of the Decree to the Western reading, which assumes its ethical interpretation, reveals the long process of theological shift under the influence of anti-Jewish polemic. The theological shift reinforced the tendency to interpret the prohibitions of the Decree in an ethical way.

The next stage of the study examined the two main interpretations of the content of the Decree: 1) the ethical explanation and; 2) the cultic explanation. The cultic explanation was the later interpretation to emerge. It resulted from a search for the original form of the Decree and drove the attention of scholars away from its ethical form to its Jewish roots. This search for the possible Jewish background of the Decree led to three options: linking the Decree a) to the Sinaitic laws of Leviticus 17–18; b) to the halakhic rules; and c) to the Noachic laws of Gen 9. Interpreters turned from the Sinaitic laws to the pre-Sinaitic forms of the covenant, and even to the Noachic laws. The flood narrative was then assumed to be the prohibition of blood consumption. Each new search attempted to relate the content of the Decree to the earliest possible background. The most recent stage of the search explored the Genesis creation-fall account.

None of these previously-suggested backgrounds provides an adequate foundation for all four prohibited matters of the Decree. The earliest prohibition of blood consumption is Gen 9:1–4, while the earliest explicit prohibition of fornication is Lev 17–18. Implicit prohibition of things polluted by idols is first mentioned in Num 25:1–3. No prohibition of things "strangled" is found anywhere in the OT. Thus, attempts to link all four prohibitions of the Decree to one common OT background have not been successful.

The present study locates the background concepts of the Decree in the creation-fall account of Gen 1–3. This became possible because of two recently developed theological concepts that provide significant premises for this study. They are the concept of "natural law," and a creation–fall–re-creation paradigm.

The first concept, "natural law," was slightly modified in light of Gen 1–3, and understood as the "natural law of God," which differs from the "natural law of nations."

The "natural law of God" provides the necessary background concepts for all four prohibitions of the Decree. These underlying concepts can be stated by three pairs of opposites: true worship versus idolatry; life versus death; undefiled marriage versus pagan cultic fornication.

The role of the creation–fall–re-creation paradigm is to show the reversal of the fall of Gen 3 and the temporal nature of the four prohibitions. Additional to this paradigm, worship motifs have been employed. Thus, this study has argued that the Genesis creation-fall account provides a common basis for the four prohibitions of the Alexandrian (ambivalent) form of the Apostolic Decree. This common basis is the irreconcilability between true and false worship. Imposing the four provisions of the Decree on Gentile converts marks their turning from false worship to true worship, as contained in the creation–fall–re-creation paradigm.

The Second Goal: Detailed Exegesis of Luke's Accounts of the Apostolic Decree

This study's second goal was to explore the literary, linguistic and historical contexts of the Decree and the grammatical and semantic structures of all three Luke's accounts of the Decree (Acts 15:1–21; 15:22–35 and 21:17–26) and the exegetical study of these passages. The exegesis revealed that the apostolic decision can be structured around two points: the Jewish ritual law was found to be unnecessary for salvation, while the Council rightly understood faith in Christ as the only instrument of salvation. The four prohibitions of the Decree were denoted as necessary for converts to observe, yet they seemed to be listed with no explanation of the reason having to be observed.

The present study argued that the reason for imposing the four prohibitions on Gentile converts was provided by the apostles, and was expressed by the Jewish interpretive method of pesher-midrash, which is employed in the first account of the Decree, Acts 15:14-21. The pesher-midrash formula was employed by James in order to give a firm Torah foundation to his proposal of the Decree. Thus, the literary form of the Decree in Acts 15 reflects the defense of the apostolic decision on the basis of the Torah, instead of reducing or totally cancelling those laws, with the exception of the four specific matters, as was believed by earlier scholars.

The present study concluded that the debate began with the issue of the validity of the ritual law for salvation. During the Jerusalem Council all laws were revised and differentiated into those belonging to the ritual law and the temple cult, and those rooted in the natural law of God in the creation-fall account. As a result, the ritual law was viewed as fulfilled in Christ and no longer necessary. True worship was established on faith in Christ and expressed with the help of midrash formed on the basis of Gen 1–3, in which the motifs of true worship were linked to the natural law of God. The reversal element of pesher-midrash served to express the possibility of reversing the fallen condition by re-creation.

The account of Gen 1–3 fits the controversies between true worship versus idolatry, between life and death, and between undefiled marriage versus pagan cultic fornication into the creation–fall–re-creation paradigm. As a result, practicing true worship established on faith in Christ (signifying a rejection of idolatry in all its forms, food sacrificed to idols, and defiled marriages with a prohibited degree of relationship), supported the reversal from the fallen condition to the re-creation initiated by God in the hearts of Gentile converts. Keeping the four prohibitions also supported converts turning from paganism to God on the practical level, with the understanding that it was the proper response of believers to the new creation, originated by God in their heart.

The present study also investigated the form of the Decree in Acts 21 and concluded that it represents an accomodation to the Jewish culture of the view that salvation is independent of the Jewish ritual law, which the church developed during the Council. This accommodation was made by returning to the previous pattern of the Mosaic ritual law in order to make the Gospel appropriate for Jewish converts in Acts 21. Though the law of Moses was no longer viewed by the church as an instrument of salvation, it provided the rites of purification necessary for entering the temple, which the majority of the Jews understood to be a holy place. This shift back to the old pattern was understood as a temporary cultural accomodation.

The midrashic structure of Acts 15:14–21, with the proposal of the Decree in vv. 19–20, is understood as the explanation formed prior to the enacting of the Decree itself. The midrashic element there, based on the creation account, revealed that the Decree's four prohibitions should be viewed as rooted in the natural law of God. This explains the cancellation of the ritual law and affirmation that the natural law of God is to be practiced by believers. The reversal element of midrash fitted the apostolic decision into the creation–fall–re-creation paradigm; expressing the reversal from false to true worship, from the fallen condition to the re-creation, and from death to life, which is initiated by God in Christ. The four prohibitions were necessary, not for salvation but for a full conversion to God, since they call for conversion from pagan worship to true worship established on Gen 1–3. The return to the old pattern in Acts 21 was understood as temporary and culturally limited.

The Third Goal: Describe the Basic Theological Concepts Rooted in Genesis 1–3 Account

The third goal of the present study was to describe basic theological concepts developed on the basis of Genesis 1–3 and show their connections to the four prohibitions of the Decree. For this purpose the diagrams of the Gen 1:24–3:24 LXX were prepared in order to help find linguistic associations, possible allusions and echoes. The diagrams highlight ten echoes of Gen 1–3 in Acts 15:

1) Consumption of the forbidden fruit (the first εἰδωλοθύτων) in Gen 3:1–7 corresponds to the prohibition of εἰδωλοθύτων in Acts 15:20; 2) God's deliberate action to save fallen humanity (ἐκάλεσεν κύριος ὁ θεὸς τὸν Αδαμ) in Gen 3:8, 9 explains Peter's words in Acts 15:7 ἀφ' ἡμερῶν ἀρχαίων ἐν ὑμῖν ἐξελέξατο ὁ θεός; 3) the phrase ἡμερῶν ἀρχαίων in Acts 15:7 is the time indicator of God's action of reconciliation undertaken in the Genesis creation-fall narrative; 4) In Gen 1 the word of God was an instrument of creation, which corresponds to Peter's λόγον τοῦ εὐαγγελίου in Acts 15:7 appointed to reach the nations and to signify the time of a new beginning; 5) Peter's concluding statement ἀλλὰ διὰ τῆς χάριτος τοῦ κυρίου Ἰησοῦ πιστεύομεν σωθῆναι in Acts 15:11 echoes units 7–9 of Gen 3, where the confession of consequences of redemption from the first sin was described; 6) The core of James' speech (καθὼς πρῶτον ὁ θεὸς ἐπεσκέψατο) in Acts 15:14 expresses that the first step toward reconciliation is always taken by God, which corresponds to Gen 3. 7) The leading role of God in salvation also is stressed in James' words in Acts 15:17, 18 (λέγει κύριος ποιῶν ταῦτα γνωστὰ ἀπ' αἰῶνος); 8) The phrase ἐγὼ ἐντέλλομαί in Genesis 2:16; 3:11, 17, in relation to the fruit prohibited for food, appears in Deut 12:10–28 in the context of blood consumption. Here ἐγὼ ἐντέλλομαί is associated with φυλάσσου. The shift from ἀπέχεσθαι in Acts 15:20 to φυλάσσεσθαι in Acts 21:25 reveals that the Decree contained commandments, some of which were related to prohibited foods; 9) the term πνικτὸς in Acts 15:20 echoes Gen 1:2; 2:7 and 6:17, where the creation of life was pictured as "breathing in" of the πνοὴν ζωῆς, and death as blocking of it; 10) the term πορνεία employed by the apostles in Acts 15:20, 29; 21:25 has to be viewed against the background of the "shame of nakedness" motifs of Genesis 3:10, 11, 21.

The present study also identified pairs of controversies implicit in Gen 1–3, which provide theological concepts which explain the apostolic decision. First is true worship versus idolatry, linked to the apostolic prohibition of εἰδωλοθύτων. Second is the life—death controversy, ψυχὴν ζῶσαν expressing life, and its reversal, which is death. Two aspects of death include: 1) the returning of life into dust, which laid a foundation for the apostolic prohibition of αἷμα, which must be drained out of slaughtered animals and covered with soil (namely, returned to dust) and 2) the returning of the "breath of life" to God, which laid the foundation of the prohibition of πνικτὸς, when the last breath was held by choking, so that it could not naturally return to God. These prohibitions belong to dietary laws based on the natural law of God, and not to the Jewish ritual law. The controversy between undefiled marriage versus pagan cultic fornication constituted the final point of the apostolic prohibition of πορνεία.

Detailed exegesis of Gen 1–3 enabled the four prohibitions to be rooted in the creation-fall narrative. Their rationale was found in the natural law of God, implicit in Gen 1–3. The prohibitions were understood as both, ethical and cultic, linked to the issue of the controversy between true versus false worship. The creation–fall–re-creation paradigm employed in this study indicated that the prohibitions would remain valid until re-creation. Mentioning of εἰδωλοθύτων and πορνεία in two passages of Revelation reveals the mingling of true and false worship in the church. The images of Revelation point to God's judgment for disobedience to the Decree and practice of false worship, also pointing to eschatological salvation and renewal for those who maintain true worship. Rev 2:25 provides the temporal limit for the keeping of the Decree (ἄχρι[ς] οὗ ἂν ἥξω), which is the time of the parousia. This agrees with Gen 3, where the curses after the fall were limited by death in individual cases and by destruction of the "serpent's head" in a general sense.

It was argued that the prohibitions of αἵματος and πνικτῶν reflected the controversy between life and death (known since Gen 3:19) and which were to illustrate the belief that only God has power over life and death. The prohibition of αἵματος was associated with two concepts: "blood represents life" and "blood redeems life." The first concept is rooted in the natural law of God, while the second was developed later as part of the ritual system. The concept "blood redeems life" was fulfilled in Christ's death and freed believers from the ritual law.

The prohibition of πνικτῶν was also understood to be related to the controversy between life and death. The creation of life was pictured as "breathing in" of the πνοὴν ζωῆς and death as blocking it. Death was understood as the reverse to creation (Gen 2:7), when the breath returns to God (Eccl 12:7), who can give it again. Killing of an animal by choking was assumed as "strangled." The violation of the natural law and deliberate eating of πνικτῶν would indicate the extreme degree of disobedience to God who controls the reversal of life and death.

Similarly the prohibition of πορνεία was rooted in the natural law of God. The principle of the creation of two separate people out of "one flesh" and then uniting two people into "one flesh" becomes the basic rationale for marriage ordained by God. Violation of this basic principle was described by the two terms πορνεία and μοιχεία. It was stated that πορνεία, which was part of cultic practices of pagan worship, is a destruction of the concept "two become one flesh."

The present study argued that the New Testament extra-Lukan occurrences of the content of the Apostolic Decree also fit the patterns of the theological concepts developed on the basis of Genesis 1:24–3:24. Extra-Lukan occurrences of the prohibitions of εἰδωλοθύτων and πορνεία, found in Pauline writings, were connected to Pauline typology and midrashic constructions built on the creation-fall narrative and linked to the issue of worship. Pauline logic reveals that idolatry deserves eternal punishment instead of the hope of re-creation in light of the creation–fall–re-creation paradigm. Also, it was shown that, after the council, Paul faced the issues (in Acts 21 and those he reflected in Romans 14) of keeping the ritual law by the believers. In those cases Paul's tolerant approach was bound to the believers who continued keeping the ritual law.

Conclusively, there were ten echoes of Gen 1–3 in the account of Acts 15; the pairs of controversies known since Gen 1–3 formed the basic theological concepts of which the four prohibitions of the Decree formed the common background; the main idea behind these pairs of controversies can be summarized as the call for true worship known since Gen 1–3. The worship motifs behind the prohibitions are to support the reversal of pagan idolatry into the patterns of true worship.

The Fourth Goal: Identify the Roles of Ritual
and Natural Law in Luke-Acts

The fourth goal was to find the roles of ritual and natural law in the creation–fall–re-creation framework throughout Luke's two-volume work. It was noted that the ritual law is a crucial theme for Luke, who widely discusses the rites of purification, temporary uncleanness connected to leprosy, death, flow of blood, and demon possession. It was argued that Luke presents Jesus' messiahship as fulfilling and superseding the ritual law associated with the temple cult. He illustrates how several types of uncleanness were healed and cleansed by Christ. For him Christ is the only true fulfillment of the temple cult and of Jewish ritual law. In carrying through this idea, Luke placed the decision of the Jerusalem Council in a setting of the natural law of God as reflected in Mosaic writings, but not in Mosaic ritual law itself.

The issue of preaching to the Gentiles was noted as another important Lukan issue, becoming prominent in Acts after Jesus' death and resurrection. For Luke, faith in Jesus cleanses and makes Gentile converts and Jewish believers equally acceptable to God. Luke emphasized that Jesus supersedes the temple cult and makes keeping of the Jewish ritual law and initiation into the temple cult unnecessary for Gentile salvation.

The issue of uncleanness for Luke focused predominantly on ritual uncleanness, while he understood permanent uncleanness to be associated with demons. Demon possession was thus assumed to be a reversible uncleanness. The demons themselves, however, were seen to be permanently unclean. Luke describes demon removal in terms of spiritual cleansing. Lukan narrative pictured humans possessed by demons as demonstrating an unnatural inclination to uncleanness, lawlessness, and violation of natural law. It was also suggested that hardening of the heart to the Gospel leads to the condition of permanent uncleanness. The role of the four prohibitions of the Decree, in view of this perspective, was to initiate a restoration to God's natural law for the Gentile converts, leading them from their previous idolatry to true worship.

The Lukan writings also revealed the changes in understanding of the Jewish feasts and levitical service by the early Church. The spiritual meaning of Passover, Pentecost and the priesthood of all believers was progressively developed. The progress of narratives brings a reader closer to the concept of, and necessity for spiritual cleansing. Luke illustrates that ritual cleansing of the ritual law was replaced by the inner cleansing of the heart in response to faith, and signified by the presence of the Holy Spirit.

The lack of discussion of the dietary laws in Luke-Acts suggested that Luke did not plan to inform readers about any changes concerning these laws. When Luke raises the issue of unclean food, it is in the context of its association with unclean matters. This study argued that Luke viewed food as standing free from the demands of the ritual law. He left food consumption subject only to those dietary laws which are rooted in natural law, known from the creation-fall narrative, to be viewed separately from the ritual law. When the ritual laws were rejected by Luke, only those dietary laws connected to the natural law of God remained valid.

Results of the Study

The research provided a new approach to the four prohibitions of the Apostolic Decree. It has confirmed that Luke's narratives were developed in order to illustrate that the ritual law was fulfilled in Christ and its role was superseded by faith in Christ. In contrast, the natural law of God, based on Gen 1–3, appears in the Lukan writings to have continuing validity, and consequently should have been viewed by the early Church as not cancelled. Its appointed role in light of the creation–fall–re-creation paradigm was to support the reversal originated by God in the heart of believers, converting them from the fallen condition to that which existed at the creation.

The fulfillment of the ritual law in Jesus' messiahship allows one to experience this reversal on a spiritual level at the moment of conversion. The issue of Jew-Gentile relationships was raised by Luke to illustrate it. The narratives explain why Gentile converts should not keep the Jewish cult and still be equally accepted into the church. Luke shows that acceptance into fellowship, in the early church, was on basis of equality before God the Creator. The four prohibitions of the Decree were selected to help the converts from the Gentiles differenciate the natural law from the ritual law in those places of the Mosaic Law where the treatment could be ambiguous. That was the logic behind the Apostolic Decree. Thus the church understood that the natural law remained valid and allowed both Jew and Gentile converts to express hope for the future physical reversal at the time of re-creation.

Findings of the present study help to reconstruct the apostolic view of true worship and its implications for contemporary Christian life. According to Acts 15:19, 20, the Decree has implication for the progress of the Gospel message, which is healthy growth of the church resulting from the process of spiritual re-creation. True worship and, consequently, re-creation become impossible when the basic laws established by God are neglected or violated. Explicit and implicit idolatry does not constitute true worship. Also fornicating and marital relationships with prohibited degree of kinship frequently approved and practiced by pagan cults tend to turn a believer back to idolatry. Consumption of food sacrificed to idols, of blood or things "strangled," which in Jewish tradition and in early patristic tradition were believed to be associated with demonic forces, could have the same effect and turn converts away from God. These assumptions reveal that the practical applications of the Decree are very important in the life of contemporary Christians.

Appendix 1

Comparative Study of Manuscripts with Lukan Accounts of the Apostolic Decree

		Different readings:	Acts 15:20	Acts 15:29	Acts 21:25
		The ambivalent readings:			
Full list of prohibitions		1. Four prohibitions (τῶν εἰδώλων καὶ τῆς πορνείας καὶ τοῦ πνικτοῦ/ῶν καὶ τοῦ αἵματος)	$\mathfrak{P}^{74}$ ℵ, C, E, L 323, 614, 945, 1175, 1241, 1505, 1739 $\mathfrak{M}$ lat sy Origen$^{lat\,(1/2)}$ Chrysostom	$\mathfrak{P}^{33,74}$ ℵ*, A*, B, C 81, 614, 1175 (co); Cl Hier^{mss}	E vg sy
	Variant readings of πνικτος	2. Use καὶ πνικτοῦ instead of καὶ τοῦ πνικτοῦ (omit article)	$\mathfrak{P}^{74}$ A, B, Ψ 33, 81 Apostolic Constitutions	$\mathfrak{P}^{74}$ ℵ², Aᶜ, E, L, Ψ 33, 323, 945, 1241, 1505, 1739 $\mathfrak{M}$ (lat) sy, CyrJ, Origen 1$^{lat\,(1/2)}$, Severian, Amphilochius, Diodore, Dydimus, Chrysostom	E
		3. Use of plural form πνικτῶν	Cl. Alex., Origen	81, 614, 1175(co) Origen 1$^{lat\,(1/2)}$, Cyr J^{mss}, Socrates, Amphilochius, Gaudentius Jerome, Cassian	
		4. Use καὶ πνικτὸν			$\mathfrak{P}^{74}$ ℵ, A, B, C, Ψ 33, 614, 945, 1505, 1739, 2818

APPENDIX 1: COMPARATIVE STUDY OF MANUSCRIPTS

	Different readings:	Acts 15:20	Acts 15:29	Acts 21:25
	The cultic reading:			
Omission	5. Three prohibitions with καὶ τοῦ πνικτοῦ (omits καὶ τῆς πορνείας)	$\mathfrak{P}^{45}$	No text	No text
	The ethical reading:			
Omissions and additions	6. Contains three prohibitions (omit καὶ τοῦ πνικτοῦ),	D gig, Ir$^{1739mg.lat}$	D 1, Ir1$^{739mg.lat}$, Tert, Hier^{mss}, Cyp, Pacian, Jerome, Augustine, Ambrosiaster	D it^d, D gig Augustine
	7. Addition of the negative form of the Golden Rule	323, 614, 945, 1739, 1891 sa; Ir$^{1739mg.lat}$ Eus^{1739mg}	D 05, D^2 614, 323, 945, 1739 sy^{h**},1891 1p w sy^{h**} sa, Eus^{1739mg}, Cyp, Ir$^{1739mg.lat}$	
	8. Addition of πράξατε φερόμενοι ἐν τῷ πνεύματι		D 05, D 1 Irenaeus$^{acc.\ to\ 1739}$ Tertullian	
	9. Addition of a phrase: Κρίναντες μηδὲν τοιοῦτο τηρεῖν αὐτούς εἰ μὴ φυλάσσεσθαι αὐτούς / Κρίναντες μηδὲν τοιοῦτο τηρεῖν αὐτούς ἀλλὰ φυλάσσεσθαι.			C, D, E, L, Ψ 36, 181, 307, 323, 453, 614, 1241, 1505, 1678 Chrysostom, Augustine Greek mss$^{acc.\ to\ Bede}$ /945, 1739, 1891

Appendix 2

Diagrams of the Passages Studied in Chapter 3

1. Basic theological concepts developed on basis of Genesis 1:24—3:24

    1.1 True worship versus idolatry in Genesis 1–3 and the apostolic prohibition of εἰδωλοθύτων

    1.1.1 Passage 1 (Gen 1:24—2:3)

    Unit one' (Gen 1:24-31)—Brief sketch of the sixth day of Creation

Part 1—Creation of the animal kingdom:

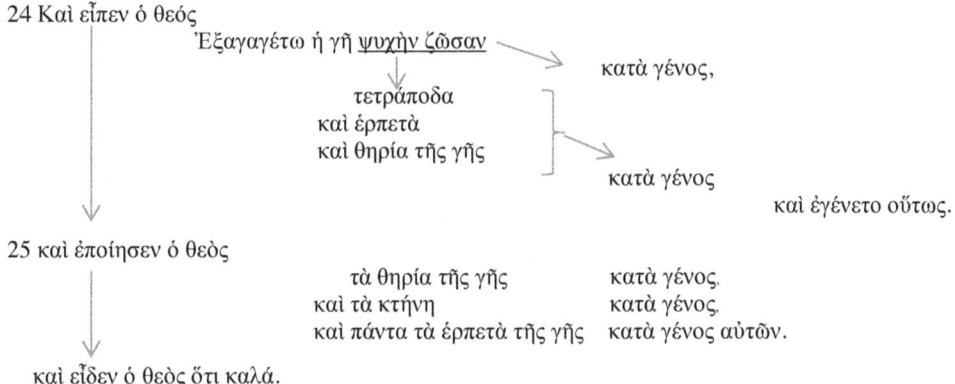

APPENDIX 2: DIAGRAMS OF THE PASSAGES STUDIED IN CHAPTER 3

Part 2—Brief sketch of the creation of human beings (Gen 1:26–31)

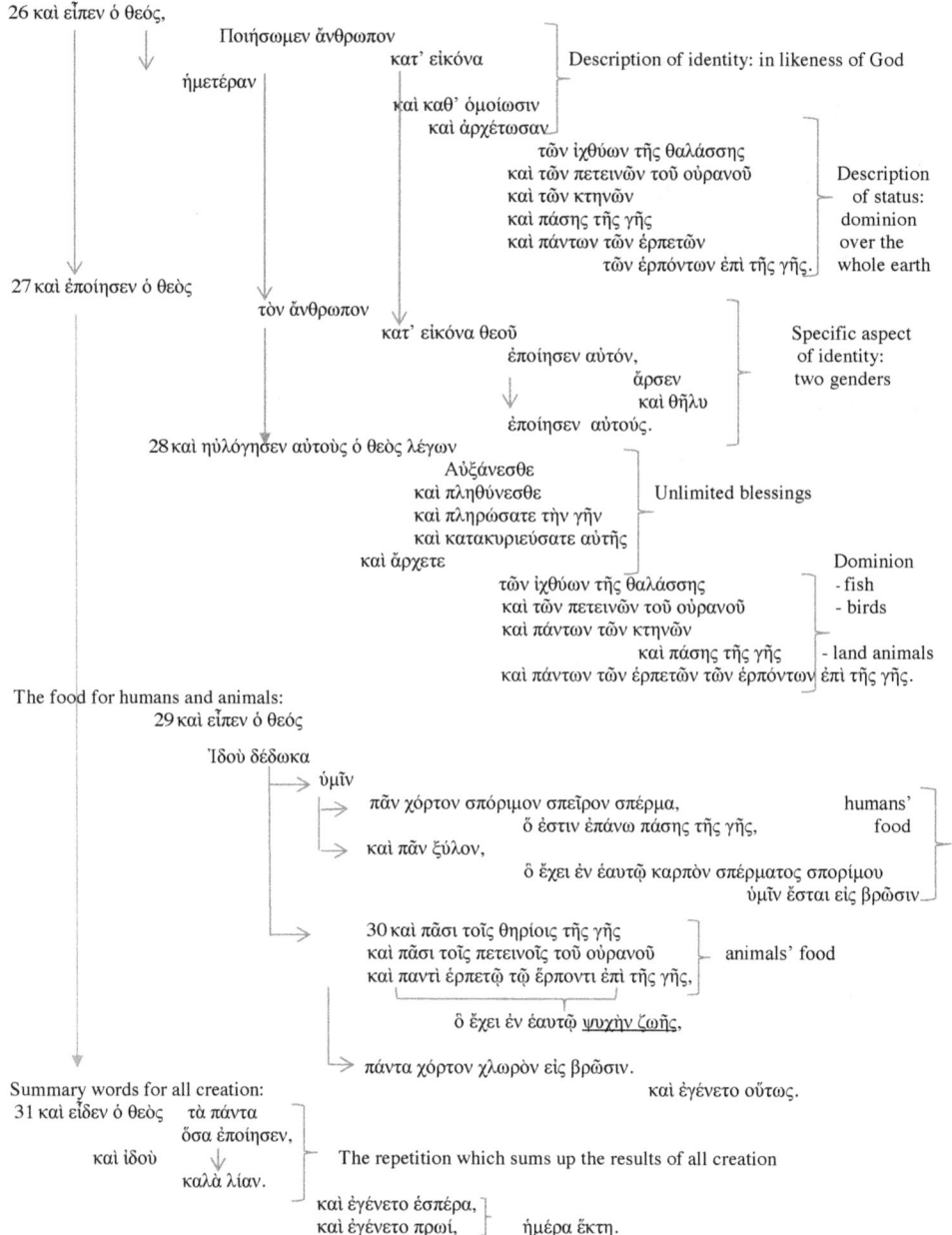

APPENDIX 2: DIAGRAMS OF THE PASSAGES STUDIED IN CHAPTER 3

The link A (Gen 2:1)—Summary of all creation account described in Gen 1:1–30

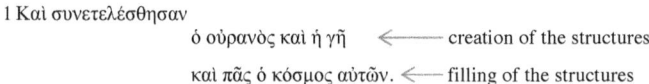

Unit two' (Gen 2:2, 3) – the first sanctification of the world.

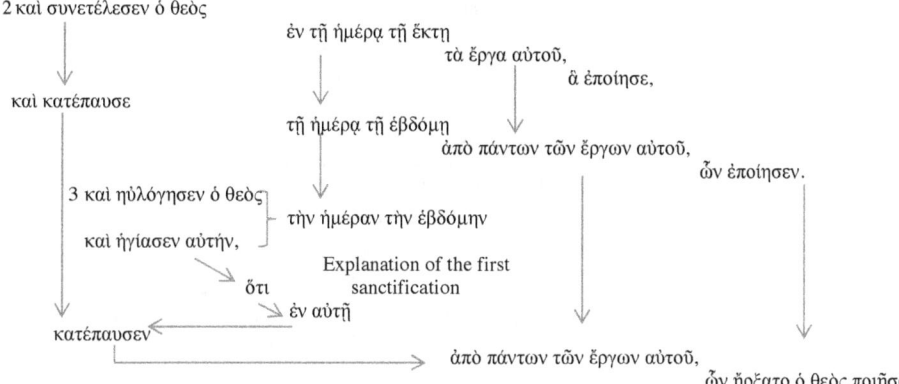

1.1.2. Passage 2 (Gen 2:4–25)—Detailed account of the creation of humans

Link B (Gen 2:4–6)—Key role of humans in the world appointed before the creation

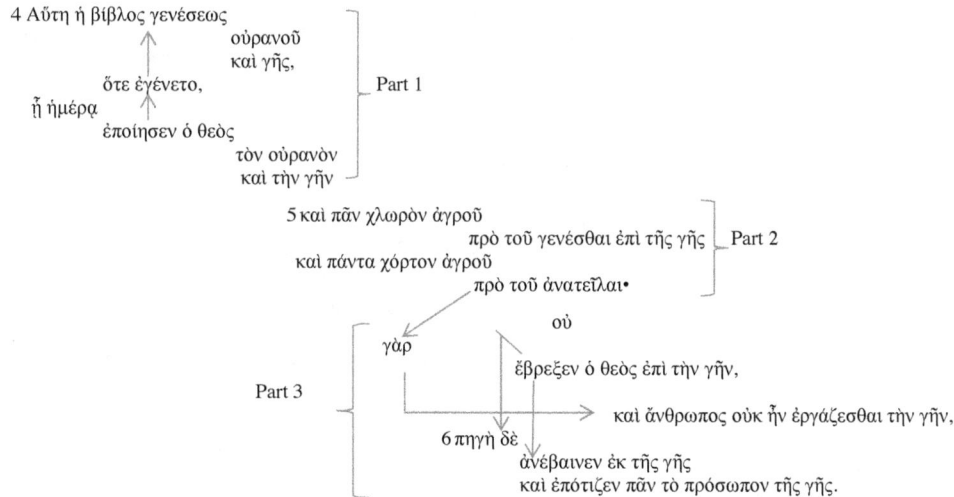

Unit one (Gen 2:7)—Process of the creation of a man

7 καὶ ἔπλασεν ὁ θεὸς τὸν ἄνθρωπον χοῦν ἀπὸ τῆς γῆς
καὶ ἐνεφύσησεν εἰς τὸ πρόσωπον αὐτοῦ πνοὴν ζωῆς,
                    καὶ ἐγένετο ὁ ἄνθρωπος εἰς ψυχὴν ζῶσαν.

APPENDIX 2: DIAGRAMS OF THE PASSAGES STUDIED IN CHAPTER 3

Unit two (Gen 2:8–15)—Creation of home and food for humans (development of Link B)

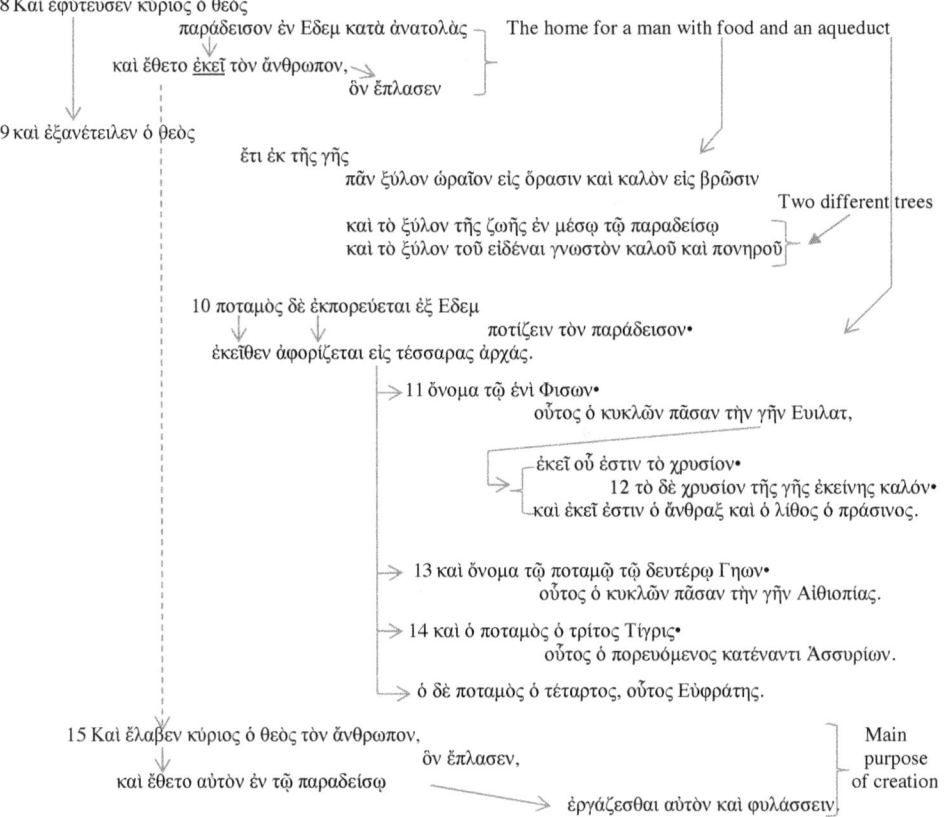

Unit three (Gen 2:16, 17)—The first covenant

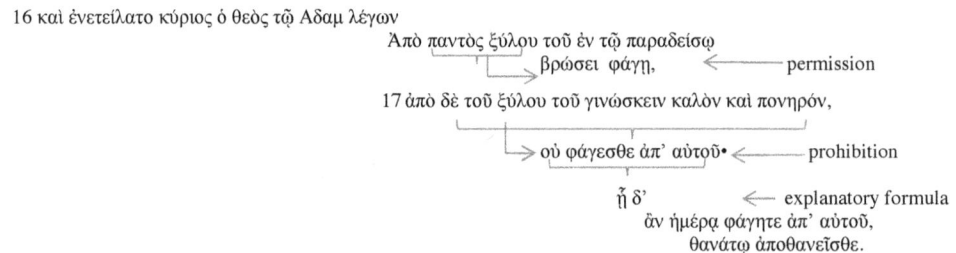

APPENDIX 2: DIAGRAMS OF THE PASSAGES STUDIED IN CHAPTER 3

Unit four—Creation of woman

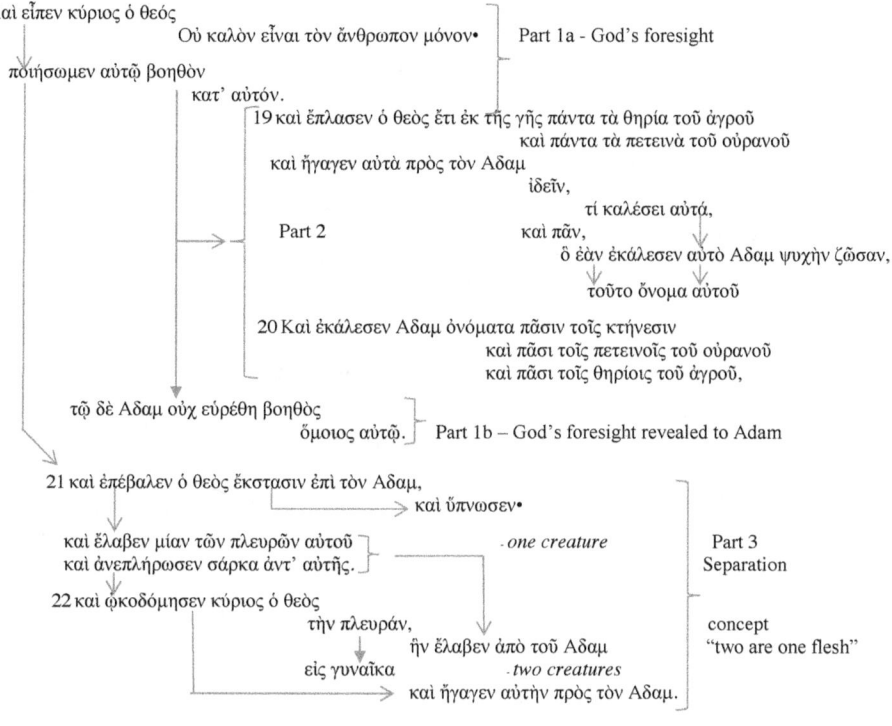

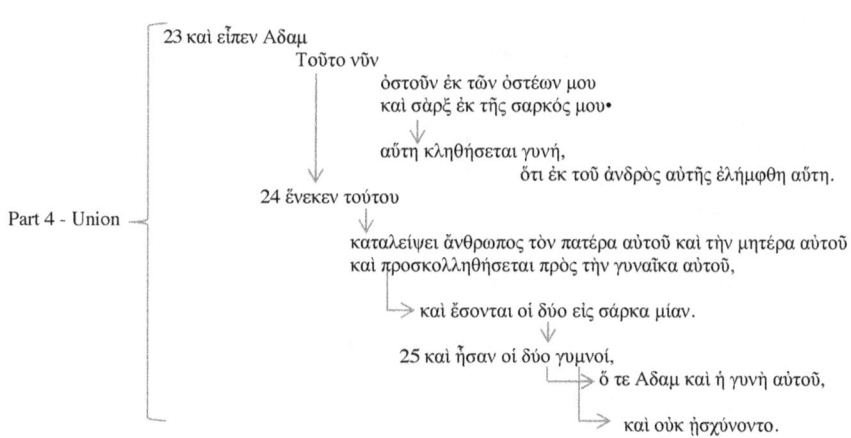

APPENDIX 2: DIAGRAMS OF THE PASSAGES STUDIED IN CHAPTER 3

1.1.3. Passage 3 (Gen 3:1-24) - The Fall narrative.

Unit five (Gen 3:1-5)—Temptation

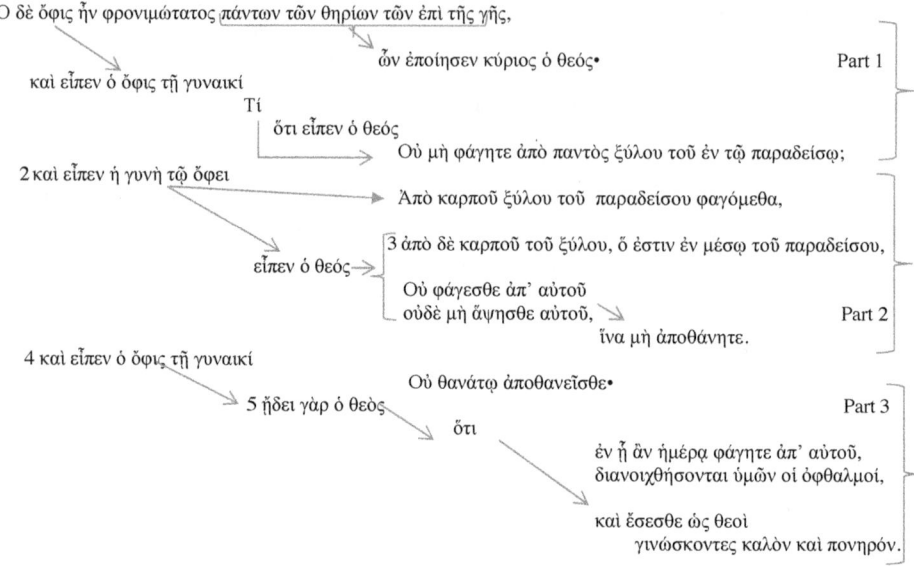

Unit six (Gen 3:6-8)—Reversal law of sin

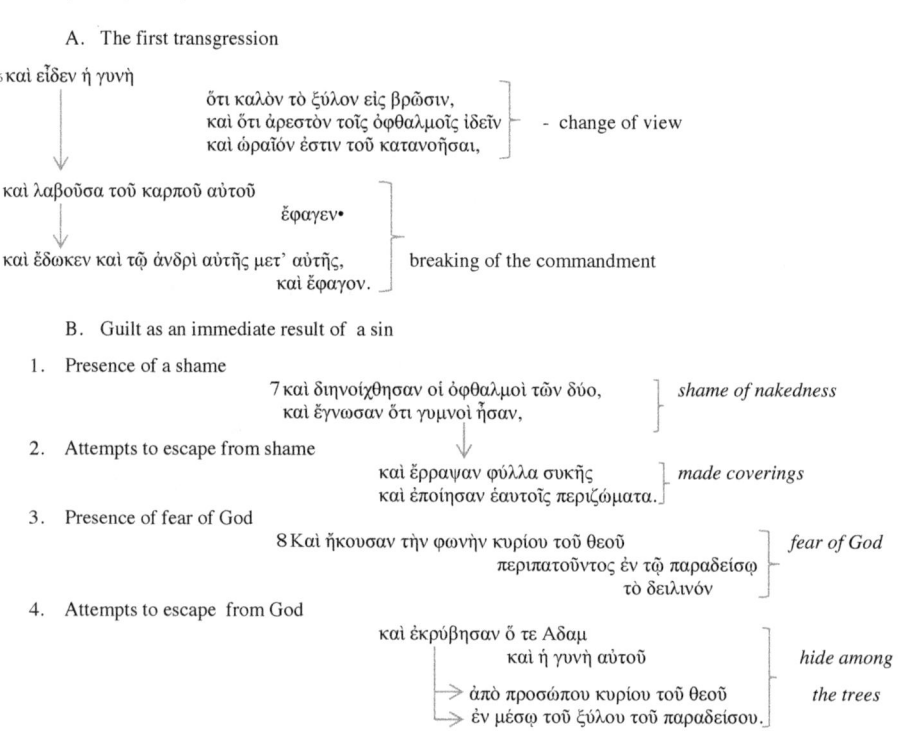

APPENDIX 2: DIAGRAMS OF THE PASSAGES STUDIED IN CHAPTER 3

Unit seven (Gen 3:9–13)—Confession of sin

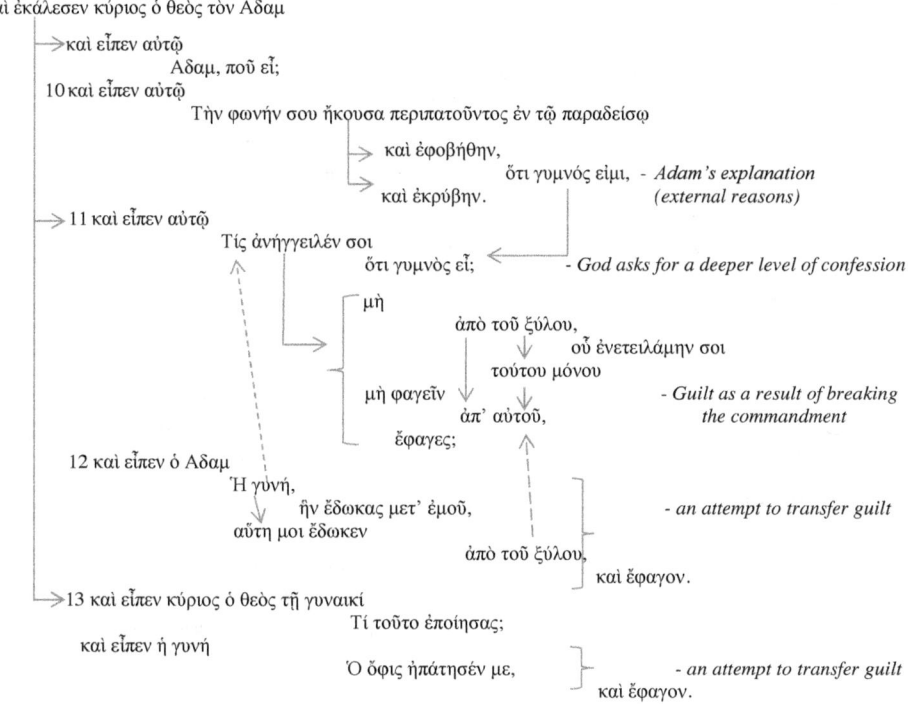

APPENDIX 2: DIAGRAMS OF THE PASSAGES STUDIED IN CHAPTER 3

Unit eight (Gen 3:14–20)—Consequences of a sin

Curse of the serpent:

14 καὶ εἶπεν κύριος ὁ θεὸς τῷ ὄφει
    Ὅτι ἐποίησας τοῦτο,
        ἐπικατάρατος σὺ
            ἀπὸ πάντων τῶν κτηνῶν
            καὶ ἀπὸ πάντων τῶν θηρίων τῆς γῆς·
        ἐπὶ τῷ στήθει σου
        καὶ τῇ κοιλίᾳ πορεύσῃ
        καὶ γῆν φάγῃ πάσας τὰς ἡμέρας τῆς ζωῆς σου.
    15 καὶ ἔχθραν θήσω
        ἀνὰ μέσον σου
        καὶ ἀνὰ μέσον τῆς γυναικὸς
        καὶ ἀνὰ μέσον τοῦ σπέρματός σου
        καὶ ἀνὰ μέσον τοῦ σπέρματος αὐτῆς·
        αὐτός σου τηρήσει κεφαλήν,
        καὶ σὺ τηρήσεις αὐτοῦ πτέρναν.

Consequences for the woman:

16 καὶ τῇ γυναικὶ εἶπεν
    Πληθύνων πληθυνῶ
        τὰς λύπας σου
        καὶ τὸν στεναγμόν σου,
            ἐν λύπαις τέξῃ τέκνα·
        καὶ πρὸς τὸν ἄνδρα σου ἡ ἀποστροφή σου,
        καὶ αὐτός σου κυριεύσει.

Consequences for the man:

17 τῷ δὲ Αδαμ εἶπεν
    Ὅτι ἤκουσας τῆς φωνῆς τῆς γυναικός σου   *Contrast: the man listened to his wife*
        καὶ ἔφαγες ἀπὸ τοῦ ξύλου,   *instead of God's commandment*
            οὗ ἐνετειλάμην σοι
            τούτου μόνου
        μὴ φαγεῖν ἀπ᾽ αὐτοῦ,

The curse of the earth

    ἐπικατάρατος ἡ γῆ ἐν τοῖς ἔργοις σου·
        ἐν λύπαις φάγῃ αὐτὴν πάσας τὰς ἡμέρας τῆς ζωῆς σου·
        18 ἀκάνθας καὶ τριβόλους ἀνατελεῖ σοι,
        καὶ φάγῃ τὸν χόρτον τοῦ ἀγροῦ.
    19 ἐν ἱδρῶτι τοῦ προσώπου σου φάγῃ τὸν ἄρτον σου
        ἕως   *The temporal limitations of curse*
        τοῦ ἀποστρέψαι σε εἰς τὴν γῆν,
            ἐξ ἧς ἐλήμφθης·
        ὅτι γῆ εἶ
        καὶ εἰς γῆν ἀπελεύσῃ.

20 καὶ ἐκάλεσεν Αδαμ τὸ ὄνομα τῆς γυναικὸς αὐτοῦ Ζωή,
    ὅτι αὕτη μήτηρ πάντων τῶν ζώντων.

APPENDIX 2: DIAGRAMS OF THE PASSAGES STUDIED IN CHAPTER 3

Unit nine (Gen 3:21-24)—Redemption

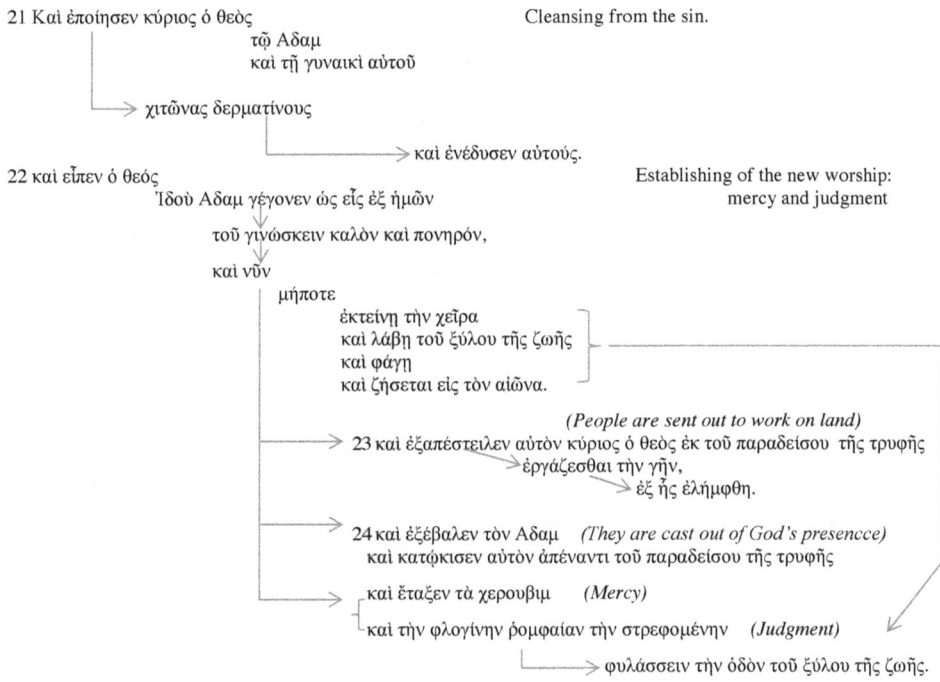

APPENDIX 2: DIAGRAMS OF THE PASSAGES STUDIED IN CHAPTER 3

1.2. The life—death controversy and the apostolic prohibition of αἷμα

1.2.1. Creation of ψυχὴν ζῶσαν as a basis for the pattern of life

1.2.2. The pattern of the creation of humans

1.2.3. The uniting role of Gen 9:1–7 and the prohibition of αἷμα

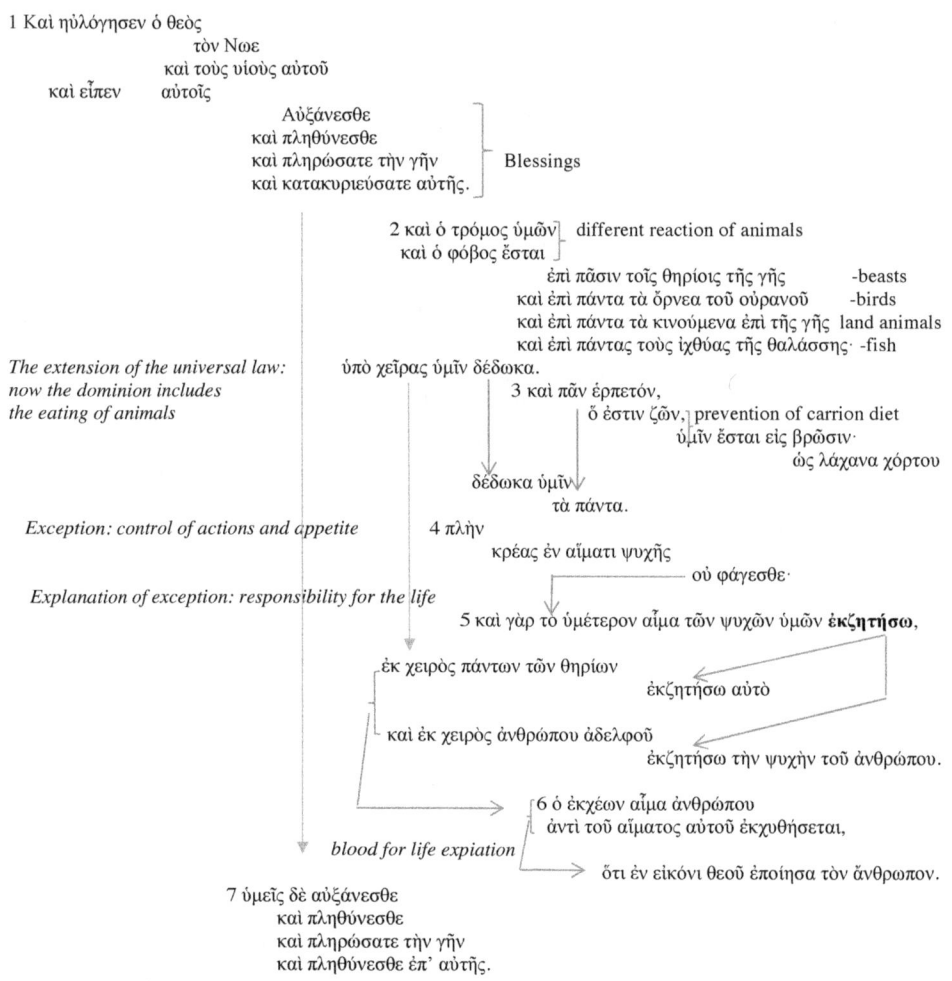

APPENDIX 2: DIAGRAMS OF THE PASSAGES STUDIED IN CHAPTER 3

1.2.4. The prohibition of αἷμα in Lev 17:10–14

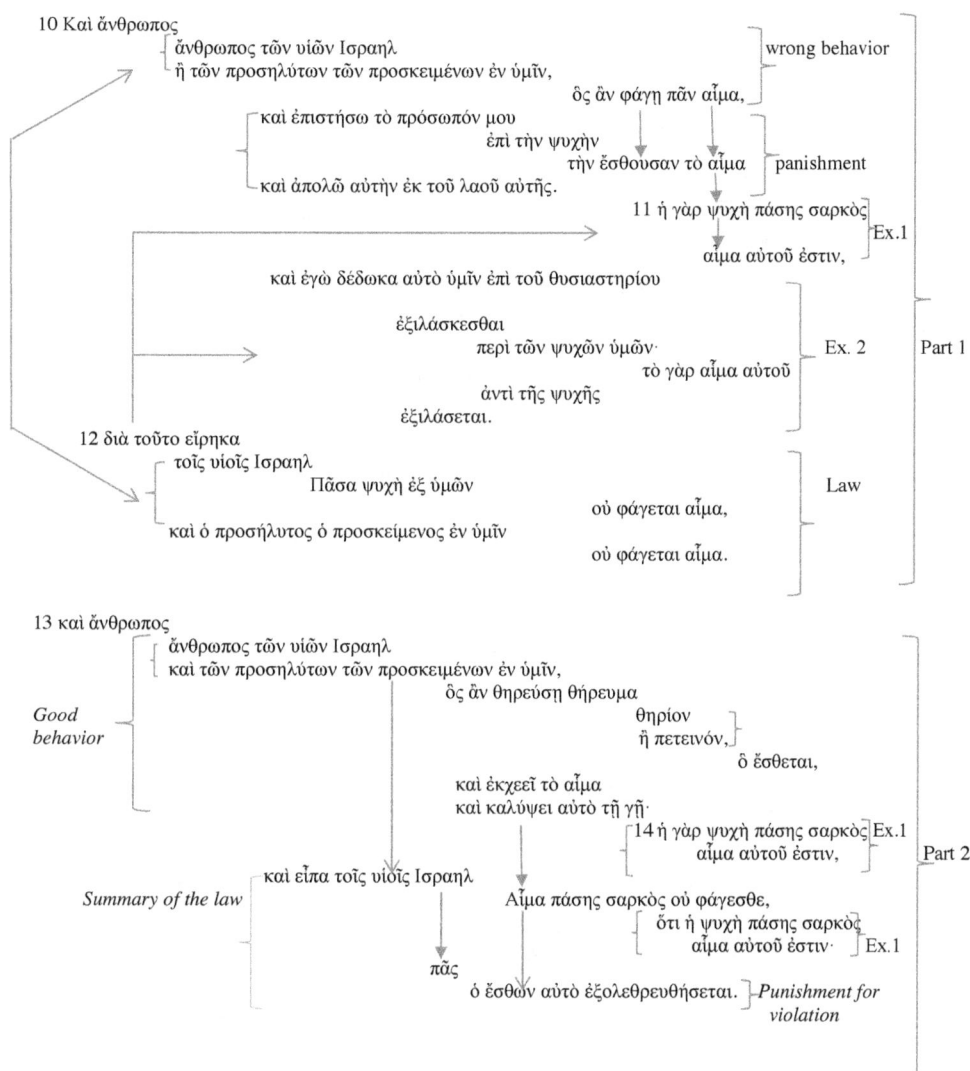

APPENDIX 2: DIAGRAMS OF THE PASSAGES STUDIED IN CHAPTER 3

1.2.5. The prohibition of αἷμα in Deut 12:20-28

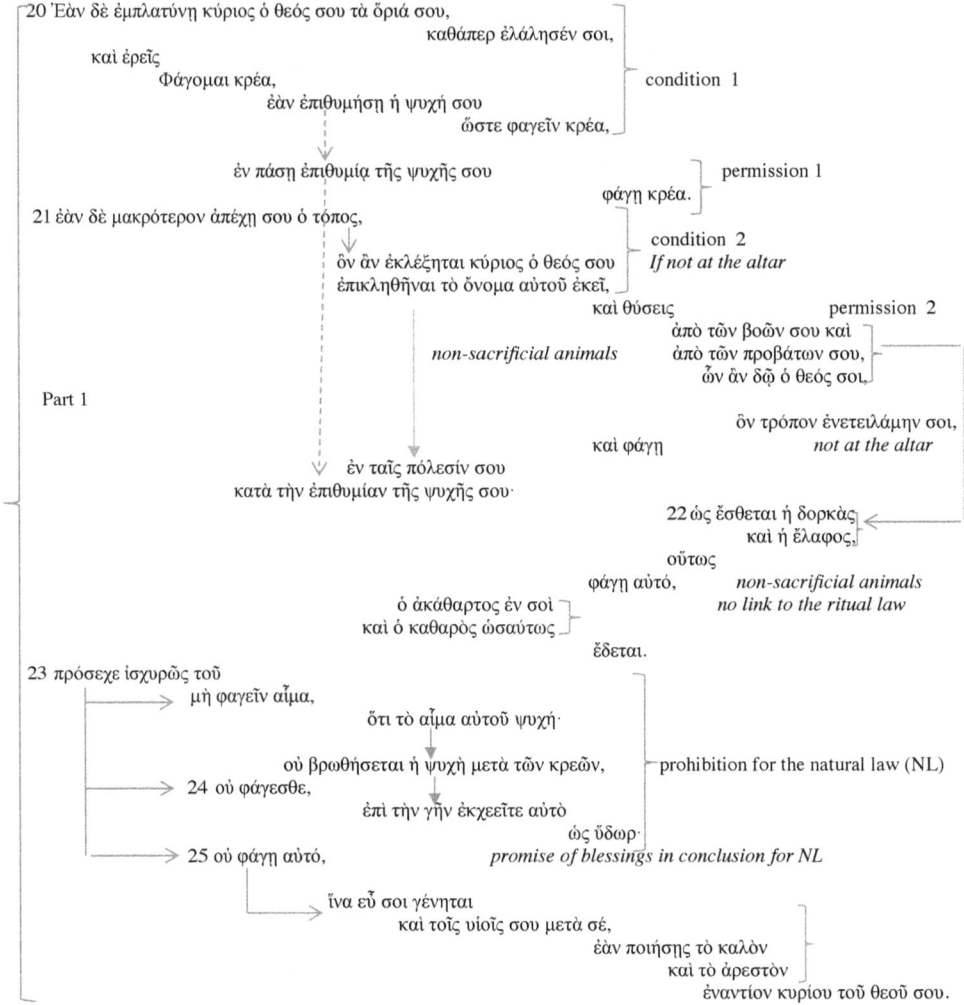

The diagram continues on the next page.

APPENDIX 2: DIAGRAMS OF THE PASSAGES STUDIED IN CHAPTER 3

Part 2
26 πλὴν τὰ ἅγιά σου,
　　　ἐὰν γένηταί σοι,
　καὶ τὰς εὐχάς σου
　　　　　λαβὼν ἥξεις εἰς τὸν τόπον,
　　　　　　　　　ὃν ἂν ἐκλέξηται κύριος ὁ θεός σου
　　　　　　　　　　ἐπικληθῆναι τὸ ὄνομα αὐτοῦ ἐκεῖ,　　*Ritual law*
　　　↓
27 καὶ ποιήσεις τὰ ὁλοκαυτώματά σου·
　　　τὰ κρέα ἀνοίσεις ἐπὶ τὸ θυσιαστήριον κυρίου τοῦ θεοῦ σου,
　　　τὸ δὲ αἷμα τῶν θυσιῶν σου προσχεεῖς πρὸς τὴν βάσιν τοῦ θυσιαστηρίου κυρίου τοῦ θεοῦ σου,
　　　τὰ δὲ κρέα φάγῃ.

Part 3
28 φυλάσσου
καὶ ἄκουε
καὶ ποιήσεις
　　　πάντας τοὺς λόγους,
　　　　οὓς ἐγὼ ἐντέλλομαί σοι,　　*general commandment for both kinds of laws*
　　　　ἵνα εὖ σοι γένηται
　　　　καὶ τοῖς υἱοῖς σου
　　　　　　δι' αἰῶνος,　　　　　　*general promise of*
　　　　　ἐὰν ποιήσῃς τὸ καλὸν　　　*eternal blessings*
　　　　　καὶ τὸ ἀρεστὸν
　　　　　　ἐναντίον κυρίου τοῦ θεοῦ σου.

305

APPENDIX 2: DIAGRAMS OF THE PASSAGES STUDIED IN CHAPTER 3

1.3. The life—death controversy and the apostolic prohibition of πνικτός

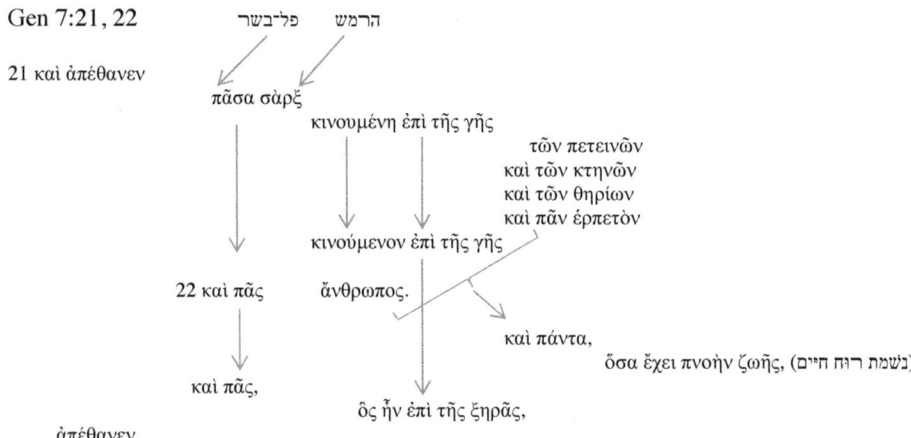

1.4. The cultic fornication and the apostolic prohibition of πορνεία

Luke 16:18—The shortest account of the final statement

18 Πᾶς ὁ ἀπολύων τὴν γυναῖκα αὐτοῦ
    καὶ γαμῶν ἑτέραν
        μοιχεύει,
καὶ ὁ ἀπολελυμένην ἀπὸ ἀνδρὸς γαμῶν
        μοιχεύει.

Matt 5:31, 32—Wider account of the final statement

31. Ἐρρέθη δέ,
    Ὃς ἂν ἀπολύσῃ τὴν γυναῖκα αὐτοῦ,
        δότω αὐτῇ ἀποστάσιον.
32. ἐγὼ δὲ λέγω ὑμῖν
    ὅτι πᾶς ὁ ἀπολύων τὴν γυναῖκα αὐτοῦ
        παρεκτὸς λόγου πορνείας
            ποιεῖ αὐτὴν μοιχευθῆναι,
    καὶ ὃς ἐὰν ἀπολελυμένην γαμήσῃ
        μοιχᾶται.

APPENDIX 2: DIAGRAMS OF THE PASSAGES STUDIED IN CHAPTER 3

Matt 19:1–12 (the full version including midrashic form of exegesis)

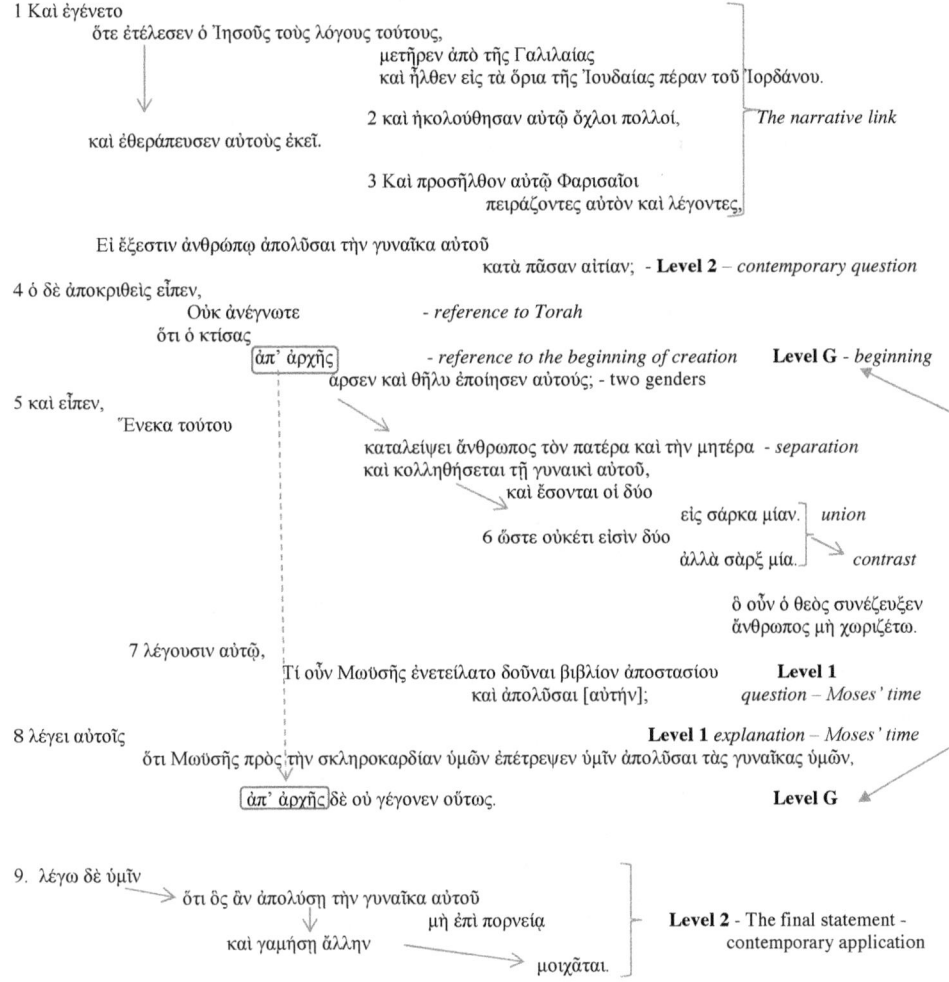

APPENDIX 2: DIAGRAMS OF THE PASSAGES STUDIED IN CHAPTER 3

2. New Testament extra-Lukan echoes of the content of the Apostolic Decree

2.1. Echoes of the Decree in the 1 Corinthians letter

2.1.1. 1 Cor 6:9–20

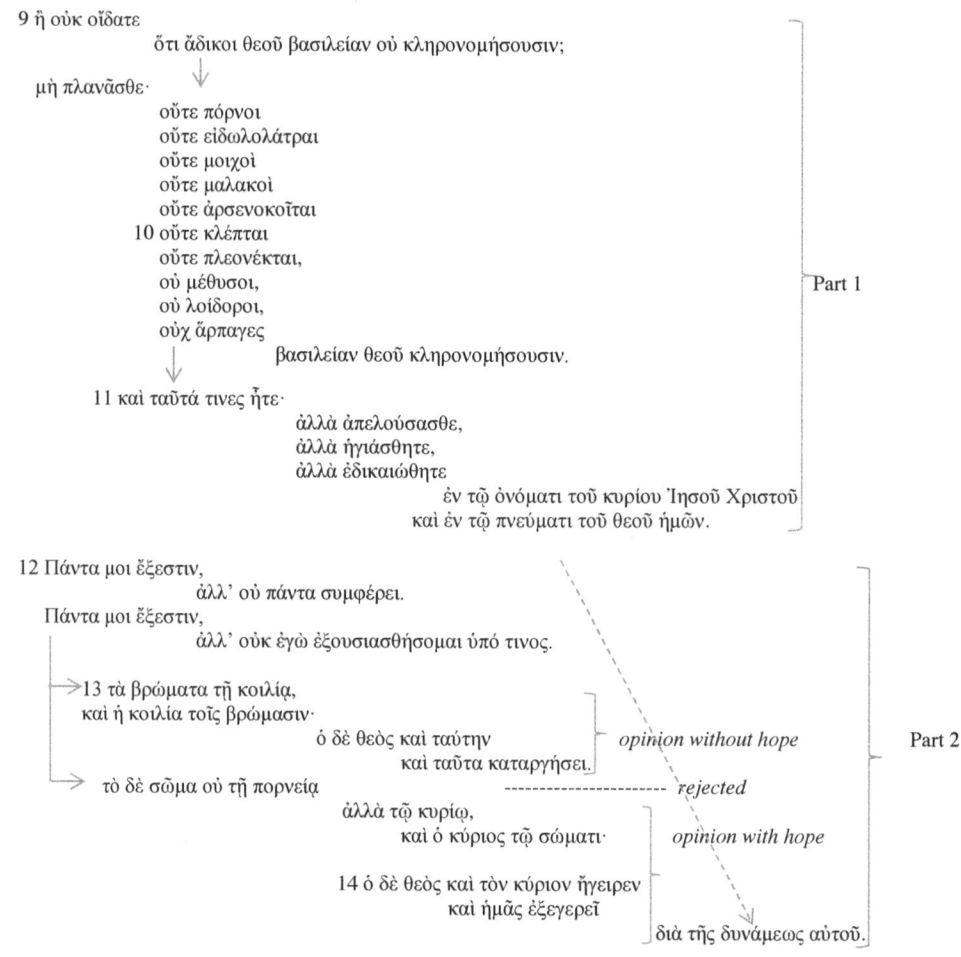

The diagram continues on the next page.

APPENDIX 2: DIAGRAMS OF THE PASSAGES STUDIED IN CHAPTER 3

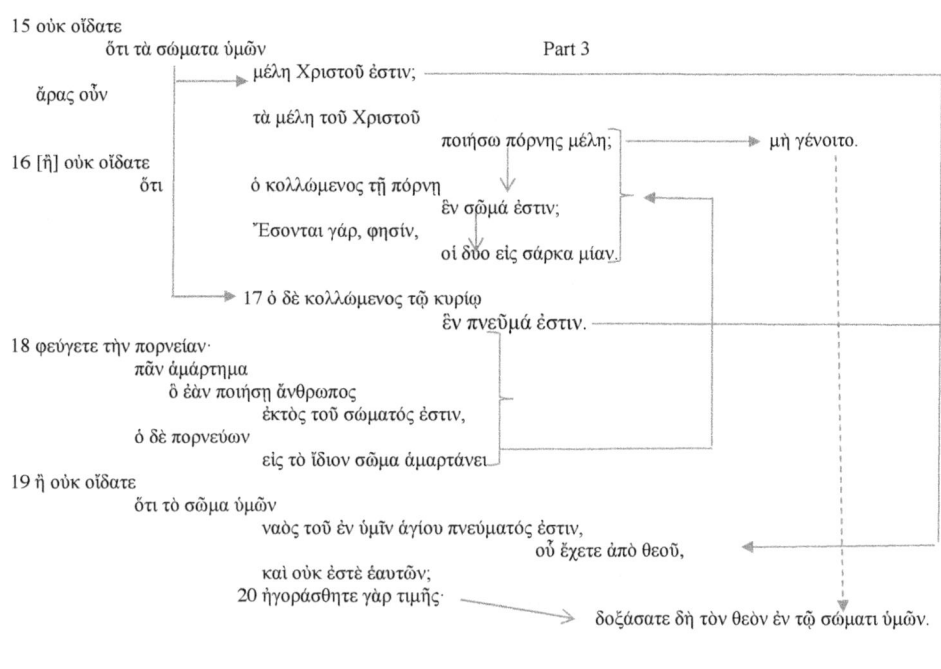

2.1.2. 1 Cor 5:1, 9–11

1 Ὅλως ἀκούεται ἐν ὑμῖν πορνεία,
    καὶ τοιαύτη πορνεία ἥτις οὐδὲ ἐν τοῖς ἔθνεσιν,
        ὥστε γυναῖκά τινα τοῦ πατρὸς ἔχειν.

9 Ἔγραψα ὑμῖν ἐν τῇ ἐπιστολῇ
    μὴ συναναμίγνυσθαι πόρνοις,
      10 οὐ πάντως
          τοῖς πόρνοις τοῦ κόσμου τούτου
          ἢ τοῖς πλεονέκταις
          καὶ ἅρπαξιν
          ἢ εἰδωλολάτραις,
            ἐπεὶ ὠφείλετε ἄρα ἐκ τοῦ κόσμου ἐξελθεῖν.
11 νῦν δὲ ἔγραψα ὑμῖν
    μὴ συναναμίγνυσθαι
        ἐάν τις ἀδελφὸς ὀνομαζόμενος
          ἢ πόρνος
          ἢ πλεονέκτης
          ἢ εἰδωλολάτρης
          ἢ λοίδορος
          ἢ μέθυσος
          ἢ ἅρπαξ,
          τῷ τοιούτῳ
    μηδὲ συνεσθίειν.

APPENDIX 2: DIAGRAMS OF THE PASSAGES STUDIED IN CHAPTER 3

2.1.3. 1 Cor 8:1–13

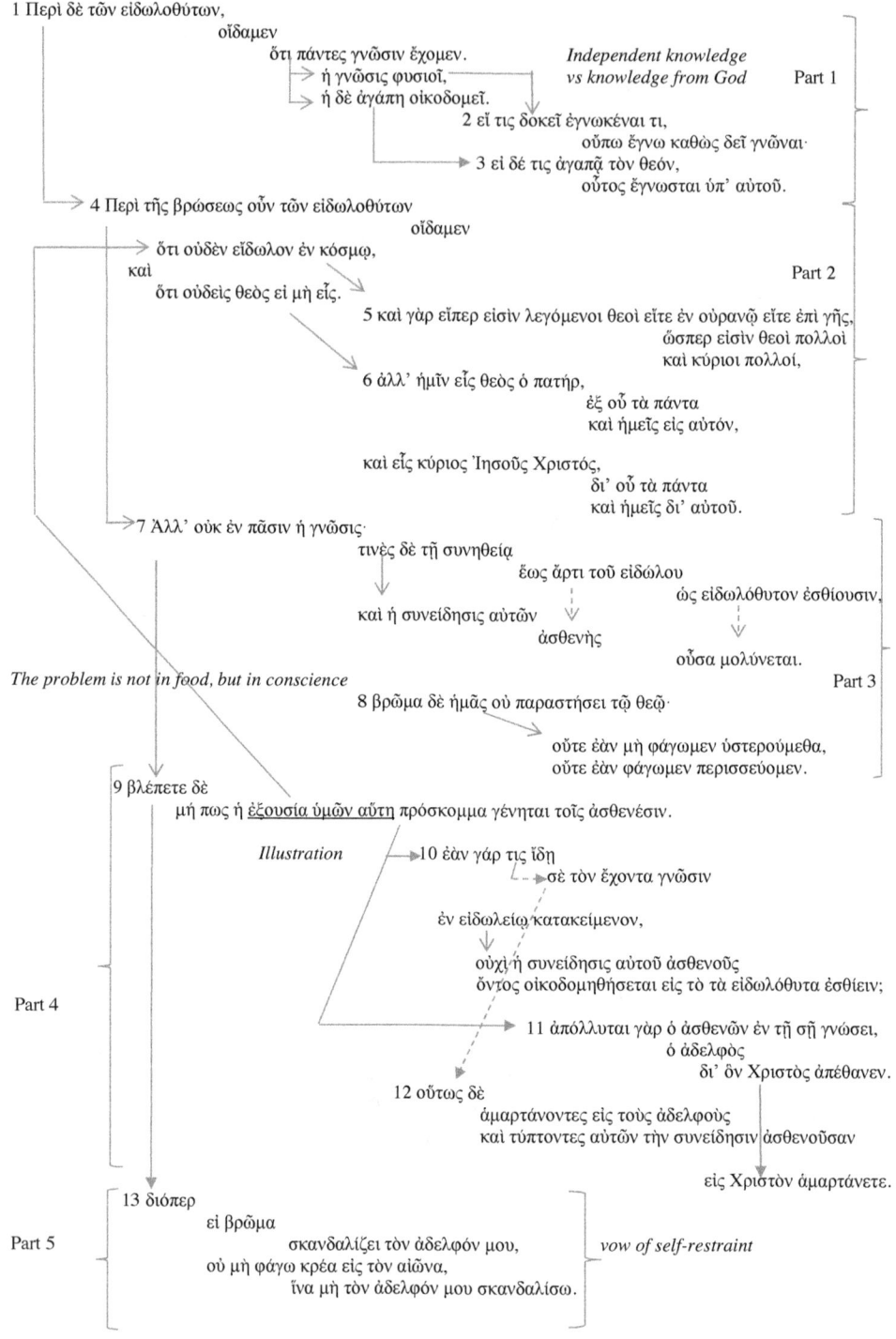

APPENDIX 2: DIAGRAMS OF THE PASSAGES STUDIED IN CHAPTER 3

2.1.4. 1 Cor 10:1–33

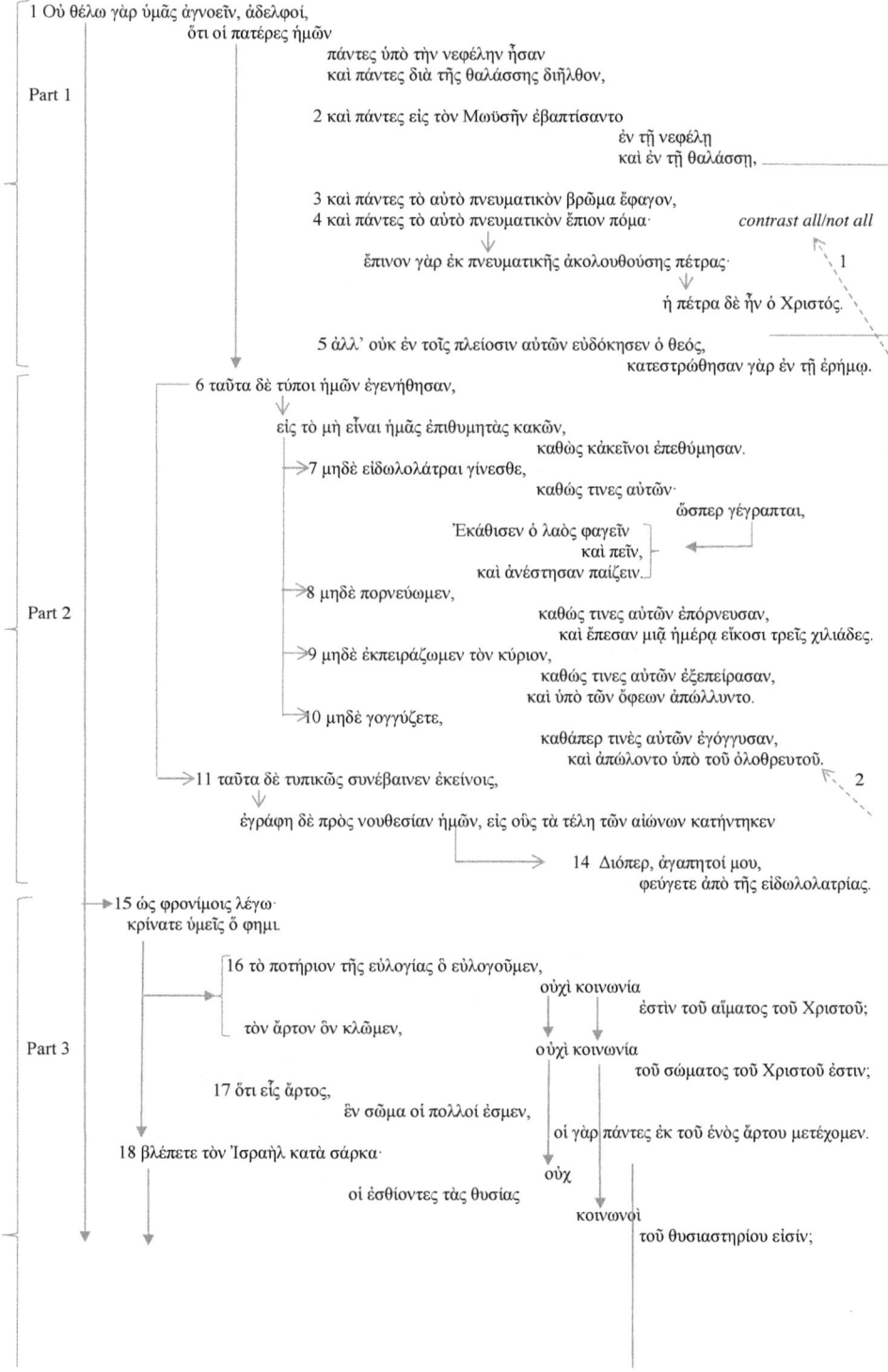

APPENDIX 2: DIAGRAMS OF THE PASSAGES STUDIED IN CHAPTER 3

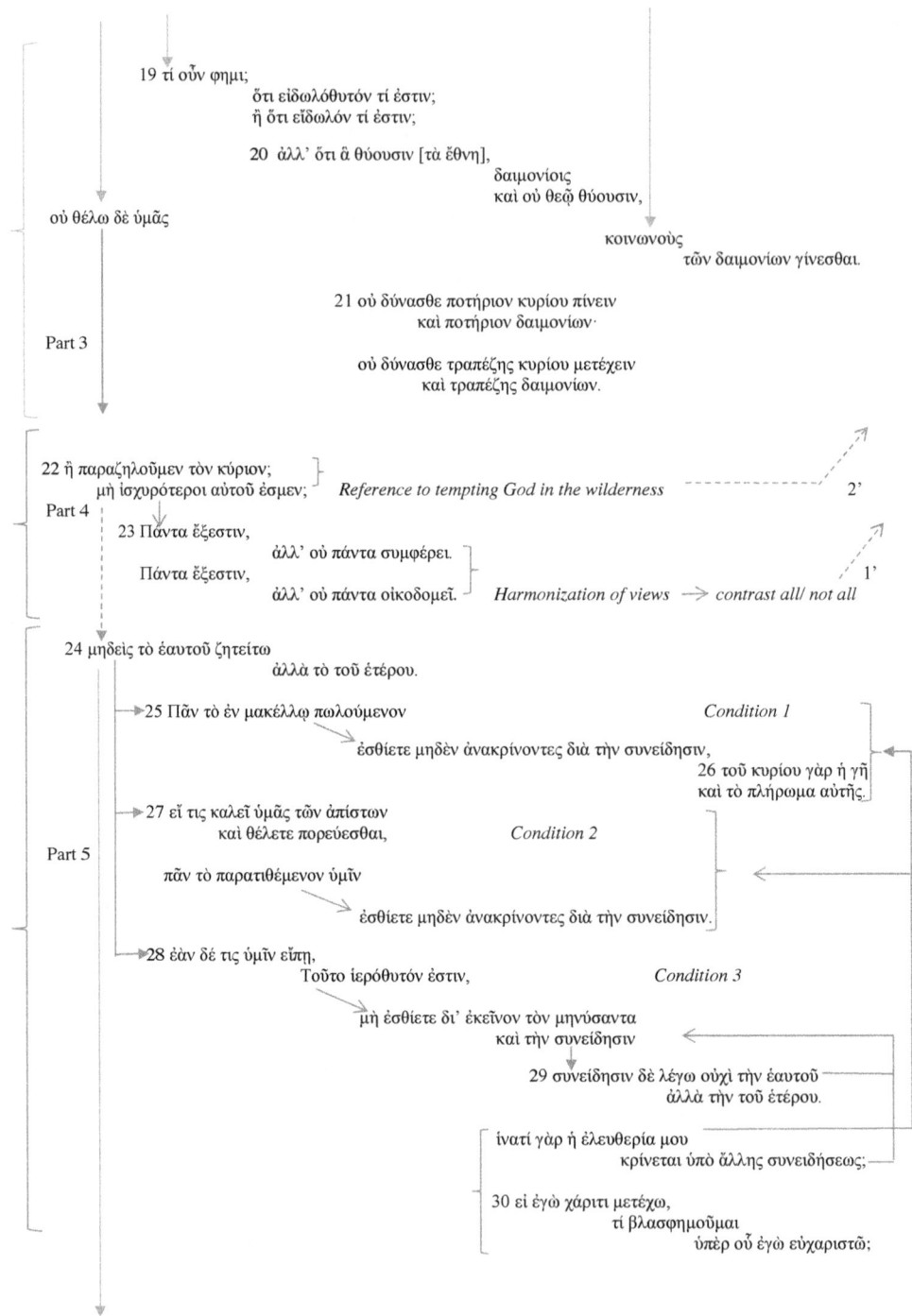

The diagram continues on the next page.

APPENDIX 2: DIAGRAMS OF THE PASSAGES STUDIED IN CHAPTER 3

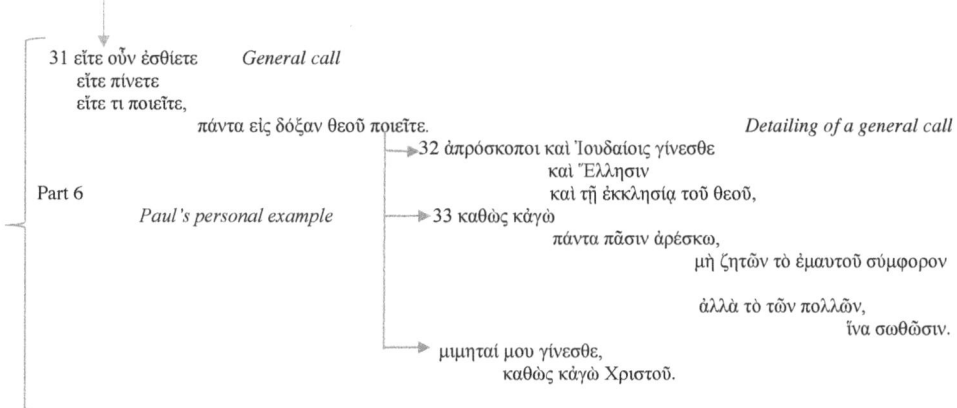

2.2. Rom 14:1–15:6

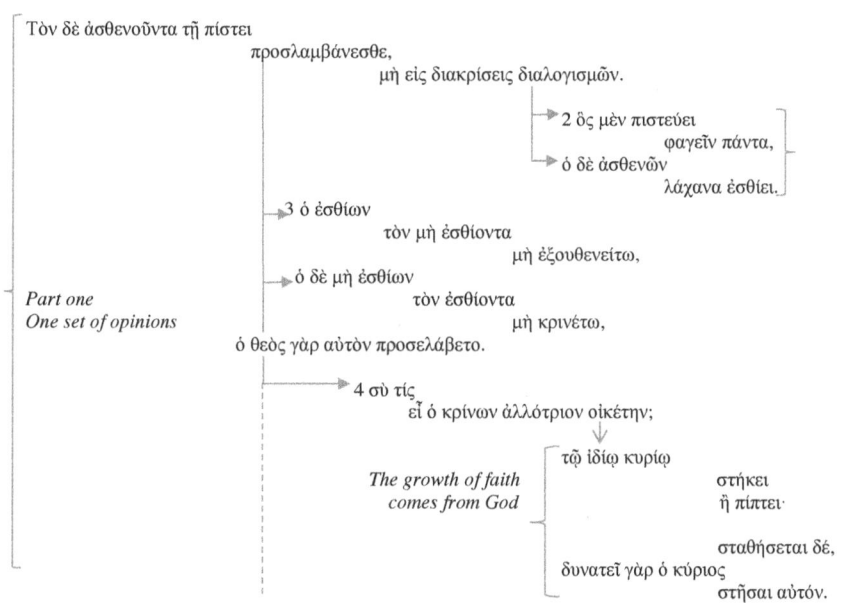

The diagram continues on the next page.

APPENDIX 2: DIAGRAMS OF THE PASSAGES STUDIED IN CHAPTER 3

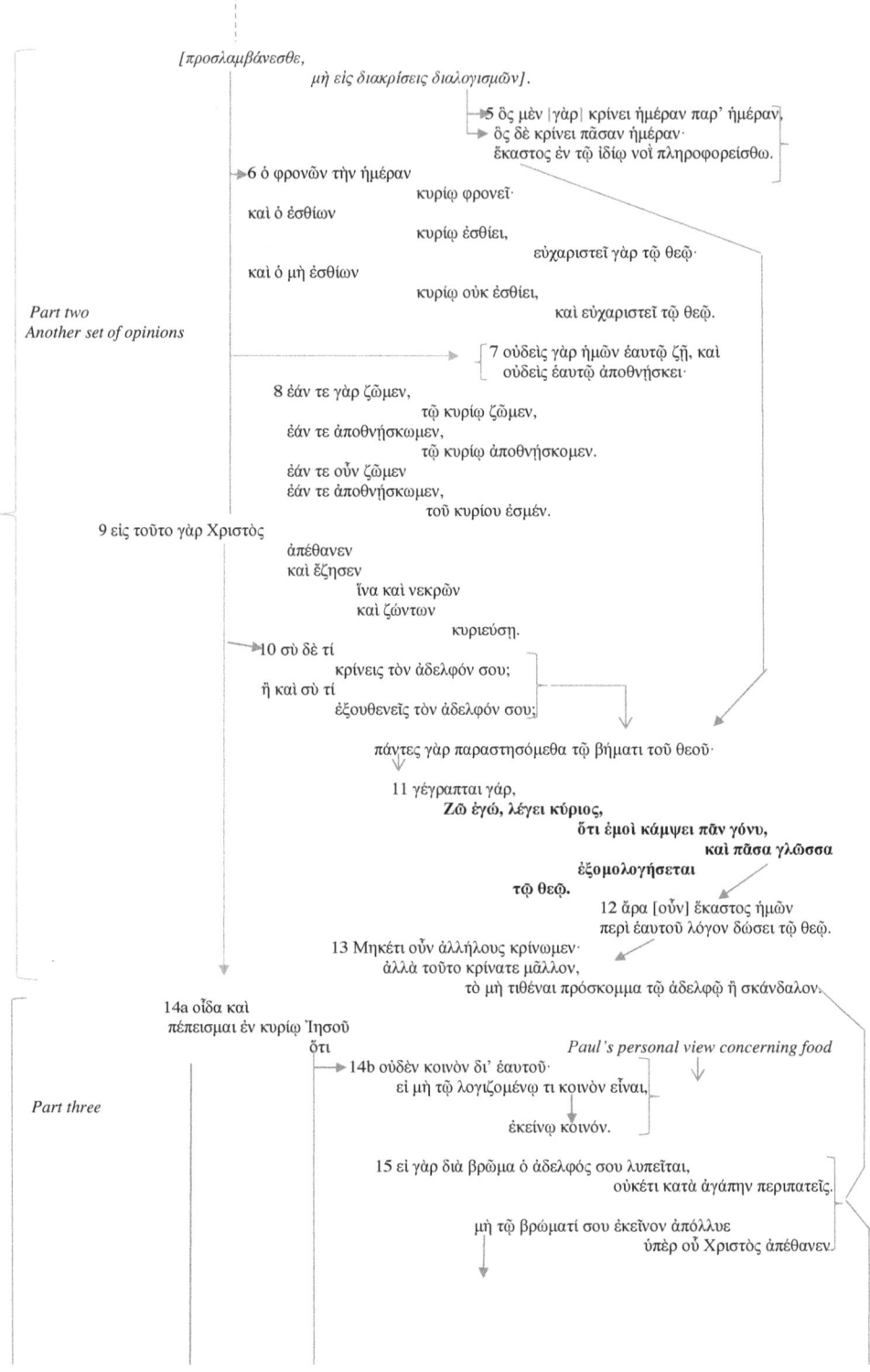

314

APPENDIX 2: DIAGRAMS OF THE PASSAGES STUDIED IN CHAPTER 3

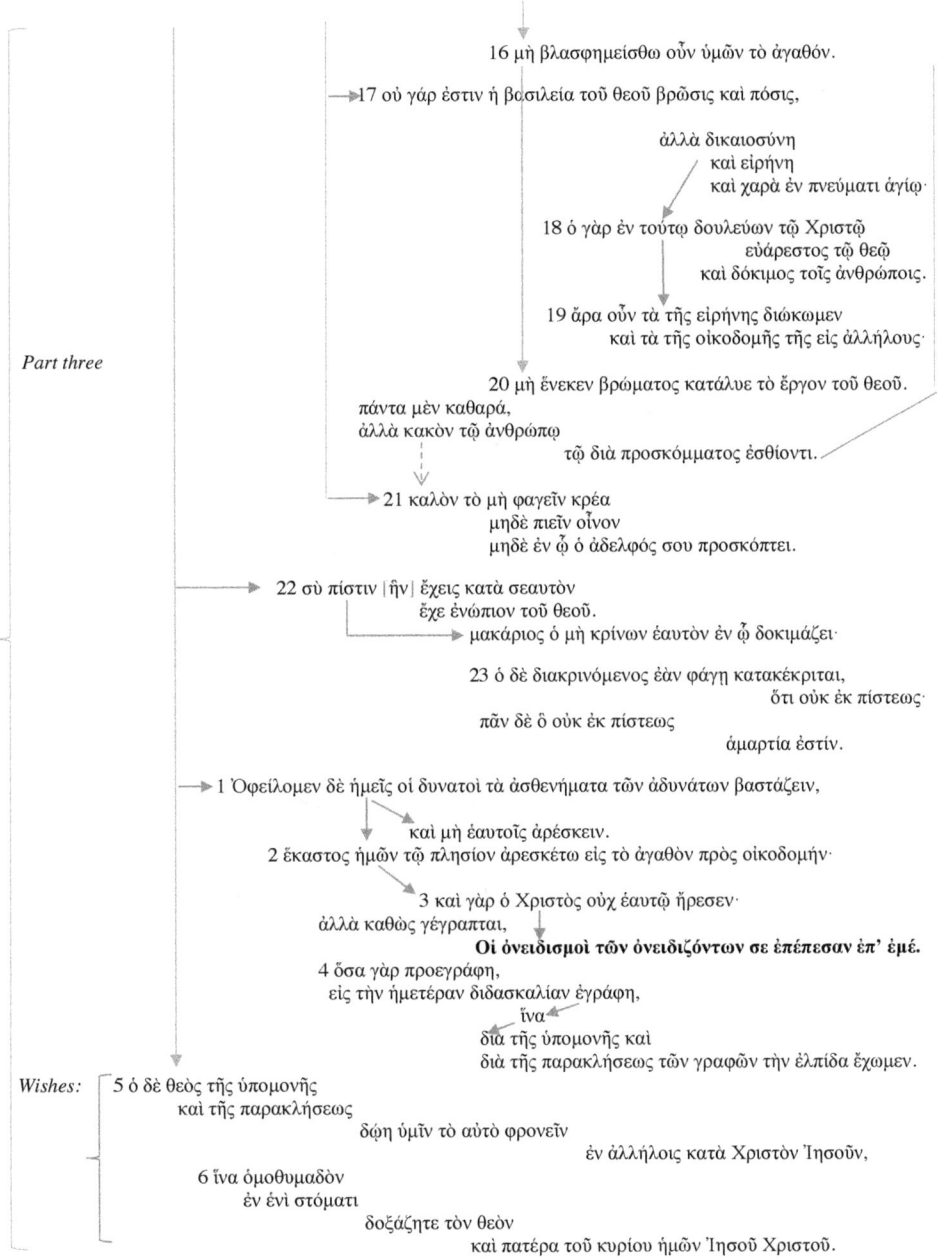

APPENDIX 2: DIAGRAMS OF THE PASSAGES STUDIED IN CHAPTER 3

2.3. Additional diagrams for passages with εἰδωλοθύτων and πορνεία in Revelation

2.3.1. Revelation 2:12–17

12 Καὶ τῷ ἀγγέλῳ τῆς ἐν Περγάμῳ ἐκκλησίας γράψον·

Τάδε λέγει ὁ ἔχων τὴν ῥομφαίαν τὴν δίστομον τὴν ὀξεῖαν·

  →13 Οἶδα ποῦ κατοικεῖς,
      ὅ που ὁ θρόνος τοῦ Σατανᾶ,
             καὶ κρατεῖς τὸ ὄνομά μου,
             καὶ οὐκ ἠρνήσω τὴν πίστιν μου
      → καὶ ἐν ταῖς ἡμέραις Ἀντιπᾶς
            ὁ μάρτυς μου
            ὁ πιστός μου,
                → ὃς ἀπεκτάνθη παρ᾽ ὑμῖν,
      ὅ που ὁ Σατανᾶς κατοικεῖ.

  →14 ἀλλ᾽ ἔχω κατὰ σοῦ ὀλίγα,
      → ὅτι ἔχεις ἐκεῖ
        κρατοῦντας τὴν διδαχὴν Βαλαάμ,
            ὃς ἐδίδασκεν τῷ Βαλὰκ
              βαλεῖν σκάνδαλον ἐνώπιον τῶν υἱῶν Ἰσραήλ,
                  → φαγεῖν εἰδωλόθυτα
                  → καὶ πορνεῦσαι·
      →15 οὕτως ἔχεις καὶ σὺ
        κρατοῦντας τὴν διδαχὴν Νικολαϊτῶν ὁμοίως.

→16 μετανόησον οὖν·
    → εἰ δὲ μή,
      ἔρχομαί σοι ταχύ,
      καὶ πολεμήσω μετ᾽ αὐτῶν ἐν τῇ ῥομφαίᾳ τοῦ στόματός μου.
→17 ὁ ἔχων οὖς ἀκουσάτω τί τὸ πνεῦμα λέγει ταῖς ἐκκλησίαις.
    → τῷ νικῶντι
      → δώσω αὐτῷ τοῦ μάννα τοῦ κεκρυμμένου, καὶ   Exod 28:21-30
      → δώσω αὐτῷ ψῆφον λευκὴν
        καὶ ἐπὶ τὴν ψῆφον
            → ὄνομα καινὸν γεγραμμένον
              ὃ οὐδεὶς οἶδεν εἰ μὴ ὁ λαμβάνων.

APPENDIX 3: DIAGRAMS OF THE PASSAGES STUDIED IN CHAPTER 4

Luke 2:41, 42

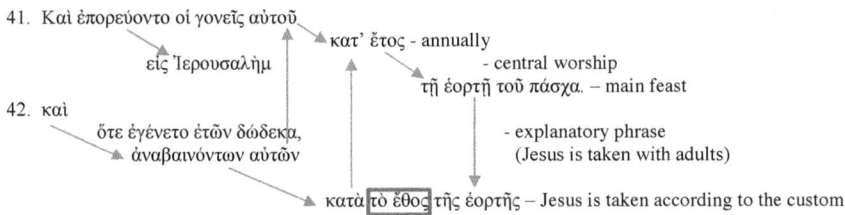

1.1.2. Luke 11:37–44—cleansing of ritual uncleanness

37 Ἐν δὲ τῷ λαλῆσαι — the interruption of speech (visible agreement with the teaching)
  ἐρωτᾷ αὐτὸν Φαρισαῖος
    ὅπως ἀριστήσῃ παρ' αὐτῷ·   Part 1
εἰσελθὼν δὲ ἀνέπεσεν.   purification issue
  38 ὁ δὲ Φαρισαῖος ἰδὼν ἐθαύμασεν — hidden disagreement
    ὅτι οὐ πρῶτον ἐβαπτίσθη πρὸ τοῦ ἀρίστου.

39 εἶπεν δὲ ὁ κύριος πρὸς αὐτόν,   — Jesus' answer to hypocrisy
  Νῦν ὑμεῖς   (disconnect of visible   Part 2
    οἱ Φαρισαῖοι   and inner sides of a person)
      → τὸ ἔξωθεν
          τοῦ ποτηρίου   Contrast:
          καὶ τοῦ πίνακος   external/internal
                          καθαρίζετε,   purification
      → τὸ δὲ ἔσωθεν   rite /hidden life
          ὑμῶν
                  → γέμει
                      ἁρπαγῆς
                      καὶ πονηρίας.   One cannot be
  40 ἄφρονες,   partially clean,
    οὐχ ὁ ποιήσας τὸ ἔξωθεν   but totally
    καὶ τὸ ἔσωθεν ἐποίησεν;   Part 3
            41 πλὴν τὰ ἐνόντα δότε ἐλεημοσύνην,
                καὶ ἰδοὺ πάντα καθαρὰ ὑμῖν ἐστιν.

42 ἀλλὰ οὐαὶ ὑμῖν
  τοῖς Φαρισαίοις,
      → ὅτι ἀποδεκατοῦτε τὸ ἡδύοσμον   source of uncleanness
          καὶ τὸ πήγανον   lack of love to others
          καὶ πᾶν λάχανον,
        καὶ παρέρχεσθε   Part 4
          τὴν κρίσιν καὶ
          τὴν ἀγάπην τοῦ θεοῦ·
                        ταῦτα δὲ ἔδει ποιῆσαι
                        κἀκεῖνα μὴ παρεῖναι.

43 οὐαὶ ὑμῖν
  τοῖς Φαρισαίοις,   Part 5
      → ὅτι ἀγαπᾶτε τὴν πρωτοκαθεδρίαν ἐν ταῖς συναγωγαῖς
          καὶ τοὺς ἀσπασμοὺς ἐν ταῖς ἀγοραῖς.   selfishness

44 οὐαὶ ὑμῖν, ...
      → ὅτι ἐστὲ ὡς τὰ μνημεῖα τὰ ἄδηλα,
          καὶ οἱ ἄνθρωποι [οἱ] περιπατοῦντες ἐπάνω   Part 6
              οὐκ οἴδασιν.
                                                         source of uncleanness

APPENDIX 3: DIAGRAMS OF THE PASSAGES STUDIED IN CHAPTER 4

1.2. Replacement of ritual cleansing with baptism

Luke 3:8—John fights against the belief that only the descendants of Abraham are clean. They are called into cleansing similar to the Gentile proselytes.

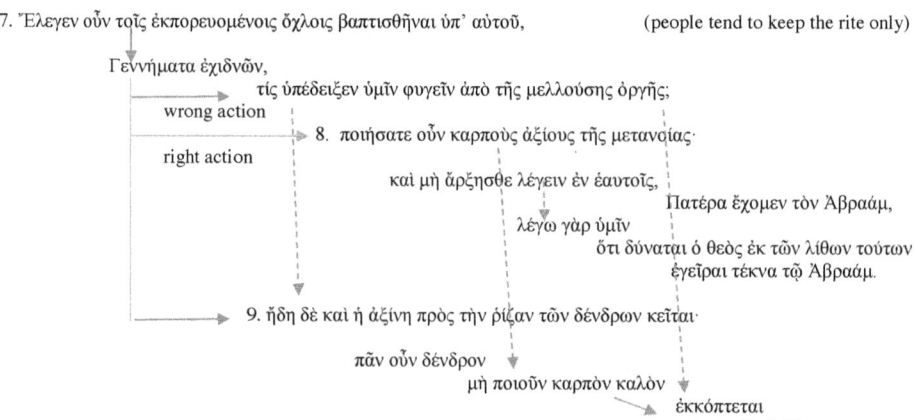

Acts 2:38, 39—Peter calls for baptism similar that of the Gentile proselytes

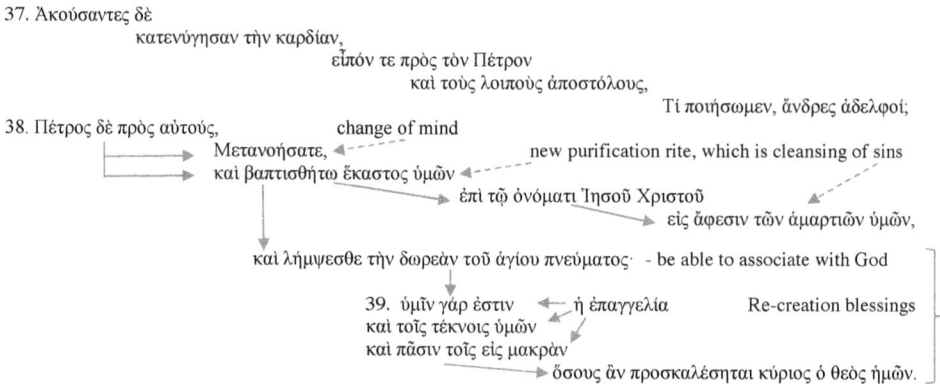

APPENDIX 3: DIAGRAMS OF THE PASSAGES STUDIED IN CHAPTER 4

1.3. Uncleanness of leprosy

Luke 5:12–14

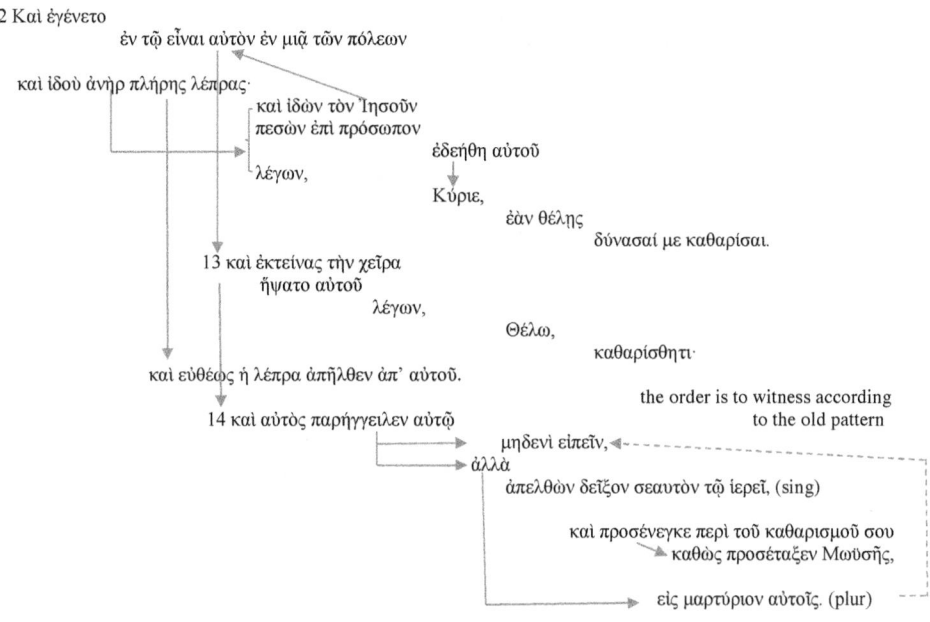

APPENDIX 3: DIAGRAMS OF THE PASSAGES STUDIED IN CHAPTER 4

Luke 17:11-19

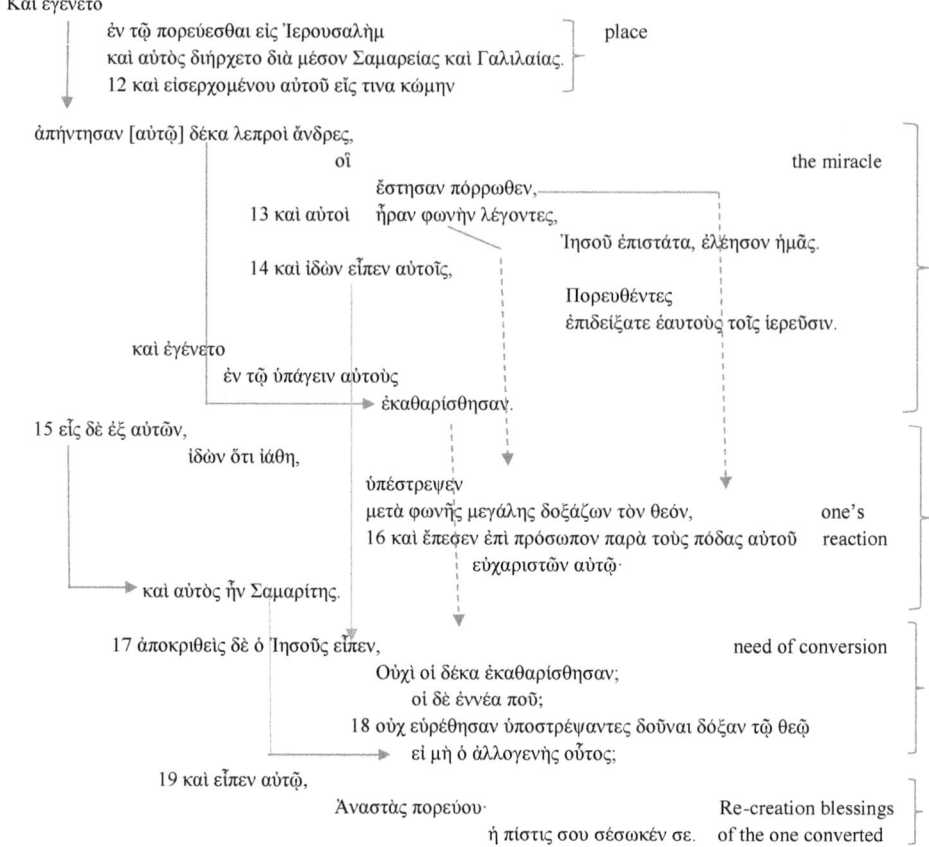

1.4. Uncleanness of a dead body

Luke 7:11-15

1.4. Uncleanness of a dead body

Luke 7:11-15

11 Καὶ ἐγένετο
 ἐν τῷ ἑξῆς ἐπορεύθη εἰς πόλιν καλουμένην Ναΐν, ⎤
 καὶ συνεπορεύοντο αὐτῷ οἱ μαθηταὶ αὐτοῦ ⎬ one crowd
 καὶ ὄχλος πολύς. ⎦

12 ὡς δὲ ἤγγισεν τῇ πύλῃ τῆς πόλεως,
 καὶ ἰδοὺ ἐξεκομίζετο τεθνηκὼς
   μονογενὴς υἱὸς τῇ μητρὶ αὐτοῦ, ⎤
   καὶ αὐτὴ ἦν χήρα, ⎬ another crowd
 καὶ ὄχλος τῆς πόλεως ἱκανὸς ἦν σὺν αὐτῇ. ⎦

13 καὶ ἰδὼν αὐτὴν
 ὁ κύριος ἐσπλαγχνίσθη ἐπ' αὐτῇ   Resurrection
 καὶ εἶπεν αὐτῇ,
   Μὴ κλαῖε.
14 καὶ προσελθὼν
 ἥψατο τῆς σοροῦ,
οἱ δὲ βαστάζοντες ἔστησαν,
 καὶ εἶπεν,
  Νεανίσκε,
  σοὶ λέγω,
   ἐγέρθητι.
15 καὶ ἀνεκάθισεν ὁ νεκρὸς
καὶ ἤρξατο λαλεῖν,

καὶ ἔδωκεν αὐτὸν τῇ μητρὶ αὐτοῦ.

16 ἔλαβεν δὲ φόβος πάντας,   spiritual lesson
 καὶ ἐδόξαζον τὸν θεὸν λέγοντες
  → ὅτι Προφήτης μέγας ἠγέρθη ἐν ἡμῖν, καὶ
  → ὅτι Ἐπεσκέψατο ὁ θεὸς τὸν λαὸν αὐτοῦ.

APPENDIX 3: DIAGRAMS OF THE PASSAGES STUDIED IN CHAPTER 4

Luke 8:40-42, 49-54—resurrection of Jairus' daughter (reverting death to life)

40. Ἐν δὲ τῷ ὑποστρέφειν τὸν Ἰησοῦν
      ἀπεδέξατο αὐτὸν ὁ ὄχλος,
          ἦσαν γὰρ πάντες προσδοκῶντες αὐτόν.
41. καὶ ἰδοὺ ἦλθεν ἀνὴρ ᾧ ὄνομα Ἰάϊρος,
    καὶ οὗτος ἄρχων τῆς συναγωγῆς ὑπῆρχεν,

      καὶ πεσὼν παρὰ τοὺς πόδας τοῦ Ἰησοῦ
        παρεκάλει αὐτὸν
          εἰσελθεῖν εἰς τὸν οἶκον αὐτοῦ,
            42. ὅτι θυγάτηρ μονογενὴς ἦν αὐτῷ
              ὡς ἐτῶν δώδεκα
              καὶ αὐτὴ ἀπέθνησκεν.

49. Ἔτι αὐτοῦ λαλοῦντος   discouraging news
    ἔρχεταί τις παρὰ τοῦ ἀρχισυναγώγου λέγων
                                ὅτι Τέθνηκεν ἡ θυγάτηρ σου,
                                μηκέτι σκύλλε τὸν διδάσκαλον.
50. ὁ δὲ Ἰησοῦς ἀκούσας ἀπεκρίθη αὐτῷ,
          Μὴ φοβοῦ,   call to
          μόνον πίστευσον,   believe
                    καὶ σωθήσεται.
51. ἐλθὼν δὲ εἰς τὴν οἰκίαν
    οὐκ ἀφῆκεν εἰσελθεῖν τινα σὺν αὐτῷ
        εἰ μὴ Πέτρον   ← election of believing
        καὶ Ἰωάννην
        καὶ Ἰάκωβον
        καὶ τὸν πατέρα τῆς παιδὸς   reaction of unbelieving
        καὶ τὴν μητέρα.
                        52. ἔκλαιον δὲ πάντες
                          καὶ ἐκόπτοντο αὐτήν.
        ὁ δὲ εἶπεν,
            → Μὴ κλαίετε,
                οὐ γὰρ ἀπέθανεν
                ἀλλὰ καθεύδει.
                        53. καὶ κατεγέλων αὐτοῦ,
                          εἰδότες ὅτι ἀπέθανεν.
54. αὐτὸς δὲ
    κρατήσας τῆς χειρὸς αὐτῆς
    ἐφώνησεν λέγων,
        → Ἡ παῖς, ἔγειρε.   similar to creation
                55. καὶ ἐπέστρεψεν τὸ πνεῦμα αὐτῆς,
                    καὶ ἀνέστη παραχρῆμα,
                    καὶ διέταξεν αὐτῇ δοθῆναι φαγεῖν.
                56. καὶ ἐξέστησαν οἱ γονεῖς αὐτῆς·

      ὁ δὲ παρήγγειλεν αὐτοῖς   order not to tell
         → μηδενὶ εἰπεῖν τὸ γεγονός   to the non-believing

APPENDIX 3: DIAGRAMS OF THE PASSAGES STUDIED IN CHAPTER 4

1.5. Uncleanness of a flow of blood

Luke 8:43–48

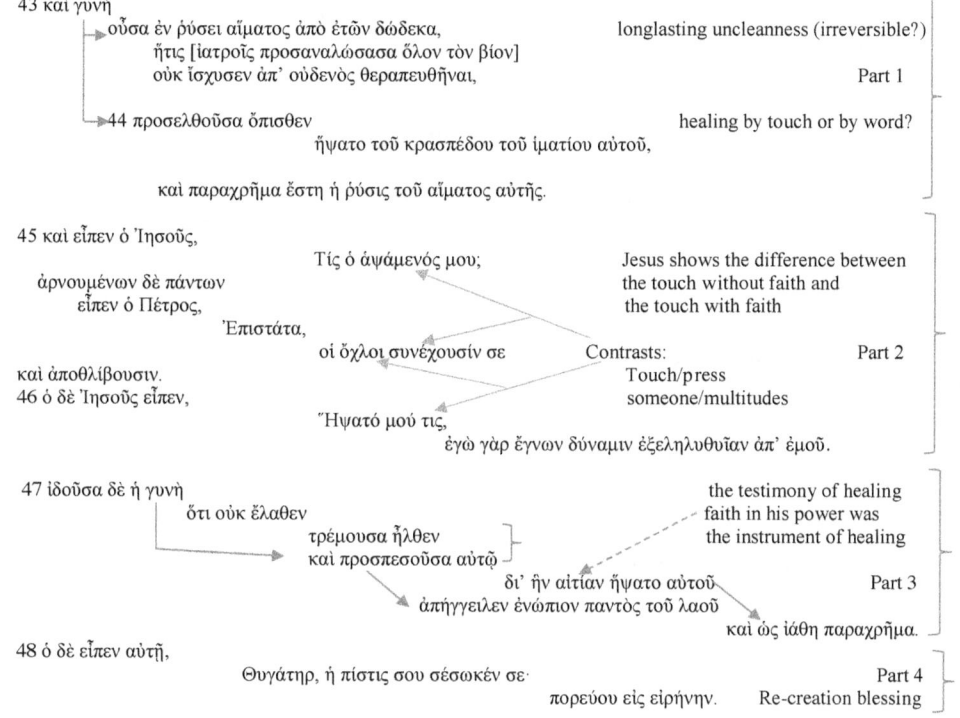

APPENDIX 3: DIAGRAMS OF THE PASSAGES STUDIED IN CHAPTER 4

1.6. Uncleanness of demon possessions

1.6.1. Luke 4:31–41

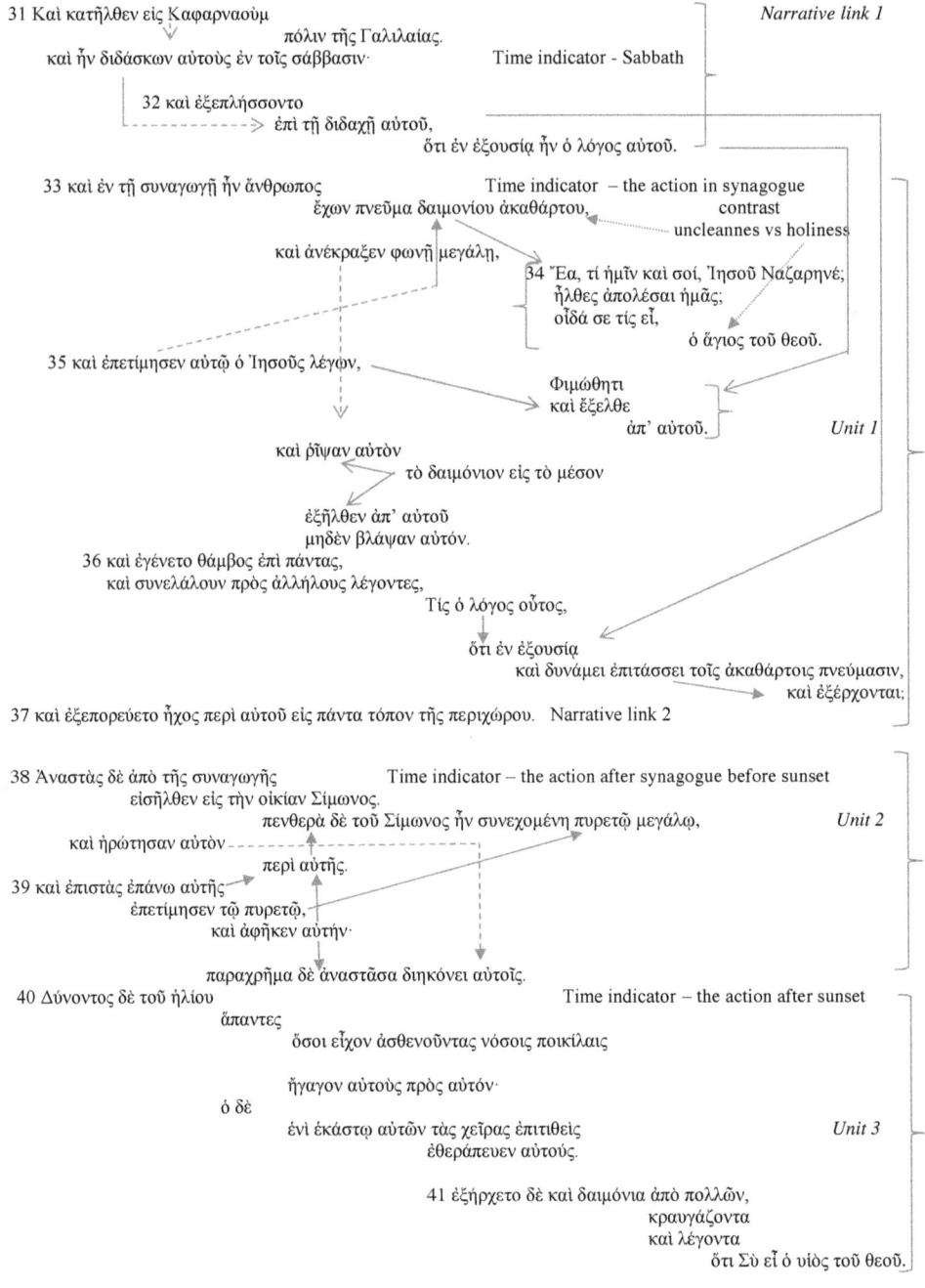

APPENDIX 3: DIAGRAMS OF THE PASSAGES STUDIED IN CHAPTER 4

1.6.2. Luke 8:26–36

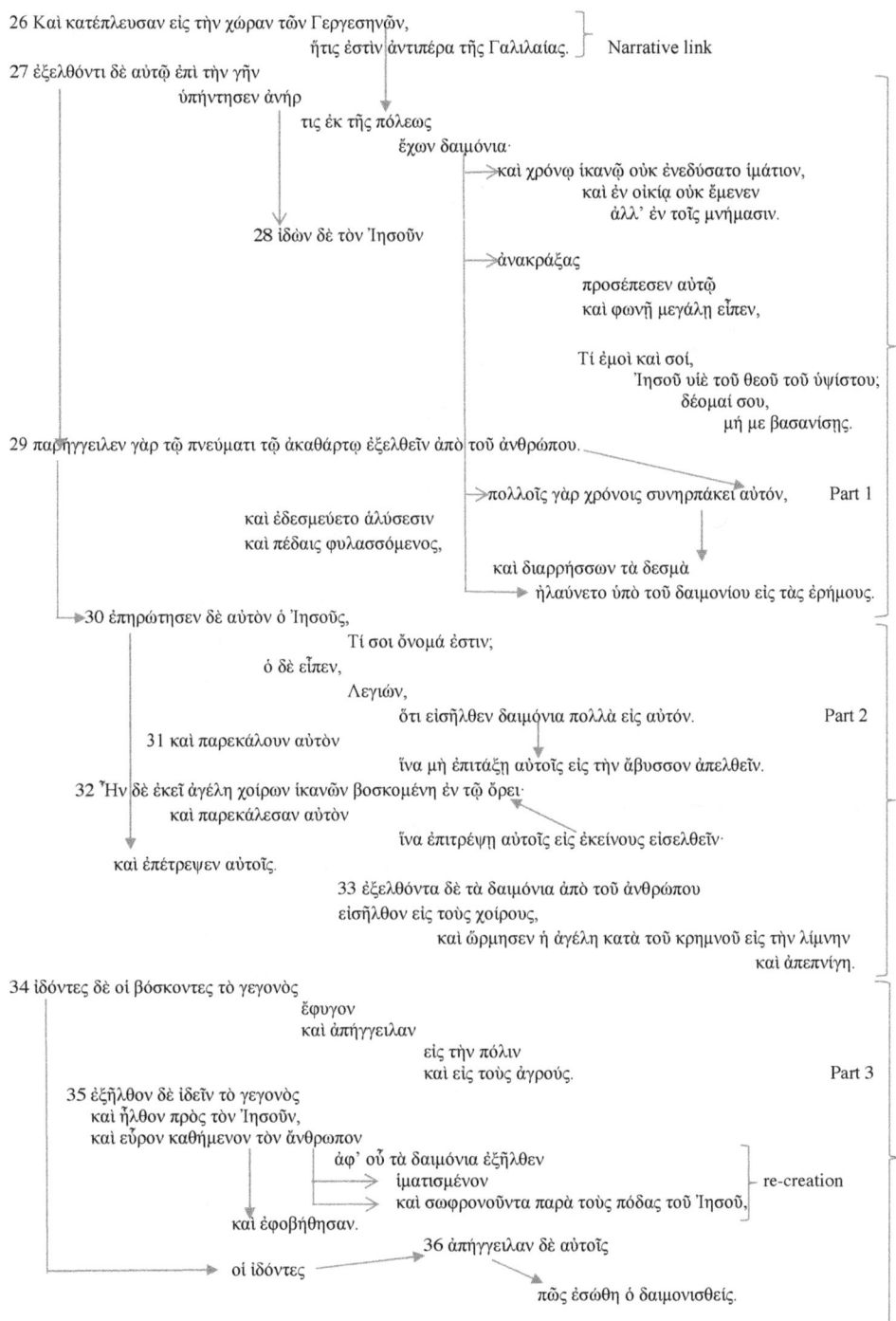

327

APPENDIX 3: DIAGRAMS OF THE PASSAGES STUDIED IN CHAPTER 4

1.6.3. Luke 11:14-26

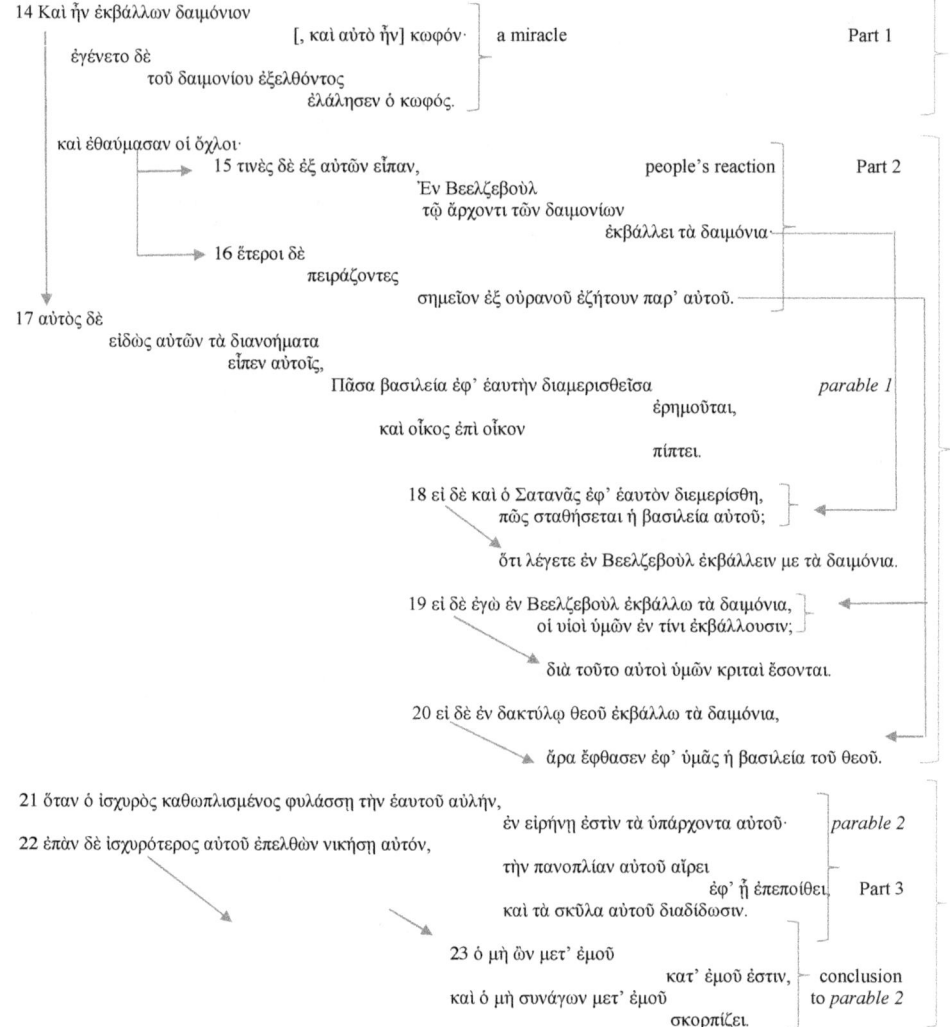

328

APPENDIX 3: DIAGRAMS OF THE PASSAGES STUDIED IN CHAPTER 4

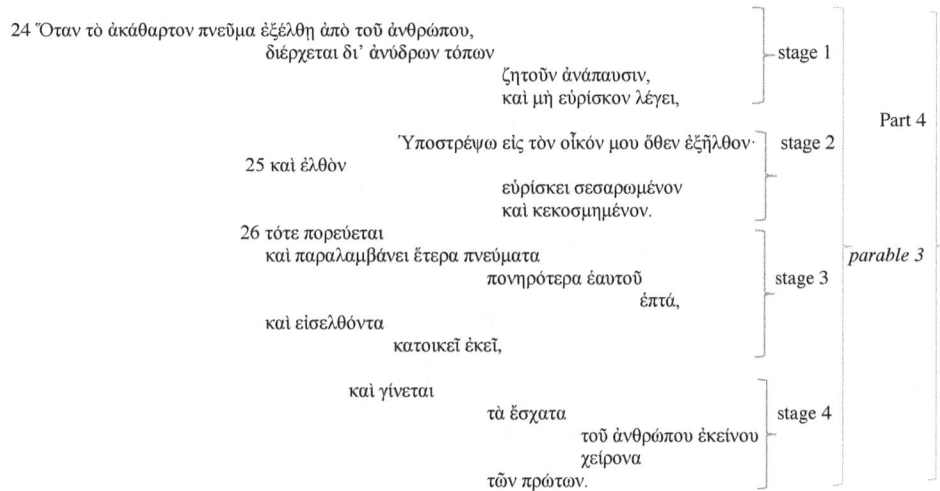

2. Uncleanness of the Gentiles

2.1. Acts 10:1-24

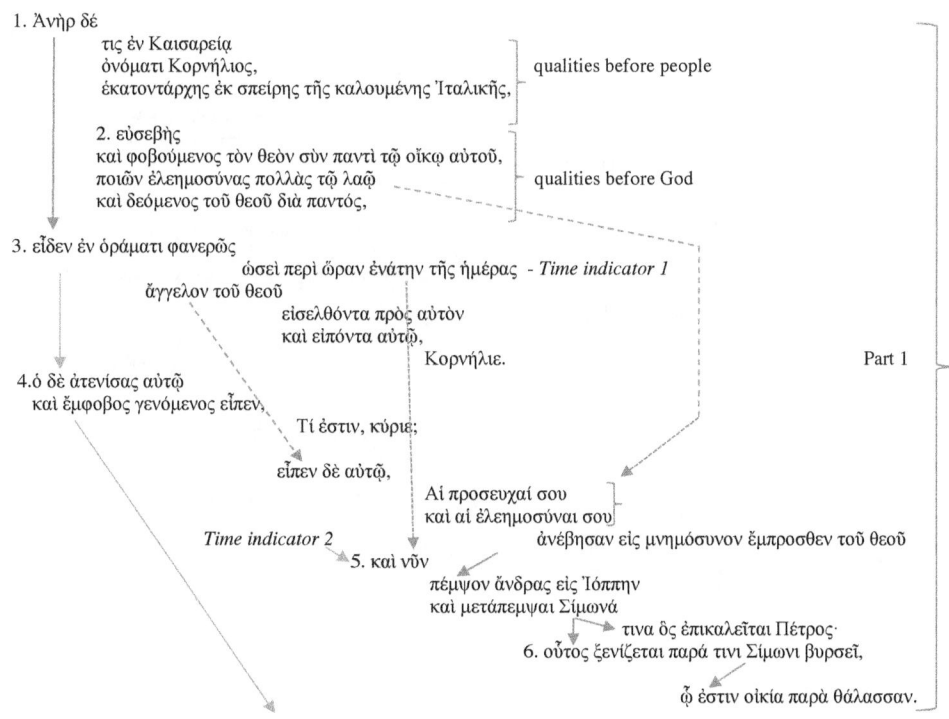

APPENDIX 3: DIAGRAMS OF THE PASSAGES STUDIED IN CHAPTER 4

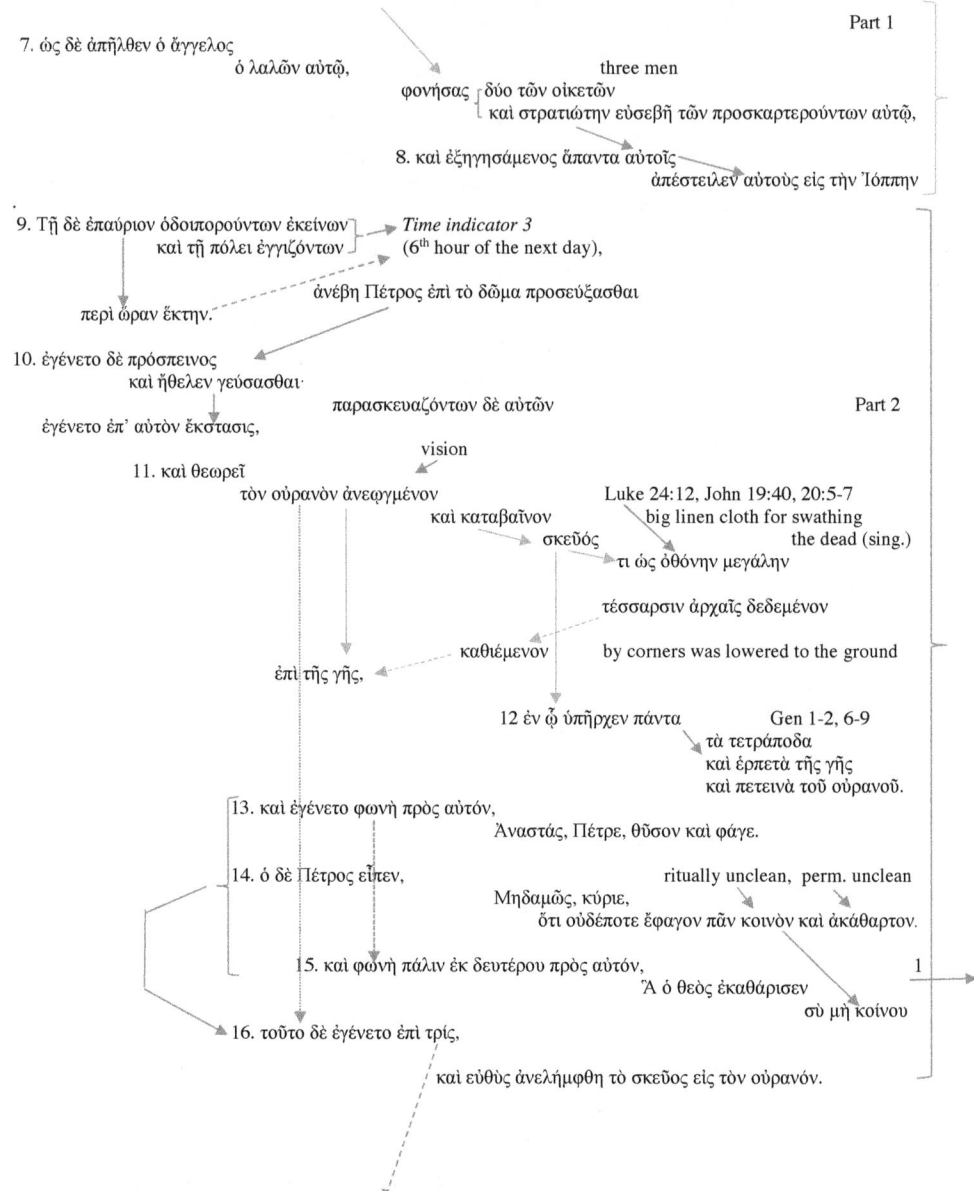

APPENDIX 3: DIAGRAMS OF THE PASSAGES STUDIED IN CHAPTER 4

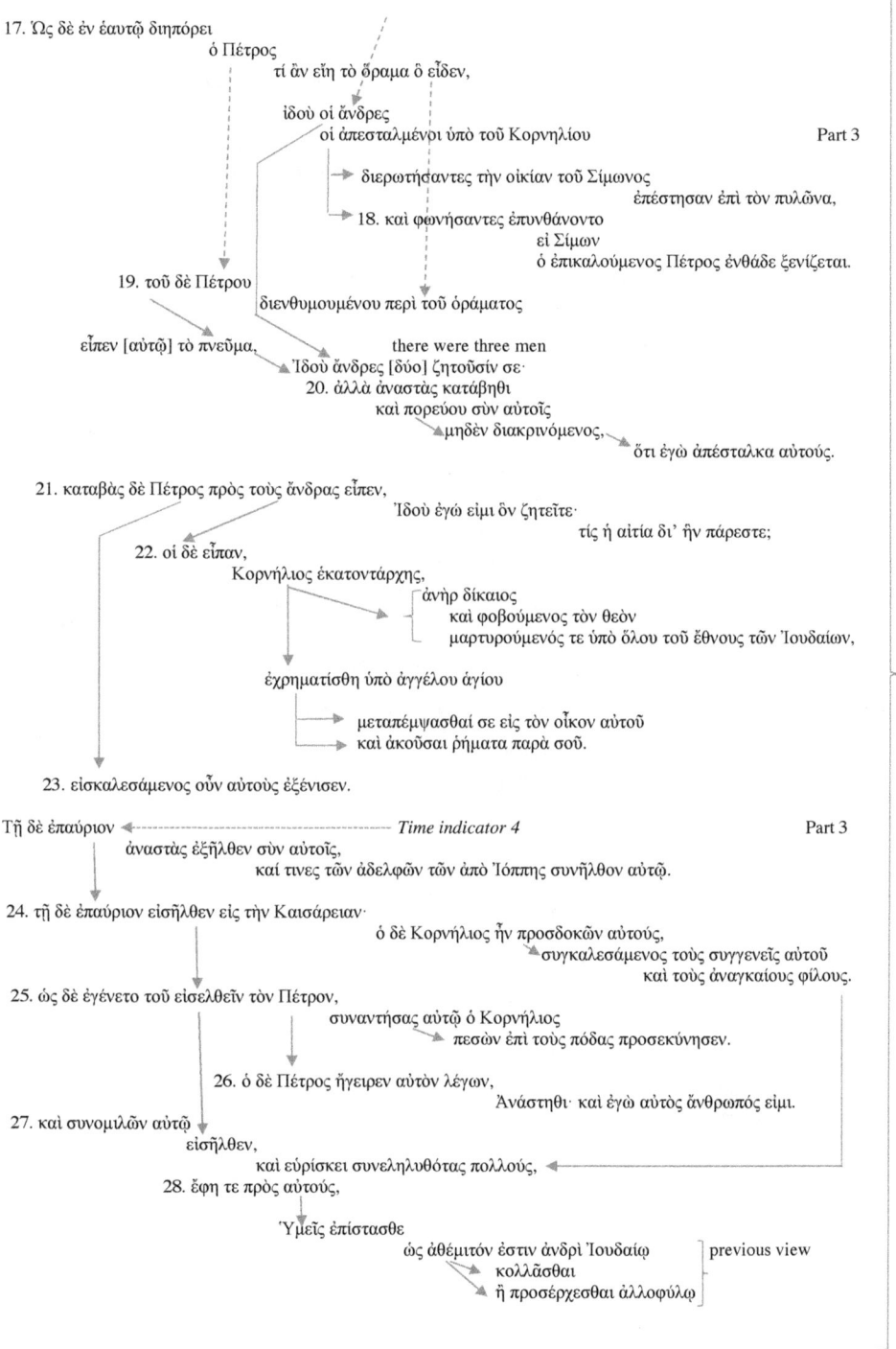

The diagram continues on the next page.

APPENDIX 3: DIAGRAMS OF THE PASSAGES STUDIED IN CHAPTER 4

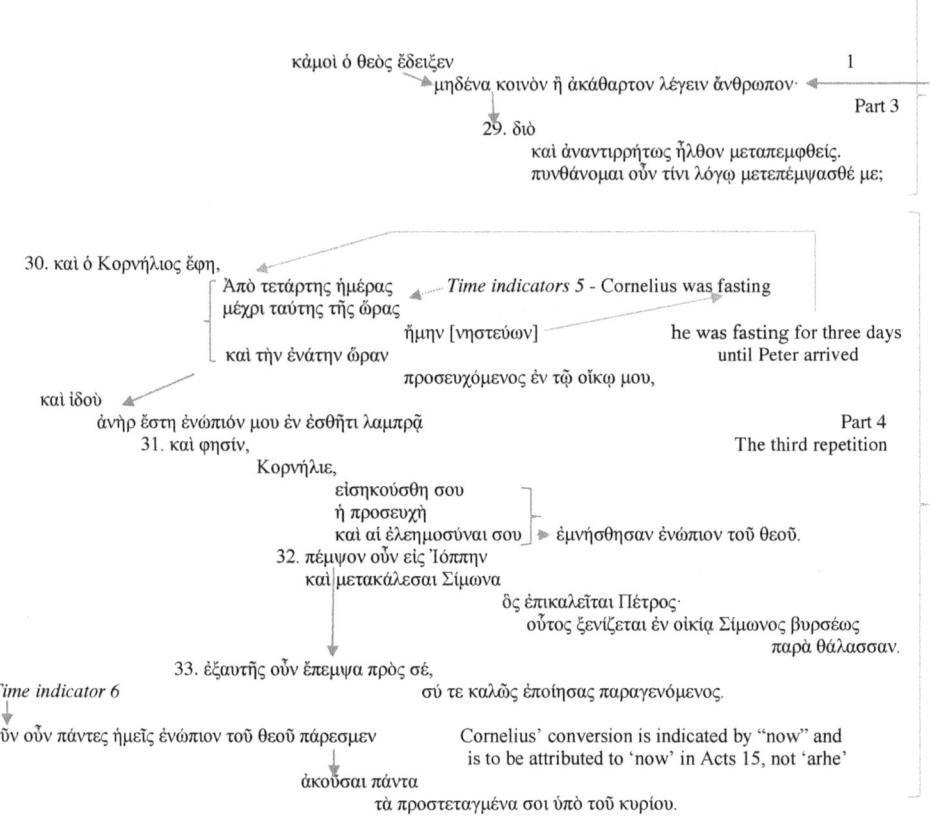

APPENDIX 3: DIAGRAMS OF THE PASSAGES STUDIED IN CHAPTER 4

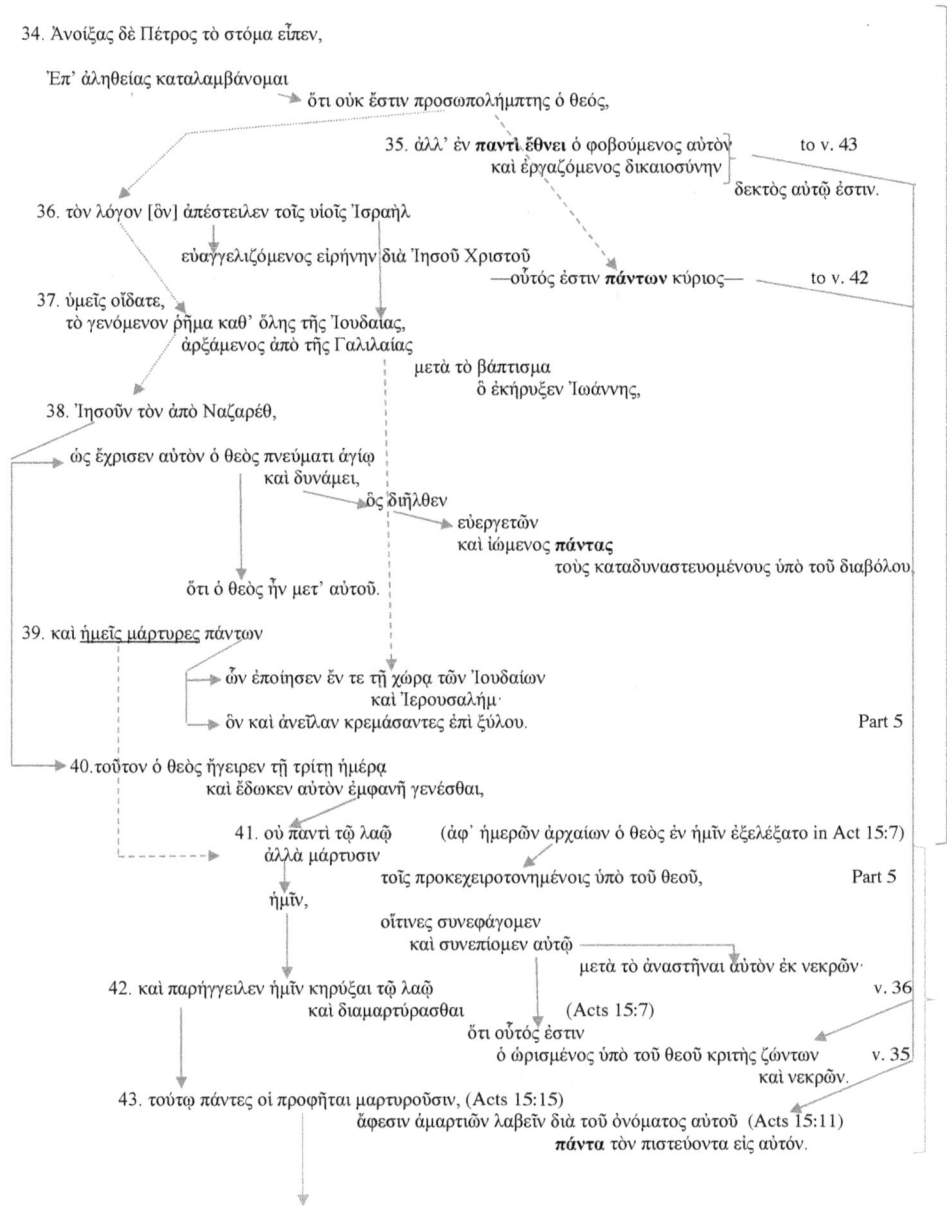

The diagram continues on the next page.

APPENDIX 3: DIAGRAMS OF THE PASSAGES STUDIED IN CHAPTER 4

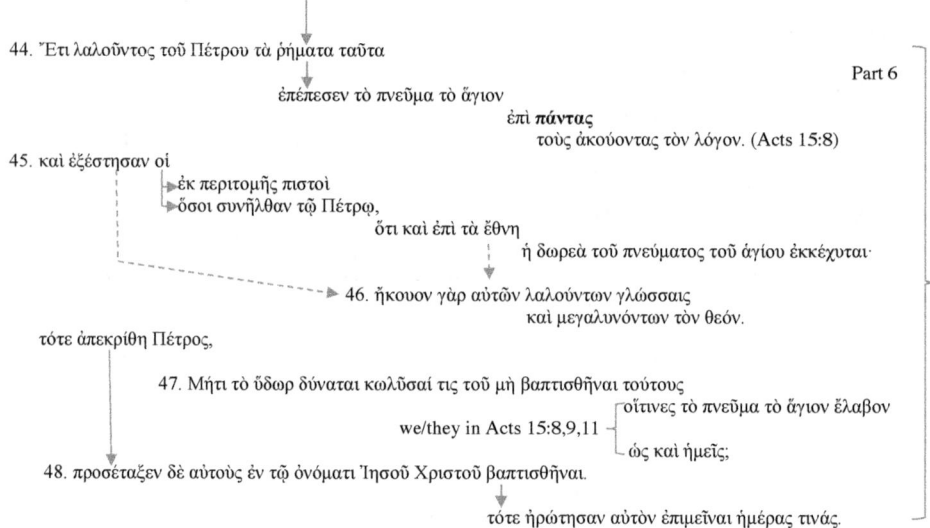

APPENDIX 3: DIAGRAMS OF THE PASSAGES STUDIED IN CHAPTER 4

2.2. Acts 11

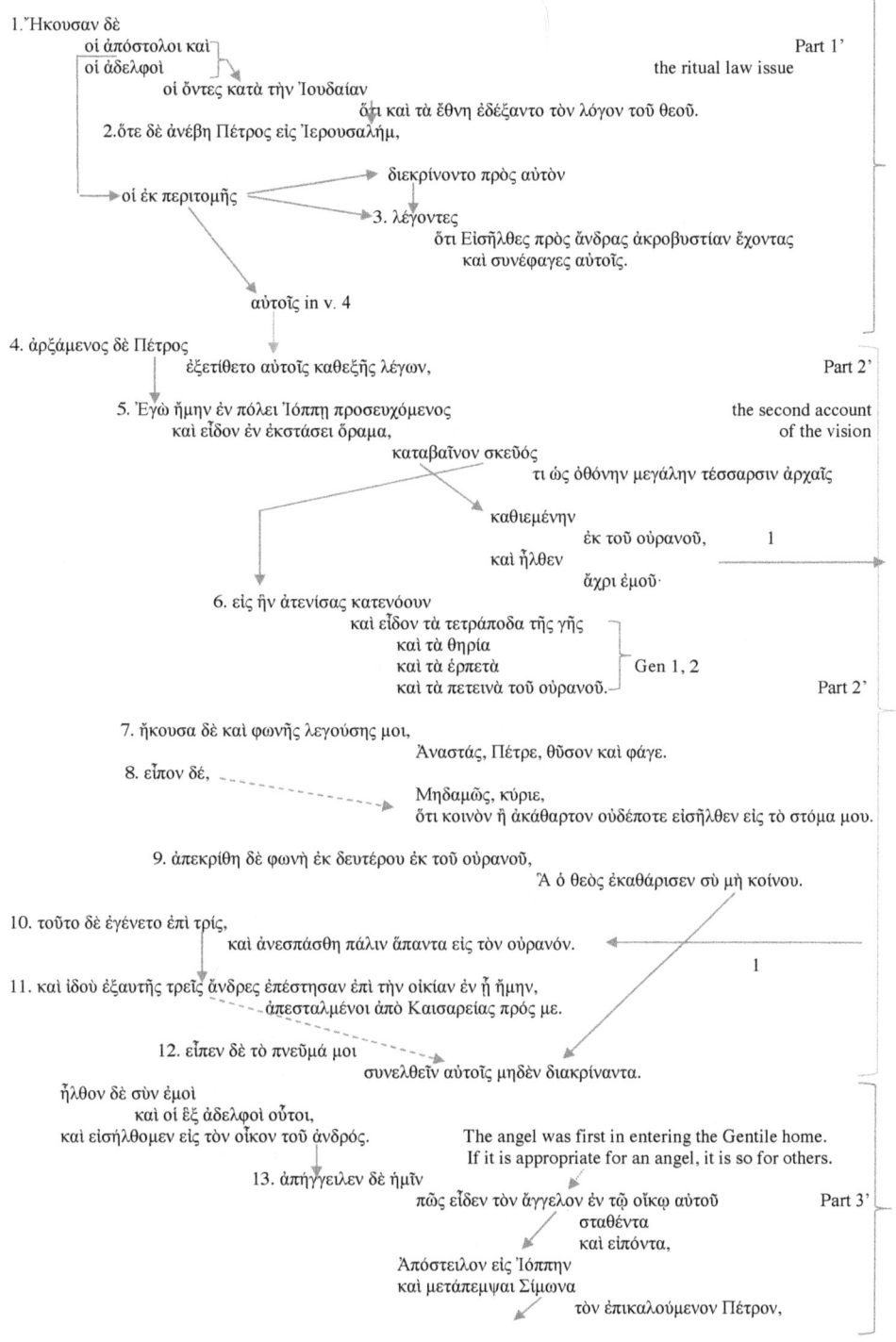

335

APPENDIX 3: DIAGRAMS OF THE PASSAGES STUDIED IN CHAPTER 4

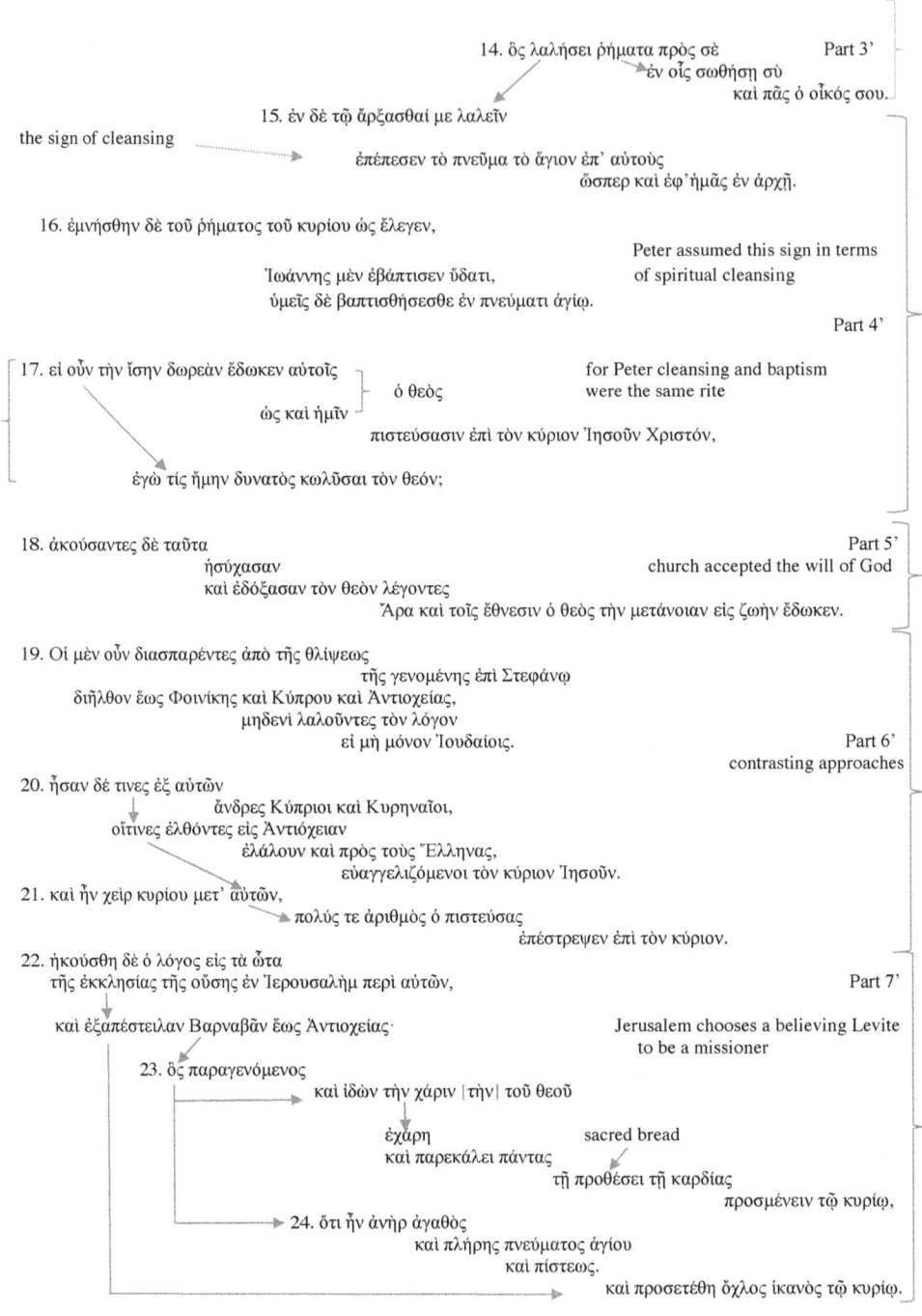

APPENDIX 3: DIAGRAMS OF THE PASSAGES STUDIED IN CHAPTER 4

2.3. The dilemma between being a believing Jew or a believing Gentile convert.

Acts 16:1-5, 13-15

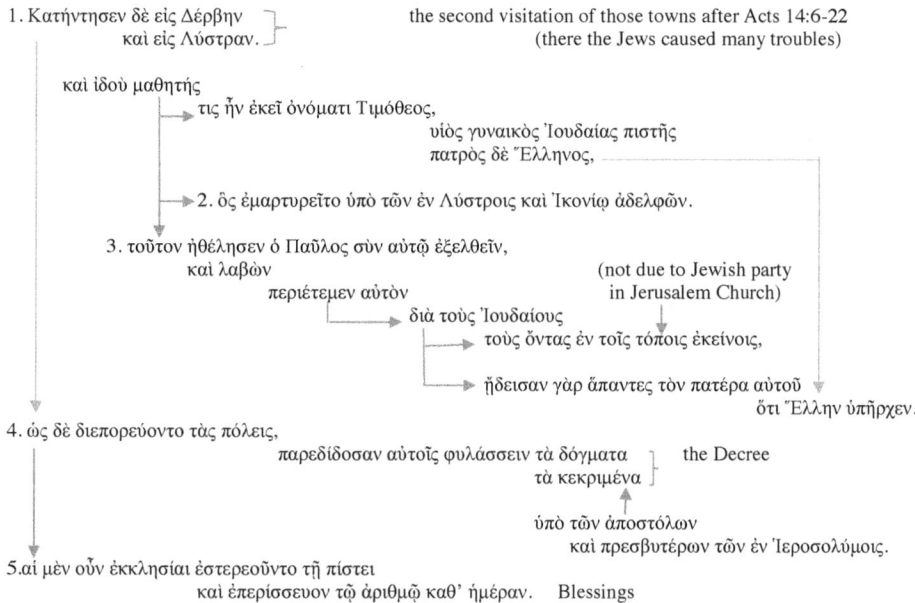

3. The changes of feasts and levitical ministry.

Luke 22:15-20

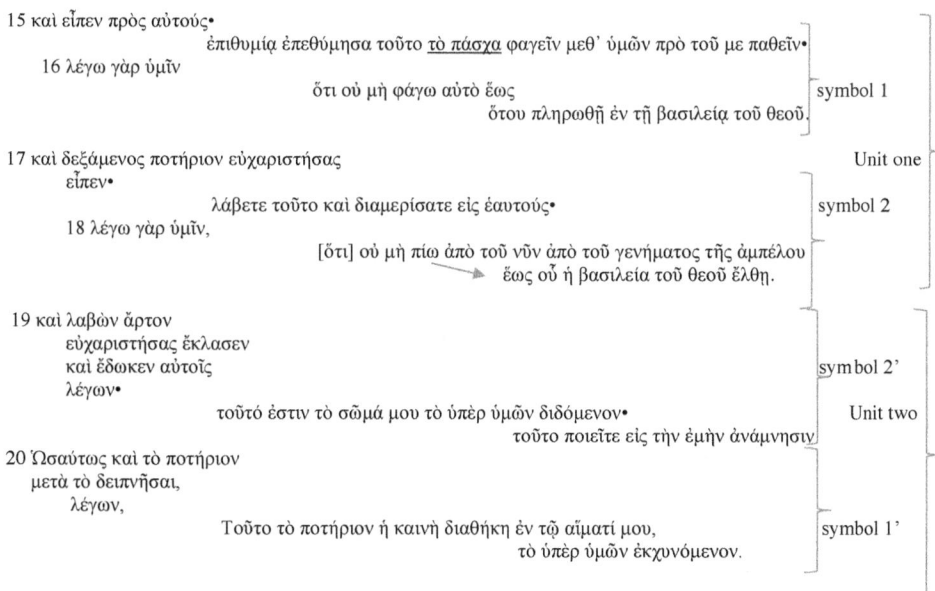

337

Bibliography

Aageson, J. W. "Typology, Correspondence, and the Application of Scripture in Romans 9-11." In *The Pauline Writings*, edited by Stanley E. Porter and Craig A. Evans, 76-97. Sheffield: Sheffield Academic, 1995.

Ajith, Fernando. *Acts: From Biblical Text to Contemporary Life*. NIV Application Commentary. Grand Rapids: Zondervan, 1998.

Aland, Barbara, and Kurt Aland, editors. *The Greek New Testament*. 28th ed. Stuttgart: Deutsche Bibelgesellschaft, 1998.

Anderson, Gary A. "Biblical Origins and the Problem of the Fall." *Pro Ecclesia* 10/1 (2001) 17-30.

———. *The Garments of Skin in Apocryphal Narrative and Biblical Commentary*. Studies in Ancient Midrash, Edited by James L. Kugel. Cambridge, MA: Harvard University Centre for Jewish Studies, 2001.

Anderson, Gary M. "Celibacy or Consummation in the Garden: Reflections on Early Jewish and Christian Interpretations of the Garden of Eden." *HTR* 82/2 (1989) 121-48.

Arrington, F. *The Acts of the Apostles: An Introduction and Commentary*. Peabody, MA: Hendrickson, 1988.

Augustine. *The Morals of the Catholic Church*. In *NPNF*, edited by Philip Schaff, 4:41-63. Grand Rapids: Eermans, 1974.

———. *On the Morals of the Manichaeans*. In *NPNF*, edited by Philip Schaff, 4:69-89. Grand Rapids: Eerdmans, 1974.

———. *Reply to Faustus the Manichaean*. In *NPNF*, edited by Philip Schaff, 4:155-345. Grand Rapids: Eerdmans, 1974.

Bacchiocchi, Samuel. *The Sabbath under Crossfire: A Biblical Analysis of Recent Sabbath/Sunday Development*. Berrien Springs, MI: Biblical Perspectives, 1999.

Badenas, Robert. *Christ the End of the Law: Romans 10.4 in Pauline Perspective*. JSNT Supplement Series 10. Sheffield: JSOT Press, 1985.

Baker, David W. "Leviticus." In *Cornerstone Biblical Commentary*, edited by Philip W. Comfort, vol. 2. Carol Stream, IL: Tyndale House, 2008.

Barker, Paul *The Triumph of Grace in Deuteronomy: Faithless Israel, Faithful Yahweh in Deuteronomy*. Milton Keynes: Paternoster, 2004.

Barrett, C. K. *A Critical and Exegetical Commentary on Acts of the Apostles: Introduction and Commentary on Acts XV-XXVIII*. ICC. Edinburgh: T. & T. Clark, 1998.

Beale, Gregory K. "Eden, the Temple, and the Church's Mission in the New Creation." *JETS*, 48 no. 1 (2005) 5-31.

Beale, G. K. *John's Use of the Old Testament in Revelation*. Sheffield: Sheffield Academic, 1998.

Beetham, Christopher A. "From Creation to New Creation: The Biblical Epic of King, Human Vicegerency, and Kingdom." In *From Creation to New Creation: Biblical Theology and Exegesis*, edited by Daniel M. Gurtner and Benjamin L. Gladd, 237–54. Peabody, MA: Hendrickson, 2013.

Belcher, Richard. *Genesis: The Beginning of God's Plan of Salvation*. The Focus on the Bible Commentary. Fearn: Christian Focus, 2012.

Black, David Alan, editor. *Rethinking New Testament Textual Criticism*. Grand Rapids: Baker Academic, 2002.

Block, Daniel. "Eden: A Temple? A Reassessment of the Biblical Evidence." In *From Creation to New Creation*, edited by Daniel Gurtner and Benjamin Gladd, 3–30. Peabody, MA: Hendrickson, 2013.

Blomberg, Craig L. *1 Corinthians*. NIV Application Commentary. Grand Rapids: Zondervan, 1994.

———. "The Law in Luke-Acts." *JSNT* 22 (1984) 53–80.

Bock, Darrell. *Acts*. BECNT. Grand Rapids: Baker Academic, 2007.

———. *Luke 1:1—9:50*. BECNT 1. Grand Rapids: Baker, 2002.

———. *Luke 9:51—24:53*. 2 BECNT 2. Grand Rapids: Baker, 2002.

Bockmuehl, Markus N. *Jewish Law in Gentile Churches: Halakhah and the Beginning of Christian Public Ethics*. Edinburgh: T. & T. Clark, 2000.

———. "Natural Law in Second Temple Judaism." *Vetus Testamentum* 45/1 (1995) 17–44.

Braulik, Georg. "Law as Gospel: Justification and Pardon According to the Deuteronomic Torah." *Interpretation* 38/1 (1984) 5–14.

Brodie, Thomas L. *The Birthing of the New Testament: The Intertextual Development of the New Testament Writings*. Sheffield: Sheffield Phoenix, 2004.

Brown, Jeannine K. "Creation's Renewal in the Gospel of John." *CBQ* 72 (2010) 275–90.

Bruce, F. F. *The Acts of the Apostles: The Greek Text with Introduction and Commentary*. 3rd ed. Leicester: Inter-Varsity, 1990.

Burchard, Christoph. "A Note on Rhēma in JosAs 17:1f, Luke 2:15,17, Acts 10:37." *NovT* 27/4 (1985) 281–95.

Butticaz, Simon. *L'identité de l'Eglise dans les Actes des apôtres: De la restauration d'Israël à la conquête universelle*. Berlin: De Gruyter, 2010.

Byrne, Brendan. *Romans*. Sacra Pagina 6. Collegeville, MN: Liturgical, 2007.

Callan, Terrance. "The Background of the Apostolic Decree (Acts 15:20, 29, 21:25)." *CBQ* 55/2 (1993) 284–97.

———. "Rhetography and Rhetology of Apocalyptic Discourse in Second Peter." In *Reading Second Peter With New Eyes: Methodological Reassessments of the Letter of Second Peter*, edited by Robert L. Webb and Duane F. Watson, 59–90. London: T. & T. Clark, 2010.

Calvin, John. *Commentary Upon the Acts of the Apostles*. Vol. 2. Translated by Christopher Fetherstone. Grand Rapids: Eerdmans, 1957.

Cassian, John. *The Twelve Books of John Cassian*. In *NPNF*, edited by Philip Schaff, 11:201–90. Grand Rapids: Eerdmans, 1973.

Chadwick, Henry. *East and West: The Making of a Rift in the Church: From Apostolic Times until the Council of Florence*. New York: Oxford University Press, 2005.

Chalmers, Aaron. "The Importance of the Noahic Covenant to Biblical Theology." *TynBul* 60/2 (2009) 207–16.

Chilton, Bruce. "Varieties and Tendencies of Midrash: Rabbinic Interpretations of Isaiah 24.23." In *Gospel Perspectives: Studies in Midrash and Historiography*, edited by R. France and D. Wenham, 3, 9–32. Sheffield: JSOT Press, 1983.

Christensen, Duane L. *Deuteronomy 1:1—21:9*. 2nd ed. WBC 6A. Nashville: T. Nelson, 2001.

Ciampa, Roy E., and Brian S. Rosner. *The First Letter to the Corinthians*. Pillar New Testament Commentary. Grand Rapids: Eerdmans, 2010.

Clarke, W. K. L. "The Use of the Septuagint in Acts." In *The Beginnings of Christianity, Part 1: The Acts of the Apostles*, edited by F. J. Foakes Jackson and Krisopp Lake, 2:66–105. London: Macmillan, 1933.

Clement. *The Instructor*. In *ANF*, edited by Alexander Roberts and James Donaldson, 2:207–298. Grand Rapids: Eerdmans, 1962.

———. *Stromata*. In *ANF*, edited by Alexander Roberts and James Donaldson, 2:299–568. Grand Rapids: Eerdmans, 1962.

Cohen, Shaye J. D. "Was Timothy Jewish (Acts 16:1–3): Patristic Exegesis, Rabbinic Law, and Matrilineal Descent." *Journal of Biblical Literature* 105/2 (1986) 251–68.

Constitutions of the Holy Apostles. In *ANF*, edited by James Donaldson, 7:387–508. Grand Rapids: Eerdmans, 1963.

Cyril. *The Catechetical Lectures*. In *NPNF*, edited by Philip Schaff, 7:6–157. Grand Rapids: Eerdmans, 1974.

Danker, F. W. *A Greek-English Lexicon of the New Testament and other Early Christian Literature*. 3rd ed. Chicago: University of Chicago Press, 2000.

Deines, Roland. *Acts of God in History: Studies Towards Recovering a Theological Historiography*. Tübingen: Mohr Siebeck, 2013.

Davids, Peter H. *The Letters of 2 Peter and Jude*. Pillar New Testament Commentary. Nottingham: Apollos, 2006.

Dibelius, Martin. *Studies in the Acts of the Apostles*. London: SCM, 1956.

Dickinson, Royce J. "The Theology of the Jerusalem Conference: Acts 15:1–35." *ResQ* 32/2 (1990) 65–83.

Didache (The Teaching of the Twelve Apostles). In *ANF*, edited by James Donaldson, 7:371–83. Grand Rapids: Eerdmans, 1963.

DiMattei, Steven. "Biblical Narratives." In *As It Is Written: Studying Paul's Use of Scripture*, edited by Stanley E. Porter and Christopher D. Stanley, 59–93. Atlanta: Society of Biblical Literature, 2008.

Douglas, Mary. *Purity and Danger: An Analysis of Concepts of Pollutions and Taboo*. London: Routledge and Kegan Paul, 1978.

Downing, Gerald F. "Freedom from the Law in Luke-Acts." *JSNT*/26 (1986) 49–52.

Dunn, James D. *The Parting of the Ways: Between Christianity and Judaism and their Significance for the Character of Christianity*. London: SCM, 1991.

Edenburg, Cynthia. "Intertextuality, Literary Competence and the Question of Readership: Some preliminary observations." *JSOT* 35/2 (2010) 131–48.

Ehrhardt, Arnold. *The Acts of the Apostles: Ten Lectures*. Manchester: Manchester University Press, 1969.

Ehrman, Bart D. *The Orthodox Corruption of Scripture: The Effect of Early Christological Controversies on the Text of the New Testament*. Oxford: Oxford University Press, 1993.

———. "The Text as Window: New Testament Manuscripts and the Social History of Early Christianity." In *The Text of the New Testament in Contemporary Research*, edited by Bart D. Ehrman and Michael W. Holmes, 361–79. Grand rapids: Eerdmans, 1995.Elledge, C.

D. "'From the Beginning It Was Not So...'": Jesus, Divorce, and Remarriage in Light of the Dead Sea Scrolls." *Perspectives in Religious Studies* 37/4 (2010) 371–389.

Ellis, E. Earle. "How the New Testament Uses the Old." In *New Testament Interpretation: Essays on Principles and Methods*, edited by H. Marshall, 199–219. Exeter: Paternoster, 1977.

———. *Prophecy and Hermeneutic in Early Christianity*. Tübingen: Mohr Siebeck, 1978.

Enns, Peter. "Creation and Re-Creation: Psalm 95 and Its Interpretation in Hebrews 3:1—4:13." *WTJ* 55/2 (1993) 255–80.

Epistle to Diognetus. In *The Apostolic Fathers*, edited by Alexander Roberts, revised by A. Cleveland Coxe, 1:23–30. 5th ed. Peabody, MA: Hendrickson, 2012.

Esler, Philip Francis. *Community and Gospel in Luke-Acts: The Social and Political Motivations of Lucan Theology*. Cambridge: Cambridge University Press, 1987.

Eusebius. "The Curch History of Eusebius." In *NPNF*, edited by Philip Schaff, 1:81–387. Grand Rapids: Eerdmans, 1976.

Evans, Craig A. "Jesus and the Spirit: On the Origin and Ministry of the Second Son of God." In *Luke and Scripture: The Function of Sacred Tradition in Luke-Acts*, 26–45. Eugene, OR: Wipf and Stock, 1993.

———. *Mark 8:27—16:20*. WBC 34B. Nashville: T. Nelson, 2001.

———. "The Old Testament in the New." In *The Face of the New Testament Studies: A Survey of Recent Research*, edited by Scot McKnight and Grant R. Osborne, 130–45. Grand Rapids: Baker Academic, 2004.

Fee, Gordon D. *Pauline Christology: An Exegetical-Theological Study*. Peabody, MA: Hendrickson, 2007.

———. "The Use of the Greek Fathers for New Testament Textual Criticism." In *The Text of the New Testament in Contemporary Research: Essays on the Status Quaestionis*, edited by Bart D. Ehrman and Michael W. Holmes, 191–207. Grand Rapids: Eerdmans, 1995.

Feldman, Emanuel. *Biblical and Post-Biblical Defilement and Mourning: Law as Theology*. New York: Ktav, 1977.

Ferguson, Everett. *Backgrounds of Early Christianity*. 3rd ed. Grand Rapids: Eerdmans, 2003.

Firmage, Edwin. *The Biblical Dietary Laws and the Concept of Holiness*. Studies in the Pentateuch 41. Leiden: Brill, 1990.

Fitzmyer, Joseph A. *The Acts of the Apostles: A New Translation with Introduction and Commentary*. AB 31. New York: Doubleday, 1998.

———. *The Gospel According to Luke (I–IX)*. AB 28. Garden City, NJ: Doubleday, 1981.

———. *Luke the Theologian: Aspects of His Teaching*. New York: Paulist, 1989.

Fonrobert, Charlotte Elisheva. "Jewish Christians, Judaizers, and Christian Anti-Judaism." In *Late Ancient Christianity*, edited by Virginia Burrus, 2:234–54. Minneapolis: Fortress, 2010.

France, R. T. "Jewish Historiography, Midrash, and the Gospels." *In Gospel Perspectives: Studies in Midrash and Historiography*, edited by R. France and D. Wenham, 3:99–128. Sheffield: JSOT Press, 1983.

Fredriksen, Paula. "Torah Observance and Christianity: the Perspective of Roman Antiquity," *Modern Theology* 11 (1995) 195–204.

Frerichs, Wendell W. "Death and Resurrection in the Old Testament." *WW* 11/1 (1991) 14–22.

Fretheim, Terence E. *God and World in the Old Testament*. Nashville: Abingdon, 2005.

Frierich, Avemarie. "Jesus and Purity." In *The New Testament and Rabbinic Literature: Supplements to the Journal for the Study of Judaism*, edited by Reimund Bieringer, Florentino García Martínez, Didier Pollefeyt and Peter J. Tomson, 255–79. Leiden: Brill, 2010.

Gager, J. *The Origins of Anti-Semitism: Attitudes toward Judaism in Pagan and Christian Antiquity*. New York: Oxford University Press, 1983.

Gane, Roy, editor. *Leviticus, Numbers*. NIV Application Commentary. Grand Rapids: Zondervan, 2004.

Garland, David E. *Luke*. Zondervan Exegetical Commentary on the New Testament 3. Grand Rapids: Zondervan, 2011.

Gasque, Ward. *A History of the Criticism of the Acts of the Apostles*. Grand Rapids: Eerdmans, 1975.

Gendy, Atef Mehanny. "Style, Content and Culture: Distinctive Characteristics in the Missionary Speeches in Acts." *Svensk Missionstidskrift* 99/3 (2011) 247–65.

Gilbert, Pierre. "He Never Meant for Us to Die: An Incursion into Genesis 1–3." *Direction* 41/1 (2012) 42–56.

Glenny, Edward W. "The Septuagint and Apostolic Hermeneutics: Amos 9 in Acts 15." *BBR* 22/1 (2012) 1–25.

Golding, Thomas A. "Pagan Worship in Jerusalem?" *BSac* 170/679 (2013) 304–16.

Gooch, Peter. *Dangerous Food: 1 Corinthians 8–10 in Its Context*. Waterloo, ON: Wilfrid Laurier University Press, 1993.

Goppelt, Leonhard. *Apostolic and Post-Apostolic Times*. London: A. & C. Black, 1970.

Goulder, M. D. "Midrash in Matthew." In *Midrash in Action and as a Literary Device*, edited by J. Duncan and M. Derrett, 2:205–10. Leiden: Brill, 1978.

Grabbe, Lester. *Leviticus*. OTG. Sheffield: Sheffield Academic Press, 1993.

Green, Gene L. *Jude and 2 Peter*. BECNT. Grand Rapids: Baker Academic, 2008.

Gurtner, Daniel M. "Luke's Isaianic Jubilee." In *From Creation to New Creation: Biblical Theology and Exegesis*, edited by Daniel M. Gurtner and Benjamin L. Gladd, 123–46. Peabody, MA: Hendrickson, 2013.

Guy, Laurie. *Introducing Early Christianity: A Topical Survey of Its Life, Beliefs, and Practices*. Downers Grove, IL: InterVarsity, 2004.

Haenchen, Ernst. *The Acts of the Apostles*. Translated by Bernard Noble and Gerald Shinn with the supervision of Hugh Anderson. Oxford: Blackwell, 1965.

Haenchen, Ernst. *Die Apostelgeschichte*. Kritisch-exegetischer Kommentar über das Neue Testament. 16th ed. Göttingen: Vandenhoeck & Ruprecht, 1977.

Halivni, David. *Midrash, Mishnah, and Gemara: The Jewish Predilection for Justified Law*. Cambridge, MA: Harvard University Press, 1986.

Harrocks, Rebecca. "Jesus' Gentile Healings: The Absence of Bodily Contact and the Requirement of Faith." In *The Body in Biblical, Christian and Jewish Texts*, edited by Joan E. Taylor, 83–101. London: T. & T. Clark, 2014.

Hartley, John. *Leviticus*. WBC 4. Waco, TX: Word, 1992.

Havrelock, Rachel. "Genesis." In *The Oxford Handbook of the Reception History of the Bible*, edited by Michael Lieb, Emma Mason, and Jonathan Roberts, 11–24. Oxford: Oxford University Press, 2011.

Hawkins, Ralph K. "The Laws of Clean and Unclean Animals in Leviticus 11: Their Nature, Theology, and Rationale: An Intertextual Study." *CBQ* 65/1 (2003) 112–13.

Hawley, Lance. "The Agenda of Priestly Taxonomy: The Conceptualisation of אָמֵט and שָׁקֶץ in Leviticus 11." *CBQ* 77/2 (2015) 231–49.
Hays, Richard B. *Echoes of Scripture in the Letters of Paul*. New Haven, CT: Yale University Press, 1989.
Heath, J. M. *Paul's Visual Piety*. Oxford: Oxford University Press, 2013.
Heil, Christoph. *Die Ablehnung der Speisegebote durch Paulus: Zur Frage nach der Stellung des Apostels zum Gesetz*. Weinheim: Beltz Athenäum, 1994.
Helyer, Larry R. "Luke and the Restoration of Israel." *JETS* 36/3 (1993) 317–29.
Hengel, Martin. *Acts and the History of Earliest Christianity*. Philadelphia: Fortress, 1979.
Hess, Lisa Maguire. "Encountering Habits of Mind at Table: Kashrut, Jews, and Christians." *Cross Currents* 62/3 (2012) 328–36.
Hirsh, Richard. "Beyond the Noahide Laws." *Reconstructionist* 67/1 (2002) 27–31.
Hogeterp, Albert. *Paul and God's Temple: A Historical Interpretation of Cultic Imagery in the Corinthian Correspondence*. Biblical Tools and Studies 2. Leuven: Peeters, 2006.
Horbury, William. *Jews and Christians in Contact and Controversy*. Edinburgh: T. & T. Clark, 1998.
Houston, Walter J. "The Laws of Clean and Unclean Animals in Leviticus 11: Their Nature, Theology, and Rationale: An Intertextual Study." *JTS* 53/1 (2002) 131–134.
Hubbard, Moyer V. *New Creation in Paul's Letters and Thought* SNTSMS 119. Cambridge: Cambridge University Press, 2005.
Hughes, Aaron W. "David Novak: An Intellectual Portrait." In *David Novak: Natural Law and Revealed Torah*, edited by Hava Tirosh-Samuelson and Aaron W Hughes, 1–18. Leiden: Brill, 2014.
Hultgren, Arland. *Paul's Letter to the Romans: A Commentary*. Grand Rapids: Eerdmans, 2011.
Ignatius. *Epistle to Hero*. In *ANF*, edited by James Donaldson, 1:113–115. Grand Rapids: Eerdmans, 1998.
———. *Epistle to the Magnesians*. In *ANF*, edited by James Donaldson, 1:59–65. Grand Rapids: Eerdmans, 1965.
———. *Epistle to the Philadelphians*. In *ANF*, edited by James Donaldson, 1:79–85. Grand Rapids: Eerdmans, 1965.
———. *Epistle to the Philippians*. In *ANF*, edited by James Donaldson, 1:116–19. Grand Rapids: Eerdmans, 1996.
Instone-Brewer, David. "Infanticide and the Apostolic Decree of Acts 15." *JETS* 52/2 (2009) 301–21.
Jacobs, Andrew S. "Jews and Christians." In *The Oxford Handbook of Early Christian Studies*, edited by Susan Harvey and David Hanter, 169–85. Oxford: Oxford University Press, 2008.
Jackson, Ryan T. *New Creation in Paul's Letters: A Study of the Historical and Social Setting of a Pauline Concept*. Tübingen: Mohr Siebeck, 2010.
Jenson, Philip, P. *Graded Holiness: a Key to the Priestly Conception of the World*. JSOT Supplement Series 106. Sheffield: JSOT Press, 1992.
Jerome. "Dialogue Against Jovinianus." In *NPNF*, edited by Philip Schaff, 6. Grand Rapids: Eerdmans, 1975.
Jervell, Jacob. *Die Apostelgeschichte*. Kritisch-exegetischer Kommentar über das Neue Testament, 17th ed. Göttingen: Vandenhoeck & Ruprecht, 1998.
———. "Law in Luke-Acts." *HTR* 64/1 (1971) 21–36.

———. *Luke and the People of God: A New Look at Luke-Acts*. Minneapolis: Augsburg, 1972.

John Chrysostom. *Homilies on the Acts of the Apostles*. In *NPNF*, edited by Philip Schaff, 11:1–328. Grand Rapids: Eerdmans, 1975.

Johnson, Luke Timothy. *The Acts of the Apostles*. Sacra Pagina 5. Collegeville, MN: Liturgical, 1992.

———. *The Gospel of Luke*. Sacra Pagina 3. Collegeville, MN: Liturgical, 1991.

Justin. *Dialogue with Trypho*. In *ANF*, edited by James Donaldson, 1:104–270. Grand Rapids: Eerdmans, 1996.

———. *The First Apology*. In *ANF*, edited by James Donaldson, 1:159–87. Grand Rapids: Eerdmans, 1996.

Kaiser, Walter C. "Davidic Promise and the Inclusion of the Gentiles (Amos 9:9–15 and Acts 15:13–18) A Test Passage for Theological Systems." *JETS* 20/2 (1977) 97–111.

Karris, Robert J. "Romans 14:1—15:13 and the Occasion of Romans." In *The Romans Debate*, edited by Karl Donfried, 75–99. Edinburgh: T. & T. Clark, 1991.

Kass, Leon R. "Why the Dietary Laws." *Commentary* 97/6 (1994) 42–48.

Keene, Thomas. "Heaven Is a Tent: The Tabernacle as an Eschatological Metaphor in the Epistle to the Hebrews." *WTJ* 72 (2010) 432.

Keener, Craig S. *Acts: An Exegetical Commentary*. 2 vols. Grand Rapids: Baker Academic, 2012, 2013.

Keener, Craig S. "Interethnic Marriages in the New Testament (Matt 1:3–6; Acts 7:29; 16:1–3; cf. 1 Cor 7:14)." *Criswell Theological Review* 6/2 (2009) 25–43.

Kitchen, Kenneth A. *On the Reliability of the Old Testament*. Grand Rapids: Eerdmans, 2003.

Kiuchi, Nobuyoshi, editor. *Leviticus*. ApOTC 3. Nottingham: Apollos, 2007.

Klawans, Jonathan. "Notions of Gentile Impurity in Ancient Judaism." *AJS Review* 20/2 (1995) 285–312.

Klinghardt, Mattheus. *Gesetz und Volk Gottes: Das lukanische Verständnis des Gesetzes nach Herkunft, Function und seinem Ort in der Geschichte des Urchristentums*. WUNT 2.32. Tübingen: Mohr Siebeck, 1988.

Kohlenberg, John R. *The Greek-English Concordance to the New Testament*. Zondervan Greek Reference Series. Grand Rapids: Zondervan, 1997.

Korpel, Mario C. A., and Johannes C. Moor. *Adam, Eve, and the Devil: A New Beginning*. Hebrew Bible Monographs 65. Sheffield: Sheffield Phoenix Press, 2014.

Korsak, Mary P. "A Fresh Look at the Garden of Eden." *Semeia* 81 (1998) 131–44.

Kubo, Sakae. *A Reader's Greek-English Lexicon of the New Testament*. Grand Rapids: Zondervan, 2010.

Kulikovsky, Andrew S. *Creation, Fall, Restoration: A Biblical Theology of Creation*. Fearn, Scotland: Christian Focus, 2009.

Lake, Kirsopp, and Henry J. Cadbury. *English Translation and Commentary*. Vol. 4 of *The Beginnings of Christianity: Part I, The Acts of the Apostles*. Edited by Foakes Jackson and Kirsopp Lake. 1933. Reprinted, Grand Rapids: Eerdmans, 1965.

Larkin, William J. "Acts." In *Cornerstone Biblical Commentary*, edited by Philip W. Comfort, vol. 12. Carol Stream, IL: Tyndale, 2006.

The Letter to Diognetus. In *ECF*, edited by John Baillie, 1:213–24. Grand Rapids: Eerdmans.

Lichtenstein, Murray H. "The Fearsome Sword of Genesis 3:24." *JBR* 134/1 (2015) 53–57.

Lierman, John D. "The New Testament Moses in the Context of Ancient Judaism." *TynBul* 53/2 (2002) 317–20.

Lieu, Judith. *Neither Jew Nor Greek? Constructing Early Christianity*. SNTW. London: T. & T. Clark, 2002.

Lipka, Hilary B. *Sexual Transgression in the Hebrew Bible*. Sheffield: Sheffield Phoenix, 2006.

Longenecker, Richard N. *Acts*. Expositor's Bible Commentary 9. Grand Rapids: Zondervan, 2008.

Lucian. *The Passing of Peregrinus*. Translated by M. A. Harmon. LCL 5. Cambridge, MA: Harvard University Press, 1972.

MacLeod, David J. "The Creation of the Universe by the Word: John 1:3–5." *BSac* 160/638 (2003) 187–201.

Maddox, Robert. *The Purpose of Luke-Acts*. Edinburgh: T. & T. Clark, 1982.

Maier, Harry O. "Heresy, Households, and the Disciplining of Diversity." In *Late Ancient Christianity*, edited by Virginia Burrus, 2:213–33. Minneapolis: Fortress, 2010.

Malcolm, Matthew R. *The World of 1 Corinthians: An Exegetical Source Book of Literary and Visual Backgrounds*. Milton Keynes: Paternoster, 2012.

Marguerat, Daniel. *The First Christian Historian: Writing the 'Acts of the Apostles'*. Translated by Ken McKinney, Gregory J. Laughery, and Richard Bauckham. Cambridge: Cambridge University Press, 2002.

Marshall, I. Howard. *Acts*. Commentary on the New Testament Use of the Old Testament. Grand Rapids: Baker Academic, 2007.

———. *Luke: Historian and Theologian*. Grand Rapids: Zondervan, 1989.

Martin, Ralph P. *James*. WBC 48. Waco, TX: Word, 1988.

Matera, Frank J. "Acts 10:34–43." *Interpretation* 41/1 (1987) 62–66.

Matson, David Lertis, and Warren S. Brown. "Tuning the Faith: The Cornelius Story in Resonance Perspective." *Perspectives in Religious Studies* 33/4 (2006) 449–65.

McCartney, Dan G. *James*. Baker Exegetical Commentary on the New Testament. Grand Rapids: Baker Academic, 2009.

McGowan, Andrew. "Food, Ritual, and Power." In *Late Ancient Christianity*, edited by Virginia Burrus, 2:145–64. Minneapolis: Fortress, 2010.

McIntosh, John A. "'For It Seemed Good to the Holy Spirit' Acts 15:28: How Did the Members of the Jerusalem Council Know This?" *Reformed Theological Review* 61/3 (2002) 131–47.

McIver, Robert K. *Intermediate New Testament Greek Made Easier*. Cooranbong: Barnard, 2015.

———. *Mainstream or Marginal? The Matthean Community in Early Christianity*. Frankfurt am Main: Peter Lang, 2012.

McLean, B. H. *New Testament Greek: An Introduction*. New York: Cambridge University Press, 2011.

McNamara, Martin. *Palestinian Judaism and the New Testament*. Good News Studies 4. Wilmington, DE: Glazier, 1983.

Meeks, Wayne A. "'And Rose Up to Play': Midrash and Paraenesis in 1 Corinthians 10.1–22." In *The Pauline Writings*, edited by Stanley E. Porter and Craig A. Evans, 124–36. Sheffield: Sheffield Academic, 1995.

Merrill, Eugene H. "Deuteronomy." In *Cornerstone Biblical Commentary*, edited by Philip W. Comfort, vol. 2. Carol Stream, IL: Tyndale, 2008.

Meshel, Naphtali. "The Form and Function of a Biblical Blood Ritual." *VT* 63/2 (2013) 276–89.

Mettinger, Tryggve N. *The Eden Narrative: A Literary and Religio-historical Study of Genesis 2–3*. Winona Lake, IN: Eisenbrauns, 2007.

Metzger, Bruce M. *The Text of the New Testament: Its Transmission, Corruption, and Restoration*. Edited by Bart D. Ehrman. 4th ed. Oxford: Oxford University Press, 2005.

———. *A Textual Commentary on the Greek New Testament*. 4th rev. ed. Stuttgart: Deutsche Bibelgesellschaft, 1994.Meyer, Jason. *The End of the Law: Mosaic Covenant in Pauline Theology*. NAC Studies in Bible and Theology. Nashville: Broadman & Holman, 2009.

Milgrom, Jacob. "Biblical Diet Laws as an Ethical System." *Interpretation* 17/3 (1963) 288–301.

———. *Leviticus 1–16: A New Translation with Introduction and Commentary*. AB 3. New York: Doubleday, 1991.

———. *Leviticus 17–22: A New Translation with Introduction and Commentary*. AB 3A. New York: Doubleday, 2000.

———. "Review of J. Moskala PhD Dissertation." *AUSS* 42 (2004) 250–51.

Miller, Chris A. "Did Peter's Vision in Acts 10 Pertain to Men or the Menu?" *BSac* 159/635 (2002) 302–17.

Minear, Paul S. *Christians and the New Creation: Genesis Motifs in the New Testament*. Louisville: Westminster John Knox, 1994.

Moo, Douglas J. "Creation and New Creation." *Bulletin for Biblical Research* 20/1 (2010) 39–60.

Morales, Michael L. *The Tabernacle Pre-Figured: Cosmic Mountain Ideology in Genesis and Exodus*. BTS 15. Leuven: Peeters, 2012.

Moskala, J. *The Laws of Clean and Unclean Animals of Leviticus 11: Their Nature, Theology, and Rationale*. Berrien Springs, MI: Adventist Theological Society, 1998.

Moulton, J. H., and G. Milligan. *Vocabulary of the Greek Testament*. 2nd ed. Peabody, MA: Hendrikson, 2004.

Mounce, William D. *The Analytical Lexicon to the Greek New Testament*. Zondervan Greek Reference Series. Grand Rapids: Zondervan, 1993.

Moyise, Steve. *Evoking Scripture: Seeing the Old Testament in the New*. London: T. & T. Clark, 2008.

Muraoka, T. *A Greek-English Lexicon of the Septuagint*. Leuven: Peeters, 2009.

Murphy, Jonathan S. "The Role of Barnabas in the Book of Acts." *BSac* 167/667 (2010) 319–41.

Murphy-O'Connor, Jerome. *Keys to First Corinthians: Revisiting the Major Issues*. New York: Oxford University Press, 2010.

Nebe, Gottfried. "Creation in Paul's Theology." In *Creation in Jewish and Christian Tradition*, edited by Henning Graf Reventlow and Hoffman Yair, 111–37. Sheffield: Sheffield Academic, 2002.

Neusner, Jacob. *Genesis Rabbah*. The Judaic Commentary to the Book of Genesis: A New American Translation, 1. Atlanta: Scholars, 1985.

Neusner, Jacob, and Bruce Chilton. *Jewish and Christian Doctrines: The Classics Compared*. New York: Routledge, 2000.

Nguyen, VanThanh. "Dismantling Cultural Boundaries: Missiological Implications of Acts 10:1—11:18." *Missiology* 40/4 (2012) 455–66.

Nixon, John. *Redemption in Genesis: The Crossroads of Faith and Reason*. Nampa, ID: Pacific, 2011.

Nolland, John, editor. *Luke 1—9:20*. WBC 35A. Waco, TX: Word, 1989.

Novak, David. "The Jewish Mission: Whether Jews Can and Should Proselytize?" *First Things* 227 (2012) 39–43.

———. "Law of Moses, Law of Nature." *First Things* 60 (1996) 45–49.
Ollenburger, Ben C. "If Mortals Die, Will They Live Again? The Old Testament and Resurrection." *Ex Auditu* 9 (1993) 29–44.
Olson, Jon C. "The Jerusalem Decree, Paul, and the Gentile Analogy to Homosexual Persons." *Journal of Religious Ethics* 40 (2012) 360–84.
O'Neill, J. C. *The Theology of Acts in Its Historical Setting*. London: SPCK, 1961.
Origen. *Against Celsus*. In *ANF*, edited by James Donaldson, 4:395–669. Grand Rapids: Eerdmans, 1956.
———. *Commentary on Matthew*. In *ANF*, edited by James Donaldson, 10:409–512. Grand Rapids: Eerdmans, 1965.
Osborne, Grant R. "2 Peter." In *Cornerstone Biblical Commentary*, edited by Philip W. Comfort, vol. 18. Carol Stream, IL: Tyndale, 2011.
Oxley, Simon. "Certainties Transformed: Jonah and Acts 10:9–35." *Ecumenical Review* 56/3 (2004) 322–26.
Pao, David W. *Acts and the Isaianic New Exodus*. Grand Rapids: Baker Academic 2002.
Pao, David W., and Echhard J. Schnabel. "Luke." In *Commentary on the New Testament Use of the Old Testament*, edited by G. K. Beale and D. A. Carson, 251–414. Grand Rapids: Backer Academic, 2007.
Parker, David C. *An Introduction to the New Testament Manuscripts and Their Texts*. New York: Cambridge University Press, 2008.
Parsons, Mikeal C. "'Nothing Defiled AND Unclean': The Conjunction's Function in Acts 10:14." *Perspectives in Religious Studies* 27/3 (2000) 263–74.
Perez, Fernandez Miguel. "Midrash and the New Testament: A Methodology for the Study of Gospel Midrash." In *The New Testament and Rabbinic Literature: Supplements to the Journal for the Study of Judaism*, edited by Reimund Bieringer, Florentino García Martínez, Didier Pollefeyt, and Peter J. Tomson, 367–84. Leiden: Brill, 2010.
Perry, John. "Are Christians the 'Aliens Who Live in Your Midst'? Torah and the Origins of Christian Ethics in Acts 10–15." *Journal of the Society of Christian Ethics* 29/2 (2009) 157–74.
Perschbacher, Wesley J. *New Testament Greek Syntax: An Illustrated Manual*. Chicago: Moody, 1995.
Pervo, Richard I. *Acts: A Commentary*. Edited by Harold W. Attridge. Minneapolis: Fortress, 2009.
Peterson, David. *The Acts of the Apostles*. Pillar New Testament Commentary. Nottingham: Apollos, 2009.
Petterson, Anthony. "Antecedents of the Christian Hope of Resurrection." *Reformed Theological Review* 59/1 (2000) 1–15.
Petzer, J. H. "The History of the New Testament—Its Reconstruction, Significance and Use in New Testament Textual Criticism." In *New Testament Textual Criticism, Exegesis, and Early Church History: A Discussion of Methods*, edited by B. Aland and J. Delobel, 18–25. Contributions to Biblical Exegisis and Theology 7. Kampen: Kok, 1994.
Phillips, Thomas E. "Creation, Sin and Its Curse, and the People of God: An Intertextual Reading of Genesis 1–12 and Acts 1–7." *Horizons in Biblical Theology* 25 (2003) 143–60.
Pierre, Paulo A. *Le probleme ecclésial des Actes à la Lumiere de deux prophéties d'Amos*. Paris: Cerf, 1985.
Pilgrim, Walter E. "Luke-Acts and a Theology of Creation." *WW* 12/1 (1992) 51–58.
Pliny. *Letters*. Translated by William Melmoth. LCL 2. London: Heinemann, 1915.

Polycarp. *The Epistle to the Philippians*. In *ANF*, edited by James Donaldson, 1:31–36. Grand Rapids: Eerdmans, 1965.

Porter, Stanley E., and Christopher D. Stanley, editors. *As It Is Written: Studying Paul's Use of Scripture*. Atlanta: Society of Biblical Literature, 2008.

Raanan, Eichler. "When God Abandoned the Garden of Eden: A Forgotten Reading of Genesis 3:24." *VT* 65 (2015) 20–32.

Räisänen, Heikki. *The Rise of Christian Beliefs: The Thought World of Early Christians*. Minneapolis: Fortress, 2010.

Reed, Stephen A. "Imagining Resurrection in the Old Testament." *Living Pulpit* 21/2 (2012) 9–13.

———. "The Role of Food as Related to Covenant in Qumran Literature." In *The Concept of the Covenant in the Second Temple Period*, edited by Stanley E. Porter and Jacqueline C. de Roo, 129–64. Atlanta: Society of Biblical Literature, 2003.

Rees, Ruth Anne. *2 Peter and Jude*. Two Horizons New Testament Commentary. Grand Rapids: Eerdmans, 2007.

Reno, Russell R. *Genesis*. Grand Rapids: Brazos, 2010.

Reynolds, J. Benjamin. "Echoes of Daniel in 1 and 2 Thessalonians," BTh/BMin (Hons) thesis, Avondale College of Higher Education, 2013.

Rich, Matthew A. "In the Beginning." *Journal for Preachers* 34/1 (2010) 23–25.

Richard, Earl J. "The Creative Use of Amos by the Author of Acts." *NovT* 24/1 (1982) 37–53.

Rius-Camps, Josep, and Jenny Read-Heimerdinger, editors. *Luke's Demonstration to Theophilus: The Gospel and the Acts of the Apostles According to Codex Bezae*. London: T. & T. Clark, 2013.

———, editors. *The Message of Acts in Codex Bezae: A Comparison with the Alexandrian Tradition*. 4 vols. London: T. & T. Clark, 2004–.

Robinson, Marilynne. "Wisdom and Light: John's Prologue as Midrash." *Christian Century* 129/8 (2012) 11–12.

Ropes, James Hardy. "Acts XV.21." *JBL* 15, nos. 1–2 (1896) 75–81.

Rosenblum, Jordan D. *Food and Identity in Early Rabbinic Judaism*. Cambridge: Cambridge University Press, 2010.

Ross, Allen. "Genesis." In *Cornerstone Biblical Commentary*, edited by Philip W. Comfort, vol. 1. Carol Stream, IL: Tyndale, 2008.

Rosser, Brian S. "Temple Prostitution in 1 Corinthians 6:12–20." *NovT* 40/4 (1998) 336–51.

Rost, Bettina. "Das Apostelkret im Verhältnis zur Mosetora: Ein Beitrag zum Gottesvolk-Verständnis bei Lukas." In *Die Apostelgeschichte I Kontext antiker und früchristlicher Historiographie*, edited by Jörg Frey, Clare K. Rothschild, and Jens Schröter, 563–604. Berlin: De Gruyter, 2009.

Royse, James R. "Scribal Tendencies in the Transmission of the Text of the New Testament." In *The Text of the New Testament in Contemporary Research: Essays on the Status Quaestionis*, edited by Bart D. Ehrman and Michael W. Holmes, 239–52. Grand Rapids: Eerdmans, 1995.

Rubin, Nissan, and Admiel Kosman. "The Clothing of the Primordial Adam as a Symbol of Apocalyptic Time in the Midrashic Sources." *HTR* 90/2 (1997) 155–74.

Rufinus. *Apology Against Jerome*. Book 2. In *NPNF*, edited by Philip Schaff, 3:460–81. Grand Rapids: Eerdmans, 1969.

Sandt, Hubertus Waltherus Maria. "An Explanation of Acts 15:6–21 in the Light of Deuteronomy 4:29–35 (LXX)." *JSNT* 46 (1992) 73–97.

Sarna, Nahum M. *Genesis*. JPS Torah Commentary. New York: Jewish Publication Society, 1989.

Savelle, Charles H. "A Reexamination of the Prohibitions in Acts 15." *BSac* 161/644 (2004) 449–68.

Scaer, Peter F. "Luke, Jesus, and the Law." In *The Law in Holy Scripture: Essays from the Concordia Theological Seminary Symposium on Exegetical Theology*, edited by Charles A. Gieschen, 97–112. St. Louis: Concordia, 2004.

Schnabel, Eckhard J. *Acts*. Zondervan Exegetical Commentary on the New Testament. Grand Rapids: Zondervan, 2012.

Scholz, Daniel J. "'Rise, Peter, Kill and Eat': Eating Unclean Food and Dining with Unclean People in Acts 10:1—11:18." *Proceedings EGL & MWBS* 22 (2002) 47–61.

Schwartz, David G. "Noahide Laws, Christian Covenants, and Jewish Expectations." *Journal of Ecumenical Studies* 27/4 (1990) 767–72.

Scott, Julius J. *Jewish Backgrounds of the New Testament*. Grand Rapids: Baker, 2000.

Shuchat, Wilfred. *The Creation According to the Midrash Rabbah*. Edited by Raphael Posner. New York: Devora, 2002.

Seifrid, Mark A. "Jesus and the Law in Acts." *JSNT* 30 (1987) 39–57.

Selengut, Charles. "Law and Ritual in Traditional Judaism." *Dialogue & Alliance* 6/3 (1992) 43–51.

Smith, Daniel Lynwood. "Interrupted Speech in Luke-Acts." *JBL* 134/1 (2015) 177–91.

Smith, Duane E. "The Divine Snake: Reading Genesis 3 in the Context of Mesopotamian Ophiomancy." *JBL* 134/1 (2015) 31–49.

Soards, Marion L. *The Speeches in Acts: Their Content, Context, and Concerns*. Louisville: Westminster John Knox, 1994.

Socrates. *Church History from A.D. 305-439*. In *NPNF*, edited by Philip Schaff, 2:1–178. Grand Rapids: Eerdmans, 1973.

Speiser, E. *Genesis*. AB 1. New York: Doubleday, 1964.

Stamps, Dennis L. "The Use of the Old Testament in the New Testament as a Rhetorical Device: A Methodological Proposal." In *Hearing the Old Testament in the New Testament*, edited by Stanley E. Porter, 9–37. Grand Rapids: Eerdmans, 2006.

Stark, Rodney. *The Triumph of Christianity: How the Jesus Movement Became the World's Largest Religion*. New York: HarperCollins, 2011.

Stein, David E. "A Rejoinder Concerning Genesis 3:6 and the NJPS Translation." *JBL* 134/1 (2015) 51–52.

Stein, Robert H. *Luke*. New American Commentary 24. Nashville: Broadman, 1992.

Stevenson, James, editor. *Creeds, Councils and Controversies: Documents Illustrating the History of the Church AD 337-461*. Cambridge: Cambridge University Press, 1989.

Stordalen, Terje. *Echoes of Eden: Genesis 2-3 and Symbolism of the Eden Garden in Biblical Hebrew Literature*. Leuven: Peeters, 2000.

Story, J. Lyle. "Luke's Instructive Dynamics for Resolving Conflicts: The Jerusalem Council." *Journal of Biblical and Pneumatological Research* 3 (2011) 99–118.

Streett, Daniel R. "As It Was in the Days of Noah: The Prophets' Typological Interpretation of Noah's Flood." *Criswell Theological Review* 5/1 (2007) 33–51.

Suggit, John N. "'The Holy Spirit and We Resolved . . .' (Acts 15:28)." *Journal of Theology for Southern Africa* 79 (1992) 38–48.

Taylor, Justin. "The Jerusalem Decrees (Acts 15.20, 29 and 21.25) and the Incident at Antioch (Gal 2.11–14)." *NTS* 47/3 (2001) 372–80.

Tertullian. *An Answer to the Jews*. In *ANF*, edited by James Donaldson, 3:151–73. Grand Rapids: Eerdmans, 1963.

———. *Apology*. LCL. London: Heinemann, 1960.

Thompson, Alan J. *The Acts of the Risen Lord Jesus*. Downers Grove, IL: InterVarsity, 2011.

Tomson, Peter J. "Divorce Halakhah in Paul and the Jesus Tradition." In *The New Testament and Rabbinic Literature*, edited by Reimund Bieringer, Florentino García Martínez, Didier Pollefeyt, and Peter J. Tomson, 289–332. Leiden: Brill, 2010.

———. "Jewish Food Laws in Early Christian Community Discourse." *Semeia* 86 (1999) 193–211.

Tigay, Jeffrey, editor. *Deuteronomy*. JPS Torah Commentary. Philadelphia: Jewish Publication Society, 1996.

Tobin, Thomas. *Paul's Rhetoric in Its Contexts: The Argument of Romans*. Peabody, MA: Hendrickson, 2004.

Toenges, Elke. "'See I Am Making All Things New': New Creation in the Book of Revelation." In *Creation in Jewish and Christian Tradition*, edited by Henning Graf Reventlow and Yair Hoffman, 139–52. JSOT Supplement Series 319. London: Sheffield Academic, 2002.

Tomson, Peter J. *Paul and the Jewish Law: Halakha in the Letters of the Apostle to the Gentiles*. Compendia Rerum Ludaicarum ad Novum Testamentarum 3. Assen: Van Gorcum, 1990.

Trites, Allison A. "The Gospel of Luke." In *Cornerstone Biblical Commentary*, edited by Philip W. Comfort, vol. 12. Carol Stream, IL: Tyndale, 2006.

VanDrunen, David. "Natural Law in Noachic Accent: A Covenantal Conception of Natural Law Drawn from Genesis 9." *Journal of the Society of Christian Ethics* 30/2 (2010) 131–49.

Vlachos, Chris A. *The Law and the Knowledge of Good and Evil: The Edenic Background of the Catalitic Operation of the Law in Paul*. Eugene, OR: Wipf & Stock, 2009.

Vogt, Peter. *Deuteronomic Theology and the Significance of Torah: A Reappraisal*. Winona Lake, IN: Eisenbrauns, 2006.

Wallace, Daniel B. *Greek Grammar: Beyond the Basics*. Grand Rapids: Zondervan, 1996.

Waltke, Bruce K. *Genesis: A Commentary*. Grand Rapids: Zondervan, 2001.

Walton, John H. *Genesis*. NIV Application Commentary. Grand Rapids: Zondervan, 2001.

Ware, James. "Paul's Hope and Ours: Recovering Paul's Hope of the Renewed Creation." *Concordia* 35/2 (2009) 129–39.

Watson, Francis. *Paul, Judaism, and the Gentiles: Beyond the New Perspective*. Grand Rapids: Eerdmans, 2007.

Wedderburn, A. J. "The 'Apostolic Decree': Tradition and Redaction." *NovT* 35/4 (1993) 362–89.

Wehnert, Jürgen. *Die Reinheit des "christlichen Gottesvolkes" aus Juden und Heiden: Studien zum historischen und theologischen Hintergrund des sogenannten Aposteldekrets*. Göttingen: VandenHoeck & Ruprecht, 1997.

Wells, L. S. A. "The Books of Adam and Eve." In *The Apocrypha and Pseudepigrapha of the Old Testament*, edited by R. H. Charles, 2:123–54. Oxford: Clarendon Press, 1913.

Wenham, Gordon. *Genesis 1–15*. WBC 1. Waco, TX: Word, 1987.

Wheaton, Byron. "As It Is Written: Old Testament Foundations for Jesus' Expectation of Resurrection." *WTJ* 70/2 (2008) 245–53.

White, Fowler R. "The Last Adam and His Seed: An Exercise in Theological Preemption." *Trinity Journal* 6/1 (1985) 60–73.

Whitlock, David B. "An Exposition of Acts 15:1–29." *Review and Expositor* 92/3 (1995) 375–78.

Wilson, Benjamin R. "'Upon a Tree' Again and Again: Redundancy and Deuteronomy 21:23 in Acts." *Neotestamentica* 47/1 (2013) 47–67.

Wilson, Stephen G. *Luke and the Law*. Society for New Testament Studies Monograph Series 50. Cambridge: Cambridge University Press, 2005.

Wood, John Halsey. "Merit in the Midst of Grace: The Covenant with Adam Reconsidered in View of the Two Powers of God." *International Journal of Systematic Theology* 10/2 (2008) 133–48.

Woods, Edward. *Deuteronomy: An Introduction and Commentary*. TOTC 56. Downers Grove, IL: InterVarsity, 2011.

Wright, David P. "Purification from Corpse-Contamination in Numbers 31:19–24." *VT* 35/2 (1985) 213–23.

Wright, N. T. *Jesus and the Victory of God*. Christian Origins and the Question of God 2. Minneapolis: Fortress, 1996.

———. *Paul: In Fresh Perspective*. Minneapolis: Fortress, 2009.

Yoon, I. David. "The Ideological Inception of Intertextuality and its Dissonance in Current Biblical Studies." *Currents in Biblical Research* 12/1 (2012) 58–76.

Young, Bread H. *Paul, the Jewish Theologian: A Pharisee among Christians, Jews, and Gentiles*. Peabody, MA: Hendrickson, 1997.

Youngblood, Ronald. *The Book of Genesis: An Introductory Commentary*. Grand Rapids: Baker, 1991.

Ziesler, J. A. "The Role of the Tenth Commandment in Romans 7." In *The Pauline Writings*, edited by Stanley E. Porter and Craig A. Evans, 137–52. Sheffield: Sheffield Academic, 1995.

References to TLG Sources

Origen of Alexandria, *Contra Celsum*, Book 8 section 30 line 3, 7, 8
    Contra Celsum, Book 8 section 29 line 26
    Commentarium in evangelium Matthaei,
    Book 11 section 12 line 58

Clemens Romanus et Clementina, *Homiliae*, Homily 7 chapter 8 section 1 line 5

Ephraem Syrus, *Sermo in secundum adventum domini nostril Iesu Christi*, page 17 line 12
    Interrogationes et responsiones, page 81 line 1.
    Institutio ad monachos, page 358 line 12.

Cyrillus Hierosolymitanus, *Catecheses ad illuminandos* 1–18. Catechesis 17
    chapter 29 line 17.

John Chrysostom, *In Acta apostolorum* (homiliae 1–55), volume 60 page 239 lines 44–46.
    In Acta apostolorum (homiliae 1–55), volume 60 page 240 lines 29–30.
    De nativitate, lines 92, 93.
    In Genesium (homiliae 1–67), volume 53 page 246 line 11
    Against the Jews, (1.5).

Didymus Caecus, *De trinitate* (lib. 2.8–27), volume 39 page 624 line 2.

Diodorus, *Fragmenta in epistulam ad Romanos*, page 100 lines 18, 25.

Epiphanius, *Panarion (Adversus haereses)*, volume 1 page 331 line 19.

Cyrillus Hierosolymitanus, *Catecheses ad illuminandos 1-18*, Catechisis 17 chapter 29 line 18.

Amphilochius, *Contra haereticos*, lines 769, 778.

Severianus, Orat, et Scr. Eccl., *Fragmenta in epistulam ad Galatas (in catenis)*, page 298 line 18.

Cyril of Alexandria, *Commentarius in xii prophetas minoris*, volume 1 page 362 line 6.
De adoratione et cultu in spiritu et veritate, volume 68 page 377 line 36.
Collectio dictorum veteris testamenti, volume 77 page 1241 line 2.

Catenae (Novum Testamentum), Catena in Acta (catena Andreae) (e cod. Oxon. coll. nov. 58), page 250 line 29.

www.ingramcontent.com/pod-product-compliance
Lightning Source LLC
Chambersburg PA
CBHW080725300426
44114CB00019B/2492